HISTORY OF THE
RISE AND INFLUENCE
OF THE SPIRIT OF
RATIONALISM IN
EUROPE

BY

WILLIAM EDWARD HARTPOLE LECKY

PART I

LONDON:

WATTS & CO.,

JOHNSON'S COURT, FLEET STREET, E.C.

1946

Printed and Published in Great Britain by C. A. Watts & Co. Limited,
5 & 6 Johnson's Court, Fleet Street, London, E.C.4

INTRODUCTORY NOTE

WILLIAM EDWARD HARTPOLE LECKY is a typical representative of nineteenth-century Rationalism. Born in 1838 of an Irish landowning family, he studied for the Protestant ministry, but was never ordained. Instead, he devoted his life to literature and became distinguished as a historian of European culture and of England and Ireland in the eighteenth century. He entered politics at the close of his life as Unionist member of Parliament for Dublin University, and died in 1903 a Privy Councillor and member of the Order of Merit.

A History of the Rise and Influence of the Spirit of Rationalism in Europe was first published in 1865 and is an important contribution to social science. Lecky was one of the first to break away from the " great man " theory of history and to recognise changes of belief as the product of impersonal and even of economic causes. Why is it that stories of the miraculous, which in the Middle Ages were universally accepted, are in the modern world received with general incredulity ? The evidence for the miraculous remains to-day what it always was; but our estimate of it has changed. The change has been effected by what Lecky calls " the spirit of the age." While he attributes the major part in the generation of this spirit to intellectual tendencies, he does not exclude social factors. " It is impossible to lay down a railway without creating an intellectual influence. It is probable that Watt and Stephenson will eventually modify the opinions of mankind as profoundly as Luther or Voltaire."

While the Reformation let loose " the germ of Rationalism," the leading Reformers were by no means Rationalists. Lecky makes an exception in the cases of Zwingli, who was inclined to toleration and sceptical about " original sin," and Socinus, the founder of the Unitarian school of thought. The real rise of Rationalism dates from the experimental philosophers of the seventeenth century. Bacon and Locke, though professing Christians, were both thoroughly Rationalist in temper and have been the bugbear of Catholic reactionaries from their day to this. Lecky traces the history of Rationalism from the age of Bacon and Locke to that of Voltaire and Rousseau, and so to the secularisation of politics which followed the French Revolution.

The work inevitably " dates." Lecky wrote eighty years ago, when it could be light-heartedly assumed that unregulated industrialism would of itself make for prosperity and peace. We know now that history never solves one problem without setting a new one, and that the conditions of world peace and prosperity in an era of mass production have still to be created. But Lecky is hardly to be blamed for failing to anticipate what few of his contemporaries foresaw. As an essay in the scientific treatment of cultural evolution the *History of Rationalism* made a mark in its day, and, provided it is read with a critical mind, may be perused with profit by our own generation.

ARCHIBALD ROBERTSON.

January 1, 1946.

iii

INTRODUCTION

DURING the fierce theological controversies that accompanied and followed the Reformation, while a judicial spirit was as yet unknown, while each party imagined itself the representative of absolute and necessary truth in opposition to absolute and fatal error, and while the fluctuations of belief were usually attributed to direct miraculous agency, it was natural that all the causes of theological changes should have been sought exclusively within the circle of theology. Each theologian imagined that the existence of the opinions he denounced was fully accounted for by the exertions of certain evil-minded men, who had triumphed by means of sophistical arguments, aided by a judicial blindness that had been cast upon the deluded. His own opinions, on the other hand, had been sustained or revived by apostles raised for the purpose, illuminated by special inspiration, and triumphing by the force of theological arguments. As long as this point of view continued, the positions of the theologian and of the ecclesiastical historian were nearly the same. Each was confined to a single province, and each, recognising a primitive faith as his ideal, had to indicate the successive innovations upon its purity. But when, towards the close of the eighteenth century, the decline of theological passions enabled men to discuss these matters in a calmer spirit, and when increased knowledge produced more comprehensive views, the historical standing-point was materially altered. It was observed that every great change of belief had been preceded by a great change in the intellectual condition of Europe, that the success of any opinion depended much less upon the force of its arguments, or upon the ability of its advocates, than upon the predisposition of society to receive it, and that that predisposition resulted from the intellectual type of the age. As men advance from an imperfect to a higher civilisation, they gradually sublimate and refine their creed. Their imaginations insensibly detach themselves from those grosser conceptions and doctrines that were formerly most powerful, and they sooner or later reduce all their opinions into conformity with the moral and intellectual standards which the new civilisation produces. Thus, long before the Reformation, the tendencies of the Reformation were manifest. The revival of Grecian learning, the development of art, the reaction against the schoolmen, had raised society to an elevation in which a more refined and less oppressive creed was absolutely essential to its well-being. Luther and Calvin only represented the prevailing wants, and embodied them in a definite form. The pressure of the general intellectual influences of the time determines the predispositions which ultimately regulate the details of belief; and though all men do not yield to that pressure with the same facility, all large bodies are at last controlled. A change of speculative opinions does not imply an increase of the data upon which those opinions rest, but a change of the habits of thought and mind which they reflect. Definite arguments are the symptoms and pretexts, but seldom the causes, of the change. Their chief merit is to accelerate the inevitable crisis. They derive their force and efficacy from their conformity with the mental habits of those to whom they are addressed. Reasoning which in one age would make no impression whatever, in the next age is received with enthusiastic applause. It is one thing to understand its nature, but quite another to appreciate its force.

And this standard of belief, this tone and habit of thought, which is the supreme arbiter of the opinions of successive periods, is created, not by the influences arising out of any one department of intellect, but by the combination of all the intellectual and even social tendencies of the age. Those who contribute most largely to its formation are, I believe, the philosophers. Men like Bacon, Descartes, and Locke have probably done more than any others to set the current of their age. They have formed a certain cast and tone of mind. They have introduced peculiar habits of thought, new modes of reasoning, new tendencies of enquiry. The impulse they have given to the higher literature has been by that literature communicated to the more popular writers, and the impress of these master-minds is clearly visible in the writings of multitudes who are totally unacquainted with their works. But philosophical methods, great and unquestionable as is their power, form but one of the many influences that contribute to the mental habits of society. Thus the discoveries of physical science, entrenching upon the domain of the anomalous and the incomprehensible, enlarging our conceptions of the range of law, and revealing the connection of phenomena that had formerly appeared altogether isolated, form a habit of mind which is carried far beyond the limits of physics. Thus the astronomical discovery, that our world is not the centre and axis of the material universe, but is an inconsiderable planet occupying to all appearance an altogether insignificant and subordinate position, and revolving with many others around a sun which is itself but an infinitesimal point in creation, in as far as it is realised by the imagination, has a vast and palpable influence upon our theological concep-

tions. Thus the commercial or municipal spirit exhibits certain habits of thought, certain modes of reasoning, certain repugnances and attractions, which make it invariably tend to one class of opinions. To encourage the occupations that produce this spirit, is to encourage the opinions that are most congenial to it. It is impossible to lay down a railway without creating an intellectual influence. It is probable that Watt and Stephenson will eventually modify the opinions of mankind almost as profoundly as Luther or Voltaire.

If these views be correct, they establish at once a broad distinction between the province of the theologian and that of the historian of opinions. The first confines his attention to the question of the truth or falsehood of particular doctrines, which he ascertains by examining the arguments upon which they rest ; the second should endeavour to trace the causes of the rise and fall of those doctrines which are to be found in the general intellectual condition of the age. The first is restricted to a single department of mental phenomena, and to those logical connections which determine the opinions of the severe reasoner ; the second is obliged to take a wide survey of the intellectual influences of the period he is describing, and to trace that connection of congruity which has a much greater influence upon the sequence of opinions than logical arguments.

Although in the present work we are concerned only with the last of these two points of view, it will be necessary to consider briefly the possibility of their co-existence ; for this question involves one of the most important problems in history —the position reserved for the individual will and the individual judgment in the great current of general causes.

It was a saying of Locke that we should not ask whether our will is free, but whether WE are free ; for our conception of freedom is the power of acting according to our will, or, in other words, the consciousness, when pursuing a certain course of action, that we might, if we had chosen, have pursued a different one. If, however, pushing our analysis still further, we ask what it is that determines our volition, I conceive that the highest principles of liberty we are capable of attaining are to be found in the two facts, that our will is a faculty distinct from our desires, and that it is not a mere passive thing, the direction and intensity of which are necessarily determined by the attraction and repulsion of pleasure and pain. We are conscious that we are capable of pursuing a course which is extremely distasteful, rather than another course which would be extremely agreeable; that in doing so we are making a continual and painful effort; that every relaxation of that effort produces the most lively pleasure; and that it is at least possible that the motive which induces us to pursue the path of self-abnegation, may be a sense of right altogether uninfluenced by prospects of future reward. We are also conscious that if our desires act powerfully upon our will, our will can in its turn act upon our desires. We can strengthen the natural powers of our will by steadily exerting it. We can diminish the intensity of our desires by habitually repressing them; we can alter, by a process of mental discipline, the whole symmetry of our passions, deliberately selecting one class for gratification and for development, and crushing and subduing the others. These considerations do not, of course, dispel the mystery which perhaps necessarily rests upon the subject of free-will. They do not solve the questions, whether the will can ever act without a motive, or what are its relations to its motives, or whether the desires may not sometimes be too strong for its most developed powers; but they form a theory of human liberty which I believe to be the highest we can attain. He who has realised, on the one hand, his power of acting according to his will, and, on the other hand, the power of his will to emancipate itself from the empire of pain and pleasure, and to modify and control the current of the emotions, has probably touched the limits of his freedom.

The struggle of the will for a right motive against the pressure of the desires is one of the chief forms of virtue; and the relative position of these two influences, one of the chief measures of the moral standing of each individual. Sometimes, in the conflict between the will and a particular desire, the former, either through its own natural strength, or through the natural weakness of its opponent, or through the process of mental discipline I have described, has obtained a supreme ascendency which is seldom or never seriously disturbed. Sometimes, through causes that are innate, and perhaps more frequently through causes for which we are responsible, the two powers exhibit almost an equipoise, and each often succumbs to the other. Between these two positions there are numerous gradations; so that every cause that in any degree intensifies the desires, gives them in some cases a triumph over the will.

The application of these principles to those constantly-recurring figures which moral statistics present is not difficult. The statistician, for example, shows that a certain condition of temperature increases the force of a passion—or, in other words, the temptation to a particular vice; and he then proceeds to argue that the whole history of that vice is strictly regulated by atmospheric changes. The vice rises into prominence with the rising temperature; it is sustained during its continuance, it declines with its decline. Year after year, the same figures and the same variations are nearly reproduced. Investigations in the most dissimilar nations only strengthen the proof; and the evidence is so ample, that it enables us, within certain limits, even to predict the future. The rivers that rise and fall with the winter torrents or the summer drought; the insect life that is called into being by the genial spring and destroyed by the returning frost; the aspect of vegetation, which pursues its appointed changes through the recurring seasons : these do not reflect more faithfully or obey more implicitly external influences, than do some great departments of the acts of man.

This is the fact which statistical tables prove, but what is the inference to be deduced from them? Not, surely, that there is no such thing as free-will, but, what we should have regarded as antecedently probable, that the degree of energy with which it is exerted is in different periods nearly the same. As long as the resistance is unaltered, the fluctuations of our desires determine the fluctuations of our actions. In this there is nothing extraordinary. It would be strange indeed if it were otherwise— strange if, the average of virtue remaining the same, or nearly the same, an equal amount of solicitation did not at different periods produce the same, or nearly the same, amount of compliance. The fact, therefore, that there is an order and sequence in the history of vice, and that influences altogether independent of human control contribute largely to its course, in no degree destroys the freedom of will, and the conclusion of the historian is perfectly reconcilable with the principles of the moralist. From this spectacle of regularity, we simply infer that the changes in the moral condition of mankind are very slow ; that there are periods when, certain desires being strengthened by natural causes, the task of the will in opposing them is peculiarly arduous ; and that any attempt to write a history of vice without taking into consideration external influences, would be miserably deficient.

Again, if we turn to a different class of phenomena, nothing can be more certain to an attentive observer than that the great majority even of those who reason much about their opinions have arrived at their conclusions by a process quite distinct from reasoning. They may be perfectly unconscious of the fact, but the ascendency of old associations is upon them ; and, in the overwhelming majority of cases, men of the most various creeds conclude their investigations by simply acquiescing in the opinions they have been taught. They insensibly judge all questions by a mental standard derived from education ; they proportion their attention and sympathy to the degree in which the facts or arguments presented to them support their foregone conclusions ; and they thus speedily convince themselves that the arguments in behalf of their hereditary opinions are irresistibly cogent, and the arguments against them exceedingly absurd. Nor are those who have diverged from the opinions they have been taught necessarily more independent of illegitimate influences. The love of singularity, the ambition to be thought intellectually superior to others, the bias of taste, the attraction of vice, the influence of friendship, the magnetism of genius—these, and countless other influences into which it is needless to enter, all determine conclusions. The number of persons who have a rational basis for their belief is probably infinitesimal ; for illegitimate influences not only determine the convictions of those who do not examine, but usually give a dominating bias to the reasonings of those who do. But it would be manifestly absurd to conclude from this, that reason has no part or function in the formation of opinions. No mind, it is true, was ever altogether free from distorting influences ; but in the struggle between the reason and the affections which leads to truth, as in the struggle between the will and the desires which leads to virtue, every effort is crowned with a measure of success, and innumerable gradations of progress are manifested. All that we can rightly infer is, that the process of reasoning is much more difficult than is commonly supposed ; and that to those who would investigate the causes of existing opinions, the study of predispositions is much more important than the study of arguments.

The doctrine, that the opinions of a given period are mainly determined by the intellectual condition of society, and that every great change of opinion is the consequence of general causes, simply implies that there exists a strong bias which acts upon all large masses of men, and eventually triumphs over every obstacle. The inequalities of civilisation, the distorting influences arising out of special circumstances, the force of conservatism, and the efforts of individual genius, produce innumerable diversities ; but a careful examination shows that these are but the eddies of an advancing stream, that the various systems are being all gradually modified in a given direction, and that a certain class of tendencies appears with more and more prominence in all departments of intellect. Individuals may resist the stream ; and this power supplies a firm and legitimate standing-point to the theologian : but these efforts are too rare and feeble to have much influence upon the general course.

To this last proposition there is, however, an important exception to be made in favour of men of genius, who are commonly at once representative and creative. They embody and reflect the tendencies of their time, but they also frequently materially modify them, and their ideas become the subject or the basis of the succeeding developments. To trace in every great movement the part which belongs to the individual and the part which belongs to general causes, without exaggerating either side, is one of the most delicate tasks of the historian.

What I have written will, I trust, be sufficient to show the distinction between the sphere of the historian and the sphere of the theologian. It must, however, be acknowledged that they have some points of contact ; for it is impossible to reveal the causes that called an opinion into being without throwing some light upon its intrinsic value. It must be acknowledged, also, that there is a theory or method of research which would amalgamate the two spheres, or, to speak more correctly, would entirely subordinate

the theologian to the historian. Those who have appreciated the extremely small influence of definite arguments in determining the opinions either of an individual or of a nation—who have perceived how invariably an increase of civilisation implies a modification of belief, and how completely the controversialists of successive ages are the puppets and the unconscious exponents of the deep undercurrent of their time—will feel an intense distrust of their unassisted reason, and will naturally look for some guide to direct their judgment. I think it must be admitted that the general and increasing tendency, in the present day, is to seek such a guide in the collective wisdom of mankind as it is displayed in the developments of history. In other words, the way in which our leading thinkers, consciously or unconsciously, form their opinions, is by endeavouring to ascertain what are the laws that govern the successive modifications of belief ; in what directions, towards what conceptions, the intellect of man advances with the advance of civilisation ; what are the leading characteristics that mark the belief of civilised ages and nations as compared with barbarous ones, and of the most educated as compared with the most illiterate classes. This mode of reasoning may be said to resolve itself into three problems. It is necessary, in the first place, to ascertain what are the general intellectual tendencies of civilisation. It is then necessary to ascertain how far those tendencies are connected, or, in other words, how far the existence of one depends upon and implies the existence of the others ; and it is necessary, in the last place, to ascertain whether they have been accompanied by an increase or diminution of happiness, of virtue, and of humanity.

My object in the present work has been, to trace the history of the spirit of Rationalism : by which I understand, not any class of definite doctrines or criticisms, but rather a certain cast of thought, or bias of reasoning, which has during the last three centuries gained a marked ascendency in Europe. The nature of this bias will be exhibited in detail in the ensuing pages, when we examine its influence upon the various forms of moral and intellectual development. At present it will be sufficient to say, that it leads men on all occasions to subordinate dogmatic theology to the dictates of reason and of conscience, and, as a necessary consequence, greatly to restrict its influence upon life. It predisposes men, in history, to attribute all kinds of phenomena to natural rather than miraculous causes ; in theology, to esteem succeeding systems the expressions of the wants and aspirations of that religious sentiment which is planted in all men ; and, in ethics, to regard as duties only those which conscience reveals to be such.

It is manifest that, in attempting to write the history of a mental tendency, some difficulties have to be encountered quite distinct from those which attend a simple relation of facts. No one can be truly said to understand any great system of belief, if he has not in some degree realised the point of view from which its arguments assume an appearance of plausibility and of cogency, the habit of thought which makes its various doctrines appear probable, harmonious, and consistent. Yet, even in the great controversies of the present day—even in the disputes between the Catholic and the Protestant—it is evident that very few controversialists ever succeed in arriving at this appreciation of the opinions they are combating. But the difficulty becomes far greater when our research extends over forms of belief of which there are no living representatives, and when we have not merely to estimate the different measures of probability subsisting in different societies, but have also to indicate their causes and their changes. To reconstruct the modes of thought which produced superstitions that have long since vanished from among us ; to trace through the obscurity of the distant past that hidden bias of the imagination which

—deeper than any strife of arguments, deeper than any change of creed—determines in each succeeding age the realised belief ; to grasp the principle of analogy or congruity according to which the conceptions of a given period were grouped and harmonised, and then to show how the discoveries of science, or the revolutions in philosophy, or the developments of industrial or political life, introduced new centres of attraction, and made the force of analogy act in new directions ; to follow out the process till the period when conclusions the reason had once naturally and almost instinctively adopted seem incongruous and grotesque, and till the whole current of intellectual tendencies is changed :—this is the task which devolves upon everyone who, not content with relating the fluctuations of opinions, seeks to throw some light upon the laws that govern them.

Probably, the greatest difficulty of such a process of investigation arises from the wide difference between professed and realised belief. When an opinion that is opposed to the age is incapable of modification and is an obstacle to progress, it will at last be openly repudiated ; and if it is identified with any existing interests, or associated with some eternal truth, its rejection will be accompanied by paroxysms of painful agitation. But much more frequently civilisation makes opinions that are opposed to it simply obsolete. They perish by indifference, not by controversy. They are relegated to the dim twilight land that surrounds every living faith ; the land, not of death, but of the shadow of death ; the land of the unrealised and the inoperative. Sometimes, too, we find the phraseology, the ceremonies, the formularies, the external aspect of some phase of belief that has long since perished, connected with a system that has been created by the wants and is thrilling with the life of modern civilisation. They resemble those images of departed ancestors, which, it is said, the ancient Ethiopians were accustomed to paint upon their bodies, as if to preserve the pleasing illusion that those could not be really dead whose lineaments were still visible among them, and were still associated with life. In order to appreciate the change, we must translate these opinions into action, must examine what would be their effects if fully realised, and ascertain how far those effects are actually produced. It is necessary, therefore, not merely to examine successive creeds, but also to study the types of character of successive ages.

It only remains for me, before drawing this introduction to a close, to describe the method I have employed in tracing the influence of the rationalistic spirit upon opinions. In the first place, I have examined the history and the causes of that decline of the sense of the miraculous, which is so manifest a fruit of civilisation. But it soon becomes evident that this movement cannot be considered by itself; for the predisposition in favour of miracles grows out of, and can only be adequately explained by, certain conceptions of the nature of the Supreme Being, and of the habitual government of the universe, which invariably accompany the earlier, or, as it may be termed, the anthropomorphic stage of intellectual development. Of the nature of this stage we have some important evidence in the history of art, which is then probably the most accurate expression of religious realisations, while the history of the encroachments of physical science upon our first notions of the system of the world, goes far to explain its decay. Together with the intellectual movement, we have to consider a moral movement that has accompanied it, which has had the effect of diminishing the influence of fear as the motive of duty, of destroying the overwhelming importance of dogmatic teaching, and of establishing the supremacy of conscience. This progress involves many important consequences; but the most remarkable of all is the decay of persecution, which, I have endeavoured to show, is indissolubly connected with a profound change in theological realisations. I have, in the last place, sought to gather fresh evidence of the operations of the rationalistic spirit in the great fields of politics and of industry. In the first, I have shown how the movement of secularisation has passed through every department of political life, how the progress of democracy has influenced and been influenced by theological tendencies, and how political pursuits contribute to the formation of habits of thought, which affect the whole circle of our judgments. In the second, I have traced the rise of the industrial spirit in Europe; its collisions with the Church; the profound moral and intellectual changes it effected; and the tendency of the great science of political economy, which is its expression.

I am deeply conscious that the present work can furnish at best but a meagre sketch of these subjects, and that to treat them as they deserve would require an amount both of learning and of ability to which I can make no pretension. I shall be content if I have succeeded in detecting some forgotten link in the great chain of causes, or in casting a ray of light on some of the obscurer pages of the history of opinions.

CONTENTS OF PART I

CHAPTER I.

THE DECLINING SENSE OF THE MIRACULOUS

ON MAGIC AND WITCHCRAFT

The Belief in Satanic Miracles, having been universal among Protestants and Roman Catholics, passed away by a silent and unreasoning process under the influence of Civilisation—Witchcraft arose from a vivid Realisation of Satanic Presence acting on the Imagination—and afterwards on the Reason—Its Existence and Importance among Savages—The Christians attributed to Magic the Pagan Miracles—Constantine and Constantius attempted to subvert Paganism by persecuting Magic—Magical character soon attributed to Christian Rites—Miracle of St. Hilarion—Persecution suspended under Julian and Jovian, but afterwards renewed—Not entirely due to Ecclesiastical Influence—Compromise between Christianity and Paganism—Prohibited Pagan Rites continue to be practised as Magic—From the Sixth to the Twelfth Century, extreme Superstition with little Terrorism, and, consequently, little Sorcery—Effects of Eclipses, Comets, and Pestilence, on the Superstition—The Cabalists—Psellus—The Revival of Literature in the Twelfth Century produced a Spirit of Rebellion which was encountered by Terrorism—which, acting on the popular Creed, produced a bias towards Witchcraft—The Black Death—Influence of the Reformation in stimulating Witchcraft—Luther—The Inquisitors—The Theology of Witchcraft—First Evidence of a Rationalistic Spirit in Europe—Wier—answered by Bodin—Rationalistic Spirit fully manifested in Montaigne—Charron—Rapid and Silent Decadence of the Belief in Witches—Opinions and Influence of La Bruyère, Bayle, Descartes, Male-

branche, and Voltaire — Gradual Cessation of the Persecution in France—In England, the First Law against Witchcraft was made under Henry VIII.—Repealed in the following Reign, but renewed under Elizabeth—Cranmer and Jewel—Reginald Scott pronounced Witchcraft a Delusion—The Law of James I.—Opinions of Coke, Bacon, Shakespeare, Browne, and Selden — English Witchcraft reached its climax in the Commonwealth—Declined immediately after the Restoration—The Three Causes were, the Reaction against Puritanism, the Influence of Hobbes, and the Baconian Philosophy as represented by the Royal Society—Charge of Sir Matthew Kale—Glanvil undertakes the Defence of the Belief—Supported by Henry More, Cudworth, Casaubon, &c.—Opposed by Webster and Wagstaafe—Baxter vainly tries to revive the Belief by Accounts of Witch Trials in America—Rapid Progress of the Scepticism—Trial of Jane Wenham—Repeal of the Laws against Witchcraft—Wesley's Summary of the History of the Movement—Great Moderation of the English Church as compared with Puritanism — Extreme Atrocity of the Witch Persecution in Scotland, and its Causes—Slow Decline of the Belief in Scotland—Conclusion -

CHAPTER II.

THE DECLINING SENSE OF THE MIRACULOUS

THE MIRACLES OF THE CHURCH

Miracles related by the Fathers and Mediæval Writers as ordinary and undoubted Occurrences—Rapid Growth of Scepticism on the Subject since the Reformation—The Sceptical Habit of Mind acts more powerfully on Contemporary than on Historical Narrations—Among the early Protestants, the Cessation of Miracles supposed to have taken place when the Fathers

CHAPTER IV.

ON PERSECUTION

I.—THE ANTECEDENTS OF

PERSECUTION

Persecution is the result, not of the personal Character of the Persecutors, but of the Principles they profess— Foundations of all Religious Systems are the Sense of Virtue and the Sense of Sin—Political and Intellectual Circumstances determine in each System their relative Importance—These Sentiments gradually converted into Dogmas, under the Names of Justification by Works and Justification by Faith— Dogmas unfaithful Expressions of Moral Sentiments—The Conception of Hereditary Guilt—Theories to account for it—The Progress of Democratic Habits Destroys it—Its dogmatic Expression the Doctrine that all Men are by Nature doomed to Damnation—Unanimity of the Fathers concerning the Non-salvability of unbaptised Infants—Divergence concerning their Fate—The Greek Fathers believed in a Limbo—The Latin Fathers denied this—Augustine, Fulgentius—Origen associates the Doctrine with that of Pre-existence— Pseudo-baptisms of the Middle Ages —The Reformation produced conflicting Tendencies on the subject, diminishing the Sense of the Efficacy of Ceremonies, increasing that of imputed Guilt—The Lutherans and Calvinists held a Doctrine that was less superstitious but more revolting than that of Catholicism—Jonathan Edwards—Dogmatic Character of early Protestantism—Rationalism appeared with Socinus—Antecedents of Italian Rationalism—Socinus Rejects Original Sin—as also does Zuinglius —Rationalistic Tendencies of this Reformer—Rapid Progress of his View of Baptism—The Scope of the Doctrine of the Condemnation of all Men extends to Adults—Sentiments of the Fathers on the Damnation of the Heathen—Great Use of this Doctrine of Exclusive Salvation in Consolidating the Power of the Church—and in abbreviating the Paroxysms of the Reformation—The Protestants almost all accepted it—Protest of Zuinglius— Opposition between Dogmatic and

RATIONALISM IN EUROPE

CHAPTER I.

ON THE DECLINING SENSE OF THE MIRACULOUS

MAGIC AND WITCHCRAFT

THERE is certainly no change in the history of the last 300 years more striking, or suggestive of more curious enquiries, than that which has taken place in the estimate of the miraculous. At present nearly all educated men receive an account of a miracle taking place in their own day, with an absolute and even derisive incredulity which dispenses with all examination of the evidence. Although they may be entirely unable to give a satisfactory explanation of some phenomena that have taken place, they never on that account dream of ascribing them to supernatural agency, such an hypothesis being, as they believe, altogether beyond the range of reasonable discussion. Yet, a few centuries ago, there was no solution to which the mind of man turned more readily in every perplexity. A miraculous account was then universally accepted as perfectly credible, probable, and ordinary. There was scarcely a village or a church that had not, at some time, been the scene of supernatural interposition. The powers of light and the powers of darkness were regarded as visibly struggling for the mastery. Saintly miracles, supernatural cures, startling judgments, visions, prophecies, and prodigies of every order, attested the activity of the one; while witchcraft and magic, with all their attendant horrors, were the visible manifestations of the other.

I propose in the present chapter to examine that vast department of miracles, which is comprised under the several names of witchcraft, magic, and sorcery. It is a subject which has, I think, scarcely obtained the position it deserves in the history of opinions, having been too generally treated in the spirit of the antiquarian, as if it belonged entirely to the past, and could have no voice or bearing upon the controversies of the present. Yet, for more than fifteen hundred years, it was universally believed that the Bible established, in the clearest manner, the reality of the crime, and that an amount of evidence, so varied and so ample as to preclude the very possibility of doubt, attested its continuance and its prevalence. The clergy denounced it with all the emphasis of authority. The legislators of almost every land enacted laws for its punishment. Acute judges, whose lives were spent in sifting evidence, investigated the question on countless occasions, and condemned the accused. Tens of thousands of victims perished by the most agonising and protracted torments, without exciting the faintest compassion ; and, as they were for the most part extremely ignorant and extremely poor, sectarianism and avarice had but little influence on the subject.[1] Nations that were completely

[1] The general truth of this statement can scarcely, I think, be questioned, though there are, undoubtedly, a few remarkable exceptions. Thus, the Templars were accused of sorcery when Philip the Beautiful wished to confiscate their property ; and the heretical opinions of the Vaudois may possibly have had something to say to the trials at Arras in 1459 ; and, indeed, the name Vauderie was at one time given to sorcery. There were, moreover, a few cases of obnoxious politicians and noblemen being destroyed on the accusation ; and during the Commonwealth there were one or two professional witch-finders in England. We have also to take into account some cases of Convent scandals, such as those of Gauffridi, Grandier, and La Cadière ; but, when all these deductions have been made, the

separated by position, by interests, and by character, on this one question were united. In almost every province of Germany, but especially in those where clerical influence predominated, the persecution raged with a fearful intensity. Seven thousand victims are said to have been burned at Trèves, six hundred by a single bishop in Bamberg, and nine hundred in a single year in the bishopric of Wurtzburg.[1] In France, decrees were passed on the subject by the Parliaments of Paris, Toulouse, Bordeaux, Rheims, Rouen, Dijon, and Rennes, and they were all followed by a harvest of blood. At Toulouse, the seat of the Inquisition, four hundred persons perished for sorcery at a single execution, and fifty at Douay in a single year. Remy, a judge of Nancy, boasted that he had put to death eight hundred witches in sixteen years. The executions that took place at Paris in a few months, were, in the emphatic words of an old writer, "almost infinite."[2] The fugitives who escaped to Spain were

there seized and burned by the Inquisition. In that country the persecution spread to the smallest towns, and the belief was so deeply rooted in the popular mind, that a sorcerer was burned as late as 1780. Torquemada devoted himself to the extirpation of witchcraft as zealously as to the extirpation of heresy, and he wrote a book upon the enormity of the crime.[1] In Flanders the persecution of witches raged through the whole of the sixteenth and the greater part of the seventeenth centuries, and every variety of torture was employed in detecting the criminals.[2] In Italy a thousand persons were executed in a single year in the province of Como ; and in other parts of the country the severity of the inquisitors at last created an absolute rebellion.[3] The same scenes were enacted in the wild valleys of Switzerland and of Savoy. In Geneva, which was then ruled by a bishop, five hundred alleged witches were executed in three months ; forty-eight were burnt at Constance or Ravensburg, and eighty in the little town of Valery in Savoy.[4] In 1670, seventy persons were condemned in

prosecutions for witchcraft will represent the action of undiluted superstition more faithfully than probably any others that could be named. The overwhelming majority of witches were extremely poor—they were condemned by the highest and purest tribunals (ecclesiastical and lay) of the time ; and as heretics were then burnt without difficulty for their opinions, there was little temptation to accuse them of witchcraft, and besides all parties joined cordially in the persecution. Grillandus, an Italian inquisitor of the fifteenth century, says—" Isti sortilegi, magici, necromantici, et similes sunt cæteris Christi fidelibus pauperiores, sordidiores, viliores, et contemptibiliores, in hoc mundo Deo permittente calamitosam vitam communiter peragunt, Deum verum infelici morte perdunt et æterni ignis incendio cruciantur." (De Sortilegiis, cap. iii.) We shall see hereafter that witchcraft and heresy represent the working of the same spirit on different classes, and therefore usually accompanied each other.

[1] See the original letter published at Bamberg in 1657, quoted in Cannaert, Procès des Sorcières, p. 145 ; see, too, Wright's Sorcery, vol. i. p. 186 ; Michelet, La Sorcière, p. 10.

[2] On French Witchcraft, see Thiers' Traité des Superstitions, tom. i. pp. 134-136 ; Madden's History of Phantasmata, vol. i. pp. 306-310 ; Garinet, Histoire de la Magie en France (passim), but especially the Remonstrance of the Parliament of Rouen, in 1670, against the pardon of witches, p. 337. Bodin's Démonomanie des Sorciers. The persecution raged with extreme violence all through the south of France. It was a brilliant suggestion of De Lancre, that the witchcraft about Bordeaux might be connected with the number of orchards—the Devil being well known to have an especial power over apples. (See the passage quoted in Garinet, p. 176.) We have a fearful illustration of the tenacity of the belief in the fact that the superstition still continues, and that blood has in consequence been shed during the present [nineteenth] century in the provinces that border on the Pyrenees. In 1807, a beggar was seized, tortured, and burned alive for sorcery by the inhabitants of Mayenne. In 1850, the Civil Tribunal of Tarbes tried a man and woman named Soubervie, for having caused the death of a woman named Bedouret. They believed that she was a witch, and declared that the priest had told them that she was the cause of an illness under which the woman Soubervie was suffering. They

accordingly drew Bedouret into a private room, held her down upon some burning straw, and placed a red-hot iron across her mouth. The unhappy woman soon died in extreme agony. The Soubervies confessed, and indeed exulted in their act. At their trials they obtained the highest possible characters. It was shown that they had been actuated solely by superstition, and it was urged that they only followed the highest ecclesiastical precedents. The jury recommended them to mercy ; and they were only sentenced to pay twenty-five francs a year to the husband of the victim, and to be imprisoned for four months. (Cordier, Légendes des Hautes Pyrénées. Lourdes, 1885, pp. 79-88.) In the Rituel Auscitain, now used in the diocese of Tarbes, it is said—"On doit reconnaître que non-seulement il peut y avoir mais qu'il y a même quelquefois des personnes qui sont véritablement possédées des esprits malins." (Ib. p. 90.)

[1] Llorente, History of the Inquisition (English Translation), pp. 129-142. Amongst other cases, more than thirty women were burnt at Calhahorra, in 1507. A Spanish monk, named Castanaga, seems to have ventured to question the justice of the executions as early as 1529 (p. 131). See also Garinet, p. 176 ; Madden, vol. i. pp. 311-315. Toledo was supposed to be the head-quarters of the magicians—probably because, in the twelfth and thirteenth centuries, mathematics, which were constantly confounded with magic, flourished there more than in any other part in Europe. Naudé, Apologie pour les Grands Hommes soupçonnez de Magie (Paris, 1625), pp. 81, 82. See also Buckle's History of Civilisation, vol. i. p. 334, note, and Simancas, De Catholicis Institutionibus, pp. 463-468.

[2] See a curious collection of documents on the subject by Cannaert, Procès des Sorcières en Belgique (Gand. 1847).

[3] Spina, De Strigibus (1522), cap. xii.; Thiers, vol. i. p. 138 ; Madden, vol. i. p. 305. Peter the Martyr, whom Titian has immortalised, seems to have been one of the most strenuous of the persecutors, Spina, Apol. c. ix.

[4] Madden, vol. i. pp. 303, 304. Michelet, La Sorcière, p. 206. Sprenger ascribes Tell's shot to the assistance of the devil. Mall. Mal. (Pars ii. c. xvi.). Savoy has

Sweden,[1] and a large proportion of them were burnt. And these are only a few of the more salient events in that long series of persecutions which extended over almost every country, and continued for centuries with unabated fury. The Church of Rome proclaimed in every way that was in her power the reality and the continued existence of the crime. She strained every nerve to stimulate the persecution. She taught by all her organs that to spare a witch was a direct insult to the Almighty, and to her ceaseless exertions is to be attributed by far the greater proportion of the blood that was shed. In 1484, Pope Innocent VIII. issued a bull, which gave a fearful impetus to the persecution, and he it was who commissioned the Inquisitor Sprenger, whose book was long the recognised manual on the subject, and who is said to have condemned hundreds to death every year. Similar bulls were issued by Julius II. in 1504, and by Adrian VI. in 1523. A long series of Provincial Councils asserted the existence of sorcery, and anathematised those who resorted to it. "The universal practice of the Church was to place magic and sorcery among the reserved cases, and at Prones, to declare magicians and sorcerers excommunicated;"[2] and a form of exorcism was solemnly inserted in the ritual. Almost all the great works that were written in favour of the executions were written by ecclesiastics. Almost all the lay works on the same side were dedicated to and sanctioned by ecclesiastical dignitaries. Ecclesiastical tribunals condemned thousands to death, and countless bishops exerted all their influence to multiply the victims. In a word, for many centuries it was universally believed that the continued existence of witchcraft formed an integral part of the teaching of the Church, and that the persecution that raged through Europe was supported by the whole stress of her infallibility.[3]

Such was the attitude of the Church of Rome with reference to this subject, but on this ground the Reformers had no conflict with their opponents. The credulity which Luther manifested on all matters connected with diabolical intervention was amazing, even for his age; and, when speaking of witchcraft, his language was emphatic and unhesitating. "I would have no compassion on these witches," he exclaimed, "I would burn them all."[1] In England the establishment of the Reformation was the signal for an immediate outburst of the superstition; and there, as elsewhere, its decline was represented by the clergy as the direct consequence and the exact measure of the progress of religious scepticism. In Scotland, where the Reformed ministers exercised greater influence than in any other country, and where the witch trials fell almost entirely into their hands, the persecution was proportionately atrocious. Probably the ablest defender of the belief was Glanvil, a clergyman of the English Establishment; and one of the most influential was Baxter, the greatest of the Puritans. It spread, with Puritanism, into the New World; and the executions in Massachusetts form one of the darkest pages in the history of America. The greatest religious leader of the last [eighteenth] century[2] was among the latest of its supporters.

If we ask why it is that the world has rejected what was once so universally and so intensely believed, why a narrative of an old woman who had been seen riding on a broomstick, or who was proved to have transformed herself into a wolf, and

---

always been especially subject to those epidemics of madness which were once ascribed to witches, and Boguet noticed that the principal wizards he had burnt were from that country. An extremely curious account of a recent epidemic of this kind in a little village called Morzines will be found in the *Relation sur une Épidémie d'Hystéro-Démonopathie en* 1861, par le Docteur A. Constans (Paris, 1863). Two French writers, Allan Kardec and Mirville, have maintained this epidemic to be supernatural.

[1] Compare Plancey, *Dict. infernal*, article *Blokula;* Hutchinson on *Witchcraft*, p. 55; Madden, vol. i. p. 354.

[2] Thiers, *Superst.* vol. i. p. 142.

[3] For ample evidence of the teaching of Catholicism

---

on the subject, see Madden's *History of Phant.* vol. i. pp. 234-248; Des Mousseaux, *Pratiques des Démons* (Paris, 1854), pp. 174-177; Thiers' *Superst.* tom. i. pp. 138-163. The two last-mentioned writers were ardent Catholics. Thiers, who wrote in 1678 (I have used the Paris edition of 1741), was a very learned and moderate theologian, and wrote under the approbation of "the doctors in the faculty of Paris:" he says—"On ne sçauroit nier qu'il y ait des magiciens ou des sorciers (car ces deux mots se prennent ordinairement dans la même signification) sans contredire visiblement les saintes lettres, la tradition sacré;eet profane, les lois canoniques et civiles et l'expérience de tous les siècles, et sans rejeter avec impudence l'autorité irréfragable et infaillible de l'Église qui lance si souvent les foudres de l'excommunication contr' eux dans ses Prônes" (p. 132). So also Garinet—"Tous les conciles, tous les synodes, qui se tinrent dans les seize premiers siècles de l'Église s'élèvent contre les sorciers; tous les écrivains ecclésiastiques les condamnent avec plus ou moins de sévérité" (p. 26). The bull of Innocent VIII. is prefixed to the *Malleus Malificarum*.

[1] *Colloquia* de fascinationibus. For the notions of Melancthon on these subjects, see Baxter's *World of Spirits*, pp. 126, 127. Calvin, also, when remodelling the laws of Geneva, left those on witchcraft intact.

[2] Wesley.

to have devoured the flocks of her neighbours, is deemed so entirely incredible,
most persons would probably be unable
to give a very definite answer to the
question. It is not because we have
examined the evidence and found it insufficient, for the disbelief always precedes,
when it does not prevent, examination.
It is rather because the idea of absurdity
is so strongly attached to such narratives,
that it is difficult even to consider them
with gravity. Yet at one time no such
improbability was felt, and hundreds of
persons have been burnt simply on the
two grounds I have mentioned.

When so complete a change takes
place in public opinion, it may be ascribed
to one or other of two causes. It may be
the result of a controversy which has
conclusively settled the question, establishing to the satisfaction of all parties a
clear preponderance of argument or fact
in favour of one opinion, and making
that opinion a truism which is accepted
by all enlightened men, even though they
have not themselves examined the evidence on which it rests. Thus, if any
one in a company of ordinarily educated
persons were to deny the motion of the
earth, or the circulation of the blood, his
statement would be received with derision, though it is probable that some of
his audience would be unable to demon-
strate the first truth, and that very few of
them could give sufficient reasons for the
second. They may not themselves be
able to defend their position, but they are
aware that, at certain known periods of
history, controversies on those subjects
took place, and that known writers then
brought forward some definite arguments
or experiments, which were ultimately
accepted by the whole learned world as
rigid and conclusive demonstrations. It
is possible, also, for as complete a change
to be effected by what is called the spirit
of the age. The general intellectual tendencies pervading the literature of a
century profoundly modify the character
of the public mind. They form a new
tone and habit of thought. They alter
the measure of probability. They create
new attractions and new antipathies, and
they eventually cause as absolute a rejection of certain old opinions as could be
produced by the most cogent and definite
arguments.

That the disbelief in witchcraft is to be
attributed to this second class of influences ; that it is the result, not of any

series of definite arguments, or of new
discoveries, but of a gradual, insensible,
yet profound modification of the habits of
thought prevailing in Europe ; that it is,
thus, a direct consequence of the progress
of civilisation, and of its influence upon
opinions ; must be evident to any one
who impartially investigates the question.
If we ask what new arguments were discovered during the decadence of the
belief, we must admit that they were
quite inadequate to account for the
change. All that we can say of the un-
satisfactory nature of confessions under
torture, of the instances of imposture that
were occasionally discovered, of the malicious motives that may have actuated
some of the accusers, might have been
said during the darkest periods of the
middle ages. The multiplication of
books and the increase of knowledge can
have added nothing to these obvious
arguments. Those who lived when the
evidences of witchcraft existed in profusion, and attracted the attention of all
classes, and of all grades of intellect,
must surely have been as competent
judges as ourselves, if the question was
merely a question of evidence. The
gradual cessation of the accusations was
the consequence, and not the cause, of
the scepticism. The progress of medical
knowledge may have had considerable
influence on the private opinions of some
writers on the subject, but it was never
influential upon the public mind, or made
the battle ground of the controversy.
Indeed, the philosophy of madness is
mainly due to Pinel, who wrote long after
the superstition had vanished ; and even
if witchcraft had been treated as a disease,
this would not have destroyed the belief
that it was Satanic, in an age when all
the more startling diseases were deemed
supernatural, and when theologians
maintained that Satan frequently acted
by the employment of natural laws. One
discovery, it is true, was made during the
discussion, which attracted great attention, and was much insisted on by the
opponents of the laws against sorcery.
It was, that the word translated " witch "
in the Levitical condemnation may be
translated " poisoner." [1] This discovery
in itself is, however, obviously insufficient

---

[1] This was first, I believe, asserted by Wier. In
England it was much maintained during the reign of
Charles II. The other side of the question was sup-
ported on the Continent by Bodin, and in England by
Glanvil, More, Casaubon, &c.

to account for the change. It does not affect the enormous mass of evidence of the workings of witchcraft, which was once supposed to have placed the belief above the possibility of doubt. It does not affect such passages as the history of the witch of Endor, or of the demoniacs in the New Testament, to which the believers in witchcraft triumphantly appealed. Assuming the existence of witches—assuming that there were really certain persons who were constantly engaged in inflicting, by diabolical agency, every form of evil on their neighbours, and whose machinations destroyed countless lives—there can be no doubt that these persons should be punished with death, altogether irrespectively of any distinct command. The truth is, that the existence of witchcraft was disbelieved before the scriptural evidence of it was questioned. A disbelief in ghosts and witches was one of the most prominent characteristics of scepticism in the seventeenth century. At first it was nearly confined to men who were avowedly freethinkers, but gradually it spread over a wider circle, and included almost all the educated, with the exception of a large proportion of the clergy. This progress, however, was not effected by any active propagandism. It is not identified with any great book or with any famous writer. It was not the triumph of one series of arguments over another. On the contrary, no facts are more clearly established in the literature of witchcraft than that the movement was mainly silent, unargumentative, and insensible; that men came gradually to disbelieve in witchcraft, because they came gradually to look upon it as absurd; and that this new tone of thought appeared, first of all, in those who were least subject to theological influences, and soon spread through the educated laity, and last of all took possession of the clergy.

It may be stated, I believe, as an invariable truth, that, whenever a religion which rests in a great measure on a system of terrorism, and which paints in dark and forcible colours the misery of men and the power of evil spirits, is intensely realised, it will engender the belief in witchcraft or magic. The panic which its teachings will create, will overbalance the faculties of multitudes. The awful images of evil spirits of superhuman power, and of untiring malignity, will continually haunt the imagination. They will blend with the illusions of age or sorrow or sickness, and will appear with an especial vividness in the more alarming and unexplained phenomena of nature.

This consideration will account for the origin of the conception of magic in those ages when belief is almost exclusively the work of the imagination. At a much later period, the same vivid realisation of diabolical presence will operate powerfully on the conclusions of the reason. We have now passed so completely out of the modes of thought which predominated in the sixteenth and seventeenth centuries, and we are so firmly convinced of the unreality of witchcraft, that it is only by a strong effort of the imagination that we can realise the position of the defenders of the belief. Yet it is, I think, difficult to examine the subject with impartiality, without coming to the conclusion that the historical evidence establishing the reality of witchcraft is so vast and so varied, that nothing but our overwhelming sense of its antecedent improbability and our modern experience of the manner in which it has faded away under the influence of civilisation can justify us in despising it. The defenders of the belief, who were often men of great and distinguished talent, maintained that there was no fact in all history more fully attested, and that to reject it would be to strike at the root of all historical evidence of the miraculous. The belief implied the continual occurrence of acts of the most extraordinary and impressive character, and of such a nature as to fall strictly within human cognisance. The subject, as we have seen, was examined in tens of thousands of cases, in almost every country in Europe, by tribunals which included the acutest lawyers and ecclesiastics of the age, on the scene and at the time when the alleged acts had taken place, and with the assistance of innumerable sworn witnesses. The judges had no motive whatever to desire the condemnation of the accused; and, as conviction would be followed by a fearful death, they had the strongest motives to exercise their power with caution and deliberation. The whole force of public opinion was directed constantly and earnestly to the question for many centuries; and, although there was some controversy concerning the details of witchcraft, the fact of its existence was long considered undoubted.

The evidence is essentially cumulative. Some cases may be explained by monomania, others by imposture, others by chance coincidences, and others by optical delusions; but, when we consider the multitudes of strange statements that were sworn and registered in legal documents, it is very difficult to frame a general rationalistic explanation which will not involve an extreme improbability. In our own day, it may be said with confidence, that it would be altogether impossible for such an amount of evidence to accumulate round a conception which had no substantial basis in fact. The ages in which witchcraft flourished were, it is true, grossly credulous; and to this fact we attribute the belief, yet we do not reject their testimony on all matters of secular history. If we considered witchcraft probable, a hundredth part of the evidence we possess would have placed it beyond the region of doubt. If it were a natural but a very improbable fact, our reluctance to believe it would have been completely stifled by the multiplicity of the proofs.

Now, it is evident that the degree of improbability we attach to histories of witches, will depend, in a great measure, upon our doctrine concerning evil spirits, and upon the degree in which that doctrine is realised. If men believe that invisible beings, of superhuman power, restless activity, and intense malignity, are perpetually haunting the world, and directing all their energies to the temptation and the persecution of mankind; if they believe that, in past ages, these spirits have actually governed the bodily functions of men, worked miracles, and foretold future events—if all this is believed, not with the dull and languid assent of custom, but with an intensely realised, living, and operative assurance; if it presents itself to the mind and imagination as a vivid truth, exercising that influence over the reason, and occupying that prominence in the thoughts of men, which its importance would demand, the antecedent improbability of witchcraft would appear far less than if this doctrine was rejected or was unrealised. When, therefore, we find a growing disposition to reject every history which involves diabolical intervention as intrinsically absurd, independently of any examination of the evidence on which it rests, we may infer from this fact the declining realisation of the doctrine of evil spirits.

These two considerations will serve, I think, to explain the history of witchcraft, and also to show its great significance and importance as an index of the course of civilisation. To follow out the subject into details would require a far greater space than I can assign to it, but I hope to be able to show, sufficiently, what have been the leading phases through which the belief has passed.

In the ruder forms of savage life, we find the belief in witchcraft universal;[1] and accompanied, in most instances, by features of peculiar atrocity. The reason of this is obvious. Terror is everywhere the beginning of religion. The phenomena which impress themselves most forcibly on the mind of the savage are not those which enter manifestly into the sequence of natural laws and which are productive of most beneficial effects, but those which are disastrous and apparently abnormal. Gratitude is less vivid than fear, and the smallest apparent infraction of a natural law produces a deeper impression than the most sublime of its ordinary operations. When, therefore, the more startling and terrible aspects of nature are presented to his mind; when the more deadly forms of disease or natural convulsion desolate his land, the savage derives from these things an intensely realised perception of diabolical presence. In the darkness of the night; amid the yawning chasms and the wild echoes of the mountain gorge; under the blaze of the comet, or the solemn gloom of the eclipse; when famine has blasted the land; when the earthquake and the pestilence have slaughtered their thousands; in every form of disease which refracts and distorts the reason; in all that is strange, portentous, and deadly, he feels and cowers before the supernatural. Completely exposed to all the influences of nature, and completely ignorant of the chain of sequence that unites its various parts, he lives in continual dread of what he deems the direct and isolated acts of evil spirits. Feeling them continually near him, he will naturally endeavour to enter into communion with them. He will strive to propitiate them with gifts. If some great calamity has fallen upon him, or if some vengeful passion has mastered his reason, he will attempt to invest himself with their authority; and his excited imagination will soon

[1] On the universality of the belief, see Herder, *Philosophy of History*, b. viii. c. 2; Maury, *Histoire de la Magie, passim.*

persuade him that he has succeeded in his desire. If his abilities and his ambition place him above the common level, he will find in this belief the most ready path to power. By professing to hold communion with and to control super-natural beings, he can exercise an almost boundless influence over those about him; and, among men who are intensely pre-disposed to believe in the supernatural, a very little dexterity or acquaintance with natural laws will support his pretensions. By converting the terror which some great calamity has produced into anger against an alleged sorcerer, he can at the same time take a signal vengeance upon those who have offended him, and in-crease the sense of his own importance. Those whose habits, or appearance, or knowledge, separate them from the multitude, will be naturally suspected of communicating with evil spirits; and this suspicion will soon become a cer-tainty, if any mental disease should aggravate their peculiarities. In this manner the influences of ignorance, imagination, and imposture will blend and co-operate in creating a belief in witchcraft, and in exciting a hatred against those who are suspected of its practice, commensurate with the terror they inspire.

In a more advanced stage of civilisa-tion, the fear of witches will naturally fade, as the habits of artificial life remove men from those influences which act upon the imagination, and as increasing know-ledge explains some of the more alarming phenomena of nature. The belief, how-ever, that it is possible, by supernatural agency, to inflict evil upon mankind, was general in ancient Greece and Rome; and St. Augustine assures us that all the sects of philosophers admitted it, with the exception of the Epicureans, who denied the existence of evil spirits. The Decem-virs passed a law condemning magicians to death. A similar law was early enacted in Greece; and, in the days of Demosthenes, a sorceress named Lamia was actually executed.[1] The philosophy of Plato, by greatly aggrandising the sphere of the spiritual, did much to foster the belief; and we find that whenever, either before or after the Christian era, that philosophy has been in the ascen-dant, it has been accompanied by a ten-dency to magic. Besides this, the

ancient civilisations were never directed earnestly to the investigation of natural phenomena; and the progress made in this respect was, in consequence, very small. On the whole, however, the per-secution seems to have been, in those countries, almost entirely free from reli-gious fanaticism. The magician was punished because he injured man, and not because he offended God.

In one respect, during the latter period of Pagan Rome, the laws against magic seem to have revived, and to have taken a somewhat different form, without, how-ever, representing any phase of a reli-gious movement, but simply a political requirement. Under the head of magic were comprised some astrological and other methods of foretelling the future; and it was found that these practices had a strong tendency to foster conspiracies against the emperors. The soothsayer often assured persons that they were destined to assume the purple, and in that way stimulated them to rebellion. By casting the horoscope of the reigning emperor, he had ascertained, according to the popular belief, the period in which the government might be assailed with most prospect of success; and had thus proved a constant cause of agitation. Some of the forms of magic had also been lately imported into the empire from Greece, and were therefore repugnant to the conservative spirit that was dominant. Several of the emperors, in consequence, passed edicts against the magicians, which were executed with considerable though somewhat spasmodic energy.[1] But, although magicians were occasion-ally persecuted, it is not to be inferred from this that everything that was com-prised under the name of magic was con-sidered morally wrong. On the contrary, many of the systems of divination formed an integral part of religion. Some of the more public modes of foretelling the future, such as the oracles of the gods, were still retained and honoured; and a law, which made divination concerning the future of the emperor high treason, shows clearly the spirit in which the others were suppressed. The emperors desired to monopolise the knowledge of the future, and consequently drew many astrologers to their courts, while they

[1] Pausanias.

[1] This very obscure branch of the subject has been most admirably treated by Maury, *Histoire de la Magie* (Paris, 1860), pp. 78-85. An extremely learned and able work, from which I have derived great assistance.

banished them from other parts of the kingdom.[1] They were so far from attaching the idea of sacrilege to practices which enabled them to foretell coming events, that Marcus Aurelius and Julian, who were both passionately attached to their religion, and who were among the best men who have ever sat upon a throne, were among the most ardent of the patrons of the magicians.

Such was the somewhat anomalous position of the magicians in the last days of Pagan Rome, and it acquires a great interest from its bearing on the policy of the Christian emperors.

When the Christians were first scattered through the Roman empire, they naturally looked upon this question with a very different spirit from that of the heathen. Inspired by an intense religious enthusiasm, which they were nobly sealing with their blood, they thought much less of the civil than of the religious consequences of magic, and sacrilege seemed much more terrible in their eyes than anarchy. Their position, acting upon some of their distinctive doctrines, had filled them with a sense of Satanic presence, which must have shadowed every portion of their belief, and have predisposed them to discover diabolical influence in every movement of the pagan. The fearful conception of eternal punishment, adopted in its most material form, had flashed with its full intensity upon their minds. They believed that this was the destiny of all who were beyond the narrow circle of their Church, and that their persecutors were doomed to agonies of especial poignancy. The whole world was divided between the kingdom of God and the kingdom of Satan. The persecuted Church represented the first, the persecuting world the second. In every scoff that was directed against their creed, in every edict that menaced their persons, in every interest that opposed their progress, they perceived the direct and immediate action of the devil. They found a great and ancient religion subsisting around them. Its gorgeous rites, its traditions, its priests, and its miracles, had pre-occupied the public mind, and presented what seemed at first an insuperable barrier to their mission. In this religion they saw the especial workmanship of the devil, and their strong predisposition to interpret every event by

a miraculous standard persuaded them that all its boasted prodigies were real. Nor did they find any difficulty in explaining them. The world they believed to be full of malignant demons, who had in all ages persecuted and deluded mankind. From the magicians of Egypt to the demoniacs of the New Testament, their power had been continually manifested. In the chosen land they could only persecute and afflict; but, among the heathen, they possessed supreme power, and were universally worshipped as divine.

This doctrine, which was the natural consequence of the intellectual condition of the age, acting upon the belief in evil spirits, and upon the scriptural accounts of diabolical intervention, had been still further strengthened by those Platonic theories which, in their Alexandrian form, had so profoundly influenced the early teachings of the Church.[1] According to these theories, the immediate objects of the devotions of the pagan world were subsidiary spirits of finite power and imperfect morality—angels, or, as they were then called, demons—who acted the part of mediators ; and who, by the permission of the supreme and inaccessible Deity, regulated the religious government of mankind. In this manner a compromise was effected between monotheism and polytheism. The religion of the state was true and lawful, but it was not irreconcilable with pure theism. The Christians had adopted this conception of subsidiary spirits ; but they maintained them to be not the willing agents, but the adversaries, of the Deity ; and the word demon, which, among the pagans, signified only a spirit below the level of a Divinity, among the Christians signified a devil.

This notion seems to have existed in the very earliest period of Christianity ; and, in the second century, we find it elaborated with the most minute and detailed care. Tertullian, who wrote in that century, assures us that the world was full of these evil spirits, whose influence might be descried in every portion of the pagan creed. Some of them belonged to that band of rebels who had been precipitated with Satan into the abyss. Others were

---

[1] Maury, ch. iv.

[1] On the doctrine of the demons, in its relation to heathen worship, see the chapter on Neo-Platonism in Maury, and the curious argument based on the Platonic theory, which occupies the greater part of the eighth book of the *De Civitate Dei*.

the angels who, in the antediluvian world, had become attached to the daughters of men ; and who, having taught them to dye wool, and to commit the still more fearful offence of painting their faces, had been justly doomed to eternal suffering.[1] These were now seeking in every way to thwart the purposes of the Almighty, and their especial delight was to attract to themselves the worship which was due to Him alone. Not only the more immoral deities of heathenism, not only such divinities as Venus, or Mars, or Mercury, or Pluto, but also those who appeared the most pure, were literally and undoubtedly diabolical. Minerva, the personification of wisdom, was a devil, and so was Diana, the type of chastity, and so was Jupiter, the heathen conception of the Most High. The spirits who were worshipped under the names of departed heroes, and who were supposed to have achieved so many acts of splendid and philanthropic heroism, were all devils who had assumed the names of the dead. The same condemnation was passed upon those bright creations of a poetic fancy, the progenitors of the mediæval fairies, the nymphs and dryads who peopled every grove and hallowed every stream.[2] The air was filled with unholy legions,[3] and the traditions of every land were replete with their exploits. The immortal lamp, which burnt with an unfading splendour in the temple of Venus ; the household gods that were transported by invisible hands through the air ; the miracles which clustered so thickly around the vestal virgins, the oracular shrines, and the centres of Roman power, were all attestations of their presence. Under the names of Sylvans and Fauns, and Dusii,

they had not only frequently appeared among mankind, but had made innumerable women the objects of their passion. This fact was so amply attested, that it appears impudence to deny it.[1] Persons possessed with devils were constantly liberated by the Christians, and tombs of the exorcists have been discovered in the catacombs. If a Christian in any respect deviated from the path of duty, a visible manifestation of the devil sometimes appeared to terrify him. A Christian lady, in a fit of thoughtless dissipation, went to the theatre, and at the theatre she became possessed with a devil. The exorcist remonstrated with the evil spirit on the presumption of its act. The devil replied apologetically that it had found the woman in its house.[2] The rites of

---

[1] *De Cultu Fœminarum*, lib. i. c. 2. This curious notion is given on the authority of the prophecy of Enoch, which was thought by some—and Tertullian seems to have inclined to their opinion—to be authoritative Scripture. St. Augustine suggests that the "angels" who were attached to the antediluvians were possibly devils—incubi, as they were called—and that the word angel in the writings attributed to Enoch, and in all parts of Scripture, signifying only messenger, may be applied to any spirit, good or bad (*De Civ. Dei,* lib. xv. cap. 23). This rule of interpretation had, as we shall see, an important influence on the later theology of witchcraft.

[2] Much the same notions were long after held about the fairies. A modern French writer states, that till near the middle of the eighteenth century, a mass was annually celebrated in the Abbey of Poissy, for the preservation of the nuns from their power (Des Mousseaux, *Pratiques des Démons,* p. 81.)

[3] One sect of heretics of the fourth century—the Messalians—went so far as to make spitting a religious exercise, in hopes of thus casting out the devils they inhaled. (Maury, p. 317.)

[1] "Hoc negare impudentiæ videatur" (St. Aug. *De Civ. Dei,* lib. xv. cap. 23). The Saint, however, proceeds to say, "Non hic aliquid audeo temere definire." See also Justin Martyr, Ap. c. v. The same notion was perpetuated through the succeeding ages, and marriage with devils was long one of the most ordinary accusations in the witch trials. The devils who appeared in the female form were generally called succubi ; those who appeared like men, incubi (though this distinction was not always preserved). The former were comparatively rare, but Bodin mentions a priest who had commerce with one for more than forty years, and another priest who found a faithful mistress in a devil for half a century: they were both burnt alive (*Démonomanie des Sorciers,* p. 107). Luther was a firm believer in this intercourse (*Ibid*). The incubi were much more common ; and hundreds, perhaps thousands, of women have been burnt on account of the belief in them. It was observed that they had a peculiar attachment to women with beautiful hair ; and it was an old Catholic belief that St. Paul alluded to this in that somewhat curious passage, in which he exhorts women to cover their heads because of the "angels" (Sprenger, *Mall Mal.* Pars i. Quæst. 4 ; and Pars ii. Quæst. 2). The incubi generally had no children, but there were some exceptions to this rule, for Nider the inquisitor assures us that the island of Cyprus was entirely peopled by their sons (*Mall. Malifi.* p. 522), and a similar parentage was ascribed to the Huns. The ordinary phenomenon of nightmare, as the name imports, was associated with this belief (see a curious passage in Bodin, p. 109). The Dusii, whose exploits St. Augustine mentions, were Celtic spirits, and are the origin of our "Deuce" (Maury, p. 189). For the much more cheerful views of the Cabalists, and other secret societies of the middle ages, concerning the intercourse of philosophers with sylphs, salamanders, etc., see that very curious and amusing book, *Le Comte de Gabalis, ou Entretiens sur les Sciences secrètes* (Paris, 1671). Lilith, the first wife of Adam, concerning whom the Rabbinical traditions are so full, who was said to suck the blood of infants, and from whose name the word lullaby (Lili Abi) is supposed by some to have been derived, was long regarded as the queen of the succubi (Plancey, *Dict. inf.,* art. *Lilith*). The Greeks believed that nightmare resulted from the presence of a demon named Ephialtes.

[2] Tertullian, *De Spectaculis,* cap. xxvi. Another woman, this writer assures us, having gone to see an actor, dreamed all the following night of a winding-sheet, and heard the actor's name ringing, with frightful reproaches, in her ears. To pass to a much later period, St. Gregory the Great, in the sixth century, mentions a nun who, when walking in a garden, began to eat without making the sign of the

paganism had in some degree pervaded all departments of life, and all were therefore tainted with diabolical influence. In the theatre, in the circus, in the market-place, in all the public festivals, there was something which manifested their presence. A Christian soldier, on one occasion, refused even to wear a festal crown, because laurels had been originally dedicated to Bacchus and Venus; and endured severe punishment rather than comply with the custom. Much discussion was elicited by the transaction, but Tertullian wrote a treatise[1] maintaining that the martyr had only complied with his strict duty.

The terror which such a doctrine must have spread among the early Christians may be easily conceived. They seemed to breathe an atmosphere of miracles. Wherever they turned they were surrounded and beleaguered by malicious spirits, who were perpetually manifesting their presence by supernatural acts. Watchful fiends stood beside every altar; they mingled with every avocation of life, and the Christians were the special objects of their hatred. All this was universally believed; and it was realised with an intensity which, in this secular age, we can scarcely conceive. It was realised as men realise religious doctrines, when they have devoted to them the undivided energies of their lives, and when their faith has been intensified in the furnace of persecution.

The bearing of this view upon the conception of magic is very obvious. Among the more civilised pagans, as we have seen, magic was mainly a civil, and in the last days of the empire, mainly a political, crime. In periods of great political insecurity it assumed considerable importance; at other periods it fell completely into the background. Its relation to the prevailing religion was exceedingly indeterminate, and it comprised many rites that were not regarded as in any degree immoral. In the early Church, on the other hand, it was esteemed the most horrible form of sacrilege effected by the direct agency of evil spirits. It included the whole system of paganism, explained all its prodigies, and gave a fearful significance to all its legends. It

assumed, in consequence, an extraordinary importance in the patristic teaching; and acted strongly and continually on the imaginations of the people.

When the Church obtained the direction of the civil power, she soon modified or abandoned the tolerant maxims she had formerly inculcated; and, in the course of a few years, restrictive laws were enacted, both against the Jews and against the heretics. It appears, however, that the multitude of pagans, in the time of Constantine, was still so great, and the zeal of the emperor so languid, that he at first shrank from directing his laws openly and avowedly against the old faith, and an ingenious expedient was devised for sapping it at its base, under the semblance of the ancient legislation. Magic, as I have said, among the Romans, included, not only those appeals to evil spirits, and those modes of inflicting evil on others, which had always been denounced as sacrilegious, but also certain methods of foretelling the future, which were not regarded as morally wrong, but only as politically dangerous. This latter department formed an offshoot of the established religion, and had never been separated from it with precision. The laws had been devised for the purpose of preventing rebellions or imposition, and they had been executed in that spirit. The Christian emperors revived these laws, and enforced them with extreme severity, but directed them against the religion of the pagans.[1] At first, that secret magic which the decemvirs had prohibited, but which had afterwards come into general use, was alone condemned; but, in the course of a few reigns, the circle of legislation expanded, till it included the whole system of paganism.

Almost immediately after his conversion, Constantine enacted an extremely severe law against secret magic. He decreed that any aruspex who entered into the house of a citizen, for the purpose of celebrating his rites, should be burnt alive, the property of his employers confiscated, and the accuser rewarded.[2] Two years later, however, a proclamation was issued which considerably attenuated the

---

cross. She had bitter cause to repent of her indecent haste, for she immediately swallowed a devil in a lettuce (*Dialogi*, lib. i. c. 4). The whole passage, which is rather long for quotation, is extremely curious.
[1] *De Coronâ.*

[1] The history of this movement has been traced with masterly ability by Maury, *Sur la Magie*, and also by Beugnot, *Destruction du Paganisme dans l'Occident.*
[2] *Codex Theodosianus*, lib. ix. tit. xvi. c. 1, 2. The pagan historian Zosimus observes, that when Constantine had abandoned his country's gods, "he made this beginning of impiety, that he looked with

force of this enactment, for it declared that it was not the intention of the Emperor to prohibit magical rites, which were designed to discover remedies for diseases, or to protect the harvests from hail, snow, or tempests.[1]

This partial tolerance continued till the death of Constantine, but completely passed away under his successor. Constantius appears to have been governed by far stronger convictions than his father. He had embraced the Arian heresy, and is said to have been much influenced by the Arian priests; and he directed his laws with a stern and almost passionate eagerness against the forms of magic which verged most closely upon the pagan worship. At the beginning of one of these laws, he complained that many had been producing tempests, and destroying the lives of their enemies by the assistance of the demons, and he proceeded to prohibit in the sternest manner, and under pain of the severest penalties, every kind of magic. All who attempted to foretell the future—the augurs, as well as the more irregular diviners—were emphatically condemned. Magicians who were captured in Rome were to be thrown to the wild beasts; and those who were seized in the provinces to be put to excruciating torments, and at last crucified. If they persisted in denying their crime, their flesh was to be torn from their bones with hooks of iron.[2] These fearful penalties were directed against those who practised rites which had long been universal; and which, if they were not regarded as among the obligations, were, at least, among the highest privileges of paganism. It has been observed as a significant fact, that in this reign the title "enemies of the human race," which the old pagan laws had applied to the

Christians, and which proved so effectual in exasperating the popular mind, was transferred to the magicians.[1]

The task of the Christian emperors in combating magic was, in truth, one of the most difficult that can be conceived; and all the penalties that Roman barbarity could devise, were unable to destroy practices which were the natural consequence of the prevailing credulity. As long as men believed that they could easily ascertain the future, it was quite certain that curiosity would at length overpower fear. As long as they believed that a few simple rites could baffle their enemies, and enable them to achieve their most cherished desires, they would most unquestionably continue to practise them. Priests might formulate their anathemas, and emperors multiply their penalties; but scepticism, and not terrorism, was the one corrective for the evil. This scepticism was nowhere to be found. The populace never questioned for a moment the efficacy of magic. The pagan philosophers were all infatuated by the dreams of Neo-Platonism, and were writing long books on the mysteries of Egypt, the hierarchy of spirits, and their intercourse with men. The Fathers, it is true, vehemently denounced magic, but they never seem to have had the faintest suspicion that it was a delusion. If Christianity had nothing to oppose to the fascination of these forbidden rites, it would have been impossible to prevent the immense majority of the people from reverting to them; but, by a very natural process, a series of conceptions were rapidly introduced into theology, which formed what may be termed a rival system of magic, in which the talismanic virtues of holy water, and of Christian ceremonies, became a kind of counterpoise to the virtue of unlawful charms. It is very remarkable, however, that, while these sacred talismans were indefinitely multiplied, the other great fascination of magic, the power of predicting the future, was never claimed by the Christian clergy. If the theory of the writers of the eighteenth century had

---

contempt on the art of foretelling" (lib. ii. c. 29); and Eusebius classifies his prohibition of prophecy with the measures directed openly against paganism (*Vita Const.* lib. i. c. 16).

[1] *Cod. Th.* lib. ix. t. xvi. l. 3.

[2] *Cod. Th.* lib. ix. t. xvi. l. 4, 5, 6. The language is curious and very peremptory—thus, we read in law 4: "Nemo haruspicem cosnulat, aut mathematicum, nemo hariolum. Augurum et vatum prava confessio conticescat. Chaldæi ac magi et ceteri quos maleficos ob facinorum magnitudinem vulgus appellat, nec ad hanc partem aliquid moliantur. Sileat omnibus perpetuo divinandi curiositas: etenim supplicium, capitis feret gladio ultore prostratus quicunque jussis obsequium denegaverit." Another law (6) concludes: "Si convictus ad proprium facinus detegentibus repugnaverit pernegando sit eculeo deditus, ungulisque sulcantibus latera perferat pœnas proprio dignas facinore." On the nature of the punishments that were employed, compare the Commentary on the law, in Ritter's edition (Leipsic, 1738), and Beugnot, tom. i. p. 143.

[1] Beugnot, tom. i. p. 148. On these laws, M. Maury well says: "De la sorte se trouvaient atteints les ministres du polythéisme les plus en crédit, les pratiques qui inspiraient à la superstition le plus de confiance.....Bien des gens ne se souciaient plus de rendre aux dieux le culte légal et consacré; mais les oracles, les augures, les présages, presque tous les païens y recouraient avec confiance, et leur en enlever la possibilité c'était les dépouiller de ce qui faisait leur consolation et leur joie" (pp. 117, 118).

been correct; if the superstitions that culminated in mediævalism had been simply the result of the knavery of the clergy; this would most certainly not have been the case. The Christian priests, like all other priests, would have pandered to the curiosity which was universal, and something analogous to the ancient oracles or auguries would have been incorporated into the Church. Nothing of this kind took place, because the change which passed over theology was the result, not of imposture, but of a normal development. No part of Christianity had a tendency to develop into an oracular system : and had such a system arisen, it would have been the result of deliberate fraud. On the other hand, there were many conceptions connected with the faith, especially concerning the efficacy of baptismal water, which, under the pressure of a materialising age, passed, by an easy and natural, if not legitimate transition, into a kind of fetishism, assimilating with the magical notions that were so universally diffused.

St. Jerome, in his life of St. Hilarion, relates a miracle of that saint which refers to a period a few years after the death of Constantius, and which shows clearly the position that Christian ceremonies began to occupy with reference to magic. It appears that a Christian, named Italicus, was accustomed to race horses against the pagan duumvir of Gaza, and that this latter personage invariably gained the victory, by means of magical rites, which stimulated his own horses, and paralysed those of his opponent. The Christian, in despair, had recourse to St. Hilarion. The saint appears to have been, at first, somewhat startled at the application, and rather shrank from participating actively in horse racing; but Italicus at last persuaded him that the cause was worthy of his intervention, and obtained a bowl of water which Hilarion himself had consecrated, and which was therefore endowed with a peculiar virtue. At length the day of the races arrived. The chariots were placed side by side, and the spectators thronged the circus. As the signal for the start was given, Italicus sprinkled his horses with the holy water. Immediately the chariot of the Christian flew with a supernatural rapidity to the goal ; while the horses of his adversary faltered and staggered, as if they had been struck by an invisible hand. The circus rang with

wild cries of wonder, of joy, or of anger. Some called for the death of the Christian magician, but many others abandoned paganism in consequence of the miracle.[1]

The persecution which Constantius directed against the magicians was of course suspended under Julian, whose spirit of toleration, when we consider the age he lived in, the provocations he endured, and the intense religious zeal he manifested, is one of the most remarkable facts in history. He was passionately devoted to those forms of magic which the pagan religion admitted, and his palace was always thronged with magicians. The consultation of the entrails, which Constantius had forbidden, was renewed at the coronation of Julian ; and it was reported among the Christians, that they presented, on that occasion, the form of a cross, surmounted by a crown.[2] During the short reign of Jovian, the same tolerance seems to have continued ; but Valentinian renewed the persecution, and made another law against "impious prayers and midnight sacrifices," which were still offered.[3] This law excited so much discontent in Greece, where it was directly opposed to the established religion, that Valentinian consented to its remaining inoperative in that province ; but, in other portions of the Empire, fearful scenes of suffering and persecution were everywhere witnessed.[4] In the East, Valens was persecuting, with impartial zeal, all who did not adopt the tenets of the Arian heresy. "The very name of philosopher," as it has been said, became " a title of proscription ;" and the most trivial offences were visited with death. One philosopher was executed, because, in a private letter, he had exhorted his wife not to forget to crown the portal of the door. An old woman perished, because she endeavoured to allay the paroxysms of a fever by magical songs. A young man, who imagined that he could cure an attack of diarrhœa by touching alternately a marble pillar and his body, while he repeated the

---

[1] *Vita Sancti Hilarionis*. This miracle is related by Beugnot. The whole life of St. Hilarion is crowded with prodigies that illustrate the view taken in the text. Besides curing about two hundred persons in a little more than a month, driving away serpents, &c., we find the saint producing rain with the same facility as the later witches.
[2] St. Gregory Nazianzen (3rd Oration against Julian).
[3] *Cod. Th.* lib. ix. t. xvi. l. 7, &c.
[4] Maury, pp. 118, 119.

vowels, expiated this not very alarming superstition by torture and by death.[1]

In reviewing these persecutions, which were directed by the orthodox and by the Arians against magicians, we must carefully guard against some natural exaggerations. It would be very unfair to attribute directly to the leaders of the Church the edicts that produced them. It would be still more unfair to attribute to them the spirit in which those edicts were executed. Much allowance must be made for the personal barbarity of certain emperors and prefects; for the rapacity that made them seek for pretexts by which they might confiscate the property of the wealthy; and for the alarm that was created by every attempt to discover the successor to the throne. We have positive evidence that one or other of these three causes was connected with most of the worst outbursts of persecution, and we know, from earlier history, that persecutions for magic had taken place on political as well as on religious grounds, long before Christianity had triumphed. We must not, again, measure the severity of the persecution by the precise language of the laws. If we looked simply at the written enactments, we should conclude that a considerable portion of the pagan worship was, at an early period, absolutely and universally suppressed. In practice, however, the law was constantly broken. A general laxity of administration had pervaded all parts of the empire, to an extent which the weakest modern governments have seldom exhibited. Popular prejudice ran counter to many of the enactments; and the rulers frequently connived at their infraction. We find, therefore, that the application of the penalties that were decreed was irregular, fitful, and uncertain. Sometimes they were enforced with extreme severity. Sometimes the forbidden rites were practised without disguise. Very frequently, in one part of the empire, persecution raged fiercely, while in another part it was unknown. When, however, all these qualifying circumstances have been admitted, it remains clear that a series of laws were directed against rites which were entirely innocuous, and which had been long universally practised, as parts of the pagan worship, for the purpose of sapping the religion from which they sprang. It

is also clear that the ecclesiastical leaders all believed in the reality of magic; and that they had vastly increased the popular sense of its enormity, by attributing to all the pagan rites a magical character. Under Theodosius, this phase of the history of magic terminated. In the beginning of his reign, that emperor contented himself with reiterating the proclamations of his predecessors; but he soon cast off all disguise, and prohibited, under the severest penalties, every portion of the pagan worship.

Such was the policy pursued by the early Church towards the magicians. It exercised in some respects a very important influence upon later history. In the first place, a mass of tradition was formed which, in later ages, placed the reality of the crime above the possibility of doubt. In the second place, the nucleus of fact, around which the fables of the inquisitors were accumulated, was considerably enlarged. By a curious, but very natural transition, a great portion of the old pagan worship passed from the sphere of religion into that of magic. The country people continued, in secrecy and danger, to practise the rites of their forefathers. They were told that, by those rites, they were appealing to powerful and malicious spirits; and, after several generations, they came to believe what they were told; without, however, abandoning the practices that were condemned. It is easier for superstitious men, in a superstitious age, to change all the notions that are associated with their rites, than to free their minds from their influence. Religions never truly perish, except by a natural decay. In the towns, paganism had arrived at the last stage of decrepitude, when Christianity arose; and, therefore, in the towns, the victory of Christianity was prompt and decisive; but, in the country, paganism still retained its vigour, and defied all the efforts of priests and magistrates to eradicate it. The invasion of the barbarians still further strengthened the pagan element, and at last a kind of compromise was effected. Paganism, as a distinct system, was annihilated, but its different elements continued to exist in a transfigured form, and under new names. Many portions of the system were absorbed by the new faith. They coalesced with the doctrines to which they bore most resemblance, gave those doctrines an extraordinary prominence in

[1] Ammianus Marcellinus, lib. xxix. c. 1, 2.

the Christian system, and rendered them peculiarly acceptable and influential. Antiquarians have long since shown that, in almost every part of the Roman Catholic faith, the traces of this amalgamation may be detected. Another portion of paganism became a kind of excrescence upon recognised Christianity. It assumed the form of innumerable superstitious rites, which occupied an equivocal position, sometimes countenanced, and sometimes condemned, hovering upon the verge of the faith, associated and intertwined with authorised religious practices, occasionally censured by councils, and habitually encouraged by the more ignorant ecclesiastics, and frequently attracting a more intense devotion than the regular ceremonies with which they were allied.[1] A third portion continued in the form of magical rites, which were practised in defiance of persecution and anathemas, and which continued, after the nominal suppression of paganism, for nearly eight centuries.[2] These rites, of course, only form *one* element, and perhaps not a very prominent one, in the system of witchcraft; but any analysis which omitted to notice them would be imperfect. All those grotesque ceremonies which Shakspeare portrayed in *Macbeth* were taken from the old paganism. In numbers of the description of the witches' sabbath, Diana and Herodias are mentioned together, as the two most prominent figures; and among the articles of accusation brought against witches, we find enumerated many of the old practices of the augurs.

In the sixth century, the victory of Christianity over paganism, considered as an external system, and the corruption of Christianity itself, were both complete; and what are justly termed the dark ages may be said to have begun. It seems, at first sight, a somewhat strange and anomalous fact that, during the period which elapsed between the sixth and the thirteenth centuries, when superstitions were most numerous, and credulity most universal, the executions for sorcery should have been comparatively rare. There never had been a time in which the minds of men were more completely imbued and moulded by supernatural conceptions, or in which the sense of Satanic power and Satanic presence was more profound and universal. Many thousands of cases of possession, exorcisms, miracles, and apparitions of the Evil One were recorded. They were accepted without the faintest doubt, and had become the habitual field upon which the imagination expatiated. There was scarcely a great saint who had not, on some occasion, encountered a visible manifestation of an evil spirit. Sometimes the devil appeared as a grotesque and hideous animal, sometimes as a black man, sometimes as a beautiful woman, sometimes as a priest haranguing in the pulpit, sometimes as an angel of light, and sometimes in a still holier form.[1] Yet, strange as it may now appear, these conceptions, though intensely believed and intensely realised, did not create any great degree of terrorism. The very multiplication of superstitions had proved their corrective. It was firmly believed that the arch-fiend was for ever hovering about the Christian; but it was also believed, that the sign of the cross, or a few drops of holy water, or the name of Mary, could put him to an immediate and ignominious flight. The lives of the saints were crowded with his devices, but they represented him as uniformly vanquished, humbled, and contemned. Satan himself, at the command of Cyprian, had again and again assailed an unarmed and ignorant maiden, who had devoted herself to religion. He had exhausted all the powers of sophistry, in obscuring the virtue of virginity; and all the resources of archangelic eloquence, in favour of a young and noble pagan who aspired to the maiden's hand; but the simple sign of the cross exposed every sophism, quenched every emotion of terrestrial love, and drove back the fiend, baffled and dismayed, to the magician who had sent him.[2] Legions of devils, drawn up in ghastly array, surrounded the church towards which St. Maur was moving, and obstructed, with menacing gestures, the progress of the saint; but a few words of exorcism scattered them in

---

[1] Many hundreds of these superstitions are examined by Thiers. A great number also are given in Scott's *Discovery of Witchcraft*.
[2] Michelet (*La Sorcière*, p. 36, *note*). See also Maury.

[1] On the appearances of the devil in the form of Christ, see the tract by Gerson in the *Malleus Malef.* (vol. ii. p. 77); and also Ignatius Lupus, in *Edict. S. Inquisitionis* (1603), p. 185.
[2] See this story very amusingly told, on the authority of Nicephorus, in Binsfeldius *De Confessionibus Maleficorum* (Trèves, 1591), pp. 465-467. St. Gregory Nazianzen mentions (Oration xviii.) that St. Cyprian had been a magician.

a moment through the air. A ponderous stone was long shown, in the church of St. Sabina at Rome, which the devil, in a moment of despairing passion, had flung at St. Dominick, vainly hoping to crush a head that was sheltered by the guardian angel. The Gospel of St. John suspended around the neck, a rosary, a relic of Christ, or of a saint, any one of the thousand talismans that were distributed among the faithful, sufficed to baffle the utmost efforts of diabolical malice. The consequence of this teaching was a condition of thought, which is so far removed from that which exists in the present day, that it is only by a strong exertion of the imagination that we can conceive it. What may be called the intellectual basis of witchcraft, existed to the fullest extent. All those conceptions of diabolical presence : all that predisposition towards the miraculous, which acted so fearfully upon the imaginations of the fifteenth and sixteenth centuries, existed ; but the implicit faith, the boundless and triumphant credulity with which the virtue of ecclesiastical rites was accepted, rendered them comparatively innocuous. If men had been a little less superstitious, the effects of their superstition would have been much more terrible. It was firmly believed that any one who deviated from the strict line of orthodoxy must soon succumb beneath the power of Satan ; but as there was no spirit of rebellion or of doubt, this persuasion did not produce any extraordinary terrorism.

Amid all this strange teaching, there ran, however, one vein of a darker character. The more terrible phenomena of nature were entirely unmoved by exorcisms and sprinklings, and they were invariably attributed to supernatural interposition. In every nation it has been believed, at an early period, that pestilences, famines, comets, rainbows, eclipses, and other rare and startling phenomena, were effected, not by the ordinary sequence of natural laws, but by the direct intervention of spirits. In this manner, the predisposition towards the miraculous, which is the characteristic of all semi-civilised nations, has been perpetuated, and the clergy have also frequently identified these phenomena with acts of rebellion against themselves. The old Catholic priests were consummate masters of these arts, and every rare natural event was, in the middle ages, an occasion for the most intense terrorism.

Thus, in the eighth century, a fearful famine afflicted France, and was generally represented as a consequence of the repugnance which the French people manifested to the payment of tithes.[1] In the ninth century a total eclipse of the sun struck terror through Europe, and is said to have been one of the causes of the death of a French king.[2] In the tenth century a similar phenomenon put to flight an entire army.[3] More than once, the apparition of a comet filled Europe with an almost maddening terror ; and, whenever a noted person was struck down by sudden illness, the death was attributed to sorcery.

The natural result, I think, of such modes of thought would be, that the notion of sorcery should be very common, but that the fear of it should not pass into an absolute mania. Credulity was habitual and universal, but religious terrorism was fitful and transient. We need not, therefore, be surprised that sorcery, though very familiar to the minds of men, did not, at the period I am referring to, occupy that prominent position which it afterwards assumed. The idea of a formal compact with the devil had not yet been formed ; but most of the crimes of witchcraft were recognised, anathematised, and punished. Thus, towards the end of the sixth century, a son of Frédégonde died after a short illness ; and numbers of women were put to the most prolonged and excruciating torments, and at last burnt or broken on the wheel, for having caused, by incantations, the death of the prince.[4] In Germany, the *Codex de Mathematicis et Maleficiis*[5] long continued in force, as did the old Salic law on the same subject in France. Charlemagne enacted new and very stringent laws condemning sorcerers to death, and great numbers seem to have perished in his reign.[6] Hail and thunder storms were almost universally attributed to their devices, though one great ecclesiastic of the ninth century —Agobard, Archbishop of Lyons—had the rare merit of opposing the popular belief.[7]

[1] Garinet, p. 38. [2] Ibid. p. 42.
[3] Buckle's *Hist.* vol. i. p. 345, *note*, where an immense amount of evidence on the subject is given.
[4] Garinet, pp. 14, 15.
[5] This was the title of the Roman code I have reviewed. Mathematicus was the name given to astrologers : as a law of Diocletian put it, "artem geometriæ disciatque exerceri publice interest. Ars autem mathematica damnábilis est et interdicta omnino."
[6] Garinet, p. 39.
[7] Garinet, p. 45. He also saved the lives of some Cabalists.

There existed, too, all through the middle ages, and even as late as the seventeenth century, the sect of the Cabalists, who were especially persecuted as magicians. It is not easy to obtain any very clear notion of their mystic doctrines, which long exercised an extraordinary fascination over many minds, and which captivated the powerful and daring intellects of Cardan, Agrippa, and Paracelsus. They seem to have comprised many traditions that had been long current among the Jews, mixed with much of the old Platonic doctrine of demons, and with a large measure of pure naturalism. With a degree of credulity, which, in our age, would be deemed barely compatible with sanity, but which was then perfectly natural, was combined some singularly bold scepticism; and, probably, a greater amount was veiled under the form of allegories than was actually avowed. The Cabalists believed in the existence of spirits of nature, embodiments or representatives of the four elements, sylphs, salamanders, gnomes, and ondines, beings of far more than human excellence, but mortal, and not untinctured by human frailty. To rise to intercourse with these elemental spirits of nature was the highest aim of the philosopher. He who would do so, must sever himself from the common course of life. He must purify his soul by fasting and celibacy, by patient and unwearied study, by deep communion with nature and with nature's laws. He must learn, above all, to look down with contempt upon the angry quarrels of opposing creeds; to see in each religion an aspect of a continuous law, a new phase and manifestation of the action of the spirits of nature upon mankind.

It is not difficult to detect the conception which underlies this teaching. As, however, no religious doctrine can resist the conditions of the age, these simple notions were soon encrusted and defaced by so many of those grotesque and material details, which invariably resulted from mediæval habits of thought, that it is only by a careful examination that their outlines can be traced. It was believed that it was possible for philosophers to obtain these spirits in literal marriage; and that such a union was the most passionate desire of the spirit-world. It was not only highly gratifying for both parties in this world, but greatly improved their prospects for the next. The sylph, though she lived for many centuries, was mortal,

and had in herself no hope of a future life, but her human husband imparted to her his own immortality, unless he was one of the reprobate, in which case he was saved from the pangs of hell by participating in the mortality of his bride. This general conception was elaborated in great detail, and was applied to the history of the Fall, and to the mythology of paganism, on both of which subjects the orthodox tenets were indignantly spurned. Scarcely anyone seems to have doubted the reality of these spirits, or that they were accustomed to reveal themselves to mankind; and the coruscations of the Aurora are said to have been attributed to the flashings of their wings.[1] The only question was, concerning their nature. According to the Cabalists, they were pure and virtuous. According to the orthodox, they were the incubi who were spoken of by St. Augustine; and all who had commerce with them were deservedly burnt.[2]

The history of the Cabalists furnishes, I think, a striking instance of the aberrations of a spirit of free-thinking in an age which was not yet ripe for its reception. When the very opponents of the Church were so completely carried away by the tide, and were engrossed with a mythological system as absurd as the wildest legends of the hagiology; it is not at all surprising that the philosophers who arose in the ranks of orthodoxy should have been extremely credulous, and that their conceptions should have been characterised by the coarsest materialism. Among the very few men who, in some slight degree, cultivated profane literature during the period I am referring to, a prominent place must be assigned to Michael Psellus. This voluminous author, though he is now, I imagine, very little read, still retains a certain position in literary history, as almost the only Byzantine writer of reputation who appeared for some

[1] Garinet, p. 35. This, however, is doubtful. Herder mentions that the Greenlanders believe the Aurora to be formed by spirits dancing and playing ball.
[2] On the Hebrew Cabala, see the learned work of M. Franck, and on the notions in the middle ages, and in the sixteenth and seventeenth centuries, *Le Comte de Gabalis*. Plancey, *Dict. infernal*, art. *Cabale*. All the heathen gods were supposed to be sylphs or other aerial spirits. Vesta was the wife of Noah—Zoroaster, her son, otherwise called Japhet. The sin of Adam was deserting the sylph for his wife, and the story of the apple was allegorical, &c. This last notion appears to have been a relic of Manichæism, and was very common among the heretics of the tenth and eleventh centuries (Matter, *Hist. du Gnosticisme*, tom. iii. pp. 259, 260). Paracelsus was one of the principal asserters of the existence of the sylphs, &c.

centuries. Towards the close of the eleventh century he wrote his dialogue on *The Operation of Demons;* which is, in a great measure, an exposition of the old Neo-Platonic doctrine of the hierarchy of spirits, but which also throws considerable light on the modes of thought prevailing in his time. He assures us that the world was full of demons, who were very frequently appearing among his countrymen, and who manifested their presence in many different ways. He had himself never seen one, but he was well acquainted with persons who had actual intercourse with them. His principal authority was a Grecian, named Marcus, who had at one time disbelieved in apparitions ; but who, having adopted a perfectly solitary life, had been surrounded by spirits whose habits and appearance he most minutely described. Having thus amassed considerable information on the subject, Psellus proceeded to digest it into a philosophical system, connecting it with the teachings of the past, and unfolding the laws and operations of the spirit world. He lays it down as a fundamental position that all demons have bodies. This, he says, is the necessary inference from the orthodox doctrine that they endure the torment of fire.[1] Their bodies, however, are not like those of men and animals, cast into an unchangeable mould. They are rather like the clouds, refined and subtle matter, capable of assuming any form, and penetrating into any orifice. The horrible tortures they endure in their place of punishment have rendered them extremely sensitive to suffering ; and they continually seek a temperate and somewhat moist warmth in order to allay their pangs. It is for this reason that they so frequently enter into men and animals. Possession appears to have been quite frequent, and madness was generally regarded as one of its results. Psellus, however, mentions that some physicians formed an exception to the prevailing opinions, attributing to physical what was generally attributed to spiritual causes, an aberration which he could only account for by the materialism which was so general in their profession. He mentions incidentally the exploits of incubi as not unknown, and enters into a long disquisition about a devil who was said to be acquainted with Armenian.

We find, then, that, all through the middle ages, most of the crimes that were afterwards collected by the inquisitors in the treatises on witchcraft were known ; and that many of them were not unfrequently punished. At the same time the executions, during six centuries, were probably not as numerous as those which often took place during a single decade of the fifteenth and sixteenth centuries. In the twelfth century, however, the subject passed into an entirely new phase. The conception of a witch, as we now conceive it—that is to say, of a woman who had entered into a deliberate compact with Satan, who was endowed with the power of working miracles whenever she pleased, and who was continually transported through the air to the Sabbath, where she paid her homage to the Evil One first appeared.[1] The panic created by the belief advanced at first slowly, but after a time with a fearfully accelerated rapidity. Thousands of victims were sometimes burnt alive in a few years. Every country in Europe was stricken with the wildest panic. Hundreds of the ablest judges were selected for the extirpation of the crime. A vast literature was created on the subject, and it was not until a considerable portion of the eighteenth century had passed away, that the executions finally ceased.[2]

I shall now endeavour to trace the general causes which produced this outburst of superstition. We shall find, I think, that in this, as in its earlier phases, sorcery was closely connected with the prevailing modes of thought on religious subjects ; and that its history is one of the most faithful indications of the laws of religious belief in their relation to the progress of civilisation.

The more carefully the history of the centuries prior to the Reformation is studied, the more evident it becomes that the twelfth century forms the great turning point of the European intellect. Owing to many complicated causes, which it would be tedious and difficult to trace, a general revival of Latin literature had then taken place, which profoundly modified the intellectual condition of

---

[1] This was a very old notion. St. Basil seems to have maintained it very strongly. Cudworth's *Int. System*, vol. ii. p 648.

[1] Maury, p. 185.
[2] The last judicial execution in Europe was, I believe, in Switzerland, in 1782 (Michelet's *Sorcière*, p. 415), the last law on the subject, the Irish Statute, which was not repealed till 1821.

Europe, and which, therefore, implied and necessitated a modification of the popular belief. For the first time for many centuries, we find a feeble spirit of doubt combating the spirit of credulity; a curiosity for purely secular knowledge replacing, in some small degree, the passion for theology; and, as a consequence of these things, a diminution of the contemptuous hatred with which all who were external to Christianity had been regarded. In every department of thought and of knowledge, there was manifested a vague disquietude, a spirit of restless and feverish anxiety, that contrasted strangely with the preceding torpor. The long slumber of untroubled orthodoxy was broken by many heresies, which, though often repressed, seemed in each succeeding century to acquire new force and consistency. Manichæism, which had for some time been smouldering in the Church, burst into a fierce flame among the Albigenses, and was only quenched by that fearful massacre in which tens of thousands were murdered at the instigation of the priests. Then it was that the standard of an impartial philosophy was first planted by Abelard in Europe, and the minds of the learned were distracted by subtle and perplexing doubts concerning the leading doctrines of the faith. Then, too, the teachings of a stern and uncompromising infidelity flashed forth from Seville and from Cordova; and the form of Averroes began to assume those gigantic proportions, which, at a later period, overshadowed the whole intellect of Europe, and almost persuaded some of the ablest men that the reign of Antichrist had begun.[1] At the same time, the passion for astrology and for the fatalism it implied revived with the revival of pagan learning, and penetrated into the halls of nobles and the palaces of kings. Every doubt, every impulse of rebellion against ecclesiastical authority, above all, every heretical

opinion, was regarded as the direct instigation of Satan, and their increase as the measure of his triumph. Yet these things were now gathering darkly all around. Europe was beginning to enter into that inexpressibly painful period in which men have learned to doubt, but have not yet learned to regard doubt as innocent; in which the new mental activity produces a variety of opinions, while the old credulity persuades them that all but one class of opinions are the suggestions of the devil. The spirit of rationalism was yet unborn; or if some faint traces of it may be discovered in the teachings of Abelard, it was at least far too weak to allay the panic. There was no independent enquiry; no confidence in an honest research; no disposition to rise above dogmatic systems or traditional teaching; no capacity for enduring the sufferings of a suspended judgment. The Church had cursed the human intellect by cursing the doubts that are the necessary consequence of its exercise. She had cursed even the moral faculty by asserting the guilt of honest error.

It is easy to perceive that, in such a state of thought, the conception of Satanic presence must have assumed a peculiar prominence, and have created a peculiar terror. Multitudes were distracted by doubts, which they sought in vain to repress, and which they firmly believed to be the suggestions of the devil. Their horror of pagans and Mahomedans diminished more and more as they acquired a relish for the philosophy of which the first, or the physical sciences of which the second, were the repositories. Every step in knowledge increased their repugnance to the coarse materialism which was prevalent, and every generation rendered the general intellectual tendencies more manifestly hostile to the Church. On the other hand, that Church presented an aspect of the sternest inflexibility. Rebellion and doubt were, in her eyes, the greatest of all crimes: and her doctrine of evil spirits and of the future world supplied her with engines of terrorism which she was prepared to employ to the uttermost. Accordingly we find that about the twelfth century the popular teaching began to assume a sterner and more solemn cast; and the devotions of the people to be more deeply tinctured by fanaticism. The old confidence which had almost toyed with Satan, and in the very exuberance of an unfaltering faith

[1] For the history of this very remarkable movement, see the able essay of Renan on Averroes. Among the Mahomedans, the panic was so great, that the theologians pronounced logic and philosophy to be the two great enemies of their profession, and ordered all books on those dangerous subjects to be burnt. Among the Christians, St. Thomas Aquinas devoted his genius to the controversy; and, for two or three centuries, most of the great works in Christendom bore some marks of Averroes. M. Renan has collected some curious evidence from the Italian painters of the fourteenth century, of the prominence Averroes had assumed in the popular mind. The three principal figures in Orgagna's picture of Hell, in the Campo Santo, at Pisa, are Mahomet, Antichrist, and Averroes.

had mocked at his devices, was exchanged for a harsh and gloomy asceticism. The aspect of Satan became more formidable, and the aspect of Christ became less engaging. Till the close of the tenth century, the central figure of Christian art had been usually represented as a very young man, with an expression of untroubled gentleness and calm resting on his countenance, and engaged in miracles of mercy. The parable of the Good Shepherd, which adorns almost every chapel in the Catacombs, was still the favourite subject of the painter; and the sterner representations of Christianity were comparatively rare. In the eleventh century all this began to change. The Good Shepherd entirely disappeared, the miracles of mercy became less frequent, and were replaced by the details of the Passion and the terrors of the Last Judgment. The countenance of Christ became sterner, older, and more mournful. About the twelfth century, this change became almost universal. From this period, writes one of the most learned of modern archæologists, "Christ appears more and more melancholy, and often truly terrible. It is, indeed, the rex tremendæ majestatis of our Dies iræ. It is almost the God of the Jews making fear the beginning of wisdom."[1] In the same age we find the scourgings and the "minutio monachi"— the practice of constant bleedings—rising into general use in the monasteries;[2] and, soon after, the Flagellants arose, whose stern discipline and passionate laments over prevailing iniquity directed the thoughts of multitudes to subjects that were well calculated to inflame their imaginations. Almost at the same time, religious persecution, which had been for many centuries nearly unknown, amid the calm of orthodoxy, was revived and stimulated. In the beginning of the thirteenth century, Innocent III. instituted the Inquisition, and issued the first appeal to princes to employ their power for the

suppression of heresy; and, in the course of the following century, the new tribunal was introduced; or, at least, executions for heresy had taken place in several great countries in Europe.

The terrorism which was thus created by the conflict between an immutable Church and an age in which there was some slight progress, and a real, though faint spirit of rebellion, gradually filtered down to those who were far too ignorant to become heretics. The priest in the pulpit or in the confessional; the monk in his intercourse with the peasant; the Flagellant, by his mournful hymns, and by the spectacle of his macerations; above all, the inquisitor, by his judgments, communicated to the lower classes a sense of Satanic presence and triumph, which they naturally applied to the order of ideas with which they were most conversant. In an age which was still grossly ignorant and credulous, the popular faith was necessarily full of grotesque superstitions, which faithfully reflected the general tone and colouring of religious teaching, though they often went far beyond its limits. These superstitions had once consisted, for the most part, in wild legends of fairies, mermaids, giants, and dragons: of miracles of saints, conflicts in which the devil took a prominent part, but was invariably defeated, or illustrations of the boundless efficacy of some charm or relic. About the twelfth century they began to assume a darker hue, and the imaginations of the people revelled in the details of the witches' Sabbath, and in the awful power of the ministers of Satan. The inquisitors traversed Europe, proclaiming that the devil was operating actively on all sides; and among their very first victims, were persons who were accused of sorcery, and who were of course condemned.[1] Such condemnations could not make the belief in the reality of the crime more unhesitating than it had been, but they had a direct tendency to multiply the accusations. The imaginations of the people were riveted upon the subject. A contagious terror was engendered. Some, whose minds were thoroughly diseased, persuaded themselves that they were in communion with Satan; all had an increasing predisposition to see Satanic agency around them.

To these things should be added a long

[1] Didron, Iconographie chretienne, Histoire de Dieu (Paris, 1843), p. 262. See, however, for the whole history of this very remarkable transition, pp. 255–273. To this I may add, that about the thirteenth century, the representations of Satan underwent a corresponding change, and became both more terrible and more grotesque (Maury, Légendes pieuses, p. 136). The more the subject is examined, the more evident it becomes that, before the invention of printing, painting was the most faithful mirror of the popular mind; and that there was scarcely an intellectual movement that it did not reflect. On the general terrorism of this period, see Michelet, Histoire de France, tom. vii. pp. 140, 141.

[2] Madden, vol. i. pp. 359–395; Cabinis, Rapports physiques et moraux, tom. ii. pp. 77–79.

[1] Garinet, p. 75.

series of social and political events, into which it is needless to enter, for they have very lately been painted with matchless vividness by an illustrious living writer.[1] A sense of insecurity and wretchedness, often rising to absolute despair, had been diffused among the people, and had engendered the dark imaginations, and the wild and rebellious passions, which, in a superstitious age, are their necessary concomitants. It has always been observed by the inquisitors that a large proportion of those who were condemned to the flames were women, whose lives had been clouded by some great sorrow ; and that music, which soothes the passions, and allays the bitterness of regret, had an extraordinary power over the possessed.[2]

Under the influences which I have attempted to trace, the notion of witchcraft was reduced to a more definite form, and acquired an increasing prominence in the twelfth and thirteenth centuries. Most of the causes that produced it, advanced by their very nature with an accelerating force, and the popular imagination became more and more fascinated by the subject. In the fourteenth century, an event occurred which was well calculated to give a fearful impulse to the terrorism ; and which may, indeed, be justly regarded as one of the most appalling in the history of humanity. I allude, of course, to the black death. A great German physician has lately investigated, with much skill and learning, the history of that time ; and he has recorded his opinion that, putting aside all exaggerated accounts, the number of those who died of the pestilence during the six years of its continuance may be estimated, by a very moderate computation, at twenty-five millions, or a fourth part of the inhabitants of Europe.[3] Many great towns lost far more than half their population ; many country districts were almost depopulated.

It would be scarcely possible to conceive an event fitted to act with a more terrific force upon the imaginations of men. Even in our own day, we know how great a degree of religious terror is inspired by a pestilence ; but, in an age when the supernatural character of disease was universally believed, an affliction of such unexampled magnitude

produced a consternation which almost amounted to madness. One of its first effects was an enormous increase of the wealth of the clergy by the legacies of the terror-stricken victims. The sect of the Flagellants, which had been for a century unknown, reappeared in tenfold numbers, and almost every part of Europe resounded with their hymns. Then, too, arose the dancing mania of Flanders and Germany, when thousands assembled with strange cries and gestures, overawing by their multitudes all authority, and proclaiming, amid their wild dances and with shrieks of terror, the power and the triumph of Satan.[1] It has been observed that this form of madness raged with an especial violence in the dioceses of Cologne and Trèves, in which witchcraft was afterwards most prevalent.[2] In Switzerland and in some parts of Germany the plague was ascribed to the poison of the Jews ; and though the Pope made a noble effort to dispel the illusion, immense numbers of that unhappy race were put to death. Some thousands are said to have perished in Mayence alone. More generally, it was regarded as a divine chastisement, or as an evidence of Satanic power ; and the most grotesque explanations were hazarded. Boots with pointed toes had been lately introduced, and were supposed by many to have been peculiarly offensive to the Almighty.[3] What, however, we have especially to observe is, that the trials for witchcraft multiplied with a fearful rapidity.[4]

In the fifteenth and sixteenth centuries they may be said to have reached their climax. The aspect which Europe then presented was that of universal anarchy and universal terrorism. The intellectual influences which had been long corroding the pillars of the Church had done their work, and a fearful moral retrogression,

---

[1] Michelet, *La Sorcière*.　　　[2] Binsfeldius, p. 155.
[3] Hecker's *Epidemics of the Middle Ages*, p. 29. Bocaccio witnessed and described this pestilence.

[1] Hecker, p. 82. The dancers often imagined themselves to be immersed in a stream of blood. They were habitually exorcised.
[2] There is still an annual festival near Trèves in commemoration of the epidemic. Madden, vol. i. p. 420.
[3] Hecker, p. 82.
[4] Ennemoser, *Hist. of Magic*, vol. ii. p. 150. I may here notice, by way of illustration, two facts in the history of art. The first is, that those ghastly pictures of the dance of death, which were afterwards so popular, and which represented an imaginative bias of such a wild and morbid power, began in the fourteenth century (Peignot, *Sur les Danses des Morts*, pp. 26-31). The second is, that in this same century the bas-reliefs on cathedrals frequently represent men kneeling down before the devil, and devoting themselves to him as his servants (Martonne, *Piété du Moyen Âge*, p. 137).

aggravated by the newly-acquired ecclesiastical wealth, accompanied the intellectual advance. Yet, over all this chaos, there was one great conception dominating unchanged. It was the sense of sin and Satan ; of the absolute necessity of a correct dogmatic system to save men from the agonies of hell. The Church, which had long been all-in-all to Christendom, was heaving in what seemed the last throes of dissolution. The boundaries of religious thought were all obscured. Conflicting tendencies and passions were raging with a tempestuous violence, among men who were absolutely incapable of enduring an intellectual suspense, and each of the opposing sects proclaimed its distinctive doctrines essential to salvation. Doubt was almost universally regarded as criminal and error as damnable ; yet the first was the necessary condition, and the second the probable consequence, of enquiry. Totally unaccustomed to independent reasoning, bewildered by the vast and undefined fields of thought, from which the opposing arguments were drawn ; with a profound sense of the absolute necessity of a correct creed, and of the constant action of Satan upon the fluctuations of the will and of the judgment ; distracted and convulsed by opposing sentiments, which an unenlightened psychology attributed to spiritual inspiration, and, above all, parched with a burning longing for certainty ; the minds of men drifted to and fro under the influence of the wildest terror. None could escape the movement. It filled all Europe with alarm, permeated with its influence all forms of thought and action, absorbed every element of national life into its ever-widening vortex.

There certainly never has been a movement which, in its ultimate results, has contributed so largely to the emancipation of the human mind from all superstitious terrors as the Reformation. It formed a multitude of churches, in which the spirit of qualified and partial scepticism that had long been a source of anarchy, might expatiate with freedom, and be allied with the spirit of order. It rejected an immense proportion of the dogmatic and ritualistic conceptions that had almost covered the whole field of religion, and rendered possible that steady movement by which theology has since then been gravitating towards the moral faculty. It, above all, diminished the prominence of clergy ; and thus prepared the way for that general secularisation of the European intellect, which is such a marked characteristic of modern civilisation. Yet, inappreciably great as are these blessings, it would be idle to deny that, for a time, the Reformation aggravated the very evils it was intended to correct. It was, for a time, merely an exchange of masters. The Protestant asserted the necessity and certainty of his distinctive doctrines, as dogmatically and authoritatively as the Catholic. He believed in his own infallibility quite as firmly as his opponent believed in the infallibility of the Pope. It is only by a very slow process that the human mind can emerge from a system of error ; and the virtue of dogmas had been so ingrained in all religious thought, by the teaching of more than twelve centuries, that it required a long and painful discipline to weaken what is not yet destroyed. The nature of truth, the limits of human faculties, the laws of probabilities, and the conditions that are essential for an impartial research, were subjects with which even the most advanced minds were then entirely unfamiliar. There was, indeed, much cultivation of logic, considered in its most narrow sense ; but there was no such thing as a comprehensive view of the whole field of mental science, of the laws and limits of the reason. There was also no conviction that the reason should be applied to every department of theology, with the same unflinching severity as to any other form of speculation. Faith always presented to the mind the idea of an abnormal intellectual condition, of the subversion or suspension of the critical faculties. It sometimes comprised more than this, but it always included this. It was the opposite of doubt and of the spirit of doubt. What irreverent men called credulity, reverent men called faith ; and although one word was more respectful than the other, yet the two words were with most men strictly synonymous. Some of the Protestants added other and moral ideas to the word, but they firmly retained the intellectual idea. As long as such a conception existed, a period of religious convulsion was necessarily a period of extreme suffering and terror ; and there can be little doubt that the Reformation was, in consequence, the most painful of all the transitions through which the human intellect has passed.

If the reader has seized the spirit of the foregoing remarks, he will already have perceived their application to the history of witchcraft. In order that men should believe in witches, their intellects must have been familiarised with the conceptions of Satanic power and Satanic presence, and they must regard these things with an unfaltering belief. In order that witchcraft should be prominent, the imaginations of men must have been so forcibly directed to these articles of belief, as to tinge and govern the habitual current of their thoughts, and to produce a strong disposition to see Satanic agency around them. A long train of circumstances, which culminated in the Reformation, had diffused through Christendom a religious terror which gradually overcast the horizon of thought, creating a general uneasiness as to the future of the Church, and an intense and vivid sense of Satanic presence. These influences were, it is true, primarily connected with abstruse points of speculative belief, but they acted in a twofold manner upon the grosser superstitions of the people. Although the illiterate cannot follow the more intricate speculations of their teachers, they can, as I have said, catch the general tone and character of thought which these speculations produce, and they readily apply them to their own sphere of thought. Besides this, the upper classes, being filled with a sense of Satanic presence, will be disposed to believe in the reality of any history of witchcraft. They will, therefore, prosecute the witches, and, as a necessary consequence, stimulate the delusion. When the belief is confined to the lower class, its existence will be languishing and unprogressive. But when legislators denounce it in their laws, and popes in their bulls ; when priests inveigh against it in their pulpits, and inquisitors burn thousands at the stake, the imaginations of men will be inflamed, the terror will prove contagious, and the consequent delusions be multiplied. Now, popes and legislators, priests and inquisitors, will do these things just in proportion to the firmness of their belief in the conceptions I have noticed, and to the intensity with which their imaginations have been directed to those conceptions by religious terrorism.

We have a striking illustration of the influence upon witchcraft, of the modes of thought which the Reformation for a time sustained in the life of Luther. No single feature was more clearly marked in his character than an intense and passionate sense of sin. He himself often described, in the most graphic language, how, in the seclusion of his monastery at Wittenberg, he had passed under the very shadow of death, how the gates of hell seemed to open beneath his feet, and the sense of hopeless wretchedness, to make life itself a burden. While oppressed by the keenest sense of moral unworthiness, he was distracted by intellectual doubt. He only arrived at the doctrines of Protestantism after a long and difficult enquiry, struggling slowly through successive phases of belief, uncheered for many years by one word of sympathy, and oscillating painfully between opposing conclusions. Like all men of vivid imagination who are so circumstanced, a theological atmosphere was formed about his mind, and became the medium through which every event was contemplated. He was subject to numerous strange hallucinations and vibrations of judgment, which he invariably attributed to the direct action of Satan. Satan became, in consequence, the dominating conception of his life. In every critical event, in every mental perturbation, he recognised Satanic power. In the monastery of Wittenberg, he constantly heard the Devil making a noise in the cloisters ; and became at last so accustomed to the fact, that he related that, on one occasion, having been awakened by the sound, he perceived that it was *only* the Devil, and accordingly went to sleep again. The black stain in the castle of Wartburg still marks the place where he flung an ink-bottle at the Devil. In the midst of his long and painful hesitation on the subject of transubstantiation, the Devil appeared to him, and suggested a new argument. In such a state of mind he naturally accepted, with implicit faith, every anecdote of Satanic miracles. He told how an aged minister had been interrupted, in the midst of his devotions, by a devil who was grunting behind him like a pig. At Torgau, the Devil broke pots and basins, and flung them at the minister's head, and at last drove the minister's wife and servants half crazy out of the house. On another occasion, the Devil appeared in the law courts, in the character of a leading barrister, whose place he is said to have filled with the utmost propriety. Fools, deformed persons, the blind and the dumb, were possessed by devils. Physicians, indeed, attempted to explain these infirmities by natural causes; but those physicians were ignorant men; they did not know all the power of Satan. Every form of disease might be produced by Satan, or by his agents, the witches; and none of the infirmities to which Luther was liable were natural, but his ear-ache was peculiarly diabolical. Hail, thunder, and plagues are all the direct consequences of the intervention of spirits. Many of those persons who were supposed to have committed suicide, had in reality been seized by the Devil and strangled by him, as the traveller is strangled by the robber. The Devil could transport men at his will through the air. He could beget children, and Luther had himself come in contact with one of them. An intense love of children was one of the most amiable characteristics of the great Reformer; but, on this occasion, he most earnestly recommended the reputed relatives to throw the child into a river, in order to free their house from the presence of a devil. As a natural consequence of these modes of thought, witchcraft did not present the slightest improbability to his mind. In strict accordance with the spirit of his age, he continually asserted the existence and the frequency of the crime, and emphatically proclaimed the duty of burning the witches.[1]

I know, indeed, few stranger, and at the same time more terrible pictures, than are furnished by the history of witchcraft during the century that preceded and the century that followed the Reformation. Wherever the conflict of opinions was raging among the educated, witchcraft, like an attendant shadow, pursued its course among the ignorant;[2] and Protestants and Catholics vied with each other in the zeal with which they prosecuted it. Never was the power of imagination—that strange faculty which casts the shadow of its images over the whole creation, and combines all the phenomena of life according to its own archetypes—more strikingly evinced. Superstitious and terror-stricken, the minds of men were impelled irresistibly towards the miraculous and the Satanic, and they

found them upon every side. The elements of imposture blended so curiously with the elements of delusion, that it is now impossible to separate them. Sometimes an ambitious woman, braving the dangers of her act, boldly claimed supernatural power, and the haughtiest and the most courageous cowed humbly in her presence. Sometimes a husband attempted, in the witch courts, to cut the tie which his church had pronounced indissoluble; and numbers of wives have, in consequence, perished at the stake. Sometimes a dexterous criminal availed himself of the panic; and, directing a charge of witchcraft against his accuser, escaped himself with impunity. Sometimes, too, a personal grudge was avenged by the accusation, or a real crime was attributed to sorcery; or a hail-storm, or a strange disease, suggested the presence of a witch. But, for the most part, the trials represent pure and unmingled delusions. The defenders of the belief were able to maintain that multitudes had voluntarily confessed themselves guilty of commerce with the Evil One, and had persisted in their confessions till death. Madness is always peculiarly frequent during great religious or political revolutions;[1] and, in the sixteenth century, all its forms were absorbed in the system of witchcraft, and caught the colour of the prevailing predisposition.[2] Occasionally, too, we find old and half-doting women, at first convinced of their innocence, but soon faltering before the majesty of justice, asking timidly, whether it is possible to be in connection with the Devil without being conscious of the fact, and at last almost persuading themselves that they had done what was alleged. Very often, the terror of the trial, the prospect of the most agonising of deaths, and the frightful tortures that were applied to the weak frame of an old and feeble woman,[3] overpowered her understanding; her brain reeled beneath the accumulated suffering, the consciousness of innocence disappeared, and the wretched victim went raving to

---

[1] Buckle's *Hist.*, vol. i. p. 424, *note*.

[2] Calmeil.

[3] For a frightful catalogue of the tortures that were employed in these cases, see Scott's *Discovery of Witchcraft* (London, 1665), pp. 11, 12. All the old treatises are full of the subject. Sprenger recommends the tortures to be continued two or three days, till the prisoner was, as he expresses it, "decenter quæstionatus" (Pars iii. Quæst. 14, 15). The tortures were all the more horrible, because it was generally believed that the witches had charms to deaden their effect.

---

[1] *Colloquia Mensalia.* Erasmus was an equally firm believer in witchcraft (Stewart's *Dissertation*, p. 57).

[2] This co-existence has been noticed by many writers; and Naudé (*Apologie*, pp. 110, 111) observes, that nearly all the heresies previous to the Reformation had been also accompanied by an outburst of sorcery.

the flames, convinced that she was about to sink for ever into perdition. The zeal of the ecclesiastics in stimulating the persecution was unflagging. It was displayed alike in Germany, France, Spain, Italy, Flanders, Sweden, England, and Scotland. An old writer who cordially approved of the rigour tells us that, in the province of Como alone, eight or ten inquisitors were constantly employed ; and he adds that, in one year, the number of persons they condemned amounted to a thousand ; and that during several of the succeeding years, the victims seldom fell below one hundred. [1]

It was natural that a body of learned men like the inquisitors, whose habits of thought were eminently retrospective, should have formed some general theories connecting the phenomena of sorcery with past events, and reducing them to a systematic form. We accordingly find that, in the course of about three centuries, a vast literature was formed upon the subject. The different forms of witchcraft were all carefully classified and associated with particular doctrines ; the whole philosophy of the Satanic was minutely investigated, and the prevailing mode of thought embodied in countless treatises, which were once regarded as masterpieces of orthodox theology.

It is very difficult for us in the present day to do justice to these works, or to realise the points of view from which they were written. A profound scepticism on all subjects connected with the Devil underlies the opinions of almost every educated man, and renders it difficult even to conceive a condition of thought in which that spirit was the object of an intense and realised belief. An anecdote which involves the personal intervention of Satan is now regarded as quite as intrinsically absurd, and unworthy of serious attention, as an anecdote of a fairy or of a sylph. When, therefore, a modern reader turns over the pages of an old treatise on witchcraft, and finds hundreds of such anecdotes related with the gravest assurance, he is often inclined to depreciate very unduly the intellect of an author who represents a condition of thought so unlike his own. The cold indifference to human suffering which these writers display gives an additional bias to his reason ; while their extraordinary pedantry, their execrable Latin,

and their gross scientific blunders, furnish ample materials for his ridicule. Besides this, Sprenger, who is at once the most celebrated, and, perhaps, the most credulous member of his class, unfortunately for his reputation, made some ambitious excursions into another field, and immortalised himself by a series of etymological blunders, which have been the delight of all succeeding scholars. [1]

But when all these qualifications have been made—and, with the exception of the last, they would all apply to any other writings of the same period—it is, I think, impossible to deny that the books in defence of the belief are not only far more numerous than the later works against it, but that they also represent far more learning, dialectic skill, and even general ability. For many centuries the ablest men were not merely unwilling to repudiate the superstition ; they often pressed forward earnestly, and with the most intense conviction, to defend it. Indeed, during the period when witchcraft was most prevalent, there were few writers of real eminence who did not, on some occasion, take especial pains to throw the weight of their authority into the scale. Thomas Aquinas was probably the ablest writer of the thirteenth century, and he assures us that diseases and tempests are often the direct acts of the Devil ; that the Devil can transport men at his pleasure through the air ; and that he can transform them into any shape. Gerson, the Chancellor of the University of Paris, and, as many think, the author of *The Imitation*, is justly regarded as one of the master-intellects of his age ; and he, too, wrote in defence of the belief. Bodin was unquestionably the most original political philosopher who had arisen since Machiavelli, and he devoted all his learning and acuteness to crushing the rising scepticism on the subject of witches. The truth is, that, in those ages, ability was no guarantee against error ; because the single

---

[1] Spina, cap. xii.

[1] " Fœmina," he assures us, is derived from Fe and minus, because women have less faith than men (p. 65). Maleficiendo is from male de fide sentiendo. For diabolus we have a choice of most instructive derivations. It comes "a dia quod est duo, et bolus quod est morsellus, quia duo occidit, scilicet corpus et animam. Et secundum etymologiam, licet Græce, interpretetur diabolus clausus ergastulo : et hoc sibi convenit cum non permittitur sibi nocere quantum vellet. Vel diabolus quasi defluens, quia defluxit, id est corruit, et specialiter et localiter " (p. 41). If the reader is curious in these matters, he will find another astounding instance of verbal criticism, which I do not venture to quote, in Bodin, *Démon.* p. 40.

employment of the reason was to develop and expand premises that were furnished by the Church. There was no such thing as an uncompromising and unreserved criticism of the first principles of teaching ; there was no such thing as a revolt of the reason against conclusions that were strictly drawn from the premises of authority. In our age, and in every other age of half belief, principles are often adopted without being fully developed. If a conclusion is drawn from them, men enquire, not merely whether the deduction is correct, but also whether its result seems intrinsically probable ; and if it does not appear so, they will reject the conclusion, without absolutely rejecting the premise. In the ages of witchcraft an inexorable logic prevailed. Men were so firmly convinced of the truth of the doctrines they were taught, that those doctrines became to them the measure of probability, and no event that seemed to harmonise with them presented the slightest difficulty to the mind. They governed the imagination, while they subdued the reason, and secular considerations never intervened to damp their assurance. The ablest men were not infrequently the most credulous ; because their ability was chiefly employed in discovering analogies between every startling narrative and the principles of their faith, and their success was a measure of their ingenuity.

It is these considerations that give the writings of the period I am referring to so great an importance in the history of opinions, and which also make it so difficult for us to appreciate their force. I shall endeavour to lay before the reader, in as concise a form as I am able, some of the leading principles they embodied ; which, acting on the imagination, contributed to produce the phenomena of witchcraft ; and, acting on the reason, persuaded men that the narratives of witches were antecedently probable.[1]

It was universally taught that innumerable evil spirits were ranging over the world, seeking the present unhappiness and the future ruin of mankind ; that these

spirits were fallen angels, who had retained many, if not all, the angelic capacities ; and that they, at all events, possessed a power and wisdom far transcending the limits of human faculties. From these conceptions many important consequences were evolved. If these spirits are for ever hovering around us, it was said, it is surely not improbable that we should meet some signs of their presence. If they delight in the smallest misfortune that can befall mankind, and possess far more than human capacities for inflicting suffering, it is not surprising that they should direct against men the energies of superhuman malice. If their highest object is to secure the ultimate ruin of man, we need not wonder that they should offer their services to those who would bribe them by the surrender of their hopes. That such a compact can be made—that it is possible for man to direct the energies of evil spirits—was established by the clearest authority. " Thou shalt not suffer a witch to live " was the solemn injunction which had been more than once repeated in the Levitical code ; and the history of the witch of Endor furnishes a detailed description of the circumstances of the crime. The Fathers had denounced magic with a unanimous and unvarying voice, and the writings of every nation bear traces of the universality of the belief. In an age which was essentially retrospective, it was impossible to name a tenet which could seem more probable, for there was none which was more closely connected with antiquity, both ecclesiastical and profane.

The popular belief, however, not only asserted the possibility and continued existence of witchcraft, it also entered into many of what we should now deem the most extravagant and grotesque details. In the first place, one of the most ordinary operations of the witch, or of the Devil acting at her command, was to cause tempests, which it was said frequently desolated the fields of a single person, leaving the rest of the country entirely untouched. If any one ventured to deny that Satan possessed, or was likely to exercise this power, he was speedily silenced by a scriptural precedent. We read in the Old Testament that the Devil, by the Divine permission, afflicted Job ; and that among the means which he employed was a tempest which destroyed the house in which the sons of

[1] The principal authority on these matters is a large collection of Latin works (in great part written by inquisitors), extending over about two centuries, and published under the title of *Malleus Maleficarum* (the title of Sprenger's book). It comprises the works of Sprenger, Nider, Basin, Molitor, Gerson, Murner, Spina, Laurentius, Bernardus, Vignitus, Grillandus, &c. I have noticed a great many other works in their places, and the reader may find reviews of many others in Madden and Plancey.

the patriarch were eating. The description, in the book of Revelation, of the four angels who held the four winds, and to whom it was given to afflict the earth, was also generally associated with this belief; for, as St. Augustine tells us, the word angel is equally applicable to good or bad spirits. Besides this, the Devil was always spoken of as the prince of the air. His immense knowledge and his immense power would place the immediate causes of atmospheric disturbances at his disposal; and the sudden tempest would, therefore, be no violation of natural laws, but simply an instance of their application by superhuman power. These considerations were, it was thought, sufficient to remove all sense of the antecedent improbability of the facts which were alleged; but every uncertainty was dispelled by the uniform teaching of the Church. At all times, the Fathers and the mediæval saints had taught, like the teachers of every other religion in the same early stage of civilisation, that all the more remarkable atmospheric changes resulted from the direct intervention of spirits.[1] Rain seems to have been commonly associated, as it still is in the Church of England, with the intervention of the Deity; but wind and hail were peculiarly identified with the Devil. If the Devil could originate a tempest, it followed, as a necessary consequence, that witches who had entered into compact with him had the same power.

The same principles of argument applied to disease. The Devil had afflicted Job with horrible diseases, and might therefore afflict others. Great pestilences were constantly described in the Old Testament as the acts of the angels; and the Devil, by the permission of the Deity and by virtue of his angelic capacities, might therefore easily produce them. The history of the demoniacs proves that devils could master and derange the bodily functions; and, therefore, to deny that they could produce disease, would be to impugn the veracity of these narratives; and the later ecclesiastical testimony on the subject, if not unanimous, was, at least, extremely strong. As, therefore, the more striking atmospheric disturbances were ascribed generally to the Devil; and, when the injury was spread over a small area, to

witches; so, the pestilences which desolated nations were deemed supernatural; and all strange and unaccountable diseases that fell upon an individual, a result of the malice of a sorcerer. If the witch could produce disease by her incantations, there was no difficulty in believing that she could also remove it.[1]

These propositions were unanimously and firmly believed. They were illustrated by anecdotes, the countless numbers of which can only be appreciated by those who have studied the literature at its source. They were indelibly graven on the minds of men by hundreds of trials and of executions, and they were admitted by almost all the ablest men in Christendom.

There were other details, however, which excited considerable discussion. One of the most striking of these was the transportation of witches through the air. That an old woman could be carried some hundreds of miles in a few minutes on a broomstick or a goat, or in any other way the Devil might select, would, in the present day, be regarded as so essentially and grotesquely absurd, that it is probable that no conceivable amount of testimony would convince men of its reality. At the period of which I am writing, this rationalistic spirit did undoubtedly exist in a few minds; for it is noticed, though with extreme contempt, by some of the writers on the subject, who treated it as a manifest mental aberration; but it had not yet assumed any importance. The measure of probability was still essentially theological; and the only question that was asked was, how far the narratives conformed with the theological conception of a spirit.

[1] There can be little doubt that a considerable amount of poisoning was mixed up with the witch cases. In ages when medical knowledge was scanty, and post-mortem examination unknown, this crime was peculiarly dreaded, and appeared peculiarly mysterious. On the other hand, it is equally certain that the witches constantly employed their knowledge of the property of herbs for the purpose of curing disease, and that they attained, in this respect, a skill which was hardly equalled by the regular practitioners. To the evidence which Michelet has collected on this matter, I may add a striking passage from Grillandus: "Quandoque vero provenit febris, tussis, dementia, phthisis, hydropsis, aut aliqua tumefactio carnis in corpore, sive apostema extrinsecus apparens: quandoque vero intrinsece apud intestina aliquod apostema sit adeo terribile et incurabile quod nulla pars medicorum id sanare et removere potest, nisi accedat alius maleficus, sive sortilegus, qui contrariis medelis et remediis ægritudinem ipsam maleficam tollat, quam facile et brevi tempore removere potest, cæteri vero medici qui artem ipsius medicinæ profitentur nihil valent et nesciunt afferre remedium" (*Mall. Mal.* vol. ii. pp. 393, 394).

[1] On the universality of this belief, in an early stage of civilisation, see Buckle's *History*, vol. i. p. 346.

On this point there seemed, at first sight, much difficulty, and considerable ingenuity was applied to elucidating it. Satan, it was remembered, had borne Christ through the air, and placed him on a pinnacle of the temple ; and therefore, said St. Thomas Aquinas, if he could do this to one body he could do it to all. The prophet Habakkuk had been transported by a spirit from Judea to Babylon, and Philip the Evangelist had been the object of a similar miracle. St. Paul had likewise been carried, perhaps in the body, into the third heaven.

This evidence was ample and conclusive ; but other perplexing difficulties arose. Nothing in the witch trials was more minutely described than the witches' Sabbath, and many hundreds of women had been burnt alive for attending it. Occasionally, however, it happened that, when a woman had been condemned on this charge by her own confession, or by the evidence of other witches, her husband came forward and swore that his wife had not left his side during the night in question. The testimony of so near a relative might, perhaps, be explained by perjury ; but other evidence was adduced which it was more difficult to evade. It was stated that women were often found lying in a state of trance, insensible to pain, and without the smallest sign of life ; that, after a time, their consciousness returned ; and that they then confessed that they had been at the witches' Sabbath. These statements soon attracted the attention of theologians, who were much divided in their judgments. Some were of opinion that the witch was labouring under a delusion of the Devil ; but they often added that, as the delusion originated in a compact, she should, notwithstanding, be burned. Others suggested a bolder and very startling explanation. That the same portion of matter cannot be in two places at once, is a proposition which rests entirely on the laws of nature ; but those laws have no existence for the miraculous ; and the miracle of transubstantiation seems to destroy all the improbability of the pluripresence of a human body. At all events, the Devil might furnish, for the occasion, a duplicate body ; in order to baffle the ministers of justice. This latter opinion became extremely popular among theologians ; and two famous Catholic miracles were triumphantly quoted in its support. St. Ambrose was, on one occasion, cele-

brating mass in a church at Milan, when he suddenly paused in the midst of the service. His head sank upon the altar, and he remained motionless, as in a trance, for the space of three hours. The congregation waited silently for the benediction. At last, the consciousness of the saint returned, and he assured his hearers that he had been officiating at Tours at the burial of St. Martin, a statement which was, of course, in a few days, verified. A similar miracle was related of St. Clement. This early saint, in the midst of a mass at Rome, was called away to consecrate a church at Pisa. His body, or an angel who had assumed its form, remained at Rome ; but the saint was at the same time present at Pisa, where he left some drops of blood upon the marble for a memorial of the miracle.[1] On the whole, the most general opinion seems to have been, that the witches were sometimes transported to the Sabbath in body, and sometimes in spirit ; and that devils occasionally assumed their forms in order to baffle the sagacity of the judges.[2]

Another important and much discussed department, was the connection between evil spirits and animals. That the Devil could assume the form of any animal[3] he

[1] Spina, *De Strigibus* (1522), cap. xi.
[2] All the phenomena of somnambulism were mixed up with the question. See, e.g., Spina, cap. x. and xi., where it is fully discussed. Many curious notions were held about somnambulism. One opinion was, that the somnambulists had never been baptised, or had been baptised by a drunken priest.
[3] This belief was probably sustained by the great use made of animals in Christian symbolism as representatives of moral qualities. In different districts different animals were supposed to be in especial connection with spirits. Delrio mentions that the ancient Irish had such a veneration for wolves that they were accustomed to pray for their salvation, and to choose them as godfathers for their children (Thiers' *Superst.* vol. ii. p. 198). Beelzebub, as is well known, was god of flies, " par ce qu'il n'y avoit pas une mouche en son temple, comme on dict qu'au Palais de Venise il n'y a pas une seule mouche et au Palais de Tolède qu'il n'y en a qu'une, qui n'est pas chose estrange ou nouvelle, car nous lisons que les Cyrénaïques, après avoir sacrifié au dieu Acaron, dieu des mouches, et les Grecs à Jupiter, surnommé Myiodes, c'est à dire mouchard, toutes les mouches s'envolaient en une nuée, comme nous lisons en Pausanias *In Arcadicis* et en *Pline* au livre xxix. cap. 6 " (Bodin, *Démon.* p. 15). Dancing bears and other intelligent animals seem to have been also connected with the Devil ; and an old council anathematised at once magicians who have abandoned their Creator, fortune-tellers, and those " qui ursas aut similes bestias ad ludum et perniciem simpliciorum circumferunt "—" for what fellowship can there be between Christ and Belial ? " (Wier, *De Præst. Dæm.* p. 557). The ascription of intelligence to animals was general through the middle ages, but it was most prominent in the Celtic race. See a curious chapter on mystic animals in Dalyell's *Superstitions of Scotland*, and also the essay of Renan on *Celtic Poetry*. Muratori (*Antiq. Ital. Diss.* xxix.) quotes an amusing

pleased, seems to have been generally admitted ; and it presented no difficulty to those who remembered that the first appearance of that personage on earth was as a serpent, and that on one occasion a legion of devils had entered into a herd of swine. St. Jerome also assures us that, in the desert, St. Antony had met a centaur and a faun—a little man with horns growing from his forehead— who were possibly devils;[1] and at all events, at a later period, the lives of the saints represent evil spirits in the form of animals as not unfrequent. Lycanthropy, however, or the transformation of witches into wolves, presented more difficulty. The history of Nebuchadnezzar, and the conversion of Lot's wife, were, it is true, eagerly alleged in support of its possibility ; but it was impossible to forget that St. Augustine appeared to regard lycanthropy as a fable, and that a canon of the Council of Ancyra had emphatically condemned the belief. On the other hand, that belief had been very widely diffused among the ancients. It had been accepted by many of the greatest and most orthodox theologians, by the inquisitors who were commissioned by the popes, and by the law courts of most countries. The evidence on which it rested was very curious and definite. If the witch was wounded in the form of an animal, she retained that wound in her human form, and hundreds of such cases were alleged before the tribunals. Sometimes the hunter, having severed the paw of his assailant, retained it as a trophy ; but when he opened his bag, he discovered in it only a bleeding hand, which he recognised as the hand of his wife.[2]

The last class of anecdotes I shall notice is that which appears to have grown out of the Catholic conception of celibacy. I mean the accounts of the influence of witchcraft upon the passions.

It is not difficult to conceive the order of ideas that produced that passionate horror of the fair sex which is such a striking characteristic of old Catholic theology. Celibacy was universally regarded as the highest form of virtue, and in order to make it acceptable, theologians exhausted all the resources of their eloquence in describing the iniquity of those whose charms had rendered it so rare. Hence the long and fiery disquisitions on the unparalleled malignity, the inconceivable subtlety, the frivolity, the unfaithfulness, the unconquerably evil propensities of women, which were the terror of one age, and which became the amusement of the next. It is not very easy to read these diatribes with perfect gravity; but they acquire a certain melancholy significance, from the fact that the teaching they represent had probably a considerable influence in predisposing men to believe in witches ; and also in producing the extreme callousness with which the sufferings of the victims were contemplated. The question why the immense majority of those who were accused of sorcery should be women, early attracted attention ; and it was generally answered, not by the sensibility of their nervous constitution, and by their consequent liability to religious monomania and epidemics, but by the inherent wickedness of the sex. There

passage from a writer of the eleventh century, concerning a dog which in that century was "moved by the spirit of Pytho."

[1] Vita S. Pauli.

[2] "L'existence des loups-garous est attestée par Virgile, Solin, Strabon, Pomponius Mela, Dionysius Afer, Varron, et par tous les Jurisconsultes et démonomanes des derniers siècles. A peine commençait-on à en douter sous Louis XIV." (Plancey, Dict. infernal, Lycanthropie). Bodin, in his chapter on Lycanthropy, and in our own day, Madden (vol. i. pp. 334-358), have collected many additional authorities. St. Augustine notices the subject with considerable hesitation, but on the whole inclines, as I have said, towards incredulity (Civ. Dei, lib. xviii. c. 17, 18). He also tells us that in his time there were some innkeepers, who were said to give their guests drugs in cheese, and thus to turn them into animals (Ibid). In the Salic laws of the fifth century there is a curious enactment "that any sorceress who has devoured a man should on conviction be fined 200 sous" (Garinet, p. 6). To come down to a later period, we find, according to Bodin, Paracelsus and Fernel, the chief physician of Henry IV., holding the belief in lycanthropy. There is probably

no country in Europe—perhaps no country in the world—in which some form of this superstition has not existed. It raged, however, especially where wolves abounded—among the Jura, in Norway, Russia, Ireland (where the inhabitants of Ossory, according to Camden, were said to become wolves once every seven years), in the Pyrenees and Greece. The Italian women usually became cats. In the East (as the Arabian Nights show) many forms were assumed. A French judge named Boguet, at the end of the sixteenth century, devoted himself especially to the subject, burnt multitudes of lycanthropes, wrote a book about them, and drew up a code in which he permitted ordinary witches to be strangled before they were burnt, but excepted lycanthropes, who were to be burnt alive (Garinet, pp. 298-302). In the controversy about the reality of the transformation, Bodin supported the affirmative, and Binsfeldius the negative side. There is a form of monomania under which men believe themselves to be animals, which is doubtless the nucleus around which the system was formed—a striking instance of the development of the miraculous. See also Bourquelot, La Lycanthropie. Among the many mad notions of the Abyssinians, perhaps the maddest is their belief that blacksmiths and potters can change themselves into hyænas, and ought therefore to be excluded from the sacrament (Hecker, Epid. p. 120).

was no subject on which the old writers expatiated with more indignant eloquence, or with more copious illustration.[1] Cato, they said, had declared that "if the world were only free from women, men would not be without the converse of the gods." Cicero had said, that "many motives will urge men to one crime, but that one passion will impel women to all crimes." Solomon, whose means of observation had in this respect been exceedingly extensive, had summed up his experience in a long series of the most crushing apophthegms. Chrysostom only interpreted the general sentiment of the Fathers, when he pronounced woman to be "a necessary evil, a natural temptation, a desirable calamity, a domestic peril, a deadly fascination, and a painted ill." Doctor after doctor echoed the same lugubrious strain, ransacked the pages of history for illustrations of the enormities of the sex, and marshalled the ecclesiastical testimonies on the subject with the most imperturbable earnestness and solemnity. Men who had most seriously formed this estimate of the great majority of women; who esteemed celibacy the highest of virtues, and every temptation to abandon it the direct consequence of Satanic presence; came, by a very natural process, to regard all the "phenomena of love" as most especially under the influence of the Devil. Hence, those wild gleams of strange and grotesque romance which, from time to time, light up the literature of witchcraft. Incubi and Succubi were for ever wandering among mankind, alluring by more than human charms the unwary to their destruction, and laying plots which were but too often successful against the virtue of the saints. Sometimes, the witches kindled in the monastic breast a more terrestrial fire; and men told, with bated breath, how, under the spell of a vindictive woman, four successive abbots in a German monastery had been wasted away by an unholy flame.[2] Occasionally, with a still more refined malice, the Evil One assumed the appearance of some noted divine, in order to bring discredit upon his character; and an astonished maiden saw, prostrate at her feet, the form of one

whom she knew to be a bishop, and whom she believed to be a saint![1] Nor was it only among those who were bound to celibacy that the deadly influences were exercised. The witches were continually disturbing, by their machinations, the joys of wedlock; and none can tell how many hundreds have died in agonies for afflicting with barrenness the marriage bed.[2]

I make no apology for having dwelt so long on a series of doctrines and arguments which the reader will probably deem very puerile, because their importance depends, not on their intrinsic value, but upon their relation to the history of opinions. The follies of the past, when they were adopted by the wisest men, are well worthy of study; and, in the case before us, they furnish, I think, an invaluable clue to the laws of intellectual development. It is often and truly said, that past ages were pre-eminently credulous, as compared with our own; yet the difference is not so much in the amount of the credulity, as in the direction which it takes. Men are always prepared to accept, on very slight evidence, what they believe to be exceedingly probable. Their

[1] See especially the long strange chapter on the subject in Sprenger.
[2] Sprenger, Pars I. Quæst. vii. At the request of St. Serenus and St. Equitius the angels performed on those saints a counteracting surgical operation (Nider, *Formic de Mal.*, c. v.).

[1] See the curious story of St. Sylvanus, Bishop of Nazareth, in Sprenger (Pars II. Quæst. 1, cap. xi.). The Devil not only assumed the appearance of this holy man, in order to pay his addresses to a lady, but when discovered, crept under a bed, suffered himself to be dragged out, and declared that he was the veritable bishop. Happily, after a time, a miracle was wrought which cleared the reputation of the calumniated prelate.

[2] As few people realise the degree in which these superstitions were encouraged by the Church which claims infallibility, I may mention that the reality of this particular crime was implied, and its perpetrators anathematised, by the provincial councils or synods of Troyes, Lyons, Milan, Tours, Bourges, Narbonne, Ferrara, St. Malo, Mont Cassin, Orleans, and Grenoble, by the Rituals of Autun, Chartres, Périgueux, Atun, Evreux, Paris, Angers, Arras, Châlons, Bologna, Troyes, Bourges, Alet, Beauvais, Meaux, Rheims, &c., and by the decrees of a long series of bishops (Thiers, *Sup. pop.*, tom. iv. ch. vii.). It was held, as far as I know without a single exception, by all the inquisitors who presided at the witch-courts, and Sprenger gives a long account of the methods which were generally employed in convicting those who were accused of the crime. Montaigne appears to have been the first who openly denied it, ascribing to the imagination what the orthodox ascribed to the Devil; and this opinion seems soon to have become a characteristic of free-thinkers in France; for Thiers (who wrote in 1678) complains that "Les esprits forts et les libertins qui donnent tout à la nature, et qui ne jugent des choses que par la raison, ne veulent pas se persuader que de nouveaux-mariés puissent par l'artifice et la malice du démon estre empêchés de se rendre le devoir conjugal" (p. 567)—a very wicked incredulity—"puisque l'Eglise, qui est conduite par le Saint-Esprit, et qui par conséquent ne peut errer, reconnoît qu'il se fait par l'opération du démon" (p. 573). The same writer shows that the belief existed in the Church in the time of Theodosius (p. 568). The last sorcerer who was burnt in France perished on this charge (Garinet, p. 256).

measure of probability ultimately determines the details of their creed, and it is
itself perpetually changing under the influence of civilisation. In the middle ages,
and in the sixteenth, and the beginning of
the seventeenth centuries, the measure of
probability was essentially theological.
Men seemed to breathe an atmosphere
that was entirely unsecular. Their intellectual and imaginative conceptions were
all coloured by theological associations;
and they accepted with cheerful alacrity
any anecdote which harmonised with their
habitual meditations. The predisposition
to believe in the miraculous was so great,
that it constructed, out of a few natural
facts, this vast and complicated system of
witchcraft; accumulated around it an
immense mass of the most varied and
circumstantial evidence; persuaded all
the ablest men for many centuries that
it was incontestably true; conducted it
unshaken through the scrutiny of the
law-courts of every European nation; and
consigned tens of thousands of victims to
a fearful and unlamented death. There
was not the smallest desire to explain
away or soften down miraculous accounts,
in order to make them harmonise with
experience, because the minds of men
were completely imbued with an order of
ideas that had no connection with experience. If we could perceive evil spirits,
untrammelled by the laws of matter,
actually hovering around us; if we could
observe them watching every action with
a deadly malignity, seeking with all
the energies of superhuman power the
misery of mankind; and darkening with
their awful aspect every sphere in which
we move; if we could see the angel of
destruction brandishing the sword of
death over the Assyrian hosts, or over
the streets of Jerusalem; and could
behold Satan transporting Christ through
the air, or the demoniacs foaming in
agony beneath his grasp, we should
probably reason on these matters in
much the same spirit as the theologians
of the fifteenth and sixteenth centuries.
Our minds would be so pervaded by these
awful images, that they would form a
measure of probability entirely different
from that which is formed by the ordinary
experience of life; a nervous consciousness of the continual presence of evil
spirits would accompany us for ever;
and would for ever predispose us to discover manifestations of their power.
The foregoing pages will, I trust, be

sufficient to elucidate the leading causes
upon which witchcraft depended. They
will show that it resulted, not from accidental circumstances, individual eccen-
tricities, or even scientific ignorance, but
from a general predisposition to see
Satanic agency in life. It grew from,
and it reflected, the prevailing modes of
religious thought; and it declined only
when those modes were weakened or
destroyed. In almost every period of the
middle ages, there had been a few men
who in some degree dissented from the
common superstitions; but their opinions
were deemed entirely incomprehensible,
and they exercised no appreciable influence upon their contemporaries. Indeed,
their doctrines being generally veiled in
the mystical form, were so perverted and
materialised, that they not unfrequently
increased the prevailing gloom. As long
as the general credulity continued, as
long as the minds of men were directed
towards the miraculous and the Satanic,
no efforts could eradicate the superstition.
In such a condition of thought, men would
always be more inclined to accept than to
reject the evidence. They would refuse
to scrutinise it with jealous suspicion;
and, though they might admit the existence of some imposture, they would never
question the substantial justice of the
belief. Not until the predisposition was
changed; not until men began to recoil
from these narratives, as palpably and
grossly improbable; not until the sense
of their improbability so overpowered the
reverence for authority, as to make them
seek in every way to evade the evidence,
and to make them disbelieve it even
when they were unable to disprove it,
could this deadly superstition be rolled
away. Its decline marks the rise, and
its destruction the first triumph, of the
spirit of rationalism in Europe.

We frequently find, in the writings of
the inquisitors, language which implies
that a certain amount of scepticism was,
even in their time, smouldering in some
minds. It was not, indeed, sufficient to
make any deep impression on public
opinion. It is identified with no great
name,[1] and produced no great book; but

[1] I should, perhaps, make one exception to this
statement—Peter of Abano, a very famous physician
and philosopher of Padua, who died in 1305. He
appears to have entirely denied the existence of demons
and of miracles; and to have attempted, by the assistance of astrology, to construct a general philosophy of
religion, casting the horoscope of each faith, and
ascribing its rise and destiny to the influence of the

it was yet sufficiently evident to elicit the anxiety of some theologians. "Those men," wrote Gerson, "should be treated with scorn, and, indeed, sternly corrected, who ridicule theologians whenever they speak of demons, or attribute to demons any effects, as if these things were entirely fabulous. This error has arisen among some learned men, partly through want of faith, and partly through weakness and imperfection of intellect......for, as Plato says, to refer everything to the senses, and to be incapable of turning away from them, is the greatest impediment to truth."[1] Sprenger also, in a long chapter, instructed theologians how to meet a spirit of vague scepticism which had arisen among certain laymen; "who had, indeed, no fixed method of reasoning, but were blindly groping in the dark, touching now on one point, and now on another." An assembly of doctors of the University of Cologne,[2] which was held in 1487, lamented, and severely and authoritatively condemned, a still more startling instance of rebellion, arising from a quarter in which it was least to be expected. When the panic was raging most fiercely in the diocese of Cologne, some priests had attempted to allay the alarm by questioning the reality of the crime. About thirty years later, Spina mentions[3] that, in some places, the innumerable executions had aroused a spirit of most acrimonious opposition. Indeed, in the north of Italy, a positive rebellion had broken out, accompanied by a tone of incredulity which that theologian piteously laments. "Most imprudent, most undevout, and most unfaithful men will not believe the things they ought to believe; and what is still more lamentable, they exert all their influence to obstruct those who are destroying the enemies of Christ." Such a conduct, Spina justly observes, was full of danger for those who were guilty of it, as they might themselves be justly punished for conniving at the crime; and it was a

distinct reflection upon the Church which was represented by the inquisitors; and upon the Pope, by whom the inquisitors were commissioned. We find, too, the clergy claiming, in a very peremptory tone, the supreme jurisdiction of these cases; and occasionally alleging the misconduct of lay judges who had suffered witches to depart unharmed. All this scepticism, however, appears to have been latent and undefined; and it was not till 1563 that it was thrown into a systematic form by John Wier, in his treatise, *De Præstigiis Dæmonum.*

Wier was a learned and able physician of Cleves. He was convinced as a doctor that many of the victims were simply lunatics; and, being a very humane man, was greatly shocked at the sufferings they endured. He was a Protestant; and therefore, perhaps, not quite as much trammelled by tradition as some of his contemporaries; though in the present day his reverence for authority would be regarded as an absolute infatuation. He had not the slightest wish to revolt against any of the first principles of the popular teaching, or even to free himself from the prevailing modes of thought. He was quite convinced that the world was peopled by crowds of demons, who were constantly working miracles among mankind; and his only object was to reconcile his sense of their ubiquity with his persuasion that some of the phenomena that were deemed supernatural, arose from disease. He was of opinion that all the witches were labouring under the delusions of the Devil. They did not make an unholy compact, or ride through the air, or arouse tempests, or produce disease, or become the concubines of Satan; but the Devil had entered into them, and persuaded them that they had done these things. The idea of possession was thus so enlarged as to absorb the idea of witchcraft. The bewitched person was truly afflicted by the Devil, but the Devil had done this directly, and not by the intervention of a witch, and had then thrown suspicion upon some old woman, in order that the greatest possible amount of suffering might be produced. Persons, he said, were especially liable to diabolical possession, when their faculties were impaired by disease, and their tempers acidulated by suffering. In an eloquent and learned chapter on "the credulity and fragility of the female sex," he showed, by the authority of the Fathers and the Greek

---

stars. He was a disciple of Averroes—perhaps the founder of Averroism, in Italy—and seems to have formed a school at Padua. When he was about eighty, he was accused of magic. It was said that he had acquired a knowledge of the seven liberal arts by seven familiar spirits whom he kept confined in a crystal; but he died before the trial was concluded, so the inquisitors were obliged to content themselves by burning his image. He was regarded as one of the greatest of magicians. Compare Naudé, *Apol.* (pp. 380–391); Renan, *Averroes* (pp. 258, 259).

[1] *Mall. Mal.* vol. ii. p. 253.
[2] Ibid. vol. i. pp. 460–468.
[3] Vol. ii. pp. 191, 299, 300.

philosophers, that women were peculiarly subject to evil influences. He also showed that the witches, in mental and moral infirmities, were pre-eminent among their sex. He argued that the word translated witch, in the Levitical law, may be translated poisoner ; and that the patristic notion of the intercourse between angels and the antediluvian women, was inadmissible. The gross improbabilities of some parts of the popular belief were clearly exhibited, and illustrated with much unnecessary learning ; and the treatise was prefaced by an earnest appeal to the princes of Europe to arrest the effusion of innocent blood.

The scepticism of this work cannot be regarded as audacious. In fact, Wier stands alone in the history of witchcraft ; and differs essentially from all the later writers on the subject. He forms a link connecting two periods ; he was as fully pervaded by the sense of the miraculous as his opponents, and he never dreamed of restricting the sphere of the supernatural. Such as it was, however, this book was the first attack of any importance on the received opinions, and excited among learned men considerable attention. Three editions were published, in a few years, at Basle and Amsterdam, which were then the centres of independent thought. It was translated into French in 1569. It was followed by a treatise, *De Lamiis*, and by a very curious catalogue of the leaders, and description of the organisation, of hell.[1] Shortly after the publication of these last works, a book appeared in reply, from the pen of Bodin, the famous author of the *Republic*, and one of the most distinguished philosophers in Europe.

Bodin was esteemed, by many of his contemporaries, the ablest man who had then arisen in France ; and the verdict has been but little qualified by later writers.[2] Amid all the distractions of a dissipated and an intriguing court, and all the labours of a judicial position, he had amassed an amount of learning so vast and so various, as to place him in the very first rank of the scholars of his nation. He has also the far higher merit of being one of the chief founders of political philosophy and political history ; and of having anticipated on these subjects many of the conclusions of our own day. In his judicial capacity he had presided at some trials of witchcraft. He had brought all the resources of his scholarship to bear upon the subject ; and he had written a great part of his *Démonomanie des Sorciers* before the appearance of the last work of Wier.

The *Démonomanie des Sorciers* is chiefly an appeal to authority, which the author deemed on this subject so unanimous and so conclusive, that it was scarcely possible for any sane man to resist it. He appealed to the popular belief in all countries, in all ages, and in all religions. He cited the opinions of an immense multitude of the greatest writers of pagan antiquity, and of the most illustrious of the Fathers. He showed how the laws of all nations recognised the existence of witchcraft ; and he collected hundreds of cases which had been investigated before the tribunals of his own or of other countries. He relates with the most minute and circumstantial detail, and with the most unfaltering confidence, all the proceedings of the witches' Sabbath, the methods which the witches employed in transporting themselves through the air, their transformations, their carnal intercourse with the Devil, their various means of injuring their enemies, the signs that lead to their detection, their confessions when condemned, and their demeanour at the stake. As for the treatise of Wier, he could scarcely find words to express the astonishment and the indignation with which he had perused it. That a puny doctor should have dared to oppose himself to the authority of all

---

[1] *Pseudomonarchia Dæmonum*—one of the principal sources of information about this subject. He gives the names of seventy-two princes, and estimates their subjects at 7,405,926 devils. It is not quite clear how much he believed on the subject.

[2] A very old critic and opponent of his views on witchcraft quaintly speaks of him as "Ce premier homme de la France, Jean Bodin, qui après avoir par une merveilleuse vivacité d'esprit, accompagnée d'un jugement solide, traicté toutes les choses divines, naturelles et civiles, se fust peut estre mescogneu pour homme, et eust esté pris infailliblement de nous pour quelque intelligence s'il n'eust laissé des marques et vestiges de son humanité dans cette démonomanie." (Naudé, *Apol.*, 127 ; 1625). Bayle (*Dict. Phil.*) pronounced Bodin to have been "one of the chief advocates of liberty of conscience of his time." In our own day, Buckle (vol. i. p. 299) has placed him as an historian above Comines, and on a level with Machiavelli ; and Hallam, speaking of the *Republic*, says, "Bodin possessed a highly philosophical mind, united with the most ample stores of history and jurisprudence. No former writer on political philosophy had been either so comprehensive in his scheme, or so copious in his knowledge ; none, perhaps, more original, more independent and fearless in his enquiries—two men alone, indeed, could be compared with him—Aristotle and Machiavel." (*Hist. of Lit.* vol. ii. p. 68.) Dugald Stewart is equally encomiastic (*Dissertation*, pp. 52–54).

ages ; that he should have such a boundless confidence in his own opinions, and such a supreme contempt for the wisest of mankind, as to carp and cavil in a sceptical spirit at the evidence of one of the most notorious of existing facts : this was, in truth, the very climax of human arrogance, the very acme of human absurdity. But, extreme as was the audacity thus displayed, the impiety was still greater. Wier "had armed himself against God." His book was a tissue of "horrible blasphemies." " No one who is ever so little touched with the honour of God, could read such blasphemies without a righteous anger." Not only had he dared to impugn the sentences of so many upright judges; not only had he attempted to save those whom Scripture and the voice of the Church had branded as the worst of criminals ; he had even ventured to publish to the world the spells and incantations he had learned from a notorious sorcerer.[1] Who could reflect without consternation on the future of Christendom after such fearful disclosures ? Who could question that the knowledge thus disseminated would multiply to an incalculable extent the number of witches, would vastly increase the power of Satan, and would be productive of countless sufferings to the innocent ? Under these circumstances, so far from relaxing the prosecutions for witchcraft and sorcery, it was necessary to continue them with a redoubled energy ; and surely, no one could be the object of a more just suspicion than a man who had written so impious a book, and who had shown such acquaintance with the secrets of so impious a profession. To pardon those whom the law of God condemned to death, was indeed beyond the province of princes. Those who were guilty of such an act had outraged the majesty of Heaven. They had virtually repudiated the Divine law, and pestilence and famine would inevitably desolate their dominions.[1] One fatal example there had been, of a king tampering with his duty in this respect. Charles IX. had spared the life of the famous sorcerer, Trois Echelles, on the condition of his informing against his colleagues ; and it is to this grievous sin that the early death of the king is most probably to be ascribed : " For the word of God is very certain, that he who suffers a man worthy of death to escape, draws the punishment upon himself, as the prophet said to King Ahab, that he should die for having pardoned a man worthy of death. For no one had ever heard of pardon being accorded to sorcerers."[2]

Such were the opinions which were promulgated, towards the close of the sixteenth century, by one of the most advanced intellects of one of the leading nations of Europe ; promulgated, too, with a tone of confidence and of triumph that shows how fully the writer could count upon the sympathies of his readers. The *Démonomanie des Sorciers* appeared in 1581. Only seven years afterwards, Montaigne published the first great sceptical work in the French language ; and, among the many subjects on which his scepticism was turned, witchcraft occupied a prominent place. It would be scarcely possible to conceive a more striking contrast, than his treatment of it presents to the works of Bodin and of Wier. The vast mass of authority which those writers loved to array, and by which they shaped the whole course of their reasoning, is calmly and unhesitatingly discarded. The passion for the miraculous, the absorbing sense of diabolical capacities, have all vanished like a dream. The old theological measure of probability has completely disappeared, and is replaced by a shrewd secular common sense. The statements of the witches were pronounced intrinsically incredible. The dreams of a disordered imagination, or the terrors of the rack, would account for many of them ; but even when it is impossible to explain away the evidence,

---

[1] Cornelius Agrippa, who had been the master of Wier. He was Advocate-General at Metz, and had distinguished himself by his efforts to prevent prosecutions for witchcraft, and by saving the life of a peasant woman whom Savin the inquisitor wished to burn. He was, consequently, generally thought to be in league with the Devil ; and it is related that, on his death-bed, he drew off from his neck a black dog, which was a demon, exclaiming that it was the cause of his perdition (Garinet, pp. 121, 122). In his early days he had studied magic, and had apparently come to the conclusion that it rested either on imposture or on a superior knowledge of the laws of nature—a conclusion which he tried to enforce in a book on the vanity of science. He was imprisoned for a year at Brussels on the charge of magic, and ceaselessly calumniated after his death. Before Wier, probably no one had done so much to combat the persecution, and his reputation was sacrificed in the cause. (See Plancey's *Dict. Infern.* art. *Agrippa*, and Thiers' *Superst.* vol. i. pp. 142, 143.) Naudé has also devoted a long chapter to Agrippa. Agrippa had not the good fortune to please any class of theologians. Among the Catholics he was regarded with extreme horror ; and Calvin, in his work *De Scandalis*, treats him as one of the chief contemners of the Gospel.

[1] Pp. 217, 228.   [2] P. 154.

it is quite unnecessary to believe it. "There are," he said, "proofs and arguments that are founded on experience and facts. I do not pretend to unravel them. I often cut them, as Alexander did the knot. After all, it is setting a high value upon our opinions to roast men alive on account of them." We may not be able to discover an adequate solution of some statements on the subject, but we should consider—and he here anticipated a mode of argument which was destined long afterwards to assume a most prominent place in theological controversy—that it is far more probable that our senses should deceive us, than that an old woman should be carried up a chimney on a broomstick ; and that it is far less astonishing that witnesses should lie, than that witches should perform the acts that were alleged.[1]

It has been justly remarked by Malebranche, that Montaigne is an example of a writer who had no pretensions to be a great reasoner ; but who nevertheless exercised a most profound and general influence upon the opinions of mankind. It is not, I think, difficult to discover the explanation of the fact. In an age which was still spell-bound by the fascinations of the past he applied to every question a judgment entirely unclouded by the imaginations of theologians, and unshackled by the dictates of authority. His originality consists, not so much in his definite opinions or in his arguments, as in the general tone and character of his mind. He was the first French author who had entirely emancipated himself from the retrospective habits of thought that had so long been universal ; who ventured to judge all questions by a secular standard, by the light of common sense, by the measure of probability which is furnished by daily experience. He was, no doubt, perfectly aware that "the laws of Plato, of the Twelve Tables, of the consuls, of the emperors, and of all nations and legislators — Persian, Hebrew, Greek, Latin, German, French, Italian, Spanish, English—had decreed capital penalties against sorcerers;" he knew that "prophets, theologians, doctors, judges, and magistrates, had elucidated the reality of the crime by many thousand violent presumptions, accusations, testimonies, convictions, repentances, and voluntary confessions, persisted in to death ;"[2] but he

was also sensible of the extreme fallibility of the human judgment ; of the facility with which the mind discovers, in the phenomena of history, a reflection of its preconceived notions ; and of the rapidity with which systems of fiction are formed in a credulous and undiscriminating age. While Catholics, Protestants, and Deists were vying with each other in their adoration of the past ; while the ambition of every scholar and of every theologian was to form around his mind an atmosphere of thought that bore no relation to the world that was about him ; while knowledge was made the bond-slave of credulity, and those whose intellects were most shackled by prejudice were regarded as the wisest of mankind, it was the merit of Montaigne to rise, by the force of his masculine genius, into the clear world of reality ; to judge the opinions of his age, with an intellect that was invigorated but not enslaved by knowledge ; and to contemplate the systems of the past, without being dazzled by the reverence that had surrounded them. He looked down upon the broad field of history, upon its clashing enthusiasms, its discordant systems, the ebb and flow of its ever-changing belief, and he drew from the contemplation a lesson widely different from his contemporaries. He did not, it is true, fully recognise those moral principles which shine with an unchanging splendour above the fluctuations of speculative opinions ; he did not discover the great laws of eternal development, which preside over and direct the progress of belief, infuse order into the seeming chaos, and reveal in every apparent aberration a purpose and a meaning ; but he, at least, obtained an intense and realised perception of the fallibility of the human intellect ; a keen sense of the absurdity of an absolute deference to the past ; and of the danger of punishing men with death on account of opinions concerning which we can have so little assurance. These things led him to suspect that witchcraft might be a delusion. The bent and character of his mind led him to believe that witchcraft was grossly improbable. He was the first great representative of the modern secular and rationalistic spirit. By extricating his mind from the trammels of the past, he had learned to judge the narratives of diabolical intervention by a standard and with a spirit that had been long unknown. The predisposition of the old theologians had been to believe that the phenomena

---

[1] Liv. iii. c. 11.　　　　　[2] Bodin, p. 252.

of witchcraft were all produced by the Devil ; and when some manifest signs of madness or of imposture were exhibited, they attempted to accommodate them to their supernatural theory. The strong predisposition of Montaigne was to regard witchcraft as the result of natural causes ; and, therefore, though he did not attempt to explain all the statements which he had heard, he was convinced that no conceivable improbability could be as great as that which would be involved in their reception. This was not the happy guess of ignorance. It was the direct result of a mode of thought which he applied to all theological questions. Fifty years earlier, a book embodying such conceptions would have appeared entirely incomprehensible, and its author would perhaps have been burnt. At the close of the sixteenth century, the minds of men were prepared for its reception, and it flashed like a revelation upon France. From the publication of the essays of Montaigne, we may date the influence of that gifted and ever enlarging rationalistic school, which gradually effected the destruction of the belief in witchcraft, not by refuting or explaining its evidence, but simply by making men more and more sensible of its intrinsic absurdity.

Thirteen years after Montaigne, Charron wrote his famous treatise on *Wisdom*. In this work he systematised many of the opinions of Montaigne, but exhibited far less genius and originality than his predecessor. Like Montaigne he looked with aversion on the miraculous ; but, like Montaigne, his scepticism arose, not from any formal examination of evidence, but from a deep sense of the antecedent improbability. That which Montaigne had thrown into the form of strong doubt, Charron almost threw into the form of a denial. All through the seventeenth century, the same modes of thought continued, slowly but steadily sapping the old belief ; but, though the industry of modern antiquaries has exhumed two or three obscure works that were published on the subject,[1] those

works never seem to have attracted any serious attention, or to have had any appreciable influence in accelerating the movement. It presents a spectacle, not of argument or of conflict, but of a silent evanescence and decay. The priests continued to exorcise the possessed, to prosecute witches, and to anathematise as infidels all who questioned the crime. Many of the lawyers, reverting to the innumerable enactments in the lawbooks, and to the countless occasions on which the subject had been investigated by the tribunals, maintained the belief with equal pertinacity ; but outside these retrospective classes, the sense of the improbability of witchcraft became continually stronger, till any anecdote which involved the intervention of the Devil was on that account generally ridiculed. This spirit was exhibited specially among those whose habits of thought were most secular, and whose minds were least governed by authority.[1] Some great scholars and writers who were fully sensible of the improbability of the belief, at the same time regarded the evidence as irresistible, and looked upon the subject with a perplexed and timid suspension of judgment. La Bruyère said that the principles on which magic rests seem vague, uncertain, and visionary ; but that many embarrassing facts have been attested by credible eye-witnesses, that it appeared equally rash to admit or to deny them, and that it was better to take a central position between the credulous who admitted all and the freethinkers who rejected all.[2] Even Bayle seems to have looked upon it in a similar spirit.[3] Descartes, though he did not, as far as I am aware, ever refer directly to the subject, probably exercised a considerable influence upon it, for the tendency of his teaching was to emancipate the mind from the power of tradition,

[1] Maury, pp. 221, 222. The principal of those writers was Naudé, whose *Apologie pour les Grands Hommes Soupçonnez de Magie*, contains much curious historical information in an extremely tiresome form. Naudé also wrote an exposure of the Rosicrucians, and a political work on *Coups d'Etat*, embodying the principles of Machiavelli. He was the first librarian of the Mazarine library, in the foundation of which he had a considerable part. Bayle (*Pensées Diverses*, § ccxli.) calls him "L'homme de France qui avoit le plus de lecture." He is said to have reconstructed some of

the dances of the ancients, and to have executed them in person before Queen Christina, in Sweden (Magnin, *Origines du Théâtre*, tom. i. p. 113). The *Apologie* was answered by a Capucin named D'Autun in a ponderous work called *L'Incrédulité Sçavante*.

[1] "Ce furent les esprits forts du commencement du dix-septième siècle qui s'efforcèrent les premiers de combattre le préjugé régnant, de défendre de malheureux fous ou d'indiscrets chercheurs contre les tribunaux. Il fallait pour cela du courage, car on risquait, en cherchant à sauver la tête du prévenu, de passer soi-même pour un affidé du diable, ou ce que ne valait pas mieux, pour un incrédule. Les libres penseurs, les libertins comme on les appelait alors, n'avaient que peu de crédit." (Maury, p. 221.)

[2] See the passage in Maury, p. 219.

[3] Ibid., p. 220.

to secularise philosophy, and to destroy the material notions that had long been associated with spirits. Malebranche mentions that in his time some of the parliaments had ceased to burn witches, and that within their jurisdiction the number of witches had declined. He inferred from this, that the contagious power of imagination had created many of the phenomena. He analysed, with much acuteness, the process of thought which produced lycanthropy; but, being a priest, he found it necessary to add, that real sorcerers should undoubtedly be put to death.[1] Voltaire treated the whole subject with a scornful ridicule; observed that since there had been philosophers in France, witches had become proportionately rare, and summed up the ecclesiastical authorities for the belief as emphatically as Sprenger or Spina, but with a very different object.[2]

In the first half of the seventeenth century, the civil power uniformly exerted its energies for the destruction of witches. It was between the publication of the works of Montaigne and of Charron that Boguet was presiding at the tribunal of St. Claude, where he is said to have burnt 600 persons, chiefly for lycanthropy. A few years later, the fifty executions at Douay, which I have already mentioned, took place; and, in 1642, Cardinal Mazarin wrote a letter to the Bishop of Evreux, congratulating him warmly on the successful zeal he had manifested on the subject.[3] Towards the middle of the century, however, the growing incredulity had reached those in power; the prosecutions for witchcraft became more rare and languid; and, in 1672, Colbert directed the magistrates to receive no accusations of sorcery, and commuted in many cases the capital punishment for the crime into a sentence of banishment. It was when some of these commutations had been made that the Parliament of Rouen drew up an extremely remarkable address to the king, protesting, in a strain of high religious fervour, against the indulgence

as directly contrary to the Word of God, to all the precedents of French law, and to all the traditions of the Christian religion.[1] After this time but few trials for sorcery took place—that of the Marshal of Luxembourg, in 1681, was, perhaps, the most remarkable—for the scepticism on the subject had already become very marked, and in the last twenty years of the seventeenth century, only seven sorcerers seem to have been burnt in France. Still later, in 1718, the Parliament of Bordeaux burnt a man upon this charge. After this period there were, indeed, one or two trials, but the prisoners were acquitted; the star of Voltaire had arisen above the horizon, and the unsparing ridicule which his followers cast upon every anecdote of witches, intimidated those who did not share in the incredulity. The formularies for exorcism still continued as they continue to the present day in Roman Catholic rituals, and they were frequently employed all through the eighteenth century; but the more educated members of the clergy for the most part allowed the subject to fall into neglect, and discouraged the attempts of some of the order to revive it. Those who still clung to the traditions of the past must have found much difficulty in accounting for the progress of the movement. That Satan should occupy such an extremely small place in the minds of men was very lamentable, but that the miraculous signs of his presence should have so completely disappeared was exceedingly perplexing. At the beginning of the present (nineteenth) century, the Abbé Fiard published a work designed to explain the difficulty. He showed that the philosophers and revolutionists of the last century were the representatives of the old sorcerers, that they acted under the direct inspiration of Satan, and that their success was entirely due to Satanic power. Lest, however, it should be said that this represented rather the moral than the miraculous influence of the Evil One, he added that many great and startling miracles had accompanied the philosophic movement, and that these miracles had not even yet ceased. The cures of Mesmer and the prophecies of Cagliostro should both be ascribed to supernatural agency; but the most startling of all the signs of diabolical presence was the ever-increasing popularity of

---

[1] *Recherche de la Vérité*, liv. ii. p. 3, c. 6.
[2] He said: "Tous les pères de l'Eglise sans exception crurent au pouvoir de la magie. L'Eglise condamna toujours la magie, mais elle y crut toujours. Elle n'excommunia point les sorciers comme des fous, qui étaient trompés, mais comme des hommes qui étaient réellement en commerce avec les diables." (*Dict. Phil.* art. *Superstition*.) This I believe to be quite true, but it was a striking sign of the times that an opponent of magic could say so, without ruining his cause.
[3] Garinet, p. 328.

ventriloquism. On this last subject, we are happily not left to our own unassisted conjectures, for some learned divines of the fourteenth century had solemnly determined that man was designed to speak by his mouth ; and that, whenever he spoke in any other way, he did so by the assistance of the Devil.[1]

The history of witchcraft in Protestant countries differs so little from its history in Catholic ones that it is not necessary to dwell upon it at much length. In both cases, a tendency towards the miraculous was the cause of the belief; and the degree of religious terrorism regulated the intensity of the persecution. In both cases, too, the rise and progress of a rationalistic spirit were the origin and the measure of its decline. In England, there appears to have been no law against sorcery till 1541, when the nation was convulsed by the first paroxysms of the Reformation. The crime had indeed been known at an earlier period, and a few executions had taken place, but they were very rare ; and, in producing them, other motives seem to have been generally mixed with superstition. Joan of Arc, the noblest of all the victims of the belief, perished by English hands, though on French soil, and under the sentence of a French bishop. Some years after, the Duchess of Gloucester, having been accused by the Cardinal of Beaufort of attempting the king's life by sorcery, was compelled to do penance, while two of her servants were executed. A few other cases have come down to us; but, although the extreme imperfection of the old criminal registers renders it very probable that there were others which are forgotten, there can be little doubt that the superstition was much less prominent in England than on the Continent.[2] Owing

partly to its insular position, and partly to the intense political life that from the earliest period animated the people, there was formed in England a fearless and self-reliant type of character essentially distinct from that which was common in Europe, eminently free from morbid and superstitious terrors, and averse to the more depressing aspects of religion. It was natural, however, that amid the conflicts of the Reformation, some of the darker superstitions should arise ; and we accordingly find Cranmer, in one of his articles of visitation, directing his clergy to seek for " any that use charms, sorcery, enchantments, witchcraft, soothsaying, or any like craft invented by the Devil." It is remarkable that the law of Henry VIII. against witchcraft was repealed in the following reign, and there was no fresh legislation about it till after the accession of Elizabeth.[1] A new law was then made, which was executed with severity ; and Jewell, when preaching before the queen, adverting to the increase of witches, expressed a hope that the penalties might be still more rigidly enforced. " May it please your grace," he added, " to understand that witches and sorcerers within these few years are marvellously increased within your grace's realm. Your grace's subjects pine away even unto the death ; their colour fadeth, their flesh rotteth, their speech is benumbed, their senses are bereft......I pray God they never practise further than upon the subject."[2] On the whole, however, these laws were far milder than those on the Continent. For the first conviction, witches who had not destroyed others by incantations or invoked evil spirits were only punished by the pillory and by imprisonment, while those who were condemned to death perished by the gallows instead of the stake. Besides this, torture, which had done so much to multiply the evidence, had always been illegal, though it has occasionally been made use of, in England, and the witchfinders were compelled to content them-

---

[1] Garinet, p. 280.

[2] The most complete authority on this subject is the chronological table of facts in Hutchinson's *Essay on Witchcraft* (1718). Hutchinson, who was a very scrupulous writer, restricted himself for the most part to cases of which he had learnt precise particulars, and he carefully gives his authorities. The number of executions he recounts as having taken place in 250 years, amounts to many thousands. Of these only about 140 were in England. This, of course, excludes those who were drowned or mobbed to death during the trial, and those who were sentenced to other than capital punishments. All the other writers I have seen, place the English executions far higher ; and it seems, I think, certain that some executions escaped the notice of Hutchinson, whose estimate is, however, probably much nearer the truth than those of most writers. See also Wright's *Sorcery*; and an article from the *Foreign Review* in " A Collection of Curious Tracts on Witchcraft," reprinted in 1838. It is quite impossible to arrive at anything like precision on this subject.

---

[1] The repeal was probably owing to the fact that witchcraft, and pulling down crosses, were combined together ; and the law had, therefore, a Popish appearance.

[2] Sermons (Parker Society), p. 1028. Strype ascribes to this sermon the law which was passed the following year (*Annals of the Ref.* vol. i. p. 11). The multitude of witches at the beginning of the reign of Elizabeth (which Strype notices) was the obvious consequence of the terrorism of the preceding reign, and of the religious changes acting in the way I have already described.

selves with pricking their victims all over in hopes of discovering the insensible spot,[1] with throwing them into the water to ascertain whether they would sink or swim, and with keeping them during several successive nights without sleep, in order to compel them to confess. These three methods were habitually employed with signal success; many women were in consequence condemned, and a considerable proportion of them were hung.

But such scenes did not take place without one noble protest. A layman named Reginald Scott published, in 1584, his *Discovery of Witchcraft*, in which he unmasked the imposture and the delusion of the system with a boldness that no previous writer had approached, and with an ability which few subsequent writers have equalled. Keenly, eloquently, and unflinchingly, he exposed the atrocious torments by which confessions were extorted, the laxity and injustice of the manner in which evidence was collected, the egregious absurdities that filled the writings of the inquisitors, the juggling tricks that were ascribed to the devil, and the childish folly of the magical charms. He also availed himself in a very dexterous manner of the strong Protestant feeling, in order to discredit statements that emanated from the Inquisition. If the question was to be determined by argument, if it depended simply or mainly upon the ability or learning of the controversialists, the treatise of Scott would have had a powerful effect; for it was by far the ablest attack on the prevailing superstition that had ever appeared, and it was written in the most popular style. As a matter of fact it exercised no appreciable influence. Witchcraft depended upon general causes, and represented the prevailing modes of religious thought. It was therefore entirely unaffected by the attempted refutation; and when James I. mounted the throne, he found the nation perfectly prepared to second him in his zeal against the witches.

James, although he hated the Puritans, had caught in Scotland much of the tone of thought concerning Satanic power which the Puritans had always encouraged, and which was exhibited to the highest perfection in the Scottish mind. He was continually haunted by the subject. He had himself written a dialogue upon it; he had confidently ascribed his stormy passage on his return from Denmark to the machinations of the witches,[1] and he boasted that the Devil regarded him as the most formidable of opponents. Soon after his accession to the throne of England, a law was enacted which subjected witches to death on the first conviction, even though they should have inflicted no injury upon their neighbours. This law was passed when Coke was Attorney-General, and Bacon a member of Parliament; and twelve bishops sat upon the Commission to which it was referred.[2] The prosecutions were rapidly multiplied throughout the country, but especially in Lancashire; and at the same time the general tone of literature was strongly tinged with the superstition. Sir Thomas Browne declared that those who denied the existence of witchcraft were not only infidels, but also, by implication, atheists.[3] Shakspeare, like most of the other dramatists of his time, again and again referred to the belief; and we owe to it that melancholy picture of Joan of Arc which is, perhaps, the darkest blot upon his genius.[4] Bacon continually in-

---

[1] It is worthy of notice that anesthesia is a recognised symptom of some of the epidemic forms of madness. Speaking of that of Morzines, Dr. Constans says: "L'anesthésie fait jamais défaut. J'ai pu pincer, piquer avec une épingle les malades, enfoncer cette épingle sous les ongles ou de toute sa longueur dans les bras, les jambes ou sur toute autre partie, sans provoquer l'apparence d'une sensation douloureuse." (*Epidémie d'Hystéro-Démonopathie en* 1861, p. 63.)

[1] This storm was the origin of one of the most horrible of the many horrible Scotch trials on record. One Dr. Fian was suspected of having aroused the wind, and a confession was wrung from him by torture, which, however, he almost immediately afterwards retracted. Every form of torture was in vain employed to vanquish his obduracy. The bones of his legs were broken into small pieces in the boot. All the torments that Scottish law knew of were successively applied. At last, the king (who personally presided over the tortures) suggested a new and more horrible device. The prisoner, who had been removed during the deliberation, was brought in, and (I quote the contemporary narrative) "his nailes upon all his fingers were riven and pulled off with an instrument, called in Scottish a turkas, which in England we call a payre of pincers, and under everie nayle there was thrust in two needels over, even up to the heads." However, notwithstanding all this, "so deeply had the devil entered into his heart, that hee utterly denied all that which he before avouched," and he was burnt unconfessed. (See a rare black letter tract, reprinted in Pitcairn's *Criminal Trials of Scotland*, vol. i. part ii. pp. 213, 223.)   [2] Madden's *Phant.* vol. i. p. 447.

[3] "I have ever believed, and do now know, that there are witches; they that doubt them do not only deny them but spirits, and are obliquely and upon consequence a sort, not of infidels, but of atheists." (*Religio Medici*, p. 24, ed. 1672.) Sir T. Browne did not, however, believe in incubi, or in lycanthropy.

[4] On the extent to which the belief was reflected in the dramatic literature of Elizabeth and James I., see Wright's *Sorcery*, vol. i. pp. 286, 296. It was afterwards the custom of Voltaire, when decrying the

veighed against the follies shown by magicians in their researches into nature; yet in one of his most important works he pronounced the three "declinations from religion" to be "heresies, idolatry, and witchcraft."[1] Selden took up a somewhat peculiar and characteristic position. He maintained that the law condemning women to death for witchcraft was perfectly just, but that it was quite unnecessary to ascertain whether witchcraft was a possibility. A woman might not be able to destroy the life of her neighbour by her incantations; but if she intended to do so, it was right that she should be hung.[2]

But, great as were the exertions made by James to extirpate witchcraft, they completely sink into insignificance before those which were made during the Commonwealth. As soon as Puritanism gained an ascendency in the country, as soon as its ministers succeeded in imparting their gloomy tenets to the governing classes, the superstition assumed a gigantic magnitude. During the few years of the Commonwealth, there is reason to believe that more alleged witches perished in England than in the whole period before and after.[3] Nor is this to be ascribed entirely to the judges or the legislators, for the judges in former reigns never shrank from condemning witches, and Cromwell was in most respects far superior to his predecessors. It was simply the natural result of Puritanical teaching acting on the mind, predisposing men to see Satanic influence in life, and consequently eliciting the phenomena of witchcraft. A panic on the subject spread through the country; and anecdotes of Satanic power soon crowded in from every side. The county of Suffolk was especially agitated, and the famous witch-finder, Matthew Hopkins, pronounced it to be infested with witches.

A commission was accordingly issued, and two distinguished Presbyterian divines were selected by the Parliament to accompany it. It would have been impossible to take any measure more calculated to stimulate the prosecution, and we accordingly find that in Suffolk sixty persons were hung for witchcraft in a single year.[1] Among others, an Anglican clergyman, named Lowes, who was now verging on eighty, and who for fifty years had been an irreproachable minister of his church, fell under the suspicion. The unhappy old man was kept awake for several successive nights, and persecuted "till he was weary of his life, and was scarce sensible of what he said or did." He was then thrown into the water, condemned, and hung. According to the story which circulated among the members of the Established Church, he maintained his innocence manfully to the end. If we believe the Puritanical account, it would appear that his brain gave way under the trial, and that his accusers extorted from him a wild romance, which was afterwards, with many others, reproduced by Baxter "for the conversion of the Sadducee and the infidel."[2]

We have seen that the conception of witchcraft, which had existed in England from the earliest period, assumed for the first time a certain prominence amid the religious terrorism of the Reformation; that its importance gradually increased as the trials and executions directed public attention to the subject; and that it, at last, reached its climax under the gloomy theology of the Puritans. It now only remains for me to trace the history of its decline.

In pursuing this task, I must repeat that it is impossible to follow the general intellectual tendencies of a nation with the degree of precision with which we may review the events or the arguments

genius of Shakspeare, to dwell constantly on such characters as the witches in Macbeth. But such scenes, though in modern times they may have an unreal and grotesque appearance, did not present the slightest improbability at the time they were written. It is probable that Shakspeare, it is certain that the immense majority even of his most highly educated and gifted contemporaries, believed with an unfaltering faith in the reality of witchcraft. Shakspeare was, therefore, perfectly justified in introducing into his plays personages who were, of all others, most fitted to enhance the grandeur and the solemnity of tragedy, when they faithfully reflected the belief of the audience.

[1] *Advancement of Learning*, xxv. 22. It is true that this book was dedicated to the king, whose writings on the subject were commended.
[2] *Table-Talk*.
[3] Hutchinson, p. 68.

[1] This is alluded to in *Hudibras*:—
  "Hath not this present Parliament
  A ledger to the devil sent
  Fully empowered to treat about
  Finding revolted witches out?
  And has not he within a year
  Hanged threescore of them in one shire?" &c.
    Second part, Canto iii.
[2] Baxter relates the whole story with evident pleasure. He says, "Among the rest, an *old reading parson* named Lowis, not far from Framlingham, was one that was hanged, who confessed that he had two imps, and that one of them was always putting him on doing mischief, and (being near the sea) as he saw a ship under sail, it moved him to send him to sink the ship, and he consented, and saw the ship sink before him." (*World of Spirits*, p. 53.) For the other view of the case, see Hutchinson, pp. 88–90.

they produced. We have ample evidence that, at a certain period of English history, there was manifested in some classes a strong disposition to regard witch stories as absurd ; but we cannot say precisely when the idea of grotesqueness was first attached to the belief, nor can we map out with exactness the stages of its progress. Speaking generally, however, there can be no doubt that it first became prominent in that great sceptical movement which followed the Restoration. The reaction against the austere rigidity of the last Government had produced among the gayer classes a sudden outburst of the most derisive incredulity. From mocking the solemn gait, the nasal twang, and the affected phraseology of the Puritans, they naturally proceeded to ridicule their doctrines : and having soon discovered in witchcraft abundant materials for their satire, they made disbelief in it one of the tests of fashion. At the same time the higher intellectual influences were tending strongly to produce a similar movement among the learned. Hobbes, who was the most distinguished of living philosophers, had directed all the energies of his scepticism against incorporeal substances, had treated with unsparing ridicule the conceptions of demons and of apparitions, and had created in his disciples a predisposition to regard them as below contempt.[1] A similar predisposition was formed by the philosophy of Bacon, which had then acquired an immense popularity. The Royal Society[2] had been just established ; a passion for natural philosophy, much resembling that which preceded the French Revolution, had become general ; and the whole force of the English intellect was directed to the study of natural phenomena, and to the discovery of natural laws. In this manner there was formed a general disposition to attribute to every event a natural cause, which was soon followed by a conviction of the absurdity of explaining phenomena by a supernatural hypothesis, and which rapidly discredited the anecdotes of witches. There does not appear to have been any very careful scrutiny of their details, yet there was a growing indisposition to be-

lieve them, as they were discordant with the modes of thought which the experimental philosophy had produced.

By the combination of these three influences a profound change was soon effected in the manner in which witchcraft was regarded. The sense of its improbability became for the first time general among educated laymen, and the number of the trials speedily diminished. In 1664, however, two women were hung in Suffolk, under a sentence of Sir Matthew Hale, who took the opportunity of declaring that the reality of witchcraft was unquestionable ; " for first, the Scriptures had affirmed so much ; and secondly, the wisdom of all nations had provided laws against such persons, which is an argument of their confidence of such a crime." Sir Thomas Browne, who was a great physician as well as a great writer, was called as a witness, and swore " that he was clearly of opinion that the persons were bewitched."[1]

Seventeen years later, the defence of the dying belief was taken up by Joseph Glanvil, a divine, who in his own day was very famous, and who, I venture to think, has been surpassed in genius by few of his successors. Among his contemporaries he was especially praised as an able scholar and dialectician, and as a writer whose style, though not untinctured by the pedantry of his age, often furnishes the noblest examples of that glorious eloquence, so rich in varied and majestic harmonies, of which Milton, Sir Thomas Browne, and the early Anglican divines were the greatest masters. To us, however, who look upon his career from the vantage ground of experience, it assumes a still higher interest, for it occupies a most important position in the history of that experimental philosophy which has become the great guiding influence of the English mind. As the works of Glanvil are far less known than they should be, and as his defence of witchcraft was intimately connected with his earlier literary enterprises, I shall make no apology for giving a general outline of his opinions.

To those who only know him as the defender of witchcraft, it may appear a somewhat startling paradox to say, that the predominating characteristic of the mind of Glanvil was an intense scepticism.

---

[1] On the opinions of Hobbes on this subject, and on his great influence in discrediting these superstitions, see Cudworth's *Intellectual System*, vol. i. p. 116.

[2] The (indirect) influence of the Royal Society on this subject is noticed by Hutchinson, and indeed most of the writers on witchcraft. See Casaubon *On Credulity*, page 191.

[1] The report of this trial is reprinted in *A Collection of Rare and Curious Tracts Relating to Witchcraft* (London, 1838).

He has even been termed by a modern critic "the first English writer who had thrown scepticism into a definite form";[1] and if we regard this expression as simply implying a profound distrust of human faculties, and not at all the rejection of any distinct dogmatic system, the judgment can hardly be disputed. And certainly, it would be difficult to find a work displaying less of the credulity and superstition that are commonly attributed to the believers in witchcraft than the treatise on *The Vanity of Dogmatising or Confidence of Opinions,*[2] in which Glanvil expounded his philosophical views. Developing a few scattered hints of Bacon, he undertook to make a comprehensive survey of the human faculties, to analyse the distorting influences that corrode or pervert our judgments, to reveal the weakness and fallibility of the most powerful intellect, and to estimate the infinity of darkness that encircles our scanty knowledge. Not only did he trace, with the most vivid and unfaltering pen, the proneness to error that accompanies the human intellect in the moments of its greatest confidence; not only did he paint in the darkest colours the tenacity and the inveteracy of prejudice; he even accepted to the fullest extent the consequence of his doctrine, and, with Descartes, enjoined a total abnegation of the opinions that have been received by education as the first condition of enquiry. He showed himself perfectly acquainted with the diversities of intellectual tone, or, as he very happily termed them, the "climates of opinion" that belong to different ages; and he devoted an entire chapter[3] to the deceptions of the imagination, a faculty which he treated with as much severity as Butler.

On the publication of this treatise Glanvil had been elected a fellow of the Royal Society, and became one of the most distinguished of the small but able minority of the clergy who cordially embraced the inductive philosophy To combat the strong antipathy with which this philosophy was regarded in the Church, and to bring theology into harmony with its principles, was the task to which he devoted the remainder of his life. Sprat, and, in a less degree, one or two other divines, were employed in the same noble cause; but the manner in which Glanvil conducted his enterprise separates him, I think, clearly from his fellow-labourers. For, while his contemporaries seem to have expected as the extreme consequences of his philosophy, on the one hand a period of passing disturbance, arising from the discovery of apparent discrepancies between science and the Bible, and on the other hand increased evidence of the faith, arising from the solution of those difficulties and from the increased perception of superintending wisdom exhibited in "the wheel-work of creation," Glanvil perceived very clearly that a far deeper and more general modification was at hand. He saw that the theological system existing in a nation is intimately connected with the prevailing modes of thought or intellectual condition; that the new philosophy was about to change that condition; and that the Church must either adapt herself to the altered tone, or lose her influence over the English mind. He saw that a theology which rested ultimately on authority, which branded doubt as criminal, and which discouraged in the strongest manner every impartial investigation, could not long co-exist with a philosophy that encouraged the opposite habits of thought as the very beginning of wisdom. He saw that while men maintained every strange phenomenon to be miraculous as long as it was unexplained, each advance of physical science must necessarily be hostile to theology; and that the passionate adoration of Aristotle, the blind pedantic reverence which accounted the simplest assertions of dead men decisive authorities, the retrospective habits of thought the universities steadily laboured to encourage, were all incompatible with the new tendencies which Bacon represented.[1] In an essay on *Anti-*

---

[1] *Biographie Universelle*—an article which is also in the *Encyclopedia Britannica.*

[2] There is a good review of this book in Hallam's *Hist. of Lit.,* vol. iii. pp. 358–362. It is, I think, by far the best thing Glanvil wrote, and he evidently took extraordinary pains in bringing it to perfection. It first appeared as a short essay; it was then expanded into a regular treatise; and still later, recast and published anew under the title of "*Scepsis Scientifica.*" This last edition is somewhat rare, the greater part of the impression having, it is said (I do not know on what authority), been destroyed in the fire of London. It was answered by Thomas White, a once famous Roman Catholic controversialist. I cannot but think that Paley was acquainted with the works of Glanvil, for their mode of treating many subjects is strikingly similar. Paley's watch simile is fully developed by Glanvil, in chap. v.

[3] Chap. xi.

[1] He compares the leading scholars of his day to the mariner who returned laden with common pebbles from

Fanatical Religion and Free Philosophy, which was designed to be a continuation of the *New Atlantis* of Bacon, he drew a noble sketch of an ideal church constructed to meet the wants of an intellectual and a critical age. Its creed was to be framed on the most latitudinarian principles, because the doctrines that could be defended with legitimate assurance were but few and simple. Its ministers were to be much less anxious to accumulate the traditions of the past than to acquire "the felicity of clear and distinct thinking," and "a large compass in their thoughts." They were to regard faith not as the opposite of reason, but as one of its manifestations. Penetrated by the sense of human weakness, they were to rebuke the spirit of dogmatic confidence and assertion, and were to teach men that, so far from doubt being criminal, it was the duty of every man "to suspend his full and resolved assent to the doctrines he had been taught, till he had impartially considered and examined them for himself."

A religious system which is thus divested of the support of authority may be upheld upon two grounds. It may be defended on the rationalistic ground, as according with conscience, representing and reflecting the light that is in mankind, and being thus its own justification; or it may be defended as a distinct dogmatic system by a train of evidential reasoning. The character of his own mind, and the very low ebb to which moral feeling had sunk in his age, induced Glanvil to prefer the logical to the moral proof, and he believed that the field on which the battle must first be fought was witchcraft, which furnished an example of miracles that were contemporary and easy to test. "For things remote or long past" (he said) "are either not believed or forgotten—whereas these being fresh and new, and attended with all the circumstances of credibility, it may

be expected they should have most success upon the obstinacy of unbelievers."[1]

The *Sadducismus Triumphatus*, which is probably the ablest book ever published in defence of the superstition, opens with a striking picture of the rapid progress of the scepticism in England.[2] Everywhere, a disbelief in witchcraft was becoming fashionable in the upper classes; but it was a disbelief that arose entirely from a strong sense of its antecedent improbability. All who were opposed to the orthodox faith united in discrediting witchcraft. They laughed at it, as palpably absurd, as involving the most grotesque and ludicrous conceptions, as so essentially incredible that it would be a waste of time to examine it. This spirit had arisen since the Restoration, although the laws were still in force, and although little or no direct reasoning had been brought to bear upon the subject. In order to combat it, Glanvil proceeded to examine the general question of the credibility of the miraculous. He saw that the reason why witchcraft was ridiculed was, because it was a phase of the miraculous and the work of the Devil; that the scepticism was chiefly due to those who disbelieved in miracles and the Devil; and that the instances of witchcraft or possession in the Bible, were invariably placed on a level with those that were tried in the law-courts of England. That the evidence of the belief was overwhelming, he firmly believed;[3]

---

[1] Preface to the *Sadducismus*.

[2] "Atheism is begun in Sadducism, and those that dare not bluntly say there is no God, content themselves (for a fair step and introduction) to deny there are spirits or witches, which sort of infidels, though they are not ordinary among the mere vulgar, yet are they numerous in a little higher rank of understandings. And those that know anything of the world, know that most of the looser gentry and the small pretenders to philosophy and wit, are generally deriders of the belief of witches and apparitions." I need hardly say that the word Atheism was, in the time of Glanvil, used in the very loosest sense: indeed, Dugald Stewart shows, that at one time the disbelievers in apostolical succession were commonly denounced as Atheists. (*Dissert.* p. 378.)

[3] See a striking passage, pp. 3, 4:—"I must premise that this, being matter of fact, is only capable of the evidence of authority and of sense, and by both these the being of witches and diabolical contracts is most abundantly confirmed. All histories are full of the exploits of those instruments of darkness, and the testimony of all ages, not only of the rude and barbarous, but of the most civilized and polished world, brings tidings of their strange performances. We have the attestation of thousands of eye and ear witnesses, and those not of the easily deceivable vulgar only, but of wise and grave discerners, and that when no interest could oblige them to agree together in a common lie; I say we have the light of all these circumstances to confirm us in the belief of

---

the Indies, imagining that that must necessarily be rare that came from afar, and he accused them of asserting, on the authority of Beza, that women have no beards, and on that of St. Augustine that peace is a blessing. He pronounced university education in general, and that of Oxford in particular, to be almost worthless. The indignation such sentiments created at Oxford is very amusingly shown in Wood's *Athenæ*, arts. *Glanvil* and *Crosse*. Crosse was a Fellow of Oxford (a D.D.), who at first vehemently assailed Glanvil in prose, but at last changed his mode of attack, and wrote comic ballads, which Wood assures us "made Glanvil and his Society ridiculous."

and this, indeed, was scarcely disputed; but, until the sense of *a priori* improbability was removed, no possible accumulation of facts would cause men to believe it. To that task he accordingly addressed himself. Anticipating the idea and almost the words of modern controversialists, he urged that there was such a thing as a credulity of unbelief; and that those who believed so strange a concurrence of delusions, as was necessary on the supposition of the unreality of witchcraft, were far more credulous than those who accepted the belief.[1] He made his very scepticism his principal weapon; and, analysing with much acuteness the *a priori* objections, he showed that they rested upon an unwarrantable confidence in our knowledge of the laws of the spirit world; that they implied the existence of some strict analogy between the faculties of men and of spirits; and that, as such analogy most probably did not exist, no reasoning based on the supposition could dispense men from examining the evidence. He concluded with a large collection of cases, the evidence of which was, as he thought, incontestable.

The *Sadducismus Triumphatus* had an extraordinary success. Numerous editions were issued, and several very able men came forward to support its views. Henry More, the famous philosopher, wrote a warm eulogium to Glanvil, and drew up a long argument in the same spirit, in which he related several additional witch cases, and pronounced the opponents of the belief to be mere " buf-

foons, puffed up with nothing but ignorance, vanity, and stupid infidelity."[1] Casaubon, the learned Dean of Canterbury, wrote to the same effect, but in more moderate language.[2] The illustrious Boyle, while noticing the weakness of the evidence of many witch stories and the necessity of great caution in collecting them, wrote to Glanvil expressing his firm belief in the story of the demon of Mascon.[3] Cudworth, perhaps the most profound of all the great scholars who have adorned the English Church, pronounced the scepticism on the subject of witches to be chiefly a consequence of the influence of Hobbes; and he added, that those who partook of that scepticism might be justly suspected of atheism.[4] Several other divines pressed forward in the same spirit; and they made witchcraft, for a time, one of the chief subjects of controversy in England. On the other side, the discussion was extremely languid. No writer, comparable in ability or influence to Glanvil, More, Cudworth, or even Casaubon, appeared to challenge the belief; nor did any of the writings on that side obtain any success at all equal to that of the *Sadducismus*. The principal writer was a surgeon named Webster, whose work is remarkable as one of the earliest instances of the systematic application of a rationalistic interpretation to the magical miracles in the Bible. According to him, the magicians in Egypt were ordinary jugglers, the witch of Endor had dressed up an accomplice to personate Samuel, the word witch in Leviticus only signified poisoner, the demoniacs were chiefly lunatics, and the Magdalene had been freed from seven vices.[5] An unknown scholar, named Wagstaafe, at Oxford, also wrote two short works on the subject;[6]

---

things done by persons of despicable power and knowledge, beyond the reach of art and ordinary nature. Standing public records have been kept of these well-attested relations, and epochas made of these unwonted events. Laws, in many nations, have been enacted against those vile practices; those among the Jews and our own are notorious. Such cases have been often determined with us, by wise and revered judges, upon clear and constructive evidence; and thousands in our own nation have suffered death for their vile compacts with apostate spirits. All this I might largely prove in their particular instances, but that it is not needful; since those that deny the being of witches do it, not out of ignorance of those heads of argument which, probably, they have heard a thousand times, but from an apprehension that such a belief is absurd, and the things impossible."

[1] "I think those that can believe all histories are romances; that all the wise could have agreed to juggle mankind into a common belief of ungrounded fables; that the sound senses of multitudes together may deceive them, and laws are built upon chimeras; that the gravest and wisest judges have been murderers, and the sagest persons fools or designing impostors; I say those that can believe this heap of absurdities are either more credulous than those whose credulity they reprehend, or else have some extraordinary evidence of their persuasion, viz., that it is absurd or impossible there should be a witch or apparition " (p. 4).

[1] His letters on the subject are prefixed to the *Sadducismus.*
[2] *On Credulity and Incredulity.* This Casaubon was son of the great Greek scholar.
[3] See his letter to Glanvil (Feb. 10, 167⅞) in Boyle's Works, vol. vi. p. 59.
[4] "As for wizards and magicians, persons who associate and confederate themselves with these evil spirits for the gratification of their own revenge, lust, ambition, and other passions; besides the Scriptures, there hath been so full an attestation given to them by persons unconcerned in all ages, that those our so confident exploders of them in this present age can hardly escape the suspicion of having some hankering towards atheism." (*Int. Syst.*, vol ii. p. 650.) See also vol. i. p. 116.
[5] Webster, *On Witches.* The identification of the Scripture demoniacs with lunatics had been made by Hobbes also.
[6] Wagstaafe was a deformed dwarfish scholar at Oxford, and was the special butt of the Oxonian wit

and one or two others appeared anonymously. The scepticism steadily increased.

A few years afterwards, a new and strenuous attempt was made to arrest it by accounts of fresh cases of witchcraft in America. The Pilgrim Fathers had brought to that country the seeds of the superstition ; and, at the time when it was rapidly fading in England, it flourished with fearful vigour in Massachusetts. Two Puritan ministers, named Cotton Mather and Parris, proclaimed the frequency of the crime ; and being warmly supported by their brother divines, they succeeded in creating a panic through the whole country. A commission was issued. A judge named Stoughton, who appears to have been a perfect creature of the clergy, conducted the trials : scourgings and tortures were added to the terrorism of the pulpit, and many confessions were obtained. The few who ventured to oppose the prosecutions were denounced as Sadducees and infidels. Multitudes were thrown into prison, others fled from the country abandoning their property, and twenty-seven persons were executed. An old man of eighty was pressed to death— a horrible sentence, which was never afterwards executed in America. The ministers of Boston and Charleston drew up an address, warmly thanking the commissioners for their zeal, and expressing their hope that it would never be relaxed.[1]

In the first year of this prosecution, Cotton Mather wrote a history of the earliest of the trials. This history was introduced to the English public by Richard Baxter, who declared in his preface that "that man must be a very obdurate Sadducee who would not believe it." Not content with having thus given the weight of his great name to the superstition, Baxter in the following year published his treatise on *The Certainty of the World of Spirits ;* in which he collected, with great industry, an immense number of witch-cases ; reverted in extremely laudatory terms to Cotton Mather and his crusade ; and denounced, in unmeasured language, all who were

sceptical upon the subject. This work appeared in 1691, when the panic in America had not yet reached its height ; and, being widely circulated beyond the Atlantic, is said to have contributed much to stimulate the prosecutions.[1] In England it produced little effect. The scepticism that was already pervading all classes was steadily and silently increasing, under the influence of an intellectual movement that was too general and too powerful for any individual genius to arrest. At the time of the Restoration the belief had been common among the most educated. In 1718, when Hutchinson wrote, it scarcely existed, except among the ignorant and a small section of the clergy.[2] Yet, in the interval, the vast preponderance of controversial literature had unquestionably been on the conservative side. During that period no less than twenty-five works[3] are known to have appeared in England in defence of the belief ; and among their authors we have seen some of the ablest men in England. The work of Baxter, notwithstanding the weight of his great name and the very definite character of his statements, appears to have remained entirely unanswered till it was reviewed by Hutchinson twenty-six years after its publication. Yet it could do no more to arrest, than the work of Scott had done to produce, the scepticism. Three witches had been executed in 1682 ; and others, it is said, endured the same fate in 1712 ; but these were the last who judicially perished in England.[4] The last trial, at least of any notoriety, was that of Jane Wenham, who was prosecuted in 1712 by some Hertfordshire clergymen. The judge entirely disbelieved in witches, and accordingly charged the jury strongly in favour of the accused, and even treated with great disrespect the rector of the parish, who declared "on his faith as a clergyman" that he believed the woman

---

(which in the seventeenth century does not appear to have been extremely brilliant). Poor Wagstaafe consoled himself by drinking whisky punch ; and having drunk too much, he died. (Wood's *Athenæ*.)

[1] Bancroft, *History of the United States*, ch. xix. Hutchinson, pp. 95-119.

[1] Hutchinson, pp. 95-119.

[2] Mr. Buckle places the scepticism a little earlier. He says : "This important revolution in our opinion was effected, so far as the educated classes are concerned, between the Restoration and Revolution : that is to say, in 1660 the majority of educated men still believed in witchcraft, and in 1688 the majority disbelieved it." (Vol. i. p. 333.) By 1718, however, the minority had become insignificant.

[3] Some of them, of course, were mere pamphlets, but a large proportion elaborate works. The catalogue is given by Hutchinson.

[4] Compare Hutchinson, p. 67, and Buckle, vol. i, p. 334. I say *judicially*, for in the *Times* of Sept. 24, 1863, there is an account of an old man who was mobbed to death in the county of Essex as a wizard.

to be a witch. The jury, being ignorant and obstinate, convicted the prisoner; but the judge had no difficulty in obtaining a remission of her sentence. A long war of pamphlets ensued, and the clergy who had been engaged in the prosecution drew up a document strongly asserting their belief in the guilt of the accused, animadverting severely upon the conduct of the judge, and concluding with the solemn words, "Liberavimus animas nostras."[1]

It is probable that this was an instance of somewhat exceptional fanaticism; and that Hutchinson, who was himself a clergyman, represented the opinions of most of the more educated of his profession, when a few years later he described witchcraft as a delusion.[2] In 1736 the laws on the subject were repealed, without difficulty or agitation; and there are very few instances of educated men regretting them. In 1768, however, John Wesley prefaced an account of an apparition that had been related by a girl named Elizabeth Hobson, by some extremely remarkable sentences on the subject:—"It is true, likewise," he wrote, "that the English in general, and indeed most of the men of learning in Europe, have given up all accounts of witches and apparitions as mere old wives' fables. I am sorry for it, and I willingly take this opportunity of entering my solemn protest against this violent compliment which so many that believe the Bible pay to those who do not believe it. I owe them no such service. I take knowledge that these are at the bottom of the outcry which has been raised, and with such insolence spread through the land, in direct opposition, not only to the Bible, but to the suffrage of the wisest and best of men in all ages and nations. They well know (whether Christians know it

or not) that the giving up of witchcraft is in effect giving up of the Bible."[1]

In reviewing the history of witchcraft in England, it is impossible to avoid observing the singularly favourable contrast which the Anglican Church presents, both to Continental Catholicism and to Puritanism. It is indeed true that her bishops contributed much to the enactment of the laws against witchcraft, that the immense majority of the clergy firmly believed in the reality of the crime, and that they continued to assert and to defend it when the great bulk of educated laymen had abandoned it. It is also true that the scepticism on the subject of witches arose among those who were least governed by the Church, advanced with the decline of the influence of the clergy, and was commonly branded as a phase and manifestation of infidelity. Yet, on the other hand, it is impossible to deny that the general moderation of the higher clergy was beyond all praise, and that even those who were most credulous were singularly free from that thirst for blood which was elsewhere so common. On the Continent, every attempt to substitute a lighter punishment for death was fiercely denounced as a direct violation of the Divine law. Indeed, some persons went so far as to question the lawfulness of strangling the witch before she was burnt. Her crime, they said, was treason against the Almighty, and therefore to punish it by any but the most agonising of deaths was an act of disrespect to Him. Besides this, the penalty in the Levitical code was stoning, and stoning had been pronounced by the Jewish theologians to be a still more painful death than the stake.[2] Nothing of this kind was found in England. There is, as far as I am aware, not a single instance of the English clergy complaining of the leniency of the laws upon the subject, or attempting to introduce torture into the trials. Their zeal in stimulating the persecution, by exorcisms and fanatical preaching, was also comparatively languid. As early as the reign of James I., the Convocation made a canon prohibiting any clergyman from exorcising a possessed person, without a licence from his bishop, and such licences

---

[1] Hutchinson, pp. 163-171. Some noble and liberal remarks.

[2] An Irish clergyman named Maxwell (who was chaplain to Lord Carteret, and a writer of considerable ability), in an essay on heathen morality, prefixed to a translation of Cumberland's *Laws of Nature*, which appeared in 1727, has the following passage on witchcraft: "Almost the whole world of mankind were sometime under Satan's domination and power by way of criminal religious subjection as being the religionists of his institution. One sort of these diabolical religionists are witches and magicians, whose existence has been so well attested by experience and by persons of unquestionable veracity, so acknowledged by heathens, by all wise laws and governments, and by the Holy Scriptures, is of theory so unexceptionably rational, and the objections against it so inconsiderable, that notwithstanding the many impostures and false stories of this kind, he that would reject them all must be a superlative believer" (p. clix.).

[1] *Journal*, 1768, Dr. Johnson spoke with a characteristic indecision on the subject of the reality of witchcraft (Boswell, August 16, 1773)

[2] Bodin, p. 217.

were scarcely ever granted.[1] Dr. Morton, a Bishop of Lichfield, in 1620, employed himself with great, and at last successful, zeal in detecting a case of imposture in a witch-story which was believed by a Catholic priest,[2] and he succeeded in saving the life of the accused. At a still earlier period, Dr. Harsenet, who was afterwards Archbishop of York, in an attack upon " Popish impostures," boldly enumerated among them most of the forms of witchcraft,[3] and appears to have been entirely incredulous on the subject. He was undoubtedly wrong in ascribing witchcraft to Catholicism, for it flourished at least as vigorously under the shadow of Puritanism ; yet the expression of so bold an opinion is well worthy of notice, and was, I believe, at the time it was written, a unique phenomenon among the English clergy.[4] Hutchinson himself wrote his history before the belief was entirely extinct.

But that which shows most strikingly the moderation of the Anglican clergy is the comparatively small amount of delusion which the history of English witchcraft presents. On the Continent there was undoubtedly much imposition ; but, for the most part, the subject presents rather the aspect of an epidemic or a mania. The religious terrorism acted on diseased imaginations, coloured every form of madness, and predisposed the minds of men to solve every difficulty by a supernatural hypothesis. In England, on the other hand, imposture appears the general characteristic. The books on the subject are full of cases of jugglers' tricks;[5] and, with the exception of the period when the Puritans were in the ascendent, it never seems to have assumed the appearance of a great and general panic. Indeed, in most of its worst manifestations, the fanaticism of Puritanism was manifested.[6]

In England that fanaticism was bridled and repressed. There was one country, however, in which it obtained an absolute ascendency. There was one country in which the Puritan ministers succeeded in moulding alike the character and the habits of the nation, and in disseminating their harsh and gloomy tenets through every section of society. While England was breaking loose from her most ancient superstitions, and advancing with gigantic strides along the paths of knowledge, Scotland still cowered with a willing submission before her clergy. Never was a mental servitude more complete, and never was a tyranny maintained with more inexorable barbarity. Supported by public opinion, the Scottish ministers succeeded in overawing all opposition, in prohibiting the faintest expression of adverse opinions, in prying into and controlling the most private concerns of domestic life ; in compelling everyone to conform absolutely to all the ecclesiastical regulations they enjoined ; and in, at last, directing the whole scope and current of legislation. They maintained their ascendency over the popular mind by a system of religious terrorism, which we can now barely conceive. The misery of man, the anger of the Almighty, the fearful power and continual presence of Satan, the agonies of hell, were the constant subjects of their preaching. All the most ghastly forms of human suffering were accumulated as faint images of the eternal doom of the immense majority of mankind. Countless miracles were represented as taking place within the land, but they were almost all of them miracles of terror. Disease, storm, famine, every awful calamity that fell upon mankind, or blasted the produce of the soil, was attributed to the direct intervention of spirits ; and Satan himself was represented as constantly appearing in a visible form upon the earth.[1] Such teaching produced its natural effects. In a land where credulity was universal, in a land where the intellect was numbed and palsied by these awful contemplations, where almost every form of

---

[1] Hutchinson : Dedication.   [2] Ibid.   [3] Ibid.
[4] I, at least, have not been able to find any other case ; but Sir Kenelm Digby, in his annotation to the passage from Sir Thomas Browne, which I have before quoted, says of the belief : " There are divines of great note, and far from any suspicion of being irreligious, that do not oppose it." The book of Dr. Harsenet is, I believe, rare ; I only know it by the copious extracts in Hutchinson. There is a notice of its author in Neal's *Hist. of the Puritans.*
[5] See Scott's *Discovery, passim.*
[6] Sir W. Scott has well noticed this influence of Puritanism on English witchcraft ; and, in comparing the different sections of the Church, he says : " On the whole, the Calvinists, generally speaking, were, of all the contending sects, the most suspicious of sorcery, the most undoubting believers in its existence, and the most eager to follow it up with what they conceived to

be the due punishment of the most fearful of crimes." (*Demonology and Witchcraft*, Letter 8.)
[1] I need hardly refer to the noble description of the Scotch Kirk in Buckle's History—a description the substantial justice of which will be questioned by no one who is acquainted with the history of Scotch witchcraft. On the multitude of miracles and apparitions of Satan that were believed, see pp. 349-369.

amusement was suppressed, and where the thoughts of men were concentrated with an undivided energy on theological conceptions, such teachings necessarily created the superstition of witchcraft. Witchcraft was but one form of the panic it produced ; it was but the reflection by a diseased imagination of the popular theology. We accordingly find that it assumed the most frightful proportions, and the darkest character. In other lands the superstition was at least mixed with much of imposture ; in Scotland it appears to have been entirely undiluted.[1] It was produced by the teaching of the clergy, and it was everywhere fostered by their persecution. Eagerly, passionately, with a thirst for blood that knew no mercy, with a zeal that never tired, did they accomplish their task. Assembled in solemn synod, the College of Aberdeen, in 1603, enjoined every minister to take two of the elders of his parish to make " a subtle and privy inquisition," and to question all the parishioners upon oath as to their knowledge of witches.[2] Boxes were placed in the churches for the express purpose of receiving the accusations.[3] When a woman had fallen under suspicion, the minister from the pulpit denounced her by name, exhorted his parishioners to give evidence against her, and prohibited anyone from sheltering her.[4] In the same spirit he exerted the power which was given him by a parochial organisation, elaborated perhaps more skilfully than any other in Europe. Under these circumstances, the witch-cases seem to have fallen almost entirely into the hands of the clergy. They were the leading commissioners. Before them the confessions were taken. They were the acquiescing witnesses, or the directors of the tortures by which those confessions were elicited.[5]

And when we read the nature of these tortures, which were worthy of an oriental imagination ; when we remember that they were inflicted, for the most part, on old and feeble and half-doting women, it is difficult to repress a feeling of the deepest abhorrence for those men who caused and who encouraged them. If the witch was obdurate, the first, and it was said the most effectual, method of obtaining confession was by what was termed " waking her." An iron bridle or hoop was bound across her face with four prongs, which were thrust into her mouth. It was fastened behind to the wall by a chain, in such a manner that the victim was unable to lie down ; and in this position she was sometimes kept for several days, while men were constantly with her to prevent her from closing her eyes for a moment in sleep.[1] Partly in order to effect this object, and partly to discover the insensible mark which was the sure sign of a witch, long pins were thrust into her body.[2] At the same time, as it was a saying in Scotland that a witch would never confess while she could drink, excessive thirst was often added to her tortures.[3] Some prisoners have been waked for five nights ; one, it is said, even for nine.[4]

The physical and mental suffering of such a process was sufficient to overcome the resolution of many, and to distract the understanding of not a few. But other and perhaps worse tortures were in reserve. The three principal that were habitually applied were the pennywinkis, the boots, and the caschielawis. The first

[1] " One of the most powerful incentives to confession was systematically to deprive the suspected witch of the refreshment of her natural sleep.....Iron collars, or witches' bridles, are still preserved in various parts of Scotland which had been used for such iniquitous purposes. These instruments were so constructed that, by means of a hoop which passed over the head, a piece of iron having four points or prongs was forcibly thrust into the mouth, two of these being directed to the tongue and palate, the others pointing outwards to each cheek. This infernal machine was secured by a padlock. At the back of the collar was fixed a ring by which to attach the witch to a staple in the wall of her cell. Thus equipped, and night and day waked and watched by some skilful person appointed by her inquisitors, the unhappy creature, after a few days of such discipline, maddened by the misery of her forlorn and helpless state, would be rendered fit for confessing anything, in order to be rid of the dregs of her wretched life. At intervals fresh examinations took place, and these were repeated from time to time until her 'contumacy,' as it was termed, was subdued. The clergy and kirk sessions appear to have been the unwearied instruments of ' purging the land of witchcraft ;' and *to them, in the first instance, all the complaints and informations were made.*" (Pitcairn, vol. i. part ii. p. 50.)

[2] Dalyell, p. 645. The " prickers" formed a regular profession in Scotland.

[3] Burt's *Letters from the North of Scotland*, vol. i, pp. 227–234.

[4] Dalyell, p. 645.

[1] The very remarkable fact, that no cases of imposture have been detected in Scotch witch-trials, is noted by Buckle (vol. ii. pp. 189, 190).
[2] Dalyell, *Darker Superstitions of Scotland*, p. 624.
[3] Ibid, p. 623.
[4] Ibid, p. 624, &c.
[5] See on this subject Pitcairn's *Criminal Trials of Scotland*, a vast repository of original documents on the subject. Pitcairn gives numbers of these confessions. He adds : " The confessions were commonly taken before presbyteries, or certain special commissioners, who usually ranked among their number the leading clergy of those districts where their hapless victims resided " (vol. iii. p. 598).

was a kind of thumbscrew ; the second was a frame in which the leg was inserted, and in which it was broken by wedges, driven in by a hammer ; the third was also an iron frame for the leg, which was from time to time heated over a brazier.[1] Fire-matches were sometimes applied to the body of the victim.[2] We read in a contemporary legal register, of one man who was kept for forty-eight hours in "vehement tortour" in the caschielawis ; and of another who remained in the same frightful machine for eleven days and eleven nights, whose legs were broken daily for fourteen days in the boots, and who was so scourged that the whole skin was torn from his body.[3] This was, it is true, censured as an extreme case, but it was only an excessive application of the common torture.

How many confessions were extorted, and how many victims perished by these means, it is now impossible to say. A vast number of depositions and confessions are preserved, but they were only taken before a single court, and many others took cognisance of the crime. We know that in 1662 more than 150 persons were accused of witchcraft ;[4] and that in the preceding year no less than fourteen commissions had been issued for the trials.[5] After these facts, it is scarcely necessary to mention how one traveller casually notices having seen nine women burning together at Leith in 1664, or how, in 1678, nine others were condemned in a single day.[6] The charges were, indeed, of the most comprehensive order, and the wildest fancies of Sprenger and Nider were defended by the Presbyterian divines.[7] In most Catholic countries, it was a griev-

ance of the clergy that the civil power refused to execute those who only employed their power in curing disease. In Scotland such persons were unscrupulously put to death.[1] The witches were commonly strangled before they were burnt, but this merciful provision was very frequently omitted. An Earl of Mar (who appears to have been the only person sensible of the inhumanity of the proceedings) tells how, with a piercing yell, some women once broke half-burnt from the slow fire that consumed them, struggled for a few moments with despairing energy among the spectators, but soon with shrieks of blasphemy and wild protestations of innocence sank writhing in agony amid the flames.[2]

The contemplation of such scenes as these is one of the most painful duties that can devolve upon the historian, but it is one from which he must not shrink, if he would form a just estimate of the past. There are opinions that may be traced from age to age by footsteps of blood ; and the intensity of the suffering they caused is a measure of the intensity with which they were realised. Scotch witchcraft was but the result of Scotch Puritanism, and it faithfully reflected the character of its parent. It is true that, before the Reformation, the people had been grossly ignorant and superstitious ; but it is also true that witchcraft in its darker forms was so rare that no law was made on the subject till 1563 ; that the law was not carried to its full severity till 1590 ; that the delusion invariably accompanied the religious terrorism which the Scotch clergy so zealously maintained ; and that those clergy, all over Scotland, applauded and stimulated the persecution.[3] The ascendency they had obtained was boundless, and in this respect their power was entirely undisputed. One

---

[1] Pitcairn.   [2] Dalyell, p. 657.
[3] Pitcairn, vol. i. part ii. p. 376. The two cases were in the same trial in 1596.
[4] Dalyell, p. 669.   [5] Pitcairn, vol. iii. p. 597.
[6] Dalyell, pp. 669, 670.
[7] For a curious instance of this, see that strange book, *The Secret Commonwealth*, published in 1691, by Robert Kirk, Minister of Aberfoil. He represents evil spirits in human form as habitually living among the Highlanders. Succubi, or, as the Scotch called them, Leannain Sith, seem to have been especially common ; and Mr. Kirk (who identifies them with the *Familiar Spirits* of Deuteronomy) complains very sadly of the affection of many young Scotchmen for the "fair ladies of this aerial order" (p. 35). Captain Burt relates a long discussion he had with a minister on the subject of old women turning themselves into cats. The minister said that one man succeeded in cutting off the leg of a cat who attacked him, that the leg immediately turned into that of an old woman, and that four ministers signed a certificate attesting the fact (vol. i. pp. 271–277). One of the principal Scotch writers on these matters was Sinclair, who was Professor of Moral Philosophy at Glasgow.

[1] Wright's *Sorcery*, vol. i. pp. 165, 166. Even to consult with witches was made capital.
[2] Pitcairn, vol. iii. p. 598. Another Earl of Mar had been himself bled to death for having, as was alleged, consulted with witches how to shorten the life of James III. (Scott's *Demonology*, Letter ix.)
[3] Sir Walter Scott seems to think that the first great outburst of persecution began when James VI. went to Denmark to fetch his bride. Before his departure he exhorted the clergy to assist the magistrates, which they did, and most especially in matters of witchcraft. The king was himself perfectly infatuated with the subject, and had this one bond of union with the ministers ; and, as Sir W. S. says, "during the halcyon period of union between kirk and king, their hearty agreement on the subject of witchcraft failed not to heat the fires against all persons suspected of such iniquity." (*Demonology*, Letter ix.) See also Linton's *Witch Stories*, p. 5.

word from them might have arrested the tortures, but that word was never spoken. Their conduct implies not merely a mental aberration, but also a callousness of feeling which has rarely been attained in a long career of vice. Yet these were men who had often shown, in the most trying circumstances, the highest and the most heroic virtues. They were men whose courage had never flinched when persecution was raging around ; men who had never paltered with their consciences to attain the favours of a king ; men whose self-devotion and zeal in their sacred calling had seldom been surpassed ; men who, in all the private relations of life, were doubtless amiable and affectionate. It is not on them that our blame should fall ; it is on the system that made them what they were. They were but illustrations of the great truth that when men have come to regard a certain class of their fellow-creatures as doomed by the Almighty to eternal and excruciating agonies, and when their theology directs their minds with intense and realising earnestness to the contemplation of such agonies, the result will be an indifference to the suffering of those whom they deem the enemies of their God, as absolute as it is perhaps possible for human nature to attain.

In Scotland the character of theology was even more hard and unpitying than in other countries where Puritanism existed, on account of a special circumstance which in some respects reflects great credit on its teachers. The Scotch Kirk was the result of a democratic movement, and for some time, almost alone in Europe, it was the unflinching champion of political liberty. It was a Scotchman, Buchanan, who first brought liberal principles into clear relief. It was the Scotch clergy who upheld them with a courage that can hardly be overrated. Their circumstances made them liberals, and they naturally sought to clothe their liberalism in a theological garb. They soon discovered precedents for their rebellions in the history of the Judges and Captains of the Jews ; and accordingly the union of an intense theological and an intense liberal feeling made them revert to the scenes of the Old Testament, to the sufferings and also the conquests of the Jews, with a peculiar affection. Their whole theology took an Old Testament cast. Their modes of thought, their very phraseology, were derived from that

source ; and the constant contemplation of the massacres of Canaan, and of the provisions of the Levitical code, produced its natural effect upon their minds.[1]

It is scarcely possible to write a history of the decline of witchcraft in Scotland, for the change of opinions was almost entirely unmarked by incidents on which we can dwell. At one period we find everyone predisposed to believe in witches. At a later period we find that this predisposition has silently passed away.[2] Two things only can, I think, be asserted on the subject with confidence—that the sceptical movement advanced much more slowly in Scotland than in England, and that the ministers were among the latest to yield to it. Until the close of the seventeenth century, the trials were sufficiently common, but after this time they became rare. It is generally said that the last execution was in 1722 ; but Captain Burt, who visited the country in 1730, speaks of a woman who was burnt as late as 1727.[3] The same very keen observer was greatly struck by the extent to which the belief still continued in Scotland, at a time when it was quite abandoned by the educated classes in England ; and he found its most ardent supporters among the Presbyterian ministers. As late as 1736, " the divines of the Associated Presbytery " passed a resolution declaring their belief in witchcraft, and deploring the scepticism that was general.[4]

I have now completed my review of the history of witchcraft, in its relation to the theologies of Rome, of England, and of Geneva. I have shown that the causes of the changes it presents must be sought, not within any narrow circle of special doctrines, but in the general intellectual and religious condition of the time. I have shown, in other words, that witchcraft resulted, not from isolated circumstances, but from modes of thought ; that it grew out of a certain intellectual temperature acting on certain theological tenets, and reflected with almost startling vividness each great intellectual change.

[1] It is rather remarkable that Bodin had also formed his theology almost exclusively from the Old Testament, his reverence for which was so great that some (Grotius and Hallam among others) have questioned whether he believed the New.

[2] The silent, unreasoning character of the decline of Scotch witchcraft has been noticed by Dugald Stewart, *Dissert.* p. 508.

[3] Burt's *Letters from the North of Scotland*, vol. i. pp. 227–234 and 271–277. I suspect Burt has misdated the execution that took place in 1722, placing it in 1727.

[4] Burton, *Hist. of Scotland*, vol. ii. p. 334.

Arising amid the ignorance of an early civilisation, it was quickened into an intenser life by a theological struggle which allied terrorism with credulity, and it declined under the influence of that great rationalistic movement which, since the seventeenth century, has been on all sides encroaching on theology. I have dwelt upon the decadence of the superstition at considerable length ; for it was at once one of the earliest and one of the most important conquests of the spirit of Rationalism. There are very few examples of a change of belief that was so strictly normal, so little accelerated by sectarian passions or individual genius, and therefore so well suited to illustrate the laws of intellectual development. Besides this, the fact that the belief when realised was always followed by persecution, enables us to trace its successive stages with more than common accuracy, while the period that has elapsed since its destruction has, in a great measure, removed the subject from the turbid atmosphere of controversy.

It is impossible to leave the history of witchcraft without reflecting how vast an amount of suffering has, in at least this respect, been removed by the progress of a rationalistic civilisation. I know that when we remember the frightful calamities that have from time to time flowed from theological divisions ; when we consider the countless martyrs who have perished in the dungeon or at the stake, the millions who have fallen in the religious wars, the elements of almost undying dissension that have been planted in so many noble nations and have paralysed so many glorious enterprises, the fate of a few thousand innocent persons who were burnt alive seems to sink into comparative insignificance. Yet it is probable that no class of victims endured suffering so unalloyed and so intense. Not for them the wild fanaticism that nerves the soul against danger, and almost steels the body against torments. Not for them the assurance of a glorious eternity, that has made the martyr look with exultation on the rising flame as on the Elijah's chariot that is to bear his soul to heaven. Not for them the solace of lamenting friends, or the consciousness that their memories would be cherished and honoured by posterity. They died alone, hated and unpitied. They were deemed by all mankind the worst of criminals. Their very kinsmen shrank from them as tainted and accursed. The superstitions they had imbibed in childhood, blending with the illusions of age, and with the horrors of their position, persuaded them in many cases that they were indeed the bondslaves of Satan, and were about to exchange their torments upon earth for an agony that was as excruciating, and was eternal. And, besides all this, we have to consider the terrors which the belief must have spread through the people at large ; we have to picture the anguish of the mother, as she imagined that it was in the power of one whom she had offended to blast in a moment every object of her affection : we have to conceive, above all, the awful shadow that the dread of accusation must have thrown on the enfeebled faculties of age, and the bitterness it must have added to desertion and to solitude. All these sufferings were the result of a single superstition, which the spirit of Rationalism has destroyed.

Chapter II.

ON THE DECLINING SENSE OF THE MIRACULOUS

THE MIRACLES OF THE CHURCH

THE same habits of mind which induced men at first to recoil from the belief in witchcraft with an instinctive and involuntary repugnance as intrinsically incredible, and afterwards openly to repudiate it, have operated in a very similar manner, and with very similar effects, upon the belief in modern miracles. The triumph, however, has not been in this case so complete, for the Church of Rome still maintains the continuance of miraculous powers ; nor has the decay been so strictly normal, for the fact that most of the Roman Catholic miracles are associated with distinctively Roman Catholic doctrines has introduced much miscellaneous controversy into the question. But, notwithstanding these considerations, the general outlines of the movement are clearly visible, and they are well deserving of a brief notice.

If we would realise the modes of thought on this subject prior to the Reformation, we must quite dismiss from our minds the ordinary Protestant notion that miracles were very rare and exceptional phenomena, the primary object of which was always to accredit the teacher of some divine truth that could not otherwise be established. In the writings of the Fathers, and especially of those of the fourth and fifth centuries, we find them not only spoken of as existing in profusion, but as being directed to the most various ends. They were a kind of celestial charity, alleviating the sorrows, healing the diseases, and supplying the wants of the faithful. They were frequent incitements to piety, stimulating the devotions of the languid, and rewarding the patience of the fervent. They were the signs of great and saintly virtue, securing universal respect for those who had attained a high degree of sanctity, or assisting them in the performance of their more austere devotions. Thus, one saint

having retired into the desert to lead a life of mortification, the birds daily brought him a supply of food, which was just sufficient for his wants ; and when a kindred spirit visited him in his retirement, they doubled the supply; and when he died, two lions issued from the desert to dig his grave, uttered a long howl of mourning over his body, and knelt down to beg a blessing from the survivor.[1] Thus, another saint, who was of opinion that a monk should never see himself naked, stood one day in despair upon the banks of a bridgeless stream, when an angel descended to assist him, and transported him in safety across the dreaded element.[2] Besides this, the power of magic was, as we have seen, fully recognised both by Christians and Pagans, and each admitted the reality of the miracles of the other, though ascribing them to the agency of demons.[3]

If we pass from the Fathers into the middle ages, we find ourselves in an atmosphere that was dense and charged with the supernatural. The demand for miracles was almost boundless, and the supply was equal to the demand. Men of extraordinary sanctity seemed naturally and habitually to obtain the power of performing them, and their lives are crowded with their achievements, which were attested by the highest sanction of the Church. Nothing could be more common than for a holy man to be lifted up from the floor in the midst of his devotions, or to be visited by the Virgin or by an angel. There was scarcely a town that could not show some relic that

[1] Paul the Hermit. See his Life by St. Jerome. The visitor of Paul was St. Antony, the first of the hermits.
[2] Ammon (Socrates, lib. iv. c. 23).
[3] See some admirable remarks on this subject in Maury, *Légendes Pieuses*, pp. 240-244 ; also Farmer, *On Demoniacs.* Middleton, *Free Enquiry*, pp. 85-87 Bingham, *Antiquities of the Christian Church*, book iii. c. 4.

had cured the sick, or some image that had opened and shut its eyes, or bowed its head to an earnest worshipper. It was somewhat more extraordinary, but not in the least incredible, that the fish should have thronged to the shore to hear St. Antony preach, or that it should be necessary to cut the hair of the crucifix at Burgos once a month, or that the Virgin of the Pillar, at Saragossa, should, at the prayer of one of her worshippers, have restored a leg that had been amputated.[1] Men who were afflicted with apparently hopeless disease started in a moment into perfect health when brought into contact with a relic of Christ or of the Virgin. The virtue of such relics radiated in blessings all around them. Glorious visions heralded their discovery, and angels have transported them through the air. If a missionary went abroad among the heathen, supernatural signs confounded his opponents, and made the powers of darkness fly before his steps. If a Christian prince unsheathed his sword in an ecclesiastical cause, apostles had been known to combat with his army, and avenging miracles to scatter his enemies. If an unjust suspicion attached to an innocent man, he had immediately recourse to an ordeal which cleared his character and condemned his accusers. All this was going on habitually in every part of Europe without exciting the smallest astonishment or scepticism. Those who know how thoroughly the supernatural element pervades the old lives of the saints may form some notion of the multitude of miracles that were related and generally believed, from the fact that M. Guizot has estimated the number of these lives, accumulated in the Bollandist Collection, at about 25,000.[2] Yet this was but one department of miracles. It does not include the thousands of miraculous images and pictures that were operating throughout Christendom,

and the countless apparitions and miscellaneous prodigies that were taking place in every country, and on all occasions. Whenever a saint was canonised, it was necessary to prove that he had worked miracles ; but except on those occasions miraculous accounts seem never to have been questioned. The most educated, as well as the most ignorant, habitually resorted to the supernatural as the simplest explanation of every difficulty.

All this has now passed away. It has passed away not only in lands where Protestantism is triumphant, but also in those where the Roman Catholic faith is still acknowledged, and where the mediæval saints are still venerated. St. Januarius, it is true, continues to liquéfy at Naples, and the pastorals of French bishops occasionally relate apparitions of the Virgin among very ignorant and superstitious peasants ; but the implicit, undiscriminating acquiescence with which such narratives were once received has long since been replaced by a derisive incredulity. Those who know the tone that is habitually adopted on these subjects by the educated in Roman Catholic countries will admit that, so far from being a subject for triumphant exultation, the very few modern miracles which are related are everywhere regarded as a scandal, a stumbling-block, and a difficulty. Most educated persons speak of them with undisguised scorn and incredulity ; some attempt to evade or explain them away by a natural hypothesis ; a very few faintly and apologetically defend them. Nor can it be said that what is manifested is merely a desire for a more minute and accurate examination of the evidence by which they are supported. On the contrary, it will, I think, be admitted that these alleged miracles are commonly rejected with an assurance that is as peremptory and unreasoning as that with which they would have been once received. Nothing can be more rare than a serious examination, by those who disbelieve them, of the testimony on which they rest. They are repudiated, not because they are unsupported, but because they are miraculous. Men are prepared to admit almost any conceivable concurrence of natural improbabilities rather than resort to the

---

[1] There is a picture of the miracle in the cathedral of Saragossa, opposite the image. It is one about which a vast amount has been written, and which the Spanish theologians are said to regard as peculiarly well established. Hume has noticed it in his Essay on Miracles.

[2] *Hist. de la Civilisation*, Leçon XVII. The Bollandist Collection was begun at Antwerp by a Jesuit named Bolland, in 1643, was stopped for a time by the French Revolution, but renewed under the patronage of the Belgian Chambers. It was intended to contain a complete collection of all the original documents on the subject. The saints are placed according to the calendar. Fifty-five large folio volumes have been published, but they only extend to the end of October. See a very beautiful

essay on the subject by Renan, *Études Religieuses*. M. Renan says: "Il me semble que pour un vrai philosophe une prison cellulaire avec ces cinquante-cinq volumes in-folio, serait un vrai paradis."

hypothesis of supernatural interference ; and this spirit is exhibited not merely by open sceptics, but by men who are sincere though perhaps not very fervent believers in their Church. It is the prevailing characteristic of that vast body of educated persons whose lives are chiefly spent in secular pursuits, and who, while they receive with unenquiring faith the great doctrines of Catholicism, and duly perform its leading duties, derive their mental tone and colouring from the general spirit of their age. If you speak to them on the subject, they will reply with a shrug and with a smile ; they will tell you that it is indeed melancholy that such narratives should be narrated in the middle of the nineteenth century ; they will treat them as palpable anachronisms, as obviously and intrinsically incredible ; but they will add that it is not necessary for all Roman Catholics to believe them, and that it is unfair to judge the enlightened members of the Church by the measure of the superstitions of the ignorant.

That this is the general tone adopted by the great majority of educated Roman Catholics, both in their writings and in their conversation, will scarcely be a matter of dispute. It is also very manifest that it is the direct product and measure of civilisation. The districts where an account of a modern miracle is received with least derision are precisely those which are most torpid and most isolated. The classes whose habits of thought are least shocked by such an account are those which are least educated and least influenced by the broad current of civilisation. If we put aside the clergy and those who are most immediately under their influence, we find that this habit of mind is the invariable concomitant of education, and is the especial characteristic of those persons whose intellectual sympathies are most extended, and who therefore represent most faithfully the various intellectual influences of their time. If you connect a nation which has long been insulated and superstitious with the general movement of European civilisation by means of railways, or a free press, or the removal of protecting laws, you will most infallibly inoculate it with this spirit.

It is further evident that this habit of thought is not a merely ephemeral movement, produced by some exceptional event, or by some transient literary fashion peculiar to our own century. All history shows that, in exact proportion to the intellectual progress of nations, the accounts of miracles taking place among them become rarer and rarer, until at last they entirely cease.[1] In this fact we have a clear indication of the decline of the old habits of thought ; for those who regard these miracles as real, ascribe their disappearance to the progress of incredulity, while those who disbelieve them maintain that they were the results of a particular direction given to the imagination, and of a particular form of imposition created and suggested by the mediæval habits of thought. In other words, the old spirit, according to one class, is the condition, and, according to the other class, the cause of the miracles; and, therefore, the cessation of miraculous narratives, when unaccompanied by an avowed change of creed, implies the decay of that spirit.

If these propositions be true—and I scarcely think that any candid person who seriously examines the subject can question them—they lead irresistibly to a very important general conclusion. They show that the repugnance of men to believe miraculous narratives is in direct proportion to the progress of civilisation and the diffusion of knowledge. It is not simply that science explains some things which were formerly deemed supernatural, such as comets or eclipses. We find the same incredulity manifested in Roman Catholic countries towards alleged miracles by saints, or relics, or images, on which science can throw no direct light, and which contain no element of improbability, except that they are miraculous. It is not simply that civilisation strengthens Protestantism at the expense of the Church of Rome. We find this spirit displayed by Roman Catholics themselves, though the uniform tendency of their theology is to destroy all notion of the antecedent improbability of modern miracles, and though the fact that these miracles are only alleged in their own church should invest them with a peculiar attraction. It is

[1] This has been noticed in an extremely ingenious fashion by Bishop Sprat :—" God never yet left Himself without a witness in the world ; and it is observable that He has commonly chosen the dark and ignorant ages wherein to work miracles, but seldom or never the times when natural knowledge prevailed ; for He knew there was not so much need to make use of extraordinary signs when men were diligent in the works of His hands and attentive to the impressions of His footsteps in His creatures." (*Hist. of Royal Society*, p. 350.)

not even that there is an increasing repugnance to an unscrutinising and blind-
fold faith. Alleged miracles are rejected
with immediate unreasoning incredulity
by the members of a church which has
done everything in its power to prepare
the mind for their reception. The plain
fact is, that the progress of civilisation
produces invariably a certain tone and
habit of thought, which makes men recoil
from miraculous narratives with an instinctive and immediate repugnance, as
though they were essentially incredible,
independently of any definite arguments,
and in spite of dogmatic teaching.
Whether this habit of mind is good or
evil, I do not now discuss; that it exists
wherever civilisation advances is, I conceive, incontestable.

We may observe, however, that it acts
with much greater force against contemporary than against historical miracles.
Roman Catholics who will reject with
immediate ridicule an account of a miracle
taking place in their own day, will speak
with considerable respect of a precisely
similar miracle that is attributed to a
mediæval saint. Nor is it at all difficult
to discover the reason of this distinction.
Events that took place in a distant past
are not realised with the same intense
vividness as those which take place among
ourselves. They do not press upon us
with the same keen reality, and are not
judged by the same measure. They come
down to us invested with a legendary
garb, obscured by the haze of years, and
surrounded by circumstances that are so
unlike our own that they refract the
imagination, and cloud and distort its
pictures. Besides this, many of these
narratives are entwined with the earliest
associations of the Roman Catholic child;
the belief in them is infused into his yet
undeveloped mind, and they are thus at
no period brought in contact with a
matured and unbiassed judgment. We
find, therefore, that although these general
habits of thought do, undoubtedly, exercise
a retrospective influence, that is not their
first or their most powerful effect.

In Protestant countries there has not
been as complete a change as that which
we have been considering, for Protestantism was only called into existence
when the old habits of thought had greatly
declined. The Reformation was created
and pervaded by the modern spirit; and
its leaders were compelled, by the exigencies of their position, to repudiate the
miraculous accounts of their time. They
could not with any consistency admit that
the Almighty had selected as the peculiar
channels of His grace, and had glorified
by countless miracles, devotions which
they stigmatised as blasphemous, idolatrous, and superstitious. We find, accordingly, that from the very beginning Protestantism looked upon modern miracles
(except those which were comprised under
the head of witchcraft) with an aversion
and distrust that contrast remarkably with
the unhesitating credulity of its opponents.
The history of its sects exhibits, indeed,
some alleged miracles, which were, apparently, the result of ignorance or enthusiasm, and a very few which were obvious
impositions. Such, for example, was the
famous voice from the wall in the reign
of Queen Mary, which proclaimed the
mass to be idolatrous, just as the crucifix
in Christ Church, at Dublin, shed tears
of blood in the following reign, because
the Protestant service was introduced into
Ireland. On the whole, however, the new
faith proved remarkably free from these
forms of deception; and its leaders
generally concurred in the belief that
miracles had ceased when Christianity
had gained a definite ascendency in the
world. The Patristic writings are full of
miraculous accounts; and most of the
reformers, and especially those in England, treated Patristic authority with
great respect; so that the line of demarcation between the miraculous and the
non-miraculous age was generally drawn
at about the period when the most eminent
of the Fathers passed away. As this was
not very long after Christianity had obtained a complete command of the civil
power, many plausible arguments could
be urged in support of the view, which
appears, in England at least, to have been
universal.

When Locke was writing his famous
Letters on Toleration, he was led to a consideration of the Patristic miracles by an
argument which seems then to have been
deemed very forcible, but which, as it
belongs to a different "climate of opinion"
from our own, would now be regarded as
both futile and irreverent. It was absolutely necessary, it was contended, under
ordinary circumstances, for the well-being
of Christianity, that it should be supported
by persecution; that is to say, that the
civil power should suppress its opponents.
When Christianity was still unrecognised
by government, it existed in an abnormal

condition ; the laws of nature were suspended in its favour, and continual miracles ensured its triumph. When, however, the conversion of Constantine placed the civil power at its disposal, the era of the supernatural was closed. The power of persecuting was obtained ; and, therefore, the power of working miracles was withdrawn. The alliance between Church and State being instituted, Christianity had arrived at its normal and final position, and exceptional assistance had become unnecessary.[1] This argument, the work of the theologians of Oxford, was not likely to stagger Locke ; but the historical question which it opened was well calculated to arrest that keen and fearless intellect, so little accustomed to bow before unsupported authority, and at the very time engaged in the defence of toleration against the entire weight of ecclesiastical tradition. He appears to have consulted Sir Isaac Newton ; for, in one of Newton's letters, we find a somewhat hesitating passage upon the subject : "Miracles," Newton wrote, " of good credit continued in the Church for about two or three hundred years. Gregorius Thaumaturgus had his name from thence, and was one of the latest who was eminent for that gift ; but of their number and frequency I am not able to give you a just account. The history of those ages is very imperfect."[2] Locke does not appear to have adopted this view. In reply to the Oxford argument, he wrote a very remarkable passage, which did not, apparently, attract at the time the attention it deserved, but which, long afterwards, obtained an extremely conspicuous place in the discussion. " This, I think," he said, " is evident, that he who will build his faith or reasonings upon miracles delivered by Church historians, will find cause to go no further than the Apostles' time, or else not to stop at Constantine's, since the writers after that period, whose word we readily take as unquestionable in other things, speak of miracles in their time, with no

less assurance than the Fathers before the fourth century ; and a great part of the miracles of the second and third centuries stand upon the credit of the writers of the fourth."[1]

After this time, the subject of the miracles of the Fathers seems to have slept until public attention was called to it by the well-known work of Middleton. That the *Free Enquiry* was a book of extraordinary merit—that it displayed great eloquence, great boldness, and great controversial dexterity, and met with no opposition at all equal to its abilities—will scarcely be denied. But, in order to appreciate its success, we should consider, besides these things, the general character of the age in which it appeared. During the half century that elapsed between Locke and Middleton, many influences that it would be tedious to examine, but to which Locke himself by his philosophy most largely contributed, had profoundly modified the theology of England. The charm and fascination which the early Fathers exercised upon the divines of the previous century had quite passed away. The Patristic works fell rapidly into neglect, and the very few who continued to study them were but little imbued with their spirit. Nothing, indeed, could be more unlike the tone of the Fathers than the cold, passionless, and prudential theology of the eighteenth century, a theology which regarded Christianity as an admirable auxiliary to the police force, and a principle of decorum and of cohesion in society, but which carefully banished from it all enthusiasm, veiled or attenuated all its mysteries, and virtually reduced it to an authoritative system of moral philosophy. There never had been a time when divines had such a keen dread of anything that appeared absurd or grotesque. The spirit that, in the previous century, had destroyed the belief in witchcraft, passed in its full intensity into their works. Common sense was the dominating characteristic of all they wrote. Generous sentiments, disinterested virtue, reverential faith, sublime speculations, had passed away. Every preacher was employed in showing that Christianity was in all respects perfectly in accordance with human reason, in eliminating or obscuring whatever could shock the feelings or offend the judgment, in representing

---

[1] This argument, in a modified form, has been reproduced by Muzarelli (a Roman theologian of some note), in his *Treatise on the Inquisition.* He cites the destruction of Ananias and Sapphira, and of Simon Magus. This class of miracles, he says, has ceased ; and the Inquisition is, in consequence, required. I know this very remarkable treatise by a translation in the fifth volume of Henrion. *Histoire de l'Eglise.*

[2] Brewster's *Life of Newton,* p. 275. There is another letter from Newton to Locke on the subject, in King's *Life of Locke,* vol. i. p. 415 ; but it is little more than a catalogue of authorities.

[1] Third letter on *Toleration,* p. 269.

religion as intended to refine and harmonise society, to embellish all the relations of life, to give a higher sanction to the dictates of human prudence, and to extend the horizon of that prudence beyond the grave. As a consequence of this state of mind, there was an increasing indisposition to accept miracles like those of the Fathers, which were not included in the evidences of Christianity, and a decreasing reverence for the writers on whose testimony they rest.

It was in the midst of this movement of thought that Middleton published his great attack upon the Patristic miracles, and brought into clear relief both the difficulties and the importance of the subject. The writings of the Fathers contain numerous accounts of miracles which they allege to have taken place in their own day and under their own notice, and which are of such a nature, and are related in such a manner, that it seems scarcely possible to avoid the conclusion that they had really taken place, or else that the Fathers deliberately palmed them off upon the credulity of their readers. The works of the first century that have come down to us are extremely scanty, and consist almost entirely of short epistles written without any historical or controversial purpose, for the encouragement or edification of believers; but, even in this century, the martyrdom of St. Polycarp supplies an account which is clearly miraculous. Justin Martyr, who wrote very early in the second century, and it is said not more than fifty years after the death of St. John, distinctly asserts the continuance of miracles in his time, and from this date the evidence is ample and unbroken. The Protestant theory is, that miracles became gradually fewer and fewer, till they at last entirely disappeared. The historical fact is, that generation after generation the miraculous accounts became more numerous, more universal, and more extraordinary. " As far as the Church historians can illustrate or throw light upon anything, there is not a single point in all history so constantly, explicitly, and unanimously affirmed by them all, as the continual succession of those powers through all ages, from the earliest Father who first mentions them down to the time of the Reformation."[1] If, then, we gave even a general credence to the historical evidence

upon the subject, we should be carried down, without pause or chasm, into the depths of the middle ages; and we should be compelled to admit that what Protestants regard as the worst superstitions of the Church of Rome were for centuries the habitual and special channels of supernatural favour. If again, in defiance of all the ordinary rules of historical criticism, we believed the assertions of the writers of the fourth century, but refused to credit the equally positive testimony of the writers of the ninth century, we should still be met by the same difficulty, though in a modified form. It may be contended, that the Fathers of the fourth century were not Roman Catholics; but it is quite certain that they were not, in the ordinary sense of the word, Protestants. It is quite certain that there existed among them many practices, forms of devotion, and doctrinal tendencies, which may not have been actually Roman Catholic, but which, at least, hung upon the extreme verge of Catholicism, which inevitably gravitated to it, and which were the germs and the embryos of mediæval theology. Now, it is precisely in connection with this department of their theology that the miraculous accounts are most numerous.

Such was the great difficulty of the question, regarded from the Protestant point of view. Middleton met it by an attack upon the veracity of the Fathers, which was so eloquent, so uncompromising, and so admirably directed, that all England soon rang with the controversy. He contended that the religious leaders of the fourth century had admitted, eulogised, and habitually acted upon principles that were diametrically opposed not simply to the aspirations of a transcendent sanctity, but to the dictates of the most common honesty. He showed that they had applauded falsehood, that they had practised the most wholesale forgery, that they had habitually and grossly falsified history, that they had adopted to the fullest extent the system of pious frauds, and that they continually employed them to stimulate the devotion of the people. These were the charges which he brought against men, around whose brows the saintly aureole had sparkled for centuries with an unfading splendour; against those great Fathers who had formed the theological systems of Europe; who had been the arbitrators of so many controversies, and the objects of the homage of

[1] Preface to the *Free Enquiry*.

so many creeds. The evidence he adduced was pointed directly at the writers of the fourth century; but he carried his argument back to a still earlier period. "When we reflect," he says, "on that surprising confidence and security with which the principal Fathers of this fourth century have affirmed as true what they themselves had either forged, or what they knew at least to be forged, it is natural to suspect that so bold a defiance of sacred truth could not be acquired or become general at once, but must have been carried gradually to that height by custom and the example of former times, and a long experience of what the credulity and superstition of the multitude would bear."[1]

It is manifest that an attack of this kind opened out questions of the gravest and widest character. It shook the estimate of the Fathers which had been general, not only in the Church of Rome, but in a great degree among the ablest of the Reformers. In the Church of England especially, the Patristic authority had been virtually regarded as almost equal in authority to that of the inspired writers. The first great theological work of the English Reformation was *The Apology*, in which Jewel justified the Reformers, by pointing out the deviations of the Church of Rome from the Patristic sentiments. It had ever been the pride of the great divines of the seventeenth century that they were the most profound students of the Patristic writings, the most faithful representatives of their spirit, and the most loyal respecters of their authority. The unsupported assertion of a Father had always been regarded as a most weighty, if not a decisive, argument in controversy. But surely this tone was idle and worse than idle, if the estimate of Middleton was correct. If the Fathers were in truth men of the most unbounded credulity and of the laxest veracity; if the sense of the importance of dogmas had, in their minds, completely superseded the sense of rectitude, it was absurd to invest them with this extraordinary veneration. They might still be reverenced as men of undoubted sincerity, and of the noblest heroism. They might still be cited as witnesses to the belief of their time, and as representing the tendencies of its intellect; but their pre-eminent authority had passed

away. But beyond all this, there were other and perhaps graver questions suggested. Under what circumstances was it permitted to reject the unanimous and explicit testimony of all ecclesiastical historians? What was the measure of their credulity and of their veracity? What again was the degree of the antecedent improbability of miracles, the criterion separating the true from the false, the amount of testimony required to substantiate them?

These were the great questions which were evoked in 1748, by this Doctor of Divinity, and they were sufficient for many years to attract the attention of the ablest enquirers in England. Among the laity, the work of Middleton seems to have met with great acceptance. Among the clergy, its impetuous, uncompromising, and sceptical tone naturally excited much alarm, and the University of Oxford signalised itself in the opposition; but it is a remarkable sign of the times that the Fathers found no abler defenders than Church and Dodwell. Gibbon, who was then a very young man, and already entangled in the arguments of Bossuet, lost his remaining faith in Protestantism during the discussion. He could not, he said, bring himself at that time to adopt the conclusions of Middleton, and he could not resist the evidence that miracles of good credit had continued in the Church after the leading doctrines of Catholicism had been introduced. He accordingly embraced those doctrines, and left the University without taking his degree. Hume investigated the subject from a philosophical point of view; he endeavoured to frame a general doctrine, determining the relation between miraculous narratives and historical testimony, the comparative improbability of the reality of miracles and of the unveracity of historians; and the result was his Essay on Miracles.[1] Farmer, repro-

<hr>

[1] Introductory Chapter.

[1] Hume's Essay was avowedly an application (right or wrong) of Tillotson's famous argument against transubstantiation. It is not so generally known that his method of reasoning had been also anticipated by Locke, who, in a very remarkable passage in his Common-place Book, contends that men should not believe any proposition that is contrary to reason, on the authority either of inspiration or of miracle, for the reality of the inspiration or of the miracle can only be established by reason. "It is harder," he says, "to believe that God should alter or put out of its ordinary course some phenomenon of the great world for once, and make things act contrary to their ordinary rule purposely, that the mind of men might do so always after, than that this is some fallacy or natural effect of which he knows not the cause, let it look ever so

ducing an old notion of Lightfoot, Webster, and Semler, and anticipating in this respect the current of German rationalism, attempted to explain the diabolical possessions of Scripture by the ordinary phenomena of epilepsy.[1] Warburton and Douglas, with probably most of the ablest of the clergy, abandoning the Patristic miracles, proceeded to establish the peculiar character and evidence of the miracles recorded by the Evangelists; and the general adoption of this tone may be said to have ushered in a new phase in the history of miracles.

It has been often remarked as a singular fact, that almost every great step which has been made by the English intellect, in connection with theology, has been made in spite of the earnest and persistent opposition of the University of Oxford. The attitude which that University preserved during the Middletonian controversy was precisely the same as that which it had exhibited towards the two great questions of the previous century. The advocates of the theory of civil liberty, in opposition to the theory of passive obedience, and the advocates of toleration as opposed to persecution, had found at Oxford their most unflinching and their most able adversaries. In our own [the nineteenth] century, when the secularisation of politics was forced upon the public mind by the discussions on the Test Act and on Catholic Emancipation, and when it had become evident to all attentive observers that this question was destined to be the battle-field of the contest between the modern spirit and tradition, the University of Oxford showed clearly that its old spirit had lost none of its intensity, though it had lost much of its influence. Still later, in 1833, a great reactionary movement emanated from the same quarter, and was directed avowedly against the habits of religious thought which modern civilisation had everywhere produced. Its supporters denounced these habits as essentially and fundamentally false. They described the history of English theology for a century and a half as a history of uninterrupted decadence. They believed, in the emphatic words of their great leader,

that "the nation was on its way to give up revealed truth."[1] After a time, the movement tended to Catholicism with a force and rapidity that it was impossible to mistake. It produced a defection which was quite unparalleled in magnitude since that which had taken place under the Stuarts; and which, unlike the former movement, was altogether uninfluenced by sordid considerations. The point which I desire to notice in connection with this defection, as illustrating the tendency I am tracing in the present chapter, is the extremely small place which the subject of Roman Catholic miracles occupied in the controversy.

If we ask, what are the grounds on which the cessation of miracles is commonly maintained, they may, I suppose, be summed up much as follows:—

Miracles, it is said, are the divine credentials of an inspired messenger announcing doctrines which could not otherwise be established. They prove that he is neither an impostor nor an enthusiast; that his teaching is neither the work of a designing intellect nor of an over-heated imagination. From the nature of the case, this could not be proved in any other way. If the Almighty designed to reveal to mankind a system of religion distinct from that which is reflected in the works of nature and written on the consciences of men, He must do so by the instrumentality of an inspired messenger. If a teacher claims to be the special organ of a divine communication revealing supernatural truths, he may be justly expected to authenticate his mission in the only way in which it can be authenticated—by the performance of supernatural acts. Miracles are, therefore, no more improbable than a revelation; for a revelation would be ineffectual without miracles. But, while this consideration destroys the common objections to the Gospel miracles, it separates them clearly from those of the Church of Rome. The former were avowedly exceptional; they were absolutely necessary; they were designed to introduce a new religion, and to establish a supernatural message. The latter were simply means of edification; they were directed to no object that could not otherwise be attained; and they were represented as taking place in a dispensation that was intended to be not of sight but of faith. Besides this,

---

strange" (King, *Life of Locke*, vol. i. pp. 230, 231). See, too, the chapter on Reason and Faith, in the *Essay on the Human Understanding*.

[1] Farmer, who was a dissenting minister, desired to destroy the difficulty arising from the fact that miracles were generally represented as attesting both truth and error. He attempted to show that there were no such things as diabolical miracles of any kind.

[1] Newman's *Anglican Difficulties*, p. 54.

miracles should be regarded as the most awful and impressive manifestations of divine power. To make them habitual and commonplace would be to degrade if not to destroy their character, which would be still further abased if we admitted those which appeared trivial and puerile. The miracles of the New Testament were always characterised by dignity and solemnity; they always conveyed some spiritual lesson, and conferred some actual benefit, besides attesting the character of the worker. The mediæval miracles, on the contrary, were frequently trivial, purposeless, and unimpressive; constantly verging on the grotesque, and not unfrequently passing the border.

Such is, I think, a fair epitome of the common arguments in favour of the cessation of miracles; and they are undoubtedly very plausible and very cogent; but, after all, what do they prove? Not that miracles have ceased; but that, SUPPOSING them to have ceased, there is nothing surprising or alarming in the fact. A man who has convinced himself of the falseness of the ecclesiastical miracles may very fairly adduce these considerations to prove that his conclusion does not impugn the Biblical narratives, or introduce confusion or incoherence into the system of Providence; but this is the full extent to which they can be legitimately carried. As an *a priori* proof, they are far too weak to withstand any serious amount of positive testimony. Miracles, it is said, are intended exclusively to accredit an inspired messenger. But, after all, what proof is there of this? It is simply an hypothesis—plausible and consistent it may be, but entirely unsupported by positive testimony. Indeed, we may go further, and say that it is distinctly opposed to your own facts. You may repudiate the unanimous belief of the early Christians that miracles were ordinary and commonplace events among all nations. You may resist the strong arguments that may be drawn from the unsurprised reception of the Christian miracles, and from the existence of the demoniacs and of the exorcists; but at least you must admit that the Old Testament relates many miracles which will not fall under your canon. The creation was a miracle, and so was the deluge, and so was the destruction of the Cities of the Plain. The Old Testament miracles are, in many respects, unlike those of the New Testament: is it impossible that

there should be another class different from either? But the ecclesiastical miracles, it is said, are often grotesque; they appear *primâ facie* absurd, and excite an irresistible repugnance. A sufficiently dangerous test in an age in which men find it more and more difficult to believe any miracles whatever! A sufficiently dangerous test for those who know the tone that has been long adopted, over an immense part of Europe, towards such narratives as the deluge, or the exploits of Samson, the speaking ass, or the possessed pigs! Besides this, a great proportion of the ecclesiastical miracles are simply reproductions of those which are recorded in the Bible; and if there are mingled with them some that appear manifest impostures, this may be a very good reason for treating these narratives with a more jealous scrutiny, but is certainly no reason for maintaining that they are all below contempt. The Bible neither asserts nor implies the revocation of supernatural gifts; and if the general promise that these gifts should be conferred may have been intended to apply only to the Apostles, it is at least as susceptible of a different interpretation. If these miracles were actually continued, it is surely not difficult to discover the beneficial purpose that they would fulfil. They would stimulate a languid piety; they would prove invaluable auxiliaries to missionaries labouring among barbarous and unreasoning savages, who, from their circumstances and habits of mind, are utterly incapable of forming any just estimate of the evidences of the religion they are expected to embrace. Even in Europe the results of the controversies of the last 300 years have not been so entirely satisfactory as to leave no room for some more decisive proofs than the ambiguous utterances of a remote antiquity. To say that these miracles are false because they are Roman Catholic is to assume the very question at issue. The controversy between Protestantism and Catholicism comprises an immense mass of complicated and heterogeneous arguments. Thousands of minds have traversed these arguments, and have found at each step their faith in Protestantism confirmed. Thousands of minds have pursued the same course with results that were diametrically opposite. The question is, whether an examination of the alleged miracles of Catholicism would not furnish a decisive criterion, or at least one of the most powerful arguments, for determining the controversy. What evidence of the truth of Catholicism could be stronger than that its distinctive doctrines had been crowned by tens of thousands of miracles, that a supernatural halo had encircled it wherever it appeared, and had cast a glory upon all its triumphs?[1] What proof of the falsehood of Catholicism could be more decisive than that it was unable to establish any of the immense mass of miracles which it had asserted, that all these were resolved and dissipated before a searching criticism, that saints had been canonised, forms of worship established, countless bulls and pastorals issued, innumerable rejoicings, pageantries, processions, and pilgrimages authoritatively instituted, public opinion all through Christendom violently and continuously agitated, on account of alleged events which had either no existence, or which were altogether misunderstood? Making every allowance for the errors of the most extreme fallibility, the history of Catholicism would on this hypothesis represent an amount of imposture probably unequalled in the annals of the human race. If, again, you say that you have formed a definite and unhesitating opinion on the subject from other arguments, I reply that, putting aside all other considerations this answer might suggest, it does not apply to the Tractarian movement we are considering. The transition from the Church of England to the Church of Rome, which was made by so many in consequence of that movement, was not abrupt or unwavering. It was, on the contrary, slow, painful, hesitating, and dubious. Some of those who made it have described themselves as trembling for months, and even

years, between the opposing creeds, their minds vibrating and oscillating to and fro : countless difficulties, colliding principles, modes of reasoning the most various, blending and neutralising sentiments of every hue, torturing their minds with doubt, and sometimes almost destroying by their conflict the very faculty of judgment. Surely one might have imagined that men in such a position would have gladly exchanged those shifting speculations that so constantly elude the grasp and bewilder the mind, and catch their colour from each changing mode of thought, for the comparatively firm and definite ground of historical criticism ! The men were admirably fitted for such criticism. They were preeminently scholars and antiquarians, and in its intellectual aspect the movement was essentially a resuscitation of the past. Nor did the age seem at first sight less suited for the enterprise. At the time of the Reformers the study of evidences, and indeed all searching investigation into the facts of the past, were unknown. When, however, Tractarianism arose, the laws of historical criticism were developed to great perfection, and they were attracting an immense proportion of the talent of Europe. In English theology, especially, they had become supreme. The attacks which Woolston and his followers had made upon the scriptural miracles had been repelled by Lardner and Paley with such unexpected vigour, with such undoubted ability, and, as it was long thought, with such unanswerable success, that all theological reasoning had been directed to this channel. Yet in the Tractarian movement the subject of modern miracles can scarcely be said to have exercised a perceptible influence. Gibbon, as we have seen, had gone over to Rome chiefly through a persuasion of their reality. Chillingworth still earlier had declared that the same reason had been one of those which had induced him to take the same step. Pascal had based his defence of Jansenism in a great measure upon the miracle of the Holy Thorn ; but at Oxford these narratives hardly excited a serious attention. What little influence they had was chiefly an influence of repulsion ; what little was written in their favour was written for the most part in the tone of an apology, as if to attenuate a difficulty rather than to establish a creed.[1]

---

[1] E.g., one of the questions of dispute is the veneration of all relics. Now St. Augustine, the ablest and most clear-headed of all the Fathers, and a man of undoubted piety, solemnly asserts that in his own diocese of Hippo, in the space of two years, no less than seventy miracles had been wrought by the body of St. Stephen, and that in the neighbouring province of Calama, where the relic had previously been, the number was incomparably greater. He gives a catalogue of what he deems undoubted miracles, which he says he had selected from a multitude so great that volumes would be required to relate them all. *In that catalogue we find no less than five cases of restoration of life to the dead* (De Civ. Dei, lib. xxii. c. 8). This statement is well known to readers of Gibbon and Middleton ; but, as far as I know, the only High Churchman who has referred to it is Mr. Ward (*Ideal of a Christian Church*, pp. 138-140), who notices it merely to lament the very different tone with which we now speak of the miraculous. This aspect of the Patristic writings has been very clearly and honestly brought out in Isaac Taylor's *Ancient Christianity*.

[1] Dr. Newman's very able essay (prefixed to Fleury's

This was surely a very remarkable characteristic of the Tractarian movement, when we remember the circumstances and attainments of its leaders, and the great prominence which miraculous evidence had long occupied in England. It was especially remarkable when we recollect that one of the great complaints which the Tractarian party were making against modern theology was, that the conception of the supernatural had become faint and dim, and that its manifestations were either explained away or confined to a distant past. It would seem as if those who were most conscious of the character of their age were unable, in the very midst of their opposition, to free themselves from its tendencies.

If we look beyond the Tractarian movement, we find a still more startling illustration of the prevailing feeling in the extraordinary strides which professed and systematised Rationalism has made in most Protestant countries. The extent to which Continental Protestantism has gravitated towards it has been recognised on all sides, and has excited the greatest hopes in some and the greatest alarm in others. It is worthy, too, of remark, that the movement has been most manifest in those countries where the leading Churches are not connected with very elaborate creeds or with liturgical services, and where the reason, being least shackled by tradition, is most free to follow the natural sequence of its developments. It is true that the word Rationalism is somewhat vague, and comprises many different modifications of belief. This consideration has constantly been urged by those who are termed orthodox Protestants in a tone of the most contemptuous scorn, but with a complete forgetfulness of the fact that for 300 years Protestantism itself was invariably assailed by the very same objection, and was invariably defended on the twofold ground that variations of belief are the necessary consequence of honest enquiry, and that amid its innumerable diversities of detail there were certain radical conceptions which gave a substantial unity to the discordant sects. Much the same general unity may be found among the various modifications of Protestant

Rationalism. Its central conception is the elevation of conscience into a position of supreme authority as the religious organ, a verifying faculty discriminating between truth and error. It regards Christianity as designed to preside over the moral progress of mankind, as a conception which was to become more and more sublimated and spiritualised as the human mind passed into new phases, and was able to bear the splendour of a more unclouded light. Religion it believes to be no exception to the general law of progress, but rather the highest form of its manifestation, and its earlier systems but the necessary steps of an imperfect development. In its eyes the moral element of Christianity is as the sun in heaven, and dogmatic systems are as the clouds that intercept and temper the exceeding brightness of its ray. The insect whose existence is but for a moment might well imagine that these were indeed eternal, that their majestic columns could never fail, and that their luminous folds were the very source and centre of light. And yet they shift and vary with each changing breeze; they blend and separate; they assume new forms and exhibit new dimensions; as the sun that is above them waxes more glorious in its power, they are permeated and at last absorbed by its increasing splendour; they recede, and wither, and disappear, and the eye ranges far beyond the sphere they had occupied into the infinity of glory that is above them.

This is not the place to enter into a critical examination of the faults and merits of Rationalism. A system which would unite in one sublime synthesis all the past forms of human belief, which accepts with triumphant alacrity each new development of science, having no stereotyped standard to defend, and which represents the human mind as pursuing on the highest subjects a path of continual progress towards the fullest and most transcendent knowledge of the Deity, can never fail to exercise a powerful intellectual attraction. A system which makes the moral faculty of man the measure and arbiter of faith must always act powerfully on those in whom that faculty is most developed. This idea of continued and uninterrupted development is one that seems absolutely to override our age. It is scarcely possible to open any really able book on any subject without encountering it in some form. It is stirring all science to its

History) is essentially an *apology* for the ecclesiastical miracles; and the miracles of the English saints, about which we have lately heard so much, never seem to have been regarded as evidential.

very depths; it is revolutionising all historical literature. Its prominence in theology is so great that there is scarcely any school that is altogether exempt from its influence. We have seen in our own day the Church of Rome itself defended in "An Essay on Development," and by a strange application of the laws of progress.

These elements of attraction do much to explain the extraordinary rapidity with which Rationalism has advanced in the present [nineteenth] century, in spite of the vagueness and obscurity it often exhibits, and the many paradoxes it has engendered. But it is well worthy of notice that the very first direction which these speculations invariably take—the very sign and characteristic of their action—is an attempt to explain away the miracles of Scripture. This is so emphatically the distinctive mark of Rationalism that with most persons it is the only conception the word conveys. Wherever it appears, it represents and interprets the prevailing disinclination to accept miraculous narratives,[1] and will resort to every artifice of interpretation in order to evade their force. Its prevalence, therefore, clearly indicates the extent to which this aversion to the miraculous exists in Protestant countries, and the rapidity with which it has of late years increased.

Everyone who has paid any attention to these subjects has a natural inclination to attribute the conclusions he has arrived at to the efforts of his own reason, acting under the influence of an unbiassed will, rather than to a general predisposition arising out of the character of his age. It is probable, therefore, that the members of the rationalistic school would very generally deny being influenced by any other considerations than those which they allege in their defence, and would point to that system of minute and critical Biblical investigation which Germany has produced as the true source of their opinions. I cannot but think that it is much less the cause than the result, and

[1] A large section of German theologians, as is well known, even regard the impossibility, or at all events the unreality, of miraculous accounts as axiomatic. Thus Strauss calmly remarks: "We may summarily reject all miracles, prophecies, narratives of angels and demons, and the like, as simply impossible and irreconcilable with the known and universal laws which govern the course of events."—Introduction to the *Life of Jesus*.

that we have a clear indication of this in the fact that a precisely similar tendency of opinions is shown in another quarter where this criticism has never been pursued. I allude to the freethinkers, who are scattered in such profusion through Roman Catholic countries. Anyone who has attentively examined that great school, which exercises so vast an influence over the literature and policy of our age, must have perceived that it is in many respects widely removed from the old Voltairian spirit. It is no longer exclusively negative and destructive, but is, on the contrary, intensely positive, and in its moral aspect intensely Christian. It clusters around a series of essentially Christian conceptions—equality, fraternity, the suppression of war, the elevation of the poor, the love of truth, and the diffusion of liberty. It revolves around the ideal of Christianity, and represents its spirit without its dogmatic system and its supernatural narratives. From both of these it unhesitatingly recoils, while deriving all its strength and nourishment from Christian ethics.

Such are, I conceive, the general outlines of this movement, which bears an obvious relationship to Protestant Rationalism, and which has been advancing through Europe with still more rapid and triumphant strides. He must indeed be wilfully blind to the course of history who does not perceive that during the last hundred years these schools have completely superseded the dogmatic forms of Protestantism as the efficient antagonists of the Church of Rome, as the centres towards which those who are repelled from Catholicism are naturally attracted. In the sixteenth and to a certain degree in the seventeenth century Protestantism exercised a commanding and controlling influence over the affairs of Europe. Almost all the great questions that agitated the minds of men were more or less connected with its progress. It exhibited, indeed, many unseemly dissensions and many grotesque extravagances; but each of its sects had a rigid and definite dogmatic system, and exercised a powerful influence on those who were around it. Whoever was dissatisfied with the teaching of the Church of Rome was almost immediately attracted and absorbed by one of these systems, and threw himself into the new dogmatism with as much zeal as he had exhibited in the old one. During the last century all this has changed. Of the many hundreds of great thinkers and writers, in every department, who have separated from the teachings and practices of Catholicism, it would be difficult to name three men of real eminence and unquestionable sincerity who have attached themselves permanently to any of the more conservative forms of Protestantism. Amid all those great semi-religious revolutions which have unhinged the faith of thousands, and have so profoundly altered the relations of Catholicism and society, Protestant Churches have made no advance and have exercised no perceptible influence. It has long been a mere truism to say that we are passing through a state of chaos, of anarchy, and of transition. During the past century the elements of dissolution have been multiplying all around us. Scarcely ever before had so large a proportion of the literature of Europe exhibited an open hostility or a contemptuous indifference towards Catholicism. Entire nations have defied its censures, and confiscated its property, and wrested every department of politics from its control. But while Catholicism has been thus convulsed and agitated to its very basis; while the signs of its disintegration are crowding upon us on every side; while the languor and feebleness it exhibits furnish a ready theme for every moralist and a problem for every philosopher, the Protestant sects have gained nothing by the decay of their ancient rival. They have still retained their ecclesiastical organisations and their ancient formularies, but the magnetism they once possessed has wholly vanished. Of all the innumerable forms into which the spirit of dogmatism crystallised after the Reformation, not one seems to have retained the power of attracting those beyond its border. Whatever is lost by Catholicism is gained by Rationalism;[1] wherever the spirit of Rationalism recedes, the spirit of Catholicism advances. Towards the close of the last [eighteenth] century, France threw off her allegiance to Christianity, endeavoured to efface all the traditions of her past, and proclaimed a new era in the religious history of mankind. She soon repented of her temerity, and retired from a position which she had found untenable. Half the nation became ultramontane Roman Catholics; the other half became indifferent or Rationalist.[1] The great majority of Continental writers have repudiated the doctrines of Catholicism, and pursue their speculations without paying the smallest deference to its authority. In the sixteenth century all such persons would have attached themselves to some definite form of Protestantism; they now assume a position which was then entirely unexampled, and would have appeared entirely inexplicable. The age of heresiarchs has passed.[2] Among very ignorant people new dogmatic systems, as Mormonism has shown, may still be successful, but among the educated classes they seem to have lost all their attraction and power. The immense missionary organisations of England succeed indeed in occasionally attracting a few isolated individuals in Roman Catholic countries to Protestantism; but we look in vain for the natural flow and current of thought which in former times impelled vast portions of society to its communion, and imparted an influence to all the great questions in Europe. The only movements which in the faintest degree reproduce the fascination of the sects of the sixteenth century are democratic and philanthropic efforts, like those of St. Simon or Mazzini. All the great intellectual problems that convulse Europe are connected with the rights of nationalities, the progress of democracy, or the dignity of labour. These have now taken the place of those dogmatic questions which in the sixteenth century formed the mainsprings of the policy of Christendom, and which in the nineteenth century have become almost uninfluential.

This is, undoubtedly, an extremely remarkable and an extremely significant contrast. Honest men will hardly deny its existence. Wise men will not shut

---

[1] Italy since the late political changes, and as a consequence of the direction given to the national sympathies by those changes, furnishes, perhaps, a slight exception; but even there the conquests of Protestantism are insignificant as compared with those of Freethinking, and it is said that among Protestants the Plymouth Brethren, who are among the least dogmatic, have also been among the most successful.

[1] I need hardly remind the reader how forcibly and eloquently this point has been brought out by Macaulay, in his Essay on Ranke's *History*.

[2] M. de Montalembert, in his *Life of Lacordaire*, has observed of Lamennais, that there is probably no instance in history of a man possessing so eminently the gifts of a great heresiarch making so little impression by his defection from the Church, and failing so completely to become the nucleus of a sect. After all, however, this was quite natural. The course which Lamennais pursued stimulated a great intellectual movement; but it was not, and was never intended to be, in the direction of a sect.

their eyes to the fact, or refuse to look steadily at its consequences. Coupled with the rationalistic movement that has taken place within Protestantism, it has inclined very many writers to conclude that the earlier forms of Protestantism were merely transitional ; that their continued existence depends, not on any life that is in them, but on the force of habit and of tradition ; that perpetual progress in the domain of belief is the natural destiny and the inevitable law of Protestantism ; and that the fate of Lot's wife is reserved for those Churches which look back on the city of dogmatism from which they fled. To assume, however, that religious life has been extirpated in Protestant Churches, because they appear to have lost the power of influencing those who are around them, is to look for it in only one form. But one conclusion we may most certainly and most safely draw from the movement we are considering. It is that the general bias of the intellect of the age is in the direction of Rationalism ; in other words, that there is a strong predisposition to value the spirit and moral element of Christianity, but to reject dogmatic systems, and more especially miraculous narratives.

We have seen that this tendency was not uninfluential in Tractarianism itself, although that system was organised as a protest and a bulwark against the tendencies of the age. Among those who are usually called orthodox Protestants, it has been clearly shown in the rapid decline of the evidential school. The pre-eminence that school obtained in England during the last [eighteenth] century is certainly not to be attributed to any general tendency towards the miraculous. Lardner and Paley and their followers acted strictly on the defensive, and were therefore compelled to meet their assailants on the ground which those assailants had selected. The spirit of scepticism, which at the Reformation extended only to the authority of particular Churches or to the justice of particular interpretations of Scripture, had gradually expanded till it included the whole domain of theology, and had produced a series of violent attacks upon the miracles. It was to repel these attacks that the evidential school arose, and the annals of religious controversy narrate few more complete victories than they achieved. Of all the English deistical works of the eighteenth century, the influence of two, and only two, survived the controversy. Hume's Essay on Miracles, though certainly not unquestioned and unassailed, cannot be looked upon as obsolete or uninfluential. Gibbon remains the almost undisputed master of his own field, but his great work does not directly involve though it undoubtedly trenches on the subject of Christian evidences. But if we except these two, it would be difficult to conceive a more complete eclipse than the English deists have undergone. Woolston and Tindal, Collins and Chubb, have long since passed into the region of shadows, and their works have mouldered in the obscurity of forgetfulness. Bolingbroke is now little more than a brilliant name, and all the beauties of his matchless style have been unable to preserve his philosophy from oblivion. Shaftesbury retains a certain place as one of the few disciples of idealism who resisted the influence of Locke ; but his importance is purely historical. His cold and monotonous though exquisitely polished dissertations have fallen into general neglect, and find few readers and exercise no influence. The shadow of the tomb rests upon them all ; a deep unbroken silence, the chill of death, surrounds them. They have long ceased to wake any interest, or to suggest any enquiries, or to impart any impulse to the intellect of England. This was the result of the English controversies of the eighteenth century, which on the conservative side consisted mainly of a discussion of miraculous evidence. It is undoubtedly very remarkable in itself, but much more so when we contrast it with what was taking place in Roman Catholic countries. Voltaire and Rousseau not only succeeded in holding their ground, but they met with no opponent whom the wildest enthusiasm could place upon their level. Their works elicited not a single refutation, I might also say not a single argument or criticism, that has come down with any authority to our own day. Diderot, Raynal, and several other members of the party have taken a place in French literature which is probably permanent, and is certainly far higher than was obtained by any of their opponents.

One might have supposed from this contrast that the evidential school, which had been crowned with such marked success, would have enjoyed a great and permanent popularity; but this expectation has not been realised. In

Germany, Kant from the beginning pronounced this mode of reasoning to be unphilosophical ;[1] in England, Coleridge succeeded in bringing it into complete disrepute ; and every year the disinclination to stake the truth of Christianity on the proof of miracles becomes more manifest. A small body of theologians continue, indeed, to persevere in the old plan, and no one will speak of their labours with disrespect ; yet they are themselves witnesses to the generality of the movement, for they complain bitterly that they are labouring in a wilderness, and that the old method has been on all sides abandoned and neglected.[2] We find, everywhere, that the prevailing feeling is to look upon the defence of Christianity as a matter not external to but part of religion. Belief is regarded, not as the result of an historical puzzle, the solution of an extremely complicated intellectual problem which presents fewest difficulties and contradictions, but as the recognition by conscience of moral truth. In other words, religion in its proofs as in its essence is deemed a thing belonging rather to the moral than the intellectual portion of human nature. Faith and not reason is its basis ; and this faith is a species of moral perception. Each dogma is the embodiment and inadequate expression of a moral truth, and is worthless except as it is vivified by that truth. The progress of criticism may shift and vary the circumstances of an historical faith, the advent of new modes of thought may make ancient creeds lifeless and inoperative, but the spirit that underlies them is eternal. The ideal and type of character will acquire new fascination when detached from the material conceptions of an early civilisation. The idolatry of dogmas will pass away ; Christianity, being rescued from the sectarianism and intolerance that have defaced it, will shine by its own moral splendour, and, sublimated above all the sphere of controversy, will resume its rightful position as an ideal and not a system, as a person and not a creed.

We find also, even among the supporters of the evidential school, a strong tendency to meet the Rationalists, as it were, halfway—to maintain that miracles are valid proofs, but that they do not necessarily

[1] On Kant's influence on German Rationalism, see Rose *On Protestantism in Germany*, pp. 183-190.
[2] See, for example, the first and second Essays in *Aids to Faith*.

imply the notion of a violation of natural law with which they had been so long associated. They are, it is said, performed simply by the application of natural means guided by supernatural knowledge. The idea of interference (it is argued) can present no difficulty to anyone who admits human liberty ;[1] for those who acknowledge that liberty must hold that man has a certain power of guiding and controlling the laws of matter, that he can of his own free will produce effects which would not have been produced without his intervention, and that in proportion as his knowledge of the laws of nature advances, his power of adapting them to his purposes is increased. That mind can influence matter is itself one of the laws of nature. That a being of supernatural knowledge and power could, by the normal exercise of his capacities, produce effects transcending both our comprehension and our capabilities, is a proposition that is eminently rational. To adapt and modify general laws to special purposes is the occupation and the characteristic of every intelligence, and to deny this power to Divine intelligence seems but little removed from atheism. It is to make the Deity the only torpid mind in the universe. There is, therefore, it is said, nothing improbable in the belief that Omniscience, by the selection of natural laws of which we are ignorant, could accomplish all those acts which we call miraculous.[2]

[1] See Mansel's "Essay on Miracles," in the *Aids to Faith*.
[2] For an exposition of this view I cannot do better than refer to an article on "The Supernatural" in the *Edinburgh Review* for October, 1862, written by the Duke of Argyle, and since republished by him in his *Reign of Law*. I select a few sentences, which contain the substance of the argument : "The reign of law in nature is indeed, as far as we can observe, universal. But the common idea of the supernatural is that which is at variance with natural law, above it or in violation of it.....Hence it would appear to follow that, to a man thoroughly possessed of the idea of natural law as universal, nothing ever could be admitted as supernatural.....But then we must understand nature as including every agency which we see entering, or can conceive from analogy capable of entering, into the causation of the world..... The power of men in respect of physical laws extends only, first, to their discovery and ascertainment, and then to their use.....A complete knowledge of all natural laws would give, if not complete power, at least degrees of power immensely greater than those which we now possess.....The relation in which God stands to those rules of His government which are called laws is, of course, an inscrutable mystery ; but those who believe that His will does govern the world must believe that, ordinarily at least, He does govern it by the choice and use of means : nor have we any certain reason to believe that He ever acts otherwise. Signs and wonders may be wrought, for aught we know, by similar instrumentality—by the selection and use of laws of which men knew nothing." That miracles were performed simply by the employ-

According to this notion, a miracle would not differ, generically, from a human act, though it would still be strictly available for evidential purposes. Miracles would thus be separated from a conception with which almost all the controversialists of the last century had identified them, and which is peculiarly repugnant to the tendencies of our age.

We have now taken a sufficiently extensive survey of the history of Miracles to enable us to arrive at a general conclusion. We have seen that ever since that revival of learning which preceded the Reformation, and dispelled the torpor and ignorance in which Europe had been for centuries immersed, the human mind has been pursuing on this subject a uniform and an unvarying course. The degrees in which different nations and churches have participated in the movement have been very various, but there is no part of Europe which has been uninfluenced by its progress. Reactionary parties have themselves reflected its character, and have at last been swept away by the advancing stream. All the weight of tradition and of learning, all the energies of conservatism of every kind, have been opposed to its progress, and all have been opposed in vain. Generation after generation the province of the miraculous has contracted, and the circle of scepticism has expanded. Of the two great divisions of these events, one has completely perished. Witchcraft and diabolical possession and diabolical disease have long since passed into the region of fables. To disbelieve them was at first the eccentricity of a few isolated thinkers ; it was then the distinction of the educated classes in the most advanced nations ; it is now the common sentiment of all classes in all countries in Europe. The countless miracles that were once associated with every holy relic and with every village shrine have rapidly and silently disappeared. Year by year the incredulity became more manifest, even where the theological profession was unchanged. Their numbers continually lessened until they at last almost ceased ; and any attempt to revive them has been treated with a general and undisguised contempt. The miracles of the Fathers are passed over with an incredulous scorn, or with a significant silence. The rationalistic

ment of unknown natural laws was maintained long since by Malebranche, and also, I think, by Butler.

spirit has even attempted to explain away those which are recorded in Scripture, and it has materially altered their position in the systems of theology. In all countries, in all churches, in all parties, among men of every variety of character and opinion, we have found the tendency existing. In each nation its development has been a measure of intellectual activity, and has passed in regular course through the different strata of society. During the last century it has advanced with a vastly accelerated rapidity ; the old lines of demarcation have been everywhere obscured, and the spirit of Rationalism has become the great centre to which the intellect of Europe is manifestly tending. If we trace the progress of the movement from its origin to the present day, we find that it has completely altered the whole aspect and complexion of religion. When it began, Christianity was regarded as a system entirely beyond the range and scope of human reason : it was impious to question ; it was impious to examine ; it was impious to discriminate. On the other hand, it was visibly instinct with the supernatural. Miracles of every order and degree of magnitude were flashing forth incessantly from all its parts. They excited no scepticism and no surprise. The miraculous element pervaded all literature, explained all difficulties, consecrated all doctrines. Every unusual phenomenon was immediately referred to a supernatural agency, not because there was a passion for the improbable, but because such an explanation seemed far more simple and easy of belief than the obscure theories of science. In the present day Christianity is regarded as a system which courts the strictest investigation, and which, among many other functions, was designed to vivify and stimulate all the energies of man. The idea of the miraculous, which a superficial observer might have once deemed its most prominent characteristic, has been driven from almost all its entrenchments, and now quivers faintly and feebly through the mists of eighteen hundred years.

The causes of this great movement are very various. It may be attributed to the success of physical science in explaining phenomena that were long deemed supernatural, and in substituting the conception of connected and unbroken law for that of capricious and isolated interference. It may be attributed, also, in a great measure to the increased severity of proof demanded under the influence of the modern critical spirit, and to the important investigations that have recently been made into the mythologies of different nations, and into the manner in which they are generated. But in addition to these, which may be regarded as the legitimate causes of the change, there is one of a somewhat different kind. The decline of the influence and realisation of dogmatic theology which characterises a secular age brings with it an instinctive repugnance to the miraculous, by diverting the mind from the class of subjects with which the miraculous is connected. When theology occupies an exceedingly prominent place in the affairs of life, and is the subject towards which the thoughts of men are naturally and violently directed, the mind will at last take a theological cast, and will judge all secular matters by a theological standard. In a period, therefore, when theology is almost co-extensive with intellectual exertion, when the whole scope of literature, policy, and art is to subserve theological interests, and when the imaginations of men are habitually inflamed by the subject of their continual meditations, it is not at all surprising that belief in existing miracles should be universal. Such miracles are perfectly congenial with the mental tone and atmosphere that is general. The imagination is constantly directed towards miraculous events, and readily forces its conceptions upon the reason. When, however, the terrestrial has been aggrandised at the expense of the theological; when, in the progress of civilisation, art and literature and government become in a great measure secularised ; when the mind is withdrawn by ten thousand intellectual influences from dogmatic considerations, and when the traces of these considerations become confused and un-realised, a new habit of thought is gradually acquired. A secular atmosphere is formed about the mind. The measure of probability is altered. Men formerly expected in every event of life something analogous to the theological notions on which they were continually meditating : they now judge everything by a secular standard. Formerly their natural impulse was to explain all phenomena by miracle ; it is now to explain them by science. This is simply the result of a general law of the human mind, which is exemplified on countless occasions in the intercourse of society. The soldier, the lawyer, and the scholar will each obtain from his special pursuit a certain cast and character of thought which he will display on all subjects, even those most remote from his immediate province. Just so an age that is immersed in theology will judge everything by a theological, that is to say a miraculous standard, and an age that is essentially secular will judge everything by a secular, that is to say a rationalistic standard. It is therefore, I conceive, no chance coincidence that the decline of the sense of the miraculous has everywhere accompanied that movement of thought which has banished dogmatic influence from so many departments of life, and so greatly restricted it in others. In the present day this tendency has become so powerful that its influence extends to every earnest thinker, even though he does not as an individual participate in the indifference to dogma from which it sprang. Whoever succeeds in emancipating himself from the special influences of education and associations by which his opinions are in the first instance determined will find the general course and current of contemporary literature the most powerful attraction to his mind. There are, it is true, a few exceptions to this rule. There are some intellects of such a repellent character that the simple fact that one class of opinions or tendencies is dominant in their neighbourhood will be sufficient to induce them to adopt the opposite. These, however, are the exceptions. With most persons who really endeavour to form their opinions by independent thought, contemporary literature exercises an attracting and controlling influence which is extremely powerful if it is not irresistible. Owing to circumstances which I shall not pause to examine, it flashes upon them with a force and directness which is not possessed by the literature of any earlier period. The general tone of thought pervading it colours all their reasonings, influences and, if they are unconscious of its action, determines all their conclusions. In the present day this influence is essentially rationalistic.

There is one other subject of great importance which is naturally suggested by the movement we have been considering. We have seen how profoundly it has altered the character of Christian Churches. It has changed not only the outward form and manifestations, but the habits of thought, the religious atmosphere which was the medium through which all events were contemplated, and by which all reasonings were refracted. No one can doubt that if the modes of thought now prevailing on these subjects, even in Roman Catholic countries, could have been presented to the mind of a Christian of the twelfth century, he would have said that so complete an alteration would involve the absolute destruction of Christianity. As a matter of fact, most of these modifications were forced upon the reluctant Church by the pressure from without, and were specially resisted and denounced by the bulk of the clergy. They were represented as subversive of Christianity. The doctrine that religion could be destined to pass through successive phases of development was pronounced to be emphatically unchristian. The ideal church was always in the past; and immutability, if not retrogression, was deemed the condition of life. We can now judge this resistance by the clear light of experience. Dogmatic systems have, it is true, been materially weakened; they no longer exercise a controlling influence over the current of affairs. Persecution, religious wars, absorbing controversies, sacred art, and theological literature, which once indicated a passionate interest in dogmatic questions, have passed away or become comparatively uninfluential. Ecclesiastical power throughout Europe has been everywhere weakened, and weakened in each nation in proportion to its intellectual progress. If we were to judge the present position of Christianity by the tests of ecclesiastical history, if we were to measure it by the orthodox zeal of the great doctors of the past, we might well look upon its prospects with the deepest despondency and alarm. The spirit of the Fathers has incontestably faded. The days of Athanasius and Augustine have passed away never to return. The whole course of thought is flowing in another direction. The controversies of bygone centuries ring with a strange hollowness on the ear. But if, turning from ecclesiastical historians, we apply the exclusively moral tests which the New Testament so invariably and so emphatically enforces, if we ask whether Christianity has ceased to produce the living fruits of love and charity and zeal for truth, the conclusion we should arrive at would be very different. If it be true Christianity to dive with a passionate charity into the darkest recesses of misery and vice, to irrigate every quarter of the earth with the fertilising stream of an almost boundless benevolence, and to include all the sections of humanity in the circle of an intense and efficacious sympathy ; if it be true Christianity to destroy or weaken the barriers which had separated class from class and nation from nation, to free war from its harshest elements, and to make a consciousness of essential equality and of a genuine fraternity dominate over all accidental differences ; if it be, above all, true Christianity to cultivate a love of truth for its own sake, a spirit of candour and of tolerance towards those with whom we differ—if these be the marks of a true and healthy Christianity, then never since the days of the Apostles has it been so vigorous as at present, and the decline of dogmatic systems and of clerical influence has been a measure if not a cause of its advance.

Chapter III.

ÆSTHETIC, SCIENTIFIC, AND MORAL DEVELOPMENTS OF RATIONALISM

THE preceding chapters will, I trust, have sufficiently shown that during the last three centuries the sense of the miraculous has been steadily declining in Europe, that the movement has been so universal that no church or class of miracles has altogether escaped its influence, and that its causes are to be sought much less in special arguments bearing directly upon the question than in the general intellectual condition of society. In this, as in all other great historical developments, we have two classes of influences to consider. There are certain tendencies or predispositions, resulting from causes that are deeply imbedded in the civilisation of the age, which create the movement, direct the stream of opinions with irresistible force in a given direction, and, if we consider only great bodies of men and long periods of time, exercise an almost absolute authority. There is also the action of special circumstances and individual genius upon this general progress, retarding or accelerating its advance, giving it in different countries and in different spheres of society a peculiar character, and for a time associating it with movements with which it has no natural connection. I have endeavoured to show that while numerous circumstances growing out of the complications of society have more or less influenced the history of the decline of the miraculous, there are two causes which dominate over all others, and are themselves very closely connected. One of these is the increasing sense of law, produced by physical sciences, which predisposes men more and more to attribute all the phenomena that meet them in actual life or in history to normal rather than to abnormal agencies ; the other is the diminution of the influence of theology, partly from causes that lie within itself, and partly from the great increase of other subjects, which inclines men to judge all matters by a secular rather than by a theological standard.

But, as we have already in some degree perceived, and as we shall hereafter see more clearly, this history of the miraculous is but a single part or aspect of a much wider movement, which in its modern phases is usually designated by the name of Rationalism. The process of thought, that makes men recoil from the miraculous, makes them modify their views on many other questions. The expectation of miracles grows out of a certain conception of the habitual government of the world, of the nature of the Supreme Being, and of the manifestations of His power, which are all more or less changed by advancing civilisation. Sometimes this change is displayed by an open rejection of old beliefs. Sometimes it appears only in a change of interpretation or of realisation ; that is to say, men generally annex new ideas to old words, or they permit old opinions to become virtually obsolete. Each different phase of civilisation has its peculiar and congenial views of the system and government of the universe to which the men of that time will gravitate ; and although a revelation or a great effort of human genius may for a time emancipate some of them from the conditions of the age, the pressure of surrounding influences will soon reassert its sway, and the truths that are unsuited to the time will remain inoperative till their appropriate civilisation has dawned.

I shall endeavour in the present chapter to trace the different phases of this development—to show how the conceptions both of the nature of the Deity and of the government of the universe are steadily modified before advancing knowledge, and to analyse the causes upon which those modifications depend.

It has been conjectured by a very high authority, that fetishism is the religion which men who are altogether uncivilised would naturally embrace ; and there certainly appears strong reason to believe that the general characteristic of the earlier stages of religious belief is to concentrate reverence upon matter, and to attribute to it an intrinsic efficacy. This fetishism, which in its rudest form consists of the worship of a certain portion of matter as matter, is shown also, though in a modified and less revolting manner, in the supposition that certain sacred talismans or signs possess an inherent efficacy altogether irrespective of the dispositions of men. Of this nature was the system of pagan magic, which attributed a supernatural power to particular herbs, or ceremonies, or words, and also the many rival but corresponding superstitions that were speedily introduced into Christianity. The sign of the cross was perhaps the earliest of these. It was adopted not simply as a form of recognition or as a holy recollection, or even as a mark of reverence, but as a weapon of miraculous power; and the writings of the Fathers are crowded with the prodigies it performed, and also with the many types and images that adumbrated its glory. Thus we are reminded by a writer in the beginning of the second century, that the sea could not be traversed without a mast, which is in the form of a cross. The earth becomes fertile only when it has been dug by a spade, which is a cross. The body of man is itself in the same holy form. So also is his face, for the eyes and nose together form a cross; a fact to which Jeremiah probably alluded when he said, "The breath of our nostrils is the anointed of the Lord."[1]

Speculations no less strange and farfetched were directed to the baptismal water. The efficacy of infant baptism, which had been introduced, if not in the Apostolic age, at least immediately after, was regarded as quite independent of

any moral virtues either in the recipient or those about him, and in the opinion of some a spiritual change was effected by the water itself, without any immediate co-operation of the Deity, by a power that had been conferred upon the element at the period of the creation.[1] The incomparable grandeur of its position in the universe was the theme of the most rapturous eloquence. When the earth was still buried in the night of chaos, before the lights of heaven had been called into being or any living creature had tenanted the eternal solitude, water existed in all the plenitude of its perfection, veiling the unshapen earth, and glorified and sanctified for ever as the chosen throne of the Deity. By water God separated the heavens from the earth. Water became instinct with life when the earth was still barren and uninhabited. In the creation of man it might appear at first sight as if its position was ignored, but even here a more mature reflection dispelled the difficulty. For in order that the Almighty should mould the earth into the human form, it was obviously necessary that it should have retained something of its former moisture; in other words, that it should have been mixed with water.[2]

Such was the direction in which the human mind drifted, with an ever-increasing rapidity, as the ignorance and intellectual torpor became more general. The same habit of thought was soon displayed in every department of theology, and countless charms and amulets came into use, the simple possession of which

---

[1] Justin Martyr, *Apol.* I. Augustine thought the wooden ark floating on the Deluge a type of the cross consecrating the baptismal waters; and Bede found a similar type in the rod of Moses stretched over the Red Sea. Another wise commentator suggested that Isaac had been saved from death, because, when ascending the mountain, he bore the "wood of sacrifice" on his shoulder. The cross, however, seldom or never appears in art before the vision of Constantine. At first it was frequently represented richly ornamented with gems or flowers. As St. Fortunatus writes:

"Arbor decora et fulgida
Ornata regis purpura,
Electa digno stipite
Tam sancta membra tangere."

The letter Tau, as representing the cross, was specially reverenced as opposed to Theta, the unlucky letter—the initial of θάνατος.

[1] See the curious argument in Tertullian, *De Baptismo,* cc. 5, 6, 7, 8.

[2] "Non enim ipsius quoque hominis figurandi opus sociantibus aquis absolutum est; de terra materia convenit, non tamen habilis nisi humecta et succida, quam scilicet ante quartum diem segregatæ aquæ in stationem suam superstite humore, limo temperant." (Tertullian, *De Baptismo,* c. iii.) From this notion of the sanctity of water grew the custom of swimming witches—for it was believed that everything unholy was repelled by it, and unable to sink into its depths (Binsfeldius, *De Confess. Mal.* p. 315)—and also probably the many legends of transformed men restored to their natural condition by crossing a stream. Among the ancient philosophers, Thales had esteemed water the origin of all things, which more than one Father considered as a kind of inspiration. Thus Minucius Felix: "Milesius Thales rerum initium aquam dixit: Deum autem eam mentem quæ ex aqua cuncta formaverit. Vides philosophi principalis nobiscum penitus opinionem consonare." (*Octavius,* c. xix.) The belief in the expiatory power of water was forcibly rebuked by Ovid:—

"Ah! nimiùm faciles, qui tristia crimina cædis
Flumineâ tolli posse putatis aquâ!"

(*Fasti,* lib. ii.)

was supposed to guarantee the owner against all evils, both spiritual and temporal. Indeed, it may be questioned whether this form of fetishism was ever more prominent in paganism than in mediæval Christianity.

When men pass from a state of pure fetishism, the next conception they form of the Divine nature is anthropomorphism, which is in some respects very closely connected with the preceding, and which, like it, is diffused in a more or less modified form over the belief of almost all uncivilised nations. Those who have ceased to attribute power and virtue to inert matter, regard the universe as the sphere of the operations of spiritual beings of a nature strictly analogous to their own. They consider every unusual phenomenon the direct and isolated act of an unseen agent, pointed to some isolated object, and resulting from some passing emotion. The thunder, the famine, and the pestilence, are the results of an ebullition of spiritual anger; great and rapid prosperity is the sign of spiritual satisfaction. But at the same time the feebleness of imagination which in this stage makes men unable to picture the Deity other than as an unseen man, makes it also impossible for them to concentrate their thoughts and emotions upon that conception without a visible representation. For while it is a matter of controversy whether or not the innate faculties of the civilised man transcend those of the savage, it is at least certain that the intellectual atmosphere of each period tells so soon and so powerfully upon all men, that long before matured age the two classes are almost as different in their capacities as in their acquirements. The civilised man not only knows more than the savage; he possesses an intellectual strength, a power of sustained and patient thought, of concentrating his mind steadily upon the unseen, of disengaging his conceptions from the images of the senses, which the other is unable even to imagine. Present to the savage the conception of an unseen Being, to be adored without the assistance of any representation, and he will be unable to grasp it. It will have no force or palpable reality to his mind, and can therefore exercise no influence over his life. Idolatry is the common religion of the savage, simply because it is the only one of which his intellectual condition will admit, and, in one form or another, it must continue until that condition has been changed.

Idolatry may be of two kinds. It is sometimes a sign of progress. When men are beginning to emerge from the pure fetishism which is probably their first stage, they carve matter into the form of an intelligent being; and it is only when it is endowed with that form that they attribute to it a Divine character. They are still worshipping matter, but their fetishism is fading into anthropomorphism. Sometimes, again, men who have once risen to a conception of a pure and spiritual being, sink, in consequence of some convulsion of society, into a lower level of civilisation. They will then endeavour to assist their imaginations by representations of the objects of their worship, and they will very soon attribute to those representations an intrinsic efficacy.

It will appear from the foregoing principles that, in the early anthropomorphic stages of society, visible images form the channels of religious devotions, and, therefore, as long as those stages continue, the true history of theology, or at least of the emotional and realised parts of theology, is to be found in the history of art. Even outside the pale of Christianity, there is scarcely any instance in which the national religion has not exercised a great and dominating influence over the national art. Thus, for example, the two ancient nations in which the æsthetic development failed most remarkably to keep pace with the general civilisation were the Persians and the Egyptians. The fire that was worshipped by the first, formed a fetish at once so simple and so sublime, that it rendered useless the productions of the chisel; while the artistic genius of Egypt was paralysed by a religion which branded all innovation as a crime, made the profession of an artist compulsory and hereditary, rendered the knowledge of anatomy impossible by its prohibition of dissection, and taught men by its elaborate symbolism to look at every natural object, not for its own sake, but as the representative of something else. Thus, again, among the nations that were especially distinguished for their keen sense of the beautiful, India and Greece are pre-eminent; but there is this important difference between them. The Indian religion ever soared to the terrible, the unnatural, and the prodigious, and consequently Indian art was so completely turned away from nature, that all faculty of accurately copying it seems to have vanished, and the simplest subject was interwoven with grotesque and fanciful inventions. The Greek religion, on the other hand, was an almost pure naturalism, and therefore Greek art was simply nature idealised, and as such has become the universal model.[1]

But it is with Christian art that we are now especially concerned, and it is also Christian art which most faithfully reflects the different stages of religious development, enabling us to trace, not merely successive phases of belief, but, what is much more important for my present purpose, successive phases of religious realisation.

The constant fall of the early Jews into idolatry, in spite of the most repeated commands and the most awful punishments, while it shows clearly how irresistible is this tendency in an early stage of society, furnished a warning which was at first not altogether lost upon the Christian Church. It is indeed true that art had so long been associated with paganism—its subjects, its symbolism, and its very tone of beauty, were so derived from the old mythology—that the Christian artists, who had probably in many cases been formerly pagan artists, introduced a considerable number of the ancient conceptions into their new sphere. But, although this fact is perfectly incontestable, and although the readiness with which pagan imagery was admitted into the symbolism of the Church forms an extremely curious and instructive contrast to the tone which most of the Fathers adopted towards the pagan deities, nearly all these instances of appropriation were singularly judicious, and the general desire to avoid anything that might lead to idolatrous worship was very manifest.

The most important and the most beneficial effect of pagan traditions upon

Christian art was displayed in its general character. It had always been a strict rule among the Greeks and Romans to exclude from sepulchral decorations every image of sadness. The funerals of the ancients were, indeed, accompanied by great displays of exaggerated and artificial lamentation ; but once the ashes were laid in the tomb, it was the business of the artist to employ all his skill in depriving death of its terror. Wreaths of flowers, Bacchic dances, hunts, or battles, all the exuberance of the most buoyant life, all the images of passion or revelry, were sculptured around the tomb, while the genii of the seasons indicated the inevitable march of time, and the masks that adorned the corners showed that life was but a player's part, to be borne for a few years with honour, and cast aside without regret.

The influence of this tradition was shown in a very remarkable way in Christianity. At first all Christian art was sepulchral art. The places that were decorated were the Catacombs ; the chapels were all surrounded by the dead ; the altar upon which the sacred mysteries were celebrated was the tomb of a martyr.[1] According to mediæval or even to modern ideas, we should have imagined that an art growing up under such circumstances would have assumed a singularly sombre and severe tone, and this expectation would be greatly heightened if we remembered the occasional violence of the persecution. The very altar-tomb around which the Christian painter scattered his ornaments with most profusion was often associated with the memory of sufferings of the most horrible and varied character, and at the same time with displays of heroic constancy that might well have invited the talents of the artist. Passions, too, were often roused to the highest point, and it would seem but natural that the great and terrible scenes of Christian vengeance should be depicted. Yet nothing of this kind appears in the Catacombs. With two doubtful exceptions, one at least being of the very latest period, there are no representations of

[1] See Winckelmann, *Hist. of Art* ; Raoul Rochette, *Cours d'Archéologie* ; and the Lectures of Barry and Fuseli. This particular characteristic of Indian art has been forcibly noticed by Mr. Ruskin in one of his Edinburgh lectures. Lessing ascribes the imperfections of Persian art to its almost exclusive employment for military subjects ; but this was itself a consequence of the small encouragement religion gave to art. On the great difference of the ideal of beauty in different nations, which has also exercised a great influence on the development of art, see some curious evidence collected by Ch. Comte, *Traité de Législation*, liv. iii. ch. 4.

[1] This is the origin of the custom in the Catholic Church of placing relics of the martyrs beneath the altars of the churches. It was also connected with the passage in the Apocalypse about the souls that were beneath the altar of God. In most early churches there was a subterranean chapel below the high altar, as a memorial of the Catacombs. A decree of the Second Council of Nice (A.D. 787) forbade the consecration of any church without relics.

martyrdoms.[1] Daniel unharmed amid the lions, the unaccomplished sacrifice of Isaac, the Three Children unscathed amid the flames, and St. Peter led to prison, are the only images that reveal the horrible persecution that was raging. There was no disposition to perpetuate forms of suffering, no ebullition of bitterness or complaint, no thirsting for vengeance. Neither the Crucifixion, nor any of the scenes of the Passion, were ever represented ; nor was the day of judgment, nor were the sufferings of the lost. The wreaths of flowers in which paganism delighted, and even some of the most joyous images of the pagan mythology, were still retained, and were mingled with all the most beautiful emblems of Christian hopes, and with representations of many of the miracles of mercy.

This systematic exclusion of all images of sorrow, suffering, and vengeance, at a time that seemed beyond all others most calculated to produce them, reveals the Early Church in an aspect that is singularly touching, and it may, I think, be added, singularly sublime. The fact is also one of extreme importance in ecclesiastical history. For, as we shall hereafter have occasion to see, there existed among some of the theologians of the Early Church a tendency that was diametrically opposite to this ; a tendency to dilate upon such subjects as the torments of hell, the vengeance of the day of judgment, and, in a word, all the sterner portions of Christianity, which at last became dominant in the Church, and which exercised an extremely injurious influence over the affections of men. But whatever might have been the case with educated theologians, it was quite impossible for this tendency to be very general as long as art, which was then the expression of popular realisations, took a different direction. The change in art was not fully shown till late in the tenth century. I have already had occasion to notice the popularity which representations of the Passion and of the day of judgment then for the first time assumed ; and it may be

[1] M. Raoul Rochette thinks that there is but one direct positive representation of a martyrdom—that of the Virgin Salome, and this is of a very late period of decadence. (*Tableau des Catacombes*, p. 187.) The same writer has collected (pp. 191, 192) a few instances from the Fathers in which representations of martyrdoms in the early basilicas are mentioned ; but they are very few, and there can be no doubt whatever of the broad contrast early Christian art in this respect bears to that of the tenth and following centuries.

added that, from this period, one of the main objects of the artists was the invention of new and horrible tortures, which were presented to the constant contemplation of the faithful in countless pictures of the sufferings of the martyrs on earth, or of the lost in hell.[1]

The next point which especially strikes us in the art of the Catacombs is the great love of symbolism it evinced. There are, it is true, a few isolated pictures of Christ and of the Virgin ; but by far the greater number of representations were obviously symbolical, and were designed exclusively as means of instruction. Of these symbols many were taken without hesitation from paganism. Thus, one of the most common is the peacock, which in the Church, as among the heathen, was selected as the emblem of immortality. Partly, perhaps, on account of its surpassing beauty, and partly from a belief that its flesh never decayed,[2] it had been adopted by the ancients as the nearest realisation of their conception of the phœnix, and at the funeral of an empress the bird was sometimes let loose from among the ashes of the deceased.[3] Orpheus drawing all men to him by his music, symbolised the attractive power of Christianity.[4] The

[1] See Raoul Rochette, *Tableau des Catacombes*, pp. 192-195 ; Didron, *Iconographie chrétienne.*
[2] Which St. Augustine said he had ascertained by experiment to be a fact, and which he seemed to regard as a miracle. (*De Civ. Dei*, lib. xxi, c. 4).
[3] See Ciampini, *Vetera Monumenta*, pars i. p. 115 ; and Maitland, *On the Catacombs.* Raoul Rochette, however, seems to regard the peacock rather as the symbol, first of all, of the apotheosis of an empress, and then generally of apotheosis, the peacock having been the bird of Juno, the empress of heaven.
[4] Orpheus is spoken of by Eusebius as in this respect symbolising Christ. The reverence that attached to him probably resulted in a great measure from the fact that among the many apocryphal prophecies of Christ that circulated in the Church, some of the most conspicuous were ascribed to Orpheus. See on this symbol, Maitland, *On the Catacombs*, p. 110 ; Raoul Rochette, *Tab. des Cat.* p. 138 ; and, for a full examination of the subject, the great work of Boldetti, *Osservazioni sopra i Cimiteri de' Santi Martyri* (Romæ, 1720), tom. i. pp. 27-29. M. Rio (*Art chrétien*, Introd. p. 36), I think rather fancifully, connects it with the descent of Orpheus to hell to save a soul. As other examples of the introduction of pagan gods into Christian art, I may mention that there is an obscure picture in one of the Catacombs, which R. Rochette supposes to represent Mercury leading the souls of the dead to judgment (*Tab. des Cat.* pp. 148-151) ; and also that Hercules, though never, I believe, represented in the Catacombs, appears more than once in the old churches, St. Augustine having identified him with Samson. (See on this representation, and generally on the connection between pagan and Christian art, that very curious and learned work, Marangoni, *Delle Cose Gentilesche e Profane trasportate ad uso delle Chiese* [Romæ, 1744], pp. 50, 51.) The sphinx also was believed by some of the early Christians (*e.g.* Clement of Alexandria) to be in some degree connected with their faith, for they supposed it to be copied from the Jewish

masks of paganism, and especially the masks of the sun and moon, which the pagans adopted as emblems of the lapse of life, continued to adorn the Christian sarcophagi, the last being probably regarded as emblems of the resurrection. The same thing may be said of the genii of the seasons.[1] Nor was this by any means the only form under which the genii were represented. The ancients regarded them as presiding over every department of nature, and many thought that a separate genius watched over the destiny of each man. This conception very naturally coalesced with that of guardian angels,[2] and the pagan representation of the genii as young winged boys, naked, and with gentle and joyous countenances, became very common in early Christian art, and passed from it into the art of later days. Even now from the summit of the baldachino of St. Peter's, the genii of paganism look down on the proudest ceremonies of Catholicism. Once or twice on the Christian sarcophagi Christ is represented in triumph, with the sky, or perhaps, more correctly, " the waters above the firmament," beneath his feet, in the form of a man extending a veil above his head, the habitual pagan representation of an aquatic deity.[3]

In addition to these symbols, which were manifestly taken from paganism, there were others mainly or exclusively produced by the Church itself. Thus, the fish was the usual emblem of Christ, chosen because the Greek word forms the initials of His name and titles,[4] and also because Christians are born by baptism in water.[5] Sometimes, but much more rarely, the stag is employed for the same purpose, because it bears the cross on its forehead, and from an old notion that it was the irreconcilable enemy of serpents, which it was supposed to hunt out and destroy.[6] Several subjects from the Bible

of a symbolical character were constantly repeated. Such were Noah in the attitude of prayer receiving the dove into his breast, Jonah rescued from the fish's mouth, Moses striking the rock, St. Peter with the wand of power, the Three Children, Daniel in the lions' den, the Good Shepherd, the dove of peace, the anchor of hope, the crown of martyrdom, the palm of victory, the ship struggling through the waves to a distant haven, the horse bounding onwards to the goal. All of these were manifestly symbolical, and were in no degree the objects of reverence or worship.

When, however, the first purity of the Christian Church was dimmed, and when the decomposition of the Roman Empire and the invasion of the barbarians overcast the civilisation of Europe, the character of art was speedily changed, and though many of the symbolical representations still continued, there was manifested by the artists a constantly increasing tendency to represent directly the object of their worship, and by the people to attach a peculiar sanctity to the image.

Of all the forms of anthropomorphism that are displayed in Catholic art, there is probably none which a Protestant deems so repulsive as the portraits of the First Person of the Trinity, that are now so common. It is, however, a very remarkable fact, which has been established chiefly by the researches of some French archæologists in the present [nineteenth] century, that these portraits are all comparatively modern, and that the period in which the superstition of Europe was most profound was precisely that in which they had no existence.[1] In an age when the

---

image of the Cherubim ; but they never reproduced it. Some later antiquaries have attributed this curious combination of the Virgin and the Lion to the advantages Egypt derives from these signs, through which the sun passes at the period of the inundation of the Nile (Caylus, *Recueil d' Antiquité*, tom. i. p. 45).

[1] Marangoni, *Delle Cose Gentilesche*, p. 45.
[2] All this is fully discussed in Marangoni.
[3] Ibid. p. 45 ; Raoul Rochette, *Tab. des Cat.*
[4] Ἰχθύς. Ἰησοῦς Χριστὸς Θεοῦ Υἱὸς Σωτήρ. The initial letters of the prophetic verses of the Sibyl of Erythra (St. Aug. *De Civ. Dei*, lib. xviii. cap. 20). The dolphin was especially selected because of its tenderness to its young.
[5] "Nos pisciculi secundum Ἰχθὺν nostrum Jesum Christum in aquâ nascimur." (Tertullian, *De Baptismo*, c. i.)
[6] Maury, *Légendes pieuses*, pp. 173-178. See, too,

Pliny, *Hist. Nat.* viii. 50; Josephus, *Antiq.* ii. 10. There is a bas-relief in the Vatican which seems to represent a stag in the act of attacking a serpent. The passage in the Psalms, about "the hart panting for the waters" (which the neophyte was accustomed to sing as he descended into the baptismal water), was mixed up with this symbol. In the middle ages, stags were invested with a kind of prophetic power. See also Ciampini, *De Sacris Ædificiis* (Romæ), p. 44 ; and the very curious chapter in Arringhi, *Roma Subterranea*, tom. ii. pp. 602-606. The stag was supposed to dread the thunder so much, that through terror it often brought forth its young prematurely, and this was associated with the passage, "The voice of thy thunder has made me afraid."

[1] This subject has been briefly noticed by Raoul Rochette in his *Discours sur l' Art du Christianisme* (1834), p. 7; and by Maury, *Légendes pieuses*; but the full examination of it was reserved for M. Didron, in his great work, *Iconographie chrétienne, Hist. de Dieu* (Paris, 1843), one of the most important contributions ever made to Christian archæology. See, too, Emeric David, *Hist. de la Peinture au Moyen Âge*, pp. 19-21.

religious realisations of Christendom were habitually expressed by visible representations—when the nature of a spirit was so inadequately conceived that artists never for a moment shrank from representing purely spiritual beings—and when that instinctive reverence which makes men recoil from certain subjects, as too solemn and sublime to be treated, was almost absolutely unknown—we do not find the smallest tendency to represent God the Father. Scenes indeed in which He acted were frequently depicted, but the First Person of the Trinity was invariably superseded by the Second. Christ, in the dress and with the features appropriated to Him in the representations of scenes from the New Testament, and often with the monogram underneath his figure, is represented creating man, condemning Adam and Eve to labour, speaking with Noah, arresting the arm of Abraham, or giving the law to Moses.[1] With the exception of a hand sometimes extended from the cloud, and occasionally encircled with a nimbus, we find in this period no traces in art of the Creator. At first we can easily imagine that a purely spiritual conception of the Deity, and also the hatred that was inspired by the type of Jupiter, would have discouraged artists from attempting such a subject, and Gnosticism, which exercised a very great influence over Christian art, and which emphatically denied the divinity of the God of the Old Testament, tended in the same direction ; but it is very unlikely that these reasons can have had any weight between the sixth and the twelfth centuries. For the more those centuries are studied, the more evident it becomes that the universal and irresistible tendency was then to materialise every spiritual conception, to form a palpable image of everything that was reverenced, to reduce all subjects within the domain of the senses. This tendency, unchecked by any sense of grotesqueness or irreverence, was shown with equal force in sculpture, painting, and legends ; and all the old landmarks and distinctions that had been made between the orthodox uses of pictures and idolatry had been virtually swept away by the resistless desire to form an image of everything that was worshipped, and to attach to that image something of the sanctity of its object. Yet amid all this no one

thought of representing the Supreme Being. In that condition of society men desired a human god, and they consequently concentrated their attention exclusively upon the Second Person of the Trinity or upon the Saints, and suffered the great conception of the Father to become practically obsolete. It continued of course in creeds and in theological treatises, but it was a void and sterile abstraction, which had no place among the realisations and no influence on the emotions of mankind. If men turned away from the Second Person of the Trinity, it was only to bestow their devotions upon saints or martyrs. With the exception, I believe, of one or two representations of the Trinity on early sarcophagi and of a single manuscript of the ninth century,[1] there exists no portrait of the Father earlier than the twelfth century ; and it was only in the fourteenth century, when the revival of learning had become marked, that these portraits became common.[2] From that time to the age of Raphael the steady tendency of Art is to give an ever-increasing pre-eminence to the Father. At first His position in painting and sculpture had been a subordinate one, and He was only represented in the least attractive occupations,[3] and commonly, through a desire to represent the co-eternity of the Persons of the Trinity, of the same age as His Son. Gradually, however, after the fourteenth century, we find the Father represented in every painting as older, more venerable, and more prominent, until at last He became the central and commanding figure,[4] exciting the highest degree of reverence, and commonly represented in different countries according

---

[1] Didron, pp. 177-182.

[1] Raoul Rochette, *Discours sur les Types de l'Art chrétien*, p. 71.
[2] Didron, pp. 227-230.
[3] See this fact worked out in detail in Didron.
[4] "On peut donc relativement à Dieu le Père partager le moyen âge en deux périodes. Dans la première, qui est antérieure au XIVe siècle, la figure du Père se confond avec celle du Fils ; c'est le Fils qui est tout-puissant et qui fait son Père à son image et ressemblance. Dans la seconde période, après le XIIIe siècle, jusqu'au XVIe, Jésus-Christ perd sa force d'assimilation iconographique et se laisse vaincre par son Père. C'est au tour du Fils à se revêtir de traits du Père, à vieillir et rider comme lui....Enfin, depuis les premiers siècles du Christianisme jusqu'à nos jours, nous voyons le Père croître en importance. Son portrait, d'abord interdit par les Gnostiques, se montre timidement ensuite et comme déguisé sous la figure de son Fils. Puis il rejette tout accoutrement étranger et prend une figure spéciale ; puis par Raphaël et enfin par l'Anglais Martin, il gagne une grave et une admirable physionomie qui n'appartient qu'à lui." (*Didron*, p. 226.)

to their ideal of greatness. In Italy, Spain, and the ultramontane monasteries of France, He was usually represented as a Pope ; in Germany, as an Emperor ; in England, and, for the most part, in France, as a King.

In a condition of thought in which the Deity was only realised in the form of man it was extremely natural that the number of divinities should be multiplied. The chasm between the two natures was entirely unfelt, and something of the Divine character was naturally reflected upon those who were most eminent in the Church. The most remarkable instance of this polytheistic tendency was displayed in the deification of the Virgin.

A conception of a divine person or manifestation of the female sex had been one of the notions of the old Jewish Cabalists ; and in the first century Simon Magus had led about with him a woman named Helena, who, according to the Catholics, was simply his mistress, but whom he proclaimed to be the incarnation of the Divine Thought.[1] This notion, under a great many different forms, was diffused through almost all the sects of the Gnostics. The Supreme Being, whom they very jealously distinguished from and usually opposed to the God of the Jews,[2] they termed the "Unknown Father," and they regarded Him as directly inaccessible to human knowledge, but as revealed in part by certain Œons or emanations, of whom the two

principal were Christ, and a female spirit termed the Divine Sophia or Ennoia, and sometimes known by the strange name of "Prounice."[1] According to some sects, this Sophia was simply the human soul, which was originally an emanation or child of the Deity, but which had wandered from its parent-source, had become enamoured of and at last imprisoned by matter, and was now struggling, by the assistance of the unfallen Œon Christ, towards its pristine purity. More commonly, however, she was deemed a personification of a Divine attribute, an individual Œon, the sister or (according to others) the mother of Christ, and entitled to equal or almost equal reverence.

In this way, long before Catholic Mariolatry had acquired its full proportions, a very large section of the Christian world had been accustomed to concentrate much attention upon a female ideal as one of the two central figures of devotion. This fact alone would in some degree prepare the way for the subsequent elevation of the Virgin ; and it should be added that Gnosticism exercised a very great and special influence over the modes of thought of the orthodox. As its most learned historian has forcibly contended, it should not be regarded as a Christian heresy, but rather as an independent system of eclectic philosophy in which Christian ideas occupied a prominent place. Nearly all heresies have aroused among the orthodox a spirit of repulsion which has produced views the extreme opposite of those of the heretic. Gnosticism, on the other hand, exercised an absorbing and attractive influence of the strongest kind. That Neo-Platonic philosophy which so deeply tinctured early theology passed, for the most part, through a Gnostic

[1] See on this subject Franck, *Sur la Kabbale*; Maury, *Croyances et Légendes de l'Antiquité* (1863), p. 338; and especially Beausobre, *Hist. du Manichéisme* (1734), tom. i. pp. 35-37. Justin Martyr, Tertullian, Irenæus, Epiphanius, and several other Fathers, notice the worship of Helena. According to them, Simon proclaimed that the angels in heaven made war on account of her beauty, and that the Evil One had made her prisoner to prevent her return to heaven, from which she had strayed. There is some reason to think that all this was an allegory of the soul.

[2] Most of the Gnostics regarded the God of the Jews or the Demiurge as an imperfect spirit presiding over an imperfect moral system. Many, however, regarded the Jewish religion as the work of the principle of Evil—the God of matter; and the Cainites made everyone who had opposed it the object of reverence, while the Ophites actually worshipped the serpent. We have, perhaps, a partial explanation of the reverence many of the Gnostics had for the serpent in the fact that this animal, which in Christianity represents the principle of Evil, had a very different position in ancient symbolism. It was the general emblem of healing (because it changes its skin), and as such appears in the statues of Æsculapius and Isis, and it was also constantly adopted as a representative animal. Thus in the Mithraic groups, that are so common in later Roman sculpture, the serpent and the dog represent all living creatures. A serpent with a hawk's head was an old Egyptian symbol of a good genius.

[1] Prounice properly signifies lasciviousness. It seems to have been applied to the Sophia considered in her fallen condition, as imprisoned in matter; but there is an extreme obscurity, which has, I think, never been cleared up, hanging upon the subject. Prounice seems to have been confounded with Beronice, the name which a very early Christian tradition gave to the woman who had been healed of an issue of blood. This woman formed one of the principal types among the Gnostics. According to the Valentinians, the twelve years of her affliction represented the twelve Œons, while the flowing blood was the force of the Sophia passing to the inferior world. See on this subject Maury, *Croyances et Légendes*, art. *Veronica*; and on the Sophia generally, Matter, *Hist. du Gnosticisme*, tom. i. pp. 275-278. M. Franck says (*La Kabbale*, p. 43) that some of the Gnostics painted the Holy Ghost as a woman; but this, I suppose, only refers to the Sophia.

medium. No sect, too, appears to have estimated more highly or employed more skilfully æsthetic aids. The sweet songs of Bardesanes and Harmonius carried their distinctive doctrines into the very heart of Syrian orthodoxy, and cast such a spell over the minds of the people that, in spite of all prohibitions, they continued to be sung in the Syrian churches till the Catholic poet St. Ephrem wedded orthodox verses to the Gnostic metres.[1] The apocryphal gospels, which were for the most part of Gnostic origin, long continued to furnish subjects for painters in orthodox churches.[2] There is even much reason to believe that the conventional cast of features ascribed to Christ, which for so many centuries formed the real object of the worship of Christendom, is derived from the Gnostic artists.[3] Besides this, Gnosticism formed the highest representation of a process of transformation or unification of religious ideas which occupied a very prominent place among the organising influences of the Church. Christianity had become the central intellectual power in the world, but it triumphed not so much

by superseding rival faiths as by absorbing and transforming them. Old systems, old rites, old images were grafted into the new belief, retaining much of their ancient character, but assuming new names and a new complexion. Thus in the symbolism of the Gnostics innumerable conceptions culled from the different beliefs of paganism were clustered around the Divine Sophia, and at least some of them passed through paintings or traditional allegories to the Virgin. The old Egyptian conception of Night the mother of day and of all things, with the diadem of stars, Isis the sister of Osiris or the Saviour, Latona the mother of Apollo, Flora the bright goddess of returning spring, to whom was once dedicated the month of May, which is now dedicated to the Virgin ; Cybele the mother of the gods, whose feast was celebrated on what is now Lady-Day, were all more or less connected with the new ideal.[1]

But while Gnosticism may be regarded as the pioneer or precursor of Catholic Mariolatry, the direct causes are to be found within the circle of the Church. If the first two or three centuries were essentially the ages of moral appreciation, the fourth and fifth were essentially those of dogmatic definitions, which were especially applied to the nature of the divinity of Christ, and which naturally and indeed necessarily tended to the continued exaltation of one who was regarded as, very literally, the Bride of God. During the Nestorian controversy the discussions on the subject assumed an almost physiological character,[2] and the emphasis with which the Church condemned the doctrines of Nestorius, who was supposed to have unduly depreciated the dignity of

---

[1] Matter, *Hist. du Gnosticisme*, tom. i. pp. 360–362.

[2] Didron, pp. 197, 198. The apocryphal gospel, however, which exercised most influence over Art was probably that of Nicodemus, which is apparently of orthodox origin, and was probably written (or at least the second part of it) against the Apollinarians. We owe to it the pictures of the Descent into Limbo that are so common in early Byzantine art. The same subject, derived from the same source, was also prominent in the mediæval sacred plays (Malone, *History of the English Stage*, p. 19).

[3] For a full discussion of this point, see Raoul Rochette's *Types de l' Art*, pp. 9–26, and his *Tableau des Catacombes*, p. 265. The opinion that the type of Christ is derived from the Gnostics (which Raoul Rochette says has been embraced by most of the Roman antiquarian) rests chiefly on the following positions :—1. That in the earliest stage of Christianity all painting and sculpture were looked upon with great aversion in the Church, and that as late as the time of Constantine portraits of Christ were very rare. 2. That the Gnostics from the beginning cultivated art, and that small images of Christ were among the most common objects of their reverence. 3. That the Gnostics were very numerous at Rome. 4. That Gnosticism exercised a great influence upon the Church, and especially upon her æsthetic development. It may be added that the Christians carefully abstained from deriving from paganism the cast of features they ascribed to Christ; and Theodoret relates that, a painter having taken Jupiter as a model in a portrait of Christ, his hand was withered, but was restored miraculously by St. Gennadius, Archbishop of Constantinople. At a later period pagan statues were frequently turned into saints. St. Augustine mentions that in his time there was no authentic portrait of Christ, and that the type of features was still undetermined, so that we have absolutely no knowledge of His appearance. "Qua fuerit ille (Christus) facie nos penitus ignoramus.... Nam et ipsius Dominicæ facies carnis innumerabilium cogitationum diversitate variatur et fingitur, quæ tamen una erat, quæcumque erat." (*De Trinitate*, lib. viii. c. 4, 5.) The type, however, was soon after formed,

---

[1] On the relation of this to Gnosticism, see Matter, *Hist. du Gnosticisme*, tom. i. pp. 88, 89–98.

[2] The strong desire natural to the middle ages to give a palpable form to the mystery of the Incarnation was shown curiously in the notion of a conception by the ear. In a hymn, ascribed to St. Thomas à Becket, occur the lines—

" Gaude Virgo, mater Christi,
Quæ per aurem concepisti,
Gabriele nuntio ;"

and in an old glass window, now, I believe, in one of the museums of Paris, the Holy Ghost is represented hovering over the Virgin in the form of a dove, while a ray of light passes from his beak to her ear, along which ray an infant Christ is descending.—Langlois, *Peinture sur Verre*, p. 147. In the breviary of the Maronites is the formulary " Verbum patris per aurem benedictæ intravit." St. Agobard says, " Descendit e cœlis missus ab arce Patris, introivit per aurem Virginis in regionem nostram." Similar expressions had been employed in the Early Church by St. Augustine and St. Ephrem. This of course was suggested by the title Logos. (Maury, *Légendes pieuses*, pp. 179, 180.)

Mary, impelled the orthodox enthusiasm in the opposite direction. The Council of Ephesus, in A.D. 431, defined the manner in which the Virgin should be represented by artists;[1] and the ever-increasing importance of painting and sculpture as the organs of religious realisations brought into clearer and more vivid relief the charms of a female ideal, which acquired an irresistible fascination in the monastic life of celibacy and solitary meditation, and in the strange mixture of gallantry and devotion that accompanied the Crusades. It was in this last period that the doctrine of the Immaculate Conception rose to prominence.[2] The lily, as the symbol of purity, was soon associated with pictures of the Virgin; and a notion having grown up that women by eating it became pregnant without the touch of man, a vase wreathed with lilies became the emblem of her maternity.

The world is governed by its ideals, and seldom or never has there been one which has exercised a more profound and, on the whole, a more salutary influence than the mediæval conception of the Virgin. For the first time woman was elevated to her rightful position, and the sanctity of weakness was recognised as well as the sanctity of sorrow. No longer the slave or toy of man, no longer associated only with the ideas of degradation and of sensuality, woman rose, in the person of the Virgin Mother, into a new sphere, and became the object of a reverential homage of which antiquity had had no conception. Love was idealised. The

moral charm and beauty of female excellence were fully felt. A new type of character was called into being : a new kind of admiration was fostered. Into a harsh and ignorant and benighted age this ideal type infused a conception of gentleness and of purity unknown to the proudest civilisations of the past. In the pages of living tenderness which many a monkish writer has left in honour of his celestial patron, in the millions who, in many lands and in many ages, have sought with no barren desire to mould their characters into her image, in those holy maidens who, for the love of Mary, have separated themselves from all the glories and pleasures of the world, to seek in fastings and vigils and humble charity to render themselves worthy of her benediction, in the new sense of honour, in the chivalrous respect, in the softening of manners, in the refinement of tastes displayed in all the walks of society : in these and in many other ways we detect its influence. All that was best in Europe clustered around it, and it is the origin of many of the purest elements of our civilisation.

But the price, and perhaps the necessary price, of this was the exaltation of the Virgin as an omnipresent deity of infinite power as well as infinite condescension. The legends represented her as performing every kind of prodigy, saving men from the lowest abysses of wretchedness or of vice, and proving at all times the most powerful and the most ready refuge of the afflicted. The painters depicted her invested with the divine aureole, judging man on equal terms with her Son, or even retaining her ascendency over Him in heaven. In the devotions of the people she was addressed in terms identical with those employed to the Almighty.[1] A reverence similar

---

[1] St. Augustine notices (*De Trinitate*) that in his time there was no authentic portrait of Mary. The Council of Ephesus wished her to be painted with the Infant Child, and this was the general representation in the Early Church. Some of the Byzantine pictures are said to have been influenced by the favourite Egyptian representations of Isis giving suck to Horus. It has been observed that in the case of Mary, as in the case of Christ, suffering and deep melancholy became more and more the prevailing expression as the dark ages rolled on, which was still further increased by the black tint the mediæval artists frequently gave her, in allusion to the description in the Song of Solomon. The first notice in writing of the resemblance of Christ to His mother is, I believe, in Nicephorus.—See Raoul Rochette, *Types de l'Art chrétien*, pp. 30-39; Pascal, *Institutions de l'Art chrétien*.

[2] Heeren, *Influences des Croisades*, pp. 204, 205. However, St. Augustine says—"Excepta itaque Sancta Virgine Maria, de qua, propter honorem Domini, nullam prorsus cum de peccatis agitur habere volo quæstionem : Unde enim scimus, quid ei plus gratiæ collatum fuerit ad vincendum omni ex parte peccatum, quæ concipere ac parere meruit eum quem constat nullum habuisse peccatum." (*De Naturâ et Gratiâ*.) Gibbon notices that the notion acquired consistency among the Mohammedans some centuries before it was adopted by the Christians. St. Bernard rejected it as a novelty. (*Decline and Fall*, ch. l. note.)

[1] Even at the present day the Psalter of St. Bonaventura—an edition of the Psalms adapted to the worship of the Virgin, chiefly by the substitution of the word *domina* for the word *dominus*—is a popular book of devotion at Rome. In a famous fresco of Orcagna, at Pisa, the Virgin is represented, with precisely the same dignity as Christ, judging mankind; and everyone who is acquainted with mediæval art has met with similar examples. An old bishop named Gilbert Massius had his own portrait painted between the Virgin giving suck to Christ and a Crucifixion. Underneath were the lines—

"Hinc lactor ab ubere,
Hinc pascor a vulnere,
Positus in medio.
Quo me vertam nescio,
In hoc dulci dubio
Dulcis est collatio.'

(Pascal, *Art chrétien*, tom. i. p. 250.)

in kind, but less in degree, was soon bestowed upon the other saints, who speedily assumed the position of the minor deities of paganism, and who, though worshipped, like them, as if ubiquitous, like them had their special spheres of patronage.

While Christendom was thus reviving the polytheism which its intellectual condition required, the tendency to idolatry that always accompanies that condition was no less forcibly displayed. In theory, indeed, images were employed exclusively as aids to worship ; but in practice, and with the general assent of the highest ecclesiastical authorities, they very soon became the objects. When men employ visible representations simply for the purpose of giving an increased vividness to their sense of the presence of the person who is addressed, and when the only distinction they make between different representations arises from the degree of fidelity or force with which they assist the imagination, these persons are certainly not committing idolatry. But when they proceed to attach the idea of intrinsic virtue to a particular image, when one image is said to work miracles and confer spiritual benefits that separate it from every other, when it becomes the object of long pilgrimages, and is supposed by its mere presence to defend a besieged city or to ward off pestilence and famine, the difference between this conception and idolatry is inappreciable. Everything is done to cast the devotion of the worshipper upon the image itself, to distinguish it from every other, and to attribute to it an intrinsic efficacy.

In this as in the former case the change was effected by a general tendency resulting from the intellectual condition of society, assisted by the concurrence of special circumstances. At a very early period the persecuted Christians were accustomed to collect the relics of the martyrs, which they regarded with much affection and not a little reverence, partly perhaps from the popular notion that the souls of the dead lingered fondly around their tombs, and partly from the very natural and praiseworthy feeling which attaches us to the remains of the good.[1]

A similar reverence was speedily transferred to pictures, which as memorials of the dead were closely connected with relics ; and the tendency to the miraculous that was then so powerful having soon associated some of them with supernatural occurrences, this was regarded as a Divine attestation of their sanctity. Two of these representations were especially prominent in the early controversies. The first was a portrait which, according to tradition, Christ had sent to Abgarus, king of Edessa,[1] and which, besides several other miracles, had once destroyed all the besieging engines of a Persian army that had invested Edessa. Still more famous was a statue of Christ, said to have been erected in a small town in Phœnicia by the woman who had been healed of an issue of blood. A new kind of herb had grown up beneath it, increased till it touched the hem of the garment of the statue, and then acquired the power of healing all disease. This statue, it was added, had been broken in pieces by Julian, who placed his own image on the pedestal, from which it was speedily hurled by a thunderbolt.[2]

In the midst of this bias the irruption and, soon after, the conversion of the barbarians were effected. Vast tribes of savages who had always been idolaters, who were perfectly incapable, from their low state of civilisation, of forming any but anthropomorphic conceptions of the Deity, or of concentrating their attention steadily on any invisible object, and who for the most part were converted, not by individual persuasion, but by the commands of their chiefs, embraced Christianity in such multitudes that their habits

[1] Thus the Council of Illiberis in its 34th canon forbade men to light candles by day in the cemeteries, for fear "of disquieting the souls of the saints." See, too, a curious passage of Vigilantius cited by St. Jerome, *Contr. Vigilant.* 8. To be buried near the tomb of a martyr was one of the most coveted privileges. See Le Blant, *Inscrip. chrétiennes de Gaule*, tom. ii. pp. 219-229.

[1] With a letter, which was accepted without hesitation by Eusebius, and which Addison, in his work on Christian Evidences, quoted as genuine. Of course, it is now generally admitted to be apocryphal. This portrait was supposed to be miraculously impressed (like that obtained by St. Veronica) on a handkerchief. It was for a long time at Constantinople, but was brought to Rome probably about A.D. 1198, and deposited in the Church of St. Sylvester in Capite, where it now is. See Marangoni, *Istoria della Cappella di Sancta Sanctorum di Roma* (Romæ, 1747), pp. 235-239 ; a book which, though ostensibly simply a history of the Acheropita, or sacred image at the Lateran, contains a fuller account of the history of the early miraculous pictures of Christ than any other I have met with.
[2] On these representations, the miracles they wrought, and the great importance they assumed in the Iconoclastic controversies, see Maimbourg, *Histoire des Iconoclastes* (1686), pp. 44-47 ; and on other early miracles attributed to images, Spanheim, *Historia Imaginum* (1686), pp. 417-420. The first of these books is Catholic, and the second the Protestant reply. See, too, Marangoni, *Sancta Sanctorum* ; and Arringhi, *Roma Subterranea*, tom. ii. pp. 452-460.

of mind soon became the dominating habits of the Church. From this time the tendency to idolatry was irresistible. The old images were worshipped under new names, and one of the most prominent aspects of the Apostolical teaching was in practice ignored.

All this, however, did not pass without protest. During the period of the persecution, when the dread of idolatry was still powerful, everything that tended in that direction was scrupulously avoided; and a few years before the First Council of Nice, a council held at Illiberis, in Spain, in a canon which has been very frequently cited, condemned altogether the introduction of pictures into the churches, "lest that which is worshipped should be painted upon the walls."[1] The Greeks, among whom the last faint rays of civilisation still flickered, were in this respect somewhat superior to the Latins, for they usually discouraged the veneration of images, though admitting that of pictures.[2] Early in the eighth century, when image-worship had become general, the sect of the Iconoclasts arose, whose long struggle against the prevailing evil, though stained with great tyranny and great cruelty, represents the fierce though unavailing attempts to resist the anthropomorphism of the age; and when the Second Council of Nice, which the Catholics now regard as œcumenical, censured this heresy and carried the veneration of images considerably further than had before been authorised, its authority was denied and its decrees contemptuously stigmatised by Charlemagne and the Gallican Church.[3] Two or three illustrious Frenchmen also made isolated efforts in the same direction.[4]

Of these efforts there is one upon which I may delay for a moment, because it is at once extremely remarkable and extremely little known, and also because it brings us in contact with one of the most rationalistic intellects of the middle ages. In describing the persecution that was endured by the Cabalists in the ninth century, I had occasion to observe that they found a distinguished defender in the person of an archbishop of Lyons, named St. Agobard. The very name of this prelate has now sunk into general oblivion,[1] or if it is at all remembered, it is only in connection with the most discreditable act of his life—the part which he took in the deposition of Lewis the Mild. Yet I question whether in the whole compass of the middle ages—with, perhaps, the single exception of Scotus Erigena—it would be possible to find another man within the Christian Church who applied himself so zealously, so constantly, and so ably to dispelling the superstitions that surrounded him. To those who have appreciated the character of the ninth century, but few words will be required to show the intellectual eminence of an ecclesiastic who, in that century, devoted one work to displaying the folly of those who attributed hail and thunder to spiritual agencies, a second to in at least some degree attenuating the popular notions concerning epilepsy and other strange diseases, a third to exposing the absurdities of ordeals, and a fourth to denouncing the idolatry of image-worship.

At the beginning of this last work Agobard collected a long series of passages from the Fathers and early Councils on the legitimate use of images. As long as they were employed simply as memorials, they were unobjectionable. But the popular devotion had long since transgressed this limit. Idolatry and anthropomorphism had everywhere revived, and devotion being concentrated on visible representations, all faith in the invisible was declining. Men, with a sacrilegious folly, ventured to apply the epithet holy to certain images,[2] offering to the work of their own hands the honour which should be reserved for the Deity, and attributing sanctity to what was destitute even of life. Nor was it any justification of this practice that the worshippers sometimes

---

[1] "Ne quod colitur et adoratur in parietibus depingatur." The Catholics maintain that this was a decree elicited by the persecution, and that its object was to prevent the profanation of Christian images by the pagans.

[2] Probably because there is no reason to believe that pictures had ever been employed as idols by the ancient Greeks or Romans.

[3] On the discussions connected with this Council, see Natalis Alexander, *Historia Eccl. Sæculi*, viii.

[4] The most celebrated being Hinckmar, Archbishop of Rheims. Baronius inveighed violently against this prelate for terming the sacred images "dolls"; but Maimbourg contends (Introduction to the *Hist. des Iconocl.*) that the expression is not to be found in any of the works of Hinckmar.

---

[1] There is an edition of his works in one volume (Paris, 1605), and another in two volumes (Paris, 1616). I have quoted from the former.

[2] "Multo autem his deteriora esse quæ humana et carnalis præsumptio fingit, etiam stulti consentiunt. In quo genere istæ quoque inveniuntur quas sanctas appellant imagines, non solum sacrilegi ex eo quod divinum cultum operibus manuum suarum exhibent, sed et insipientes sanctitatem eis quæ sine anima sunt imaginibus tribuendo."—p. 233.

disclaimed the belief that a divine sanctity resided in the image itself,[1] and asserted that they reverenced in it only the person who was represented ; for if the image was not divine, it should not be venerated. This excuse was only one of the devices of Satan,[2] who was ever seeking, under the pretext of honour to the saints, to draw men back to the idols they had left. No image could be entitled to the reverence of those who, as the temples of the Holy Ghost, were superior to every image, who were themselves the true images of the Deity. A picture is helpless and inanimate. It can confer no benefit and inflict no evil. Its only value is as a representation of that which is least in man—of his body and not his mind. Its only use is as a memorial to keep alive the affection for the dead ; if it is regarded as anything more, it becomes an idol, and as such should be destroyed. Very rightly then did Hezekiah grind to powder the brazen serpent in spite of its sacred associations, because it had become an object of worship. Very rightly too did the Council of Illiberis and the Christians of Alexandria[3] forbid the introduction of representations into the churches, for they foresaw that such representations would at last become the objects of worship, and that a change of faith would only be a change of idols ; nor could the saints themselves be more duly honoured than by destroying ignominiously their portraits when those portraits had become the objects of superstitious reverence.[4]

It will, I think, be admitted that these sentiments are exceedingly remarkable when we consider the age in which they were expressed, and the position of the person who expressed them. No Protestant fresh from the shrines of Loretto or Saragossa ever denounced the idolatry practised under the shadow of Catholicism with a keener or more incisive eloquence than did this mediæval saint. But although it is extremely interesting to detect the isolated efforts of illustrious individuals to rise above the general conditions of their age, such efforts have usually but little result. Idolatry was so intimately connected with the modes of thought of the middle ages, it was so congruous with the prevailing conception of the government of the universe, and with the materialising habits that were displayed upon all subjects, that no process of direct reasoning could overthrow it, and it was only by a fundamental change in the intellectual condition of society that it was at last subverted.

It must, however, be acknowledged that there is one example of a great religion, reigning for the most part over men who had not yet emerged from the twilight of an early civilisation, which has nevertheless succeeded in restraining its votaries from idolatry. This phenomenon, which is the pre-eminent glory of Mahometanism, and the most remarkable evidence of the genius of its founder, appears so much at variance with the general laws of historic development, that it may be well to examine for a moment its causes. In the first place, then, it must be observed that the enthusiasm by which Mahometanism conquered the world was mainly a military enthusiasm. Men were drawn to it at once, and without conditions, by the splendour of the achievements of its disciples, and it declared an absolute war against all the religions it encountered. Its history therefore exhibits nothing of the process of gradual absorption, persuasion, compromise, and assimilation, that was exhibited in the dealings of Christianity with the barbarians. In the next place, one

---

[1] "Dicit forsitan aliquis non se putare imagini quam adorat aliquid inesse Divinum, sed tantummodo pro honore ejus cujus effigies est, tali eam veneratione donare. Cui facile respondetur, quia si imago quam adorat Deus non est nequaquam veneranda est."—p. 237.

[2] "Agit hoc nimirum versutus et callidus humani generis inimicus, ut, sub prætextu honoris sanctorum, rursus idola introducat, rursus per diversas effigies adoretur."—p. 252.

[3] Speaking of the conduct of some Alexandrian Christians, who only admitted the sign of the cross into their churches, he says:—" O quam sincera religio ! crucis vexillum ubique pingebatur non aliqua vultus humani similitudo. (Deo scilicet hæc mirabiliter etiam ipsis forsitan nescientibus disponente) si enim sanctorum imagines hi qui dæmonum cultum reliquerant venerari juberentur, puto quod videretur eis non tam idola reliquisse quam simulachra mutasse."—p. 237.

[4] "Quia si serpentem æneum quem Deus fieri præcepit, quoniam errans populus tanquam idolum colere cœpit, Ezechias religiosus rex, cum magna pietatis laude contrivit : multo religiosius sanctorum imagines (ipsis quoque sanctis faventibus, qui ob sui honorem cum divinæ religionis contemptu eas adorari more idolorum indignantissime ferunt) omni genere conterendæ et usque ad pulverem sunt eradendæ ; præsertim cum non illas fieri Deus jusserit, sed humanus sensus excogitaverit."—p. 243. "Nec iterum ad sua latibula fraudulenta recurrat astutia, ut dicat se non imagines sanctorum adorare sed sanctos ; clamat enim Deus, 'Gloriam meam alteri non dabo, nec laudem meam sculptilibus.'"—pp. 254, 255. See too the noble concluding passage on the exclusive worship of Christ, breathing a spirit of the purest Protestantism.

of the great characteristics of the Koran is the extreme care and skill with which it labours to assist men in realising the unseen. Descriptions the most minutely detailed, and at the same time the most vivid, are mingled with powerful appeals to those sensual passions by which the imagination in all countries, but especially in those in which Mahometanism has taken root, is most forcibly influenced. In no other religion that prohibits idols is the strain upon the imagination so slight.[1]

In the last place, the prohibition of idols was extended to every representation of men and animals, no matter how completely unconnected they might be with religion.[2] Mahomet perceived very clearly that in order to prevent his disciples from worshipping images, it was absolutely necessary to prevent them from making any ; and he did this by commands which were at once so stringent and so precise, that it was scarcely possible to evade them. In this way he preserved his religion from idolatry ; but he made it the deadly enemy of art. How much art has lost by the antagonism it is impossible to say. Certainly the wonderful proficiency attained by the Spanish Moors in architecture, which was the only form of art that was open to them, and, above all, the ornamentation of the Alhambra, and the Alcazar of Seville, in which, while the representations of animal life are carefully excluded, plants and flowers and texts from the Koran and geometrical figures are woven together in a tracery of the most exquisite beauty,[3] seem to

imply the possession of æsthetic powers that have seldom been surpassed.

Mahometanism sacrificed art, but it cannot be said that Christianity during the middle ages was altogether favourable to it. The very period when representations of Christ, or the saints, were regarded as most sacred, was precisely that in which there was no art in the highest sense of the word, or at least none applied to the direct objects of worship. The middle ages occasionally, indeed, produced churches of great beauty ; mosaic work for their adornment was cultivated with considerable zeal in the fifth century, and again, after the establishment in the eleventh century of a school of Greek artists at Monte Cassino, with considerable success ;[1] similar skill was shown in gold church ornaments,[2] and in the illumination of manuscripts ;[3] but the habitual

from the vegetable world in the Alhambra is unrivalled in beauty, the lions which support one of the fountains, and which form, I believe, the solitary instance of a deviation from the command of the Prophet, might rank with the worst productions of the time of Nicolas of Pisa.

[1] According to tradition, the earliest specimen of Christian mosaic work is a portrait of Christ, preserved in the Church of St. Praxede of Rome, which St. Peter is said to have worn round his neck, and to have given at Rome to Pudens, his host, the father of St. Praxede. The finest specimens of the mosaics of the fifth and sixth centuries are at Ravenna, especially in the church of St. Vitale, which was built by the Greeks, who were the great masters of this art. Ciampini, who is the chief authority on this subject, thinks (*Vetera Monumenta*, pars i., Romæ, 1690, p. 84) that the art was wholly forgotten in Rome for the three hundred years preceding the establishment of the Monte Cassino school in 1066 ; but Marangoni assigns a few wretched mosaics to that period (*Ist. Sanct.* pp. 180–182). A descriptive catalogue of those at Rome has lately been published by Barbet de Jouy, and a singularly interesting examination of their history by M. Vitet (*Études sur l'Histoire de l'Art*, tom. i.). For a general view of the decline of art, see the great history of D'Agincourt.

[2] The art of delicate carving on gold and silver was chiefly preserved in the middle ages by the reverence for relics, for which the most beautiful works were designed. Rouen was long famed for its manufacture of church ornaments, but these were plundered, and for the most part destroyed, by the Protestants, when they captured the city in 1562. The luxurious habits of the Italian states were favourable to the goldsmiths, and those of Venice were very celebrated. A large proportion of them are said to have been Jews. Francia, Verrocchio, Perugino, Donatello, Brunelleschi, and Ghiberti were all originally goldsmiths. M. Didron has published a manual of this art. The goldsmiths of Limoges had the honour of producing a saint, St. Eloi, who became the patron of the art. Carved ivory diptychs were also very common through the middle ages, and especially after the eighth century.

[3] Much curious information on the history of illumination and miniature painting is given in Cibrario, *Economia Politica del Medio Evo*, vol. ii. pp. 337–346. Peignot says that from the fifth to the tenth century the miniatures in manuscripts exhibited an extremely high perfection, both in drawing and in colouring, and that from the tenth to the fourteenth the drawing

---

[1] It is quite true, as Sale contends, that Mahomet did not introduce polygamy, and therefore that the fact of his permitting it could not have been one of the motives urging Asiatics to embrace the new religion ; but it is also true that Mahomet and his disciples, more skilfully than any other religionists, blended sensual passions with religion, associated them with future rewards, and converted them into stimulants of devotion.

[2] Some of the early Christians appear to have wished to adopt this course, which would have been the only effectual means of repressing idolatry. In an apocryphal work, called *The Voyages of St. John*, which was circulated in the Church, there was a legend that St. John once found his own portrait in the house of a Christian, that he thought at first it was an idol, and, even when told its true character, severely blamed the painter. (Beausobre, *Hist. du Manichéisme*.) A passage in the invective of Tertullian against Hermogenes has been quoted as to the same effect : "Pingit illicite, nubit assidue, legem Dei in libidinem defendit, in artem contemnit, bis falsarius et cauterio et Stylo." Clemens Alexandrinus was of opinion that ladies broke the second commandment by using looking-glasses, as they thereby made images of themselves.—Barbeyrac, *Morale des Pères*, c. v. § 18.

[3] See on this subject a striking passage from Owen Jones, quoted in Ford's *Spain*, vol. i. p. 304. It is remarkable that, while the ornamentation derived

veneration of images, pictures, and talismans was far from giving a general impulse to art. And this fact, which may at first sight appear perplexing, was in truth perfectly natural. For the æsthetic sentiment and a devotional feeling are so entirely different, that it is impossible for both to be at the same moment predominating over the mind, and very unusual for both to be concentrated upon the same object. The sensation produced by a picture gallery is not that of religious reverence, and the favourite idols have in no religion been those which approve themselves most fully to the taste.[1] They have rather been pictures that are venerable from their extreme antiquity, or from the legends attached to them, or else representations of the most coarsely realistic character. Painted wooden statues the size of life have usually been the favourite idols, but these are so opposed to the genius of true art that—with the exception of Spain, where religious feeling has dominated over every other consideration, and where three sculptors of very great ability, named Juni, Hernandez, and Montañes, have devoted themselves to their formation—they have scarcely ever exhibited any high artistic merit, and never the very highest. The mere fact, therefore, of pictures or images being destined for worship, is likely to be rather prejudicial than otherwise to art. Besides this, in an idolatrous period the popular reverence speedily attaches to a particular type of countenance, and even to particular gestures or dresses ; and all innovation, and therefore all improvement, is resisted.

These reasons apply to the art of the middle ages in common with that of all other periods of virtual or avowed idolatry. There was, however, another consideration, acting in the same direction, which was peculiar to Christianity. I mean the low estimate of physical beauty that characterised the monastic type of religion. Among the Greeks, beauty of every order[1] was the highest object of worship. In art especially no subject was tolerated in which deformity of any kind was manifested. Even suffering was habitually idealised. The traces of mental anguish upon the countenance were exhibited with exquisite skill, but they were never permitted so to contort the features as to disturb the prevailing beauty of the whole.[2] The glory of the human body was the central conception of art, and nakedness was associated rather with dignity than with shame. God, it was emphatically said, was naked.[3] To represent an emperor naked, was deemed the highest form of flattery, because it was to represent his apotheosis. The athletic games which occupied so large a place in ancient life, contributed greatly to foster the admiration of physical strength, and to furnish the most admirable models to the sculptors.[4]

It is easy to perceive how favourable such a state of feeling must have been to the development of art, and no less easy to see how contrary it was to the spirit of a religion which for many centuries made the suppression of all bodily passions the central notion of sanctity. In this respect philosophers, heretics, and saints were unanimous. Plotinus, one of the most

---

deteriorated, but revived with the revival of painting (*Essai sur l'Histoire du Parchemin*, p. 76). Glass painting and miniature painting were both common long before Cimabue, and probably exercised a great influence over the early artists.

[1] See on this subject, and generally on the influence of mediæval modes of thought upon art, Raoul Rochette, *Cours d'Archéologie*, one of the very best books ever written on art. (It has been translated by Mr. Westropp.) The history of miracles strikingly confirms the position in the text. As Marangoni says: "Anzi ella è cosa degna di osservazione che l' Altissimo per ordinario opera molto più prodigi nelle Immagini sagre nelle quali non spicca l' eccellenza dell' arte o alcuna cosa superiore all' umana."—*Istoria della Cappella di Sancta Sanctorum*, p. 77.

[1] Even animal beauty. It is one of the most subtle, and, at the same time, most profoundly just, criticisms of Winckelmann, that it was the custom of the Greeks to enhance the perfection of their ideal faces by transfusing into them some of the higher forms of animal beauty. This was especially the case with Jupiter, the upper part of whose countenance is manifestly taken from that of a lion, while the hair is almost always so arranged as to increase the resemblance. There are many busts of Jupiter, which, if all but the forehead and hair were covered, would be unhesitatingly pronounced to be images of lions. Something of the bull appears in like manner in Hercules ; while in Pan (though not so much with a view to beauty as to harmony) the human features always approach as near as human features can to the characteristics of the brute. As M. Raoul Rochette has well observed, this is one of the great distinctive marks of Greek sculpture. The Egyptians often joined the head of an animal to the body of a man without making any effort to soften the incongruity ; but beauty being the main object of the Greeks, in all their composite statues—Pan, Centaurs, hermaphrodites—the two natures that are conjoined are fused and blended into one harmonious whole.

[2] See the *Laocoon* of Lessing. It is to this that Lessing ascribes the famous device of Timanthes in his Sacrifice of Iphigenia—drawing the veil over the face of Agamemnon—which Pliny so poetically explains.

[3] " Deus nudus est."—Seneca, *Ep.* xxxi.

[4] Raoul Rochette, *Cours d'Archéologie*, pp. 269, 270. See also Fortoul, *Études d'Archéologie.*

eminent of the Neo-Platonic philosophers, was so ashamed of the possession of a body, that he refused to have his portrait taken on the ground that it would be to perpetuate his degradation. Gnosticism and Manicheism, which in their various modifications obtained a deeper and more permanent hold in the Church than any other heretical systems, maintained as their cardinal tenet the essential evil of matter; and some of the Cathari, who were among the latest Gnostics, are said to have even starved themselves to death in their efforts to subdue the propensities of the body.[1] Of the orthodox saints, some made it their especial boast that for many years they had never seen their own bodies, others mutilated themselves in order more completely to restrain their passions, others laboured with the same object by scourgings and fastings, and horrible penances. All regarded the body as an unmingled evil, its passions and its beauty as the most deadly of temptations. Art, while governed by such sentiments, could not possibly arrive at perfection,[2] and the passion for representations of the Crucifixion, or the deaths of the martyrs, or the sufferings of the lost, impelled it still further from the beautiful.

It appears, then, that, in addition to the generally low intellectual condition of the middle ages, the special form of religious feeling that was then dominant, exercised an exceedingly unfavourable influence upon art. This fact becomes very important when we examine the course that was taken by the European mind after the revival of learning.

Idolatry, as I have said, is the natural form of worship in an early stage of civilisation; and a gradual emancipation from material conceptions one of the most invariable results of intellectual progress. It appears therefore natural, that when nations have attained a certain point,

they should discard their images; and this is what has usually occurred. Twice, however, in the history of the human mind, a different course has been adopted. Twice the weakening of the anthropomorphic conceptions has been accompanied by an extraordinary progress in the images that were their representatives, and the æsthetic feeling having dominated over the religious feeling, superstition has faded into art.

The first of these movements occurred in ancient Greece. The information we possess concerning the æsthetic history of that nation is so ample, that we can trace very clearly the successive phases of its development.[1] Putting aside those changes that are interesting only in an artistic point of view, and confining ourselves to those which reflect the changes of religious realisation, Greek idolatry may be divided into four distinct stages. The first was a period of fetishism, in which shapeless stones, which were possibly aërolites, and were, at all events, said to have fallen from heaven, were worshipped. In the second, painted wooden idols dressed in real clothes became common.[2] After this, a higher art which was popularly ascribed to Dædalus arose, but, like the Egyptian and later Byzantine art, it was at first strictly religious, and characterised by an intense aversion to innovation. Then came the period in which increasing intellectual culture, and the prevalence of philosophical speculations, began to tell upon the nation, in which the religious reverence was displaced, and concentrated rather on the philosophical conception of the Deity than upon the idols in the temples, and in which the keen sense of beauty, evoked by a matured civilisation, gave a new tone and aspect to all parts of religion.[3] The images were not then broken, but they were gradually regarded simply as the embodiments of the beautiful. They began to exhibit little or no religious feeling, no spirit of reverence or

---

[1] Matter, *Hist. du Gnosticisme*, tom. iii. p. 264.

[2] The period in which the ascetic ideal of ugliness was most supreme in art was between the sixth and twelfth centuries. Many of the Roman mosaics during that period exhibit a hideousness which the inexpertness of the artists was quite insufficient to account for, and which was evidently imitated from the emaciation of extreme asceticism.—See Vitet, *Études sur l'Histoire de l'Art*, tom. i. pp. 268–279. Concerning the art of the middle ages, besides the works that have come down to us, we have a good deal of evidence in a book by a bishop of the thirteenth century, named Durandus, called *Rationale Divinorum Officiorum*. A great deal of curious learning on mediæval art is collected by the Abbé Pascal in his *Institutions de l'Art chrétien*; but, above all, in the *Iconographie chrétienne* of Didron.

[1] See an extremely clever sketch of the movement in Raoul Rochette, *Cours d'Archéologie*; and Winckelmann, *Hist. of Art*.

[2] According to Winckelmann, wooden statues with marble heads, called ἀκρόλιθοι, continued as late as the time of Phidias. From the painted wooden statues was derived the custom of painting those in marble and bronze. Heyne, who has devoted a very learned essay to Greek sculpture, thinks the statues of Dædalus were in wood (*Opuscula Academica*, tom. v. p. 339); but this appears very doubtful. Pausanias says he saw a statue ascribed to Dædalus which was of stone.

[3] According to Pliny (*Hist. Nat.* xxxiv. 19), the sculptor Myron first departed from the ancient types.

self-abasement, but a sense of harmony and gracefulness, a conception of ideal perfection which has perhaps never been equalled in other lands. The statue that had once been the object of earnest prayer was viewed with the glance of the artist or the critic. The temple was still full of gods, and those gods had never been so beautiful and so grand ; but they were beautiful only through the skill of the artist, and the devotion that once hallowed them had passed away. All was allegory, poetry, and imagination. Sensual beauty was typified by naked Venus ; unconscious loveliness, and untried or natural chastity, by Diana. Minerva, with her downcast eyes and somewhat stern features, represented female modesty and self-control. Ceres, with her flowing robes and her golden sheaf, was the type of the genial summer ; or, occasionally with dishevelled hair, and a countenance still troubled with the thought of Proserpine, was the emblem of maternal love. Each cast of beauty—after a brief period of unmingled grandeur, even each form of sensual frailty—was transported into the unseen world. Bacchus nurtured by a girl, and with the soft delicate limbs of a woman, was the type of a disgraceful effeminacy. Apollo the god of music, and Adonis the lover of Diana, represented that male beauty softened into something of female loveliness by the sense of music or the first chaste love of youth, which the Christian painters long afterwards represented in St. Sebastian or St. John. Hercules was the chosen type of the dignity of labour. Sometimes he appears in the midst of his toils for man, with every nerve strained, and all the signs of intense exertion upon his countenance. Sometimes he appears as a demigod in the Assembly of Olympus, and then his muscles are rounded and subdued, and his colossal frame softened and harmonised as the emblem at once of strength and of repose. In very few instances do we find any conceptions that can be regarded as purely religious, and even those are of a somewhat Epicurean character. Thus Jupiter, Pluto, and Minos are represented with the same cast of countenance, and the difference is chiefly in their expression. The countenance of Pluto is shadowed by the passions of a demon ; the brow of Minos is bent with the inexorable sternness of a judge. Jupiter alone presents an aspect of unclouded calm : no care can darken, and

no passion ruffle, the serenity of the king of heaven.[1]

It was in this manner that the Greek mythology passed gradually into the realm of poetry, and that the transition was effected or facilitated by the visible representations that were in the first instance the objects of worship. A somewhat similar change was effected in Christian art at the period of the revival of learning, and as an almost immediate result of the substitution of Italian for Byzantine art.

There are few more striking contrasts than are comprised in the history of the influence of Grecian intellect upon art. In the early period of her history Greece had arrived at the highest point of æsthetic perfection to which the human intellect has yet attained. She bequeathed to us those forms of almost passionate beauty which have been the wonder and the delight of all succeeding ages, and which the sculptors of every land have recognised as the ideal of their efforts. At last, however, the fountain of genius became dry. Not only creative power, but even the very perception and love of the beautiful, seem to have died out, and for many centuries the Greek Church, the Greek empire, and the Greek artists proved the most formidable obstacles to æsthetic development.[2] It was from this quarter that the Iconoclasts issued forth to wage their fierce warfare against Christian sculpture. It was in the Greek Church that was most fostered the tradition of the deformity of Christ, which was as fatal to religious art as it was offensive to religious feeling.[3] It was in Greece,

---

[1] See Winckelmann and Ottfried Müller.

[2] This influence is well noticed by M. Rio, in a book called *The Poetry of the Christian Art.* An exception, however, should be made in favour of Greek architects, to whom Italy owed its first great ecclesiastical structure, the church of St. Vitale at Ravenna (which Charlemagne copied at Aix-la-Chapelle), and at a later period St. Mark's at Venice, and several other beautiful edifices. The exile of the Greek artists during the Iconoclast persecution, and the commercial relations of Venice, Pisa, and Genoa, account for the constant action of Greece on Italy through the middle ages. I have already noticed the skill of the Byzantine artists in mosaic work.

[3] Of which Justin Martyr, Tertullian, and Cyril of Alexandria, were the principal advocates. The last declared that Christ had been "the ugliest of the sons of men." This theory furnished Celsus with one of his arguments against Christianity. The opposite view was taken by Jerome, Ambrose, Chrysostom, and John Damascene. With a view of supporting the latter opinion, there was forged a singularly beautiful letter, alleged to have been written to the Roman Senate by Lentulus, who was proconsul in Judæa before Herod, and in which the following passage occurs : "At this time there appeared a man, who is still living—a man

too, that arose that essentially vicious, conventional, and unprogressive style of painting which was universal in Europe for many centuries, which trammelled even the powerful genius of Cimabue, and which it was reserved for Giotto and Massacio to overthrow. This was the uniform tendency of modern Greece. It was the extreme opposite of that which had once been dominant, and it is a most remarkable fact that it was at last corrected mainly by the masterpieces of Greek antiquity. It is now very generally admitted that the proximate cause of that ever-increasing course of progress which was pursued by Italian art from Cimabue to Raphael, is chiefly to be found in the renewed study of ancient sculpture begun by Nicolas of Pisa towards the close of the twelfth century, and afterwards sustained by the discoveries at Rome.

The Church of Rome, with the sagacity that has usually characterised her, adopted and fostered the first efforts of revived art, and for a time she made it essentially Christian. It is impossible to look upon the pictures of Giotto and his early successors without perceiving that a religious feeling pervades and sanctifies them. They exhibit, indeed, a keen sense of beauty; but this is always subservient to the religious idea; it is always sub-

dued and chastened and idealised. Nor does this arise simply from the character of the artists. Christian art had, indeed, in the angelic friar of Fiesole, one saint who may be compared with any in the hagiology. That gentle monk, who was never known to utter a word of anger or of bitterness, who refused without a pang the rich mitre of Florence, who had been seen with tears streaming from his eyes as he painted his crucified Lord, and who never began a picture without consecrating it by a prayer,[1] forms one of the most attractive pictures in the whole range of ecclesiastical biography. The limpid purity of his character was reflected in his works, and he transmitted to his disciple Gozzoli something of his spirit, with (I venture to think) the full measure of his genius.

But on this, as on all other occasions, even the higher forms of genius were ultimately regulated by the law of supply and demand. There was a certain religious conception abroad in the world. That conception required a visible representation, and the painter appeared to supply the want. The revival of learning had broken upon Europe. The study of the classics had given an impulse to every department of intellect, but it had not yet so altered the condition of society as to shake the old belief. The profound ignorance that reigned until the twelfth century had been indeed dispelled. The grossness of taste, and the incapacity for appreciating true beauty, which accompanied that ignorance, had been corrected; but the development of the imagination preceded, as it always does precede, the development of the reason. Men were entranced with the chaste beauty of Greek literature before they were imbued with the spirit of abstraction, of free criticism, and of elevated philosophy, which it breathes. They learned to admire a pure style or a graceful picture before they learned to appreciate a refined creed or an untrammelled philosophy. All through Europe, the first effect of the revival of learning was to produce a general efflorescence of the beautiful. A general discontent with the existing forms of belief was not produced till much later. A material, sensuous, and anthropomorphic faith was still adapted to the intellectual condition of the age, and therefore

endowed with wonderful power—his name is Jesus Christ. Men say that He is a mighty prophet; but His disciples call Him the Son of God. He calls the dead to life, and frees the sick from every form of disease. He is tall of stature, and His aspect is sweet and full of power, so that they who look upon Him may at once love and fear Him. The hair of His head is of the colour of wine; as far as the ears it is straight and without glitter, and from the ears to the shoulders it is curled and glossy, and from the shoulders it descends over the back, divided into two parts after the manner of the Nazarenes. His brow is pure and even; his countenance without a spot, but adorned with a gentle glow; his expression bland and open; his nose and mouth are of perfect beauty; his beard is copious, forked, and of the colour of his hair; his eyes are blue and very bright. In reproving and threatening, He is terrible; in teaching and exhorting, gentle and loving. The grace and majesty of his appearance are marvellous. No one had ever seen Him laugh, but rather weeping. His carriage is erect; his hands well formed and straight; his arms of passing beauty. Weighty and grave in speech, He is sparing of words. He is the most beautiful of the sons of men." Nearly all archæologists have inferred from the representations of the fourth century that this description was then in existence. Dean Milman, however, argues from the silence of St. John Damascene, and of the disputants at the Second Council of Nice, that it is of a much later date. See on this whole subject, Emeric David, *Hist. de la Peinture*, pp. 24–26; and Didron, *Iconographie chrétienne*, pp. 251–276. I may add, that as late as 1649 a curious book (*De Formâ Christi*) was published on this subject at Paris by a Jesuit, named Vavassor, which represents the controversy as still continuing.

[1] The same thing is related of the Spanish sculptor Hernandez, and of the Spanish painter Juannes.— Ford's *Spain*, vol. ii. p. 271.

painting was still the special organ of religious emotions. All the painters of that period were strictly religious, that is to say, they invariably subordinated considerations of art to considerations of religion. The form of beauty they depicted was always religious beauty, and they never hesitated to disfigure their works with loathsome or painful images if they could in that manner add to their religious effect.

To these general considerations we should add the important influence of Dante, who may be regarded as the most faithful representative of that brief moment in which the renewed study of the pagan writings served only to ennoble and refine, and not yet to weaken, the conceptions of theology. No other European poet realised so fully the sacred character antiquity attributed to the bard. In the great poems of Greece and Rome, human figures occupied the foreground, and even when supernatural machinery was introduced, it served only to enhance the power or evoke the moral grandeur of mortals. Milton, indeed, soared far beyond the range of earth; but when he wrote, religious conceptions no longer took the form of palpable and material imagery, and even the grandest representations of spiritual beings under human aspects appeared incongruous and unreal. But the poem of Dante was the last apocalypse. It exercised a supreme ascendency over the imagination at a time when religious imagery was not so much the adjunct as the essence of belief, when the natural impulse of every man was to convert intellectual conceptions into palpable forms, and when painting was in the strictest sense the normal expression of faith. Scarcely any other single influence contributed so much, by purifying and feeding the imagination, to give Christian art a grandeur and a religious perfection, and at the same time a sombre and appalling aspect. "Dipped in the gloom of earthquake and eclipse," the pencil of the great poet loved to accumulate images of terror and of suffering, which speedily passed into the works of the artists, enthralled and fascinated the imaginations of the people, and completed a transformation that had long been in progress. At first, after the period of the Catacombs, the painters expatiated for the most part upon scenes drawn from the Book of Revelation, but usually selected in such a manner as to inspire

any sentiment rather than terror. The lamb, which, having been for some centuries the favourite symbol of Christ, was at last condemned by a council in 692,[1] the mystic roll with its seven seals, the New Jerusalem with its jewelled battlements, or Bethlehem transfigured in its image, constantly recurred. But many circumstances—of which the panic produced by the belief that the world must end with the tenth century, and the increased influence of asceticism arising from the permission accorded to the monks of establishing their communities in the cities,[2] were probably the chief—contributed to effect a profound change. The churches, in their ornaments, in their general aspect, and even in their forms,[3] became the images of death, and painting was tending rapidly in the same direction, when the *Inferno* of Dante opened a new abyss of terrors to the imaginations of the artists, and became the representative, and in a measure the source, of an art that was at once singularly beautiful, purely religious, and deeply imbued with terrorism and with asceticism.

These were the characteristics of the first period of revived art, and they harmonised well with the intellectual condition of the day. After a time, however, the renewed energies of the European mind began to produce effects that were far more important. A spirit of unshackled criticism, a capacity for refined abstractions, a dislike to materialism in faith, and to asceticism in practice, a disposition to treat with unceremonious ridicule imposture and ignorance in high

[1] The object of this council (which was held at Constantinople, and is known under the title "In Trullo") was to repress the love of allegory that was general; and a very learned historian of art thinks that it first produced pictures of the Crucifixion. (Emeric David, *Hist. de la Peinture*, pp. 59-61.) Its decree was afterwards either withdrawn or neglected, for lambs soon reappeared, though they never regained their former ascendency in art: but after Constantine they for nearly three centuries had superseded every other symbol. (Rio, *Art. chrétien*, Intro. p. 49.) Ciampini says that the council which condemned them was a pseudo-council—not sanctioned by the Pope. (*Vetera Monumenta*, pars i. p. 28. See, too, Marangoni, *Istoria della Cappella di Sancta Sanctorum*, p. 159.)

[2] At first they were strictly forbidden to remain in the towns. Even the priest-ridden Theodosius made a law (which, however, he afterwards revoked) commanding all who had embraced the profession of monks to betake themselves to "vast solitudes" and "desert places." (*Cod. Theod.* lib. xvi. tit, 3, c. 1.)

[3] That is, by the introduction of the cross, which was the first innovation on the old basilica architecture, and in many of the churches by a slight inclination of the extremity from the straight line, it is said, to represent the verse, "Jesus *bowed his head* and gave up the ghost."

places, an impatience of the countless ceremonies and trivial superstitions that were universal, and a growing sense of human dignity, were manifested on all sides, and they adumbrated clearly a coming change. The movement was shown in the whole tone of literature, and in the repeated and passionate efforts to attain a more spiritual creed that were made by the precursors of the Reformation. It was shown at least as forcibly in the rapid corruption of every organ of the old religion. They no longer could attract religious fervour; and as their life was gone, they degenerated and decayed. The monasteries, once the scenes of the most marvellous displays of ascetic piety, became the seats of revelry, of licentiousness, and of avarice. The sacred relics, and the miraculous images that had so long thrilled the hearts of multitudes, were made a source of unholy traffic, or of unblushing imposition. The indulgences, which were intended to assuage the agonies of a despairing conscience, or to lend an additional charm to the devotions of the pious, became a substitute for all real religion. The Papal See itself was stained with the most degrading vice, and the Vatican exhibited the spectacle of a pagan court without the redeeming virtue of pagan sincerity. Wherever the eye was turned, it encountered the signs of disorganisation, of corruption, and of decay. For the long night of mediævalism was now drawing to a close, and the chaos that precedes resurrection was supreme. The spirit of ancient Greece had arisen from the tomb, and the fabric of superstition crumbled and tottered at her touch. The human mind, starting beneath her influence from the dust of ages, cast aside the bonds that had enchained it, and, radiant in the light of recovered liberty, remoulded the structure of its faith. The love of truth, the passion for freedom, the sense of human dignity, which the great thinkers of antiquity had inspired, vivified a torpid and down-trodden people, blended with those sublime moral doctrines and with those conceptions of enlarged benevolence which are at once the glory and the essence of Christianity, introduced a new era of human progress, with new aspirations, habits of thought, and conditions of vitality, and, withdrawing religious life from the shattered edifices of the past, created a purer faith, and became the promise of an eternal development.

This was the tendency of the human intellect, and it was faithfully reflected in the history of art. As the old Catholic modes of thought began to fade, the religious idea disappeared from the paintings, and they became purely secular, if not sensual, in their tone. Religion, which was once the mistress, was now the servant, of art. Formerly the painter employed his skill simply in embellishing and enhancing a religious idea. He now employed a religious subject as the pretext for the exhibition of mere worldly beauty. He commonly painted his mistress as the Virgin. He arrayed her in the richest attire, and surrounded her with all the circumstances of splendour. He crowded his pictures with nude figures, with countenances of sensual loveliness, with every form and attitude that could act upon the passions, and not unfrequently with images drawn from the pagan mythology. The creation of beauty became the single object of his art. His work was a secular work, to be judged by a secular standard.

There can be no doubt that this secularisation of art was due to the general tone of thought that had been produced in Europe. The artist seeks to represent the conceptions of his time, and his popularity is the proof of his success. In an age in which strong religious belief was general, and in which it turned to painting as to the natural organ of its expression, such a style would have been impossible. The profanity of the painters would have excited universal execration, and all the genius of Titian or Michael Angelo would have been unable to save their works from condemnation. The style became popular, because educated men ceased to look for religion in pictures ; or in other words, because the habits of thought that made them demand material representations of the objects of their belief had declined.

This was the ultimate cause of the entire movement. There were, however, two minor causes of great importance, which contributed largely to the altered tone of art, while they at the same time immeasurably increased its perfection— one of them relating especially to colour, and the other to form.

The first of these causes is to be found in the moral condition of Italian society. The age was that of Bianca di Cappello, and of the Borgias. All Italian literature and all Italian manners were of the laxest character, and the fact was neither concealed nor deplored. But that which especially distinguished Italian immorality is, that growing up in the midst of all the forms of loveliness, it assumed from the first an æsthetic character, united with the most passionate and yet refined sense of the beautiful, and made art the special vehicle of its expression. This is one of the peculiar characteristics of later Italian painting,[1] and it is one of the chief causes of its artistic perfection. For sensuality has always been extremely favourable to painting,[2] the main object of the artist being to exhibit to the highest possible degree the beauty and the attractive power of the human body. Twice in the history of art national sensuality has thrown itself into national art, and in each case with the same result. The first occasion was in ancient Greece, at the time when Apelles derived a new inspiration from the voluptuous loveliness of Lais, and when the goddess of beauty, glowing with the fresh charms of Phryne or Theodota, kindled a transport of no religious fervour in the Athenian mind. The second occasion was in the Italian art of the sixteenth century.

The rapid progress of a sensual tone

[1] German pictures are often indecent, but never sensual. It is all the difference between Swift and Don Juan. The nude figure as painted by Van der Werff is ivory—as painted by Titian or Correggio, it is life. Spanish art tried much to be religious and respectable; and, like the Vergognosa at Pisa, put her hands before her eyes in the midst of the wickedness that surrounded her. But I am afraid she sometimes looked through her fingers. This aspect of Italian art has been most vividly exhibited in the writings of Stendhal (H. Beyle).

[2] It is perhaps true, as modern critics say, that the transition of Greek art from Phidias to Praxiteles was a decline. It is certainly true that that transition was from the representation of manly strength, and the form of beauty that is most allied to it, to the representation of beauty of a sensual cast—from an art of which Minerva was the central figure, to an art of which Venus was the type—or (as the German critics say) from the ascendency of the Doric to the ascendency of the Ionic element. But this decadence, if it really took place, is not, I think, inconsistent with what I have stated in the text; for sculpture and painting have each their special perfections, and the success of the artist will in a great degree depend upon his appreciation of the peculiar genius of the art he pursues. Now sculpture is as far superior to painting in its capacity for expressing strength and masculine beauty, as painting is superior to sculpture in expressing warmth and passionate beauty. All the efforts of a Grecian chisel never equalled the voluptuous power of the brush of Titian; and, on the other hand, painting has tried in vain to rival the majesty and the force of sculpture. If there be an exception to this last proposition, it is one which proves the rule, for it is furnished by Michael Angelo, the greatest modern sculptor, in the most sculptor-like frescoes in the world. It should be added, however, that landscape painting is in no sense the creature of sensuality, and Mr. Ruskin has with some force claimed it as a special fruit of Christianity.

in most of the schools of Italian art is a fact which is too manifest to be questioned or overlooked; but there is one school which may be regarded especially as its source and representative. This school was that of the Venetian painters, and it reflected very visibly the character of its cradle. Never perhaps was any other city so plainly formed to be the home at once of passion and of art. Sleeping like Venus of old upon her parent wave, Venice, at least in the period of her glory, comprised within herself all the influences that could raise to the highest point the æsthetic sentiment, and all that could lull the moral sentiment to repose. Wherever the eye was turned, it was met by forms of strange and varied and entrancing beauty, while every sound that broke upon the ear was mellowed by the waters that were below. The thousand lights that glittered around the gilded domes of St. Mark, the palaces of matchless architecture resting on their own soft shadows in the wave, the long paths of murmuring water, where the gondola sways to the lover's song, and where dark eyes lustrous with passion gleam from the overhanging balconies, the harmony of blending beauties, and the languid and voluptuous charm that pervades the whole, had all told deeply and fatally on the character of the people. At every period of their history, but never more so than in the great period of Venetian art, they had been distinguished at once for their intense appreciation of beauty and for their universal, unbridled, and undisguised licentiousness.[1] In the midst of such a society it was very natural that a great school of sensual art should arise, and many circumstances conspired in the same direction. Venice was so far removed from the discoveries of the ancient statues, that it was never influenced by what may be termed the learned school of art, which eventually sacrificed all sense of beauty to anatomical studies; at the same time, the simultaneous appearance of a constellation of artists of the very highest order, the luxurious habits that provided these artists with abundant patrons, the discovery of oil painting,[2] which attained its highest

[1] On the amazing vice of Venice, and on the violent but unsuccessful efforts of the magistrates to arrest it, see much curious evidence in Sabatier, Hist. de la Législation sur les Femmes publiques (Paris, 1828).
[2] It is generally said to have been invented in the beginning of the fifteenth century by Van Eyck, who died in 1440; but the claim of Van Eyck is not undis-

perfection under the skill of the Venetian colourists, perhaps even the rich merchandise of the East, accustoming the eye to the most gorgeous hues,[1] had all in different ways their favourable influence upon art. The study of the nude figure, which had been the mainspring of Greek art, and which Christianity had so long suppressed, rose again, and a school of painting was formed, which for subtle sensuality of colouring had never been equalled, and, except by Correggio, has scarcely been approached. Titian in this as in other respects was the leader of the school, and he bears to modern much the same relation as Praxiteles bears to ancient art. Both the sculptor and the painter precipitated art into sensuality, both of them destroyed its religious character, both of them raised it to high æsthetic perfection, but in both cases that perfection was followed by a speedy decline.[2] Even in Venice there was one great representative of the early religious school, but his influence was unable to stay the stream. The Virgin of Bellini was soon exchanged for the Virgin of Titian—the ideal of female piety for the ideal of female beauty.

A second influence which contributed to the secularisation, and at the same time to the perfection, of art, was the discovery of many of the great works of pagan sculpture. The complete disappearance of these during the preceding centuries may be easily explained by the religious and intellectual changes that had either accompanied or speedily followed the triumph of Christianity. The priests, and especially the monks, being firmly convinced that pagan idols were all tenanted by demons, for some time made it one of their principal objects to break them in pieces, and cupidity proved scarcely less destructive than fanaticism. Among the ancient Greeks, as is well known, marble had never obtained the same ascendency in sculpture as among ourselves. Great numbers of statues were made of bronze, and a large proportion of the masterpieces of the most illustrious artists were of ivory or of gold. No features are more wonderful in the history of the Greek states than the immense sums they consented to withdraw from all other objects, to expend upon the cultivation of beauty, and the religious care with which these precious objects were preserved unharmed amid all the vicissitudes of national fortune, amid war, rebellion, and conquest. This preservation was in part due to the intense æsthetic feeling that was so general in antiquity, but in part also to the catholicity of spirit that usually accompanied polytheism, which made men regard with reverence the objects and ceremonies even of worships that were not their own, and which was especially manifested by the Romans, who in all their conquests respected the temples of the vanquished as representing under many forms the aspiration of man to his Creator. Both of these sentiments were blotted out by Christianity. For about 1,500 years the conception that there could be anything deserving of reverence or respect, or even of tolerance, in the religions that were external to the Church, was absolutely unknown in Christendom, and at the same time the ascetic theories I have noticed destroyed all perception of beauty, or at least of that type of beauty which sculpture represented. The bronze statues were converted into coinage, the precious metals were plundered,[1] the marble was turned into lime, mutilated or forgotten. When Christianity arose, the colossal statue of Jupiter, in gold and ivory, which was deemed the masterpiece of Phidias, and the greatest of all the achievements of art, still existed at Olympia. Our last notice of it is during the reign of Julian. At Rome, the invasion of the Barbarians, the absolute decadence of taste that followed their ascendency,

---

puted. It was introduced into Italy about 1452 by a Sicilian painter named Antonello. (Rio, *Art chrétien*, tom. i. p. 354.)

[1] At an earlier period, oriental robes exercised an influence of a different kind upon art. In the thirteenth century, when they began to pour into France, the ornamentation, and especially the tracery, of the windows of many of the French cathedrals are said to have been copied accurately from these patterns. See a very curious essay on painted glass by Thevenot (Paris, 1837). I may add that, at the time of Augustus, the importation of Indian dresses had told powerfully on Roman art, producing the paintings known as arabesque, and (as Vitruvius complains) diverting the artists from the study of the Greek model. In the middle ages both Venice and Florence were famous for their dyers.

[2] Praxiteles is said to have definitely given the character of sensuality to Venus, who had previously floated between several ideals of beauty, and also to have been the especial author of the effeminate type of Apollo. Phryne, who was then the great model of voluptuous beauty—she who, having been condemned to death, was absolved on account of her exceeding loveliness—was his mistress. His contemporary Polycles greatly strengthened the sensual movement by introducing into art the hermaphrodite. See Rio, *Art chrétien*, Introd. pp. 17–21; O. Müller, *Manuel d'Archéologie*, tom. i. pp. 156–157.

[1] Constantine himself set the example in this respect. See the admiring remarks of Eusebius, *Vita Const.* lib. iii. caps. 5, 6.

and those great conflagrations which more than once reduced vast districts to ruin, completed the destruction of the old traditions, while most of the statues that had been transported to Constantinople, and had survived the fury of the monks, were destroyed by the Iconoclasts, the Crusaders, or the Mahometans.

Towards the close of the twelfth century, as we have already seen, Nicolas of Pisa for the first time broke the slumber of mediæval art by the skill he had derived from the works of antiquity. There was then, however, no ancient model of the highest class known, and the principal subject of his study is said to have been a pagan sarcophagus of third or fourth rate merit, which had been employed for the burial of the mother of the famous Countess Matilda, and which was then in the Cathedral, and is now in the Campo Santo, of Pisa. Giotto, Massacio, and their contemporaries, all pursued their triumphs without the assistance of any great ancient model. Poggio, who wrote at the beginning of the fifteenth century, was only able to enumerate six statues within the walls of Rome. Rienzi and Petrarch gave some slight impulse to archæological collections, and during the latter half of the fifteenth century the exertions of the Medici, and of a long series of popes, sustained by the passionate admiration for antiquity that followed the revival of learning, produced vast works of excavation, which were rewarded by the discovery of numerous statues.[1] Art immediately rose to an unparalleled perfection, and an unbounded and almost universal enthusiasm was created. Paul II., indeed, in 1468, directed a fierce persecution against the artists at Rome,[2] but as a general rule his successors were warm patrons of art, and Julius II. and Leo X. may even be regarded as the most munificent of their munificent age. All the artists of Rome and Florence made the remains of pagan antiquity their models. Michael Angelo himself proclaimed the Torso Belvedere his true master.[3] The dis-

tinctive type and tone of Christianity was thus almost banished from art, and replaced by the types of paganism.

Such was the movement which was general in Italian art; but it did not pass unchallenged, and it was retarded by one most remarkable reaction. Under the very palace of the Medici, and in the midst of the noblest collections of pagan art, a great preacher arose who perceived clearly the dangerous tendency, and who employed the full force of a transcendent genius to arrest it. The influence of Savonarola upon painting has been so lately and so fully described by an able living historian of art,[1] that it is not necessary to dwell upon it at length. It is sufficient to say that during the last few years of the fifteenth century a complete religious revival took place in Tuscany, and that Savonarola, who was much more than a brilliant orator, perceived very clearly that in order to make it permanent it was necessary to ally it with the tendencies of the age. He accordingly, like all successful religious revivalists of ancient and modern times, proceeded to identify religion with liberty and with democracy, by his denunciations of the tyranny of the Medici and by the creation of great lending societies, for the purpose of checking the oppressive usury that had become general. He endeavoured to secure the ascendency of his opinions over the coming generation by guiding the education of the children, and by making them the special objects of his preaching. He attempted above all to purify the very sources of Italian life, by regenerating the sacred music, and by restoring painting to its pristine purity. Week after week he launched from the pulpit the most scathing invectives against the artists who had painted prostitutes in the character of the Virgin, who under the pretext of religious art had pandered to the licentiousness of their age, and who had entirely forgotten their dignity as the teachers of mankind. As these invectives were not inspired by the fanaticism of the old Iconoclasts, but proceeded from one who possessed to the highest degree the Tuscan perception of the beautiful, they produced an impression that was altogether unparalleled. Almost all the

---

[1] When this impulse had ceased in Italy, it was still in some degree continued by the explorations of the French in Greece, where a French consulate was formed about 1630. See Vitet, *Études sur l'Histoire de l'Art*, tom. i. p. 94.

[2] See the description in Platina.

[3] And was accordingly in sculpture (as in painting) singularly unfortunate in catching the moral expression of Scripture subjects. His Moses—half prize-fighter, half Jupiter Tonans—is certainly the extreme antithesis to "the meekest man in all the world." His

colossal statue of David after his victory over Goliath (it would be as rational to make a colossal statue of a Lilliputian) would be perfect as an Achilles.

[1] Rio—I think the best part of his book.

leading painters of Italy were collected at
Florence, and almost all, under the influence of Savonarola, attempted to revive the religious character of art. The
change was immediately exhibited in the
painting of Italy, and the impression
Savonarola made upon the artists was
shown by the conduct of many of them
when the great reformer had perished in
the flames. Botticelli cast aside his
pencil for ever. Baccio della Porta[1] retired broken-hearted into a monastery.
Perugino (perhaps the greatest of all the
purely religious painters of Catholicism)
glided rapidly into scepticism, and on his
death-bed refused disdainfully the assistance of a confessor. Raphael, who had
derived all the religious sentiment of his
early paintings from Perugino, was the
first to vindicate the orthodoxy of Savonarola by inserting his portrait among those
of the doctors of the Church, in the fresco
of the Dispute of the Sacrament.

After the death of Savonarola the
secularisation of art was portentously
rapid. Even Raphael, who exhibits the
tendency less than his contemporaries,
never shrank from destroying the religious character of his later works by
the introduction of incongruous images.
Michael Angelo, that great worshipper
of physical force, probably represented
the influence to the highest degree.
Austere, pure, and majestic as he undoubtedly was, no great artist was ever
more destitute of the peculiar tenderness
of Christian sentiment, and it was also
reserved for him to destroy the most
fearful of all the conceptions by which
the early painters had thrilled the people.
By making the Last Judgment a study of
naked figures, by the introduction of
Charon and his boat, and by the essentially pagan character of his Christ, he
most effectually destroyed all sense of the
reality of the scene, and reduced it to the
province of artistic criticism. This fresco
may be regarded as the culmination of
the movement. There were of course at
a later period some great pictures, and
even some religious painters; but painting never again assumed its old position
as the normal and habitual expression of
the religious sentiments of the educated.
In the first period of mediævalism it had
been exclusively religious, and æsthetic
considerations were almost forgotten. In
the second period the two elements co-

existed. In the last period the religious
sentiment disappeared, and the conception of beauty reigned alone. Art had
then completed its cycle. It never afterwards assumed a prominent or commanding influence over the minds of men.
It is worthy of remark that a transition
very similar to that we have traced in
painting took place about the same time
in architecture. The architect, it is true,
does not supply actual objects of worship,
and in this respect his art is less closely
connected than that of the painter with
the history of anthropomorphism ; but, on
the other hand, the period in which men
require a visible material object of worship, is also that in which their religious
tone and sentiment are most dependent
upon imposing sensuous displays. Christianity has created three things which
religious poetry has ever recognised as
the special types and expressions of its
religious sentiment. These are the church
bell, the organ, and the Gothic cathedral.
The first is said to have been invented by
Paulinus, a bishop of Nola in Campania,
about the year 400.[1] The second appears
to have been first used in the Greek
Church, and to have passed into the
Western Empire in the seventh or eighth
century.[2] The third arose under the
revived sense of beauty of the twelfth
century, and preceded by a little the
resurrection of painting. The new pictures and the new churches were both
the occasions of ebullitions of the most
passionate devotion. When Cimabue
painted one of his famous Virgins, the
people of Florence gathered around it as
to a religious festival, they transported
it with prayers and thanksgivings to the
Church, and filled the streets with hymns
of joy, because a higher realisation of a
religious conception had flashed upon
them. Just so those majestic cathedrals

---

[1] Better known as Fra Bartolomeo.

[1] Anderson, *Hist. of Commerce*, vol. ii. p. 36. There
is a very curious collection of passages from the *Acts
of the Saints*, in which bells are alluded to (but none of
them apparently earlier than the beginning of the
seventh century) in an out-of-the-way quarter. (Suarez,
De Fide, lib. ii. c. 16.) See, too, Colgan's *Acta Sanctorum Hiberniæ*, tom. i. p. 149.
[2] Anderson, vol. i. p. 30. There had before been
known a water organ, called an hydraulicon. There
was also a wind instrument which some have placed
among the antecedents of the organ, but which seems
to have been almost exactly the same as a Scotch bag-
pipe. I am sorry to say Julian had the bad taste to
praise it in one of his epigrams. (See Burney, *Hist. of
Music*, vol. ii. pp. 65-67.) There is a curious series of
papers on the musical instruments in the middle ages,
by Coussemaker, in the *Annales archéologiques* (edited
by Didron), tom. iv. They have since, I believe, been
published separately.

that arose almost simultaneously through-out Europe became at once the channel of the enthusiasm of Christendom ; the noblest efforts of self-sacrifice were made to erect them, and they were universally regarded as the purest expression of the religious feeling of the age. That this estimate was correct, that no other build-ings the world has seen are so admirably calculated to produce a sensation of blended awe and tranquillity, to harmonise or assuage the qualms of passion, to lull to sleep the rebellious energies of the intellect, to create around the mind an artificial, unworldly, but most impressive atmosphere, to represent a Church which acts upon the imagination by obscurity and terrorism, and by images of solemn and entrancing beauty, will be admitted by all who have any perception of the character, or any knowledge of the his-tory of art. Whenever these modes of feeling have been very general, Gothic architecture has been the object of rap-turous admiration. Whenever these modes of feeling were very rare, Gothic archi-tecture has sunk into neglect and dis-favour.[1]

[1] We have a very striking example of this in both the buildings and the criticisms of the eighteenth century. What (e.g.) should we now say to an imagi-native writer who, speaking of York Minster, assured us, as Smollett does, "that the external appearance of an old cathedral cannot but be displeasing to the eye of every man who has any idea of propriety and pro-portion"; who could only describe Durham Cathedral as "a huge gloomy pile"; and who acknowledged that he associated the idea of a church with a spire espe-cially with that of a man impaled (see *Humphrey Clinker*)? Thus too Hutcheson, in one of the ablest English works on the philosophy of the beautiful, applies himself elaborately to proving that the ancient preference of Gothic to Roman architecture is not inconsistent with the universality of the sense of beauty, but is only an aberration caused by historical associa-tions. "Education may make an inattentive Goth imagine that his countrymen have attained the perfec-tion of architecture, and an aversion to their enemies the Romans may have joined some disagreeable ideas to their very buildings and excited them to their demolition." (*An Enquiry concerning Beauty*, secs. vi. vii.) Everyone, I should think, who was well acquainted with the literature of the eighteenth century, must have been struck with the contempt for Gothic architecture pervading it ; but the extent to which this was carried was never fully shown till the publication, a few years ago, of an exceedingly curious book by the Abbé Corblet, called *L'Architecture du Moyen Âge jugée par les écrivains des deux derniers Siècles* (Paris, 1859). This learned antiquary has shown that, during the last half of the seventeenth century, and during the whole of the eighteenth century, there was scarcely a single writer, no matter what may have been his religious opinions, who did not speak of Gothic archi-tecture not merely without appreciation, but with the most supreme and unqualified contempt. The list includes, among others, Fénélon, Bossuet, Molière, Fleury, Rollin, Montesquieu, La Bruyère, Helvétius, Rousseau, Mengs, and Voltaire. Goethe at one time opposed, but afterwards yielded to, the stream. Milan Cathedral was the special object of ridicule. Gothic

I do not intend to follow at length the vicissitudes of architecture, or to trace the successive phases of its secularisation. It is sufficient to observe, that about the time when the dense ignorance that had overspread Europe was dispelled, there arose a form of architecture which was exclusively and emphatically Christian, which has been universally admitted to be beyond all others the most accordant with the spirit of mediæval religion, and in which the highest sense of beauty was subordinated to the religious sentiment. At the time when the moral and intel-lectual chaos that preceded the Reforma-tion was universal, and when painting had been secularised and had passed entirely into the worship of beauty, archi-tecture exhibited a corresponding de-cadence. The old Gothic style was every-where discarded, and it was supplanted under the influence of Brunelleschi[1] by a style which some persons may deem more beautiful, but which is universally ad-mitted to be entirely devoid of a religious character. The gorgeous, gay, and beautifully proportioned edifices that then rose to fashion were, in fact, avowedly formed from the model of the great temples of antiquity, and the beauty to which they aspired was purely classic. Cologne Cathedral, the last of the great mediæval works, remained unfinished while the whole energies of Europe were concentrated upon the church of St. Peter at Rome. The design of this great work

architecture was then almost universally ascribed to the Goths of the fifth century, and Bishop Warburton suggested that they had derived the idea from the overarching boughs of their native forests. Some, however, and among others Barry, regarded it as an imperfect imitation of Greek architecture. Many of the criticisms were very curious. Thus, Dupuis thought the zodiacs on the cathedrals were a remnant of the worship of Mithra. Another critic found a connection between the shape of the ogive and the eggs of Isis. A third, named Montluisant, explained all the sculptures on the front of Notre Dame de Paris by the science of the philosopher's stone : God the Father, holding an angel in each hand, is the Deity, calling into existence the incombustible sulphur and the mercury of life. The flying dragon biting its tail is the philosopher's stone, composed of the fixed and the volatile substances, the former of which devours the latter, &c., &c. (*Œuvres de St.-Foix*, tom. iii. pp. 245, 246.) It is to the Catholic revival of the present [nineteenth] century that we mainly owe the revival of Gothic architecture.
[1] It is true that the Greek traditions had always lingered in Italy, and that pure Gothic never succeeded in gaining an ascendency there as in other countries. The exterior of the little church of Sta. Maria della Spina, at Pisa, which was designed by Nicolas of Pisa, is perhaps the best specimen of purely Italian origin, for Milan Cathedral is said to be due to German archi-tects ; but this fact, while it accounts for Italy having been the great assailant of the Gothic, did not prevent its influence from being cosmopolitan.

was confided to Michael Angelo, who had been the chief agent in the secularisation of painting, and the spirit in which he undertook it was clearly expressed in his famous exclamation, that he would suspend the Pantheon in the air.

Of all the edifices that have been raised by the hand of man, there is perhaps none that presents to the historian of the human mind a deeper interest than St. Peter's, and there is certainly none that tells a sadder tale of the frustration of human efforts and the futility of human hopes. It owes its greatest splendour to a worldly and ambitious pontiff,[1] who has not even obtained an epitaph beneath its dome. It was designed to be the eternal monument of the glory and the universality of Catholicism, and it has become the most impressive memorial of its decay. The most sublime associations that could appeal to the intellect or the religious sentiment cluster thickly around it, but an association of which none had dreamed has consecrated it, and will abide with it for ever. The most sacred relics of the Catholic faith are assembled within its walls. The genius of Michael Angelo, Raphael, Bramante, Cellini, Thorwaldsen, and Canova, has adorned it. Mosaics of matchless beauty reproduce the greatest triumphs of Christian painting, and mingle their varied hues with those gorgeous marbles that might have absorbed the revenues of a kingdom. Beneath that majestic dome, which stands like the emblem of eternity, and dwarfs the proudest monuments below, rest the remains of those who were long deemed the greatest of the sons of men. There lie those mediæval pontiffs who had borne aloft the lamp of knowledge in an evil and benighted age, who had guided and controlled the march of nations, and had been almost worshipped as the representatives of the Almighty. There too the English traveller pauses amid many more splendid objects at the sculptured slab which bears the names of the last scions of a royal race, that for good or for ill had deeply influenced the destiny of his land. But inexpressibly great as are these associations, in the eyes of the theologian the recollection of Luther, and the indulgences, and the Reformation will tower above them all; while to the philosophic historian St. Peter's possesses an interest of a still higher order.

[1] Julius II

For it represents the conclusion of that impulse, growing out of the anthropomorphic habits of an early civilisation, which had led men for so many centuries to express their religious feelings by sensuous images of grandeur, of obscurity, and of terrorism. It represents the absorption of the religious by the æsthetic element, which was the sure sign that the religious function of architecture had terminated. The age of the cathedrals had passed. The age of the printing press had begun.

I have dwelt at considerable length upon this aspect of the history of art, both because it is, I think, singularly fascinating in itself, and because it reflects with striking fidelity the religious developments of the time. When the organs of a belief are entirely changed, it may be assumed that there is some corresponding change in the modes of thought of which they are the expression, and it cannot be too often repeated that before printing was invented, and while all conceptions were grossly anthropomorphic, the true course of ecclesiastical history is to be sought much more in the works of the artists than of the theologians. It is now admitted by most competent judges, that the true causes of the Reformation are to be found in the deep change effected in the intellectual habits of Europe by that revival of learning which began about the twelfth century in the renewed study of the Latin classics, and reached its climax after the fall of Constantinople in the diffusion of the knowledge of Greek and of the philosophy of Plato by the Greek exiles. This revival ultimately produced a condition of religious feeling which found its expression in some countries in Protestantism, and in other countries in the prevalence among the educated classes of a diluted and rationalistic Catholicism entirely different from the gross and absorbing superstition of the middle ages. Which of these two forms was adopted in any particular country depended upon many special political or social, or even geographical considerations; but, wherever the intellectual movement was strongly felt, one or other appeared. It is surely a remarkable coincidence, that while the literature of antiquity was thus on a large scale modifying the mediæval modes of thought, the ancient sculptures should on a smaller scale have exercised a corresponding influence upon the art that was their expression. And, although the æsthetic movement was necessarily confined to the upper classes and to the countries in which civilisation was most prominent, it represented faithfully a tendency that in different forms was still more widely displayed. It represented the gradual destruction of the ascendency which the Church had once exercised over every department of intellect, the growing difference in realised belief between the educated and the ignorant, and the gradual disappearance of anthropomorphic or idolatrous conceptions among the former.

The aspect, however, of the subject which is peculiarly significant, is, I think, to be found in the nature of the transition which religious art underwent. The sense of beauty gradually encroached upon and absorbed the feeling of reverence. This is a form of religious decay which is very far from being confined to the history of art. The religion of one age is often the poetry of the next. Around every living and operative faith there lies a region of allegory and of imagination into which opinions frequently pass, and in which they long retain a transfigured and idealised existence after their natural life has died away. They are, as it were, deflected. They no longer tell directly and forcibly upon human actions. They no longer produce terror, inspire hopes, awake passions, or mould the characters of men, yet they still exercise a kind of reflex influence, and form part of the ornamental culture of the age. They are turned into allegories. They are interpreted in a non-natural sense. They are invested with a fanciful, poetic, but most attractive garb. They follow instead of controlling the current of thought, and being transformed by far-fetched and ingenious explanations, they become the embellishments of systems of belief that are wholly irreconcilable with their original tendencies. The gods of heathenism were thus translated from the sphere of religion to the sphere of poetry. The grotesque legends and the harsh doctrines of a superstitious faith are so explained away, that they appear graceful myths foreshadowing and illustrating the conceptions of a brighter day. For a time they flicker upon the horizon with a softly beautiful light that enchants the poet, and lends a charm to the new system with which they are made to

blend ; but at last this too fades away. Religious ideas die like the sun ; their last rays, possessing little heat, are expended in creating beauty.

There can be no question that the steady tendency of the European mind, not merely in the period that elapsed between the revival of learning in the twelfth century and the Reformation, but also in that between the Reformation and our own day, has been to disengage itself more and more from all the conceptions which are connected either with fetishism or with anthropomorphism. The evidence of this meets us on all sides. We find it among the Catholics, in the steady increase in Catholic countries of a purely rationalistic public opinion, in the vast multiplication of rationalistic writings, and also in the profound difference in the degree of reverence attached even by fervent Catholics to images and talismans, in cities like Paris, which are in the centre of the intellectual movement of the age, and in cities like Seville or Naples, which have long been excluded from it. Among the Protestants the same tendency is displayed with equal force in the rapid destruction of what is termed the sacramentarian principle. This is manifest in the steady and almost silent evanescence of that doctrine of consubstantiation which was once asserted with such extreme emphasis as the distinctive mark of the great Lutheran sect, but which is now scarcely held, or if held is scarcely insisted on ;[1] in the decadence of the High Church party, which in the seventeenth century comprised the overwhelming majority of the Anglican clergy, but which in the nineteenth century, notwithstanding a concurrence of favourable circumstances and the exertions of a leader of extraordinary genius, never included more than a minority ;[2] in the constant alteration of

[1] Indeed in Prussia, and some other parts of Germany, the Calvinists and Lutherans have actually coalesced. The tendency to assimilation appears to have been strongly felt as early as the middle of the seventeenth century, and Bishop Bedell exerted himself strongly to promote it. (See some interesting particulars in his *Life*, by Usher.) On the recent amalgamation of the Lutherans and Calvinists in Germany, and on its relation to rationalism, there are some remarks worth reading in Amand Saintes' *Hist. du Rationalisme en Allemagne.*

[2] The principles of parties change so much more than their names that it is not easy to get an accurate notion of their strength at different periods. Shortly after the accession of William III., the Low Church clergy, according to Macaulay (*History of England,* vol. iii. p. 741), scarcely numbered a tenth part of the priesthood. On their strength in the present controversy, see some curious statistics in Conybeare's Essay on

the proportion between Anglicans and Dissenters, to the detriment of the former; and in the rapid development of continental Protestantism into rationalism.

The dominating cause of this movement is, as I have said, to be found mainly in that process of education which is effected by the totality of intellectual influences, and which produces both a capacity and a disposition to rise above material conceptions, and to sublimate all portions of belief. There is, however, one separate branch of knowledge which has exercised such a deep, and at the same time such a distinct, influence upon it, that it requires a separate notice. I mean the progress of physical science modifying our notions of the government of the universe.

In the early Church the interests of theology were too absorbing to leave any room for purely secular studies. If scientific theories were ever discussed, it was simply with a view to elucidating some theological question, and the controversy was entirely governed by the existing notions of inspiration. On this subject two doctrines prevailed, which did not by any means exclude each other, but were both somewhat different from those that are now professed—one of them being allegorical, the other intensely literal. The first, which had been extremely popular among the Jewish commentators, rested upon the belief, that besides the direct and manifest meaning of a scriptural narrative, which was to be ascertained by the ordinary modes of exegesis, there was an occult meaning, which could be discovered only by the eye of faith, or at all events by human ingenuity, guided by the defined doctrines of the Church. Thus, while the historian was apparently relating a very simple narrative, or enforcing a very simple truth, his real and primary object might be to unfold some Christian mystery, of which all the natural objects he mentioned were symbols.

This notion, which in modern times has been systematised and developed with great ingenuity by Swedenborg in his "Doctrine of Correspondences," was the origin of many of those extremely far-fetched, and, as they would now appear, absurd, interpretations of Scripture that are so numerous in the Fathers, and several of which I have already had occasion to notice. Supposing it to be

true, a very important question arose concerning the comparative authority of the historical and the spiritual meanings.

Origen, as is well known, made the principle of allegorical interpretation the basis of a system of free-thinking, sometimes of the boldest character. Manichæism having violently assailed the Mosaic Cosmogony, he cordially accepted the assault as far as it was directed against the literal interpretation, turned into absolute ridicule, as palpable fables, the stories of the serpent and the trees of life and of knowledge, and contended that they could only be justified as allegories representing spiritual truths.[1] Origen, however, verged far too closely upon heresy to be regarded as a representative of the Church ; and the prevailing though not very clearly defined opinion among the orthodox seems to have been, that the literal and the allegorical interpretations should be both retained.

Perhaps the clearest illustration of this doctrine is to be found in a short treatise of St. Augustine in defence of Genesis against the Manichæans, which is very remarkable when we remember that its author was not more distinguished for his great abilities than for the precision and logical character of his mind. In this work, St. Augustine reviews and answers at length the objections which the Manichæans had brought against each separate portion of the six days' work. Having done this, he proceeds to lay down the principle, that besides the literal meaning, there was a spiritual meaning which was veiled in the form of allegory. Thus the record of the six days' creation contained, not merely a description of the first formation of the material world, but also a prophetic sketch of the epochs into

[1] See Beausobre, *Hist. du Manichéisme*, tom i. pp. 286-288. Barbeyrac, *Morale des Pères*, ch. vii., has collected a number of wonderful extravagances of interpretation into which the love of allegory led Origen. One of the most curious writings of the ancient Church bearing on this subject has been lately printed in the *Spicilegium Solesmense* (curante Dom. J. B. Pitra). It is the *Clavis* of St. Melito, who was Bishop of Sardis, it is said, in the beginning of the second century, and consists of a catalogue of many hundreds of birds, beasts, plants, and minerals, that were symbolical of Christian virtues, doctrines, and personages.
A modern High Churchman writes : "I believe that a geologist deeply impressed with the mystery of baptism—that mystery by which a new creature is formed by means of water and fire—would never have fallen into the absurdities of accounting for the formation of the globe solely by water or solely by fire. He would not have maintained a Vulcanian or a Neptunian theory. He would have suspected that the truth lay in the union of both."—Sewell, *Christian Morals*, p. 323.

Church Parties. The failure of the movement was very candidly confessed by the leader, in his *Anglican Difficulties*.

which the history of mankind was to be divided ; the sixth day being the Christian dispensation, in which the man and woman, or Christ and the Church, were to appear upon earth.[1] Nor did it foreshadow less clearly the successive stages of the Christian life. First of all the light of faith streams upon the mind which is still immersed in the waves of sin ; then the firmament of discipline divides things carnal from things spiritual ; then the regenerated soul is raised above the things of earth, and prepared for the production of virtue ; spiritual intelligences rise like the planets in their various orders in the firmament of discipline, good works spring from the waves of trial as the fish from the sea, the purified mind itself produces its own graces, till, sanctified thought being wedded to sanctified action, as Eve to Adam, the soul is prepared for its coming rest.[2] In the same way, when the serpent was condemned to creep along the earth, this meant that temptation comes commonly by pride and sensuality.[3] When it was condemned to eat earth, this probably signified the vice of curiosity, plunging into the unseen. When it is related that there was a time when no rain fell upon the earth, but that a mist, rising from the ground, watered its face, we should understand that prophets and apostles were once unnecessary, for every man bore the spring of revelation in his own breast. The literal narrative was true, and so was the spiritual signification ; but if in the first anything was found which could not be literally interpreted in a manner consonant either with the doctrines of the Church or with the dignity of the Creator, the passage was to be treated as an enigma, and its true import was to be sought in the spiritual meaning.[4] Some touches of description were inserted solely with a view to that meaning. Thus, when in the summary of the creation that is said to have been effected in one day which was really effected in six, and when the " green herbs " are specially singled out among created things, these expressions,

which, taken literally, would be pointless or inaccurate, are intended merely to direct the mind to particular portions of the allegory.

Together with the method of interpretation laid down in this and in other works of the early Church, there was another different, though, as I have said, not necessarily antagonistic one, of an intensely literal character. Theologians were accustomed to single out any incidental expressions that might be applied in any way to scientific theories, even though they were simply the metaphors of poetry or rhetoric, or the ordinary phrases of common conversation, and to interpret them as authoritative declarations, superseding all the deductions of mere worldly science. The best known example of this is to be found in those who condemned the opinions of Galileo, because it had been said that the " sun runneth about from one end of heaven to the other," and that " the foundations of the earth are so firmly fixed that they cannot be moved." It may be well, however, to give an illustration of an earlier date of the extent to which this mode of interpretation was carried.

Among the very few scientific questions which occupied a considerable amount of attention in the early Church, one of the most remarkable was that concerning the existence of the Antipodes. The Manichæans had chanced to stumble on the correct doctrine,[1] and consequently the Fathers opposed it. Although, however, the leaders of the Church were apparently unanimous in denying the existence of the Antipodes, it appears that the contrary opinion had spread to a considerable extent among the less noted Christians, and some fear was entertained lest it should prove a new heresy.

About the year A.D. 535, in the reign of Justinian, there was living in a monastery of Alexandria an old monk named Cosmas, to whom the eyes of many were then turned. He had been in his youth a merchant, and in that profession had travelled much, especially in the regions of India and of Ethiopia. He was also noticed for his keen and inquisitive mind, and for his scientific attainments, and since he had embraced a religious life he had devoted himself zealously to the relations between Scripture and science. At the earnest request of some of the theo-

---

[1] The Church being wedded to Christ, " Bone of his bone, and flesh of his flesh," that is to say, participating alike of his strength and of his purity. (*De Genesi, contra Manichæos,* lib. i. c. 23.)

[2] Lib. v. cap. 25. This notion of marriage representing the union of the two main elements of life is very beautifully developed by Swedenborg, in a book on *Coniugal Affection.*

[3] The chest signifying pride, and the stomach sensuality.

[4] Lib. ii. cap. 2.

[1] Beausobre, *Hist. du Manichéisme,* tom. i. p. 246.

logians of his time, he determined, though now somewhat broken in health, and suffering especially, as he tells us, from "a certain dryness both of the eyes and of the stomach," to employ the remainder of his life in the composition of a great work, which was not only to refute the "anile fable" of the Antipodes, but was to form a complete system of the universe, based upon the teaching of Revelation.

This book is called the *Topographia Christiana*, or *Christian Opinion concerning the World.*[1] Independently of its main interest, as probably the most elaborate work on the connection between science and the Bible which the early Church has bequeathed us, it is extremely curious on account of its many digressions concerning life and manners in the different nations Cosmas had visited. It opens in a tone of great confidence. It is "a Christian topography of the universe, established by demonstrations from Divine Scripture, concerning which it is not lawful for a Christian to doubt."[2] In a similar strain the writer proceeds to censure with great severity those weak-minded Christians who had allowed the subtleties of Greek fables, or the deceitful glitter of mere human science, to lead them astray, forgetting that Scripture contained intimations of the nature of the universe of far higher value and authority than any to which unassisted man could attain, and seeking to frame their conceptions simply by the deductions of their reason. Such, Cosmas assures us, is not the course he would pursue. "To the law and to the testimony" was his appeal, and he doubted not that he could evolve from their pages a system far more correct than any that pagan wisdom could attain.

The system of the universe of which remarks to this effect form the prelude may be briefly stated. According to Cosmas, the world is a flat parallelogram. Its length, which should be measured from east to west, is the double of its breadth, which should be measured from north to south. In the centre is the earth we inhabit, which is surrounded by the ocean, and this again is encircled by another earth, in which men lived before the deluge, and from which Noah was transported in the ark. To the north of the world is a high conical mountain, around which the sun and moon continually revolve. When the sun is hid behind the mountain, it is night; when it is on our side of the mountain, it is day. To the edges of the outer earth the sky is glued. It consists of four high walls rising to a great height and then meeting in a vast concave roof, thus forming an immense edifice of which our world is the floor. This edifice is divided into two stories by the firmament which is placed between the earth and the roof of the sky. A great ocean is inserted in the side of the firmament remote from the earth. This is what is signified by the waters that are above the firmament. The space from these waters to the roof of the sky is allotted to the blest; that from the firmament to our earth to the angels, in their character of ministering spirits.

The reader will probably not regard these opinions as prodigies of scientific wisdom; but the point with which we are especially concerned is the manner they were arrived at. In order to show this, it will be necessary to give a few samples of the arguments of Cosmas.

In the account of the six days' creation, it will be remembered, the whole work is summed up in a single sentence, "This is the book of the generation of the heaven and the earth." These expressions are evidently intended to comprise everything that is contained in the heaven and the earth. But, as Cosmas contended, if the doctrine of the Antipodes were correct, the sky would surround and consequently contain the earth, and therefore it would only be said, "this is the book of the generation of the sky."[1] This very simple argument was capable of great extension, for there was scarcely any sacred writer who had not employed the phrase "the heaven and the earth" to include the whole creation, and who had not thus implied that one of them did not include the other. Abraham, David, Hosea, Isaiah, Zechariah, and many others, were cited. Even Melchisedec had thus uttered his testimony against the Antipodes. If we examine the subject a little further, we are told that the earth

---

[1] This work is published in the Benedictine edition of the Greek Fathers (Paris, 1706), tom. ii. I have quoted the Benedictine Latin translation. In his preface, Montfaucon has collected a long chain of passages from the Fathers denying the existence of the Antipodes.

[2] Lib. i. prologus 2.

[1] "Ait, 'Hic est liber generationis cœli et terræ,' quasi omnia iis contineantur, et universa quæ in eis sunt cum illis significentur   Nam si secundum fucatos illos Christianos cœlum tantummodo universa contineat, terram cum cœlo non nominasset, sed dixisset 'Hic est liber generationis cœli.'" (P. 126.)

is fixed firmly upon its foundations, from which we may at least infer that it is not suspended in the air ; and we are told by St. Paul, that all men are made to live upon the " face of the earth," from which it clearly follows that they do not live upon more faces than one, or upon the back. With such a passage before his eyes, a Christian, we are told, should not "even speak of the Antipodes."

Such arguments might be considered a conclusive demonstration of the falseness of the Manichæan doctrine. It remained to frame a correct theory to fill its place. The first great point of illumination that meets us in this task, consists in the fact that St. Paul more than once speaks of the earth as a tabernacle.[1] From this comparison some theologians, and Cosmas among the number, inferred that the tabernacle of Moses was an exact image of our world. This being admitted, the paths of science were greatly simplified. The tabernacle was a parallelogram twice as long from east to west, as from north to south, and covered over as a room. Two remarkable passages, mistranslated in the Septuagint, in one of which Isaiah is made to compare the heavens to a vault, and in the other of which Job speaks of the sky as glued to the earth, completed the argument,[2] and enabled the writer to state it almost with the authority of an article of faith.[3]

It is easy to perceive how fatal such systems of interpretation must have been to scientific progress. It is indeed true that Cosmas belongs to a period when the intellectual decadence had already begun, that he was himself à writer of no very great abilities, and that some of the more eminent Fathers had treated the subject of the Antipodes with considerable good sense, contending that it was not a matter connected with salvation.[4]

But still, from the very beginning, the principles of which this book forms an extreme example were floating through the Church. The distinction between theology and science was entirely unfelt. The broad truth which repeated experience has now impressed on almost every unprejudiced student, that it is perfectly idle to quote a passage from the Bible as a refutation of any discovery of scientific men, or to go to the Bible for information on any scientific subject, was altogether undreamed of,[1] and in exact proportion to the increase of European superstition did the doctrine of inspiration dilate till it crushed every department of the human intellect. Thus, when in the middle of the eighth century an Irish saint, named St. Virgilius, who was one of the very few men who then cultivated profane sciences, ventured in Bavaria to assert the existence of the Antipodes, the whole religious world was thrown into a paroxysm of indignation, St. Boniface heading the attack, and Pope Zachary, at least for a time, encouraging it. At last men sailed to the Antipodes, and they then modified their theological opinions on the subject. But a precisely similar contest recurred when the Copernican system was promulgated. Although the discovery of Copernicus was at first uncensured, and his book— which was published in 1543—dedicated to Pope Paul III., as soon as its views had acquired some weight among the learned, the suspicions of the Roman theologians were aroused, and the opinion of the motion of the earth was authoritatively censured, first of all in the person of Copernicus and two of his disciples,[2] and seventeen years later by

---

[1] Cosmas inferred this from fanciful interpretations of Heb. viii. 1, 2 ; ix. 1, 2, 11, 12, 24.

[2] These were Isaiah xl, 22, and Job xxxviii. 38. The first was translated δ στήσας τὸν οὐρανὸν ὡς καμάραν. The second, οὐρανὸν δὲ εἰς γῆν ἔκλίνε, κέχυται δὲ ὥσπερ γῆ κονία, κεκόλληκα δὲ αὐτὸν ὥσπερ λίθῳ κύβον.

[3] "Sic igitur et nos quemadmodum Hesaias figuram primi cœli prima die conditi cum terra facti, cum terra universum complectendi ad fornicis figuram adornati statuimus esse. Ac quemadmodum in Job dictum est cœlum conglutinatum esse terræ, ita quoque nos dicimus. Itemque cum ex Moyse didicerimus terram magis quoad longitudinem extendi, id nos quod fatemur gnari, scilicet Scripturæ divinæ credendum." (P. 129.)

[4] This very liberal opinion had been expressed by Basil and Ambrose.

---

[1] This doctrine began to dawn upon a few minds during the Copernican controversy. Those who desire to trace its history may read with interest some opinions on the subject that were collected and answered by a contemporary writer on the question between Galileo and the Church (Libertus Fromundus, Vesta, sive Anti-Aristarchi Vindex : Antverpiæ, 1634). As I shall have occasion again to quote Fromundus, I may mention that he was a professor and doctor of theology at Louvain, that he was the author of a work on meteorology, in which he combated very forcibly the notion that atmospheric changes were the results of spiritual intervention, which Bodin had lately been defending ; and that he was on the whole by no means a superstitious man, except on the subject of comets, of the prophetic character of which he was, I believe, a strenuous advocate. He wrote, in conjunction with a theologian named Fieni, a book about comets, which I have never been fortunate enough to meet with. He was one of the principal defenders of the immobility of the earth, and his works are full of curious information on the theological aspect of the subject. He died in 1653.

[2] The first condemnation was in 1616, and was

the condemnation and the imprisonment of Galileo.

It is, indeed, marvellous that science should ever have revived, amid the fearful obstacles theologians cast in her way. Together with a system of Biblical interpretation so stringent, and at the same time so capricious, that it infallibly came into collision with every discovery that was not in accordance with the unaided judgments of the senses, and therefore with the familiar expressions of the Jewish writers, everything was done to cultivate a habit of thought the direct opposite of the habits of science. The constant exaltation of blind faith, the countless miracles, the childish legends, all produced a condition of besotted ignorance, of grovelling and trembling credulity that can scarcely be paralleled except among the most degraded barbarians. Innovation of every kind was regarded as a crime ; superior knowledge excited only terror and suspicion. If it was shown in speculation, it was called heresy. If it was shown in the study of nature, it was called magic. The dignity of the Popedom was unable to save Gerbert from the reputation of a magician,[1] and the magnificent labours of

Roger Bacon were repaid by fourteen years' imprisonment, and many others of less severe but unremitting persecution. Added to all this, the overwhelming importance attached to theology diverted to it all those intellects which in another condition of society would have been employed in the investigations of science. When Lord Bacon was drawing his great chart of the field of knowledge, his attention was forcibly drawn to the torpor of the middle ages. That the mind of man should so long have remained tranced and numbed seemed, at first sight, an objection to his theories, a contradiction to his high estimate of human faculties. But his answer was prompt and decisive. A theological system had lain like an incubus upon Christendom, and to its influence, more than to any other single cause, the universal paralysis is to be ascribed.[1]

At last the revival of learning came, the regeneration of physical science speedily followed it, and it soon effected a series of most important revolutions in our conceptions.

The first of these was to shake the old view of the position of man in the universe. To an uncivilised man, no proposition appears more self-evident than that our world is the great central object of the universe. Around it the sun and moon appear alike to revolve, and the stars seem but inconsiderable lights destined to garnish its firmament. From this conception there naturally followed a crowd of superstitions which occupy a conspicuous place in the belief of every early civilisation. Man being the centre of all things, every startling phenomenon has some bearing upon his acts. The eclipse, the comet, the meteor, and the tempest, are all intended for him. The whole history of the universe centres upon him, and all the dislocations and perturbations it exhibits are connected with his history.[2]

provoked by the book of a Carmelite, named Foscarini, in defence of the Copernican view. The cardinals of the Congregation of the Index, whose function it is to pronounce authoritatively in the name of the Church on the orthodoxy of new books, then issued a decree, of which the following is the principal part : " Quia ad notitiam Sanctæ Congregationis pervenit falsam illam doctrinam Pythagoricam, divinæque Scripturæ omnino adversantem, de mobilitate terræ et immobilitate solis, quam Nicolaus Copernicus *Revolutionibus Orbium cælestium*, et Didacus Astunica in *Job*, etiam docent, jam divulgari et multis recipi, sicuti videre est ex quâdam epistolâ impressâ cujusdam P. Carmelitæ, cujus titulus *Letera del R. P. Maestro Paolo Foscarini sopra l'Opinione dei Pythagorici e del Copernico*, &c., in quâ dictus pater ostendere conatur præfatam doctrinam de immobilitate solis in centro mundi et mobilitate terræ consonam esse veritati, et non adversari Sacræ Scripturæ : ideo, ne ulterius hujusmodi opinio in perniciem Catholicæ veritatis serpat, censuit dictos hic Copernicum *de Revolut. Orbium* et Didacum Astunicam in *Job* suspendendos esse donec corrigantur. Librum vero P. Paulli Foscarini Carmelitæ omnino prohibendum, atque omnes alios libros pariter idem docentes prohibendos."—Fromundus, *Anti-Aristarchus, sive Orbis Terræ immobilis. In quo Decretum S. Congregationis S. R. E. Cardinal.* 1616 *adversus Pythagorico-Copernicanos editum defenditur* (Antverpiæ, 1631), p. 18.
[1] Sylvester II. He was the first Frenchman who sat on the throne of Peter, the reputed author of Gallican opinions, and it is said the ablest mathematician and mechanician of his time. He died in 1003. Among other things, he invented a kind of clock. He had also a statue, like that of Roger Bacon, which answered all his questions. According to the popular legend, he was in communion with the devil, who raised him successively to the sees of Rheims, Ravenna, and Rome ; and promised that he should never die till he had been at Jerusalem, which Gerbert construed as a

promise of immortality. But, like that made to Henry IV. of England, it proved to be a cheat, and the Pope felt the hand of death upon him while officiating in the Chapel of Jerusalem, in the Basilica of St, Croce. The legend goes on to say that, struck by remorse, he ordered his body to be cut in pieces, to be placed on a car driven by oxen, and to be buried wherever they stopped of themselves, he being unworthy to rest in the church of God. But, to show that pardon may be extended even to the most guilty, the oxen stopped at the door of the Lateran. Whenever, it is said, a pope is about to die, the tomb of Sylvester grows moist, and the bones of the old magician clatter below. (See Gregorovius, *On the Tombs of the Popes ;* and the original account in Matthew of Westminster, anno 998.)
[1] *Novum Organon.*
[2] Even the sun and stars were supposed to shine with

The science which especially corrects these notions is astronomy, but for a considerable period it rather aggravated them, for it was at first inseparably blended with astrology. It is an extremely ingenious and, at least as far as the period of the revival of learning is concerned, an extremely just observation of M. Comte, that this last study marks the first systematic effort to frame a philosophy of history by reducing the apparently capricious phenomena of human actions within the domain of law.[1] It may, however, perhaps, be also regarded as one of the last struggles of human egotism against the depressing sense of insignificance which the immensity of the universe must produce. And certainly it would be difficult to conceive any conception more calculated to exalt the dignity of man than one which represents the career of each individual as linked with the march of worlds, the focus towards which the influences of the most sublime of created things continually converge.[2] But, notwithstanding this temporary aberration, there can be no doubt of the ultimate tendency of a science which proves that our world is but an infinitesimal fraction in creation, and which, by demonstrating its motion, shows that it is as undistinguished by its position as by its magnitude. The mental importance of such a discovery can hardly be overrated. Those who regard our earth as the centre of the material universe will always attribute to it a similar position in the moral scheme, and when the falsehood of the first position is demonstrated, the second appears incongruous or a difficulty.[3]

It has been reserved for the present [nineteenth] century and for a new science to add to the discovery of Copernicus and Galileo another which has not yet been fully realised, but is no doubt destined to exercise a similar and a commanding influence over all future systems of belief : I mean the discoveries of geology relating to the preadamite history of the globe. To those who regard the indefinite as the highest conception of the infinite, the revelation of eternity is written on the rocks as the revelation of immensity upon the stars. But to more scientific minds the most important effect of geology has not been that it throws back to an incalculable distance the horizon of creation, nor yet that it has renovated and transformed all the early interpretations of the Mosaic cosmogony ; but that it has conclusively disproved what was once the universal belief concerning the origin of death. That this fearful calamity appeared in the universe on account of the transgression of man, that every pang that convulses the frame of any created being, every passion or instinct or necessity that contributes to the infliction of suffering, is but the fruit of the disobedience in Paradise, was long believed with unfaltering assurance, and is even now held by many who cannot be regarded as altogether uneducated. And this general proposition became a great archetype, a centre around which countless congenial beliefs were formed, a first principle or measure of probability guiding the predispositions of men in all their enquiries. If all death and all pain resulted from the sin of Adam, it was natural to give every particular instance of death or pain a special signification ; and if these, the greatest of terrestrial imperfections, were connected with the history of man, it was natural to believe that all minor evils were no less so. But geology has now

<hr/>

a feebler light since the Fall (St. Isidore, *De Ordine Creaturarum*, cap. v.). On the effects of man's sin on the vegetable world, see St. Augustine, *De Genesi*, lib. i. cap. 13.
[1] I have already mentioned the bold attempt of Peter of Abano, in the beginning of the fourteenth century, to construct, by the aid of astrology, a philosophy of religions. Cardan, too, cast the horoscope of Christ, and declared that all the fortunes of Christianity were predicted by the stars. Vanini adopted a somewhat similar view. (Durand, *Vie de Vanini*, pp. 93-99.) Pomponazzi attempted to explain the phenomena of magic by the influence of the stars (*Biog. Univ.* art. *Pomponazzi*); and Bodin, in the very greatest political work of the sixteenth century, having raised the question whether it is possible to discover any principle of order presiding over the development of societies, maintains that such a principle can only be revealed by astrology. (*République*, liv. iv. c. 2.)
[2] As a poet expresses it :—
  "The warrior's fate is blazoned in the skies ;
  A world is darkened when a hero dies."
[3] Whatever may be thought of its justice, there cannot be two opinions about the exquisite beauty of

the suggestion by which Dr. Chalmers sought to meet this difficulty—that the parable of the shepherd leaving the ninety-nine sheep to seek that which had gone astray, is but a description of the act of the Deity seeking to reclaim the single world that had revolted against Him, as though it were of more importance than all that had remained faithful. It may be added that astronomy itself furnishes a striking illustration of the danger of trusting too implicitly to our notions of the fitness of things. The ancient astronomers unanimously maintained that the motions of the celestial bodies must necessarily be circular and uniform, because they regarded that as the most perfect kind of movement ; and the persistence with which this notion was held, till it was overthrown by Kepler, was one of the chief obstacles to astronomical progress.

proved decisively that a profound error
lurks in these conclusions. It has proved
that countless ages before man trod this
earth death raged and revelled among its
occupants, that it so entered into the
original constitution of things that the
agony and the infirmity it implies were
known as at present when the mastodon
and the dinotherium were the rulers of
the world. To deny this is now impossible ; to admit it is to abandon one
of the root-doctrines of the past.

A second kind of influence which
scientific discoveries have exercised upon
belief has been the gradual substitution
of the conception of law for that of supernatural intervention. This substitution I
have already had occasion to refer to
more than once, but I trust the reader
will pardon me for reverting to it for a
moment, in order to show with more
precision than I have hitherto done the
extent and nature of the change. It is
the especial characteristic of uncivilised
men that their curiosity and, still more,
their religious sentiments, are very rarely
excited by those phenomena which fall
obviously within the range of natural
laws, while they are keenly affected by all
that appear abnormal. It is indeed true
that this expression " natural law " has to
the uncivilised man only a very vague and
faint signification, that he has no conception of the close connection subsisting
between different classes of phenomena,
and that he frequently attributes each
department even of those which are most
regular to the action of special presiding
spirits ; yet still certain phenomena are
recognised as taking place in regular
sequences, while others appear capricious,
and the latter are associated especially
with divine intervention. Thus comets,
meteors, and atmospheric phenomena
were connected with religious ideas long
after the sun and the stars. Thus, too,
games of chance were from a very early
period prohibited, not simply on account
of the many evils that result from them,
but as a species of blasphemy, being an
appeal on trivial matters to the adjudication of the Deity.[1] Man being unable to

calculate how the die will fall, it was
believed that this is determined by a
divine interposition, and accordingly the
casting of lots became one of the favourite
means of approaching the Deity.[1]

From this habit of associating religious
feelings chiefly with the abnormal, two
very important consequences ensued, one
of them relating to science and the other
to theology. In the first place, as long
as abnormal and capricious phenomena
are deemed the direct acts of the Deity,
all attempts to explain them by science
will be discouraged ; for such attempts
must appear an irreverent prying into the
divine acts, and, if successful, they
diminish the sources of religious emotion.[2]
In the second place, it is evident that the
conception of the Deity in an early period
of civilisation must be materially different
from that in a later period. The consciousness of the divine presence in an
unscientific age is identified with the idea
of abnormal and capricious action ; in a
scientific age it is consistent with that of
regular and unbroken law. The forms of
religious emotion being very different,
the conceptions of the Deity around which
they centre must be equally so. The one
conception consists mainly of the ideas of
interference, of miracle, of change, and
of caprice ; the other of regularity, of
immutability, of prescience, and of moral
perfection.

The first science that rose to perfection
at the period I am referring to was
astronomy, which early attained a great
prominence on account of the revival of
astrology that had been produced in the
fourteenth century by the renewed study
of the works of pagan antiquity, and
perhaps still more by the profound influence the Arabian intellect then exercised on Christendom. The great work
of Copernicus, the almost simultaneous
appearance of Kepler, Galileo, and Tycho
Brahe, and the invention and rapid improvement of the telescope, soon introduced

---

[1] See a clear view of the old opinions on this subject
in Barbeyrac, *De la Nature du Sort* (Amsterdam, 1714),
who sustained an ardent controversy on the subject
with a Dutch divine. The first writer, I believe, who
clearly and systematically maintained that lots were
governed by purely natural laws was an English
Puritan minister named Gataker, in a work *On the
Nature and Use of Different Kinds of Lots* (London,
1619)—a well-reasoned and curious book, teeming with
quaint learning.

[1] Hence the term "sortes" was applied to oracles.
Hence, too, such words as "sortilegi," "sorcerers."

[2] Thus De Maistre, speaking of the ancients, says :
—" Leur physique est à peu près nulle. Car non-
seulement ils n'attachaient aucun prix aux expériences
physiques, mais ils les méprisaient, et même ils y attachaient je ne sais quelle légère idée d'impiété ; *et ce
sentiment confus venait de bien haut.*" (*Soirées de St.-
Pétersbourg*, 5me entretien.) This is the true spirit of
superstition. Speaking of earthquakes, Cosmas says :
—" Quod vero terra moveatur id non a vento fieri
dicimus ; non enim fabulas comminiscimur ut illi, sed
illud jussu Dei fieri pronuntiamus, *nec curiose rem
perquirimus*, ait quippe Scriptura per Davidem, ' Qui
respicit terram et facit eam tremere,' &c."—p. 115.

the conception of natural law into what had long been the special realm of superstition. The Theory of Vortices of Descartes, although it is now known to have no scientific value, had, as has been truly said, a mental value of the very highest order, for it was the first attempt to form a system of the universe by natural law and without the intervention of spiritual agents.[1] Previously the different motions of the heavenly bodies had been for the most part looked upon as isolated, and the popular belief was that they, as well as all atmospheric changes, were effected by angels.[2] In the Talmud a special angel was assigned to every star and to every element, and similar notions were general throughout the middle ages.[3] The belief in the existence of a multitude of isolated and capricious phenomena naturally suggested the belief in angels to account for them, and on the other hand the association of angels with phenomena that obtruded themselves constantly on the attention produced a vivid sense of angelic presence, which was shown in the countless legends of angelic manifestations. All this passed away before the genius of Descartes and of Newton. The reign of law was recognised as supreme, and the conceptions that grew out of the earlier notion of the celestial system waned and vanished.

For a long time, however, comets continued to be the refuge of the dying superstition. Their rarity, the eccentricity of their course, the difficulty of ascertaining their nature, and the grandeur and terror of their aspect, had all contributed to impress men with an extraordinary sense of their supernatural character. From the earliest ages they had been regarded as the precursors of calamity, and, men being accustomed to regard them in that light, a vast mass of evidence was soon accumulated in support of the belief. It was shown that comets had preceded the death of such rulers as Cæsar, or Constantine the Great, or Charles V. Comets were known to have appeared before the invasion of Greece by Xerxes, before the Peloponnesian War, before the civil wars of Cæsar and Pompey, before the fall of Jerusalem, before the invasion of Attila, and before a vast number of the greatest famines and pestilences that have afflicted mankind.[1] Many hundreds of cases of this kind were collected, and they furnished an amount of evidence which was quite sufficient to convince even somewhat sceptical minds, at a time when the supernatural character of comets harmonising with the prevailing notions of the government of the universe appeared antecedently probable. Some theologians indeed, while fully acknowledging the ominous character of these apparitions, attempted to explain them in a somewhat rationalistic manner. According to their view, comets were masses of noxious vapour—exhaled, some said from the earth, and others from the sky—which by tainting the atmosphere produced pestilence. Kings were indeed especially liable to succumb beneath this influence, but this was only because their labours and their luxurious habits rendered them weaker than other men.[2] Usually, however, comets were simply regarded as supernatural warnings sent to prognosticate calamity. Two or three great men made vain efforts to shake the belief. Thus, during one of the panics occasioned by a great comet, Paracelsus wrote forcibly against the popular notions,[3] which he assailed on theological grounds as forming a species of fatalism, and as being inconsistent with the belief in Providence. In the midst of a similar panic in 1680, Bayle made a similar effort; but, in obedience to the spirit of the age, he adopted not a theological but a philosophical point of view. He displayed with consummate skill the weakness of a process of reasoning which rested on an arbitrary selection of chance coincidences, and he made the subject the text for an admirable book on the gradual consolidation of superstitions.[4] But theo-

---

[1] This was originally a remark of St. Simon, but it has been adopted and made great use of by M. Comte and some of his disciples. See that very able book, Littré, *Vie de Comte.*

[2] Roccamora, *De Cometis*, p. 17; St. Isidore, *De Ordine Creaturarum.*

[3] Maury, *Légendes pieuses*, pp. 17-18. Angels were sometimes represented in old Christian painting and sculpture bearing along the stars (and especially the Star of Bethlehem) in their hands. See, *e.g.*, a very curious old bas-relief round the choir of Notre Dame at Paris.

[1] The fullest statement of the evidence of the prophetic character of comets I have met with is in Raxo, *De Cometis* (1578). The author was a Spanish physician.

[2] Roccamora, *De Cometis* (Romæ, 1670), pp. 238-239.

[3] In a letter to Zuinglius.

[4] And, flying off at a tangent from his main subject, for an admirable dissertation on the relation between religion and morals. With the greatest possible admiration for the *Critical Dictionary*, which will be always regarded as one of the most stupendous monuments of erudition and of critical acumen ever bequeathed by a single scholar, I cannot but think that the original genius of Bayle shines still more brightly

logy and philosophy were alike impotent till science appeared to assist them. Halley predicted the revolution of comets, and they were at once removed to the domain of law, and one of the most ancient of human superstitions was destroyed.

The process which took place in astronomy furnishes but a single though perhaps an extreme example of that which, in the seventeenth century, took place in every field of science. Everywhere the rapid conquests of the new spirit were substituting the idea of natural law for that of supernatural interference, and persuading men that there must be a natural solution even where they were unable to discover it. The writings of Bacon, although their influence has, I think, been considerably exaggerated, partly through national pride, and partly because men have accepted too readily the very unfair judgments Bacon expressed of his contemporaries,[1] probably contributed more than any other single cause to guide the movement, and have, in England at least, become almost supreme. Chemistry disengaged itself from alchemy, as astronomy had done from astrology. The Academy del Cimento was established in Tuscany in 1657, the Royal Society in London in 1660, and the

in the *Contrains-les d'Entrer*, in some of the *Pensées diverses sur les Comètes*, and in two or three of his *Nouvelles Lettres*.
[1] The age of Bacon was certainly not as benighted and ignorant on scientific matters as he always represented it. On the contrary, when we remember that it was the age of Copernicus, Galileo, Tycho Brahe, Kepler, and Gilbert, it would be difficult to name one that was more distinguished. A large portion of the scientific revival in Europe may be justly ascribed to these great men; and the only apology that can be offered for the representations of Bacon is that, notwithstanding his great genius, he was totally unable to grasp their discoveries. The Copernican system—the greatest discovery of the age—he rejected to the last. The important discoveries of Gilbert about the magnet he treated not only with incredulity but with the most arrogant contempt. In measuring his influence, we have to remember that it was certainly not dominant outside England till that union between the English and French intellects that immediately preceded the French Revolution. Then, indeed, his philosophy exercised an immense and salutary influence upon the Continent; but Europe had not been sleeping till then. In Great Britain itself Bacon produced no perceptible effect upon the great school of literature and science that grew up beyond the Tweed; and even in England, where he had been almost omnipotent, two of the very greatest men stood apart from his disciples. The whole method and mental character of Newton was opposed to that of Bacon, and, as his biographer, Sir David Brewster, very forcibly contends, there is not the slightest reason to believe that Newton owed anything to his predecessor; while Harvey avowedly owed his great discovery to that doctrine of final causes which Bacon stigmatised as "barren, like a virgin consecrated to God that can bear no fruit."

Academy of Sciences at Paris in 1666. The many different sciences that were simultaneously cultivated not merely rescued many distinct departments of nature from superstition, but also by their continual convergence produced the conception of one all-embracing scheme of law, taught men habitually to associate the divine presence with order rather than with miracle, and accustomed them to contemplate with admiring reverence the evidence of design displayed in the minutest animalcule and in the most short-lived ephemera, and also the evidence of that superintending care which adapts a sphere of happiness for the weakest of created beings.

A very important consequence of this change was that theological systems lost much of their harsh and gloomy character. As long as men drew their notions of the Deity from what they regarded as the abnormal, their attention was chiefly concentrated upon disasters, for these are for the most part exceptional, while the principal sources of happiness are those which are most common. Besides, it is one of the most unamiable characteristics of human nature that it is always more impressed by terror than by gratitude. Accordingly the devotion of our ancestors was chiefly connected with storms and pestilences and famine and death, which were regarded as penal inflictions, and which consequently created an almost maddening terror. All parts of belief assumed a congenial hue till the miserable condition of man and the frightful future that awaited him became the central ideas of theology. But this, which in an early phase of civilisation was perfectly natural, soon passed away when modern science acquired an ascendency over theological developments: for the attention of men was then directed chiefly to those multitudinous contrivances which are designed for the well-being of all created things, while the terrorism once produced by the calamities of life was at least greatly diminished when they were shown to be the result of general laws interwoven with the whole system of the globe, and many of which had been in operation before the creation of man.

Another branch of scientific progress which I may notice on account of its influence upon speculative opinions is the rapid growth of a morphological conception of the universe. According to the great philosophers of the seventeenth century, our world was a vast and complicated mechanism called into existence and elaborated instantaneously in all its parts by the creative fiat of the Deity. In the last century, however, and still more in the present [nineteenth] century, the progress of chemistry, the doctrine of the interchange and indestructibility of forces, and the discoveries of geology, have greatly altered this conception. Without entering into such questions as that of the mutability of species, which is still pending, and which the present writer would be altogether incompetent to discuss, it will be admitted that in at least a large proportion of the departments of science the notion of constant transformation, constant progress under the influence of natural law from simple to elaborate forms, has become dominant. The world itself, there is much reason to believe, was once merely a vapour, which was gradually condensed and consolidated, and its present condition represents the successive evolutions of countless ages. This conception, which exhibits the universe rather as an organism than a mechanism, and regards the complexities and adaptations it displays rather as the results of gradual development from within than of an interference from without, is so novel, and at first sight so startling, that many are now shrinking from it with alarm, under the impression that it destroys the argument from design, and almost amounts to the negation of a Supreme Intelligence. But there can, I think, be little doubt that such fears are, for the most part, unfounded.[1] That matter is governed by mind, that the contrivances and elaborations of the universe are the products of intelligence, are propositions which are quite unshaken, whether we regard these contrivances as the results of a single momentary exercise of will, or of a slow, consistent, and regulated evolution. The proofs of a pervading and developing intelligence and the proofs of a co-ordinating and combining intelligence, are both untouched, nor can any conceivable progress of science in this direction destroy them. If the famous suggestion, that all animal and vegetable life is produced by a natural process of evolution from a single vital germ, were a demonstrated truth, we should still be able to point to

[1] See the remarks on the consistence of morphological conceptions with the doctrine of final causes in Whewell's *History of Scientific Ideas.*

the evidences of intelligence displayed in the measured and progressive development, in those exquisite forms so different from what blind chance could produce, and in the manifest adaptation of surrounding circumstances to the living creature, and of the living creature to surrounding circumstances. The argument from design would indeed be changed ; it would require to be stated in a new form, but it would be fully as cogent as before. Indeed it is, perhaps, not too much to say, that the more fully this conception of universal evolution is grasped, the more firmly a scientific doctrine of Providence will be established, and the stronger will be the presumption of a future progress.

The effects of this process which physical science is now undergoing are manifested very clearly in the adjacent field of history, in what may be termed the morphological conception of opinions —that is to say, in the belief that there is a law of orderly and progressive transformation to which our speculative opinions are subject, and the causes of which are to be sought in the general intellectual condition of society. As the main object of this whole book is to illustrate the nature and progress of this conception, it is not necessary to dwell upon it at present, and I advert to it simply for the purpose of showing its connection with the discoveries of science.

It will be remarked that in this, as in most other cases, the influence physical sciences have exercised over speculative opinions has not been of the nature of a direct logical proof displacing an old belief, but rather the attracting influence of a new analogy. As I have already had occasion to observe, an impartial examination of great transitions of opinions will show that they have usually been effected not by the force of direct arguments, not by such reasons as those which are alleged by controversialists and recorded in creeds, but by a sense of the incongruity or discordance of the old doctrines with other parts of our knowledge. Each man assimilates the different orders of his ideas. There must always be a certain keeping or congruity or analogy between them. The general measure of probability determines belief, and it is derived from many departments of knowledge. Hence it is that whenever the progress of enquiry introduces a new series of conceptions into physical science, which represents one aspect of the relations of the Deity to man, these conceptions, or at least something like them, are speedily transferred to theology, which represents another.

It must, however, be acknowledged, that there are some influences resulting from physical science which are deeply to be deplored, for they spring neither from logical arguments nor from legitimate analogies, but from misconceptions that are profoundly imbedded in our belief, or from fallacies into which our minds are too easily betrayed. The increased evidence of natural religion furnished by the innumerable marks of creative and co-ordinating wisdom which science reveals, can hardly be over-estimated,[1] nor can it be reasonably questioned that a world governed in all its parts by the interaction of fixed natural laws implies a higher degree of designing skill than a chaos of fortuitous influences irradiated from time to time by isolated acts of spiritual intervention. Yet still so generally is the idea of divine action restricted to that of miracle, that every discovery assigning strange phenomena their place in the symmetry of nature has to many minds an irreligious appearance, which is still further strengthened by the fact, that while physical science acquiesces in the study of laws as the limit of its research, even scientific men sometimes forget that the discovery of law is not an adequate solution of the problem of causes. When all the motions of the heavenly bodies have been reduced to the dominion of gravitation, gravitation itself still remains an insoluble problem. Why it is that matter attracts matter we do not know—we perhaps never shall know. Science can throw much light upon the laws that preside over the development of life ; but what life is, and what is its ultimate cause, we are utterly unable to say. The mind of man, which can track the course of the comet and measure the velocity of light, has hitherto proved incapable of explaining the existence of

the minutest insect or the growth of the most humble plant. In grouping phenomena, in ascertaining their sequences and their analogies, its achievements have been marvellous ; in discovering ultimate causes it has absolutely failed. An impenetrable mystery lies at the root of every existing thing. The first principle, the dynamic force, the vivifying power, the efficient causes of those successions which we term natural laws, elude the utmost efforts of our research. The scalpel of the anatomist and the analysis of the chemist are here at fault. The microscope, which reveals the traces of all-pervading, all-ordaining intelligence in the minutest globule, and displays a world of organised and living beings in a grain of dust, supplies no solution of the problem. We know nothing or next to nothing of the relations of mind to matter, either in our own persons or in the world that is around us ; and to suppose that the progress of natural science eliminates the conception of a first cause from creation, by supplying natural explanations, is completely to ignore the sphere and limits to which it is confined.

It must be acknowledged also, that as the increasing sense of law appears to many the negation of the reality, or at all events of the continuity, of the divine action, so an increased sense of the multiplicity of the effects of matter not unfrequently leads to a negation of the existence of mind. The mathematician so often cited, who maintained that the soul must be extension, and the fiddler who was convinced that it must be harmony, are scarcely exaggerated representatives of the tendency manifested by almost everyone who is much addicted to a single study to explain by it all the phenomena of existence. Nearly every science when it has first arisen has had to contend with two great obstacles—with the unreasoning incredulity of those who regard novelty as necessarily a synonym for falsehood, and with the unrestrained enthusiasm of those who, perceiving vaguely and dimly a new series of yet undefined discoveries opening upon mankind, imagine that they will prove a universal solvent. It is said that when, after long years of obstinate disbelief, the reality of the great discovery of Harvey dawned upon the medical world, the first result was a school of medicine which regarded man simply as an hydraulic machine, and found the principle of every

---

[1] Laplace, who has done more than anyone else to systematise arguments from probability, and who will certainly not be accused of any desire to subordinate science to theology, states the argument for design derived from the motions of the planetary bodies in the following almost bewildering terms : "Des phénomènes aussi extraordinaires ne sont point dus à des causes irrégulières. En soumettant au calcul leur probabilité, on trouve qu'il y a plus de deux cents mille milliards à parier contre un qu'ils ne sont point l'effet du hasard."—*Système du Monde*, liv. v. c. 6.

malady in imperfections of circulation.[1]
The same history has been continually reproduced. That love of symmetry which
makes men impatient to reduce all phenomena to a single cause, has been the
parent of some of the noblest discoveries,
but it has also, by the imperfect classifi-
cations it has produced, been one of the
most prolific sources of human error.
In the present day, when the study of the
laws of matter has assumed an extraordinary development, and when the relations between the mind and the body are
chiefly investigated with a primary view
to the functions of the latter, it is neither
surprising nor alarming that a strong
movement towards materialism should be
the consequence.

But putting aside these illegitimate
consequences, it appears that in addition
to the general effects of intellectual
advancement upon theological opinions
in enabling men more readily to conceive
the invisible, and thus rescuing them
from idolatry, and in enabling them to
spiritualise and elevate their ideal, and
thus emancipating them from anthropomorphism, that particular branch of intellectual progress which is comprised under
the name of physical science has exercised a distinct and special influence,
which has been partly logical but more
generally the assimilating influence of
analogy. It has displaced man's early
conception of the position of his world in
the universe, and of the relation of the
catastrophes it exhibits to his history.
It has substituted a sense of law for a
predisposition to the miraculous, and
taught men to associate the Deity with
the normal rather than with the abnormal.
It has in a great degree divested calamity
of its penal character, multiplied to an
incalculable extent the evidences of the
divine beneficence, and at the same time
fostered a notion of ordered growth
which has extended from the world of
matter to the world of mind.

These have been its chief effects upon
belief. It has also exercised a considerable influence upon the systems of Biblical interpretation by which that belief is
expressed. The first great impulse to
rationalistic Biblical criticism was probably given by the antagonism that was
manifested between the discovery of
Galileo and Scripture as it was interpreted by the host of theologians who
argued after the fashion of Cosmas.
New facts were discovered and therefore
a new system of interpretation was required, and men began to apply their
critical powers to the sacred writings for
the purpose of bringing them into conformity with opinions that had been
arrived at independently by the reason.
Each new discovery of science that bore
upon any Scriptural question, each new
order of tendencies evoked by the advance
of civilisation, produced a repetition of the
same process.

Probably the earliest very elaborate
example of this kind of interpretation was
furnished by a French Protestant, named
La Peyrère, in a book which was published in 1655.[1] The author, who fully
admitted though he endeavoured to restrict
the sphere of the miraculous, had been
struck by some difficulties connected with
the ordinary doctrine of Original Sin,
and by some points in which science
seemed to clash with the assertions of the
Old Testament ; and he endeavoured to
meet them by altogether isolating the
Biblical history from the general current
of human affairs. Adam, he maintained,
was not the father of the human race but
simply the progenitor of the Jews, and
the whole antediluvian history is only
that of a single people. Thus the
antiquity which the Eastern nations
claimed might be admitted, and the principal difficulties attending the Deluge
were dissolved. It was altogether a
mistake to suppose that death and sickness and suffering were the consequences
of the transgression. Adam had by this
act simply incurred spiritual penalties,
which descended upon the Jews. "In
the day thou eatest thou shalt die" could
not have been meant literally, because it
was not literally fulfilled ; nor can the
curse upon the serpent, because motion
of the serpent along the ground is precisely that which its conformation implies.
The existence of men who were not of
the family of Adam is shadowed ob-
scurely in many passages, but appears
decisively in the history of Cain, who
feared to wander forth lest men should
kill him, and who built a city at a time
when, according to the common view, he
was almost alone in the world.[2] The ming-

---

[1] Lemoine, *Le Vitalisme de Stahl*, p. 6.

[1] *Systema Theologicum ex Præ-Adamitarum Hypo-
thesi*, pars i. The second part never appeared.
[2] Some of La Peyrère's arguments on this point are
curiously far-fetched. Thus he asks why Abel should
have kept sheep if there were no robbers to be feared,

ling of the sons of God and the daughters of men means the intermarriage between the two races. The Deluge is an absolute impossibility if regarded as universal, but not at all surprising if regarded as a partial inundation.

Proceeding to the history of a later period, La Peyrère in the first place denies the Mosaic authorship of the Pentateuch. In defence of this position he urges the account of the death of Moses, and he anticipates several of those minute criticisms which in our own day have acquired so great a prominence. The phrase " These are the words which Moses spake beyond Jordan," the notice of the city which is called " Jair to the present day," the iron bedstead of Og still shown in Rabbath, the difficulties about the conquest of the Idumeans, and a few other passages, seem to show that the compilation of these books was long posterior to the time of Moses, while certain signs of chronological confusion which they evince render it probable that they are not homogeneous, but are formed by the fusion of several distinct documents. It should be observed, too, that they employ a language of metaphor and of hyperbole which has occasionally given rise to misapprehensions, special instances of providential guidance being interpreted as absolute miracles. Thus, for example, the wool of the Jewish flocks was quite sufficient to furnish materials for clothing in the desert ; and the assertion that the clothes of the Jews waxed not old is simply an emphatic expression of that extraordinary providence which preserved them from all want for forty years in the wilderness. At the same time, La Peyrère does not deny that the Jewish history is full of miracles, but he maintains very strongly that these were only local, and that the general course of the universe was never disturbed to effect them. The prolongation of the day at the command of Joshua was not produced by any alteration in the course of the earth or sun, but was simply an atmospheric phenomenon such as is sometimes exhibited in the Arctic regions.

The darkness at the crucifixion was also local ; the retrogression of the shadow on the sundial in the reign of Hezekiah did not result from a disturbance of the order of the heavenly bodies ; the light that stood over the cradle of Christ was a meteor, for a star could not possibly mark out with precision a house.

The author of this curious book soon after its publication became a Roman Catholic, and in consequence recanted his opinions ; but the school of Biblical interpretation of which he was perhaps the first founder continues actively to the present day. To trace its history in detail does not fall within the plan of the present work. It will be sufficient to say that there are two natural theories by which men have endeavoured to explain the rise of religions, and that each of these theories has in particular ages or countries or conditions of thought exercised a supreme ascendency.[1] The first method, which attributes religions to special and isolated causes, found its principal ancient representative in Euhemerus, who maintained that the pagan gods were originally illustrious kings, deified after death either by the spontaneous reverence of the people or by the cunning of the rulers,[2] and whose work, being translated by Ennius, is said to have contributed largely to that diffusion of scepticism in Rome which preceded the rise of Christianity. To this class of criticism belong also all attempts to explain miracles by imposture, or by optical delusions, or by the misconception of some natural phenomenon, or by any other isolated circumstance. The other method, which is called mythical, and which was adopted among the ancients by the Pythagoreans, the Neo-Platonists, and the Gnostics, regards different dogmatic systems as embodying religious sentiments or great moral conceptions that are generally diffused among mankind, or as giving a palpable and (so to speak) material form to the aspirations of the societies in which they spring up. Thus, while fully admitting that special circumstances have an important influence over the rise of opinions, the interpreters of this school seek the true efficient cause in the general intellectual atmosphere that is prevalent. They do not pretend to

and where Cain got the weapon with which he killed his brother. The existence of a race of men not descended from Adam was very strenuously maintained, towards the close of the last [eighteenth] century, by an eccentric member of the Irish Parliament, named Dobbs, in a very strange book called *A Short View of Prophecy.* It has also been advocated in America, with a view to the defence of negro slavery. Mr. Dobbs thought there was a race resulting from an intrigue of Eve with the Devil.

[1] See Denis, *Hist. des Idées morales dans l' Antiquité.*
[2] Locke, in his *Treatise on Government*, adopts very fully the theory of Euhemerus about the origin of the pagan divinities.

explain in detail how different miracles came to be believed, but they assert that in a certain intellectual condition phenomena which are deemed miraculous will always appear, and that the general character of those phenomena will be determined by the prevailing predisposition. The first of these schools of interpretation was general in the seventeenth and eighteenth centuries, and has been especially favoured by nations like the ancient Romans, or like the modern English and French, who are distinguished for a love of precise and definite conclusions ; while the second has been most prominent in the present [nineteenth] century, and in Germany.

It must, however, be admitted that the energy displayed in framing natural explanations of miraculous phenomena bears no proportion to that which has been exhibited in a criticism that is purely disintegrating and destructive. Spinoza, whose profound knowledge not only of the Hebrew language, but also of Rabbinical traditions and of Jewish modes of thought and expression, made him peculiarly competent for the task, set the example in his *Tractatus Theologico-Politicus*,[1] and Germany soon after plunged with great energy into the same career. But the fact which must, I think, especially strike the impartial observer is that these criticisms, in at least the great majority of cases, are carried on with a scarcely disguised purpose of wresting the Bible into conformity with notions that have been independently formed. The two writers who have done most to supply the principles of the movement are Lessing and Kant. The first emphatically asserts that no doctrine should be accepted as part of Scripture which is not in accordance with "reason," an expression which in the writings of modern German critics may be not unfairly regarded as equivalent to the general scope and tendency of modern thought.[2] The

doctrine of Kant is still more explicit According to him,[1] every dogmatic system, or, as he expresses it, every "ecclesiastical belief," should be regarded as the vehicle or envelope of "pure religion," or, in other words, of those modes of feeling which constitute natural religion. The ecclesiastical belief is necessary, because most men are unable to accept a purely moral belief unless it is, as it were, materialised and embodied by grosser conceptions. But the ecclesiastical belief being entirely subordinate to pure religion, it followed that it should be interpreted simply with a view to the latter—that is to say, all doctrines and all passages of Scripture should be regarded as intended to convey some moral lesson, and no interpretation, however natural, should be accepted as correct which collides with our sense of right.

The statement of this doctrine of Kant may remind the reader that in tracing the laws of the religious progress of societies I have hitherto dwelt only on one aspect of the subject. I have examined several important intellectual agencies which have effected intellectual changes, but have as yet altogether omitted the laws of moral development. In endeavouring to supply this omission, we are at first met by a school which admits, indeed, that the true essence of all religion is moral, but at the same time denies that there can be in this respect any principle of progress. Nothing, it is said, is so immutable as morals. The difference between right and wrong was always known, and on this subject our conceptions can never be enlarged. But if in the term moral be included not simply the broad difference between acts which are positively virtuous and those which are positively vicious, but also the prevailing ideal or standard of excellence, it is quite certain that morals exhibit as constant a progress as intellect, and it is probable that this progress has exercised as important an influence upon society. It is one of the most familiar facts that there are certain virtues that are higher than others, and that many of these belong exclusively to a highly developed civilisation.[2] Thus, that the love of truth

---

[1] Spinoza was, as far as I know, the first writer who dwelt much on the possible or probable falsification of some portions of the Old Testament by the insertion of wrong vowel-points, a subject which was a few years since investigated in a work on *Hebrew Interpolations*, by Dr. Wall, of Dublin University. Some of the remarks of Spinoza about the Jewish habit of speaking of the suggestions of their own minds as inspiration are still worth reading, but with these exceptions the value of the *Tractatus Theologico-Politicus* seems to me to be chiefly historical.

[2] See, on Lessing's views, a clear statement in Amand Sainte's *Hist. critique du Rationalisme en Allemagne*. Strauss, in the Introduction to his *Life of Jesus*, gives a vivid sketch of the progress of

German Rationalism, and the manner in which he there treats the subject of miracles illustrates very clearly the wide use made of the term "reason" in German criticism.

[1] See his *Religion within the Limits of the Reason*.

[2] This fact has been well noticed in some of the writings of Archbishop Whately.

is a virtue is a proposition which, stated simply, would have been probably accepted with equal alacrity in any age, but if we examine the extent to which it is realised we find a profound difference. We find that in an early period, while all the virtues of an uncompromising partisan are cordially recognised, the higher virtue, which binds men through a love of conscientious enquiry to endeavour to pursue an eclectic course when party and sectarian passions rage fiercely around them, is not only entirely unappreciated, but is almost impossible ; that it is even now only recognised by a very few who occupy the eminences of thought ; and that it must therefore be recognised by the multitude in proportion as they approach the condition of those few. Thus, the pursuit of virtue for its own sake is undoubtedly a higher excellence than the pursuit of virtue for the sake of attaining reward or avoiding punishment ; yet the notion of disinterested virtue belongs almost exclusively to the higher ranks of the most civilised ages, and exactly in proportion as we descend in the intellectual scale is it necessary to elaborate the system of rewards and punishments.

Humanity again, in theory, appears to be an unchangeable virtue, but if we examine its applications we find it constantly changing. Bull-baiting and bear-baiting and cock-fighting, and countless amusements of a similar kind, were once the favourite pastimes of Europe, were pursued by all classes even the most refined and the most humane, and were universally regarded as perfectly legitimate.[1] Men of the most distinguished excellence are known to have delighted in them. Had anyone challenged them as barbarous, his sentiments would have been regarded not simply as absurd, but as incomprehensible. There was, no doubt, no controversy upon the subject.[2]

Gradually, however, by the silent pressure of civilisation, a profound change passed over public opinion. It was effected, not by any increase of knowledge or by any process of definite reasoning, but simply by the gradual elevation of the moral standard. Amusements that were once universal passed from the women to the men, from the upper to the lower classes, from the virtuous to the vicious, till at last the Legislature interposed to suppress them, and a thrill of indignation is felt whenever it is discovered that any of them have been practised. The history of the abolition of torture, the history of punishments, the history of the treatment of the conquered in war, the history of slavery—all present us with examples of practices which in one age were accepted as perfectly right and natural, and which in another age were repudiated as palpably and atrociously inhuman. In each case the change was effected much less by any intellectual process than by a certain quickening of the emotions, and consequently of the moral judgments ; and if in any country we find practices at all resembling those which existed in England a century ago, we infer with certainty that that country has not received the full amount of civilisation. The code of honour which first represents and afterwards reacts upon the moral standard of each age is profoundly different. The

[1] For a full view of the extent to which these amusements were carried on and diversified in England, see Strutt's *Sports and Pastimes of the English People.* Sir Thomas More was accustomed to boast of his skill in throwing the "cock stele"; and, to the very last, bull-baiting was defended warmly by Canning, and with an almost passionate earnestness by Windham.

[2] As Macaulay, with characteristic antithesis, says :— "If the Puritans suppressed bull-baiting, it was not because it gave pain to the bull, but because it gave pleasure to the spectators." The long unsuccessful warfare waged by the Popes against Spanish bull-fighting forms a very curious episode in ecclesiastical history ; but its origin is to be found in the number of men who had been killed. An old theologian mentions that, in the town of Concha, a bull that had killed seven men became the object of the highest reverence, and the people were so gratified that a painting represent-

ing the achievement was immediately executed for the public square (Concina, *De Spectaculis,* p. 283). The writers who denounced Spanish bull-fighting contrasted it specially with that of Italy, in which the bull was bound by a rope, and which was therefore innocent (*Ibid.* p. 285). Bull-fighting was prohibited under pain of excommunication by Pius V., in 1567. In 1575, Gregory XIII. removed the prohibition except as regards ecclesiastics, who were still forbidden to frequent bull-fights, and as regards festal days, on which they were not to be celebrated. Some Spanish theologians having agitated much on this subject, Sixtus V., in 1586, confirmed the preceding bull. At last, in 1596, Clement VIII., moved by the remonstrance of the Spanish king and the discontent of the Spanish people, removed all prohibitions (in Spain) except those which rested on the monks, only enjoining caution. At present bull-fights are usually performed on festal days, and form part of most great religious festivals, especially those in honour of the Virgin ! On this curious subject full details are given in Thesauro, *De Pœnis Ecclesiasticis* (Romæ, 1640), and in Concina, *De Spectaculis* (Romæ, 1752). Among the Spanish opponents of bull-fighting was the great Jesuit Mariana. It is curious enough that perhaps the most sanguinary of all bull-fights was in the Coliseum of Rome, in 1333, when the Roman nobles descended into the arena and eighteen were killed (Cibrario, *Economia Politica,* vol. i. pp. 196-197) ; but the Pope was then at Avignon. Michelet has noticed that while bull-fighting was long extremely popular in Rome, the Romagna, and Spoleto, it never took root in Naples, notwithstanding the long domination of the Spaniards.

whole type of virtue in a rude warlike people is distinct from that of a refined and peaceful people, and the character which the latter would admire the former would despise. So true is this, that each successive stratum of civilisation brings with it a distinctive variation of the moral type. In the words of an illustrious historian, " if the archæologist can determine the date of a monument by the form of its capital, with much greater certainty can the psychological historian assign to a specific period a moral fact, a predominating passion, or a mode of thought, and can pronounce it to have been impossible in the ages that preceded or that followed. In the chronology of art the same forms have sometimes been reproduced, but in the moral life such a recurrence is impossible : its conceptions are fixed in their eternal place in the fatality of time."[1]

There is, however, one striking exception to this law in the occasional appearance of a phenomenon which may be termed moral genius. There arise from time to time men who bear to the moral condition of their age much the same relations as men of genius bear to its intellectual condition. They anticipate the moral standard of a later age, cast abroad conceptions of disinterested virtue, of philanthropy, or of self-denial that seem to bear no relation to the spirit of their time, inculcate duties and suggest motives of action that appear to most men altogether chimerical. Yet the magnetism of their perfections tells powerfully upon their contemporaries. An enthusiasm is kindled, a group of adherents is formed, and many are emancipated from the moral condition of their age. Yet the full effects of such a movement are but transient. The first enthusiasm dies away, surrounding circumstances resume their ascendency, the pure faith is materialised, encrusted with conceptions that are alien to its nature, dislocated, and distorted till its first features have almost disappeared. The moral teaching, being unsuited to the time, becomes inoperative until its appropriate civilisation has dawned, or at most it faintly and imperfectly filters through an accumulation of dogmas, and thus accelerates in some measure the arrival of the condition it requires.

From the foregoing considerations it is

not difficult to infer the relations of dogmatic systems to moral principles. In a semi-barbarous period, when the moral faculty or the sense of right is far too weak to be a guide of conduct, dogmatic systems interpose and supply men with motives of action that are suited to their condition, and are sufficient to sustain among them a rectitude of conduct that would otherwise be unknown. But the formation of a moral philosophy is usually the first step of the decadence of religions. Theology, then ceasing to be the groundwork of morals, sinks into a secondary position, and the main source of its power is destroyed. In the religions of Greece and Rome this separation between the two parts of religious systems was carried so far that the inculcation of morality at last devolved avowedly and exclusively upon the philosophers, while the priests were wholly occupied with soothsaying and expiations.

In the next place, any historical faith, as it is interpreted by fallible men, will contain some legends or doctrines that are contrary to our sense of right. For our highest conception of the Deity is moral excellence, and consequently men always embody their standard of perfection in their religious doctrines ; and as that standard is at first extremely imperfect and confused, the early doctrines will exhibit a corresponding imperfection. These doctrines being stereotyped in received formularies, for a time seriously obstruct the moral development of society, but at last the opposition to them becomes so strong that they must give way ; they are then either violently subverted or permitted to become gradually obsolete.

There is but one example of a religion which is not necessarily subverted by civilisation, and that example is Christianity. In all other cases the decay of dogmatic conceptions is tantamount to a complete annihilation of the religion, for although there may be imperishable elements of moral truth mingled with those conceptions, they have nothing distinctive or peculiar. The moral truths coalesce with new systems, the men who uttered them take their place with many others in the great pantheon of history, and the religion having discharged its functions is spent and withered. But the great characteristic of Christianity, and the great moral proof of its divinity, is that it has been the main source of the moral development of Europe, and that it

[1] Michelet.

has discharged this office not so much by the inculcation of a system of ethics, however pure, as by the assimilating and attractive influence of a perfect ideal. The moral progress of mankind can never cease to be distinctively and intensely Christian as long as it consists of a gradual approximation to the character of the Christian Founder. There is, indeed, nothing more wonderful in the history of the human race, than the way in which that ideal has traversed the lapse of ages, acquiring a new strength and beauty with each advance of civilisation, and infusing its beneficent influence into every sphere of thought and action. At first men sought to grasp by minute dogmatic definitions the divinity they felt. The controversies of the Homoousians or Monophysites or Nestorians or Patripassians, and many others whose very names now sound strange and remote, then filled the Church. Then came the period of visible representations. The handkerchief of Veronica, the portrait of Edessa, the crucifix of Nicodemus, the paintings of St. Luke,[1] the image traced by an angel's hand, which is still venerated at the Lateran, the countless visions narrated by the saints, show the eagerness with which men sought to realise as a palpable and living image their ideal. This age was followed by that of historical evidences, the age of Sebonde and his followers. Yet more and more with advancing years, the moral ideal stood out from all dogmatic conceptions, and it is no exaggeration to say, that at no former period was it so powerful, or so universally acknowledged, as at present. This is a phenomenon altogether unique in history; and to those who recognise in the highest type of excellence the highest revelation of the Deity, its importance is too manifest to be overlooked.

I trust the reader will pardon the tedious length to which this examination, which I would gladly have abridged, has extended. For the history of rationalism is quite as much a history of moral as of intellectual development, and any conception of it that ignores the former

must necessarily be mutilated and false. Nothing, too, can, as I conceive, be more erroneous or superficial than the reasonings of those who maintain that the moral element of Christianity has in it nothing distinctive or peculiar. The method of this school, of which Bolingbroke may be regarded as the type, is to collect from the writings of different heathen writers certain isolated passages embodying precepts that were inculcated by Christianity; and when the collection had become very large, the task was supposed to be accomplished. But the true originality of a system of moral teaching depends not so much upon the elements of which it is composed, as upon the manner in which they are fused into a symmetrical whole, upon the proportionate value that is attached to different qualities, or, to state the same thing by a single word, upon the type of character that is formed. Now it is quite certain that the Christian type differs not only in degree, but in kind, from the Pagan one.

In applying the foregoing principles to the history of Christian transformations, we should naturally expect three distinct classes of change. The first is the gradual evanescence of doctrines that clash with our moral sense. The second is the decline of the influence of those ceremonies, or purely speculative doctrines, which, without being opposed to conscience, are at least wholly beyond its sphere. The third is the substitution of the sense of right for the fear of punishment as the main motive to virtue.

I reserve the consideration of the first of these three changes for the ensuing chapter, in which I shall examine the causes of religious persecution, and shall endeavour to trace the history of a long series of moral anomalies in speculation which prepared the way for that great moral anomaly in practice. The second change is so evident, that it is not necessary to dwell upon it. No candid person who is acquainted with history can fail to perceive the difference between the amount of reverence bestowed in the present day, by the great majority of men, upon mere speculative doctrines or ritualistic observances, and that which was once general. If we examine the Church in the fourth and fifth centuries, we find it almost exclusively occupied with minute questions concerning the manner of the co-existence of the two natures in Christ. If we examine it in

---

[1] As Lami and Lanzi have shown, this legend probably resulted from a confusion of names; a Florentine monk, named Luca, of the eleventh century, being, there is much reason to believe, the chief author of the "portraits by St. Luke." They are not, however, all by the same hand, or of exactly the same age, though evidently copied from the same type. Others think they are Byzantine pictures brought to Italy during the time of the Iconoclasts and of the Crusades.

the middle ages, we find it absorbed in ritualism and pilgrimages. If we examine it at the Reformation, we find it just emerging beneath the pressure of civilisation from this condition; yet still the main speculative test was the doctrine concerning the Sacrament, which had no relation to morals; and the main practical test, on the Continent at least, was the eating of meat on Fridays.[1] In the present day, with the great body of laymen, such matters appear simply puerile, because they have no relation to morals.

The third change is one which requires more attention, for it involves the history of religious terrorism—a history of the deepest but most painful interest to all who study the intellectual and moral progress of Europe.

It would be difficult, and perhaps not altogether desirable, to attain in the present day to any realised conception of the doctrine of future punishment as it was taught by the early Fathers, and elaborated and developed by the mediæval priests. That doctrine has now been thrown so much into the background, it has been so modified and softened and explained away, that it scarcely retains a shadow of its ancient repulsiveness. It is sufficient to say that it was generally maintained that eternal damnation was the lot which the Almighty had reserved for an immense proportion of his creatures; and that that damnation consisted not simply of the privation of certain extra-

ordinary blessings, but also of the endurance of the most excruciating agonies. Perhaps the most acute pain the human body can undergo is that of fire; and this, the early Fathers assure us, is the eternal destiny of the mass of mankind. The doctrine was stated with the utmost literalism and precision. In the two first apologies for the Christian faith it was distinctly asserted. Philosophy, it was said, had sometimes enabled men to look with contempt upon torments, as upon a transient evil; but Christianity presented a prospect before which the stoutest heart must quail, for its punishments were as eternal as they were excruciating.[1] Origen, it is true, and his disciple Gregory of Nyssa, in a somewhat hesitating manner, diverged from the prevailing opinion, and strongly inclined to a figurative interpretation, and to the belief in the ultimate salvation of all;[2] but they were alone in their opinion. With these two exceptions, all the Fathers proclaimed the eternity of torments, and all defined those torments as the action of a literal fire upon a sensitive body.[3] When the pagans argued that a body could not remain for ever unconsumed in a material flame, they were answered by the analogies of the salamander, the asbestos, and the volcano; and by appeals to the Divine Omnipotence, which was supposed to be continually exerted to prolong the tortures of the dead.[4]

We may be quite sure that neither in the early Church, nor in any other period,

---

[1] In France especially the persecution on this ground was frightful. Thus, Bodin tells us that in 1539 the magistrates of Angers burnt alive those who were proved to have eaten meat on Friday if they remained impenitent, and hung them if they repented. (*Démon. des Sorciers*, p. 216.) In England the subject was regarded in a very peculiar light. Partly because Anglicanism clung closely to the Fathers, and partly because England was a maritime country, fasting was not only encouraged, but strictly enjoined; and a long series of laws and proclamations were accordingly issued between 1548 and the Restoration, enjoining abstinence on Wednesdays and Fridays, and throughout Lent; "considering that due and godly abstinence is a mean to virtue, and to subdue men's bodies of their souls and spirits; and considering, also, *especially*, that fishers, and men using the trade of fishing in the sea, may thereby the rather be set on work." See a list of these laws in Hallam's *Const. Hist.* vol. i. A homily also enjoins fasting on the same complex ground. There are some very good remarks on the tendency of theologians to condemn more severely error than immorality, and in condemning different errors to dwell most severely on those which are purely speculative, in Bayle, *Pensées diverses*, cxcix. He says: "Si un docteur de Sorbonne avoit la hardiesse de chanceler tant soit peu sur le mystère de l'Incarnation....il couroit risque du feu de la Grève; mais s'il se contentoit d'avancer quelques propositions de morale relâchée, comme le fameux Escobar, on se contenteroit de dire que cela n'est pas bien, et peut-être on verroit la censure de son livre."

[1] "Sic et Epicurus omnem cruciatum doloremque deprætiat modicum quidem contemptibilem pronuntiando magnum vero non diuturnum. Enimvero nos qui sub Deo omnium speculatore dispungimur, quique æternam ab eo pœnam providemus merito soli innocentiæ occurrimus et pro scientiæ plenitudine et pro magnitudine cruciatus non diuturni verum sempiterni." (Tertullian, *Apol.* cap. xlv.)
[2] The opinions of this last Father on the subject, which are very little known, are clearly stated in that learned book, Dallæus, *De Pœnis et Satisfactionibus* (Amsterdam, 1649), lib. iv. c. 7. For Origen's well-known opinions, see *Ibid.* lib. iv. c. 6.
[3] A long chain of quotations establishing this will be found in Swinden, *On the Fire of Hell* (London, 1727); and in Horberry's *Enquiry concerning Future Punishment* (London, 1744).
[4] See the long argument based on these grounds in St. Aug. *De Civ. Dei*, lib. xxi. cc. 1-9. Minutius Felix treats the same subject in a somewhat ferocious passage: "Ipse rex Jupiter per torrentes ripas et atram voraginem jurat religiose: destinatam enim sibi cum suis cultoribus pœnam præscius perhorrescit: nec tormentis aut modus ullus aut terminus. Illic sapiens ignis membra urit et reficit: carpit et nutrit sicut ignes fulminum corpora tangunt nec absumunt: sicut ignes Ætnæ et Vesuvii et ardentium ubique terrarum flagrant nec erogantur: ita pœnale illud incendium non damnis ardentium pascitur sed inexesa corporum laceratione nutritur." (*Octavius*, cap. xxxv.)

was this doctrine universally realised.
There must have been thousands who,
believing, or at least professing, that there
was no salvation except in the Church,
and that to be excluded from salvation
meant to be precipitated into an abyss of
flames, looked back nevertheless to the
memory of a pagan mother, who had
passed away, if not with a feeling of
vague hope, at least without the poignancy of despair. There must have been
thousands who, though they would perhaps have admitted with a Father that the
noblest actions of the heathen were but
" splendid vices," read nevertheless the
pages of the great historians of their
country with emotions that were very
little in conformity with such a theory.
Nor, it may be added, were these persons
those whose moral perceptions had been
least developed by contemplating the
gentle and tolerant character of the
Christian Founder. Yet still the doctrine
was stamped upon the theology of the
age, and, though it had not yet been
introduced into art, it was realised to a
degree which we at least can never reproduce ; for it was taught in the midst
of persecution and conflict, and it flashed
upon the mind with all the vividness of
novelty. Judaism had had nothing like
it. It seems now to be generally admitted that the doctrine of a future life,
which is often spoken of as a central conception of religion, was not included in
the Levitical revelation, or at least was so
faintly intimated that the people were
unable to perceive it.[1] During the captivity, indeed, the Jews obtained from
their masters some notions on the subject,
but even these were very vague, and the
Sadducees, who rejected the new doctrine
as an innovation, were entirely uncon-
demned. Indeed, it is probable that the
chosen people had less clear and correct

knowledge of a future world than any
other tolerably civilised nation of antiquity.
Among the early popular traditions of the
pagans, there were, it is true, some faint
traces of a doctrine of hell, which are said
to have been elaborated by Pythagoras,[1]
and especially by Plato, who did more
than any other ancient philosopher to
develop the notion of expiation ;[2] but
these, at the period of the rise of Christianity, had little or no influence upon the
minds of men ; nor had they ever presented the same characteristics as the
doctrine of the Church. For among the
pagans future torture was supposed to be
reserved exclusively for guilt, and for
guilt of the most extreme and exceptional
character. It was such culprits as
Tantalus, or Sisyphus, or Ixion, that
were selected as examples, and, excepting
in the mysteries,[3] the subject never seems
to have been brought very prominently
forward. It was the distinctive doctrine
of the Christian theologians, that sufferings more excruciating than any the
imagination could conceive were reserved
for millions, and might be the lot of the
most benevolent and heroic of mankind.
That religious error was itself the worst
of crimes, was before the Reformation
the universal teaching of the Christian
Church. Can we wonder that there were
some who refused to regard it as an
evangel?

If we pursue this painful subject into
the middle ages, we find the conception
of punishment by literal fire elaborated
with more detail. The doctrine, too, of a
purgatory even for the saved had grown
up. Without examining at length the
origin of this last tenet, it may be sufficient to say that it was a natural continuation of the doctrine of penance ; that
the pagan poets had had a somewhat
similar conception, which Virgil introduced into his famous description of the
regions of the dead ; that the Manichæans
looked forward to a strange process of
purification after death ;[4] and that some
of the Fathers appear to have held that

---

[1] This fact had been noticed by several early English
divines (Barrow and Berkeley among the number); but
it was brought into especial relief by Warburton, who,
as is well known, in his *Divine Legation*, based a
curious argument in favour of the divine origin of the
Levitical religion upon the fact that it contained no
revelation of a future world. Archbishop Whately,
who strongly took up the view of Warburton concerning the fact, has, in one of his *Essays on the
Peculiarities of the Christian Religion*, applied it very
skilfully to establishing the divine origin, not indeed of
Judaism, but of Christianity, because Christianity does
contain a revelation of the future world. Both these
writers contend that the well-known passage in Job
does not refer to the resurrection. The subject has
been dwelt on from another point of view by Chubb,
Voltaire, Strauss, and several other writers. On the
growth of the doctrine among the Jews, see Mackay's
Religious Development of the Greeks and Hebrews,
vol. ii. pp. 286-297.

[1] Denis, *Histoire des Idées morales dans l'Antiquité*,
tom. i. pp. 18, 19.
[2] *Ibid.* pp. 104-106.
[3] On the place representations of Tartarus had in
the mysteries, see Magnin, *Origines du Théâtre*,
tom. i. pp. 81-84.
[4] The Manichæans are said to have believed that the
souls of the dead were purified in the sun; that they
were then borne in the moon to the angels ; and that
the phases of the moon were caused by the increase or
diminution of the freight. (Beausobre, *Hist. critique
du Manichéisme*, tom. i. pp. 243-244.)

at the day of judgment all men must pass through a fire, though apparently rather for trial than for purification, as the virtuous and orthodox were to pass unscathed, while bad people and people with erroneous theological opinions were to be burnt.[1] Besides this, the doctrine perhaps softened a little the terrorism of eternal punishment, by diminishing the number of those who were to endure it; though, on the other hand, it represented extreme suffering as reserved for almost all men after death. It may be added that its financial advantages are obvious and undeniable.

There was in the ninth century one striking example of a theologian following in the traces of Origen, and, as far as I know, alone in the middle ages, maintaining the figurative interpretation of the fire of hell. This was John Scotus Erigena, a very remarkable man, who, as his name imports,[2] and as his contemporaries inform us, was an Irishman, and who appears to have led, for the most part, that life of a wandering scholar for which his countrymen have always been famous. His keen wit, his great and varied genius, and his knowledge of Greek, soon gained him an immense reputation. This last acquirement was then extremely rare, but it had been kept up in the Irish monasteries some time after it had disappeared from the other seminaries of Europe. Scotus threw himself with such ardour into both of the great systems of Greek philosophy, that some have regarded him principally as the last representative of Neo-Platonism, and others as the founder of Scholasticism.[3] He displayed on all questions a singular disdain for authority, and a spirit of the boldest free thought, which, like Origen, with whose works he was probably much imbued, he defended by a

lavish employment of allegories. Among the doctrines he disbelieved, and therefore treated as allegorical, was that of the fire of hell.[1]

Scotus, however, was not of his age. The material conceptions of mediævalism harmonised admirably with the material doctrine: and after the religious terrorism that followed the twelfth century, that doctrine attained its full elaboration. The agonies of hell seemed then the central fact of religion, and the perpetual subject of the thoughts of men. The whole intellect of Europe was employed in illustrating them. All literature, all painting, all eloquence, was concentrated upon the same dreadful theme. By the pen of Dante and by the pencil of Orcagna, by the pictures that crowded every church, and the sermons that rang from every pulpit, the maddening terror was sustained. The saint was often permitted in visions to behold the agonies of the lost, and to recount the spectacle he had witnessed. He loved to tell how by the lurid glare of the eternal flames he had seen millions writhing in every form of ghastly suffering, their eyeballs rolling with unspeakable anguish, their limbs gashed and mutilated and quivering with pain, tortured by pangs that seemed ever keener by the recurrence, and shrieking in vain for mercy to an unpitying heaven. Hideous beings of dreadful aspect and of fantastic forms hovered around, mocking them amid their torments, casting them into cauldrons of boiling brimstone, or inventing new tortures more subtle and more refined. Amid all this a sulphur stream was ever seething, feeding and intensifying the waves of fire. There was no respite, no alleviation, no hope. The tortures were ever varied in their character, and they never palled for a moment upon the sense. Sometimes, it was said, the flames while retaining their intensity withheld their light. A shroud of darkness covered the scene, but a ceaseless shriek of anguish attested the agonies that were below.[2]

---

[1] Dallæus, *De Pœnis et Satisfactionibus*, lib. iv. c. 9. Some of the ancients had a notion about fire being the portal of the unseen world. Herodotus (lib. v. c. 92) tells a curious story about Periander, a tyrant of Corinth, who invoked the shade of his wife; but she refused to answer his questions, alleging that she was too cold; for though dresses had been placed in her tomb, they were of no use to her, as they had not been burnt.

[2] Scoti was at first the name of the Irish; it was afterwards shared and finally monopolised by the inhabitants of Scotland. Erigena means born in Erin —the distinctive name of Ireland. There is an amusing notice of Scotus Erigena in Matthew of Westminster (an. 880).

[3] He is regarded in the first light by M. Guizot in his *History of Civilisation;* and in the second by M. St.-René Taillandier, in his able and learned treatise on Scotus.

[1] On the doctrines of Scotus, and especially on that about hell, see Taillandier, *Scot. Érigène*, pp. 176-180; Ampère, *Hist. littéraire de la France*, tom. iii. p. 95; Alexandri *Hist. Eccles.* tom. vi. pp. 361-363. According to this last writer, Scotus admitted literal torments for the devil, but not for man.

[2] The details of many of these visions are given in their full force in Swinden; and in Plancey, *Dictionnaire infernal*, art. *Enfer*. Dean Milman, in his *Hist. of Latin Christianity*, has noticed this passion for detailed pictures of hell (which seems to date from St Gregory the Great) with his usual force and justice.

It is useless to follow the subject into detail. We may reproduce the ghastly imagery that is accumulated in the sermons and in the legends of the age. We may estimate the untiring assiduity with which the Catholic priests sought in the worst acts of human tyranny, and in the dark recesses of their own imaginations, new forms of torture, to ascribe them to the Creator. We can never conceive the intense vividness with which these conceptions were realised, or the madness and the misery they produced. For those were ages of implicit and unfaltering credulity ; they were ages when none of the distractions of the present day divided the intellect, and when theology was the single focus upon which the imagination was concentrated. They were ages, too, when the modern tendency to soften or avoid repulsive images was altogether unknown, and when, in the general paralysis of the reason, every influence was exerted to stimulate the imagination. Wherever the worshipper turned, he was met by new forms of torture, elaborated with such minute detail, and enforced with such a vigour and distinctness, that they must have clung for ever to the mind, and chilled every natural impulse towards the Creator. How, indeed, could it be otherwise ? Men were told that the Almighty, by the fiat of his uncontrolled power, had called into being countless millions whom He knew to be destined to eternal, excruciating, unspeakable agony ; that He had placed millions in such a position that such agony was inevitable ; that He had prepared their place of torment, and had kindled its undying flame ; and that, prolonging their lives for ever, in order that they might be for ever wretched, He would make the contemplation of their sufferings one of the elements of the happiness of the redeemed.[1] No other religious teachers had ever proclaimed such tenets, and as long as they were realised intensely the benevolent precepts and the mild and gentle ideal of the New Testament could not possibly be influential. The two things were hopelessly incongruous. The sense of the divine goodness being destroyed, the whole fabric of natural religion crumbled in the dust. From that time religion was necessarily diverted from the moral to the dogmatic, and became an artificial thing of relics and ceremonies, of credulity and persecution, of asceticism and terrorism. It centred entirely upon the priests, who supported it mainly by intimidation.

I have already, when examining the phenomena of witchcraft, noticed the influence of this doctrine upon the imagination, which it has probably done more to disease than almost all other moral and intellectual agencies combined. I shall hereafter touch upon its effects, upon the intellectual history of Europe, upon the timidity and disingenuousness of enquiry —the distrust, and even hatred, of intellectual honesty it encouraged. There is, however, a still more painful effect to be noticed. That the constant contemplation of suffering, especially when that contemplation is devoid of passion, has a tendency to blunt the affections, and thus destroy the emotional part of humanity, is one of the most familiar facts of common observation. The law holds good even in men, like surgical operators, who contemplate pain solely for the benefit of others. The first repulsion is soon exchanged for indifference, the indifference speedily becomes interest, and the interest is occasionally heightened to positive enjoyment. Hence the anecdotes related of surgeons who have derived the most exquisite pleasure from the operations of their profession, and of persons who, being unable to suppress a morbid delight in the contemplation of suffering, have determined to utilise their defect, and have become the most unflinching operators in the hospitals. Now it is sufficiently manifest that upon this emotional part of humanity depends by far the greater number of kind acts that are done in the world, and especially the prevailing ideal and standard of humanity. There are, no doubt, persons who are exceedingly benevolent through a sense of duty, while their temperament remains entirely callous. There are even cases in which the callousness of temperament increases in proportion to the active benevolence, for it is acquired in contemplating suffering for the purpose of relieving it, and, as Bishop Butler reminds us, " active habits are strengthened, while passive impressions are weakened, by repetition." But the overwhelming majority are in these matters governed by their emotions. Their standard and their acts depend upon the liveliness of

---

[1] St. Thomas Aquinas says, " Ut beatitudo sanctorum eis magis complaceat et de ea uberiores gratias Deo agant datur eis ut pœnam impiorum perfecte videant." (*Summa, Suppl.*, quæst. xciv. art. 1.)

their feelings. If this be so, it is easy to conceive what must have been the result of the contemplations of mediævalism. There is a fresco in the great monastery of Pavia which might be regarded as the emblem of the age. It represents a monk with clasped hands, and an expression of agonising terror upon his countenance, straining over the valley of vision where the sufferings of the lost were displayed, while the inscription above reveals his one harrowing thought, "Quis sustinebit ne descendam moriens?"

In such a state of thought, we should naturally expect that the direct and powerful tendency of this doctrine would be to produce a general indifference to human sufferings, or even a bias towards acts of barbarity. Yet this only gives an inadequate conception of its effects. For not only were men constantly expatiating on these ghastly pictures, they were also constantly associating them with gratitude and with joy. They believed that the truth of Christianity implied the eternal torture of a vast proportion of their fellow creatures, and they believed that it would be a gross impiety to wish that Christianity was untrue. They had collected with such assiduity, and had interpreted with such a revolting literalism, every rhetorical passage in the Bible that could be associated with their doctrine, that they had firmly persuaded themselves that a material and eternal fire formed a central truth of their faith, and that, in the words of an Anglican clergyman, "the hell described in the Gospel is not with the same particularity to be met with in any other religion that is or hath been in the whole world."[1] Habitually treating the language of parable as if it was the language of history, they came to regard it as very truly their ideal of happiness, to rest for ever on Abraham's bosom, and to contemplate for ever the torments of their brother in hell. They felt with St. Augustine that "the end of religion is to become like the object of worship," and they represented the Deity as confining his affection to a small section of his creatures, and inflicting on all others the most horrible and eternal suffering.

Now it is undoubtedly true, that when doctrines of this kind are intensely realised, they will prove most efficacious in dispelling the apathy on religious

subjects which is the common condition of mankind. They will produce great earnestness, great self-sacrifice, great singleness of purpose. Loyola, who had studied with profound sagacity the springs of enthusiasm, assigned in his spiritual exercises an entire day to be spent in meditating upon eternal damnation, and in most great religious revivals the doctrine has occupied a prominent place. It is also undoubtedly true, that in a few splendid instances the effect of this realisation has been to raise up missionary teachers of such heroic and disinterested zeal, that their lives are among the grandest pages in the whole range of biography. But although this may be its effect upon some singularly noble natures, there can be little question that in the vast majority of cases its tendency will be to indurate the character, to diffuse abroad a callousness and insensibility to the suffering of others that will profoundly debase humanity. If you make the detailed and exquisite tortures of multitudes the habitual object of the thoughts and imaginations of men, you will necessarily produce in most of them a gradual indifference to human suffering, and in some of them a disposition to regard it with positive delight. If you further assure men that these sufferings form an integral part of a revelation which they are bound to regard as a message of good tidings, you will induce them to stifle every feeling of pity, and almost to encourage their invincibility as a virtue. If you end your teaching by telling them that the Being who is the ideal of their lives, confines his affection to the members of a single Church, that He will torture for ever all who are not found within its pale, and that his children will for ever contemplate those tortures in a state of unalloyed felicity, you will prepare the way for every form of persecution that can be directed against those who are without. He who most fully realised these doctrines, would be the most unhappy or the most unfeeling of mankind. No possible prospect of individual bliss could reconcile a truly humane man who followed the impulse of his humanity, to the thought that those who were external to his faith were destined to eternal fire. No truly humane man could avoid wishing, that rather than this should be the case, he and all others should sleep the sleep of annihilation. When the doctrine was intensely realised and implicitly

[1] Swinden, p. 129.

believed, it must, therefore, have had one or other of two effects. It must have produced an intensity of compassion that would involve extreme unhappiness and would stimulate to extreme heroism, or it must have produced an absolute callousness and a positive inclination to inflict suffering upon the heretic. It does not require much knowledge of human nature to perceive that the spirit of Torquemada must be more common than that of Xavier.

That this was actually the case must be evident to anyone who is not wilfully blind to the history of Christendom. I have mentioned that writer who in the second century dilated most emphatically on the doctrine of eternal punishment by fire as a means of intimidation. In another of his works he showed very clearly the influence it exercised upon his own character. He had written a treatise dissuading the Christians of his day from frequenting the public spectacles. He had collected on the subject many arguments, some of them very powerful, and others extremely grotesque ; but he perceived that to make his exhortations forcible to the majority of his readers, he must point them to some counter attraction. He accordingly proceeded—and his style assumed a richer glow and a more impetuous eloquence as he rose to the congenial theme—to tell them that a spectacle was reserved for them, so fascinating and so attractive that the most joyous festivals of earth faded into insignificance by the comparison. That spectacle was the agonies of their fellow countrymen, as they writhe amid the torments of hell. "What," he exclaimed, "shall be the magnitude of that scene ? How shall I wonder ? How shall I laugh ? How shall I rejoice ? How shall I triumph when I behold so many and such illustrious kings, who were said to have mounted into heaven, groaning with Jupiter their god in the lowest darkness of hell ! Then shall the soldiers who had persecuted the name of Christ burn in more cruel fire than any they had kindled for the saints.......Then shall the tragedians pour forth in their own misfortune more piteous cries than those with which they had made the theatre to resound, while the comedian's powers shall be better seen as he becomes more flexible by the heat. Then shall the driver of the circus stand forth to view all blushing in his flaming chariot, and the

gladiators pierced, not by spears, but by darts of fire.......Compared with such spectacles, with such subjects of triumph as these, what can prætor or consul, quæstor or pontiff, afford ? And even now faith can bring them near, imagination can depict them as present." [1]

I have quoted this very painful passage not so much as an instance of the excesses of a morbid disposition embittered by persecution, as because it furnishes a striking illustration of the influence of a certain class of realisations on the affections. For in tracing what may be called the psychological history of Europe, we are constantly met by a great contradiction, which can only be explained by such considerations. By the confession of all parties, the Christian religion was designed to be a religion of philanthropy, and love was represented as the distinctive test or characteristic of its true members. As a matter of fact, it has probably done more to quicken the affections of mankind, to promote pity, to create a pure and merciful ideal, than any other influence that has ever acted on the world. But while the marvellous influence of Christianity in this respect has been acknowledged by all who have mastered the teachings of history, while the religious minds of every land and of every opinion have recognised in its Founder the highest conceivable ideal and embodiment of compassion as of purity, it is a no less incontestable truth

---

[1] "Quæ tunc spectaculi latitudo? Quid admirer? Quid rideam? ubi gaudeam? ubi exultem, spectans tot et tantos reges, qui in cœlum recepti nuntiabantur cum ipso Jove et ipsis suis testibus in imis tenebris congemescentes ! Item præsides persecutores dominici nominis sævioribus quam ipsi flammis sævierunt insultantibus contra Christianos liquescentes ! quos præterea sapientes illos philosophos coram discipulis suis una conflagrationibus erubescentes, quibus nihil ad Deum pertinere suadebant, quibus animas aut nullas aut non in pristina corpora redituras affirmabant ! Etiam poetas non ad Rhadamanthi nec ad Minois sed ad inopinati Christi tribunal palpitantes. Tunc magis tragœdi audiendi magis scilicet vocales in sua propria calamitate. Tunc histriones cognoscendi solutiores multo per ignem. Tunc spectandus auriga in flammea rota totus rubens; tunc xystici contemplandi non in gymnasiis sed in igne jaculati; nisi quod ne tunc quidem illos velim visos, ut qui malim ad eos potius conspectum insatiabilem conferre qui in dominum desævierunt. Hic est ille dicam fabri aut quæstuariæ filius, sabbati destructor, Samarites et dæmonium habens. Hic est quem a Juda redemistis, hic est ille arundine et colaphis diverberatus, sputamentis decoratus, felle et aceto potatus. Hic est quem clam discentes subripuerunt ut resurrexisse dicatur, vel hortulanus detraxit ne lactucæ suæ frequentia commeantium læderentur. Ut talia spectes, ut talibus exultes, quis tibi prætor, aut consul, aut quæstor, aut sacerdos de suâ liberalitate præstabit? Et tamen hæc jam quodammodo habemus per fidem, spiritu imaginante repræsentata." (Tertullian, *De Spectac.* cap. xxx.)

that for many centuries the Christian priesthood pursued a policy, at least towards those who differed from their opinions, implying a callousness and absence of the emotional part of humanity which has seldom been paralleled, and perhaps never surpassed. From Julian, who observed that no wild beasts were so ferocious as angry theologians, to Montesquieu, who discussed as a psychological phenomenon the inhumanity of monks, the fact has been constantly recognised. The monks, the Inquisitors, and in general the mediæval clergy, present a type that is singularly well defined, and is in many respects exceedingly noble, but which is continually marked by a total absence of mere natural affection. In zeal, in courage, in perseverance, in self-sacrifice, they towered far above the average of mankind ; but they were always as ready to inflict as to endure suffering. These were the men who chanted their Te Deums over the massacre of the Albigenses or of St. Bartholomew, who fanned and stimulated the Crusades and the religious wars, who exulted over the carnage, and strained every nerve to prolong the struggle, and, when the zeal of the warrior had begun to flag, mourned over the languor of faith, and contemplated the sufferings they had caused with a satisfaction that was as pitiless as it was unselfish. These were the men who were at once the instigators and the agents of that horrible detailed persecution that stained almost every province of Europe with the blood of Jews and heretics, and which exhibits an amount of cold, passionless, studied and deliberate barbarity unrivalled in the history of mankind.[1]

Now, when a tendency of this kind is habitually exhibited among men who are unquestionably actuated by the strongest sense of duty, it may be assumed that it is connected with some principle they have adopted, or with the moral atmosphere they breathe. It must have an intellectual or logical antecedent, and it must have what may be termed an emotional antecedent. By the first, I understand certain principles or trains of reasoning which induce men to believe that it is their duty to persecute. By the second, I understand a tendency or disposition of feeling that harmonises with persecution, removes the natural reluctance on the subject, and predisposes men to accept any reasoning of which persecution is the conclusion. The logical antecedents of persecution I shall examine in the next chapter. The most important emotional antecedent is, I believe, to be found in the teaching concerning the future world. It was the natural result of that teaching, that men whose lives present in many respects examples of the noblest virtue, were nevertheless conspicuous for ages as prodigies of barbarity, and proved absolutely indifferent to the sufferings of all who dissented from their doctrines. Nor was it only towards the heretic that this inhumanity was displayed ; it was reflected more or less in the whole penal system of the time. We have a striking example of this in the history of torture. In ancient Greece, torture was never employed except in cases of treason. In the best days of ancient Rome, notwithstanding the notorious inhumanity of the people, it was exclusively confined to the slaves. In mediæval Christendom it was made use of to an extent that was probably unexampled in any earlier period, and in cases that fell under the cognisance of the clergy it was applied to every class of the community.[1] And what strikes us most in considering the mediæval tortures is not so much their diabolical barbarity, which it is indeed impossible to exaggerate, as the extraordinary variety, and what may be termed the artistic skill, they displayed. They represent a condition of thought in

---

[1] We shall have ample evidence of this in the next chapter. At present it is sufficient to say that the use of the *slow* fire in burning heretics was in many districts habitual. In that curious book, the *Scaligeriana* (a record of the conversation of Joseph Scaliger, by an intimate friend who lived in his house), we have a horrible description of one of these executions in Guienne : "J'avois environ seize ans que je vis brusler un Jacobin qui fermoit la bouche aux Papistes : on le dégrada et on le brusla à petit feu, le liant avec des cordes mouillées par les aisselles près la potence, et là on mettoit le feu dessous tellement qu'il estoit demy consumé avant qu'il fut mort." (Art. Heretici. See, too, art. Sorciers, and Cousin's account of the execution of Vanini.)

[1] In cases of heresy and treason, but the first were of course by far the most common. As one of the old authorities on the subject says : "In crimine hæresis omnes illi torquendi sunt qui in crimine læsæ majestatis humanæ torqueri possunt ; quia longe gravius est divinum quam temporalem lædere majestatem, ac proinde nobiles, milites, decuriones, doctores, et omnes qui quantâlibet prærogativâ præfulgent in crimine hæresis et in crimine læsæ majestatis humanæ torqueri possunt....quo fit quod minores viginti quinque annis propter suspicionem hæresis et læsæ majestatis torqueri possunt, minores etiam quatuordecim annis terreri et habenâ vel ferulâ cædi. (Suarez de Paz, *Praxis Ecclesiastica et Sæcularis* [1619], p. 158.)

which men had pondered long and carefully on all the forms of suffering, had
compared and combined the different
kinds of torture, till they had become the
most consummate masters of their art,
had expended on the subject all the resources of the utmost ingenuity, and had
pursued it with the ardour of a passion.
The system was matured under the
mediæval habit of thought, it was
adopted by the Inquisitors, and it received
its finishing touches from their ingenuity.[1]
In every prison the crucifix and the rack
stood side by side, and in almost every
country the abolition of torture was at
last effected by a movement which the
Church opposed, and by men whom she
had cursed. In England, it is true,
torture had always been illegal, though it
had often been employed, especially in
ecclesiastical cases;[2] but almost every
other country illustrates the position I
have stated. In France, probably the
first illustrious opponent of torture was
Montaigne, the first of the French
sceptics ; the cause was soon afterwards
taken up by Charron and by Bayle ; it
was then adopted by Voltaire, Montesquieu, and the Encyclopædists ; and it
finally triumphed when the Church had
been shattered by the Revolution.[3] In

Spain, torture began to fall into disuse
under Charles III., on one of the few
occasions when the Government was in
direct opposition to the Church.[1] In Italy
the great opponent of torture was
Beccaria, the friend of Helvétius and of
Holbach, and the avowed exponent of
the principles of Rousseau.[2] Translated
by Morellet, commented on by Voltaire
and Diderot, and supported by the whole
weight of the French philosophers, the
work of Beccaria flew triumphantly over
Europe, and vastly accelerated the movement that produced it. Under the influence of that movement, the Empress
of Russia abolished torture in her dominions, and accompanied the abolition
by an edict of toleration. Under the
same influence, Frederick of Prussia,
whose adherence to the philosophical
principles was notorious, took the same
step, and his example was speedily followed by Duke Leopold of Tuscany.
Nor is there, upon reflection, anything
surprising in this. The movement that
destroyed torture was much less an intellectual than an emotional movement. It
represented much less a discovery of the
reason than an increased intensity of
sympathy. If we asked what positive
arguments can be adduced on the subject,
it would be difficult to cite any that was
not perfectly familiar to all classes at
every period of the middle ages.[3] That
brave criminals sometimes escaped, and
that timid persons sometimes falsely declared themselves guilty ; that the guiltless frequently underwent a horrible

[1] The extraordinary ingenuity of the mediæval tortures, and the extent to which they were elaborated by
the clergy, is well shown in an article on torture by
Villegille, in *Lacroix, le Moyen Âge et la Renaissance*
(Paris, 1848), tom. iii. The original works on the
subject are very numerous, and possess a great but
painful interest. Perhaps the fullest is Marsilius' (a
lawyer of Bologna) *Tractatus de Quæstionibus* (1529
and 1537—both editions in black letter). Marsilius
boasted that he was the inventor of the torture that
consisted of depriving the prisoner of all sleep—a
torture which was especially used in the States of
the Church: "In Statu Ecclesiastico hi duo modi
magis in usu sunt, ut et tormentum taxillorum, et
vigiliæ per somni subtractionem, quem modum
invenisse asserit Marsilius." (*Chartaria, Praxis
Interrogandorum Reorum* [Romæ, 1618], p. 198.).
Besides these works, there are full accounts of the
nature of the tortures in Simancas' *De Catholicis
Institutionibus*, Eymericus' *Directorium Inquisitorum*,
and many other works to which they refer.
[2] On the extent to which it was employed by the
Catholics, under Mary, in the trials of Protestants, see
Strutt's *Manners of the English People*, vol. iii. p. 46 ;
and on the extent to which it was employed by Protestants in the trials of Catholic priests, see Hallam,
Const. Hist. (ed. 1827), vol. i. p. 159 ; and the evidence
collected in Milner's *Letters to a Prebendary*. Bishops
Grindal and Coxe suggested the application of torture
to the Catholic priests. Froude, *Hist.*, vol. vii. pp. 418,
419. See, too, Barrington *On the Statutes*, pp. 80, and
440, 441.
[3] The suppression of one department of torture was
effected in France as early as 1780, and was one of the
measures of reform conceded to the revolutionary
party. All torture, however, was not abolished till
the Revolution was actually triumphant, and the
abolition was one of the first acts of the democrats.
(See Loiseleur, *Sur les Peines.*) Besides the essays of

Montaigne, torture was denounced in the *Sagesse* of
Charron, in the *Contrains-les d'Entrer* of Bayle, and
in many parts of the writings of Voltaire (see, *e.g.*, art.
Torture, in *Phil. Dict.*) and his contemporaries.
[1] Buckle's *Hist.*, vol. ii. p. 140, note. Luis Vives, a
rather famous Spanish philosopher, in his Annotations
to St. Augustine, had protested against torture as early
as the first half of the sixteenth century. His opinions
on this subject were vehemently denounced by a bishop
named Simancas, in a very remarkable book called *De
Catholicis Institutionibus ad præcavendas et extirpan-
das Hæreses* (1569), to which I shall have occasion
hereafter to refer. Simancas observes that "Inquisi-
tores Apostolici sæpissime reos torquere solent" ; he
defends the practice with great energy, on the authority
of theologians ; and he gives a very vivid description of
different modes of torture the Inquisitors employed in
their dealings with heretics (pp. 297-309). See also, on
this horrible subject, Llorente, *Hist. of Inquisition*.
Simancas notices that, in other countries, criminals
were in his day tortured in public, but in Spain in
secret (p. 305).
[2] On the influence of Beccaria, see Loiseleur, pp. 335-
338. Morellet's translation passed through seven
editions in six months.
[3] There is, perhaps, one exception to this. Beccaria
grounded much of his reasoning on the doctrine of the
social compact. I cannot, however, think that this
argument had much influence in producing the change.

punishment, and that the moral influence of legal decisions was seriously weakened ; [1]—these arguments, and such as these, were as much truisms in the eleventh and twelfth centuries as they are at present. Nor was it by such means that the change was effected. Torture was abolished because in the progress of civilisation the sympathies of men became more expansive, their perceptions of the sufferings of others more acute, their judgments more indulgent, their actions more gentle. To subject even a guilty man to the horrors of the rack, seemed atrocious and barbarous, and therefore the rack was destroyed. It was part of the great movement which abolished barbarous amusements, mitigated the asperities and refined the manners of all classes. Now it is quite certain that those who seriously regarded eternal suffering as the just punishment of the fretfulness of a child, could not possibly look upon torture with the same degree and kind of repulsion as their less orthodox neighbours. It is also certain, that a period in which religion, by dwelling incessantly on the legends of the martyrs, or on the agonies of the lost, made the combination of new and horrible forms of suffering the habitual employment of the imagination, was of all others that in which the system of torture was likely to be most atrocious. It may be added, that the very frame of mind that made men assail the practice of torture, made them also assail the mediæval doctrine of future punishment. The two things grew out of the same condition of society. They flourished together, and they declined together.

The truth is that in every age the penal code will in a great degree vary with the popular estimate of guilt. Philosophers have written much on the purely preventive character of legal punishments ; but it requires but little knowledge of history, or even of human nature, to show that a code constructed altogether on such a principle is impossible. It is indeed true that all acts morality condemns do not fall within the province of the legislator, and that this fact is more fully appreciated as civilisation advances.[2] It

is true, too, that in an early stage, the severity of punishments results in a great measure from the prevailing indifference to the infliction of suffering. It is even true that the especial prominence or danger of some crime will cause men to visit it for a time with penalties that seem to bear no proportion to its moral enormity. Yet it is, I think, impossible to examine penal systems without perceiving that they can only be efficient during a long period of time, when they accord substantially with the popular estimate of the enormity of guilt. Every system, by admitting extenuating circumstances and graduated punishments, implies this, and every judgment that is passed by the public is virtually an appeal to an ideal standard. When a punishment is pronounced excessive, it is meant that it is greater than was deserved. When it is pronounced inadequate, it is meant that it is less than was deserved. Even regarding the law simply as a preventive measure, it is necessary that it should thus reflect the prevailing estimate of guilt, for otherwise it would come into collision with that public opinion which is essential to its operation. Thus, towards the close of the last [eighteenth] century, both murder and horse-stealing were punished by death. In the first case juries readily brought in verdicts, the public sanctioned those verdicts, and the law was efficacious. In the second case the criminals were almost usually acquitted; and when they were executed, public opinion was shocked and scandalised. The reason of this was that men looked upon death as a punishment not incommensurate with the guilt of murder, but exceedingly disproportionate to that of theft. In the advance of civilisation, there is a constant tendency to mitigate the severity of penal codes, for men learn to realise more intensely the suffering they are inflicting; and they at the same time become more sensible of the palliations of guilt. When, however, such a doctrine concerning the just reward of crime as I have noticed is believed and realised, it must inevitably have the effect of retarding the progress.

Such, then, were the natural effects of the popular teaching on the subject of

---

[1] It is worthy of notice that St. Augustine perceived very clearly the evil of torture, and stated the case against it with his usual force and terseness : "Cum quæritur utrum sit nocens cruciatur et innocens luit pro incerto scelere certissimas pœnas." (*De Civ. Dei*, lib. xix. cap. 6); but he concluded that it was necessary.
[2] The tendency of all penal systems constructed

under the influence of the clergy to make the legal code coextensive with the moral code, and to make punishments as much as possible of the nature of expiation, is well known. As a modern instance of this, Sweden is perhaps the most remarkable. See the striking book of Mr. Laing, upon its present condition.

future punishment which was universal during the middle ages, and during the sixteenth and the greater part of the seventeenth century. How completely that teaching has passed away must be evident to anyone who will take the pains of comparing old theological literature with modern teaching. The hideous pictures of material fire and of endless torture which were once so carefully elaborated and so constantly enforced, have been replaced by a few vague sentences on the subject of " perdition," or by the general assertion of a future adjustment of the inequalities of life ; and a doctrine which grows out of the moral faculty, and is an element in every truly moral religion, has been thus silently substituted for a doctrine which was the greatest of all moral difficulties. The eternity of punishment is, indeed, still strenuously defended by many ; but the nature of that punishment, which had been one of the most prominent points in every previous discussion on the subject, has now completely disappeared from controversy. The ablest theologians once regarded their doctrine as one that might be defended, but could not possibly be so stated as not at first sight to shock the feelings. Leibnitz argued that offences against an Infinite Being acquired an infinite guilt, and therefore deserved an infinite punishment. Butler argued that the analogy of nature gave much reason to suspect that the punishment of crimes may be out of all proportion with our conceptions of their guilt. Both, by their very defences, implied that the doctrine was a grievous difficulty. As, however, it is commonly stated at present, the doctrine is so far from being a difficulty, that any system that was without it would be manifestly imperfect, and it has accordingly long since taken its place as one of the moral evidences of Christianity.

This gradual and silent transformation of the popular conceptions is doubtless chiefly due to the habit of educing moral and intellectual truths from our own sense of right, rather than from traditional teaching, which has accompanied the decline of dogmatic theology, and which first became conspicuous in the seventeenth century. Descartes, who was the chief reviver of moral philosophy, may be regarded as its leading originator ; for the method which he applied to metaphysical enquiries was soon applied (consciously or unconsciously) to moral subjects. Men, when seeking for just ideas of right and wrong, began to interrogate their moral sense much more than the books of theologians, and they soon proceeded to make that sense or faculty a supreme arbiter, and to mould all theology into conformity with its dictates. At the same time the great increase of secular influences, and the rapid succession of innovations, made theologians yield with comparative facility to the pressure of their age.

But besides this general rationalistic movement, there was another tendency which exercised, I think, a real though minor influence on the movement, and which is also associated with the name of Descartes. I mean the development of a purely spiritual conception of the soul. The different effects which a spiritual or a material philosophy has exercised on all departments of speculation, form one of the most interesting pages in history. The ancients—at least the most spiritual schools—seem to have generally regarded the essence of the soul as an extremely subtle fluid, or substance, quite distinct from the body ; and, according to their view, and according to the views that were long afterwards prevalent, this excessive subtlety of essence constituted immateriality. For the soul was supposed to be of a nature totally different from surrounding objects, simple, incapable of disintegration, and emancipated from the conditions of matter. Some of the Platonists verged very closely upon, and perhaps attained, the modern idea of a soul, whose essence is purely intellectual; but the general opinion was, I think, that which I have described. The distinct and, as it was called, immaterial nature of the soul, was insisted on by the ancients with great emphasis as the chief proof of its immortality. If mind be but a function of matter, if thought be but " a material product of the brain," it seems natural that the dissolution of the body should be the annihilation of the individual. There is, indeed, an instinct in man pointing to a future sphere, where the injustices of life shall be rectified, and where the chain of love that death has severed shall be linked anew, which is so closely connected with our moral nature that it would perhaps survive the rudest shocks of a material philosophy ; but to minds in which the logical element is most prominent, the psychological argument will always appear the most satisfactory. That there exists in man an indivisible being connected with, but essentially distinct from, the body, was the position which Socrates dwelt upon as one of the chief foundations of his hopes in the last hours of his life, and Cicero in the shadow of age; and the whole moral system of the school of Plato was based upon the distinction. Man, in their noble imagery, is the horizon-line where the world of spirit and the world of matter touch. It is in his power to rise by the wings of the soul to communion with the gods, or to sink by the gravitation of the body to the level of the brute. It is the destiny of the soul to pass from state to state; all its knowledge is but remembrance, and its future condition must be determined by its present tendency. The soul of that man who aspires only to virtue, and who despises the luxury and the passions of earth, will be emancipated at last from the thraldom of matter, and, invisible and unshackled, will drink in perfect bliss in the full fruition of wisdom. The soul of that man who seeks his chief gratification in the body, will after death be imprisoned in a new body, will be punished by physical suffering, or, visible to the human eye, will appear upon earth in the form of a ghost to scare the survivors amid their pleasures.[1]

Such were the opinions that were held by the school of Plato, the most spiritual of all the philosophers of antiquity. When Christianity appeared in the world, its first tendency was very favourable to these conceptions, for it is the effect of every great moral enthusiasm to raise men above the appetites of the body, to present to the mind a supersensual ideal, and to accentuate strongly the antagonism by which human nature is convulsed. We accordingly find that in its earlier and better days the Church assimilated especially with the philosophy of Plato, while in the middle ages Aristotle was supreme; and we also find that the revival of Platonism accompanied the spiritualising movement that preceded the Reformation. Yet there were two doctrines that produced an opposite tendency. The pagans asserted the immateriality of the soul, because they believed that the body must perish for ever; and some of the Christians, in

denying this latter position, were inclined to reject the distinction that was based upon it. But above all, the firm belief in punishment by fire, and the great prominence the doctrine soon obtained, became the foundation of the material view. The Fathers were early divided upon the subject.[1] One section, comprising the ablest and the best, maintained that there existed in man an immaterial soul, but that that soul was invariably associated with a thin, flexible, but sensitive body, visible to the eye. Origen added that the Deity alone could exist as a pure spirit unallied with matter.[2] The other school, of which Tertullian may be regarded as the chief, utterly denied the existence in man of any incorporeal element, maintained that the soul was simply a second body, and based this doctrine chiefly on the conception of future punishment.[3] Apparitions were at that time regarded as frequent. Tertullian mentions a woman who had seen a soul, which she described as "a transparent and lucid figure in the perfect form of a man."[4] St. Antony saw the soul of Ammon carried up to heaven. The soul of a Libyan hermit named Marc was borne to heaven in a napkin. Angels also were not unfrequently seen, and

[1] This theory is developed in the *Phædo*. The Greeks had an extreme fear of the dead, and consequently a strong predisposition to see ghosts.

[1] "Not one of them (the early Fathers) entertained the same opinion as the majority of Christians do at the present day, that the soul is perfectly simple, and entirely destitute of all body, figure, form, and extension. On the contrary, they all acknowledge it to contain something corporeal, although of a different kind and nature from the bodies of this mortal sphere. But yet they are divided into two opinions. For some contend that there are two things in the soul—spirit, and a very thin and subtle body in which this spirit is clothed.... Those who follow Plato and the Platonists (*i.e.* Clement, Origen, and their disciples), adopt the Platonic doctrine respecting the soul also, and pronounce it to be most simple in itself, but yet always invested with a subtle body. But the others, who keep far aloof from Plato, and consider his philosophy to be prejudicial to Christian principles, repudiate this doctrine of his as well, and maintain that the soul altogether is nothing more than a most subtle body.... They very frequently assail the Platonists with bitter invectives, for inculcating that the soul is of a nature most simple, and devoid of all concretion."—Note by Mosheim to Cudworth's *Intell. System* (Harrison's ed.), vol. iii. p. 325. Mr. Hallam says: "The Fathers, with the exception, perhaps the single one, of Augustine, had taught the corporeity of the thinking substance." (*Hist. of Lit.*)

[2] Cudworth, vol. iii. p. 318. The same Father based his doctrine of the soul in a great measure on apparitions. (*Intell. System*, vol. iii. p. 330.)

[3] "Corporalitas animæ in ipso evangelio relucebit. Dolet apud inferos anima cujusdam, et punitur in flammâ et cruciatur in linguâ et de digito animæ felicioris implorat solatium roris."—Tertullian, *De Anima*, cap. vii.

[4] *Ibid.* cap. ix. I should mention that this book was written after Tertullian had become a Montanist, but there is no reason to believe that this had anything to say to his psychology.

were universally believed to have cohabited with the daughters of the antediluvians.

Under the influence of mediæval habits of thought every spiritual conception was materialised, and what at an earlier and a later period was deemed the language of metaphor, was generally regarded as the language of fact. The realisations of the people were all derived from painting, sculpture, or ceremonies that appealed to the senses, and all subjects were therefore reduced to palpable images.[1] The angel in the last judgment was constantly represented weighing the souls in a literal balance, while devils clinging to the scales endeavoured to disturb the equilibrium. Sometimes the soul was portrayed as a sexless child, rising out of the mouth of the corpse.[2] But above all, the doctrine of purgatory arrested and enchained the imagination. Every church was crowded with pictures representing the souls of those who had just died as literal bodies writhing with horrible contortions in a literal fire. The two doctrines were strictly congruous, and each supported the other. Men who believed in a "physical soul," readily believed in a physical punishment. Men who materialised their view of the punishment, materialised their view of the sufferers.

We find, however, some time before the Reformation, evident signs of a desire on the part of a few writers to rise to a purer conception of the soul. The pantheistic writings that flowed from the school of Averroes, reviving the old Stoical notion of a soul of nature, directed attention to the great problem of the connection between the worlds of matter and of mind. The conception of an all-pervading spirit which "sleeps in the stone, dreams in the animal, and wakes in the man;"[3] the belief that the hidden vital principle which produces the varied forms of organisation, is but the thrill of the Divine essence that is present in them all —this belief, which had occupied so noble a place among the speculations of antiquity, reappeared; and was, perhaps, strengthened by the rapid progress of

mysticism, which may be regarded as the Christian form of pantheism. Coalescing at first with some lingering traditions of Gnosticism, mysticism appeared in the thirteenth century in the sect of the Bégards, and especially in the teaching of David de Dianant, Ortlieb, and Amaury de Bene; and in the following century, under the guidance of Eckhart, Tauler, Suso, and Ruysbroek, it acquired in Germany an extraordinary popularity, to which the strong religious feeling elicited by the Black Death, and the reaction that had begun against the excessive aridity of scholasticism, both contributed.[1] The writings ascribed to Dionysius the Areopagite, which have always been the Bible of mysticism, and which had been in part translated by Scotus Erigena, and also some of the works of Scotus himself, rose to sudden favour, and a new tone was given to almost all classes of theological reasoners. As the philosophical aspect of this tone of thought, an order of investigation was produced, which was shown in curious enquiries about how life is first generated in matter. The theory of spontaneous generation, which Lucretius had made the basis of a great portion of his system, and on which the philosophers of the eighteenth century laid so great stress, was strongly asserted,[2] and all the mysteries of generation treated with a confidence that elicits a smile,[3] not unmixed with melancholy when we think how completely these great questions of the nature and origin of life, which may be almost said to form the basis of all

---

[1] See on this subject Maury, *Légendes pieuses*, pp. 125–127.

[2] Maury, *Légendes pieuses*, p. 124. There is an example of this in the Triumph of Death, by Orcagna, at Pisa. In the Greek churches the souls of the blest were sometimes represented as little children clasped in the mighty hand of God. (Didron, *Iconographie*, p. 216.)

[3] Schelling.

---

[1] See Schmidt, *Études sur le Mysticisme allemand du XIVe siècle*, in the *Mémoires des Sciences morales et politiques de l'Institut de France*, tom. ii.

[2] The following passage from Vives is interesting both as giving a concise view of the notions prevailing about spontaneous generation, and on account of the very curious notion in it about mice: "De viventibus alia generationem habent spontaneum, ut muscæ, culices, formicæ, apes: quæ nec sexum ullum habent. Alia ex commixtione sexuum producunt, ut homo, equus, canis, leo. Sunt quæ ambiguam habent procreationem, ut mures; nam eorum alii ex sordibus sine concubitu, alii ex concubitu proveniunt." (*De Anima*, lib. i.) Van Helmont, as is well known, gave a recipe for producing mice. St. Augustine, after taking great pains to solve different objections to the goodness of Providence, oddly enough selects the existence of mice as an impenetrable one which faith alone can grasp: "Ego vero fateor me nescire mures et ranæ quare creati sunt, aut muscæ, aut vermiculæ." (*De Genesi, contra Manichæos*, c. xvi.)

[3] Thus, Melanchthon deals, in a tone of most absolute assurance, with the great question of the cause of the difference of sex: "Mares nascuntur magis in dextrâ parte matricis, et a semine quod magis a dextro testiculo oritur. Fœmellæ in sinistrâ matricis parte nascuntur." (Melanchthon, *De Anima*, p. 420.) This theory originated, I believe, with Aristotle, and was afterwards repeated by numerous writers.

real knowledge, have eluded our investigations, and how absolutely the fair promise of the last century has in this respect been unfulfilled. From enquiries about the genesis of the soul, it was natural to proceed to examine its nature. Such enquiries were accordingly earnestly pursued, with the assistance of the pagan writers; and the conclusions arrived at on this point by different schools exercised, as is always the case, a very wide influence upon their theological conceptions. I cannot doubt, that when at last Descartes maintained that thought is the essence of the soul, and that the thinking substance is therefore so wholly and generically different from the body, that none of the forms or properties of matter can afford the faintest image of its nature, he contributed much to that frame of mind which made men naturally turn with contempt from ghosts, visible demons, and purgatorial fires.[1] It is true that the Cartesian doctrine was soon in a measure eclipsed, but it at least destroyed for ever the old notion of an inner body.[2]

From the time of Descartes, the doctrine of a material fire may indeed be said to have steadily declined.[3] The sceptics of the seventeenth and eighteenth centuries treated it with great contempt, and in England, at least, the last great con-

troversy on the subject in the Church, seems to have taken place during the first half of the eighteenth century. Swinden, Whiston, Horberry, Dodwell, and in America Jonathan Edwards, discussed it from different points of view,[1] and attested the rapid progress of the scepticism. Towards the close of the century the doctrine had passed away; for though there was no formal recantation or change of dogmas, it was virtually excluded from the popular teaching, though it even now lingers among the least educated Dissenters, and in the Roman Catholic manuals for the poor.

I have dwelt at length upon this very revolting doctrine, because it exercised, I believe, an extremely important influence on the modes of thought and types of character of the past. I have endeavoured to show how its necessary effect was to chill and deaden the sympathies, to predispose men to inflict suffering, and seriously to retard the march of civilisation. It has now virtually passed away, and with it the type of character that it did so much to form. Instead of the old stern Inquisitor, so unflinching in his asceticism, so heroic in his enterprises, so remorseless in his persecution—instead of the men who multiplied and elaborated the most hideous tortures, who wrote long cold treatises on their application, who stimulated and embittered the most ferocious wars, and who watered every land with the blood of the innocent— instead of this ecclesiastical type of character, we meet with an almost feminine sensibility, and an almost morbid indisposition to inflict punishment. The pre-eminent characteristic of modern Christianity is the boundless philanthropy it displays. Philanthropy is to our age what asceticism was to the middle ages, and what polemical discussion was to the sixteenth and seventeenth centuries. The emotional part of humanity, the humanity of impulse, was

---

[1] The sharp line Descartes tried to draw between the body and the soul explains his doctrine of animals, which has often been grossly misunderstood. Thought, he contended, is the essence of the soul, and all that is not thought (as life and sensibility) is of the body. In denying that brutes had souls, he denied them the power of thought, but left them all besides. This distinction in its full rigidity would now be maintained by very few; and Stahl gave psychology an impulse in quite another direction by his doctrine (which was that of Aristotle), that the soul includes the vital principle— all that separates living from dead bodies. He thus founded the psychology of animals, and in a great measure fused psychology and medicine. There is a clear statement on this point in Maine de Biran, *Nouveaux Rapports physiques et moraux.* There is at present a remarkable revival of the doctrine of Stahl in France, in the writings of Tissot, Boullier, Charles, and Lemoine.

[2] A doctrine, however, something like that of the old Fathers, but applied to the bodies of the blest, has been lately advocated in two very ingenious American books —Hitchcock's *Religion of Geology,* and *Lectures on the Seasons.* The author has availed himself of Reichenbach's theories of "odic light," &c.

[3] Descartes himself gives us the opinion of his contemporaries on the subject: "Bien que la commune opinion des théologiens soit que les damnés sont tourmentés par le feu des enfers, néanmoins leur sentiment n'est pas pour cela qu'ils sont déçus par une fausse idée que Dieu leur a imprimée, d'un feu qui les consume, mais plutôt qu'ils sont véritablement tourmentés par le feu; parce que 'comme l'esprit d'un homme vivant, bien qu'il ne soit pas corporel, est néanmoins détenu dans le corps, ainsi Dieu par sa toute-puissance peut aisément faire qu'il souffre les atteintes du feu corporel après la mort.'" (*Réponses aux six Objections.*)

[1] This was, as far as I know, the last of the great controversies concerning the locality of hell—a question which had once excited great attention. The common opinion which St. Thomas had sanctioned was that it was in the centre of the earth. Whiston, however, who denied the eternity of punishment, contended that it was the tail of a comet; while Swinden (whose book seems to have made a considerable sensation, and was translated into French) strenuously contended that it was the sun. According to Plancey (*Dict. infernal,* art. Enfer), some early theologians not only held this, but explained the spots in the sun by the multitude of the souls.

never so developed, and its development, in Protestantism at least, where the movement has been most strikingly evinced, has always been guided and represented by the clergy. Indeed, this fact is recognised quite as much by their opponents as by their admirers. A certain weak and effeminate sentimentality, both intellectual and moral, is the quality which every satirist of the clergy dwells upon as the most prominent feature of their character. Whether this quality, when duly analysed, is as despicable as is sometimes supposed, may be questioned ; at all events, no one would think of ascribing it to the ecclesiastics of the school of Torquemada, of Calvin, or of Knox.

The changes that take place from age to age in the types of character in different professions, though they are often every evident, and though they form one of the most suggestive branches of history, are of course not susceptible of direct logical proof. A writer can only lay the general impressions he has derived from the study of the two periods before the judgments of those whose studies have resembled his own. It is more, therefore, as an illustration than as a proof, that I may notice, in conclusion, the striking contrast which the history of punishments exhibits in the two periods of theological development. We have seen that the popular estimate of the adequacy of the penalties that are affixed to different crimes must in a great measure vary with the popular realisations of guilt. We have seen, too, that the abolition of torture was a movement almost entirely due to the opponents of the Church, and that it was effected much less by any process of reasoning than by the influence of certain modes of feeling which civilisation produced. Soon, however, we find that the impulse which was communicated by Voltaire, Beccaria, and the Revolution, passed on to the orthodox, and it was only then that it acquired its full intensity. The doctrine of a literal fire having almost ceased to be a realised conception, a growing sense of the undue severity of punishments was everywhere manifested ; and in most countries, but more especially in England, there was no single subject on which more earnestness was shown. The first step was taken by Howard. Nowhere perhaps in the annals of philanthropy do we meet a picture of more unsullied and fruitful beneficence

than is presented by the life of that great Dissenter, who, having travelled over more than 40,000 miles in works of mercy, at last died on a foreign soil a martyr to his cause. Not only in England, but over the whole of Europe, his exertions directed public opinion to the condition of prisons, and effected a revolution, the results of which can never be estimated. Soon after followed the mitigation of the penal code. In England the severity of that code had long been unexampled ; and as crimes of violence were especially numerous, the number of executions was probably quite unparalleled in Europe. Indeed, Fortescue, who was chief justice under Henry VI., notices the fact with curious complacency, as a plain proof of the superiority of his countrymen. "More men," he tells us, "are hanged in Englonde in one year than in Fraunce in seven, because the English have better hartes. The Scotchmenne, likewise, never dare rob, but only commit larcenies."[1] In the reign of Henry VIII., when an attempt was made to convert the greater part of England into pasture land,[2] and when the suppression of the monasteries had destroyed the main source of charity, and had cast multitudes helplessly upon the world, Holingshed estimates the executions at the amazing number of 72,000, or 2,000 a year.[3] This estimate is utterly incredible, but even at the end of the reign of Elizabeth, and notwithstanding the poor-law which had been enacted, the annual executions are said to have been about 400.[4] In the middle of the eighteenth century, however, though the population had greatly increased, they had fallen to less than one hundred.[5] A little before this time Bishop Berkeley, following in the steps that had been traced by More in his *Utopia*, and by Cromwell in one of his speeches, raised his voice in favour of substituting other punishments for death.[6] But all through

[1] Barrington, *On the Statutes* (London, 1769), p. 461.
[2] Sir Thomas More, in his *Utopia* (book. i.), gives a frightful description of the misery and the crimes resulting from the ejectments necessitated by this change. He speaks of twenty men hung on one gibbet.
[3] Barrington, pp. 461, 462. It should be added that Mr. Froude utterly rejects this estimate.
[4] *Ibid.*
[5] Barrington says this was the case when he wrote, which was in 1766.
[6] He asks "whether we may not, as well as other nations, contrive employment for our criminals ; and whether servitude, chains, and hard labour for a term of years, would not be a more discouraging as well as a more adequate punishment for felons than even death itself." (*Querist*, No. 54.)

the reign of George III. the code was aggravated, and its severity was carried to such a point, that when Romilly began his career, the number of capital offences was no less than 230.[1] It was only at the close of the last [eighteenth] and in the beginning of the present [nineteenth] century, that this state of things was changed. The reform in England, as over the rest of Europe, may be ultimately traced to that Voltairean school of which Beccaria was the representative, for the impulse created by the treatise *On Crimes and Punishments* was universal, and it was the first great effort to infuse a spirit of philanthropy into the penal code, making it a main object of legislation to inflict the smallest possible amount of suffering. Beccaria is especially identified with the cause of the abolition of capital punishment, which is slowly but steadily advancing towards its inevitable triumph. In England, the philosophical element of the movement was nobly represented by Bentham, who in genius was certainly superior to Beccaria, and whose influence, though perhaps not so great, was also European. But while conceding the fullest merit to these great thinkers, there can be little doubt that the enthusiasm and the support that enabled Romilly, Mackintosh, Wilberforce, and Brougham to carry their long series of reforms through Parliament, was in a very great degree owing to the untiring exertions of the Evangelicals, who, with a benevolence that no disappointment could damp, and with an indulgence towards crime that sometimes amounted even to a fault, cast their whole weight into the cause of philanthropy. The contrast between the position of these religionists in the destruction of the worst features of the ancient codes, and the precisely opposite position of the mediæval clergy, is very remarkable. Sectarians will only see in it the difference between rival churches, but the candid historian will, I think, be able to detect the changed types of character that civilisation has produced ; while in the difference that does undoubtedly in this respect exist between Protestantism and Catholicism, he will find one of the results of the very

[1] See Romilly's *Life* for many statistics on the subject.

different degrees of intensity with which those religions direct the mind to the debasing and indurating conceptions I have reviewed.

It has been said that the tendency of religious thought in the present day " is all in one direction—towards the identification of the Bible and conscience." It is a movement that may be deplored, but can scarcely be overlooked or denied. Generation after generation the power of the moral faculty becomes more absolute, the doctrines that oppose it wane and vanish, and the various elements of theology are absorbed and recast by its influence. The indifference of most men to dogmatic theology is now so marked, and the fear of tampering with formularies that are no longer based on general conviction is with some men so intense, that general revisions of creeds have become extremely rare ; but the change of belief is not the less profound. The old words are indeed retained, but they no longer present the old images to the mind, or exercise the old influence upon life. The modes of thought and the types of character which those modes produce are essentially and universally transformed. The whole intellectual atmosphere, the whole tenour of life, the prevailing enthusiasms, the conceptions of the imagination, are all changed. The intellect of man moves onward under the influence of regular laws in a given direction, and the opinions that in any age are realised and operative, are those which harmonise with its intellectual condition. I have endeavoured in the present chapter to exhibit the nature of some of these laws, the direction in which some of these successive modifications are tending. If the prospect of constant change such an enquiry exhibits should appear to some minds to remove all the landmarks of the past, there is one consideration that may serve in a measure to reassure them. That Christianity was designed to produce benevolence, affection, and sympathy, being a fact of universal admission, is indefinitely more certain than that any particular dogma is essential to it ; and in the increase of these moral qualities we have therefore the strongest evidence of the triumph of the conceptions of its Founder.

CHAPTER IV.

ON PERSECUTION

I.—THE ANTECEDENTS OF PERSECUTION

WHEN it is remembered that the Founder of Christianity summed up human duties in the two precepts of love to God and love to man, and illustrated the second precept by a parable representing the sentiment of a common humanity destroying all the animosities of sectarianism, the history of persecution in the Christian Church appears as startling as it is painful. In the eighteenth century, when the minds of men were for the first time very sensible of the contrast, it was commonly explained by imputing interested motives to the clergy, and in all the writings of Voltaire and his school hypocrisy was represented as the usual concomitant of persecution. This notion may now be said to have quite passed away. While it is undoubtedly true that some persecutions, and even some that were very atrocious, have sprung from purely selfish motives, it is almost universally admitted that these are far from furnishing any adequate explanation of the facts. The burnings, the tortures, the imprisonments, the confiscations, the disabilities, the long wars and still longer animosities that for so many centuries marked the conflicts of great theological bodies, are chiefly due to men whose lives were spent in absolute devotion to what they believed to be true, and whose characters have passed unscathed through the most hostile and searching criticism. In their worst acts the persecutors were but the exponents and representatives of the wishes of a large section of the community, and that section was commonly the most earnest and the most unselfish. It has been observed, too, since the subject has been investigated with a passionless judgment, that persecution invariably accompanied the realisation of a particular class of doctrines, fluctuated with their fluctuations, and may therefore be fairly presumed to represent their action upon life.

In the last chapter I have, I trust, done something towards the solution of the difficulty. I have shown that the normal effect of a certain class of realisations upon the character would be to produce an absolute indifference to the sufferings of those who were external to the Church, and consequently to remove that reluctance to inflict pain which is one of the chief preservatives of society. I have now to trace the order of ideas which persuaded men that it was their duty to persecute, and to show the process by which those ideas passed away. The task is a painful one, for the doctrines I must refer to are those which are most repugnant to our moral sense, and in an age in which they are not realised or believed the bare statement of them is sufficient to shock the feelings of many : at the same time, a clear view of their nature and influence is absolutely essential to an understanding of the past.

There are two moral sentiments which seem universally diffused through the human race, and which may be regarded as the nuclei around which all religious systems are formed. They are the sense of virtue, leading men to attach the idea of merit to certain actions which they may perform ; and the sense of sin, teaching men that their relation to the Deity is not that of claimants but of suppliants. Although in some degree antagonistic, there probably never was a religious mind in which they did not co-exist, and they may be traced as prominent elements in the moral development of every age and creed, but at the same time their relative importance is far from being the same. There are certain ages in which the sense of virtue has been the mainspring of religion ; there are other ages in which this position is occupied by the sense of sin. This may be partly owing to the differences in the original constitutions of different races, or to those influences of surrounding nature which act so early upon the mind that it is scarcely possible to distinguish them from natural tendencies ; but it is certainly in a great measure due to the political and intellectual circumstances that are dominant. When prosperity and victory and dominion have long continued to elate, and when the virtues that contribute most to political greatness, such as fortitude and self-reliance, are cultivated, the sense of human dignity will become the chief moral principle, and every system that opposes it will be distasteful. But when, on the other hand, a religious system emanates from a suffering people, or from a people that is eminently endowed with religious sentiment, its character will be entirely different. It will reflect something of the circumstances that gave it birth ; it will be full of pathos, of humility, of emotion ; it will lead men to aspire to a lofty ideal, to interrogate their conscience with nervous anxiety, to study with scrupulous care the motives that actuate them, to distrust their own powers, and to throw themselves upon external help.

Now, of all systems the world has ever seen, the philosophies of ancient Greece and Rome appealed most strongly to the sense of virtue, and Christianity to the sense of sin. The ideal of the first was the majesty of self-relying humanity ; the ideal of the other was the absorption of the manhood into God. It is impossible to look upon the awful beauty of a Greek statue, or to read a page of Plutarch, without perceiving how completely the idea of excellence was blended with that of pride. It is equally impossible to examine the life of a Christian saint, or the painting of an early Christian artist, without perceiving that the dominant conception was self-abnegation and self-distrust. In the earliest and purest days of the Church this was chiefly manifested in the devotional frame of mind which was habitual, and in the higher and more delicate moral perception that accompanied it. Christianity then consisted much more of modes of emotion than of intellectual propositions. It was not till about the third century that the moral sentiments which at first constituted it were congealed into an elaborate theology, and were in consequence necessarily perverted. I say necessarily perverted, because a dogma cannot be an adequate or faithful representative of a

mode of feeling. Thus while the sense of virtue and the sense of sin have always co-existed, though in different degrees, in every religious mind, when expressed in a dogmatic form, under the names of Justification by Faith and Justification by Works, they became directly opposed to one another ; and while each doctrine grew in the first instance out of the moral faculty, each was at last developed to consequences from which that faculty indignantly revolts. As the result of one doctrine, men constructed a theory in which the whole scheme of religion was turned into a system of elaborate barter, while the attitude of self-distrust and humility produced by the sensitiveness of an awakened conscience was soon transformed into a doctrine according to which all the virtues and all the piety of the heathen contained nothing that was pleasing to the Almighty, or that could ward off the sentence of eternal damnation.

In considering, however, the attitude which mankind occupied towards the Almighty in the early theology of the Church, we have another important element to examine : I mean the conception of hereditary guilt. To a civilised man, who regards the question abstractedly, no proposition can appear more self-evident than that a man can only be guilty of acts in the performance of which he has himself had some share. The misfortune of one man may fall upon another, but guilt appears to be entirely personal. Yet, on the other hand, there is nothing more certain than that the conceptions both of hereditary guilt and of hereditary merit pervade the belief and the institutions of all nations, and have under the most varied circumstances clung to the mind with a tenacity which is even now but beginning to relax. We find them in every system of early punishment which involved children in the destruction of a guilty parent, in every account of curses transmitted through particular families or particular nations, in every hereditary aristocracy, and in every legend of an early fall. All these rest upon the idea that there is something in the merit or demerit of one man that may be reflected upon his successors altogether irrespectively of their own acts. It would perhaps be rash to draw with much confidence any law concerning the relations of this idea to different conditions of society from the history of Christendom, but, as far as we may judge, it seems to be strongest in ages when civilisation is very low, and on the whole to decline, but not by any means steadily and continuously, with the intellectual advance. There seems to be a period in the history of every nation when punishments involving the innocent child with the guilty parent are acquiesced in as perfectly natural, and another period when they are repudiated as manifestly unjust. We find, however, that in a portion of the middle ages, when the night of barbarism was in part dispelled, a vast aristocratical system was organised which has probably contributed more than any other single cause to consolidate the doctrine of hereditary merit. For the essence of an aristocracy is to transfer the source of honour from the living to the dead, to make the merits of living men depend not so much upon their own character and actions as upon the actions and position of their ancestors ; and as a great aristocracy is never insulated, as its ramifications penetrate into many spheres, and its social influence modifies all the relations of society, the minds of men become insensibly habituated to a standard of judgment from which they would otherwise have recoiled. If in the sphere of religion the rationalistic doctrine of personal merit and demerit should ever completely supersede the theological doctrine of hereditary merit or demerit, the change will, I believe, be largely influenced by the triumph of democratic principles in the sphere of politics.

The origin of this widely diffused habit of judging men by the deeds of their ancestors is one of the most obscure and contested points in philosophy. Some have seen in it a dim and distorted tradition of the Fall ; others have attributed it to that confusion of misfortune with guilt which is so prominent in ancient beliefs. Partly in consequence of the universal conviction that guilt deserves punishment, and partly from the notion that the events which befall mankind are the results not of general laws but of isolated acts directed to special purposes, men imagined that whenever they saw suffering they might infer guilt. They saw that the effects of an unrighteous war will continue long after those who provoked it have passed away ; that the virtue or vice, the wisdom or folly, of the parent will often determine the fortunes of the children and that each generation has probably more power over the destiny of that which succeeds it than over its own. They saw that there was such a thing as transmitted suffering, and they therefore concluded that there must be such a thing as transmitted guilt. Besides this, patriotism and Church feeling, and every influence that combines men in a corporate existence, makes them live to a certain degree in the past, and identify themselves with the actions of the dead. The patriot feels a pride or shame in the deeds of his forefathers very similar to that which springs from his own. Connected with this, it has been observed that men have a constant tendency, in speaking of the human race, to forget that they are employing the language of metaphor, and to attribute to it a real objective existence distinct from the existence of living men. It may be added, too, that that retrospective imagination which is so strong in some nations, and which is more or less exhibited in all, leads men to invest the past with all the fascination of poetry, to represent it as a golden age incomparably superior to their own, and to imagine that some great catastrophe must have occurred to obscure it.

These considerations, and such as these, have often been urged by those who have written on the genesis of the notion of hereditary guilt. Fortunately, however, their examination is unnecessary for my present purpose, which is simply to ascertain the expression of this general conception in dogmatic teaching, and to trace its influence upon practice. The expression is both manifest and emphatic. According to the unanimous belief of the Early Church, all who were external to Christianity were doomed to eternal damnation, not only on account of their own transgression, but also on account of the transmitted guilt of Adam, and therefore even the new-born infant was subject to the condemnation until baptism had united it to the Church.

The opinion which was so graphically expressed by the theologian who said " he doubted not there were infants not a span long crawling about the floor of hell " is not one of those on which it is pleasing to dilate. It was one, however, which was held with great confidence in the Early Church, and if in times of tranquillity it became in a measure unrealised, whenever any heretic ventured to impugn it it was most unequivocally enforced.

At a period which is so early that it is impossible to define it, infant baptism was introduced into the Church ; it was adopted by all the heretics as well as by the orthodox ; it was universally said to be for " the remission of sins " ; and the whole body of the Fathers, without exception or hesitation, pronounced that all infants who died unbaptised were excluded from heaven. In the case of unbaptised adults a few exceptions were admitted,[1] but the sentence on infants was inexorable. The learned English historian of Infant Baptism states that, with the exception of a contemporary of St. Augustine named Vincentius, who speedily recanted his opinion as heretical, he has been unable to discover a single instance of an orthodox member of the Church expressing the opposite opinion before Hinckmar, who was Archbishop of Rheims in the ninth century.[2] In the time of this prelate, a bishop who had quarrelled with his clergy and people ventured to prohibit baptism in his diocese ; and Hinckmar, while severely condemning the act, expressed a hope that it would not be visited on the infants who died when the interdict was in force. With this exception the unanimity seems to have been unbroken. Some of the Greek Fathers, indeed, imagined that there was a special place assigned to infants where there was neither suffering nor enjoyment, while the Latins inferred from the hereditary guilt that they must descend into a place of torment ; but both agreed that they could not be saved. The doctrine was so firmly rooted in the Church, that even Pelagius, who was one of the most rationalistic intellects of his age, and who entirely denied the reality of hereditary guilt, retained infant baptism, acknowledged that it was for the remission of sins, and did not venture to deny its necessity. It was on this point that he was most severely pressed by his opponents, and St. Augustine says that

he was driven to the somewhat desperate resource of maintaining that baptism was necessary to wash away the guilt of the pettishness of the child ![1] Once, when severely pressed as to the consequences of the doctrine, St. Augustine was compelled to acknowledge that he was not prepared to assert dogmatically that it would have been better for these children not to have been born, but at the same time he denied emphatically that a separate place was assigned them, and in one of his sermons against the Pelagians he distinctly declared that they descended into "everlasting fire."[2] Origen and many of the Egyptians explained the doctrine by the theory of pre-existence.[3] Augustine associated it with that of imputed righteousness, maintaining that guilt and virtue might be alike imputed ;[4] and this view seems to have been generally adopted. Among the writings of the Fathers there are few which long possessed a greater authority than a short treatise *De Fide*, which is one of the clearest and most forcible extant epitomes of the Patristic faith, and which till the time of Erasmus was generally ascribed to St. Augustine, though it is now known to have been written, in the beginning of the sixth century, by St. Fulgentius.[5] In this treatise we find the following very distinct statement of the doctrine : " Be assured," writes the saint, " and doubt not, that not only men who have obtained the use of their reason, but also little children who have begun to live in their mothers' womb and have there died, or who, having been just born, have passed away from the world without the sacrament of holy baptism, administered in the name of the Father, Son, and Holy Ghost, must be punished by the eternal torture of undying fire ; for although they have committed no sin by their own will, they have nevertheless drawn with them the condemnation of original sin, by their carnal conception and nativity."[6] It will be remembered

---

[1] Martyrdom—or, as it was termed, the baptism of blood—being the chief. Some, however, relying on the case of the penitent thief, admitted a "baptism of perfect love," when a baptism by water could not be obtained. This consisted, of course, of extraordinary exercises of faith. Catechumens also, who died during the preparation for baptism, were thought by some to be saved. See Lamet et Fromageau, *Dict. des Cas de Conscience*, tom. i. p. 208.

[2] Wall's *History of Infant Baptism*, vol. ii. p. 211. St. Thomas Aquinas afterwards suggested the possibility of the infant being saved who died within the womb : "God may have ways of saving it for aught we know."

[1] Wall, vol. i. pp. 282, 283. It is gratifying to know that St. Augustine, in answering this argument, distinctly declared that the crying of a baby is not sinful, and therefore does not deserve eternal damnation.

[2] *Ibid.* vol. ii. pp. 192–206—a full view of St. Augustine's sentiments on the subject.

[3] Hieronym. *Epist.* lib. ii. ep. 18.

[4] *Ibid.* ep. 28.

[5] He was born about A.D. 467. (*Biog. Univ.*)

[6] "Firmissime tene, et nullatenus dubites, non solum homines jam ratione utentes, verum etiam parvulos, qui, sive in uteris matrum vivere incipiunt et ibi moriuntur, sive jam de matribus nati sine sacramento

that these saints, while maintaining that infants whose existence was but for a moment descended into eternal fire on account of an apple that was eaten four thousand years before they were born, maintained also that the creation and the death of those infants were the direct, personal, and uncontrolled acts of the Deity.

All through the middle ages we trace the influence of this doctrine in the innumerable superstitious rites which were devised as substitutes for regular baptism. Nothing, indeed, can be more curious, nothing can be more deeply pathetic, than the record of the many ways by which the terror-stricken mothers attempted to evade the awful sentence of their Church. Sometimes the baptismal water was sprinkled upon the womb ; sometimes the stillborn child was baptised, in hopes that the Almighty would antedate the ceremony ; sometimes the mother invoked the Holy Spirit to purify by His immediate power the infant that was to be born ; sometimes she received the Host or obtained absolution, and applied them to the benefit of her child. These and many similar practices[1] con-

sancti baptismatis quod datur in nomine Patris et Filii et Spiritus Sancti de hoc sæculo transeunt, ignis æterni sempiterno supplicio puniendos ; quia etsi peccatum propriæ actionis nullum habuerunt, originalis tamen peccati damnationem carnali conceptione et nativitate traxerunt."—*De Fide*, § 70. So also St. Isidore : " Pro soli originali reatu luunt in inferno nuper nati infantuli pœnas, si renovati per lavacrum non fuerint." (*De Sentent.* lib. i. c. 22.) St. Avitus, being of a poetical turn of mind, put the doctrine into verse :—

" Omnibus id vero gravius, si fonte lavacri
Divini expertem tenerum mors invida natum
Præcipitat, durâ generatum sorte, gehennæ,
Qui mox ut matris cessarit filius esse
Perditionis erit : tristes tunc edita nolunt
Quæ flammis tantum genuerunt pignora matres."
　　　　　　　—*Ad Fuscinam Sororem.*

For several other testimonies of the later Fathers to the same effect, see Natalis Alexander, *Historia Ecclesiastica* (Paris, 1699), tom. v. pp. 130–131.

[1] For a very full account of these curious superstitions, see the chapter on " Baptism " in Thiers' *Superstitions*, and also a striking memoir in the first volume of *Le Moyen Âge*, by Lacroix. We can now hardly realise a condition of thought in which the mind was concentrated so strongly upon the unborn fœtus ; but we should remember that, besides the doctrine of baptism, there were two subjects much discussed in the early Church which tended to produce an order of realisations to which we are not accustomed. Some of the early writers, and especially the Nestorians, had agitated questions concerning the time when the divinity of Christ was united to the fœtus in the womb, that had filled the Church with curious physiological speculations. Besides this, one of the earliest struggles of the Church was for the suppression of the custom of destroying the offspring in the womb, and which was extremely common among the pagans, and which they do not seem to have regarded as at all a crime.

tinued all through the middle ages, in spite of every effort to extirpate them, and the severest censures were unable to persuade the people that they were entirely ineffectual. For the doctrine of the Church had wrung the mother's heart with an agony that was too poignant even for that submissive age to bear. Weak and superstitious women, who never dreamed of rebelling against the teaching of their clergy, could not acquiesce in the perdition of their offspring, and they vainly attempted to escape from the dilemma by multiplying superstitious practices, or by attributing to them a more than orthodox efficacy. But the vigilance of the theologians was untiring. All the methods by which these unhappy mothers endeavoured to persuade themselves that their children might have been saved are preserved in the decrees of the Councils that anathematised them.

At last the Reformation came. In estimating the character of that great movement we must carefully distinguish its immediate objects from its ultimate effects. The impulse of which it was in part the cause, and in part the consequence, at last issued in a diffusion of a rationalistic spirit which no Church, however retrograde or dogmatic, has been able to exclude. The essence of that spirit is to interpret the articles of special creeds by the principles of universal religion—by the wants, the aspirations, and the moral sentiments which seem inherent in human nature. It leads men, in other words, to judge what is true and what is good, not by the teachings of tradition, but by the light of reason and of conscience ; and where it has not produced an avowed change of creed it has at least produced a change of realisations. Doctrines which shock our sense of right have been allowed gradually to become obsolete, or if they are brought forward they are stated in language which is so

Tertullian (*Apol.* c. 9) and the author of the Epistle ascribed to St. Barnabas appear to have been among the first to denounce this pagan practice. Another illustration of the estimate in which baptism was held is furnished by the notion that bodily distempers followed irregular baptism. I have already referred to the belief that somnambulists had been baptised by a drunken priest ; but perhaps the most curious example was in a great epidemic attack of St. Vitus's dance, which appeared in the Netherlands in 1375. The common people then believed that the disease resulted from unchaste priests having baptised the children, and their fury was so great that it was with difficulty that the lives of the ecclesiastics were saved. (Hecker *Epidemics of the Middle Ages*, pp. 153, 154.)

colourless and ambiguous, and with so many qualifications and exceptions, that their original force is almost lost. This, however, was the ultimate, not the immediate, effect of the Reformation, and most of the Reformers were far from anticipating it. They designed to construct a religious system which should be as essentially dogmatic, distinct, and exclusive as that which they assailed, but which should represent more faithfully the teachings of the first four centuries. The Anabaptist movement was accompanied by so many excesses and degenerated so constantly into anarchy that it can scarcely be regarded as a school of religious thought, but it had at least the effect of directing the minds of theologians to the subject of infant baptism. The Council of Trent enunciated very clearly the doctrine of Rome. It declared the absolute necessity of baptism for salvation ; it added, to guard against every cavil, that baptism must be by literal water,[1] and it concluded with the usual formulary of a curse. Among the Protestants two opposite tendencies were manifest. One of the first objects of the Reformers was to oppose or restrict the doctrine that ceremonies possessed an intrinsic merit independently of the disposition of the worshipper, and it was not difficult to perceive that this doctrine had been favoured by infant baptism more than by any other single cause. On the other hand, the Protestant taught even more clearly than the Catholic the doctrine of imputed righteousness, and was therefore more disposed to dwell upon the doctrine of imputed guilt. The Lutherans, in the Confession of Augsburg, asserted the absolute necessity of baptism quite as emphatically as the Tridentine theologians,[2] and in one respect many of the Protestants went beyond the Roman Catholics ; for they taught explicitly that the penalty due to original sin was " eternal fire," whereas the Church of Rome had never formally condemned the notion of a third place which the Greek Fathers had originated, which some of the schoolmen had revived, and which about the time of the Reformation was

very general among the Catholics.[1] Calvin was in some respects more favourable to unbaptised infants than the disciples of Luther, for he taught that the children of believers were undoubtedly saved, that the intention to baptise was as efficacious as the ceremony, and that, although infant baptism should be retained, the passage in the discourse to Nicodemus, which had previously been universally applied to it, was susceptible of a different interpretation.[2] But these doctrines arose simply from the reluctance of Calvin and his followers to admit the extraordinary efficacy of a ceremony, and not at all from any moral repugnance to the doctrine of transmitted guilt. No school declared more constantly and more emphatically the utter depravity of human nature, the sentence of perdition attaching to the mere possession of such a nature, and the eternal damnation of the great majority of infants. A few of the enthusiastic advocates of the doctrine of reprobation even denied the universal salvation of baptised infants, maintaining that the Almighty might have predestinated some of them to destruction. All of them maintained that the infants who were saved were saved on account of their connection with Christianity, and not on account of their own innocence. All of them declared that the infant came into the world steeped in guilt, and under the sentence of eternal condemnation. Jonathan Edwards, who was probably the ablest as he was one of the most unflinching of the defenders of Calvinism, has devoted to this subject all the resources

[1] Wall. The notion of a limbo had been so widely diffused that Sarpi says the Tridentine Fathers at one time hesitated whether they should not condemn as heretical the Lutheran proposition that unbaptised infants went into " eternal fire." We find Pascal, however, stating the doctrine in a very repulsive form : " Qu'y a-t-il de plus contraire aux règles de notre misérable justice que de damner éternellement un enfant incapable de volonté pour un péché où il paroît avoir eu si peu de part qu'il est commis six mille ans avant qu'il fut en être ? Certainement rien ne nous heurte plus rudement que cette doctrine, et cependant sans ce mystère le plus incompréhensible de tous nous sommes incompréhensibles à nous-mêmes." (Pensées, cap. iii. § 8.) I have little doubt, however, that the more revolting aspect of the doctrine was nearly obsolete in the Church at the time of the Reformation. In the twelfth century St. Bernard had said : " Nihil ardet in inferno nisi propria voluntas."

[2] According to Wall, Calvin was the very first theologian who denied that the passage, " Except a man be born of water and of the spirit," &c., applied to baptism. (Vol. ii. p. 180.) Jeremy Taylor strongly supported Calvin's view : " The water and the spirit in this place signify the same thing ; and by water is meant the effect of the spirit cleansing and purifying the soul, as appears in its parallel place of Christ baptising with the spirit and with fire." (Liberty of Prophesying, § 18.)

[1] A great deal of controversy had been excited in the middle ages about a Jew, who, being converted to Christianity in a desert, where there was no water, and being as was supposed in a dying state, was baptised with sand. There were also some cases of women baptising their children with wine. For full details about these, see Thiers' Traité des Superstitions.

[2] Arts. ii. and ix.

of his great ingenuity. No previous writer developed more clearly the arguments which St. Augustine had derived from the death of infants, and from the pangs that accompany it ; but his chief illustrations of the relations of the Deity to His creatures are drawn from those scenes of massacre when the streets of Canaan were choked with the multitude of the slain, and when the sword of the Israelite was for ever bathed in the infant's blood.[1]

So far, then, the Reformation seems to have made little or no change. The doctrine of Catholicism, harsh and repulsive as it appears, does not contrast at all unfavourably with those of the two great founders of dogmatic and conservative Protestantism. At a period when passions ran high, and when there was every disposition to deepen the chasm between Catholicity and the Reformed Churches—at a period therefore when any tendency to rebel against the Catholic doctrine of transmitted guilt would have been clearly manifested—that doctrine was in all essentials fully accepted. Questions concerning the nature of the sacraments, the forms of Church government, the meaning of particular passages of Scripture, the due order and subordination of different portions of theological systems, were discussed with the most untiring and acrimonious zeal. All Europe was convulsed with controversy, and the most passionate enthusiasm was evoked. But the whole stress and energy of this enthusiasm flowed in a dogmatic channel. It was not the revolt of the reason claiming a supreme authority in the domain of thought ; it was not the rebellion of the moral faculty against doctrines that collided with its teaching : or if such elements existed they were latent and unavowed, and their position in the first ebullitions of Protestantism was entirely subordinate. The germ of Rationalism had indeed been cast abroad, but more than a century was required to develop it. There was no subtlety of interpretation connected with the eucharistic formularies that did not excite incomparably more interest than the broad questions of morality. Conscience was the last tribunal to which men would have referred as the supreme authority of their creed. There was much doubt as to what

historical authorities were most valuable, but there was no doubt that the ultimate basis of theology must be historical.

To this statement there are, however, two eminent exceptions. Two theologians, who differed widely in their opinions and in their circumstances, were nevertheless actuated by the same rationalistic spirit, were accustomed to form their notions of truth and goodness by the decisions of their own reason and conscience, and, disregarding all the interpretations of tradition, to mould and adapt their creed to their ideal. These theologians were Socinus and Zuinglius, who may be regarded as the representatives of Rationalism in the first period of Protestantism.

The school of thought which Lælius Socinus contributed to plant at Vicenza, and which his more illustrious nephew, in conjunction with other Italians, spread through the greater part of Europe, was the natural result of a long train of circumstances that had been acting for centuries in Italy. The great wealth of the Italian republics, their commercial relations with men of all nations and of all creeds, the innumerable memorials of paganism that are scattered over the land, and the high æsthetic development that was general, had all in different ways and degrees contributed to produce in Italy a very unusual love of intellectual pursuits and a very unusual facility for cultivating them. Upon the fall of Constantinople, when the Greek scholars were driven into exile, bearing with them the seeds of an intellectual renovation, Italy was more than any other country the centre to which they were attracted. In the Italian princes they found the most munificent and discerning patrons, and in the Italian universities the most congenial asylums. Padua and Bologna were then the great centres of freethought. A series of professors, of whom Pomponatius appears to have been the most eminent, had pursued in these universities speculations as daring as those of the eighteenth century, and had habituated a small but able circle of scholars to examine theological questions with the most fearless scrutiny. They maintained that there were two spheres of thought, the sphere of reason and the sphere of faith, and that these spheres were entirely distinct. As philosophers, and under the guidance of reason, they elaborated theories of the boldest and

[1] See Jonathan Edwards on *Original Sin*—one of the most revolting books that have ever proceeded from the pen of man.

most unflinching scepticism; as Catholics, and under the impulse of faith, they acquiesced in all the doctrines of their Church.[1] The fact of their accepting certain doctrines as a matter of faith did not at all prevent them from repudiating them on the ground of reason; and the complete separation of the two orders of ideas enabled them to pursue their intellectual speculations by a method which was purely secular, and with a courage that was elsewhere unknown. Even in Catholicism a dualism of this kind could not long continue, but it was manifestly incompatible with Protestantism, which at least professed to make private judgment the foundation of belief. Faith considered as an unreasoning acquiescence disappeared from theology, and the order of ideas which reason had established remained alone. As a consequence of all this, the Reformation in Italy was almost confined to a small group of scholars, who pushed its principles to their extreme limits, with an unflinching logic, with a disregard for both tradition and consequences, and above all with a secular spirit that was elsewhere unequalled. With the peculiar tenets connected with the name of Socinus we are not now concerned, for the question of theological method is distinct from that of theological doctrines. It is, however, sufficiently manifest that although Socinus laid a far greater stress on the authority of Revelation than his followers, the prevailing

sentiment which actuated him was a desire to subordinate traditional tenets to the dictates of reason and of conscience, and that his entire system of interpretation was due to this desire. It is also evident that it was this spirit that induced him to discard with unqualified severity the orthodox doctrines of the sinfulness of error and of the transmission of guilt.[1]

It may appear at first sight a strange paradox to represent the career of Zuinglius as in any degree parallel to that of Socinus. Certainly the bold and simple-minded pastor of Zurich, who bore with such an unflinching calm the blaze of popularity and the storms of controversy, and perished at last upon the battle-field, forms in most respects a glaring contrast to the timid Italian who spent his life in passing from court to court, and from university to university, shrinking with nervous alarm from all opposition and notoriety, and instilling almost furtively, into the minds of a few friends whom his gentle manners had captivated, the great principles of religious toleration. Certainly, too, nothing could be further from the mind of Zuinglius than the doctrines which are known as Socinianism, nor did the antecedents of the two Reformers bear any resemblance. Yet there can, I think, be no doubt that the dominant predisposition of Zuinglius also was to interpret all tenets according to the *a priori* conceptions of reason and conscience. Though a man of much more than common ability he had but slight pretensions to learning, and this, in an age when men are endeavouring to break loose from tradition, has sometimes proved a positive and a most important advantage. The tendency of his mind was early shown in the position he assumed on the eucharistic controversy. There was no single subject in which the leading Reformers wavered so much, none on which they found so great a difficulty in divesting themselves of their old belief. The voice of reason was clearly on one side, the weight of tradition inclined to the other, and the language of Scripture was susceptible of either interpretation. Luther never advanced beyond consubstantiation; Calvin only arrived at his final views after a long series of oscillations; the English Reformers can scarcely be said to have ever arrived at

---

[1] See, on the career of Pomponatius, Matter, *Histoire des Doctrines morales des trois derniers Siècles*, tom. i. pp. 51–67. Pomponatius was born at Mantua in 1462, and died in 1524. His principal work is on *The Immortality of the Soul.* He was protected by Leo X. (*Biog. Univ.*) Vanini said that the soul of Averroes had passed into Pomponatius. The seventeenth century furnishes some striking examples of this separation of the philosophical and theological points of view. Thus Charron, who as a philosopher wrote one of the most sceptical books of his age, was a priest, and author of a treatise on *Christian Evidences.* Pascal, too, while devoting his life to the defence of religion, accepted with delight the Pyrrhonism of Montaigne, maintained in the most emphatic language the utter vanity of philosophy, and denied that reason could establish even the outlines of morals. Huet, the great Bishop of Avranches, defended the same position in his posthumous *Traité philosophique de la foiblesse de l'esprit humain.* Bayle, in his *Réponses au Provincial;* and Leibnitz, in his *La Foi et la Raison,* have collected much information about this school of thought. See, too, Cousin's work on Pascal. In our own day, similar views have been maintained by Lamennais, in his *Essai sur l'Indifférence,* and in a less degree by Dr. Newman. Luther himself had maintained that a proposition may be true in theology and false in philosophy—an opinion which the Sorbonne condemned: "Sorbona pessime definivit idem esse verum in philosophia et theologia, impieque damnavit eos qui contrarium docuerint." (Amand Saintes, *Hist. du Rationalisme en Allemagne,* p. 29.)

[1] Neander, *Hist. of Dogmas,* vol. ii. pp. 657, 658.

any definite conclusions. Zuinglius alone, from the very beginning, maintained with perfect confidence the only doctrine which accords with the evidence of the senses, stated it in language of transparent precision, and clung to it with unwavering tenacity. The same tendency was shown still more clearly in his decisions on those points in which tradition clashes with conscience. It is surely a most remarkable fact that in the age of such men as Luther and Calvin, as Melanchthon and Erasmus, Zuinglius, who in intellectual power was far inferior to several of his contemporaries, should almost alone have anticipated the rationalistic doctrine of the seventeenth century concerning the innocence of error, and the tolerance that should be accorded to it. On the subject of original sin he separated himself with equal boldness from the other leaders of the Reformation, maintaining that it was nothing more than a malady or evil tendency, and that it did not in any degree involve guilt.[1]

It was thus that two of the leaders of the Reformation were induced by the rationalistic character of their minds to abandon the notion of transmitted guilt, and the doctrine concerning unbaptised infants which was connected with it. If the current of opinions has since then been flowing in the same direction, this is entirely due to the increased diffusion of a rationalistic spirit, and not at all to any active propagandism or to any definite arguments. Men have come instinc-

tively and almost unconsciously to judge all doctrines by their intuitive sense of right, and to reject or explain away or throw into the background those that will not bear the test, no matter how imposing may be the authority that authenticates them. This method of judgment, which was once very rare, has now become very general. Every generation its triumph is more manifest, and entire departments of theology have receded or brightened beneath its influence.[1] How great a change has been effected in the doctrine concerning unbaptised children must be manifest to anyone who considers how completely the old doctrine has disappeared from popular teaching, and what a general and intense repugnance is excited by its simple statement. It was once deemed a mere truism; it would now be viewed with horror and indignation: and if we desired any further proof of the extent of this change we should find it in the position which the Quakers and the Baptists have assumed in Christendom. It is scarcely possible to conceive any sects which in the Early Church would have been regarded with more unmingled abhorrence, or would have been deemed more unquestionably outside the pale of salvation. It is no exaggeration to say that the feeling of repugnance with which men now look upon the polygamy of the Mormons presents but a very faint image of that which the Fathers would have manifested towards those who systematically withheld from their children that baptism which was unanimously pronounced to be essential to their salvation. Yet the Quakers and the Baptists have now obtained a place among the most respected sections of the Church, and in the eyes of very many Protestants the peculiarities of the second, at least, are not sufficiently serious to justify any feeling of repulsion or to prevent the most cordial co-operation. For a great change has silently swept over Christendom; without controversy and without disturbance an old doctrine has passed away from among the realisations of mankind.

---

[1] Neander, *Hist. of Dogmas*, vol. ii. pp. 658, 659. Bossuet made a violent attack upon this notion of Zuinglius, which he regarded with extreme horror, because, as he plaintively observes, supposing it to be true, then "le péché originel ne damne personne, pas même les enfants des païens." (*Variations protestantes*, liv. ii. c. 21.) The remarks of Bossuet are especially worthy of attention on account of the great clearness with which he maintains the universality of the belief in the damnable nature of original sin in all sections of the Christian Church. He has, however, slightly overstated the doctrine of Zuinglius. The Reformer distinctly declared original sin to be simply a disease, and not properly a sin. From his language in his *Treatise on Baptism*, it was inferred that he asserted the salvation of pagan infants. However, in 1526, he wrote a short treatise *On Original Sin*, in which he said that his former work had been misrepresented; that he maintained indeed that the word "sin" was only applied to our original malady by a figure of speech; that he was quite sure that that malady never in itself damned Christian children, but that he was not equally sure that it never damned pagan children. He inclined, however, strongly to the belief that it did not: "De Christianorum natis certi sumus eos peccato originali non damnari, de aliorum non itidem; quamvis, ut ingenue fateor, nobis probabilior videtur sententia quam docuimus, non temere pronunciandum esse de gentilium quoque natis et eis qui opus legis faciunt ex lege intus digito Dei scripta." (P. 28.)

[1] Chillingworth treated the subject with his usual admirable good sense: "This is certain, that God will not deal unjustly with unbaptised infants; but how in particular He will deal with them concerns not us, and so we need not much regard it." (*Religion of Protestants*, chap. vii.) Jeremy Taylor strongly rejected both original sin, in the sense of transmitted guilt, and the damnation of infants that was inferred from it.

But the scope of the doctrine we are considering was not confined to unbaptised children; it extended also to all adults who were external to the Church. If the whole human race existed under a sentence of condemnation which could only be removed by connection with Christianity, and if this sentence was so stringent that even the infant was not exempt from its effects, it was natural that the adult heathen, who added his personal transgressions to the guilt of Adam, should be doomed at last to perdition. Nor did the Fathers who constructed the early systems of theology at all shrink from the consequence. At a time when the Christian Church formed but an infinitesimal fraction of the community, at a time when almost all the members who composed it were themselves converts from paganism, and reckoned among the pagans those who were bound to them by the closest ties of gratitude and affection, the great majority of the Fathers deliberately taught that the entire pagan world was doomed to that state of punishment which they invariably described as literal and undying fire. In any age and under any circumstances such a doctrine must seem inexpressibly shocking, but it appears most peculiarly so when we consider that the convert who accepted it, and who with a view to his own felicity proclaimed the system of which he believed it to form a part to be a message of good tidings, must have acquiesced in the eternal perdition of the mother who had borne him, of the father upon whose knees he had played, of the friends who were associated with the happy years of childhood and early manhood, of the immense mass of his fellow-countrymen, and of all those heroes and sages who by their lives or precepts had first kindled a moral enthusiasm within his breast. All these were doomed by one sweeping sentence. Nor were they alone in their condemnation. The heretics, no matter how trivial may have been their error, were reserved for the same fearful fate. The Church, according to the favourite image of the Fathers, was a solitary ark floating upon a boundless sea of ruin. Within its pale there was salvation; without it salvation was impossible. "If anyone out of Noah's ark could escape the deluge," wrote St. Cyprian, "he who is out of the Church may also escape." "Without this house," said Origen, "that is without

the Church, no one is saved." "No one," said St. Augustine, "cometh to salvation and eternal life except he who hath Christ for his head, but no one can have Christ for his head except he that is in His body the Church."[1] "Hold most firmly," added St. Fulgentius, "and doubt not that not only all pagans but also all Jews, heretics, and schismatics who depart from this present life outside the Catholic Church are about to go into eternal fire, prepared for the devil and his angels."[2] So prominent and so unquestionable was this doctrine deemed, that the Council of Carthage, in the fourth century, made it one of the test-questions put to every bishop before ordination.[3]

This doctrine has had a greater influence than perhaps any other speculative opinion upon the history of mankind. How different it is from the conceptions to which the great teachers of antiquity had arrived must be evident to anyone who knows how fondly they cherished the doctrine of the immortality of the soul, how calmly they contemplated the approach of death,[4] and how hope-

[1] I take these references from Palmer, *On the Church* (vol. i. pp. 11-13, 3rd ed.), where there is much evidence on the subject collected. Mr. Palmer contends that the Fathers are unanimous on the subject, but Barbeyrac shows that at least two, and those of the earliest (Justin Martyr and Clemens Alexandrinus), admitted the possible salvation of the pagans (*Morale des Pères*, ch. xi. § 11), and that the first expressly said that Socrates and Heraclitus in the sight of God were Christians. See, too, Tennemann, *Manuel de l'Histoire de la Philosophie*, tom. i. pp. 314, 315. I am afraid, however, there is no doubt that the great majority of the Fathers took the other view. Minucius Felix thought the dæmon of Socrates was a devil. (*Octavius*, ch. xxvi.)

[2] *De Fide*, § 81; and again, still more explicitly: "Omni enim homini qui Ecclesiæ Catholicæ non tenet unitatem, neque baptismus neque eleemosyna quamlibet copiosa, neque mors pro nomine Christi suscepta proficere poterit ad salutem, quamdiu eo vel hæretica vel schismatica pravitas perseverat quæ ducit ad mortem," (§ 22.)

[3] Palmer, *On the Church*, vol. i. p. 13. And again the Synod of Zerta in A.D. 412: "Whosoever is separated from the Catholic Church, however innocently he may think he lives, for this crime alone that he is separated from the unity of Christ will not have life, but the wrath of God remaineth on him." This statement is said to have been drawn up by St. Augustine. See Hawarden's *Charity and Truth*, pp. 39-40 (Dublin, 1809).

[4] I know nothing in the world sadder than one of the sayings of Luther on this matter. I quote it from that beautiful old translation of *The Table Talk* by Bell: "It were a light and an easy matter for a Christian to suffer and overcome death if he knew not that it were God's wrath; the same title maketh death bitter to us. But an heathen dieth securely away; he neither seeth nor feeleth that it is God's wrath, but meaneth it is the end of nature and is natural. The epicurean says it is but to endure one evil hour." A distinguished living antiquarian, comparing the heathen and the mediæval representations of death, observes: "Dans la société païenne, toute composée du sensualisme et de licence

fully they looked forward to the future. Never can men forget that noble Greek who, struck down by an unrighteous sentence, summoned around him his dearest disciples, and having reasoned with them on the immortality of the soul and the rewards of virtue and the goodness of the gods, took with a gentle smile the cup of death, and passed away thanking the god of healing who had cured him of the disease of life. That "the just man should take confidence in death,"[1] that he who has earnestly, though no doubt imperfectly, tried to do his duty has nothing to fear beyond the grave, had been the consoling faith of all the best minds of antiquity. That the bold, unshackled, and impartial search for truth is among the noblest and, therefore, among the most innocent employments of mankind, was the belief which inspired all the philosophies of the past. Nor was it merely or mainly in the groves of Athens that this spirit was manifested. It should never be forgotten that the rationalist has always found the highest expression of his belief in the language of the prophet, who declared that the only service the Almighty required was a life of justice, of mercy, and of humility ; of the wise man, who summed up the whole duty of man in the fear of God and the observance of His commandments ; of the apostle, who described true religion as consisting of charity and of purity ; and of that still greater Teacher, who proclaimed true worship to be altogether spiritual, and who described the final adjudication as the separation of mankind according to their acts and not according to their opinions.

But, however this may be, the doctrine of salvation in the Church alone was unanimously adopted when Christianity passed from its moral to its first dogmatic stage, and on two occasions it conferred an inestimable benefit upon mankind. At a time when Christianity was struggling against the most horrible persecutions, and also against the gross con-

ceptions of an age that could obtain but a very partial idea of its elevated purity, the terrorism of this doctrine became an auxiliary little in harmony indeed with the spirit of a philanthropic religion, but admirably suited to the time, and powerful enough to nerve the martyr with an unflinching courage, and to drive the doubter speedily into the Church. Again, when the ascendency of the new faith had become manifest, it seemed for a time as if its administrative and organising function would have been destroyed by the countless sects that divided it. The passion for allegory and the spirit of eclecticism that characterised the Eastern converts, the natural subtlety of the Greek mind, and still more the disputatious philosophy of Aristotle, which the Greek heretics introduced into the Church, and which Nestorianism planted in the great school of Edessa,[1] had produced so many and such virulent controversies that the whole ecclesiastical fabric seemed dislocated, and intellectual anarchy was imminent. The conception of an authoritative Church was not yet fully formed, though men were keenly sensible of the importance of dogma. It is computed that there were about ninety heresies in three centuries.[2] Such questions as the double procession of the Holy Ghost, the proper day for celebrating Easter, the nature of the light upon Mount Tabor, or the existence in Christ of two independent but perfectly coincident wills, were discussed with a ferocity that seems almost to countenance the suggestion of Butler, that communities like individuals may be insane. But here again the doctrine of exclusive salvation exercised a decisive influence. As long as it was held and realised, the diversities of private judgment must have waged a most unequal warfare with the unity of authority. Men could not long rest amid the conflict of opposing arguments ; they could not endure that measure of doubt which is the necessary accompaniment of controversy. All the fractions of Christianity soon gravitated to one or two great centres, and a spiritual despotism

---

on se gardait bien de représenter la mort comme quelque chose de hideux ; il ne paraît même point que le squelette ait été alors le symbole de l'impitoyable divinité. Mais quand le christianisme eut conquis le monde, quand une éternité malheureuse dut être la punition des fautes commises ici-bas, la mort, qui avait semblé si indifférente aux anciens, devint une chose dont les conséquences furent si terribles pour le chrétien qu'il fallut les lui rapporter à chaque instant en frappant ses yeux des images funèbres." (Jubinal, *Sur les Danses des Morts*, p. 8.)
[1] Plato.

[1] It is remarkable that Aristotle, whom the schoolmen placed almost on a level with the Fathers, owes his position entirely to the early heretics ; that the introduction of his philosophy was at first invariably accompanied by an increase of heresy ; and that the Fathers, with scarcely an exception, unequivocally denounced it. See much curious evidence of this in Allemand - Lavigerie, *École chrétienne d'Édesse* (Thèse présentée à la Faculté des Lettres de Paris, 1850.)
[2] Middleton's *Free Enquiry*, Introd. p. 86.

was consolidated which alone could control and temper the turbulent elements of mediæval society, could impose a moral yoke upon the most ferocious tyrants, could accomplish the great work of the abolition of slavery in Europe, and could infuse into Christendom such a measure of pure and spiritual truth as to prepare men for the better phase that was to follow it.

All this was done by the doctrine of exclusive salvation. At the Reformation, when the old Church no longer harmonised with the intellectual condition of Europe, and when the spirit of revolt was manifested on all subjects and in all countries, the doctrine was for the most part unchallenged ; and although it undoubtedly produced an inconceivable amount of mental suffering, it had at least the effect of terminating rapidly the anarchy of transition. The tenacity with which it was retained by the Reformers is of course partly due to the difficulty of extricating the mind from old theological modes of thought ; but it was, I think, still more the result of that early tendency to depreciate the nature and the works of man which threw them naturally upon dogmatic systems. There were, indeed, few subjects on which they were so unanimous. " The doctrine of salvation in the Church," writes a learned living author, " was held by all the Lutherans and Reformed, and by the sects which separated from them, as well as by the Romish and other Churches. Luther teaches that remission of sins and sanctification are only obtained in it ; and Calvin says, ' Beyond the bosom of the Church, no remission of sins is to be hoped for, nor any salvation.' The Saxon Confession, presented to the Synod of Trent A.D. 1551, the Helvetic, Confession, the Belgic, the Scottish—all avow that salvation is only to be had in the Church. The Presbyterian divines assembled at Westminster, A.D. 1647, in their ' Humble Advice concerning a Confession of Faith ' (c. 25), declare that ' the visible Church, which is also Catholique and universal under the Gospel (not confined to one nation, as before under the Law), consists of all those throughout the world that profess the true religion ......out of which there is no ordinary possibility of salvation.' The Independents admitted the same."[1] Nor was

the position of the Anglican Church at all different. The Athanasian Creed was given an honoured place among her formularies, and the doctrine which that creed distinctly asserts was implied in several of the services of the Church, and was strongly maintained by a long succession of her divines.[1] Among the leading Reformers, Zuinglius, and Zuinglius alone, openly and unequivocally repudiated it. In a Confession of Faith which he wrote just before his death, and which marks an important epoch in the history of the human mind, he described in magnificent language that future " assembly of all the saintly, the heroic, the faithful, and the virtuous," when Abel and Enoch, Noah and Abraham, Isaac and Jacob, will mingle with " Socrates, Aristides, and Antigonus, with Numa and Camillus, Hercules and Theseus, the Scipios and the Catos," and when every upright and holy man who has ever lived will be present with his God.[2] In our age, when the doctrine of exclusive salvation seldom excites more than a smile, such language appears but natural, but when it was first written it excited on all sides amazement and indignation. Luther on reading it said he despaired of the salvation of Zuinglius : Bossuet quotes the passage as a climax to his charges against the Swiss Reformer, and quotes it as if it required no comment, but was in itself sufficient to hand down its author to the contempt and indignation of posterity.

I shall now proceed to examine the more remote consequences of the doctrine of exclusive salvation, in order to trace the connection between its decline and some other remarkable features of the rationalistic movement. In the first place, it is manifest that the conceptions I have reviewed are so directly opposed to our natural sense of what is right and just, to all the conclusions at which those great teachers arrived who evolved their doctrines from their own moral nature, that they must establish a permanent opposition between dogmatic theology and natural religion. When the peace of the Church has long been undisturbed, and when the minds of men are not directed with very strong interest to

[1] Palmer, *On the Church*, vol. i. p. 13.

[1] See a great deal of evidence of this in Palmer.
[2] This passage is given in full by Bossuet, *Variations protestantes*, liv. ii. c. 19. The original Confession was published by Bullinger, in 1536, with a very laudatory preface.

dogmatic questions, conscience will act insensibly upon the belief, obscuring or effacing its true character. Men will instinctively endeavour to explain it away, or to dilute its force, or to diminish its prominence. But when the agitation of controversy has brought the doctrine vividly before the mind, and when the enthusiasm of the contest has silenced the revolt of conscience, theology will be developed more and more in the same direction, till the very outlines of natural religion are obliterated. Thus we find that those predestinarian theories which are commonly identified with Calvin, though they seem to have been substantially held by St. Augustine, owe their reception mainly to the previous action of the doctrine of exclusive salvation upon the mind. For the one objection to the metaphysical and other arguments the Calvinist can urge, which will always appear conclusive to the great majority of mankind, is the moral objection. It is this objection, and this alone, which enables men to cut through that entangling maze of arguments concerning freewill, foreknowledge, and predetermination, in which the greatest intellects both of antiquity and of modern days have been hopelessly involved, and which the ablest metaphysicians have pronounced inextricable. Take away the moral argument : persuade men that when ascribing to the Deity justice and mercy they are speaking of qualities generically distinct from those which exist among mankind— qualities which we are altogether unable to conceive, and which may be compatible with acts that men would term grossly unjust and unmerciful: tell them that guilt may be entirely unconnected with a personal act, that millions of infants may be called into existence for a moment to be precipitated into a place of torment, that vast nations may live and die, and then be raised again to endure a never-ending punishment, because they did not believe in a religion of which they had never heard, or because a crime was committed thousands of years before they were in existence : convince them that all this is part of a transcendently perfect and righteous moral scheme, and there is no imaginable abyss to which such a doctrine will not lead. You will have blotted out those fundamental notions of right and wrong which the Creator has engraven upon every heart; you will have extinguished the lamp of conscience;

you will have taught men to stifle the inner voice as a lying witness, and to esteem it virtuous to disobey it. But even this does not represent the full extent of the evil. The doctrine of exclusive salvation not only destroys the moral objection to that ghastly system of religious fatalism which Augustine and Calvin constructed, it directly leads to it by teaching that the ultimate destiny of the immense majority of mankind is determined entirely irrespectively of their will. Millions die in infancy; millions live and die in heathen lands ; millions exist in ranks of society where they have no opportunities for engaging in theological research ; millions are so encumbered by the prejudices of education that no mental effort can emancipate them from the chain. We accordingly find that predestinarianism was in the first instance little more than a development of the doctrine of exclusive salvation. St. Augustine illustrated it by the case of a mother who had two infants. Each of these is but "a lump of perdition ;" neither has ever performed a moral act. The mother overlies one, and it perishes unbaptised ; the other is baptised, and is saved.

But the doctrine of Augustine and Ambrose never seems to have been pushed in the Early Church to the same extremes, or to have been stated with the same precision, as it afterwards was by the Reformers.[1] The mild and sagacious Erasmus soon perceived in this one of the principal evils of the Reformation, and he wrote a treatise in defence of freewill, which elicited from Luther one of the most unequivocal and certainly one of the most revolting declarations of fatalism in the whole compass of theology. "The human will," said Luther, "is like a beast of burden. If God mounts it, it

[1] The doctrine of double predestination was, however, maintained in the ninth century by a monk named Gotteschalk, who was opposed by Hinckmar, Archbishop of Rheims, in the spirit of a theologian, and by Scotus Erigena in the spirit of a freethinker. For an account of this once-famous controversy see the learned work of M. St.-René Taillandier, Scot Érigène et la Philosophie scholastique (Strasbourg, 1843), pp. 51–58; and for a contemporary view of the opinions of Gotteschalk, see a letter by Amulo, Archbishop of Lyons (the immediate successor of Agobard), printed with the works of Agobard (Paris, 1666). According to Amulo, Gotteschalk not only held the doctrines of reprobation and particular redemption, but even declared that the Almighty rejoiced and exulted over the destruction of those who were predestinated to damnation. Gotteschalk was condemned to be degraded from the priesthood, to be imprisoned, and to be scourged. (Llorente, Hist. de l'Inquisition, tom. i. p. 20.)

wishes and goes as God wills; if Satan mounts it, it wishes and goes as Satan wills. Nor can it choose the rider it would prefer, or betake itself to him, but it is the riders who contend for its possession."[1] "This is the acme of faith, to believe that He is merciful who saves so few and who condemns so many; that He is just who at His own pleasure has made us necessarily doomed to damnation; so that, as Erasmus says, He seems to delight in the tortures of the wretched, and to be more deserving of hatred than of love. If by any effort of reason I could conceive how God could be merciful and just who shows so much anger and iniquity, there would be no need for faith."[2] "God foreknows nothing subject to contingencies, but he foresees, foreordains, and accomplishes all things by an unchanging, eternal, and efficacious will. By this thunderbolt freewill sinks shattered in the dust."[3]

Such were the opinions of the greatest of the Reformers. The doctrine of Calvin and his school was equally explicit. According to them, the Fall, with all its consequences, was predetermined ages before the Creation, and was the necessary consequence of that predetermination. The Almighty, they taught, irrevocably decided the fate of each individual long before He called him into existence, and has predestined millions to His hatred and to eternal damnation. With that object He gave them being—with that object He withholds from them the assistance that alone can correct the perversity of the nature with which He created them. He will hate them during life, and after death He will cast them into the excruciating torments of undying fire, and will watch their agonies without compassion through the countless ages of eternity.[1]

It is needless to comment upon such teaching as this. That it makes the Deity the direct author of sin,[2] that it subverts all our notions of justice and of mercy, that the simple statement of it is inexpressibly shocking and revolting, can hardly be denied by its warmest supporters. Indeed, when we combine this teaching with the other doctrines I have considered in the present chapter, the whole may be regarded as unequalled in the religious history of mankind. In our age such tenets have retired from the blaze of day; they are found only in the obscure writings of obscure men. Since

---

[1] "Sic humana voluntas in medio posita est ceu jumentum, si insederit Deus vult et vadit quo vult Deus, ut Psalmus dicit: 'Factus sum sicut jumentum et ego semper tecum.' Si insederit Satan vult et vadit quo vult Satan; nec est in ejus arbitrio ad utrum sessorem currere aut eum quærere, sed ipsi sessores certant ob ipsum obtinendum et possidendum." (*De Servo Arbitrio*, pars. i. sec. 24.)

[2] "Hic est fidei summus gradus, credere illum esse clementem qui tam paucos salvat tam multos damnat, credere justum qui sua voluntate nos necessario damnabiles facit, ut videatur, referente Erasmo, delectari cruciatibus miserorum, et odio potius quam amore dignus. Si igitur possem ulla ratione comprehendere quomodo is Deus misericors et justus, qui tantam iram et iniquitatem ostendit, non esset opus fide." (*Ibid.* sec. 23.)

[3] "Est itaque et hoc imprimis necessarium et salutare Christiano nosse, quod Deus nihil præscit contingiter, sed quod omnia incommutabilia et æterna, intallibilique voluntate et prævidet et præponit et facit. Hoc fulmine sternitur et conteritur penitus liberum arbitrium." (Sec. 10.) I give these sections according to Vaughan's translation (1823), for in the original edition (1526) there are no divisions, and the pages are not numbered. Melanchthon, in the first edition of his *Commonplaces*, expressed extreme predestinarian views, but omitted them in later editions. Luther, in his old age, said he could not review with perfect satisfaction any of his works except, perhaps, his *Catechism* and his *De Servo Arbitrio* (Vaughan's Preface, p. 57). There is a full notice of this book in one of Sir W. Hamilton's essays.

[1] On Calvin's views, see especially his *De Æterna Dei Prædestinatione*, and his *Institut. Christ.* lib. iii. c. 21-23. But perhaps their clearest and most emphatic statement is in a work of Beza, *De Æterna Dei Prædestinatione contra Sebastianum Castellionem* (published in the *Opuscula* of Beza, Genevæ, 1658). The pointed objections on the score of moral rectitude of his rationalistic opponent brought the enormities of the Calvinistic doctrine into the fullest relief. There is a curious old translation of this work, under the title of *Beza's Display of Popish Practices, or Patched Pelagianism*, translated by W. Hopkinson (London, 1578). Beza especially insists on the unfairness of accusing Calvinists of asserting that God so hated some men that He predestinated them to destruction; the truth being that God of His free sovereignty predestinated them to destruction, and therefore to His hatred; so that "God is not moved with the hatred of any that He should drive him to destruction, but He hath hated whom He hath predestinated to destruction." Another point on which Jonathan Edwards especially has insisted (in his *Freedom of Will*) is that there can be no injustice in punishing *voluntary* transgression, and that the transgressions of the reprobate are voluntary; men having been since Adam created with wills so hopelessly corrupt that without Divine assistance they must *inevitably* be damned, and God having in the majority of cases resolved to withhold that assistance. The fatality, therefore, does not consist in man being compelled to do certain things whether he wishes it or not, but in his being brought into the world with such a nature that his wishes necessarily tend in a given direction.

[2] Calvinists, indeed, often protest against this conclusion; but it is almost self-evident, and the ablest writer of the school admits it in a sense which is quite sufficiently large for his opponents: "If by the author of sin is meant the permitter or not hinderer of sin, and at the same time a disposer of the state of events in such a manner for wise, holy, and most excellent ends and purposes that sin, if it be permitted or not hindered, will most certainly and infallibly follow; I say, if this be all that is meant, I do not deny that God is the author of sin." (Jonathan Edwards, *Freedom of Will*, p. 369.) The predestination of the fall of Adam, whose will was not hopelessly corrupt, has of course its own peculiar difficulties.

Jonathan Edwards they have had no exponent of undoubted genius, and no distinguished writer could venture without a serious loss of reputation openly to profess them. Such language as was employed on this subject by men like Luther, Calvin, and Beza, while in the zenith of their popularity, would not now be tolerated for a moment outside a small and uninfluential circle. The rationalistic spirit has so pervaded all our habits of thought, that every doctrine which is repugnant to our moral sense excites an intense and ever-increasing aversion; and as the doctrine of exclusive salvation, which prepared the mind for the doctrine of reprobation, is no longer realised, the latter appears peculiarly revolting.

Another very important subject upon which the doctrine of exclusive salvation has exercised great influence, is the relation between dogmas and morals. The older theologians invariably attributed to dogmas an intrinsic efficacy which was entirely independent of their effect upon life. Thus we have already had occasion to observe, that in the Early Church no controversies were deemed so important as those which concerned the connection between the two natures in Christ, and that at the Reformation the acceptance or rejection of transubstantiation was made the habitual test of orthodoxy. On the other hand, the politician, in a secular age, is inclined to value religious systems solely according to their influence upon the acts of mankind. He sees that religious controversies have often dislocated the social system, have presented an insuperable obstacle to the fusion of the different elements of a nation, have produced long and sanguinary wars, and have diverted a large proportion of intellect and energy from enterprises that are conducive to the welfare of society. These he considers the evils of theology, which are compensated for by the control that it exercises over the passions of mankind, by the high sense of duty it diffuses, by the consolations it affords in age, in suffering, and in sorrow, and by the intensity of the philanthropy it inspires. His object therefore is to encourage a system in which the moral restraint shall be as great as possible, and the dogmatic elements shall be few and torpid. The rationalist occupies a central position between the two. Like the early theologian, he denies that the measure of theological excellence is entirely utili-

tarian; like the politician, he denies that dogmas possess an intrinsic efficacy. He believes that they are intended to act upon and develop the affective or emotional side of human nature, that they are the vehicles by which certain principles are conveyed into the mind which would otherwise never be received, and that when they have discharged their functions they must lose their importance. In the earlier phases of society men have never succeeded in forming a purely spiritual and moral conception of the Deity, and they therefore make an image which they worship. By this means the conception of the Deity is falsified and debased, but the moral influence of worship is retained: a great evil is the price of an inestimable benefit. As, however, men obtain with increasing civilisation a capacity for forming purer and more moral conceptions, idolatry becomes an unmingled evil, and is in consequence at last abandoned. Just in the same way a purely moral religion, appealing to a disinterested sense of duty and perception of excellence, can never be efficacious in an early condition of society. It is consequently materialised, associated with innumerable ceremonies, with elaborate creeds, with duties that bear no relation to moral sentiments, with an ecclesiastical framework, and with a copious legendary. Through all this extraneous matter the moral essence filters down to the people, preparing them for the higher phases of development. Gradually the ceremonies drop away, the number of doctrines is reduced, the ecclesiastical ideal of life and character is exchanged for the moral ideal; dogmatic conceptions manifest an increased flexibility, and the religion is at last transfigured and regenerated, radiant in all its parts with the pure spirit that had created it.

It is manifest that according to this view there exists a certain antagonism between the dogmatic and the moral elements of a religious system, and that their relative influence will depend mainly on the degree of civilisation; an amount of dogmatic pressure which is a great blessing in one age being a great evil in another. Now, one of the most obvious consequences of the doctrine of exclusive salvation is that it places the moral in permanent subordination to the dogmatic side of religion. If there be a Catholic faith "which except a man believe he cannot be saved," it is quite natural that men should deem it "before *all* things" necessary to hold it. If the purest moral life cannot atone for error, while a true religion has many means of effacing guilt, the mind will naturally turn to the doctrinal rather than to the practical side. The extent to which this tendency has been manifested in the Church of Rome is well known. Protestant controversialists have often drawn up long and perfectly authentic lists of celebrated characters who were stained with every crime, and who have nevertheless been among the favourites of the Church, who have clung to her ordinances with full orthodox tenacity, who have assuaged by her absolution every qualm of conscience, and who have at last, by endowing a monastery or undergoing a penance or directing a persecution against heretics, persuaded themselves that they had effaced all the crimes of their lives. In Protestantism this combination of devotion and immorality, which is not to be confounded with hypocrisy, appears more rare. Lives like that of Benvenuto Cellini, in which the most atrocious crimes alternate with ecstasies of the most rapturous and triumphant piety, are scarcely ever to be met with; yet it would be rash to say that the evil is unknown. The tenacity with which Protestant nations cling to the orthodox tenets of the Reformation can scarcely, I think, be said to bear any fixed proportion to the national morality, and Sweden, which of all Protestant countries has been most conspicuous for its prolonged legislation against heterodoxy, is said to be equally conspicuous for the scandalous amount of illegitimacy among the people.[1]

These are the contradictions that result from the doctrine of exclusive salvation among those who do not belong to a high order of sanctity, and who gladly purchase a license for the indulgence of their passions by an assiduous cultivation of what they deem the more important side of their faith. A very much more general tendency, and one which has exercised a far more pernicious influence upon the history of mankind, is displayed by those whose zeal is entirely unselfish. Being convinced that no misfortune can be so great as heresy, and that the heretic is doomed to eternal misery, they have habitually supported their creed by imposture and falsehood. That they should do this is quite natural. Whatever may be the foundation of the moral law, it is certain that in the eyes of the immense majority of mankind there are some overwhelming considerations that will justify a breach of its provisions. If some great misfortune were to befall a man who lay on a sick bed, trembling between life and death; if the physician declared that the knowledge of that misfortune would be certain death to the patient, and if concealment were only possible by a falsehood, there are very few moralists who would condemn that falsehood. If the most ardent denouncer of "pious frauds" were to meet an assassin in pursuit of an innocent man, and were able by misdirecting the pursuer to save the fugitive, it may be safely predicted that the lie would be unscrupulously uttered. It is not very easy to justify these things by argument, or to draw a clear line between criminal and innocent falsehood; but that there are circumstances which justify untruth has always been admitted by the common sentiment of mankind, and has been distinctly laid down by the most eminent moralists.[1] When therefore a man believes that those who adopt an erroneous opinion will be consigned to perdition, when he not only believes this but realises it as a living and operative truth, and when he perceives that it is possible either by direct falsehood or by the suppression or distortion of truth to strengthen the evidences of his faith, he usually finds the

[1] See Laing's *Sweden*, pp. 108–141, where this question is minutely examined. This is a mere question of figures. The following passage from another work of the same writer is less susceptible of decisive proof, and is, I am inclined to think, somewhat overstated, but is nevertheless very suggestive: "The Swiss people present to the political philosopher the unexpected and most remarkable social phenomenon of a people eminently moral in conduct yet eminently irreligious: at the head of the moral state in Europe, not merely for absence of numerous or great crimes, or of disregard of right, but for ready obedience to law, for honesty, fidelity to their engagements, for fair-dealing, sobriety, industry, orderly conduct, for good government, useful public institutions, general well-being, and comfort; yet at the bottom of the scale for religious feeling, observances, or knowledge, especially in the Protestant cantons, in which prosperity, well-being, and morality seem to be, as compared to the Catholic cantons, in an inverse ratio to the influence of religion on the people....It is a very remarkable social state, similar, perhaps, to that of the ancient Romans, in whom morality and social virtue were also sustained without the aid of religious influences." (Laing's *Notes of a Traveller*, pp. 146–147.) Dr. Arnold said, I think

truly, that the popular notion about the superior prosperity of the Protestant over the Catholic cantons is greatly exaggerated: it exists in some cases and not in others.

[1] Thus, not to quote Roman Catholic authorities, Jeremy Taylor, in the *Ductor Dubitantium*, lib. iii, c. 2, lays down several cases of justifiable falsehood.

temptation irresistible. But there are two very important distinctions between the hypothetical cases I have mentioned and the pious frauds of theologians. The first are the results of isolated moral judgments, while the latter are systematised and raised to the dignity of a regular doctrine. The first, again, spring from circumstances that are so extremely rare and exceptional that they can scarcely have any perceptible influence upon the general veracity of the person who utters them, while the second induce a habit of continual falsehood. The Fathers laid down as a distinct proposition that pious frauds were justifiable and even laudable,[1] and if they had not laid this down they would nevertheless have practised them as a necessary consequence of their doctrine of exclusive salvation. Immediately all ecclesiastical literature became tainted with a spirit of the most unblushing mendacity. Heathenism was to be combated, and therefore prophecies of Christ by Orpheus and the Sibyls were forged, lying wonders were multiplied, and ceaseless calumnies poured upon those who, like Julian, opposed the faith. Heretics were to be convinced, and therefore interpolations of old writings or complete forgeries were habitually opposed to the forged Gospels. The veneration of relics and the monastic system were introduced, and therefore innumerable miracles were attributed to the bones of saints or to the prayers of hermits, and were solemnly asserted by the most eminent of the Fathers.[2] The tendency

was not confined to those Eastern nations which had been always almost destitute of the sense of truth; it triumphed wherever the supreme importance of dogmas was held. Generation after generation it became more universal; it continued till the very sense of truth and the very love of truth seemed blotted out from the minds of men.

That this is no exaggerated picture of the condition at which the middle ages arrived, is known to all who have any acquaintance with its literature; for during that gloomy period the only scholars in Europe were priests and monks, who conscientiously believed that no amount of falsehood was reprehensible which conduced to the edification of the people. Not only did they pursue with the grossest calumny every enemy to their faith, not only did they encircle every saint with a halo of palpable fiction, not only did they invent tens of thousands of miracles for the purpose of stimulating devotion—they also very naturally carried into all other subjects the indifference to truth they had acquired in theology. All their writings, and more especially their histories, became tissues of the wildest fables, so grotesque and at the same time so audacious, that they were the wonder of succeeding ages. And the very men who scattered these fictions broadcast over Christendom, taught at the same time that credulity was a virtue and scepticism a crime. As long as the doctrine of exclusive salvation was believed and realised, it was necessary for the peace of mankind that they should be absolutely certain of the truth of what they believed; in order to be so certain, it was necessary to suppress adverse arguments; and in order to effect this object, it was necessary that there should be no critical or sceptical spirit in Europe. A habit of boundless credulity was therefore a natural consequence of the doctrine of exclusive salvation; and not only did this habit naturally produce a luxuriant crop of falsehood, it was itself the negation of the spirit of truth. For the man who really loves truth cannot possibly subside into a condition of con-

---

[1] See on this subject the evidence collected in Middleton's *Free Enquiry;* the curious panegyric on the habit of telling lies in St. Chrysostom *On the Priesthood;* the remarks of Coleridge in *The Friend,* and of Maury (*Croyances et Légendes,* p. 268). St. Augustine, however, is in this respect an exception. In his treatise *Contra Mendacium* he strongly denounced the tendency, and especially condemns the Priscillianists, among whom it appears to have been very common, and also certain Catholics who thought it justifiable to pretend to be Priscillianists for the purpose of discovering the secrets of that sect. The most revolting aspect of this subject is the notion that heretics are so intensely criminal as to have no moral rights—a favourite doctrine in Catholic countries where no Protestant or sceptical public opinion exists. Thus the Spanish Bishop Simancas—"Ad pœnam quoque pertinet et hæreticorum odium, quod fides illis data servanda non est. Nam si tyrannis, piratis, et cæteris prædonibus quia corpus occidunt fides servanda non est, longe minus hæreticis pertinacibus qui occidunt animas." (*De Catholicis Institutionibus,* p. 365.)

[2] Since the last note was written, this subject has been discussed at some length by Dr. Newman, in his *Apologia pro Vita sua.* I do not, however, find anything to alter in what I have stated. Dr. Newman says (Appendix, p. 77): "The Greek Fathers thought that, when there was a *justa causa,* an untruth need not be a lie. St. Augustine took another view, though

with great misgiving, and, whether he is rightly interpreted or not, is the doctor of the great and common view that all untruths are lies, and that there can be *no* just cause of untruth.... Now, as to the just cause, the Greek Fathers make them such as these—self-defence, charity, *zeal for God's honour,* and the like." It is plain enough that this last would include all of what are commonly termed pious frauds.

tented credulity. He will pause long before accepting any doubtful assertion, he will carefully balance opposing arguments, he will probe every anecdote with scrupulous care, he will endeavour to divest himself of every prejudice, he will cautiously abstain from attributing to probabilities the authority of certainties. These are the essential characteristics of the spirit of truth, and by their encouragement or suppression we can judge how far a system of doctrine coincides with that spirit.

We have seen that there were three ways in which the indissoluble association of salvation with a particular form of belief produced or promoted the absolute indifference to truth and the boundless credulity that characterised the ages in which theology was supreme. It multiplied to an enormous extent pious frauds, which were perpetrated without scruple because they were supposed to produce inestimable benefits to mankind. It rendered universal that species of falsehood which is termed misrepresentation, and which consists mainly of the suppression of all opposing facts ; and it crushed that earnestness of enquiry which is at once the essential characteristic of the love of truth, and the sole bulwark against the encroachments of error. There was, however, yet another way, which, though very closely connected with the foregoing, is sufficiently distinct to claim a separate consideration.

A love of truth, by the very definition of the terms, implies a resolution under all circumstances to approach as nearly as possible to its attainment, or in other words, when demonstration is impossible, to adopt the belief which seems most probable. In this respect there is an important difference between speculative and practical life. He who is seeking for truth is bound always to follow what appears to his mind to be the stress of probabilities ; but in action it is sometimes wise to shape our course with a view to the least probable contingency ; because we have to consider not merely the comparative probabilities of success afforded by different courses, but also the magnitude of the results that would ensue. Thus, a man is justly regarded as prudent who insures his house against fire, though an absolute and unrequited loss is the most probable consequence of his act ; because the loss he would suffer in the more probable contingency is in-

considerable, and the advantage he would derive from the insurance in the less probable contingency is very great. From this consideration Pascal—who with Fermat was the founder of what may be termed the scientific treatment of probabilities—derived a very ingenious argument in defence of his theological opinions, which was afterwards adopted by an English mathematician named Craig.[1] They contended, that when a religious system promises infinite rewards and threatens infinite punishments, it is the part of a wise man to sacrifice the present to embrace it, not merely if he believes the probabilities to preponderate in its favour, but even if he regards its truth as extremely improbable, provided the probabilities against it are not infinite. Now, as long as such an argument is urged simply with a view of inducing men to adopt a certain course of action, it has no necessary connection with morals, and should be judged upon prudential grounds.[2] But the case becomes widely different when to adopt the least probable course means to acknowledge a Church which demands as the first condition of allegiance an absolute and heartfelt belief in the truth of what it teaches. When this is the case the argument of Pascal means, and only can mean, that men should by the force of will compel themselves to believe what they do not believe by the force of reason ; that they should exert all their efforts, by withdrawing their attention from one side and concentrating it upon the other, and by the employment of the distorting influences of the affections, to disturb the results of their judgment. Nor is this merely the speculation of some isolated mathematicians ; it is a principle that is constantly acted on in every society which is governed by the doctrine we are considering.[3] Mere sophisms or imperfect reasoning have a comparatively

[1] In a very curious book called *Theologiæ Christianæ Principia Mathematica*. (Londini, 1699.)

[2] The reader may find a review of it made on those grounds in Laplace, *Théorie des Probabilités*. It is manifest that, if correct, obedience would be due to any impostor who said he dreamed that he was a Divine messenger, provided he put his promises and threatenings sufficiently high.

[3] Thus in the seventeenth century the following was a popular Catholic argument. Protestants admit that Catholics may be saved, but Catholics deny that Protestants can ; therefore it is better to become a Catholic. Considering that this argument was designed, by playing on superstitious terrors, and by obscuring the sense of the Divine goodness, to induce men to tamper with their sense of truth, and

small place in the history of human error; the intervention of the will has always been the chief cause of delusion. Under the best circumstances we can but imperfectly guard against its influence; but wherever the doctrine of exclusive salvation is held, it is reduced to a system and regarded as a virtue.

Certainly, whatever opinion may be held concerning the general tendencies of the last three centuries, it is impossible to deny the extraordinary diffusion of a truthful spirit, as manifested both in the increased intolerance of what is false and in the increased suspicion of what is doubtful. This has been one of the general results of advancing civilisation to which all intellectual influences have converged, but the improvement may be said to date more especially from the writings of the great secular philosophers of the seventeenth century. These philosophers destroyed the old modes of thought, not by the force of direct polemical discussion, but by introducing a method of enquiry and a standard of excellence incompatible with them. They taught men to esteem credulity discreditable, to wage an unsparing war against their prejudices, to distrust the verdicts of the past, and to analyse with cautious scrutiny the foundation of their belief. They taught them, above all, to cultivate that love of truth for its own sake which is perhaps the highest attribute of humanity; which alone can emancipate the mind from the countless influences that enthral it, and guide the steps through the labyrinth of human systems; which shrinks from the sacrifice of no cherished doctrine, and of no ancient tie; and which, recognising in itself the reflex of the Deity, finds in itself its own reward.

The conspicuous place which Bacon, Descartes, and Locke have obtained in the history of the human mind, depends much less on the originality of their doctrines or their methods than on the skill with which they developed and diffused

them. Long before Descartes, St. Augustine had anticipated the "cogito ergo sum"; but that which St. Augustine had thrown out as a mere truism, or, at best, as a passing suggestion, Descartes converted into the basis of a great philosophy. Half a century before Bacon, Leonardo da Vinci had exhibited the superiority of the inductive method, and had clearly stated its principles; but even if Leonardo had published his work, it may be safely asserted that the magnificent development of Bacon was necessary to make that method supreme in science. Each of these great men attacked with vast ability and marvellous success some intellectual vice which lay at the very root of the old habits of thought. Descartes taught that the beginning of all knowledge was the rejection of every early prejudice, and a firm resolution to bring every opinion to the test of individual judgment. Locke taught the necessity of mapping out the limits of human faculties, and by his doctrine concerning innate ideas, and above all by his masterly analysis of Enthusiasm, he gave the death-blow to the opinions of those who would remove a certain class of mental phenomena altogether from the jurisdiction of the reason.[1] Bacon, whose gigantic intellect made excursions into every field, was pre-eminently noted for his classification of the *idola* or distorting influences that act on the mind, and for his constant injunction to correct theory by confronting it with facts. Descartes also, in addition to the vast intrinsic value of his works, had the immense merit of doing more than any previous writer to divorce philosophy from erudition, and to make it an appeal to the reasoning powers of ordinary men. The schoolmen, though they had carried philosophical definition almost to the highest conceivable point of perfection, had introduced a style of disquisition so pedantic and monotonous, so full of subtle distinctions and endless repetitions, that all but the most patient students were re-

considering too that its success depended mainly on the timidity, self-distrust, and modesty of the person to whom it was addressed, it may probably be esteemed as thoroughly base and demoralising as any that it is even possible for the imagination to conceive. Yet it was no doubt very effective, and was perfectly in harmony with the doctrine we are considering. Selden asked, "Is their Church better than ours, because it has less charity?" and Bedell, in a passage which Coleridge justly pronounced one of the most beautiful in English prose, compared the two Churches in this respect to the rival mothers before Solomon.

[1] It has been observed by a very able French critic (M. Littré) that the increasing tendency, as civilisation advances, to substitute purely psychological for miraculous solutions is strikingly illustrated by a comparison of *Orestes* with *Hamlet*. The subject of both pieces is essentially the same—a murdered king, a guilty wife, a son distracted between his duty to his dead father and to his living mother; but while the Greek found it necessary to bring the Furies upon the scene to account for the mental paroxysms of Orestes, the Englishman deemed the natural play and conflict of the emotions amply sufficient to account for the sufferings of Hamlet.

pelled by their works ; while their constant appeal to authority, and the fact that they wrote only in Latin, excluded those who were but little learned from the discussion. The great prominence academic præ-lections obtained about the time of the Reformation contributed, I imagine, largely to introduce a simpler and more popular style. Rather more than sixty years before the *Method* of Descartes, Ramus, in his *Dialectics*, had set the example of publishing a philosophical work in French, and Bruno had thrown some of his dreamy speculations into Italian ; but neither of these men was sufficiently able to form a new epoch in the history of philosophy, and their ends were not calculated to encourage imitators —the first having been murdered by the Catholics on the night of St. Bartholomew, and the second burnt alive at Rome by the Pope. Descartes more than anyone else was the author of what may be called the democratic character of philosophy, and this is not the least of his merits. The influence of Locke and Bacon, again, was especially powerful as a corrective of the old tendency to fiction, on account of a certain unimaginative character that was exhibited by the philosophies of both—a character that was perfectly congenial to the intellect of Locke, but very remarkable in the case of Bacon, among whose great faculties imagination occupied an almost dispro-portionate prominence. That this feature of the Baconian philosophy is at present exercising a decidedly prejudicial influ-ence on the English intellect, by pro-ducing an excessive distaste for the higher generalisations, and for all specu-lations that do not lead directly to prac-tical results, has been maintained by many Continental writers, and by at least three of the most eminent English ones.[1] It is, indeed, quite true that Bacon never went in this respect so far as some of his disciples. He certainly never made utility the sole object of science, or at least never restricted utility to material advantages. He asserted in the noblest language the superiority of abstract truth to all the fruits of invention,[2] and would never have

called those speculations useless which form the intellectual character of an age. Yet, on the other hand, it must be ac-knowledged that the general tone of his writings, the extraordinary emphasis which he laid upon the value of experi-ments, and above all upon the bearing of his philosophy on material comforts, re-presents a tendency which was very naturally developed into the narrowest utilitarianism. Those who regarded natural science simply as the minister to the material comforts of mankind were the disciples of Bacon, in much the same sense as Condillac and his followers were the disciples of Locke : they did not accurately represent the doctrines of their master, but they represented the general tendency of his teaching.

But, whatever may be thought of the influence which the inductive philosophy now exercises on the English mind, there can be no doubt that both that philosophy and the essay of Locke were peculiarly fatal to the mediæval modes of thought on account of the somewhat plodding character they displayed. By enlarging the domain of the senses, by making ex-perience the final test of truth, and by greatly discouraging the excursions of theorists, they checked the exuberance of the European imagination, imparted an air of grotesqueness to the wild fictions that had so long been received, and taught men to apply tests both to their traditions and to their emotions which divested them of much of their apparent mystery. It was from the writings of Locke and Bacon that Voltaire and his followers drew the principles that shat-tered the proudest ecclesiastical fabrics of Europe, and it is against these philo-sophers that the ablest defenders of mediæval theology have exhibited the most bitter animosity.[1]

---

[1] Coleridge, Buckle, and Mill.

[2] "And yet (to speak the whole truth), just as we are deeply indebted to light because it enables us to enter on our way, to exercise arts, to read, to distinguish one another, and nevertheless the sight of light is itself more excellent and beautiful than the manifold uses of it ; so, assuredly, the very contemplation of things as they are, without superstition or imposture, without

error or confusion, is in itself more worthy than all the produce of discoveries." (*Novum Organon.*)

[1] Thus De Maistre, the great apostle of modern Ultramontanism, assures us that "dans l'étude de la philosophie, le mépris de Locke est le commencement de la sagesse"; and that "*l'Essai sur l'Entendement humain* est très-certainement, et soit qu'on le nie ou qu'on en convienne, tout ce que le défaut absolu de génie et de style peut enfanter de plus assommant." (*Soirées de St.-Pétersbourg,* 6me Entretien.) Bacon he calmly terms "un charlatan," and, speaking of his greatest works, says : "Le livre *De la Dignité et de l'Accroissement des Sciences* est donc un ouvrage parfaitement nul et méprisable....Quant au *Novum Organon,* il est bien plus condamnable encore, puisque, indépendamment des erreurs particulières dont il four-mille, le but général de l'ouvrage le rend digne d'un Bedlam." (*Examen de la Philosophie de Bacon.*) In the same way, though in very different language, the

It was thus that the great teachers of the seventeenth century, who were themselves but the highest representatives of the tendencies of their age, disciplined the minds of men for impartial enquiry, and having broken the spell that so long had bound them, produced a passionate love of truth which has revolutionised all departments of knowledge. It is to the impulse which was then communicated that may be traced the great critical movement which has renovated all history, all science, all theology—which has penetrated into the obscurest recesses, destroying old prejudices, dispelling illusions, rearranging the various parts of our knowledge, and altering the whole scope and character of our sympathies. But all this would have been impossible but for the diffusion of a rationalistic spirit obscuring or destroying the notion of the guilt of error. For, as we have seen, whenever the doctrine of exclusive salvation is generally believed and realised, habits of thought will be formed around it that are diametrically opposed to the spirit of enquiry and absolutely incompatible with human progress. An indifference to truth, a spirit of blind and at the same time wilful credulity will be encouraged, which will multiply fictions of every kind, will associate enquiry with the ideas of danger and of guilt, will make men esteem that impartiality of

Tractarian party, and especially Dr. Newman (both before and after his conversion), have been ceaselessly carping at the psychology of Locke and the inductive philosophy of Bacon.

judgment and study which is the very soul of truth an unholy thing, and will so emasculate their faculties as to produce a general torpor on every subject. For the different elements of our knowledge are so closely united that it is impossible to divide them into separate compartments, and to make a spirit of credulity preside over one compartment while a spirit of enquiry is animating the others. In the middle ages theology was supreme, and the spirit of that theology was absolute credulity, and the same spirit was speedily diffused through all forms of thought. In the seventeenth century the pre-eminence of theology was no longer decisive, and the great secular writers introduced a love of impartiality and of free research which rapidly passed from natural science and metaphysics into theology, and destroyed or weakened all those doctrines which were repugnant to it. It was between the writings of Bacon and Locke that Chillingworth taught, for the first or almost for the first time in England, the absolute innocence of honest error. It was between the writings of Bacon and Locke that that latitudinarian school was formed which was irradiated by the genius of Taylor, Glanvil, and Hales, and which became the very centre and seedplot of religious liberty. It was between the same writings that the writ *De Hæretico comburendo* was expunged from the Statute Book, and the soil of England for the last time stained with the misbeliever's blood !

HISTORY OF THE
RISE AND INFLUENCE

OF THE SPIRIT OF

RATIONALISM IN
EUROPE

BY

WILLIAM EDWARD HARTPOLE LECKY

PART II

LONDON:
WATTS & CO.,
JOHNSON'S COURT, FLEET STREET, E.C.
1946

CONTENTS OF PART II

CHAPTER VI.

THE INDUSTRIAL HISTORY OF
RATIONALISM

RATIONALISM IN EUROPE

CHAPTER IV.

(continued)

ON PERSECUTION

II.—THE HISTORY OF PERSECUTION

THE considerations I have adduced in the first part of this chapter will be sufficient to show how injurious have been the effects of the doctrine of exclusive salvation. We have still, however, one consequence to examine, before which all others fade into insignificance. I mean, of course, religious persecution. This, which is perhaps the most fearful of all the evils that men have inflicted upon their fellows, is the direct practical result of the principles we have hitherto considered in their speculative aspect. If men believe with an intense and realising faith that their own view of a disputed question is true beyond all possibility of mistake, if they further believe that those who adopt other views will be doomed by the Almighty to an eternity of misery which, with the same moral disposition but with a different belief, they would have escaped, these men will, sooner or later, persecute to the full extent of their power. If you speak to them of the physical and mental suffering which persecution produces, or of the sincerity and unselfish heroism of its victims, they will reply that such arguments rest altogether on the inadequacy of your realisation of the doctrine they believe. What suffering that man can inflict can be comparable to the eternal misery of all who embrace the doctrine of the heretic? What claim can human virtues have to our forbearance, if the Almighty punishes the mere profession of error as a crime of the deepest turpitude? If you encountered a lunatic who, in his frenzy, was inflicting on multitudes around him a death of the most prolonged and excruciating agony, would you not feel justified in arresting his career by every means in your power—by taking his life if you could not otherwise attain your object? But if you knew that this man was inflicting not temporal but eternal death, if he was not a guiltless though dangerous madman, but one whose conduct you believed to involve the most heinous criminality, would you not act with still less compunction or hesitation?[1] Arguments from expediency, though they may induce men under some special circumstances to refrain from persecuting, will never make them adopt the principle of toleration. In the first place, those who believe that the religious service of the heretic is an act positively offensive to the Deity will always feel disposed to put down that act if it is in their power, even though they cannot change the mental disposition from which it springs. In the next place, they will soon perceive that the intervention of the civil ruler can exercise almost as much influence upon belief as upon profession. For although there is indeed a certain order and sequence in the history of opinions, as in the phases of civilisation it reflects,

---

[1] As St. Thomas Aquinas says, "Si falsarii pecuniæ vel alii malefactores statim per seculares principes juste morti traduntur, multo magis hæretici statim, ex quo de hæresi convincuntur, possunt non solum excommunicari sed et juste occidi." (*Summa*, pars. ii. qu. **xi.** art. iii.)

which cannot be altogether destroyed, it is not the less true that man can greatly accelerate, retard, or modify its course. The opinions of ninety-nine persons out of every hundred are formed mainly by education, and a Government can decide in whose hands the national education is to be placed, what subjects it is to comprise, and what principles it is to convey. The opinions of the great majority of those who emancipate themselves from the prejudices of their education are the results in a great measure of reading and of discussion, and a Government can prohibit all books and can expel all teachers that are adverse to the doctrines it holds. Indeed, the simple fact of annexing certain penalties to the profession of particular opinions, and rewards to the profession of opposite opinions, while it will undoubtedly make many hypocrites, will also make many converts. For anyone who attentively observes the process that is pursued in the formation of opinions must be aware that, even when a train of argument has preceded their adoption, they are usually much less the result of pure reasoning than of the action of innumerable distorting influences which are continually deflecting our judgments. Among these one of the most powerful is self-interest. When a man desires very earnestly to embrace a certain class of doctrines, either in order to join a particular profession, or to please his friends, or to acquire peace of mind, or to rise in the world, or to gratify his passions, or to gain that intellectual reputation which is sometimes connected with the profession of certain opinions, he will usually attain his desire. He may be firmly resolved to make any sacrifice rather than profess what he does not believe, yet still his affections will endow their objects with a magnetism of which he is perhaps entirely unconscious. He will reason not to ascertain what is true, but to ascertain whether he can conscientiously affirm certain opinions to be true. He will insensibly withdraw his attention from the objections on one side, and will concentrate it with disproportionate energy upon the other. He will preface every conclusion by an argument, but the nature of that argument will be determined by the secret bias of his will. If, then, a Government can act upon the wishes of a people, it can exercise a considerable influence upon their reason.

Such are some of the arguments by which the persecutor in the earlier stages of Christian history might have defended his acts. And surely the experience of later times has fully corroborated his view by showing that, in the great conflicts between argument and persecution, the latter has been continually triumphant. Persecution extirpated Christianity from Japan ; it crushed the fair promise of the Albigenses ; it rooted out every vestige of Protestantism from Spain. France is still ostensibly, and was long in truth, the leading champion of Catholicity, but the essential Catholicity of France was mainly due to the massacre of St. Bartholomew and the revocation of the Edict of Nantes. England is justly esteemed the chief pillar of Protestantism, yet the English people remained long poised indecisively between the two creeds till the skilful policy and the coercive laws of Elizabeth determined its vacillations. At the Reformation almost every Government prohibited one or other religion ; and whereas the members of the State religion formed at first but a doubtful and wavering majority, and sometimes not even a majority, a few generations produced substantial unanimity ; and since the policy of coercion has been generally abandoned, and the freest scope been given for discussion, the relative position of Protestants and Catholics has not been perceptibly changed.

Before such broad and patent facts as these, the few exceptions that may be adduced can have no great weight, and even those exceptions, when carefully examined, will often be found far less real than is supposed. Thus, for example, the case of Ireland is continually cited. The Irish Catholics, we are told, were subject at first to a system of open plunder, and then to a long detailed legal persecution[1] which was designed to make them abandon their faith. All the paths of honour and wealth were monopolised by Protestants, while shackles of every description hampered the Catholics in all the relations of life. Yet these only clung the closer to their faith on account of the storms that assailed it. That very acute observer, Arthur Young, declared at the close of the penal laws, that the relative

[1] For their details see Parnell, *Penal Laws*. In common parlance, the "penal laws" date from the treaty of Limerick, but the legislative assaults on Irish Catholicism began with Elizabeth.

proportion of Catholics to Protestants had not been at all reduced—if anything rather the reverse—and that those who denied this admitted that, at the past rate of conversions, 4,000 years would be required to make Ireland Protestant. In the Irish Parliament it was stated that 71 years of the penal system had only produced 4,055 converts.

This statement may at first sight appear to furnish an extremely strong argument, but it completely omits the most important element of Irish ecclesiastical history. In Ireland the old faith marked the division between two races, it was the symbol of the national spirit, it was upheld by all the passions of a great patriotic struggle, and its continuance simply attests the vitality of a political sentiment. When every other northern nation abandoned Catholicism, the Irish still retained it out of antipathy to their oppressors, and in every great insurrection the actuating spirit was mainly political. Of all the outbreaks against the English power, that of 1641 was probably the most passionate and most vindictive. In that rebellion one Englishman of distinction was exempt from the hostility that attached to his race. He was treated with the most respectful and even affectionate deference, and when he died he was borne to the grave with all the honours the rebel army could afford. That Englishman was Bishop Bedell, the councillor of Sarpi and of De Dominis, and the founder of proselytism in Ireland.[1]

Such was the spirit that was displayed by the Irish Catholics in the midst of one of their most ferocious outbreaks ; and surely no one who is acquainted with the history of Ireland since the Union will imagine that the repeal of the persecuting code has in any degree mitigated their zeal. While their influence in the State has been immeasurably augmented, while their number has increased with a rapidity that was only broken by the frightful famine and emigration that more than decimated their ranks, the sectarian spirit that actuates them has become continually more conspicuous. It may indeed be truly said that of all civilised countries Ireland is that in which public opinion is governed most habitually by theological considerations, and in which the most momentous secular interests are most continually subordinated to the conflicts of rival clergy. The causes of this deplorable condition I have not now to investigate. It is sufficient to say that it exists in spite of the abrogation of the persecuting laws. If there was one secular question which the Irish Catholics pursued with an intense and genuine ardour, it was the struggle for the repeal of the Union. For a long series of years they maintained that struggle with a combination of enthusiasm, of perseverance, and of self-sacrifice, such as has been seldom evinced in a political contest, and they invariably based their claim on the broad principle that the form of government in any country should be determined by the majority of its inhabitants. But no sooner had that principle come into collision with the Church, no sooner had its triumph menaced the security of the Vatican and wrested two provinces from the Pope, than all this was changed. The teaching of Davis and of O'Connell was at once forgotten. The bond that had so long connected the Irish Catholics with liberalism was broken, and the whole party pressed forward, with an alacrity that would be ludicrous if it were not pitiable, to unite themselves with the most retrogressive politicians in Europe, and to discard and trample on the principles they had so long and so enthusiastically maintained.

These considerations show that the intense energy of Irish Catholicism cannot be altogether attributed to religious persecution. Much the same qualification may be applied to the case of the English dissenters. The Anglican Church, it is sometimes said, persecuted with great cruelty those who separated from her ecclesiastical government; yet, nevertheless, the dissenters became so powerful that they shattered both the Church and the Crown, and brought the king and the Archbishop of Canterbury to the scaffold. But this is a palpable misrepresentation. The extreme servility which the English Church manifested to the most tyrannical of sovereigns, and the bitter persecution it directed against all adverse communions, had together made Puritanism the representative and the symbol of

---

[1] The very curious life of Bedell, by his son-in-law Alexander Clogy, which was written in 1641–2, and which formed the basis of the narrative of Burnet, was printed from the MSS. in the British Museum in 1862. We have an amusing instance of the uncompromising Protestantism of Bedell in the fact that when the insurgents who retained him prisoner gave him permission to perform the Anglican service freely with his friends, he availed himself of that permission to celebrate the thanksgiving for the 5th of November.

democracy. The rebellion was simply
the outburst of political liberalism, intensified, indeed, but by no means created,
by the exasperation of the dissenters. It
represented the hatred of political tyranny
much more than the hatred of episcopacy.
After two or three fluctuations a period
arrived when the Church of England was
greatly depressed, and the Toleration Act
was passed, which, though very defective
in theory, accorded a large measure of
practical liberty to all classes of dissenters.
Those who maintain that persecution can
only strengthen the system against which
it is directed, might have expected that
this Act would have produced a diminution
of dissent, or, at least, a relaxation of its
principles. But the result was precisely
opposite. About the time when the Act
was passed, the dissenters were estimated at rather more than one twenty-
third of the population of England ; less
than a century after they were estimated
at one-fourth.[1] In zeal the Methodists
will bear comparison with the Puritans,
and if the animosity between Anglicans
and dissenters is mitigated, this has not
been because dissent has been attracted
to the Church, but because the Church
has been penetrated by the doctrines of
dissent.

The foregoing arguments appear to me
to prove, not, indeed, that persecution is
a good thing, or even that it can invariably effect the object for which it is
employed, but that it has, as a matter of
fact, exercised an enormous influence
over the belief of mankind. The two
main causes of theological changes seem
to be the appearance from time to time
of great religious teachers, and the succession of the phases of civilisation. The
first cast abroad the seeds of religious
truth ; the second provide the different
atmospheres by which those seeds are in
turn developed. But, while this law is
producing a continual modification of
opinions, which is more or less felt
through the entire community, it leaves
free scope for the operation of many minor
influences, which cause in the same
period a considerable diversity of realised
belief, and a still greater diversity of profession. Of these influences the intervention of government is probably the
most powerful. It is certainly far more
powerful than any direct polemical discussion. Millions of devoted Catholics

[1] See a note in Buckle, *History of Civilisation*, vol. i.
p 385.

and millions of devoted Protestants would,
at the present hour, repudiate indignantly
their present belief but for the coercive
enactments of former rulers ; and there is
scarcely a country in which the prevailing
faith is not in some degree due to bygone
legislation. But whether or not this be
true is, in reality, immaterial to my argument ; for, however strongly the reader
may deny the efficacy of persecution upon
belief, it is certain that until lately it was
deemed indisputable. It is also certain
that, in ages when the doctrine of exclusive salvation is fully realised, the
spirit of faith will be so exalted that the
ruler will never question for a moment
the justice of his belief. Now, when men
are firmly convinced that the highest of
all possible objects is to promote the
interests of their faith, and that by the
employment of force they can most fully
attain that object, their persecution will
be measured by their power and their
zeal.[1]

These are the general logical antecedents of persecution, and they are quite
sufficient to account for all its atrocities,
without imputing any sordid motives to
the persecutor. There is, however, one
other consideration that exercised a very
important influence in the same direction
—I mean the example of the Jewish legislators. When we now read of such scenes
as the massacres of Canaan, the slaughter
of the priests of Baal, or the forcible
reforms of Josiah, they can scarcely be
said to present themselves to the mind as
having any very definite application to
the present. Those who do not regard
them as the natural products of an imperfect civilisation, regard them at least
as belonging to a dispensation so entirely
exceptional as to be removed altogether
from the ordinary conditions of society.
But in the early Church, and in the sixteenth century, they were looked upon in
a very different light. The relations of
an established religion to the State were
mainly derived from the Old Testament.
The Jewish was deemed a type of the
Christian Church, and the policy that
was commended in the one was regarded
as at least not blamable in the other.

[1] This was the opinion expressed by Charles James
Fox. "The only foundation for toleration," he said,
"is a degree of scepticism, and without it there can be
none. For if a man believes in the saving of souls, he
must soon think about the means ; and if by cutting off
one generation he can save many future ones from hell
fire, it is his duty to do it." (Rogers, *Recollections*,
p. 49.)

Now the Levitical code was the first code of religious persecution that had ever appeared among mankind. It pronounced idolatry to be not simply an error, but a crime, and a crime that must be expiated with blood.[1]

The opinions of the Fathers on the subject were divided. Those who wrote when a pagan or heretical power was supreme were the champions of toleration. Those who wrote when the Church was in the ascendency usually inclined to persecution. Tertullian during the pagan[2] and Hilary of Poitiers during the Arian[3] persecution, were the most conspicuous advocates of the duty of absolute and complete toleration, and several passages tending, though less strongly, in the same direction, emanated from other Fathers during seasons of adversity.[4] It should, however, be mentioned that Lactantius, in the reign of Constantine, asserted the iniquity of persecution quite as strongly as any previous writer,[5] and

also that the later Fathers, while defending the milder forms of coercion, seldom or never wished death to be the penalty of heresy. In this respect the orthodox seem to have been for a time honourably distinguished from the Arians. On one occasion in the reign of the Arian emperor Valens, no less than eighty Catholic ecclesiastics are said to have been imprisoned in a ship at sea and treacherously burnt.[1]

Still, from the very moment the Church obtained civil power under Constantine, the general principle of coercion was admitted and acted on both against the Jews, the heretics, and the pagans. The first had at this time become especially obnoxious, on account of a strong Judaising movement which had produced one or two heresies and many apostasies, and they were also accused of assailing "with stones and other manifestations of rage" those who abandoned their faith. Constantine provided against these evils by a law, in which he condemned to the flames any Jew who threw stones at a Christian convert, and at the same time rendered it penal for any Christian to become a Jew[2]. Against the Arian and Donatist heretics, his measures were more energetic. Their churches were destroyed, their assemblies were forbidden, their bishops banished, their writings burnt, and all who concealed those writings threatened with death. Some of the Donatists were actually condemned to death, but the sentence was remitted, and any blood that was at this time shed seems to have been due to the excessive turbulence of the Circumcelliones, a sect of Donatists whose principles and acts appear to have been perfectly incompatible with the tranquillity of the State.[3]

---

[1] On the influence of this command on Christian persecution, see Bayle, Contrains-les d'entrer, pt. ii. ch. iv., and some striking remarks in Renan, Vie de Jésus, pp. 412-413; to which I may add as an illustration the following passage of Simancas: "Hæretici pertinaces publice in conspectu populi comburendi sunt; et id fieri solet extra portas civitatis: quemadmodum olim, in Deut. cap. xvii., idolatra educebatur ad portas civitatis, et lapidibus obruebatur." (De Cathol. Instit. p. 375.) Taylor, in noticing this argument, finely says that Christ, by refusing to permit his apostles to call down fire like Elias on the misbeliever, clearly indicated his separation from the intolerance of Judaism. (Liberty of Prophesying, sec. 22.)

[2] Apol. cap. xxiv.

[3] Ad Auxentium.

[4] The reader may find a full statement of the passages from the Fathers favourable to toleration in Whitby, On Laws against Heretics (1723, published anonymously); Taylor, Liberty of Prophesying; Bayle, Contrains-les d'entrer, and many other books. The other side of the question has been developed, among other writers, by Palmer, On the Church; Muzzarelli, Simancas, Paramo, and all the other old writers on the Inquisition. There is, I think, an impartial view of the whole subject in Milman, History of Christianity. See, too, Blackstone's Commentaries, b. iv. ch. iv.

[5] Inst. lib. v. c. xx. Lactantius embraced Christianity during the persecution of Diocletian, but it appears almost certain that his Institutions were mainly written, or at least published, at Trèves during the reign of Constantine, and he never abandoned the tolerant maxims he proclaimed. This was especially creditable to him, as he was tutor to the son of Constantine, and consequently singularly tempted to avail himself of the arm of power. Unfortunately, this very eloquent writer, who was certainly one of the ablest in the early Church, possessed comparatively little influence on account of his passion for paradox. He maintained that no Christian might engage in warfare, or execute a capital sentence; he was one of the strongest asserters of the opinion that God the Father had a figure (a controversy raised by Origen), and he was accused of denying the personality of the Holy Ghost. "Lactantius," said Jerome, "quasi quidam fluvius eloquentiæ Tullianæ, utinam tam nostra confirmare potuisset, quam facile aliena destruxit!" (Epist. lib. ii. epist. 14.) The works of Lactantius were condemned by a Council presided over by Pope

Gelasius in the 5th century. See Alexandri Hist. Ecclesiastica (Paris, 1699), tom. iv. pp. 100-103; Ampère, Hist. littéraire de la France, tom. i. pp. 218-223. Some of the peculiar notions of Lactantius appeared at a later period among the Waldenses.

[1] Socrates, lib. iv. c. xyi. The Donatists were also fierce persecutors, and Nestorius showed his sentiments clearly enough when he said to the Emperor, "Give me the earth purged from heretics, and I will give you heaven." The Spanish Arians seem to have originated the intense intolerance that has been perpetuated from generation to generation in Spain.

[2] Cod. Theod. lib. xvi. tit. 8. The apostate "sustinebit meritas pœnas." Constantius afterwards made the penalty confiscation of goods. A Jew who married a Christian incurred the penalty of death. See, on this department of legislation, Bedarride, Hist. des Juifs, pp. 16-20.

[3] Milman, History of Christianity, vol. ii. pp. 372-375. See also the review of these measures in Palmer, On the Church, vol. ii. p. 250. The first law that has

The policy of Constantine towards the pagans is involved in considerable obscurity, and I have already in a former chapter sketched its principal features. During the first years of his reign, while the ascendency of Christianity was very doubtful, and while the pagan Licinius was still his colleague in the empire, he showed marked tolerance towards the adherents of the old superstitions, and when his law against private or magical sacrifices had created a considerable panic among them, he endeavoured to remove the impression by a proclamation in which he authorised in the most express terms the worship in the temples.[1] Besides this, he still retained the old imperial title of Pontifex Maximus,[2] and does not appear to have altogether discarded the functions it implied. As, however, his position became more strong, and especially after the defeat of Licinius in 324, he gradually changed his policy. By forbidding the prefects and governors to pay any respect to the idols, he placed the government of the provinces in Christian hands.[3] About 330, he went still further, and if we may believe the unanimous testimony of the ecclesiastical historians, he prohibited the temple worship. This enactment has not come down to us, but the prohibition is expressly and unequivocally asserted by both Eusebius, Sozomen, and Theodoret,[4] and Libanius tells us that the penalty of holding converse with the old gods was death.[5]

Eusebius notices some temples that were at this time closed, and speaks of similar measures as being very common ; but, at the same time, we have decisive evidence that the pagan worship was connived at in many and probably most parts of the empire, that temples were dedicated, and the ceremonies performed without molestation or concealment.[1] It is only by taking into account the extreme laxity of the administration of law at this period of Roman history, that we can estimate aright the position of the pagans. The government was strongly hostile to their faith, but was as yet restrained by their numbers ; the habitual policy was therefore gradually to destroy their political importance, and by laws directed ostensibly against magic to suppress those portions of worship which were not indeed the essentials, but formed what may be called the religious luxuries of paganism. Other and more stringent laws were made, but they were generally in abeyance, or at least their execution depended upon political circumstances, or upon the disposition of the governors. Constantius made laws distinctly prohibiting every form of pagan worship,[2] but yet there is no fact more certain than that this worship continued till the period of Theodosius.[3]

It is not necessary to follow in detail the persecuting laws of the first century of the Church's power, and indeed such a task would be intolerably tedious, on account of the activity that was displayed in this department of legislation.

come down to us, in which the penalty of death is annexed to the simple profession of a heresy, is law 9 *De Hæreticis* in the Theodosian Code. It was made by Theodosius the Great, and was applicable only to some sects of Manichæans. It is worthy of notice that this is also the first law in which we meet the title of "Inquisitors of the Faith." Optatus in the reign of Constantine advocated the massacre of the Donatists, on the ground of the Old Testament precedents (see Milman).

[1] "Addite aras publicas atque delubra, et consuetudinis vestræ celebrate solemnia : nec enim prohibemus preteritæ usurpationis officia libera luce tractari."— *Cod. Th.* lib. ix. tit. 16, cc. i. ii.

[2] The first emperor who refused it was Gratian (Zosimus, book iv.).

[3] Eusebius, *Vita Const.* lib. ii. cc. xliv. xlv.

[4] See Eusebius, *Vita Const.* lib. ii. cc. xliv. xlv., lib. iv. c. xxiii.; Theodoret, lib. vi. c. xxi.; Sozomen, lib. iii. c. xvii. Eusebius repeats this assertion over and over again ; see Milman, *History of Christianity*, vol. ii. pp. 460-464 (ed. 1840).

[5] Speaking of his youth, Libanius says : "Plus apud Deos quam apud homines in terra conversabatur, tametsi lex prohiberet, quam audenti violare capitis pœna fuit. Veruntamen cum illis ipsis vitam agens et iniquam legem et impium legislatorem deridebat." (*De Vita sua*, Libanii *Opera* [ed. 1627], vol. ii. p. 11.) However, in his oration *Pro Templis*, Libanius says distinctly that Constantine did not disturb the worship of the temples. It is hard to reconcile these two passages with each other, and the last with the state-

ments of Eusebius ; but I suppose the fact is that the law was made, but was generally suffered to be inoperative.

[1] See a great deal of evidence of this in Beugnot, *Décadence du Polythéisme.* But it is absurd to speak of Constantine, as M. Beugnot does, as an apostle of tolerance. "Connivance," as Burke once said, "is the relaxation of tyranny, and not the definition of liberty." One of Constantine's proclamations of tolerance seems to have been posterior to the prohibition of public sacrifices.

[2] *Cod. Th.* xvi. 10, 2-4. The terms of one of these laws seem to imply that Constantine had made a similar enactment : "Cesset superstitio : sacrificiorum aboleatur insania. Nam quicunque *contra legem divi Principis Parentis nostri*, et hanc nostræ mansuetudinis jussionem, ausus fuerit sacrificia celebrare, competens in eum vindicta et præsens sententia exeratur." For a full discussion of this very perplexing subject, see Milman, *Hist. of Christianity*, and Gibbon, ch. xxi.

[3] Thus, for example, the pagan Zosimus tells us expressly that in the beginning of the reign of Theodosius his co-religionists were still at liberty to worship in the temples. The history is in a great measure a repetition of that of the persecution which the Christians had themselves endured. Generally they had been allowed freely to celebrate their worship, but from time to time, either through popular indignation or imperial suspicions, there were sudden outbursts of fearful persecution.

The Theodosian Code, which was compiled under Theodosius the Younger, contains no less than sixty-six enactments against heretics, besides many others against pagans, Jews, apostates, and magicians. It is sufficient to say that at first the Arian measures seem to have been rather more severe than the Catholic ones, but that the scope of the latter was steadily enlarged, and their severity increased, till they reached a point that has seldom been surpassed. First the pagans were deprived of offices in the State; then their secret sacrifices were prohibited; then every kind of divination was forbidden; then the public sacrifices were suppressed; and finally the temples were destroyed, their images broken, and the entire worship condemned.[1] The enforcement of these measures in the country districts was the last, the most difficult, and the most melancholy scene of the drama. For in those days, when means of communication were very few and ignorance was very general, it was quite possible for a religious movement to gain a complete ascendency in the towns while the peasants were scarcely aware of its existence. In their calm retreats the paroxysms of change were seldom felt. They still continued with unfaltering confidence to worship the old gods when a new faith had attracted the educated to its banner, or when scepticism was withering the beliefs of the past. Multitudes had probably scarcely realised the existence of Christianity when the edict arrived which doomed their temples to destruction. Libanius, who, as the minister of Julian, had exhibited a spirit of tolerance even more remarkable than that of his master, pleaded the peasants' cause with courage, dignity, and pathos. The temple, he said, was to them the very eye of nature, the symbol and manifestation of a present Deity, the solace of all their troubles, the holiest of all their joys. If it were overthrown, their dearest associations would be annihilated. The tie that linked them to the dead would be severed. The poetry of life, the consolation of labour, the source of faith, would be destroyed.[2] But these pleas were unavailing. Under Theodosius the Great all the temples were razed to the ground, and all forms of pagan and heretical worship absolutely prohibited.[3]

Such was the persecuting spirit displayed by the Christians of the fourth and fifth centuries. It is both interesting and important to observe how far it was the consequence of a theological development, and what were the stages of that development. The noble protests against persecution which the persecuted prelates had uttered form indeed a striking contrast to the measures I have related; but, unfortunately, new circumstances produce new opinions, and when the bias of the will is altered, a change will soon be manifested in the judgment. Still, in justice to the persecutors, it must be admitted that they were but the logical exponents of principles that had before existed in the Church. These principles were the doctrine of exclusive salvation, and the conceptions of the guilt of error and of ecclesiastical authority. It is very remarkable, too, that even before Constantius some theologians had begun to deduce their rule of conduct towards heretics from the penal enactments of the Levitical law. To excommunicate the heretic was, they said, to consign him to eternal damnation; and they were justified in inflicting this frightful punishment upon those who rebelled against their authority, because the ancient idolater had been punished with death.[1] From such a doctrine there was but a step to persecution. The premises were already formed; it only remained to draw the obvious conclusion.

There cannot, I think, be much doubt that the minds of the leaders of the Church were so prepared by these modes of thought that the eulogies which

extremely slight difference that separated them from the orthodox) were allowed to celebrate their worship till A.D. 525, when the Bishop of Rome succeeded in procuring their suppression. (Taylor, *Liberty of Prophesying*, epistle dedicatory.)

[1] "Neither let those who refuse to obey their bishops and priests think within themselves that they are in the way of life and of salvation, for the Lord God says in Deuteronomy, 'Whoever will act presumptuously, and will not hear the priest or the judge, whoever he may be in those days, he shall die, and the people will hear and fear, and do no more presumptuously.' God commanded those to be slain who would not obey the priests or the judges set over them for a time. Then, indeed, they were slain with the sword while the carnal circumcision still remained; but now, since the spiritual circumcision has begun amid the servants of God, the proud and contumacious are killed when they are cast out of the Church. For they cannot live without it; for the house of God is one, and there can be salvation for no one except in the Church." (Cyprian, *Epis.*, Book i. ep. 11.) That excommunication is a severer penalty than death, and that the Church, having the power of inflicting the first, may also inflict the second, was one of the arguments of Bellarmine in favour of persecution, and was answered by Taylor, *Liberty of Prophesying*, sec. 14.

[1] See the laws *De Templis*.   [2] *Pro Templis*.
[3] It is said, however, that, notwithstanding these laws, the Novatians (probably on account of the

Eusebius unceasingly lavishes upon the persecuting edicts of Constantine were a faithful expression of their sentiments. But the writer who was destined to consolidate the whole system of persecution, to furnish the arguments of all its later defenders, and to give to it the sanction of a name that long silenced every pleading of mercy, and became the glory and the watchword of every persecutor, was unquestionably Augustine, on whom more than on any other theologian—more perhaps even than on Dominic and Innocent—rests the responsibility of this fearful curse. A sensualist and a Manichæan, a philosopher and a theologian, a saint of the most tender and exquisite piety, and a supporter of atrocious persecution, the life of this Father exhibits a strange instance of the combination of the most discordant agencies to the development of a single mind, and of the influence of that mind over the most conflicting interests. Neither the unbridled passions of his youth, nor the extravagances of the heresy he so long maintained, could cloud the splendour of his majestic intellect, which was even then sweeping over the whole field of knowledge, and acquiring in the most unpropitious spheres new elements of strength. In the arms of the frail beauties of Carthage, he learned to touch the chords of passion with consummate skill ; and the subtleties of Persian metaphysics, the awful problems of the origin of evil and of the essence of the soul which he vainly sought to fathom, gave him a sense of the darkness around us that coloured every portion of his teaching. The weight and compass of his genius, his knowledge both of men and of books, a certain aroma of sanctity that imparted an inexpressible charm to all his later writings, and a certain impetuosity of character that overbore every obstacle, soon made him the master intellect of the Church. Others may have had a larger share in the construction of her formularies—no one since the days of the apostles infused into her a larger measure of his spirit. He made it his mission to map out her theology with inflexible precision, to develop its principles to their full consequences, and to co-ordinate its various parts into one authoritative and symmetrical whole. Impatient of doubt, he shrank from no conclusion, however unpalatable ; he seemed to exult in trampling human instincts in the dust,

and in accustoming men to accept submissively the most revolting tenets. He was the most staunch and enthusiastic defender of all those doctrines that grow out of the habits of mind that lead to persecution. No one else had developed so fully the material character of the torments of hell, no one else had plunged so deeply into the speculations of predestinarianism, very few had dwelt so emphatically on the damnation of the unbaptised. For a time he shrank from, and even condemned, persecution ; but he soon perceived in it the necessary consequence of his principles. He recanted his condemnation ; he flung his whole genius into the cause ; he recurred to it again and again, and he became the framer and the representative of the theology of intolerance.[1]

Strange indeed has been the destiny of this man ! The most illustrious of his contemporaries, in a few centuries, lost their ascendency. Their names, indeed, still continued in honour, their works were read by monkish scholars, but changing modes of thought and feeling soon isolated them from the sympathies of mankind. Alone by the power of his genius, Augustine traversed the lapse of ages with unfading influence ; but he survived to be the watchword of the most opposing doctrines, the promoter alike of the best and worst sentiments of our nature. From his teaching concerning imputed righteousness, predestinarianism, and good works, the Protestants drew their most powerful weapons. In the intolerant rigidity of his doctrines, in his exaltation of authority, and in the imperious character of his genius, Catholicism recognised her most faithful type. Both sects found in his writings the purest expressions of their religious sentiments, and both sheltered their intolerance beneath his name.

The arguments by which Augustine supported persecution were, for the most part, those which I have already stated. Some of them were drawn from the doctrine of exclusive salvation, and others from the precedents of the Old Testament. It was merciful, he contended, to punish heretics, even by death, if this could save them or others from the eternal

---

[1] See his *Retract.* lib. ii. c. v.; *Epist.* xciii. (in some editions xlviii.) cxxvii. clxxxv.; *Contra Gaudentium*, c. xxv.; *Contra Epist. Parmeniani*, c. vii. There are many other passages on the subject scattered through his writings.

suffering that awaited the unconverted. Heresy was described in Scripture as a kind of adultery ; it was the worst species of murder, being the murder of souls ; it was also a form of blasphemy ; and on all these grounds might justly be punished. If the New Testament contained no examples of the apostles employing force, this was simply because in their time no prince had embraced Christianity. But had not Elijah slaughtered with his own hand the prophets of Baal ? Did not Hezekiah, and Josiah, and the king of Nineveh, and Nebuchadnezzar after his conversion, destroy by force idolatry within their dominions ; and were they not expressly commended for their piety ? St. Augustine also seems to have originated the application of the words, " Compel them to enter in," to religious persecution.[1]

It is, however, worthy of remark, that although Augustine defended the measures that had been taken against the Donatists, and although he maintained that heresy was the worst of crimes, and that it should be punished according to its enormity, he still, with an amiable inconsistency, exerted himself much to prevent the penalty from being capital. He exhorted, he even commanded as a bishop, those in authority to restrict it to banishment ; he threatened, that if they refused to do so, the bishops would cease to inform against heretics ; and he laboured not unsuccessfully to save the lives of some who were condemned.[2] In this respect the manner in which heretics and pagans were treated presents a remarkable contrast. In a passage which occurs in one of his letters to the Donatists, St. Augustine informs us of two striking facts. The first is, that, in his time, the sentence of death was incurred by anyone who celebrated the rites of the religion which had a few centuries before been universal in the empire. The second is, that this sentence was unanimously applauded in the Christian Church.[1]

The reluctance of the clergy to sanction the death of heretics for a long time coexisted with the most earnest desire to suppress their worship by force, and to banish their teachers from the empire. The first execution of heretics in which ecclesiastics took any part seems to have been in A.D. 385, when some Priscillianists were put to death at the instigation of two obscure bishops named Ursatius and Ithacus. St. Ambrose, though one of the most active in procuring the suppression of the Jewish and pagan worship, protested strongly against this act ; and St. Martin of Tours denounced it with almost passionate vehemence as an atrocious crime, and refused to hold any communion with the offending bishops.[2] The indignation that was excited on this occasion resulted, perhaps, hardly so much from the fact that heretics had been put to death, as from the part the bishops had taken in the transaction ; for from an early period there was an opinion diffused through the Church, of which Tertullian and Lactantius were the principal exponents, that a Christian should under no circumstances slay his fellow-men, either by bringing a capital charge, or by acting as a judge, a soldier, or an executioner. When the triumph of Christianity had been attained, it was of course necessary that this rule—which, indeed, had never been generally adopted in its full stringency—should be relaxed as regards laymen, but it still continued in the case of priests. All ecclesiastics who delivered up a culprit to the civil power, without supplicating the judges that he should not be punished by death or mutilation, were regarded as guilty of a gross irregularity, and were in consequence liable to ecclesiastical censures. At first this

---

[1] *Epist.* l. *Bonifacio.*
[2] See especially *Epist.* c. clviii. clix. clx. On the other hand, Augustine bases the right of punishing heresy on the enormity of the crime, which he considered greater than any other. (*Contra Gaudentium*, lib. i. c. xix.) He assimilates heresy to blasphemy, and says that blasphemy is justly punished by death. (*Epist.* cv., otherwise cixvi.) He adduces as applicable precedents all the worst Old Testament persecutions, and he defends the condemnation of some Donatists to death by Constantine, on the ground of justice, though he applauds on the ground of mercy the remission of the sentence. (*Contra Parmenianum*, lib. i. c. viii.) His general view seems to have been that heretics might justly be punished by death, but that the orthodox should not exact strict justice. However, he vacillated a good deal, and both moderate and extreme persecutors find much in their defence in his writings. Religious liberty he emphatically cursed. "Quid est enim pejor, mors animæ quam libertas erroris?" (*Epist.* clxvi.)

[1] "Quis enim nostrum, quis vestrum non laudat leges ab imperatoribus datas contra sacrifica paganorum? Et certe longe ibi pœna severior constituta est ; illius quippe impietatis capitale supplicium est." (*Epist.* xciii., in some editions xcviii.) See Gibbon, ch. xxviii.

[2] Ampère, *Hist. littéraire de la France*, tom. i. pp. 310, 320 ; Milman, vol. iii. p. 60 ; Taylor, *Liberty of Prophesying*, sec. 14. St. Martin, however, was one of the most active in destroying the pagan temples, and was accustomed in that employment to range over his diocese at the head of a perfect army of monks. (See Gibbon.)

rule was the expression of a pure philanthropy, and was intended to save the life
of the accused, but it at last degenerated
into an act of the most odious hypocrisy.
Boniface VIII. decided that a bishop
might safely deliver up a culprit, though
he was certain his intercession would
not be attended to ; and the same form of
supplication continued to be employed by
the Inquisitors, though they had themselves condemned the heretic to death,
and though Innocent VIII. had excommunicated any magistrate who either
altered their sentence, or delayed more
than six days in carrying it into execution.[1]

During the latter half of the fourth
century, there were two causes which
contributed especially to the increased
severity of the persecution. The first was
the great development of the corporate
action of the clergy, as evinced by the
multitude of Councils. A large proportion
of these, and among others those of
Ephesus and Constantinople, which were
esteemed œcumenical, called upon the
civil power to banish or otherwise punish
the heretics,[2] and their decrees had a considerable influence upon the government.
The second cause was the establishment
and rapid growth of the monastic system,
which called into existence a body of men
who, in self-denial, in singleness of purpose, in heroic courage, and, at the same
time, in merciless fanaticism, have seldom
been surpassed. Abandoning every tie of
home and friendship, discarding all the
luxuries and most of what are deemed
the necessaries of life, scourging and
macerating their bodies, living in filth
and loneliness and desolation, wandering
half-starved and half-naked through the
deserts with the wild beasts for their only
companions, the early monks almost extinguished every natural sentiment, and
emancipated themselves as far as is possible from the conditions of humanity.[3]
Ambition, and wealth, and ease, and all

the motives that tell most powerfully
upon mankind, were to them unmeaning
words. No reward could bribe them, no
danger could appal them, no affection
could move them. They had learned to
embrace misery with a passionate love.
They enjoyed a ghastly pleasure in multiplying forms of loathsome penance, and
in trampling upon every natural desire.
Their imaginations, distempered by self-
inflicted sufferings, peopled the solitude
with congenial spirits, and transported
them at will beyond the horizon of the
grave. To promote the interests of their
Church was the only passion that remained, and to gratify it there was no
suffering that they were not ready to
endure or to inflict. The pagan historians
have given us a graphic description of the
zeal they manifested in destroying the
temples. Sometimes a bishop led the
enterprise from which the civil authorities
recoiled, and one prelate, named Mar-
cellus, perished in a conflict with the
peasants who were defending with despairing courage the altars of their gods.
A few years of such zeal sufficed, and
paganism as a distinct system perished
in the empire.

After the suppression of paganism in
the Roman Empire, a period of many
centuries occurred during which religious
persecution was very rare. The principle
was indeed fully admitted, and whenever
the occasion called for it, it was applied ;
but heresies scarcely ever appeared, and
the few that arose were exceedingly insignificant. A few heretics whose doctrines were merged in the charge of
magic, two or three who were burnt by
Alexius Comnenus, some more who were
burnt in France in the beginning of the
eleventh century, and some Cathari and
sectaries with kindred views who were
burnt at Cologne[1] or in Italy, seem to

---

[1] The history of this has been written in a very
striking book called *La Tolérance ecclésiastique et
civile*, by Thadeus de Trautsmandorff. The author
was a canon of Olmutz, and afterwards Bishop of
Königgratz in Bohemia. The work appeared in
Latin, at Pavia, in 1783, and was translated into
French in 1796. It is one of the most remarkable
books in favour of tolerance produced by any priest
in the eighteenth century. See, too, on the form of intercession employed by the inquisitors, Limborch, *Historia Inquisitionis* (Amsterdam, 1692), pp. 365-367,
372.
[2] On the influence of the Councils, see Palmer *On
the Church*, vol. ii. p. 333 ; Muzzarelli, *Sur l'Inquisition*.
[3] *Vide* St. Jerome, passim.

[1] Natalis Alexander, *Historia Ecclesiastica*, tom.
vii. p. 337. The following are all the cases Simancas
could collect : "Antiquissima est pœna ignis adversus
impios et hæreticos, ut ex actis Chalcedonensis Concilii
satis constare potest. Illic enim episcopus Alexandrinus dixisse traditur : 'Si Eutyches præter dogmata
ecclesiæ sapit non solum pœna dignus est sed et igne.'
Anatolium quoque hæreticum igni vivum combusserunt,
ut Nicephorus prodidit, lib. xviii. *Eccl. Hist.* c. 4.
Gregorius quoque, lib. i. Dialogorum, refert Basilium
magum Romæ fuisse combustum et rem gestam laudat.
Et propter impiam atque scelestam disciplinam Tem-
plarii concremati fuerunt....Et Basilius hæreticus
communi suffragio combustus fuit, sicuti Zonaras
retulit in imperio Alexii Comneni ; alibi quoque
hæretici jam olim vivi cremati sunt, quemadmodum
Paulus Æmilius, lib. vi. *De Rebus Francorum*, retulit.
Item constitutionibus Siculus cavetur ut vivi hæretici
in conspectu populi comburantur, flammarum commissi

have been all or nearly all who perished for heresy during several centuries before the Albigenses. Catholicism was then perfectly in accordance with the intellectual wants of Europe. It was not a tyranny, for the intellectual latitude it permitted was fully commensurate with the wants of the people. It was not a sect or an isolated influence acting in the midst of Europe and forming one weight in the balance of power, but rather an all-pervasive energy animating and vivifying the whole social system. A certain unity of type was then manifested, which has never been restored. The corporations, the guilds, the feudal system, the monarchy, the social habits of the people, their laws, their studies, their very amusements, all grew out of ecclesiastical teaching, embodied ecclesiastical modes of thought, exhibited the same general tendencies, and presented countless points of contact or of analogy. All of them were strictly congruous. The Church was the very heart of Christendom, and the spirit that radiated from her penetrated into all the relations of life, and coloured the institutions it did not create. In such a condition of society, heresies were almost impossible. For while the particular form that a heresy assumes may be dependent upon circumstances that are peculiar to the heresiarch, the existence and success of heretical teaching always proves that the tone of thought or measure of probability prevailing at the time has begun to diverge from the tone of thought or measure of probability of orthodoxy. As long as a church is so powerful as to form the intellectual condition of the age, to supply the standing-point from which every question is viewed, its authority will never be disputed. It will reflect so perfectly the general conceptions of the people, that no difficulties of detail will seriously disturb it. This ascendency was gained by mediæval Catholicity more completely than by any other system before or since, and the stage of civilisation that resulted from it was one of the most important in the evolution of society. By consolidating the heterogeneous and anarchical elements that succeeded the downfall of the Roman Empire; by infusing into Christendom the conception of a bond of unity that is superior to the divisions of nationhood,

and of a moral tie that is superior to force; by softening slavery into serfdom, and preparing the way for the ultimate emancipation of labour, Catholicism laid the very foundations of modern civilisation. Herself the most admirable of all organisations, there was formed beneath her influence a vast network of organisations, political, municipal, and social, which supplied a large proportion of the materials of almost every modern structure.

But though in many respects admirable and useful, this stage was manifestly transitory. It could only exist by the suppression of all critical spirit, by a complete paralysis of the speculative faculties. It was associated with conceptions of the government of the universe, the history of the past, and the prospects of the future, that were fundamentally false, and must necessarily have been dissolved by advancing knowledge. As soon as the revival of learning commenced, as soon as the first pulsations of intellectual life were felt, the movement of decomposition began. From that moment Catholicism, aiming at an impossible immobility, became the principle of retrogression. From that moment she employed all the resources that her position and her great services had given her, to arrest the expansion of the human mind, to impede the circulation of knowledge, and to quench the lamp of liberty in blood. It was in the course of the twelfth century that this change was manifested, and in the beginning of the next century the system of coercion was matured. In 1208, Innocent III. established the Inquisition. In 1209, De Montfort began the massacre of the Albigenses. In 1215, the Fourth Council of the Lateran enjoined all rulers, "as they desired to be esteemed faithful, to swear a public oath that they would labour earnestly, and to the full extent of their power, to exterminate from their dominions all those who were branded as heretics by the Church."[1]

[1] The fourth Council of the Lateran is esteemed œcumenical in the Church of Rome, and exercised very great influence both on this account and because it was the council which first defined the doctrine of transubstantiation. Its decree on Persecution, however, had been anticipated by the Council of Avignon, in 1209, which enjoined all bishops to call upon the civil power to exterminate heretics (Rohrbacher, *Hist. de l'Église catholique*, tom. xvii. p. 220). The bull of Innocent III. threatened any prince who refused to extirpate heretics from his realm with excommunication, and with the forfeiture of his dominions. See the text in Eymericus, *Directorium Inquisitorum* (Romæ, 1578), p. 60.

judicio. Quod legibus quoque Hispanis constitutum et consuetudine jam pridem receptum est." (*De Catholicis Institutionibus* [Romæ, 1575], pp. 363, 364.)

It is in itself evident, and it is abundantly proved by history, that the virulence theologians will display towards those who differ from them, will depend chiefly on the degree in which the dogmatic side of their system is developed. " See how these Christians love one another !" was the just and striking exclamation of the heathen in the first century. " There are no wild beasts so ferocious as Christians who differ concerning their faith," was the equally striking and probably equally just exclamation of the heathen in the fourth century. And the reason of this difference is manifest. In the first century there was, properly speaking, scarcely any theology, no system of elaborate dogmas authoritatively imposed upon the conscience. Neither the character of the union of two natures in Christ, nor the doctrine of the atonement, nor the extent of the authority of the Church, had been determined with precision, and the whole stress of religious sentiment was directed towards the worship of a moral ideal, and the cultivation of moral qualities. But in the fourth century men were mainly occupied with innumerable subtle and minute questions of theology, to which they attributed a transcendent importance, and which in a great measure diverted their minds from moral considerations. However strongly the Homoousians and Homoiousians were opposed to each other on other points, they were at least perfectly agreed that the adherents of the wrong vowel could not possibly get to heaven, and that the highest conceivable virtues were futile when associated with error. In the twelfth century, when persecution recommenced, the dogmatic or ecclesiastical element had been still further aggrandised by the immense development of ecclesiastical ceremonies, and the violence with which it was defended was proportionately unscrupulous. The reluctance to shed blood which had so honourably distinguished the Fathers completely passed away, or, if we find any trace of it, it is only in the quibble by which the Church referred the execution of her mandates to the civil magistrate, who, as we have seen, was not permitted to delay that execution for more than six days, under pain of excommunication. Almost all Europe, for many centuries, was inundated with blood, which was shed at the direct instigation or with the full approval of the ecclesiastical authorities, and under the pressure of a public opinion that was directed by the Catholic clergy, and was the exact measure of their influence.

That the Church of Rome has shed more innocent blood than any other institution that has ever existed among mankind, will be questioned by no Protestant who has a competent knowledge of history. The memorials, indeed, of many of her persecutions are now so scanty, that it is impossible to form a complete conception of the multitude of her victims, and it is quite certain that no powers of imagination can adequately realise their sufferings. Llorente, who had free access to the archives of the Spanish Inquisition, assures us that by that tribunal alone more than 31,000 persons were burnt, and more than 290,000 condemned to punishments less severe than death.[1] The number of those who were put to death for their religion in the Netherlands alone, in the reign of Charles V., has been estimated by a very high authority at 50,000,[2] and at least half as many perished under his son.[3] And when to these memorable instances we add the innumerable less conspicuous executions that took place, from the victims of Charlemagne to the free-thinkers of the seventeenth century, when we recollect that after the mission of Dominic the area of the persecution comprised nearly the whole of Christendom,

---

[1] Llorente, *Hist. de l'Inquisition*, tom. iv. pp. 271, 272. This does not include those who perished by the branches of the Spanish Inquisition in Mexico, Lima, Carthagena, the Indies, Sicily, Sardinia, Oran, and Malta. Llorente having been himself at one time secretary in the Inquisition, and having during the occupation by the French had access to all the secret papers of the tribunal, will always be the highest authority. One would fain hope, however (and it is very probable), that these figures are overstated, and Prescott has detected two or three instances of exaggeration in the calculations on which they are based. (*Ferdinand and Isabella*, vol. iii. pp. 492, 493.) It appears from Mariana (*De Rebus Hispaniæ*, xxiv. 17) that 2,000 persons were burnt by the Spanish Inquisition under Torquemada alone. An old historian, named Bernaldez, says that 700 were burnt at Seville between 1482–1489 ; and an inscription placed over the door of the Inquisition of Seville in 1524, declares that nearly 1,000 persons had been burnt since the expulsion of the Jews in 1492. (Llorente, tom. i. pp. 273–275.)

[2] Sarpi, *Hist. of Council of Trent.* Grotius says 100,000.

[3] " Upon the 16th of February, 1568, a sentence of the Holy Office condemned *all the inhabitants* of the Netherlands *to death* as heretics. From this universal doom only a few persons especially named were excepted. A proclamation of the king, dated ten days later, confirmed this decree of the Inquisition and ordered it to be carried into instant execution.... Three millions of people, men, women, and children, were sentenced to the scaffold in three lines." (Motley's *Rise of the Dutch Republic*, vol. ii. p. 155.)

and that its triumph was in some districts so complete as to destroy every memorial of the contest, the most callous nature must recoil with horror from the spectacle. For these atrocities were not perpetrated in the brief paroxysms of a reign of terror, or by the hands of obscure sectaries, but were inflicted by a triumphant Church, with every circumstance of solemnity and deliberation. Nor did the victims perish by a rapid and painless death, but by one which was carefully selected as among the most poignant that man can suffer. They were usually burnt alive. They were burnt alive not unfrequently by a slow fire.[1] They were burnt alive after their constancy had been tried by the most excruciating agonies that minds fertile in torture could devise.[2]

[1] One of the advantages of this being that the victim had more time for repentance. The following edifying anecdote is from Eymericus: "In Cathalonia, in civitate Barchinon, fuerunt tres hæretici, ut impenitentes œd non relapsi, traditi brachio sæculari; et cum unus eorum qui erat sacerdos fuisset igni expositus, et ex uno latere jam aliqualiter adustus, clamavit quod educeretur, quia volebat abjurare, et pœnitebat. Et sic factum est: verum si bene vel male, nescio." (*Directorium Inquisitorum*, p. 335.) Castellio notices in his time the bitter complaints of some zealous theologians "si quem videant strangulari, ac non vivum lentâ flammâ torreri." (Cluten, *De Hæreticis persequendis* [1610]: Preface of Martin Bellius.) See for a very horrible instance (produced, however, by aggravated circumstances), Sessa, *De Judæis* (Turin, 1717), p. 96. I may mention here that Eymericus was an Inquisitor in Arragon about 1368. His *Directorium* was printed at Barcelona as early as 1503; it passed through a great many editions, and with the *Commentaries* of Pegna was long the standing guide of the Inquisition. The admiring biographer of Eymericus sums up his life dwelling upon posterity in one happy sentence: "Hæc magna est et postrema viri laus, eum acri odio hæreticos omnes habuisse." Independently of its value as throwing light upon the Inquisition in its earlier stages, this book is remarkable as giving a singularly clear view of the heresies of the time. I have not met anywhere else with so satisfactory a review of the opinions of Averroes. In addition to the brief sketch prefixed to the *Directorium*, there is a full history of the life of Eymericus (which was rather remarkable) in Touron, *Hist. des Hommes illustres de l'ordre de Saint Dominique*.

[2] The tortures of the Inquisition I have noticed in the last chapter; but I may add that this mode of examination was expressly enjoined by Pope Innocent IV. in a bull, beginning "Teneatur præterea potestas seu rector omnes hæreticos quos captos habuerit cogere citra membri diminutionem et mortis periculum tanquam vere latrones et homicidas animarum, et fures Sacramentorum Dei et fidei Christianæ, errores suos expresse fateri et accusare alios hæreticos." Clement IV. issued a bull nearly in the same terms (Eymericus, Appendix, p. 9). It was decided by the Inquisitors that even a heretic who confessed his guilt might be tortured to discover his accomplices (Carena, *De Inquisitione* [Lugduni, 1649], pp. 69–73). The rule was that the tortures were not to be *repeated*, but it was decided that they might be *continued* through three days: "Si quæstionatus decenter noluerit fateri veritatem....poterit ad terrorem, vel etiam ad veritatem, secunda dies vel tertia assignari ad continuandum tormenta, non ad iterandum, quia iterari non debent, nisi novis supervenientibus indiciis contra eum, quia tunc possunt; sed

This was the physical torment inflicted on those who dared to exercise their reason in the pursuit of truth; but what language can describe, and what imagination can conceive, the mental suffering that accompanied it? For in those days the family was divided against itself. The ray of conviction often fell upon a single member, leaving all others untouched. The victims who died for heresy were not, like those who died for witchcraft, solitary and doting women, but were usually men in the midst of active life, and often in the first flush of youthful enthusiasm, and those who loved them best were firmly convinced that their agonies upon earth were but the prelude of eternal agonies hereafter.[1] This was especially the case with weak women, who feel most acutely the sufferings of others, and around whose minds the clergy had most successfully wound their toils. It is horrible, it is appalling to reflect what the mother, the wife, the sister, the daughter of the heretic must have suffered from this teaching. She saw the body of him who was dearer to her than life, dislocated and writhing and quivering with pain; she watched the slow fire creeping from limb to limb till it had swathed him in a sheet of agony, and when at last the scream of anguish had died away, and the tortured body was at rest, she was told that all this was acceptable to the God she served, and was but a faint image of the sufferings He would inflict through eternity upon the dead. Nothing was wanting to give emphasis to the doctrine. It rang from every pulpit. It was painted over every altar. The Spanish heretic was led to the flames in a dress covered with representations of devils and of frightful tortures to remind the spectators to the very last of the doom that awaited him.

All this is very horrible, but it is only a small part of the misery which the persecuting spirit of Rome has produced. For,

continuari non prohibentur." (Eymericus, p. 314.) Paramo, a Sicilian Inquisitor, assures us that the Inquisition was, like the good Samaritan, pouring into its wounded country the wine of a wholesome severity mingled with the oil of mercy. He was also of opinion that it resembled the Jewish tabernacle, in which the rod of Aaron and the manna (of mercy) lay side by side. (*De Origin. Inq.* p. 153.)

[1] The following is part of the sentence pronounced upon the relapsed heretic: "Tu in reprobum sensum datus, maligno spiritu ductus pariter et seductus, præeligisti torqueri diris et perpetuis cruciatibus in infernum, et hic temporalibus ignibus corporaliter consumari, quam adhærendo consilio saniori ab erroribus damnabilibus ac pestiferis resilire." (Eymericus, p. 337.)

judging by the ordinary measure of human courage, for every man who dared to avow his principles at the stake, there must have been many who believed that by such an avowal alone they could save their souls, but who were nevertheless scared either by the prospect of their own sufferings, or of the destitution of their children,[1] who passed their lives in one long series of hypocritical observances and studied falsehoods, and at last, with minds degraded by habitual deception, sank hopeless and terror-stricken into the grave.[2] And besides all these things, we have to remember that the spirit which was manifested in acts of detailed persecution had often swept over a far wider sphere, and produced sufferings not perhaps so excruciating, but far more extensive. We have to recollect those frightful massacres, perhaps the most fearful the world has ever seen: the massacre of the Albigenses, which a pope had instigated, or the massacre of St. Bartholomew, for which a pope returned solemn thanks to Heaven. We have to recollect those religious wars which reproduced themselves century after century with scarcely diminished fury, which turned Syria into an Aceldama, which inundated with blood the fairest lands of Europe, which blasted the prosperity and paralysed the intellect of many a noble nation, and which planted animosities in Europe that two hundred years have been unable altogether to destroy. Nor should we forget the hardening effects that must have been produced on the minds of the spectators who at every royal marriage in Spain were regaled by the public execution of heretics, or who were summoned to the great square of Toulouse to contemplate the struggles of four hundred witches in the flames. When we add together all these various forms of suffering, and estimate all their aggravations, when we think that the victims of these persecutions were usually men who were not only entirely guiltless, but who proved themselves by their very deaths to be endowed with most transcendent and heroic virtues, and when we still further consider that all this was but part of one vast conspiracy to check the development of the human mind, and to destroy that spirit of impartial and unrestricted enquiry which is the very first condition of progress as of truth; when we consider all these things, it can surely be no exaggeration to say that the Church of Rome has inflicted a greater amount of unmerited suffering than any other religion that has ever existed among mankind. To complete the picture, it is only necessary to add that these things were done in the name of the Teacher who said: "By this shall all men know that ye are my disciples, that ye love one another."

But while the pre-eminent atrocity of the persecutions of the Church of Rome is fully admitted, nothing can be more grossly disingenuous or untrue than to represent persecution as her peculiar taint. She persecuted to the full extent of the power of her clergy, and that power was very great. The persecution of which every Protestant Church was guilty was measured by the same rule, but clerical influence in Protestant countries was

[1] It was the invariable rule to confiscate the entire property of the impenitent heretic, a rule which Paramo justifies on the ground that the crime of the heretic is so great that something of his impurity falls upon all related to him, and that the Almighty (whom he blasphemously terms the First Inquisitor) deprived both Adam and his descendants of the Garden of Eden. The children of the heretic were thus left absolutely destitute, and with a stigma upon them that in the fifteenth and sixteenth centuries was sufficient to shut them out from all sympathy, from all charity, and from all hope. The thought that those who were most dear to him would probably be abandoned either to starvation or to the life of the prostitute was doubtless one of the most acute pangs of the martyr, and the hope of preventing such a catastrophe one of the most powerful inducements to recant. In this rule we have also an explanation of those trials of dead men for heresy which the Catholic clergy so frequently instituted. Protestants sometimes regard these simply as displays of impotent malice. Nothing, however, can be more false. They had the very intelligible object of robbing the children of the dead. "Juste enim proceditur contra defunctos hæreticos. Primo, ut memoria ejus damnatur. Secundo, ut bona illius per fiscum ab hæredibus defuncti nou a quibuslibet aliis possessoribus auferantur." (Paramo, *De Orig. et Progressu Sancti Inquisitionis* [Madrid, 1598], p. 588.) The confiscation of the goods of the heretic was authorised by a bull of Innocent III. (on the ground that children are in the Divine judgments often punished for the offences of their fathers), and again by Alexander IV. (Eymericus, pp. 58, 59, 64.) The following passage from an old ecclesiastical lawyer gives a vivid picture of the ferocity displayed towards the children of heretics: "Ipsi filii hæreticorum adeo sunt effecti a jure incapaces et inhabiles ad succedendum patri, quod illi etiam in uno nummo succedere non possunt; immo semper debent in miseria et egestate sordescere sicut filii reorum criminis læsæ majestatis humanæ, adeo quod nihil aliud eis sit relinquendum, nisi sola vita quæ ex misericordia largitur, et tales esse debent in hoc mundo ut eis vita sit supplicium et mors solatium." (Farinacius, *De Delictis et Pœnis*, p. 205: Venice, 1519.) However, it was provided that children who betrayed their parents preserved their inheritance. On the laws resulting from these notions, see Prescott, *Ferdinand and Isabella*, vol. i. pp. 262, 263.

[2] Before operating in any district, the Inquisitors always made a proclamation offering pardon under certain conditions to those who confessed and retracted their heresies within thirty or forty days. Mariana says that when this proclamation was made, on the first establishment of the Inquisition in Andalusia, 17,000 recantations followed. (*De Rebus Hispaniæ*, lib. xxiv. c. 17.)

comparatively weak. The Protestant persecutions were never so sanguinary as those of the Catholics, but the principle was affirmed quite as strongly, was acted on quite as constantly, and was defended quite as pertinaciously by the clergy. In Germany, at the time of the Protestation of Spires, when the name of Protestant was assumed, the Lutheran princes absolutely prohibited the celebration of mass within their dominions. In England, a similar measure was passed as early as Edward VI.[1] On the accession of Elizabeth, and before the Catholics had given any signs of discontent, a law was made prohibiting any religious service other than the Prayer Book ; the penalty for the third offence being imprisonment for life ; while another law imposed a fine on anyone who abstained from the Anglican service. The Presbyterians through a long succession of reigns were imprisoned, branded, mutilated, scourged, and exposed in the pillory. Many Catholics under false pretences were tortured and hung. Anabaptists and Arians were burnt alive.[2] In Ireland,

the religion of the immense majority of the people was banned and proscribed, and when in 1626 the Government manifested some slight wish to grant it partial relief, nearly all the Irish Protestant bishops, under the presidency of Usher, assembled to protest in a solemn resolution against the indulgence. " The religion of Papists," they said, " is superstitious, their faith and doctrine erroneous and heretical ; their Church in respect of both apostatical. To give them therefore a toleration, or to consent that they may freely exercise their religion, and profess their faith and doctrine, is a grievous sin."[1] In Scotland, during nearly the whole period that the Stuarts were on the throne of England, a persecution rivalling in atrocity almost any on record was directed by the English Government, at the instigation of the Scotch bishops, and with the approbation of the English Church, against all who repudiated episcopacy. If a conventicle was held in a house, the preacher was liable to be put to death. If it was held in the open air, both minister and people incurred the same fate. The Presbyterians were hunted like criminals over the mountains. Their ears were torn from the roots. They were branded with hot irons. Their fingers were wrenched asunder by the thumbkins. The bones of their legs were shattered in the boots. Women were scourged publicly through the streets. Multitudes were transported to Barbadoes, infuriated soldiers were let loose upon them, and encouraged to exercise all their ingenuity in torturing them.[2] Nor was it only the British Government, or the zealous advocates of episcopacy, who manifested this spirit. When the Reformation triumphed in Scotland, one of its first fruits was a law prohibiting any priest from celebrating, or any worshipper from hearing mass, under pain of the confiscation of his goods for the first offence, of exile for the second, and of death for the third.[3] That the Queen of Scotland should be permitted to hear mass in her own private chapel, was

[1] Hallam, *Const. Hist.*
[2] Hallam, *Const. Hist.* And then in 1562 it was enacted, that all who had ever graduated at the universities or received holy orders, all lawyers, all magistrates, must take the oath of supremacy when tendered to them, under pain of forfeiture or imprisonment during the royal pleasure ; and if after three months they refused to take the oath when again tendered to them, they were guilty of high treason and condemned to death. Now the discontent of the Catholics might be a very good reason for making them take the oath of allegiance, which is simply a test of loyalty. It might even be a reason for making the oath of supremacy obligatory on those who for the future aspired to offices of importance—in other words, for excluding the Catholics from such offices ; but to pass a retrospective law which made almost every educated Roman Catholic, if he refused to take an oath which was absolutely and confessedly irreconcilable with the doctrines of his Church, liable to be punished with death, was as sweeping a measure of persecution as any that history records. And this was done many years before the bull which deposed Elizabeth. The misconceptions which ignorance, and worse than ignorance, accumulated around this subject have been so completely dispelled by Hallam and Macaulay that I will only add one remark. The principal apology which was published for the policy of Elizabeth towards the Catholics was Bishop Bilson's *Christian Subjection*, in 1585. In that work the coercive laws were openly justified on the ground of the absolute sinfulness of toleration (pp. 16–29). Nor was it merely the public profession of error which was rightly prohibited. This distinction the Bishop indignantly repudiates. " No corner is so secret," he says, addressing the Catholics, " no prison so close, but your impiety there suffered doth offend God, infect others, and confirm your own frowardness. If your religion be good, why should it lack churches? If it be naught, why should it have chambers ? A Christian prince may not pardon or wink at your falsehood " (p. 26). See also on the duty of intolerance, pp. 16–29. Milner, in his *Letters to a Prebendary*, has collected much evidence on the subject. There is much truth as well as bitter eloquence

in the taunt of an old persecuted Puritan when he denounced Anglicanism as " the Church that is planted in the blood of her mother."
[1] Elrington, *Life of Usher*, vol. i. p. 73.
[2] For the circumstances of the persecution in Scotland, see Wodrow's *History*; and for a summary of the laws against Nonconformists in England, Neal's *History of the Puritans*, vol. ii. pp. 695–696.
[3] Buckle, *Hist.*, vol. ii. p. 231 ; McKenzie, *Laws of Scotland*.

publicly denounced as an intolerable evil. "One mass," exclaimed Knox, "is more fearful to me than if 10,000 armed enemies were landed in any part of the realm."[1] In France, when the government of certain towns was conceded to the Protestants, they immediately employed their power to suppress absolutely the Catholic worship, to prohibit any Protestant from attending a marriage or a funeral that was celebrated by a priest, to put down all mixed marriages, and to persecute to the full extent of their power those who had abandoned their creed.[2] In Sweden, all who dissented from any article of the Confession of Augsburg were at once banished.[3] In Protestant Switzerland numerous Anabaptists perished by drowning ; the freethinker Gentilis by the axe ; Servetus, and a convert to Judaism, by the flames.[4] In America, the colonists who were driven from their own land by persecution, not only proscribed the Catholics, but also persecuted the Quakers— the most inoffensive of all sects—with atrocious severity.[5] If Holland was somewhat more tolerant, it was early remarked, that while the liberty allowed there was unusually great, the power accorded to the clergy was unusually small.[6] As late as 1690 a synod was held at Amsterdam, consisting partly of Dutch and partly of French and English ministers who were driven to Holland by persecution, and in that synod the doctrine that the magistrate has no right to crush heresy and idolatry by the civil power, was unanimously pronounced to be "false, scandalous, and pernicious."[7] When Descartes went to Holland, the reformed clergy directed against him all the force of their animosity, and the accusation by which they endeavoured to stir up the civil power against the author of the most sublime of all modern proofs of the existence of the Deity, was atheism.[8] The right of the civil magistrate to punish heresy was maintained by the Helvetic, Scottish, Belgic, and Saxon Confessions.[1] Luther, in reply to Philip of Hesse, directly asserted it ;[2] Calvin, Beza, and Jurieu, all wrote books on the lawfulness of persecution. Knox, appealing to the Old Testament, declared that those who were guilty of idolatry might justly be put to death.[3] Cranmer and Ridley, as well as four other bishops, formed the commission in the reign of Edward VI. for trying and condemning Anabaptists. The only two exceptions to this spirit among the leaders of the Reformation, seem to have been Zuinglius and Socinus. The first was always averse to persecution.[4] The second was so distinctively the apostle of toleration, that this was long regarded as one of the peculiar doctrines of his sect.[5] With

except one of which Linnæus was the victim. Some good people in Sweden desired, it is said, to have his system of botany suppressed, because it was based upon the discovery of the sexes of the plants, and was therefore calculated to inflame the minds of youth. (Gioja, *Filosofia della Statistica*, tom. ii. p. 389.)

[1] Palmer, *On the Church*, vol. i. p. 380.

[2] And also in reply to the Wittenberg theologians. At an earlier period, when his translation of the New Testament was proscribed, he had advocated toleration. For a full view of his sentiments, see Henry's *Life of Calvin*, vol. ii. pp. 232-242.

[3] McCrie's *Life of Knox*, p. 246. It is in his *Appellation* that this great apostle of murder most fully expounded his views: "None provoking the people to idolatrie oght to be exempted from the punishment of death....The whole tribes did in verie dede execute that sharp judgment against the tribe of Benjamin for a lesse offense than for idolatrie. And the same oght to be done wheresoever Christ Jesus and his Evangill is so receaved in any realme province or citie that the magistrates and people have solemnly avowed and promised to defend the same, as under King Edward of late days was done in England. In such places, I say, it is not only lawful to punish to the death such as labour to subvert the true religion, but the magistrates and people are bound to do so onless they wil provoke the wrath of God against themselves....And therefore, my Lordes, to return to you, [seeing that God hath armed your handes with the sworde of justice, seeing that His law most streatly commandeth idolaters and fals prophetes to be punished with death, and that you be placed above your subjects to reigne as fathers over their children, and further seeing that not only I, but with me manie thousand famous, godlie, and learned persons, accuse your Byshoppes and the whole rabble of the Papistical clergie of idolatrie, of murther, and of blasphemie against God committed : it appertaineth to your Honours to be vigilant and carefull in so weightie a matter. The question is not of earthly substance, but of the glorie of God, and of the salvation of yourselves." (Knox's *Works*, Laing's edition, vol. iv. pp. 500-515.) In 1572 the two houses of Convocation implored Elizabeth to put Mary Queen of Scots to death, alleging among other reasons that she had endeavoured to seduce God's people to idolatry, and that according to the Old Testament all who did so should be put to death. (Froude's *Hist. of England*, vol. x. pp. 360-362.)

[4] This is noticed by Hallam and other writers.

[5] Thus, for example, Jurieu, the great antagonist of Bossuet, the most eminent French minister in Holland (he was pastor of Rotterdam), and certainly one of the most distinguished Protestants of his day, calls

[1] McCrie, *Life of Knox* (ed. 1840), p. 246.

[2] Much evidence of this is collected in Buckle, vol. i. pp. 509-523.

[3] Macaulay, *Essays*, vol. ii. p. 140; Laing, *Sweden*.

[4] The religious policy of the Swiss Protestants has lately been well treated by M. Barni in his very interesting work, *Les Martyrs de la libre pensée*.

[5] See Bancroft's *History of America*.

[6] Temple, *On the United Provinces*.

[7] Bayle, art. *Augustine*, note H. See, too, on the general intolerance of the Dutch clergy, Hallam, *Hist. of Lit.*, vol. iii. p. 289.

[8] *Biog. Univ.*, art. *Descartes*; Voltaire (*Lettres philosophiques*, xiv.). Considering the writings of Descartes, this is perhaps the most preposterous accusation ever brought against a philosopher, if we

these exceptions, all the most eminent
Reformers advocated persecution, and in
nearly every country where their boasted
Reformation triumphed, the result is to
be mainly attributed to coercion.[1] When
Calvin burnt Servetus for his opinions on
the Trinity, this, which, in the words of
a great modern historian, "had perhaps
as many circumstances of aggravation as
any execution for heresy that ever took
place,"[2] was almost unanimously applauded by all sections of Protestants.[3]
Melanchthon, Bullinger, and Farel wrote
to express their warm approbation of the
crime. Beza defended it in an elaborate
treatise. Only one man of eminence
ventured openly to oppose it, and that
man, who may be regarded as the first
avowed champion of complete religious
liberty, was also one of the most eminent
of the precursors of rationalism. He
wrote under the name of Martin Bellius,
but his real name was Chatillon, or, as it
was generally latinised, Castellio.[4]

Castellio was a Frenchman, a scholar
of remarkable acquirements, and a critic
of still more remarkable boldness. He
had been at one time a friend of Calvin,
and had filled a professorship at Geneva,
but the daring spirit which he carried
into every sphere soon scandalised the
leaders of the Reformation. Having
devoted himself early to Biblical criticism,
he had translated the Bible into Latin,
and in the course of his labours he came
to the conclusion that the Song of Solomon was simply a Jewish love song, and
that the allegory that was supposed to
underlie it was purely imaginary.[1] A
still graver offence in the eyes of the
Geneva theologians was his emphatic
repudiation of the Calvinistic doctrine of
predestination. He assailed it not so
much by any train of arguments, or by
an appeal to authority, as on the broad
grounds of its repugnance to our sense of
right, and he developed its moral atrocity
in a manner that elicited from Beza a
torrent of almost frantic invective. Driven
from Geneva, he at last obtained a professorship at Basle, where he denounced
the murder of Servetus, and preached for
the first time in Christendom the duty
of absolute toleration, based upon the
rationalistic doctrine of the innocence of
error. The object of doctrines, he said,
is to make men better, and those which
do not contribute to this end are absolutely unimportant. The history of dogmas
should be looked upon as a series of
developments, contributing to the moral
perfection of mankind. First of all,
polytheism was supreme. Christ came
and effected the ascendency of monotheism, in which Jews, Turks, and

universal toleration, "Ce dogme socinien, le plus dan-
gereux de tous ceux de la secte socinienne, puisqu'il va
à ruiner le christianisme et à établir l'indifférence des
religions." (*Droits des deux Souverains en matière de
Religion, la Conscience et l'Expérience* [Rotterdam,
1687], p. 14.) This work (which was published anonymously) was written in reply to the *Contrains-les
d'entrer* of Bayle, with the rather unnecessary object
of showing that the French Protestants repudiated the
tolerant maxims of that great writer.

[1] I commend the following passage to the special
attention of my readers: "Peut-on nier que le paganisme est tombé dans le monde par l'autorité des
empereurs romains? On peut assurer sans témérité
que le paganisme seroit encore debout, et que les trois
quarts de l'Europe seroient encore payens, si Constantin et ses successeurs n'avoient emploié leur autorité
pour l'abolir. Mais, je vous prie, de quelles voies
Dieu s'est-il servi dans ces derniers siècles pour rétablir
la véritable religion dans l'Occident? Les rois de
Suède, ceux de Danemarck, ceux d'Angleterre, les
magistrats souverains de Suisse, des Païs-Bas, des
villes libres d'Allemagne, les princes électeurs, et autres
princes souverains de l'empire, n'ont-ils pas emploié
leur autorité pour abattre le Papisme?....En vérité il
faut être bien téméraire pour condamner des voies dont
la Providence s'est constamment servi pour établir la
véritable religion; excepté le premier établissement du
christianisme, et sa conservation, dans laquelle Dieu a
voulu qu'il y eût un miracle sensible; c'est pourquoi il
n'a pas voulu que l'autorité s'en mêlât; excepté, dis-je,
cet endroit de l'histoire de l'Eglise, on voit constamment partout que Dieu fait entrer l'autorité pour
établir la véritable religion et pour ruiner les fausses."
(*Droits des deux Souverains*, pp. 280-282.)

[2] Hallam, *Hist. of Literature*, vol. i. p. 554.

[3] See the collection of approbations quoted by Beza,
De Hæreticis; McKenzie, *Life of Calvin*, pp. 79-89;
and the remarks in Coleridge, *Notes on English
Divines*, vol. i. p. 49.

[4] His name was originally Chatillon or Chateillon,
which, after the fashion of the age, he latinised into
Castellio; but, at the beginning of his career, some one
having called him by mistake Castalio, he was so
charmed by the name, which, by reminding him of the
Castalian fount, seemed a good augury for his literary
career, that he adopted it. See, for a full account of
his life, Bayle, art. *Castalio*, and Henry, *Life of*

Calvin; and, for a short notice, Hallam, *Hist. of
Literature*, vol. i. p. 557. Besides the works I have
noticed in the text, Castalio translated the dialogues
of the famous Socinian Ochino, and an anonymous
German work of the mystical school of Tauler, edited
the Sibylline verses (his preface is given to the recent
edition by Alexander [Paris, 1846]), wrote a defence of
his translation of the Bible (which translation seems to
have been an indifferent performance), and published
some minor essays or dialogues.

[1] From which he somewhat rashly concluded that it
ought not to be retained in the Bible. "For my part,"
said Niebuhr, when a young German pastor expressed
his scruples about reading what he believed to be simply
a love song, "I should deem the Bible itself imperfect
if it did not include an expression of the deepest and
strongest passion of humanity." The history of the
interpretations of the Song of Solomon would be long
and curious: from the Jewish Cabalists—who, regarding
heaven as the union of man with the Deity by love, and
death as the "kiss of God," esteemed the Song of
Solomon the highest expression of this transcendental
union—to the somewhat fantastic criticisms of M.
Renan.

Christians all agree. Christianity again introduced a specific type of character, of which universal charity and beneficence were the leading features. Questions concerning the Trinity, or predestination, or the sacraments, are involved in great and perhaps impenetrable obscurity, and have no moral influence, and ought in consequence not to be insisted upon. "To discuss the difference between the Law and the Gospel, gratuitous remission of sins or imputed righteousness, is as if a man were to discuss whether a prince was to come on horseback, or in a chariot, or dressed in white or in red."[1] To persecute for such questions is absurd, and not only absurd but atrocious. For if the end of Christianity be the diffusion of a spirit of beneficence, persecution must be its extreme antithesis ; and if persecution be an essential element of a religion, that religion must be a curse to mankind.[2]

Such new and startling sentiments as these, coming from a writer of considerable eminence, attracted much attention, and aroused great indignation. Both Calvin and Beza replied in a strain of the fiercest invective. Calvin especially, from the time when Castellio left Geneva, pursued him with untiring hatred, laboured hard to procure his expulsion from Basle, denounced him in the preface to an edition of the New Testament[3] as

"one who had been chosen by Satan to deceive the thoughtless and indifferent," and attempted to blast his character by the grossest calumnies. In the friendship of Socinus, Castellio found some compensation for the general hatred of which he was the object, and he appears to have inclined greatly to the doctrines of his friend. Separated alike from the Protestants and the Catholics, his prospects in life were blighted, he sank into a condition of absolute destitution, and is said to have been almost reduced to literal starvation, when death relieved him of his sufferings. A few kindly sentences of Montaigne,[1] who pronounced his closing scene to have been a disgrace to mankind, have in some degree rescued this first apostle of toleration from oblivion.

Some years after the murder of Servetus, Beza, in relating its circumstances, declared that Castellio and Socinus were the only men who had opposed it ;[2] and although this statement is not strictly true,[3] it but very little exaggerates the unanimity that was displayed. When we recollect the great notoriety of this execution, and also its aggravated character,

longe copiosius quam a me recensentur facis in libello duorum foliorum et quidem perparvorum."
[1] *Essais*, liv. i. ch. 34.   [2] Beza, *Vita Calvini.*
[3] It is sufficiently refuted by Beza himself in his answer to Castellio, when he speaks of those who objected to the burning of Servetus (he calls them "emissaries of Satan"), as amounting to a sect. He also specifies two or three writers, of whom the principal seems to have been Clebergius. I have never been able to meet with the work of this author, but Beza represents him as objecting absolutely to all forms of persecution, and basing this objection on the absolute innocence of honest error ; which doctrine again he rested on the impossibility of ascertaining certainly religious truths, as demonstrated by the continuance of controversy. The following passages quoted by Beza are extremely remarkable for the age : "De controversiis nondum certo constat ; si enim constaret disputari defuisset." "Nonne Deus eos amabit qui id quod verum esse putant defenderint bonâ fide ? Etiam si forte erraverint, nonne eis veniam dabit ?" (Beza, pp. 65, 93.) Hallam has also exhumed three or four books or pamphlets that were written at the same time in favour of toleration. Acontius (Acanacio) seems to have been one of the most distinguished of these authors. Hallam says (*Hist. of Literature*) his book is "perhaps, the first wherein the limitation of fundamental articles of Christianity to a small number is laid down at considerable length. He instances among doctrines which he does not reckon fundamental, those of the Real Presence and of the Trinity." Acontius was born at Trent. He adopted sceptical or indifferent opinions, verging on Socinianism ; he took refuge in England, and received a pension from Elizabeth. There is a full notice of him in an anonymous French history of Socinianism of very great research (1723), ascribed to Guichard or to Lamy (pp. 261-264). The hand of Socinus was suspected in some of these works. That of Bellius was by some ascribed to him. So, too, was a work now attributed to an author named Minos Celso, concerning whom scarcely anything is known, except that, like Socinus, he was born at Sienna. (See *Biog. Univ.*, arts. *Servetus* and *Celso*.)

[1] On which Beza comments : "Hac impietate quid tandem magis impium aut diabolicum ipsæ unquam inferiorum portæ exhalarunt." (*De Hæreticis a Civili Magistratu puniendis : Libellus adversus Martini Bellii farraginem et Novorum Academicorum sectam* [1554], p. 58.)
[2] "Quis non putet Christum aliquem esse Molochum aut ejus generis aliquem Deum si sibi vivos homines immolari, comburique velit ? Quis velit servire Christo eâ conditione, ut si in aliquâ re inter tot controversias ab iis dissideat, qui habent in alios potestatem, vivus comburatur ipsius Christi jussu crudelius quam in tauro Phalaridis, etiamsi in mediis flammis Christum magnâ voce concelebret, et se in eum pleno ore credere vociferetur ?" (Preface of Martin Bellius in Joachim Cluten's *De Hæreticis persequendis*, ed. 1610.) This work consists of a collection of passages from different authors (two of them by Castellio) in favour of toleration.
[3] See Bayle and Henry. Castellio, when publishing his edition of the Bible, made the preface the vehicle of a warm appeal for toleration (which is given in Cluten). Calvin, among other things, accused him of stealing wood for his fire—an accusation which was solemnly refuted. Bayle has collected much evidence to show that Castellio was a man of spotless character, singularly loved by those about him, intensely amiable, keenly sensible of the attacks of which he was the object. Castellio has himself made a collection of the epithets Calvin in one short work heaped upon him : "Vocas me subinde in Gallico libello : blasphemum, calumniatorem, malignum, canem latrantem, plenum ignorantiæ et bestialitatis, sacrarum literarum impurum corruptorem, Dei prorsus derisorem, omnis religionis contemptorem, impudentem, impurum canem, impium, obscœnum, torti perversique ingenii, vagum, balatronem, nebulonem vero appellas octies ; et hæc omnia

so general an approbation seems to show
clearly not only that the spirit of early
Protestantism was as undoubtedly intolerant as the spirit of Catholicism,
which is an unquestionable fact, but also
that it flinched as little from the extreme
consequences to which intolerance leads.
It seems to show that the comparative
mildness of Protestant persecutions results much more from the circumstances
under which they took place, than from
any sense of the atrocity of burning the
heretic. And, indeed, while the Romish
persecutions were undoubtedly unrivalled in magnitude, it must be admitted that there are some aspects
under which they contrast not unfavourably with the Protestant ones. Catholicism was an ancient Church. She had
gained a great part of her influence by
vast services to mankind. She rested
avowedly upon the principle of authority.
She was defending herself against aggres-
sion and innovation. That a Church so
circumstanced should endeavour to stifle
in blood every aspiration towards a purer
system, was indeed a fearful crime, but
it was a crime which was not altogether
unnatural. She might point to the price-
less blessings she had bestowed upon
humanity, to the slavery she had destroyed, to the civilisation she had founded,
to the many generations she had led with
honour to the grave. She might show
how completely her doctrines were interwoven with the whole social system, how
fearful would be the convulsion if they
were destroyed, and how absolutely incompatible they were with the acknow-
ledgment of private judgment. These
considerations would not make her blame-
less, but they would at least palliate her
guilt. But what shall we say of a Church
that was but a thing of yesterday, a
Church that had as yet no services to
show, no claims upon the gratitude of
mankind, a Church that was by profession the creature of private judgment,
and was in reality generated by the
intrigues of a corrupt court, which,
nevertheless, suppressed by force a
worship that multitudes deemed necessary
to their salvation, and by all her organs,
and with all her energies, persecuted
those who clung to the religion of their
fathers? What shall we say of a religion
which comprised at most but a fourth
part of the Christian world, and which
the first explosion of private judgment
had shivered into countless sects, which

was, nevertheless, so pervaded by the
spirit of dogmatism that each of these
sects asserted its distinctive doctrines
with the same confidence, and persecuted
with the same unhesitating virulence, as
a Church that was venerable with the
homage of more than twelve centuries?
What shall we say of men who, in the
name of religious liberty, deluged their
land with blood, trampled on the very
first principles of patriotism, calling in
strangers to their assistance, and openly
rejoicing in the disasters of their country,
and who, when they at last attained their
object, immediately established a religious
tyranny as absolute as that which they
had subverted? These were the attitudes
which for more than a century Protestantism uniformly presented, and so strong and
so general was its intolerance that for
some time it may, I believe, be truly said
that there were more instances of partial
toleration being advocated by Roman
Catholics than by orthodox Protestants.
Although nothing can be more egre-
giously absurd than to represent the
Inquisition as something unconnected
with the Church, although it was created
by a Pope, and introduced into the chief
countries of Europe by the sovereigns
who were most devoted to the Church,
and composed of ecclesiastics, and directed to the punishment of ecclesiastical
offences, and developed in each country
according to the intensity of Catholic
feeling, and long regarded as the chief
bulwark of Catholicity—although all the
atrocities it perpetrated do undoubtedly
fall upon the blood-stained Church that
created it—it is nevertheless true that one
or two popes endeavoured to moderate its
severities, and reproved the excesses of
Torquemada in language that is not
without something of evangelical mildness. Erasmus, too, at all times endeavoured to assuage the persecution,
and Erasmus lived and died in communion with the Church. Sir Thomas
More, though he was himself a persecutor, at least admitted the abstract excellence of toleration, and extolled it in
his *Utopia*. Hôpital, and Lord Balti-
more the Catholic founder of Maryland,
were the first two legislators who uniformly upheld religious liberty when in
power, and Maryland continued the solitary refuge for the oppressed of every
Christian sect, till the Protestant party
who were in the ascendant in its legislature basely enacted the whole penal code

against the co-religionists of the founder of the colony. But among the Protestants it may, I believe, be safely affirmed, that there was no example of the consistent advocacy or practice of toleration in the sixteenth century that was not virulently and generally denounced by all sections of the clergy,[1] and scarcely any till the middle of the seventeenth century. Indeed, even at the close of the seventeenth century, Bossuet was able to maintain that the right of the civil magistrate to punish religious error was one of the points on which both churches agreed ; and he added that he only knew two bodies of Christians who denied it. They were the Socinians and the Anabaptists.[2]

It is often said that Protestantism in its earlier days persecuted, because it had inherited something of the principles of Rome ; but that persecution was entirely uncongenial with its character, and was therefore in course of time abandoned. In a certain sense, this is undoubtedly true. Protestantism received the doctrine of persecution from Rome just as it received the Athanasian Creed or any other portion of its dogmatic teaching. The doctrine of private judgment is inconsistent with persecution just as it is inconsistent with the doctrine of exclusive salvation, and with the universal practice of all sections of early Protestants in their dealings with error. If man is bound to form his opinions by his private judgment, if the exercise of private judgment is both a duty and a right, it is absurd to prescribe beforehand the conclusion to which he must arrive, to brand honest error as criminal, and to denounce the spirit of impartiality and of scepticism as offensive to the Deity. This is what almost all the Protestant leaders did in the sixteenth and seventeenth centuries, and what a very large proportion of them still do, and it was out of this conception of the guilt of error that persecution arose. Nothing can be more erroneous than to represent it merely as a weapon which was employed in a moment of conflict, or as the outburst of a natural indignation, or as the unreasoning observance of an old tradition. Persecution among the early Protestants was a distinct and definite doctrine, digested into elaborate treatises, indissolubly connected with a large portion of the received theology, developed by the most enlightened and far-seeing theologians, and enforced against the most inoffensive as against the most formidable sects. It was the doctrine of the palmiest days of Protestantism. It was taught by those who are justly esteemed the greatest of its leaders. It was manifested most clearly in those classes which were most deeply imbued with its dogmatic teaching. The Episcopalians generally justified it by appealing to St. Augustine, and Calvin and the Scotch Puritans by appealing to the Old Testament ; but in both cases the dominating and controlling cause was the belief in exclusive salvation and in the guilt of error, and in all countries the first dawning of tolerance represents the rise of that rationalistic spirit which regards doctrines simply as the vehicles of moral sentiments, and which, while it greatly diminishes their value, simplifies their character and lessens their number.

The evidence I have accumulated will be sufficient to show how little religious liberty is due to Protestantism considered as a dogmatic system. It might appear also to show that the influence of the Reformation upon its progress was

---

[1] If this language should appear startling to any reader, I commend to his attention the following passage from an historian who was accustomed to weigh well his expressions : "At the end of the sixteenth century the simple proposition, that men for holding or declaring heterodox opinions in religion should not be burned alive or otherwise put to death, was itself little else than a sort of heterodoxy ; and though many privately must have been persuaded of its truth, the Protestant churches were as far from acknowledging it as that of Rome. No one had yet pretended to assert the general right of religious worship, which, in fact, was rarely or never conceded to the Romanists in a Protestant country, though the Huguenots shed oceans of blood to secure the same privilege for themselves." (Hallam, *Hist. of Literature*, vol. i. p. 560.) The same judicious historian elsewhere says : "Persecution is the deadly original sin of the Reformed churches, that which cools every honest man's zeal for their cause in proportion as his reading becomes more extensive." (*Const. Hist.*, vol. i. ch. 2.)

[2] "La discipline de nos Réformés permet aussi le recours au bras séculier en certains cas, et on trouve parmi les articles de la discipline de l'Église de Genève que les ministres doivent déférer au magistrat les incorrigibles qui méprisent les peines spirituelles, et en particulier ceux qui enseignent de nouveaux dogmes sans distinction. Et encore aujourd'hui celui de tous les auteurs Calvinistes qui reproche le plus aigrement à l'Eglise romaine la cruauté de sa doctrine, en demeure d'accord dans le fond, puisqu'il permet l'exercice de la puissance du glaive dans les matières de la religion et de la conscience (Jurieu, *Syst.* ii. chs. 22-23, &c.) ; chose aussi qui ne peut être révoquée en doute sans énerver et comme estropier la puissance publique ; de sorte qu'il n'y a point d'illusion plus dangereuse que de donner la souffrance pour un caractère de la vraie Église, et je ne connois parmi les Chrétiens que les Sociniens et les Anabaptistes qui s'opposent à cette doctrine." (*Variations protestantes*, liv. x. ch. 56.) The Anabaptists, however, were not always so tolerant, and one of the earliest rallying cries of the insurgents of Munster was : "Que tous non rebaptisez fussent mis à mort comme payens et meschans." (Sleidan, liv. x.)

but small. Such a conclusion would, however, be altogether erroneous, for although that influence was entirely indirect, it was not the less powerful. To the Reformation is chiefly due the appearance of that rationalistic spirit which at last destroyed persecution. By the events that followed the Reformation, the adherents of different religious creeds became so mingled, that it was the interest of a large proportion of the members of every church to advocate toleration. At the Reformation, too, the doctrine of the celibacy of the clergy was assailed, and the ministers of the new churches, being drawn into more intimate communion with society, were placed in circumstances far more fitted to develope the kindly affections than the circumstances of the Catholic priests; while in England, at least, the accomplishments of a scholar and the refinement of a gentleman, blending with the pure and noble qualities of a religious teacher, have produced a class type which is scarcely sullied by fanaticism, and is probably, on the whole, the highest as it is the most winning that has ever been attained. Besides this, the Reformation produced a number of churches, which possessed such an amount of flexibility that they have been able to adapt themselves to the requirements of the age, while Catholicism continues to the present day the bitter enemy of toleration. The influence of the first three facts is, I think, sufficiently obvious. A short sketch of the history of toleration in France and England will clearly establish the fourth.

In order to understand the history of religious liberty, there are two distinct series of facts to be considered. There is a succession of intellectual changes which destroy the conceptions on which persecution rests, and a succession of political events which are in part the consequence of those changes, but which also react powerfully upon their cause. The intellectual basis of French toleration is to be found in that great sceptical movement which originated towards the close of the sixteenth century, and which at last triumphed in the Revolution. In no other country had that movement been so powerful, not only on account of the great ability with which it was conducted, but also from the curious fact that its first three leaders represented three entirely different casts of mind, and acted in consequence upon three different sections of

society. The scepticism of Montaigne was that of a man of the world; the scepticism of Descartes was that of a philosopher; the scepticism of Bayle was that of a scholar. Montaigne, looking with an impartial eye on the immense variety of opinions that were maintained with equal confidence by men of equal ability, and judging all subjects by a keen, worldly, and somewhat superficial common sense, arrived at the conclusion that it was hopeless seeking to ascertain what is true; that such a task transcended the limits of human powers; and that it was the part of a wise man to remain poised with an indifferent mind between opposing sects. As a consequence of this he taught for the first time, or almost for the first time, in France, the innocence of error and the evil of persecution. Descartes had a far greater confidence in human faculties, but he had also a far greater distrust of the ordinary judgments of experience. He taught men that the beginning of all wisdom is absolute, universal scepticism; that all the impressions of childhood, all the conclusions of the senses, all of what are deemed the axioms of life, must be discarded, and from the simple fact of consciousness the entire scheme of knowledge must be evolved. Like many of the greatest philosophers, Descartes did not pause to apply his principles to practical life, but their influence was not the less great. The scepticism which he made the beginning of wisdom, and the purely rational process by which that scepticism was at last dispelled, were alike inconsistent with a system which esteemed doubt a sin, and which enforced conviction by the brand.

The intellect of Bayle was very different from those of his predecessors, and was indeed in some respects almost unique. There have been many greater men, but there never perhaps was one who was so admirably fitted by his acquirements and his abilities, and even by the very defects of his character, to be a perfect critic. With the most profound and varied knowledge he combined to an almost unrivalled extent that rare faculty of assuming the standing-point of the system he was discussing, and of developing its arguments as they would have been developed by its most skilful advocate. But while he possessed to the highest degree that knowledge and that philosophical perception which lay bare the hidden springs of past beliefs, he appeared to be almost absolutely destitute of the creative power, and almost absolutely indifferent to the results of controversy. He denied nothing. He inculcated nothing. He scarcely exhibited any serious preference. It was his delight to bring together the arguments of many discordant teachers, to dissect and analyse them with the most exquisite skill, and then to develope them till they mutually destroyed one another. His genius was never so conspicuous as when lighting up the wrecks of opposing systems, exhuming the shattered monuments of human genius to reveal their nothingness and their vanity. In that vast repertory of obscure learning from which Voltaire and every succeeding scholar have drawn their choicest weapons, the most important and the most insignificant facts, the most sublime speculations to which man can soar, and the most trivial anecdotes of literary biography, lie massed together in all the irony of juxtaposition, developed with the same cold but curious interest, and discussed with the same withering sardonic smile. Never perhaps was there a book that evinced more clearly the vanity of human systems or the disintegrating power of an exhaustive enquiry. To such a writer nothing could be more revolting than an exclusive worship of one class of opinions, or a forcible suppression of any of the elements of knowledge. Intellectual liberty was the single subject which kindled his cold nature into something resembling enthusiasm. In all he wrote he was its earnest and unwavering advocate, and he diffused his own passion among the scholars and antiquarians of whom he was the chief. He had also the merit of doing more than any previous writer to break the spell which St. Augustine had so long cast over theology. The bitter article on the life of that saint was well adapted as a prelude to an attack upon his opinions.

But while the immense learning and the extraordinary ability of the *Dictionary* of Bayle render it one of the most important pioneers of religious liberty, there was another work in which the same author applied himself more directly to the advocacy of toleration. I mean that treatise on the text "Compel them to enter in," in which, abandoning for once the negative and destructive criticism in which he delighted, he undertook to elucidate the bases of a rational belief. This book may, I believe, without exaggeration, be regarded as one of the most valuable contributions to theology during the seventeenth century, and as forming more than any other work the foundation of modern rationalism.[1] While the famous argument of Tillotson against transubstantiation is stated as forcibly as by Tillotson, and the famous argument of Chillingworth on the necessity of private judgment as the basis even of an infallible Church as forcibly as by Chillingworth, the main principles of Kant's great work on the relations of the Bible to the moral faculty are fully anticipated, and are developed in a style that is as remarkable for its clearness as that of the German philosopher is for its obscurity. At the beginning of this work Bayle disclaims any intention of entering into a critical examination of the passage that he had taken as his motto. His refutation of the persecutor's interpretation rests not on any detailed criticism, but on a broad and general principle. There are certain intellectual and moral truths which are universal among mankind, and which, being our earliest and most vivid intuitions, cannot be questioned without universal scepticism.[2] Thus, for example, the axiom that the whole is greater than a part, represents the highest kind of certainty to which we can possibly attain, and no message purporting to be a revelation can be received in contradiction to it. For the reality of such a revelation, and the justice of such an interpretation, must necessarily be established by a process of reasoning, and no process of reasoning can be so evident as the axiom. In the same way, the fundamental differences between right and wrong are so stamped upon the mind, that they may be taken as the ultimate tests of all ethical teaching. No positive enactments can supersede them. No interpretation of a Divine revelation that violates them can be acknowledged as correct.[3] The intuition by which we know what is right and what is wrong, is clearer than any chain

[1] Bayle, who was a great coward about his books, published this under the title "*Contrains-les d'entrer, traduit de l'Anglois du Sieur Jean Fox de Bruggs*, par M. J. F. : à Cantorberry, chez Thomas Litwel."

[2] See, for a full development of this, ch. i.

[3] "Sans exception il faut soumettre toutes les lois morales à cette idée naturelle d'équité qui, aussi bien que la lumière métaphysique, illumine tout homme venant au monde." And therefore he concludes "que tout dogme particulier, soit qu'on l'avance comme contenu dans l'Écriture, soit qu'on le propose autrement, est faux lorsqu'il est réfuté par les notions claires et distinctes de la lumière naturelle, principalement à l'égard de la morale" (ch. i.).

of historic reasoning ; and, admitting the reality of a revelation, if the action of the moral faculty were suspended, we should have no means of deciding from what source that revelation had emanated. In judging therefore a moral precept, we should dissociate it as far as possible from all special circumstances that are connected with our passions and our prejudices, and, having reduced it to its simplest and most abstract form, should reject it without hesitation if repugnant to our moral faculty. We should do this even if we can discover no second meaning. But, if tested by this rule, it will appear grossly immoral to compel men to profess a religion they do not believe, and therefore such a course cannot be enjoined by the Deity. Nor is it less irrational than immoral. For one of the first and most obvious consequences of persecution, is to prevent that comparison of the opinions of many classes which is absolutely essential for the discovery of truth. We believe perhaps that our neighbours are immersed in damnable error, but they believe the same thing of us. We may be firmly persuaded of the truth of the opinions we have been taught, but we know that each new research encroaches upon the domain of prejudice, and that the more the horizon of our minds extends, the more necessary we find it to revise both our principles and our arguments. And indeed, when we consider the feebleness of our faculties, the extent to which our conceptions are coloured by the atmosphere in which we live, and above all the infinite nature of the Being to whom we aspire, it is impossible to avoid suspecting that all our conceptions on this subject must be partial and distorted, that our attempts to classify religious opinions into absolute truth and falsehood are almost necessarily futile, that different men according to the measure of their faculties obtain some faint glimpses of different aspects of the Divine nature, and that no one has a right to arrogate to himself the possession of such an amount of perfect truth as to render it unnecessary for him to correct and enlarge his views by comparing them with those even of the most ignorant of mankind.[1]

It is not necessary for my purpose to pursue in detail the arguments by which Bayle expanded these principles, or to notice the many important consequences he deduced from them. What I have written will be sufficient to show the general character of his defence of toleration. It will show that Bayle, like Montaigne and Descartes, was tolerant because he was rationalistic, and was rationalistic because he was sceptical. Keenly sensible of the weakness of our faculties, and of the imperfection of all dogmatic systems, he resolved to subordinate those systems to the teachings of natural religion, and he therefore protested against a practice which presupposes a degree of certainty that does not exist, and which is repugnant to the dictates of conscience.

The intellectual movement of which these three writers were the representatives, and in a great degree the cause, was clearly reflected in the policy of the two wisest, if not greatest, rulers France has ever possessed. By the Edict of Nantes, Henry IV., whose theological zeal was notoriously languid, solemnly established the principle of toleration. By entering into a war in which his allies were chiefly Protestants, and his enemies Catholics, Richelieu gave a new direction to the sympathies of the people, instituted lines of demarcation which were incompatible with the old spirit of sect, and prepared the way for the general secularisation of politics. The reaction which took place under Louis XIV., although it caused intolerable suffering, and, indeed, partly in consequence of that suffering, had eventually the effect of accelerating the movement. The *dragonnades*, and the revocation of the Edict of Nantes, formed the most conspicuous events of a period which was pre-eminently disastrous to France, and the effects of those measures upon French prosperity were so rapid and so fatal that popular indignation was roused to the highest point.

---

[1] "Tout homme aiant éprouvé qu'il est sujet à l'erreur, et qu'il voit ou croit voir en vieillissant la fausseté de plusieurs choses qu'il avoit cru véritable, doit être toujours disposé à écouter ceux qui lui offrent des instructions en matière même de religion. Je n'en excepte pas les Chrétiens ; et je suis persuadé que s'il nous venoit une flotte de la terre australe, où il y eut des gens qui fissent connoître qu'ils souhaitoient de conférer avec nous sur la nature de Dieu et sur le culte que l'homme lui doit, aiant appris que nous avons sur cela des erreurs damnables, nous ne ferions pas mal de les écouter, non-seulement parce que ce seroit le moien de les désabuser des erreurs où nous croirions qu'ils seroient, mais aussi parce que nous pourrions profiter de leurs lumières, et que nous devons nous faire de Dieu une idée si vaste et si infinie que nous pouvons soupçonner qu'il augmentera nos connoissances à l'infini, et par des degrés et des manières dont la variété sera infinie." (Part i. ch. 5.)

The ruin of the French army, the taxation that ground the people to the dust, the paralysis of industry, the intellectual tyranny, and the almost monastic austerity of the court, had all combined to increase the discontent, and, as is often the case, the whole weight of this unpopularity was directed against each separate element of tyranny. The recoil was manifested in the wild excesses of the Regency, a period which presents, in many respects, a very striking resemblance to the reign of Charles II. in England. In both cases the reaction against an enforced austerity produced the most unbridled immorality ; in both cases this was increased by the decay of those theological notions on which morality was at that time universally based ; in both cases the court led the movement ; and in both cases that movement resulted in a revolution, which in the order of religion produced toleration, and in the order of politics produced an organic change. That vice has often proved an emancipator of the mind, is one of the most humiliating, but, at the same time, one of the most unquestionable, facts in history. It is the special evil of intolerance that it entwines itself around the holiest parts of our nature, and becomes at last so blended with the sense of duty, that, as has been finely said, "Conscience, which restrains every other vice, becomes the prompter here."[1] Two or three times in the history of mankind, its destruction has involved a complete dissolution of the moral principles by which society coheres, and the cradle of religious liberty has been rocked by the worst passions of humanity.

When the moral chaos that followed the death of Louis XIV. was almost universal, when all past beliefs were corroded and vitiated, and had degenerated into empty names or idle superstitions, a great intellectual movement arose, under the guidance of Voltaire and Rousseau, which was designed to reconstruct the edifice of morality, and which, after a brief but fierce struggle with the civil power, obtained a complete ascendency on the Continent. The object of these writers was not to erect a new system of positive religion, but rather to remove those systems which then existed, and to prove the adequacy of natural religion to the moral wants of mankind. The first of these tasks was undertaken especially by Voltaire. The second was more congenial to the mind of Rousseau. Both writers exercised a great influence upon the history of toleration ; but that influence, if not directly opposed, was at least very different. Voltaire was at all times the unflinching opponent of persecution. No matter how powerful was the persecutor, no matter how insignificant was the victim, the same scathing eloquence was launched against the crime, and the indignation of Europe was soon concentrated upon the oppressor. The fearful storm of sarcasm and invective that avenged the murder of Calas, the magnificent dream in the *Philosophical Dictionary* reviewing the history of persecution from the slaughtered Canaanites to the latest victims who had perished at the stake, the indelible stigma branded upon the persecutors of every age and of every creed, all attested the intense and passionate earnestness with which Voltaire addressed himself to his task. On other subjects a jest or a caprice could often turn him aside. When attacking intolerance, he employed, indeed, every weapon, but he employed them all with the concentrated energy of a profound conviction. His success was equal to his zeal. The spirit of intolerance sank blasted beneath his genius. Wherever his influence passed, the arm of the Inquisitor was palsied, the chain of the captive riven, the prison door flung open. Beneath his withering irony persecution appeared not only criminal but loathsome, and since his time it has ever shrunk from observation, and masked its features under other names. He died, leaving a reputation that is indeed far from spotless, but having done more to destroy the greatest of human curses than any other of the sons of men.

Rousseau had probably quite as strong a sense of the evil of religious persecution as Voltaire, but by a remarkable process of reasoning he justified its worst excesses. He saw very plainly that the intolerance of the past was not due to any accidental circumstances or to any interested motives, but was the normal product of the doctrine of exclusive salvation. He maintained that reciprocity was the condition of toleration—that is to say, that a dominant party is only justified in according toleration where there is some reasonable probability that it will continue when the relative position of the

[1] Grattan.

parties is changed. From these two principles he inferred the necessity of the widest intolerance. He told the believers in the doctrine of exclusive salvation that it was their manifest duty to persecute all who differed from them. He told the philosophers that it was necessary to banish all who held the doctrine of exclusive salvation, because that principle was incompatible with the tranquillity of society.[1] This opinion was very natural at a time when the experiment of absolute toleration had scarcely ever been tried, and in the writings of one who was essentially a theorist. We now know that religious liberty has an admirable influence in reducing opinions to their proper level ; that it invariably acts upon and modifies doctrines which seem subversive of society ; and that, while it leaves the professions of men unchanged, it profoundly alters their realisations. This Rousseau did not perceive, and his blindness was shared by many of his contemporaries. In the French Revolution especially we find the two tendencies—an intense love of religious liberty and a strong bias towards intolerance—continually manifested. In that noble enactment which removed at a single stroke all civil disabilities from Protestants and Jews, we have a splendid instance of the first. In the exile, the spoliation, and, too often, the murder, of Catholic priests, we have a melancholy example of the second. Still it must be admitted in palliation of these excesses that they took place in a paroxysm of the wildest popular excitement, when the minds of men were exasperated to the highest degree by an atrocious and long-continued tyranny, when the very existence of the State was menaced by foreign invaders, and when the bulk of the priesthood were openly conspiring against the liberties of their country. It should also be remembered that the priests had to the very last declared themselves the implacable enemies of religious liberty. At all events, the spirit of tolerance soon re-

gained the ascendency ; and when the elements of revolution had been at last consolidated into a regular government, France found herself possessed of a degree of religious liberty which had never been paralleled in any other Roman Catholic country, and which has been barely equalled in the most advanced Protestant ones. As this liberty grew out of the social and intellectual condition which was attained at the Revolution, it was not dependent upon any political combination, and the long series of political changes which have taken place during the last half-century have only fortified and developed it.

The inference to be drawn from this sketch is that the growth of religious liberty in France was at all times directly opposed to the Church, and that its triumph was a measure of her depression. Once, however, in the present century, an attempt was made, under the leadership of Lamennais, to associate Catholicity with the movement of modern civilisation, and it was supported by all the advantages of great genius and great piety, combined with circumstances that were in some respects singularly propitious. The issue of that attempt is profoundly instructive. It is shown in the abandonment of Catholicity by the greatest of its modern champions. It is shown still more strikingly in the solemn and authoritative condemnation of religious liberty by a pope, who justly attributed it to the increasing spirit of rationalism. " We arrive now," wrote Gregory XVI., " at another most fruitful cause of evils, with which we lament that the Church is at present afflicted; namely, indifferentism, or that pernicious opinion which is disseminated everywhere by the artifice of wicked men, according to which eternal salvation may be obtained by the profession of any faith, if only practice be directed by the rule of right and uprightness.......From this noxious fountain of indifferentism flows that absurd and erroneous opinion, or rather that form of madness, which declares that liberty of conscience should be asserted and maintained for everyone. For which most pestilential error, that full and immoderate liberty of opinions paves the way which, to the injury of sacred and civil government, is now spread far and wide, and which some with the utmost impudence have extolled as beneficial to religion. But 'what,' said Augustine,

[1] " Ceux qui distinguent l'intolérance civile et l'intolérance théologique, se trompent à mon avis. Ces deux intolérances sont inséparables. Il est impossible de vivre en paix avec des gens qu'on croit damnés ; les aimer seroit haïr Dieu qui les punit : il faut absolument qu'on les ramène ou qu'on les tourmente....On doit tolérer toutes les religions qui tolèrent les autres, autant que leurs dogmes n'ont rien de contraire aux devoirs du citoyen ; mais quiconque ose dire, ' Hors de l'Église point de salut,' doit être chassé de l'Etat, à moins que l'État ne soit l'Eglise, et que le prince ne soit le Pontife." (*Contrat social*, liv. iv. c. 8.)

'is more deadly to the soul than the liberty of error?'......From this cause, too, arises that never sufficiently to be execrated and to be detested liberty of publication of all books which the populace relish, which some are most ardently extending and promoting.......And yet, alas! there are those who are so carried away by impudence that they audaciously assert that the deluge of errors flowing from this source is amply counterbalanced by an occasional book which, amid the transport of iniquity, defends religion and truth.......What sane man would permit poison to be publicly scattered about, sold, and even drunk, because there is a remedy by which its effects may possibly be counteracted?"[1]

If we compare the history of English toleration with the history I have just sketched, we shall find some striking points of resemblance; but also some differences which illustrate very happily the nature of the superiority of Protestantism over Catholicism. Among Protestants, as among Catholics, the advance of the spirit of rationalism was, as I have said, the necessary antecedent of the victory of toleration. As long as men believed that those who rejected certain opinions were excluded from salvation, they continued to persecute. When the number of what were deemed fundamental doctrines was very great, the persecution was very severe. When the progress of latitudinarianism diminished the number, the circle of toleration was proportionately enlarged; when the government fell into the hands of classes who did not believe or did not realise the doctrine of exclusive salvation, the persecution entirely ceased. Other influences, such as the conflict of interests, the progress of political liberty, the softening of manners, or the benevolent feelings of individual divines, did no doubt affect the movement; but their agency was so subsidiary that, speaking generally, it may be safely asserted, that as the doctrine of exclusive salvation was the source of that fearful mass of suffering which we have reviewed, so the spirit of rationalism which destroyed that doctrine was the measure of religious liberty. It is also true that in Protestant countries as well as in Catholic ones the great majority of the clergy were the

[1] Bull delivered at Sta. Maria Maggiore on the Feast of the Assumption, 1832. The whole bull is given by Lamennais, *Affaires de Rome*, pp. 318-357.

bitter enemies of the movement, that they defended entrenchment after entrenchment with a desperate tenacity, and that some of the noblest triumphs of toleration are the memorials of their depression. But at this point the history of the religions divides, and two very important distinctions attest the superiority of Protestantism. Its flexibility is so great that it has been able cordially to coalesce with a tendency which it long resisted, whereas the Church of Rome is even now exhausting its strength by vain efforts to arrest a spirit with which it is unable to assimilate. Besides this, as I have already noticed, toleration, however incompatible with some of the tenets which Protestants have asserted, is essentially a normal result of Protestantism, for it is the direct, logical, and inevitable consequence of the due exercise of private judgment. When men have appreciated the countless differences which the exercise of that judgment must necessarily produce, when they have estimated the intrinsic fallibility of their reason, and the degree in which it is distorted by the will, when, above all, they have acquired that love of truth which a constant appeal to private judgment at last produces, they will never dream that guilt can be associated with an honest conclusion, or that one class of arguments should be stifled by authority. In the seventeenth century, when the controversies with Catholicism had brought the central principle of Protestantism into clear relief, and when the highest genius of Europe still flowed in the channels of divinity, this love of truth was manifested in the greatest works of English theology to a degree which very few departments of literature have ever equalled. Hooker, unfolding with his majestic eloquence the immutable principles of eternal law; Berkeley, the greatest modern master of the Socratic dialogue, asserting the claims of free thought against those who vainly boasted that they monopolised it, and pursuing with the same keen and piercing logic the sophisms that lurked in the commonplaces of fashion and in the obscurest recesses of metaphysics; Chillingworth, drawing with a bold and unfaltering hand the line between certainties and probabilities, eliminating from theology the old conception of faith considered as an unreasoning acquiescence, and teaching that belief should always be strictly "proportionable to the credibility of its motives;"—these and such as these, even when they were themselves opposed to religious liberty, were its real founders. Their noble confidence in the power of truth, their ceaseless struggle against the empire of prejudice, their comprehensive views of the laws and limits of the reason, their fervent passionate love of knowledge, and the majesty and dignity of their sentiments, all produced in England a tone of thought that was essentially opposed to persecution, and made their writings the perennial source by which even now the most heroic natures are invigorated. A nation was not far from a just estimate of religious controversies when it had learnt to hold with Milton that "opinion in good men is but knowledge in the making"; and that, "if a man believes things only because his pastor says so, or the assembly so determines, without knowing other reason, though his belief be true, yet the very truth he holds becomes his heresy."[1] It was not far from religious liberty when it could receive the noble language of Chillingworth: "If men do their best endeavours to free themselves from all errors, and yet fail of it through human frailty, so well I am persuaded of the goodness of God, that if in me alone should meet a confluence of all such errors of all the Protestants in the world that were thus qualified, I should not be so much afraid of them all, as I should be to ask pardon for them."[2]

There does not appear to have been any general movement in England in favour of religious liberty till the time of the Great Rebellion. The tyranny of Laud had then disgusted most men with the system he pursued; the rapid vicissitudes of politics had made all parties endure the bitterness of persecution, and the destruction of the old government had raised some of the ablest Englishmen to power. It would have been strange, indeed, if this great question had been untouched at a period when Cromwell was guiding the administration, and Milton the intellect, of England, and when the enthusiasm of liberty had thrilled through every quarter of the land. The Catholics, indeed, were ruthlessly proscribed, and Drogheda and Wexford tell but too plainly the light in which they were regarded. The Church of

England, or, as it was then termed, "prelacy," was also legally suppressed, though Cromwell very frequently connived at its worship; but with these exceptions the toleration was very large. There was a division on the subject between the Independents and the Presbyterians. The former, with Cromwell himself, desired the widest liberty of conscience to be extended to all Christians, short of the toleration of "Popery and Prelacy," and in 1653 they succeeded in inducing the Parliament to pass a Bill to that effect. Supported by the Independents, Cromwell went still further, and gave the Jews once more a legal footing in England, permitted them to celebrate their worship, and protected their persons from injury. The Presbyterians, on the other hand, constantly laboured to thwart the measures of the Protector. They desired that those only should be tolerated who accepted the "fundamentals" of Christianity, and they drew up a list of these "fundamentals," which formed as elaborate and exclusive a test as the articles of the Church they had defeated.[1] Baxter, however, although he pronounced universal toleration to be "soul murder,"[2] and struggled vigorously against the policy of the Independents, was, on the whole, somewhat more liberal than his co-religionists, and it should be recorded to his special honour that he applauded the relief that was granted to the Jews, when most of the

[1] A full description of them is given in Neal's *History of the Puritans*. In 1648 the Presbyterians tried to induce the Parliament to pass a law by which anyone who persistently taught anything contrary to the main propositions comprised in the doctrines of the Trinity and the Incarnation should be punished with death, and all who taught Popish, Arminian, Antinomian, Baptist, or Quaker doctrines, should be imprisoned for life, unless they could find sureties that they would teach them no more. (Neal, vol. ii. pp. 338-340.) The Scotch were unwearied in their efforts to suppress liberty of conscience, and in 1645 their Parliament addressed the English Parliament: "The Parliament of this kingdom is persuaded that the piety and wisdom of the honourable houses will never admit toleration of any sects or schisms contrary to our solemn league and covenant '; and at the same time published a solemn "declaration against toleration of sectaries and liberty of conscience." (*Ibid.* pp. 211-222.) Among the notions started by the Anabaptists was that of a sleep of the soul between death and judgment, against which Calvin wrote a book with the barbarous title of *Psychopannychia*. This very harmless notion was one of those which, when obstinately persisted in, the Presbyterians of 1648 wished to punish with an indefinite period of imprisonment. (Neal, vol. ii. p. 339.)
[2] "Popery, Mahometanism, infidelity, and heathenism are the way to damnation; but liberty to preach up and to practise them is the means to make men Papists, Mahometans, Infidels, and Heathens; therefore this liberty is the way to men's damnation." (*Holy Commonwealth*, 2nd Preface.)

[1] *Areopagitica.*
[2] *Religion of Protestants*, p. 44 (ed. 1742).

Presbyterians, under the leadership of Prynne, were denouncing it.

The three principal writers who at this time represented the movement of toleration, were Harrington, Milton, and Taylor—the first of whom dealt mainly with its political, and the other two with its theological, aspect. Of the three, it must be acknowledged that the politician took by far the most comprehensive view. He perceived very clearly that political liberty cannot subsist where there is not absolute religious liberty, and that religious liberty does not consist simply of toleration, but implies a total abolition of religious disqualifications. In these respects he alone among his contemporaries anticipated the doctrines of the nineteenth century. "Where civil liberty is entire," he wrote, "it includes liberty of conscience. Where liberty of conscience is entire, it includes civil liberty."[1] "Liberty of conscience entire, or in the whole, is where a man, according to the dictates of his own conscience, may have the free exercise of his religion, without impediment to his preferment or employment in the State."[2]

But if Harrington took the widest view of the rights of conscience, Milton was certainly the advocate who was most likely to have advanced the cause, both on account of his high position in the Commonwealth, and because his opinions on the subject were, for the most part, embodied in a tract, which probably represents the very highest point that English eloquence has attained. The *Paradise Lost* is, indeed, scarcely a more glorious monument of the genius of Milton than the *Areopagitica*. If, even at the present day, when the cause for which it was written has long since triumphed, it is impossible to read it without emotion, we can hardly doubt that when it first appeared it exercised a mighty influence over the awakening movement of liberty. Milton advocated tolerance on several distinct grounds. In defence of truth he deemed persecution

wholly unnecessary, " For truth is strong next to the Almighty. She needs no policies or stratagems or licensings to make her victorious. These are the shifts and the defences that error uses against her power."[1] But if persecution is unnecessary in the defence of truth, it has a fearful efficacy in preventing men from discovering it ; and when it is so employed, as infallibility does not exist among mankind, no man can assuredly decide. For truth is scattered far and wide in small portions among mankind, mingled in every system with the dross of error, grasped perfectly by no one, and only in some degree discovered by the careful comparison and collation of opposing systems.[2] To crush some of these systems, to stifle the voice of argument, to ban and proscribe the press, or to compel it only to utter the sentiments of a single sect, is to destroy the only means we possess of arriving at truth ; and as the difficulty of avoiding error is under the most favourable circumstances very great, it may be presumed that the doctrines which it is necessary to hold are but few, and where the error is not fundamental it should not be suppressed by law. All the differences that divide Protestants are upon matters not bearing on salvation, and therefore all classes— Socinians, Arians, and Anabaptists, as well as others—should be tolerated.[3] The Catholics, however, Milton rigidly excludes from the smallest measure of tolerance, and the reason he gives is very remarkable. The intriguing policy of its priesthood might at that time, at least, furnish a plausible ground, but Milton, though evidently believing it to be so, expressly refuses to base his decision upon it. His exclusion of Catholics rests upon a distinct religious principle. The worship

---

[1] *Political Aphorisms*, 23–24.
[2] *A System of Politics*, ch. vi. Passages very similar occur in the *Oceana*, and, indeed, all through the writings of Harrington. The following is, I think, a very remarkable instance of political prescience : " If it be said that in France there is liberty of conscience in part, it is also plain that while the hierarchy is standing this liberty is falling, and that if ever it comes to pull down the hierarchy, it pulls down that monarchy also. Wherefore the monarchy and hierarchy will be beforehand with it, if they see their true interest." (*System of Politics*, ch. vi.)

[1] *Areopagitica.*
[2] " Truth, indeed, came once into the world with her Divine Master, and was a perfect shape most glorious to look on ; but when He ascended, and his Apostles after Him were laid asleep, then straight arose a wicked race of deceivers, who, as the story goes of the Egyptian Typhon with his conspirators, how they dealt with the good Osiris, took the virgin Truth, hewed her lovely form into a thousand pieces, and scattered them to the four winds. From that time ever since the sad friends of Truth, such as durst appear, imitating the careful search that Isis made for the mangled body of Osiris, went up and down gathering up limb by limb, still as they could find them. We have not yet found them all, Lords and Commons, nor ever shall do till her Master's second coming." (*Areopagitica.*)
[3] See his tract, *Of true Religion, Heresy, Schism, Toleration*, published in 1673. He does not, however, seem to have understood the Socinian heresy exactly as it is now understood.

of the Catholics is idolatrous, and the Old Testament forbids the toleration of idolatry.[1]

The last name I have mentioned is Taylor, whose *Liberty of Prophesying* is, if we except *The Religion of Protestants*, unquestionably the most important contribution of the Anglican Church towards toleration.[2] It is scarcely possible to read it without arriving at an invincible conviction that it expressed the genuine sentiments of its author Its argument is based upon latitudinarian principles, which appear more or less in all his writings, and its singularly indulgent tone towards the Catholics, its earnest advocacy of their claims to toleration,[3] which would hardly have been expected from so uncompromising a Protestant as the author of *The Dissuasive from Popery*, was certainly not intended to propitiate the Puritans. Besides this, the whole book is animated with a warmth and tenderness of charity, a catholicity of temper biassing the judgment in favour of mercy, which could scarcely have been counterfeited. This was indeed at all times the most amiable characteristic of Taylor. His very style—like the murmur of a deep sea, bathed in the sun—so richly coloured by an imagination that was never disunited from the affections, and at the same time so sweetly cadenced, so full of gentle and varied melodies, reflects his character; and not the less so because of a certain want of nervousness and consistency, a certain vagueness and almost feebleness which it occasionally displays. The arguments on which he based his cause are very simple. He believed that the great majority of theological propositions cannot be clearly deduced from Scripture, and that it is therefore not necessary to hold them. The Apostles' Creed he regarded as containing the doctrines which can certainly be established, and, therefore, as comprising all that are fundamental. All errors on questions beyond these do not affect salvation, and ought, in consequence, to be tolerated. As far, therefore, as he was a sceptic, Taylor was a rationalist, and as far as he was a rationalist he was an advocate of toleration. Unfortunately for his reputation, he wrote *The Liberty of Prophesying* in exile, and, to a certain extent, abandoned its principles when his Church regained her ascendency.[1]

All through the period of the Restoration, the movement of toleration continued. The vast amount of scepticism existing in the country caused the governing class to look with comparative indifference upon doctrinal differences, and the general adoption of the principles of Bacon and of Descartes, by the ablest writers, accelerated the movement, which began to appear in the most unexpected quarters.[2] The expression of that movement in the Anglican Church is to be found in the latitudinarian school, which followed closely in the steps of Chillingworth. Like the Independents and Presbyterians of the Commonwealth, like the greater number of the opponents of the execution of Servetus, the members of this school usually based their advocacy of tolerance on the ground of the distinction between fundamentals and non-fundamentals, and the degree in which they restricted or expanded the first depended mainly on their scepticism. Glanvil, who was, perhaps, the most uncompromising of these writers, having,

---

[1] "As for tolerating the exercise of their (the Catholics') religion, supposing their State activities not to be dangerous, I answer that toleration is either public or private, and the exercise of their religion as far as it is idolatrous can be tolerated neither way: not publicly, without grievous and unsufferable scandal given to all conscientious beholders; not privately, without great offence to God, declared against all kind of idolatry though secret. Ezech. viii. 7, 8, and verse 12, &c., and it appears by the whole chapter, that God was no less offended with those secret idolatries than with those in public, and no less provoked than to bring on and hasten his judgments on the whole land for them also." (*Of true Religion*, &c.) It is of course open to supposition, and not very improbable, that this passage, being written after the Restoration, when Catholicism had become a serious menace to the liberty of England, emanated rather from the politician than from the theologian.

[2] Chillingworth published *The Religion of Protestants* in 1637, one year before he took orders—which last step he had many scruples about.

[3] Sec. 22. He desires that they should be absolutely tolerated, unless, indeed, they openly preach such doctrines as the non-observance of faith with heretics, or that a pope can absolve subjects from the oath of allegiance, or that an heretical prince may be slain by his people.

[1] On which Coleridge remarks, I think a little too severely: "If Jeremy Taylor had not in effect retracted after the Restoration, if he had not, as soon as the Church had gained power, most basely disclaimed and disavowed the principle of toleration, and apologised for the publication by declaring it to have been a *ruse de guerre*, currying pardon for his past liberalism by charging, and most probably slandering, himself with the guilt of falsehood, treachery, and hypocrisy, his character as a man would have been almost stainless." (*Notes on English Divines*, vol. i. p. 209.)

[2] *E.g.*, in Quakerism—that strange form of distorted rationalism, which, while proclaiming doctrines absolutely subversive of national independence, and occasionally producing extraordinary extravagances of conduct, maintained in the most unequivocal language the absolute inefficiency of mere religious ceremonies, the possibility of salvation in any Church, and the injustice of every form of persecution.

in his treatise *On the Vanity of Dogmatising*, preached almost universal scepticism, proceeded in consequence to advocate almost universal toleration. He drew up a catalogue of necessary articles of belief, which was of such a nature that scarcely anyone was excluded, and he contended that no one should be punished for errors that are not fundamental. The effects of the tendency were soon manifested in the laws, and in 1677 the power of consigning heretics to death was withdrawn from the Church.

It appears, then, that the first stage of toleration in England was due to the spirit of scepticism encroaching upon the doctrine of exclusive salvation. But what is especially worthy of remark is, that the most illustrious of the advocates of toleration were men who were earnestly attached to positive religion, and that the writings in which they embodied their arguments are even now among the classics of the Church. *The Religion of Protestants* and *The Liberty of Prophesying* are justly regarded as among the greatest glories of Anglicanism, and Glanvil, Owen, and Hales are still honoured names in theology. This is well worthy of notice when we consider the unmixed scepticism of those who occupied a corresponding position in France; but there is another circumstance which greatly heightens the contrast. At the very period when the principle of toleration was first established in England by the union of the spirit of scepticism with the spirit of Christianity, the greatest living anti-Christian writer was Hobbes, who was perhaps the most unflinching of all the supporters of persecution. It was his leading doctrine that the civil power, and the civil power alone, has an absolute right to determine the religion of the nation, and that, therefore, any refusal to acquiesce in that religion is essentially an act of rebellion.

But while the rationalistic spirit had thus found a firm footing within the Church, it was strongly opposed and generally overborne by the dogmatic spirit which was represented by the great majority of the clergy, and which radiated with especial energy from Oxford. Taylor, as we have seen, recoiled before the prevailing intolerance. Glanvil sank into considerable discredit, from which, however, he in some degree emerged by his defence of witchcraft.

Heretics were no longer liable to be burnt, but all through the reign of Charles II., and during the greater part of the reign of James, the Dissenters endured every minor form of persecution. At last, James, irritated by the penal laws that oppressed his co-religionists, determined to proclaim toleration with a high hand. That he did this solely with a view to the welfare of his own Church, and not at all from any love of toleration, may be inferred with considerable certainty from the fact that he had himself been one of the most relentless of persecutors; but it is not impossible, and, I think, not altogether improbable, that he would have accepted a measure of toleration which relieved the Roman Catholics, without embarking in the very hazardous enterprise of establishing Catholic ascendency. The sequel is too well known to require repetition. Every educated Englishman knows how the great majority of the clergy, in spite of the doctrine of passive obedience they had taught, and of the well-known decision of Taylor that even an illegal ordinance should be accepted, refused to read the declaration; how their attitude endeared them to the people, and accelerated the triumph of the Revolution; how they soon imprudently withdrew from and opposed the movement they had produced; how upon the achievement of the Revolution they sank into a condition of almost unequalled political depression; and how the consequence of that depression was the Toleration Act, which, though very imperfect according to our present notions, is justly regarded as the Magna Charta of religious liberty. Those who defended it were of the same class as the previous advocates of toleration. Somers and the other leading Whigs were members of the Anglican Church. Locke was in religion the avowed disciple of Chillingworth, and in politics the highest representative of the principles of Harrington; and it was on the double ground of the sanctity of an honest conviction, and of the danger of enlarging the province of the civil magistrate, that he defended toleration against the theologians of Oxford.[1] While the Toleration Act and the establishment of the Scotch Kirk gave virtual freedom of worship to all Protestants, the abrogation of the censorship established freedom

---

[1] His opponent was Archdeacon Proast, whose pamphlets were printed in the University.

of discussion. The battle was thus won. Intolerance became an exception and an anomaly, and it was simply a question of time how soon it should be expelled from its last entrenchments.

We have seen that the spirit of intolerance was at first equally strong in the Church of Rome and in the reformed churches, and that its extinction both in Catholic and Protestant countries was due to the spirit of rationalism. We have seen that in both cases the clergy were the untiring enemies of this the noblest of all the conquests of civilisation, and that it was only by a long series of anti-ecclesiastical revolutions that the sword was at last wrung from their grasp. We have seen, too, that while the Church of Rome was so constituted that an anti-ecclesiastical movement where she ruled invariably became anti-Christian, the flexibility of Protestantism was so great that rationalism found free scope for action within its pale. Discarding more and more their dogmatic character, and transforming themselves according to the exigencies of the age, the churches of the Reformation have in many cases allied themselves with the most daring speculations, and have in most cases cordially coalesced with the spirit of toleration. When a country which is nominally Roman Catholic is very tolerant, it may be inferred with almost absolute certainty that the social and intellectual influence of the Church is comparatively small ; but England and America conclusively prove that a nation may be very tolerant, and at the same time profoundly Protestant. When in a Roman Catholic country the human intellect on the highest of subjects pursues its course with unshackled energy, the freethinker is immediately severed from the traditions, the worship, the moralising influences of his Church ; but Germany has already shown, and England is beginning to show, that the boldest speculations may be wedded to a Protestant worship, and may find elements of assimilation in a Protestant creed. It is this fact which is the most propitious omen of the future of Protestantism. For there is no such thing as a theological antiseptic. Every profound intellectual change the human race has yet undergone, has produced at least some modification of all departments of speculative belief. Much that is adapted to one phase of civilisation becomes useless or pernicious in another.

The moral element of a religion appeals to forms of emotion which are substantially unchanged by time, but the intellectual conceptions that are associated with it assume their tone and colour from the intellectual atmosphere of the age. Protestantism as a dogmatic system makes no converts, but it has shown itself capable of blending with and consecrating the prevailing rationalism. Compare the series of doctrines I have reviewed in the present chapter with the habitual teaching of modern divines, and the change is sufficiently apparent. All those notions concerning the damnation of unbaptised infants, or of the heathen, or of the heretic, which once acted so great a part in the history of Christendom, are becoming rapidly unrealised and inoperative, where they are not already openly denied. Nor has it been otherwise with persecution. For centuries the Protestant clergy preached it as a duty ; when driven from this position, they almost invariably defended its less atrocious forms, disguising it under other names. At last this passed away. Only a few years ago six ladies were exiled from Sweden because they had embraced the Roman Catholic faith ;[1] but a striking example soon proved how uncongenial were such measures with the Protestantism of the nineteenth century. An address drawn up by some of the most eminent English opponents of Catholicism, and signed by the Archbishop of Canterbury, protested against the act as an outrage to the first principles of Protestantism.

The history which I have traced in the present chapter naturally leads to some reflections on the ultimate consequences of the rationalistic method of investigation as distinguished from the system of coercion. The question, What is truth ? has certainly no prospect of obtaining a speedy answer ; but the question, What is the spirit of truth ? may be discussed with much greater prospect of agreement. By the spirit of truth, I mean that frame of mind in which men who acknowledge their own fallibility, and who desire above all things to discover what is true, should

[1] *Annuaire des Deux Mondes*, 1858, p. 463. In the previous year an attempt had been made by the Government to moderate the fierce intolerance of the Swedish law ; but the Bill, though adopted by the Houses of the Middle Class and of the Peasants, was rejected by those of the Nobles and of the Clergy. A slight—unfortunately very slight—modification was effected in 1860.

adjudicate between conflicting arguments. As soon as they have distinctly perceived that reason, and reason alone, should determine their opinions, that they never can be legitimately certain of the truth of what they have been taught till they have both examined its evidence and heard what can be said against it, and that any influence that introduces a bias of the will is necessarily an impediment to enquiry, the whole theory of persecution falls at once to the ground. For the object of the persecutor is to suppress one portion of the elements of discussion; it is to determine the judgment by an influence other than reason; it is to prevent that freedom of enquiry which is the sole method we possess of arriving at truth. The persecutor never can be certain that he is not persecuting truth rather than error, but he may be quite certain that he is suppressing the spirit of truth. And indeed it is no exaggeration to say that the doctrines I have reviewed represent the most skilful, and at the same time most successful, conspiracy against that spirit that has ever existed among mankind. Until the seventeenth century, every mental disposition which philosophy pronounces to be essential to a legitimate research was almost uniformly branded as a sin, and a large proportion of the most deadly intellectual vices were deliberately inculcated as virtues. It was a sin to doubt the opinions that had been instilled in childhood before they had been examined. It was a virtue to hold them with unwavering, unreasoning credulity. It was a sin to notice and develop to its full consequences every objection to those opinions, it was a virtue to stifle every objection as a suggestion of the devil. It was sinful to study with equal attention and with an indifferent mind the writings on both sides, sinful to resolve to follow the light of evidence wherever it might lead, sinful to remain poised in doubt between conflicting opinions, sinful to give only a qualified assent to indecisive arguments, sinful even to recognise the moral or intellectual excellence of opponents. In a word, there is scarcely a disposition that marks the love of abstract truth, and scarcely a rule which reason teaches as essential for its attainment, that theologians did not for centuries stigmatise as offensive to the Almighty. By destroying every book that could generate discussion, by diffusing through every field

of knowledge a spirit of boundless credulity, and, above all, by persecuting with atrocious cruelty those who differed from their opinions, they succeeded for a long period in almost arresting the action of the European mind, and in persuading men that a critical, impartial, and enquiring spirit was the worst form of vice. From this frightful condition Europe was at last rescued by the intellectual influences that produced the Reformation, by the teaching of those great philosophers who clearly laid down the conditions of enquiry, and by those bold innovators who, with the stake of Bruno and Vanini before their eyes, dared to challenge directly the doctrines of the past. By these means the spirit of philosophy or of truth became prominent, and the spirit of dogmatism, with all its consequences, was proportionately weakened. As long as the latter spirit possessed an indisputable ascendency, persecution was ruthless, universal, and unquestioned. When the former spirit became more powerful, the language of anathema grew less peremptory. Exceptions and qualifications were introduced; the full meaning of the words was no longer realised; persecution became languid; it changed its character; it exhibited itself rather in a general tendency than in overt acts; it grew apologetical, timid, and evasive. In one age the persecutor burnt the heretic; in another, he crushed him with penal laws; in a third, he withheld from him places of emolument and dignity; in a fourth, he subjected him to the excommunication of society. Each stage of advancing toleration marks a stage of the decline of the spirit of dogmatism and of the increase of the spirit of truth.

Now, if I have at all succeeded in carrying the reader with me in the foregoing arguments, it will appear plain that the doctrine of exclusive salvation represents a point from which two entirely different systems diverge. In other words, those who reject the doctrine cannot pause there. They will inevitably be carried on to a series of doctrines, to a general conception of religion that is radically and fundamentally different from the conception of the adherent of the doctrine. I speak, of course, of those who hold one or other opinion with realising earnestness. Of these it may, I believe, be truly said, that according to their relation to this doctrine they will be divided into different classes, with different types of character, different standards of excellence, different conceptions of the whole spirit of theology. The man who with realising earnestness believes the doctrine of exclusive salvation, will habitually place the dogmatic above the moral element of religion; he will justify, or at least very slightly condemn, pious frauds or other immoral acts that support his doctrines ; he will judge men mainly according to their opinions, and not according to their acts ; he will lay greater stress on those duties that grow out of an ecclesiastical system than on those which grow out of the moral nature of mankind ; he will obtain the certainty that is necessary to his peace by excluding every argument that is adverse to his belief ; and he will above all manifest a constant tendency to persecution. On the other hand, men who have been deeply imbued with the spirit of earnest and impartial enquiry, will invariably come to value such a disposition more than any particular doctrines to which it may lead them ; they will deny the necessity of correct opinions ; they will place the moral far above the dogmatic side of their faith ; they will give free scope to every criticism that restricts their belief ; and they will value men according to their acts, and not at all according to their opinions. The first of these tendencies is essentially Roman Catholic. The second is essentially rationalistic.

It is impossible, I think, to doubt that, since Descartes, the higher thought of Europe has been tending steadily in this second direction, and that sooner or later the spirit of truth will be regarded in Christendom, as it was regarded by the philosophers of ancient Greece, as the loftiest form of virtue. We are indeed still far from that point. A love of truth that seriously resolves to spare no prejudice and accord no favour, that prides itself on basing every conclusion on reason or conscience, and in rejecting every illegitimate influence, is not common in one sex, is still rarer in the other, and is very far indeed from being the actuating spirit of all who boast most loudly of their freedom from prejudice. Still it is to this that we are steadily approximating ; and there probably never before was a period since the triumph of Christianity when men were judged so little according to their belief, and when history, and even ecclesiastical history, was written with such earnest, such scrupulous impar-

tiality. In the political sphere the victory has almost been achieved. In the social sphere, although the amalgamation of different religious communities is still very imperfect, and although a change of religion by one member of a family not unfrequently produces a rupture and causes a vast amount of the more petty forms of persecution, the improvement has been rapid and profound. The fierce invectives which Protestant and Catholic once interchanged, are now for the most part confined to a small and select circle of the more ardent disciples of either creed ; and it is commonly admitted among educated men, that those who, under the sense of duty, and at the cost of great mental suffering, have changed their religion, ought not to be pronounced the most culpable of mankind, even though they have rejected the opinions of their censor. This is at least a vast improvement since the time when the term "miscreant" or misbeliever was first made a synonym for the most atrocious of criminals, and when apostasy was universally regarded as the worst of crimes. Already, under the same influences, education at the Universities has in a great measure lost its old exclusive character ; and members of different creeds having been admitted within their pale, men are brought in contact with representatives of more than one class of opinions at a time when they are finally deciding what class of opinions they will embrace. There cannot, I think, be much doubt that the same movement must eventually modify profoundly the earlier stages of education. If our private judgment is the sole rule by which we should form our opinions, it is obviously the duty of the educator to render that judgment as powerful, and at the same time to preserve it as unbiassed, as possible. To impose an elaborate system of prejudices on the yet undeveloped mind, and to entwine those prejudices with all the most hallowed associations of childhood, is most certainly contrary to the spirit of the doctrine of private judgment. A prejudice may be true or false ; but if private judgment is to decide between opinions, it is, as far as that judgment is concerned, necessarily an evil, and especially when it appeals strongly to the affections. The sole object of man is not to search for truth ; and it may be, and undoubtedly often is, necessary for other purposes to instil into the mind of the child certain opinions, which he will have hereafter to reconsider. Yet still it is manifest that those who appreciate this doctrine of private judgment as I have described it, will desire that those opinions should be few, that they should rest as lightly as possible upon the mind, and should be separated as far as possible from the eternal principles of morality.

Such seem the general outlines of the movement around us. Unhappily it is impossible to contemplate it without feeling that the Protestantism of Chillingworth is much less a reality to be grasped than an ideal to which, at least in our age, we can most imperfectly approximate. The overwhelming majority of the human race necessarily accept their opinions from authority. Whether they do so avowedly, like the Catholics, or unconsciously, like most Protestants, is immaterial. They have neither time nor opportunity to examine for themselves. They are taught certain doctrines on disputed questions as if they were unquestionable truths, when they are incapable of judging, and every influence is employed to deepen the impression. This is the true origin of their belief. Not until long years of mental conflict have passed can they obtain the inestimable boon of an assured and untrammelled mind. The fable of the ancient[1] is still true. The woman even now sits at the portal of life, presenting a cup to all who enter in which diffuses through every vein a poison that will cling to them for ever. The judgment may pierce the clouds of prejudice. In the moments of her strength she may even rejoice and triumph in her liberty, yet the conceptions of childhood will long remain latent in the mind, to reappear in every hour of weakness, when the tension of the reason is relaxed, and when the power of old associations is supreme.[2] It is not surprising that very few should possess the courage and the perseverance to encounter the mental struggle. The immense majority either never examine the

This is especially the result of some diseases. Thus, *e.g.*, there is a case on record of an ignorant woman repeating, in a delirium, certain words which were recognised as Hebrew and Chaldaic. When she returned to consciousness she knew nothing of these words, she had no notion of their meaning ; and being told that they were Hebrew and Chaldaic, she could recollect no possible way in which she could have acquired them. A searching investigation into her antecedents was instituted ; and it was found that when a girl she had been servant to a clergyman who was accustomed to walk up and down his passage reading those languages. The words were hidden in the mind, were reproduced by disease, and were forgotten when the disease had passed. (Carpenter, *Human Physiology*, p. 808.) It is said that a momentary review of numbers of long-forgotten incidents of life is the last phenomenon of consciousness before the insensibility that precedes drowning. But not only are facts retained in the memory of which we are unconscious, the mind itself is also perpetually acting—pursuing trains of thought automatically, of which we have no consciousness. Thus it has been often observed, that a subject which at night appears tangled and confused, acquires a perfect clearness and arrangement during sleep. Thus the schoolboy knows that verses learnt by heart just before sleep are retained with much greater facility than those which are learnt at any other time ; thus, in the course of recollection, two facts will often rise in succession which appear to have no connection whatever ; but a careful investigation will prove that there is some forgotten link of association which the mind had pursued, but of which we are entirely unconscious. It is in connection with these facts that we should view that reappearance of opinions, modes of thought, and emotions belonging to a former stage of our intellectual history, that is often the result of the automatical action of the mind when volition is altogether suspended. It is especially common (or, at least, especially manifest) in languor, in disease, and, above all, in sleep. M. Maury, who has investigated the subject with his usual great ability, has shown that in sleep hyperæsthesia of the memory is very common ; that not only facts, but processes of thought that belong altogether to the past, are reproduced ; and that a frequent dreamer will often be brought under the influence of vices in which he had once indulged, but by which in his waking hours he is rarely or never overcome. There can be little doubt that when we are actively reasoning this automatic action of the mind still continues, but the ideas and trains of thought that are thus produced are so combined and transformed by the reason, that we are unconscious of their existence. They exist, nevertheless, and form (or greatly contribute to) our mental bias. It is impossible to review this most suggestive subject without suspecting that the saying, "habit is a second nature," represents more than a metaphor, that the reason is much more closely connected with the will than is generally imagined ; and that the origin of most of those opinions we attribute to pure reasoning, is more composite than we suppose. This important subject was first incidentally pointed out by Leibnitz. After his time, it seems, except in as far as it was connected with the animism of Stahl, to have been almost unnoticed till very recently. Sir W. Hamilton (in his *Essays*) has treated it from a psychological, and Drs. Laycock (*The Brain and the Mind*) and Carpenter (*Human Physiology*, pp. 799–819) from a medical, point of view. Mr. Morell, following in the steps of Stahl, has availed himself of it (*Mental Philosophy*) to explain the laws of generation, ascribing the formation of the fœtus to the unconscious action of the soul ; and M. Maury (*Le Sommeil et les Rêves*) has shown its connection with the phenomena of sleep. See, too, De Quincey's *Opium-Eater*, pp. 259–261, ed. 1864 ; Tissot, *Sur la Vie ;* and Saisset, *L'Ame et la Vie.*

[1] Cebes.
[2] This very painful recurrence, which occupies such an important place in all religious biographies, seems to be attached to an extremely remarkable and obscure department of mental phenomena which has only been investigated with earnestness within the last few years, and which is termed by psychologists "latent consciousness," and by physiologists "unconscious cerebration" or the "reflex action of the brain." That certain facts remain so hidden in the mind, that it is only by a strong act of volition they can be recalled to recollection, is a fact of daily experience ; but it is now fully established that a multitude of events which are so completely forgotten that no effort of will can revive them, and that their statement calls up no reminiscence, may nevertheless be, so to speak, imbedded in the memory, and may be reproduced with intense vividness under certain physical conditions.

opinions they have inherited, or examine them so completely under the dominating influence of the prejudice of education, that whatever may have been the doctrines they have been taught, they conclude that they are so unquestionably true, that nothing but a judicial blindness can cause their rejection. Of the few who have obtained a glimpse of higher things, a large proportion cannot endure a conflict to which old associations and, above all, the old doctrine of the guilt of error, lend such a peculiar bitterness; they stifle the voice of reason, they turn away from the path of knowledge, they purchase peace at the expense of truth. This is, indeed, in our day, the most fatal of all the obstacles to enquiry. It was not till the old world had been reduced to chaos that the Divine voice said, " Let there be light"; and in the order of knowledge, as in the order of nature, dissolution must commonly precede formation. There is a period in the history of the enquirer when old opinions have been shaken or destroyed, and new opinions have not yet been formed, a period of doubt, of terror, and of darkness, when the voice of the dogmatist has not lost its power, and the phantoms of the past still hover over the mind, a period when every landmark is lost to sight, and every star is veiled, and the soul seems drifting helpless and rudderless before the destroying blast. It is in this season of transition that the temptations to stifle reason possess a fearful power. It is when contrasting the tranquillity of past assurance with the feverish paroxysms that accompany enquiry, that the mind is most likely to abandon the path of truth. It is so much easier to

assume than to prove; it is so much less painful to believe than to doubt; there is such a charm in the repose of prejudice, when no discordant voice jars upon the harmony of belief; there is such a thrilling pang when cherished dreams are scattered, and old creeds abandoned, that it is not surprising that men should close their eyes to the unwelcome light. Hence the tenacity exhibited by systems that have long since been disproved. Hence the oscillation and timidity that characterise the research of most, and the indifference to truth and the worship of expediency that cloud the fair promise of not a few.

In our age these struggles are diffused over a very wide circle, and are felt by men of many grades of intellect. This fact, however, while it accounts for the perturbation and instability that characterise a large portion of contemporary literature, should materially lighten the burden of each individual enquirer. The great majority of the ablest intellects of the century have preceded him, and their genius irradiates the path. The hands of many sympathisers are extended to assist him. The disintegration around him will facilitate his course. He who, believing that the search for truth can never be offensive to the God of truth, pursues his way with an unswerving energy, may not unreasonably hope that he may assist others in their struggle towards the light, and may in some small degree contribute to that consummation when the professed belief shall have been adjusted to the requirements of the age, when the old tyranny shall have been broken, and the anarchy of transition shall have passed away.

CHAPTER V.

THE SECULARISATION OF POLITICS

THE evidence I have collected in the preceding chapters will be sufficient to exhibit the nature of the rationalistic movement, and also the process by which it has been developed. To establish the first, I have reviewed a long series of theological conceptions which the movement has weakened or transformed. To establish the second, I have shown that the most important changes were much less the results of direct controversy than of the attraction of the prevailing modes of thought, which themselves represented the convergence of a great variety of theological influences. In the remainder of this work, I propose to trace more fully than I have yet had occasion to do, the relations of the rationalistic movement to the political and economical history of Europe, or, in other words, to show on the one hand how the theological development has modified political and economical theories; and, on the other hand, how the tendencies produced by these have reacted upon theology.

But, before entering upon this field, it will perhaps not be altogether unnecessary to remind the reader once more of the main principle upon which the relevance of this species of narrative depends. It is that the speculative opinions which are embraced by any large body of men are accepted, not on account of the arguments upon which they rest, but on account of a predisposition to receive them. This predisposition depends with many persons entirely upon the circumstances of their position, that is to say, upon the associations of childhood, friendship, or interest, and is of such a nature as altogether to dispense with arguments. With others, it depends chiefly upon the character of their minds, which induces them to embrace one class of arguments rather than another. This intellectual character, again, results partly from natural and innate peculiarities, and partly from the totality of influences that act upon the mind. For the mind of man is no inert receptacle of knowledge, but absorbs and incorporates into its own constitution the ideas which it receives. In a healthy condition, increased knowledge implies an increased mental capacity, and each peculiar department of study not merely comprises a peculiar kind of information, but also produces a peculiar ply and tendency of judgment. All minds are more or less governed by what chemists term the laws of elective affinity. Like naturally tends to like. The predominating passion of every man colours the whole train of his reasoning, and in every subject he examines he instinctively turns to that aspect which is most congruous to his favourite pursuit.

If this be so, we should naturally expect that politics, which occupy so large a place in the minds of men, should at all times have exercised a considerable influence on the tone of thought from which theological opinions arise, and that a general tendency to restrict the province of theology should have resulted in a secularisation of politics. In the present chapter, I shall examine the stages of that secularisation and the minor changes that are connected with it. The subject will naturally divide itself into two parts. We shall first see how theological interests gradually ceased to be a main object of political combinations; and afterwards, how, by the repudiation of the divine right of kings and the assertion of the social contract, the basis of authority was secularised.

If we take a broad view of the course of history, and examine the relations of great bodies of men, we find that religion and patriotism are the chief moral influences to which they have been subject, and that the separate modifications and mutual interaction of these two agents may almost be said to constitute the moral history of mankind. For some centuries before the introduction of Christianity, patriotism was in most countries the presiding moral principle, and religion occupied an entirely subordinate position. Almost all those examples of heroic self-sacrifice, of passionate devotion to an unselfish aim, which antiquity affords, were produced by the spirit of patriotism. Decius and Regulus, Leonidas and Harmodius, are the pagan parallels to Christian martyrs.[1] Nor was it only in the great crises of national history that this spirit was evoked. The pride of patriotism, the sense of dignity which it inspires, the close bond of sympathy produced by a common aim, the energy and elasticity of character which are the parents of great enterprises, were manifested habitually in the leading nations of antiquity. The spirit of patriotism pervaded all classes. It formed a distinct type of character, and was the origin both of many virtues and of many vices.

If we attempt to estimate the moral condition of such a phase of society, we must in some respects place it extremely high. Patriotism has always proved the best cordial of humanity, and all the sterner and more robust virtues were matured to the highest degree by its power. No other influence diffuses abroad so much of that steady fortitude which is equally removed from languor and timidity on the one hand, and from feverish and morbid excitement upon the other. In nations that have been long pervaded by a strong and continuous political life, the pulse beats high and steadily, habits of self-reliance are formed which enable men to confront danger with a calm intrepidity, and to retain a certain sobriety of temperament amid the most trying vicissitudes. A capacity for united action, for self-sacrifice, for long and persevering exertion, becomes general. A high, though sometimes rather capricious, standard of honour is formed, and a stern simplicity of habits encouraged. It is probable that in the best days of the old classic republics the passions of men were as habitually under control, national tastes as simple and chastened, and acts of heroism as frequent and as grand, as in the noblest periods of subsequent history. Never did men pass through life with a more majestic dignity, or meet death with a more unfaltering calm. The full

sublimity of the old classic type has never been reproduced in its perfection, but the spirit that formed it has often breathed over the feverish struggles of modern life, and has infused into society a heroism and a fortitude that have proved the invariable precursors of regeneration.

All this was produced among nations that were notoriously deficient in religious feeling, and had, indeed, degraded their religion into a mere function of the State. The disinterested enthusiasm of patriotism had pervaded and animated them, and had called into habitual action many of the noblest moral capacities of mankind.

To this picture there is, however, a melancholy reverse. If the Roman civilisation exhibited to a very high degree the sterner virtues, it was pre-eminently deficient in the gentler ones. The pathos of life was habitually repressed. Suffering and weakness met with little sympathy or assistance. The slave, the captive, the sick, the helpless, were treated with cold indifference, or with merciless ferocity. The hospital and the refuge for the afflicted were unknown. The spectacle of suffering and of death was the luxury of all classes. An almost absolute destruction of the finer sensibilities was the consequence of the universal worship of force. The existence of the gods was, indeed, recognised, but the ideals of excellence were not sought on the heights of Olympus, but in the annals of Roman prowess. There was little sense of the superhuman, no conception of sin, no desire to rise above the things of earth ; pride was deemed the greatest of virtues, and humility the most contemptible of weaknesses. The welfare of the State being the highest object of unselfish devotion, virtue and vice were often measured by that standard, and the individual was habitually sacrificed to the community.

But perhaps the greatest vice of the old form of patriotism was the narrowness of sympathy which it produced. Outside the circle of their own nation all men were regarded with contempt and indifference, if not with absolute hostility. Conquest was the one recognised form of national progress, and the interests of nations were, therefore, regarded as directly opposed. The intensity with which a man loved his country was a measure of the hatred which he bore to those who were without it. The enthusiasm which produced the noblest

---

[1] It is worthy of notice, that the first development of sculpture, which in almost all other nations was religious, in Rome appears to have been patriotic—the objects of representation being not the gods, but the true national ideals, the heroes of Rome. (See O. Müller, *Manuel d'Archéologie*, vol. i. pp. 251-252.)

virtues in a narrow circle was the direct and powerful cause of the strongest international antipathies.

In Judæa the religious system occupied a more prominent position than among the Greeks or Romans, but it had been indissolubly connected with national interests, and the attachment to it was in reality only a form and aspect of patriotism. Whatever opinion may be held as to whether a future life was intended to be among the elements of the Levitical revelation, there can be no question that the primary incentives which that revelation offered were of a patriotic order. The devotion of the people to their religious system was to be the measure of their national prosperity. When their faith burnt with a strong and unsullied flame, every enemy succumbed beneath their arms; but whenever idolatry had corrupted their devotions, a hostile army encircled Mount Moriah. All the traditions of their religion were identified with splendid national triumphs. The rescue from Egypt, the conquest of Canaan, and the massacre of its inhabitants, the exploits of the inspired warriors who had broken the chains of a foreign master, the destruction of the hosts of the Assyrian, were all legends interweaving in the Jewish mind the association of the Church and of the State. The spirit of sect, or an attachment not to abstract principles, but to a definite and organised ecclesiastical institution, is a spirit essentially similar to patriotism, but is directed to a different object, and is therefore, in most cases, hostile to it. In Judæa the spirit of patriotism and the spirit of sect were united; each intensified the other, and the exclusive intolerance which is the result of each existed with double virulence.

Such was the condition of the Pagan and Jewish world when the sublime doctrine of universal brotherhood was preached to mankind. After eighteen hundred years men are only beginning to realise it, and at the time when it was first proclaimed it was diametrically opposed to the most cherished prejudices of the age.

In Judæa the spirit of an exclusive patriotism not only pervaded the national mind, but was also at this period an intensely active moral principle. In the Roman Empire patriotism was little more than an intellectual conception; society was in a condition of moral dissolution, and disinterested enthusiasm was extremely rare. The fortunes of the infant Church were, probably, in no slight measure determined by these circumstances. In Judæa it was rejected with indignant scorn. In the Roman Empire it obtained a marvellous triumph, but it triumphed only by transforming itself under the influence of the spirit of sect. The passion for the visible and material which in that age it was impossible to escape—which encrusted the teachings of the Church with an elaborate and superstitious ritualism, designed to appeal to and enthral the senses, and converted its simple moral principles into a complicated creed—acted with equal force upon its government, and transformed it into a highly centralised monarchy, pervaded by a spirit of exclusiveness very similar to that which had animated the old Roman republic. The spirit of sect was, indeed, far stronger and more virulent than the most envenomed spirit of nationality. The ancient patriot regarded nations that were beyond his border with indifference, or with a spirit of rivalry; but the priest declared everyone who rejected his opinions to be a criminal.

From this period for many centuries Catholicism, considered as an ecclesiastical organisation, was the undisputed mistress of Europe; national feelings scarcely ever came into collision with its interests, and the whole current of affairs was directed by theology. When, however, the first breathings of the spirit of Rationalism were felt in Europe, when, under the influence of that spirit, dogmatic interests began to wane, and their paramount importance to be questioned, a new tendency was manifested. The interests of the Church were subordinated to those of the State. Theology was banished from department after department of politics, until the whole system of government was secularised.

The period in which political affairs were most completely governed by theological considerations was unquestionably the age of the Crusades. It was no political anxiety about the balance of power, but an intense religious enthusiasm, that impelled the inhabitants of Christendom towards the city which was at once the cradle and the symbol of their faith. All interests were then absorbed, all classes were governed, all passions subdued or coloured, by religious fervour. National animosities that had raged for centuries were pacified by its power. The intrigues of statesmen and the jealousies of kings disappeared beneath its influence. Nearly two millions of lives are said to have been sacrificed in the cause. Neglected governments, exhausted finances, depopulated countries were cheerfully accepted as the price of success. No wars the world had ever before seen were so popular as these, which were at the same time the most disastrous and the most unselfish.

Long before the Reformation, such wars as the Crusades had become impossible, and the relative prominence of secular policy had materially increased. This was in part the result of the better organisation of the civil government, which rendered unnecessary some of the services the Church had previously rendered to the community. Thus, when the general tolerance of private wars had produced a condition of anarchy that rendered all the relations of life insecure, the Church interposed and proclaimed in the eleventh century the "Truce of God," which was the first effective barrier to the lawlessness of the barons. Her bishops became the arbitrators of every quarrel, and succeeded in a great measure in calming the ferocity of the age. But when this object was in part attained, and when the regal power was consolidated, the Truce of God, in spite of many attempts to revive it,[1] fell rapidly into desuetude, and the preservation of tranquillity passed from the ecclesiastical to the civil government. This is but a single example of a process that was continually going on during the latter half of the middle ages. The Church had formerly exercised nearly every function of the civil government, on account of the inefficiency of the lay governors, and every development of secular administration, while it relieved the ecclesiastics of a duty, deprived them of a source of power.

But, besides the diminution of influence that resulted from this cause, the Church for many centuries found a strenuous antagonist in the regal power. The famous history of the investitures, and the equally remarkable, though less famous, ordinance by which in 1319 all bishops were expelled from the Parliament of Paris, are striking examples of the energy with which the conflict was sustained. Its issue depended mainly on the superstition of the people. In a profoundly superstitious age neither skill nor resolution could resist the effects of an excommunication or an interdict, and the most illustrious monarchs of the middle ages succumbed beneath their power. But some time before the Reformation their terror was in a great measure destroyed. The rapid growth of the industrial classes, which were at all times separated from theological tendencies, the revival of a spirit of bold and unshackled enquiry, and the discredit that had fallen upon the Church on account of the rival popes, and of the corruption of the monasteries, were the chief causes of the emancipation. The Reformation was only possible when the old superstitions had been enfeebled by the spirit of doubt, and diluted by the admixture of secular interests. Kings then availed themselves gladly of the opportunity of throwing off the restraints of the Papacy. Patriots rebelled against the supremacy of a foreign power. The lay classes welcomed a change by which the pressure of the clergy was lightened.

A comparison of the religious wars produced by the Reformation with the Crusades shows clearly the great change that had passed over the spirit of Europe. The Crusades had been purely religious. They represented solely the enthusiasm of the people for dogmatic interests, and they were maintained for more than two centuries by an effort of unexampled self-sacrifice. In the religious wars, on the other hand, the secular and ecclesiastical elements were very evenly balanced. The object sought was political power, but difference of religious belief formed the lines of demarcation separating the hostile coalitions, and created the enthusiasm by which the struggle was maintained. The spirit of the theologian was sufficiently powerful to inundate Europe with blood, but only when united with the ambition of the politician. Yet dogmatic agreement still formed the principle of alliance, and all co-operation with heretics was deemed a sin.

This phase of opinions continued for more than a century after the Reformation. It passed away under the pressure of advancing civilisation, but not before the ministry of Richelieu ; for although Francis I. had made an alliance with the

[1] It was confirmed as part of the general law of the Church by Alexander III. in 1179. See Ducellier, *Hist. des Classes Laborieuses en France*, pp. 87-89, 127, 128.

Turks, and a few other sovereigns had exhibited a similar indifference to the prevailing distinctions, their policy was rarely successful. Even at the last, the change was only effected with considerable difficulty, and Italy, Spain, Germany, and the Netherlands swarmed with writings denouncing the alliance of the French with the Swedes as little short of an apostasy from Christianity. A book entitled *Mars Gallicus,* and published in 1635, under the pseudonym of Alexander Patricius Armacanus, was especially singled out as the most conclusive demonstration of the sinfulness of alliances with heretics, and it marks the first dawn of the reputation of one who was destined to exercise a deep and lasting influence over the fortunes of the Church. It was written by Jansenius, who owed to it his promotion to the bishopric of Ypres.[1] But the genius of Richelieu, seconded by the intellectual influences of the age, prevailed over every difficulty; and the Peace of Westphalia is justly regarded as closing the era of religious wars. The invasion of Holland by Louis XIV. was near becoming one, and religious fanaticism has more than once lent its aid to other modern struggles;[2] but wars like those which once distracted Europe have become almost impossible. Among all the elements of affinity and repulsion that regulate the combinations of nations, dogmatic interests, which were once supreme, can scarcely be said to exist. Among all the possible dangers that cloud the horizon, none appears more improbable than a coalition formed upon the principle of a common belief, and designed to extend the sphere of its influence. Such coalitions were once the most serious occupations of statesmen. They now exist only in the speculations of the expounders of prophecy.

It was in this way that, in the course of a few centuries, the foreign policy of all civilised nations was completely and finally secularised. Wars that were once regarded as simple duties became absolutely impossible. Alliances that were once deemed atrocious sins became habitual and unchallenged. That which had long been the centre around which all other interests revolved, receded and disappeared, and a profound change in the actions of mankind indicated a profound change in their belief.

I have already noticed the decline of that religious persecution, which was long the chief sign and measure of ecclesiastical influence over the internal policy of nations. There is, however, one aspect of the Inquisition which I have not referred to, for it belongs to the subject of the present chapter—I mean its frequent hostility to the civil power.

Before the thirteenth century, the cognisance of heresy was divided between the bishop and the civil magistrate. The Church proclaimed that it was a crime more deadly than any civil offence, and that it should be punished according to its enormity; the bishop accused the heretic, and the magistrate tried and condemned him. During the earlier part of the middle ages, this arrangement, which had been that of the Theodosian Code, was accepted without difficulty. The civil government was then very submissive, and heretics almost unknown, the few cases that appeared being usually resolved into magic. When, however, at the close of the twelfth century, a spirit of rebellion against the Church had been widely diffused, the Popes perceived that some more energetic system was required, and among the measures that were devised, the principal was the Inquisition, which was intended not merely to suppress heresy, but also to enlarge the circle of ecclesiastical jurisdiction.

This new tribunal[1] was placed in the hands of the two religious orders of St. Dominic and St. Francis, and its first object was to monopolise the trials of cases of heresy. The bishop of the diocese had a certain position in the local tribunal, but it was generally little more than honorary, and was entirely subordinate to that of the chief Inquisitor. The civil government was only represented by an " Assessor," and by some minor officers appointed by the Inquisitor himself, and its function was merely to execute those whom the ecclesiastics had condemned. A third of the confiscated goods was bestowed upon the district where the trial took place, which in its turn was to bear the expenses of the confinement of the prisoners. To crown all,

---

[1] *Avis aux Réfugiés,* p. 56 (ed. 1692).
[2] *E.g.,* the recent invasion of Morocco by the Spaniards. On the religious character Louis XIV. tried to give the invasion of Holland, see Michelet, *Louis XIV.*

[1] The relations of the Inquisition and the civil power have been admirably sketched by Sarpi, in a short work called *Discorso dell' Origine dell' Uffizio dell Inquisitione,* which I have closely followed.

the society was centralised by the appointment of an Inquisitor-General at Rome,
with whom all the branches of the tribunal were to be in constant communication.

It is obvious that this organisation, in
addition to its religious importance, had
a very great political importance. It
transferred to ecclesiastics a branch of
jurisdiction which had always been regarded as belonging to the civil power,
and it introduced into every country
where it was acknowledged a corporation
of extraordinary powers entirely dependent
on a foreign potentate. The Inquisitors
early found a powerful, though somewhat
encroaching, friend in the Emperor
Frederick II., who in 1224 issued four
edicts at Padua, in which he declared
himself their protector, commanded that
all obstinate heretics should be burnt, and
all penitent heretics imprisoned for life,
and delegated the investigation of the
crime to the ecclesiastics, though the
power of pronouncing the condemnation
was reserved to the secular judge. In
the first half of the thirteenth century
the new tribunal was introduced into
Lombardy, the Marches, Romagna, Tuscany, the Balearic Isles, Arragon, and
some of the cities of France and Germany.
In Naples, however, the hostility of the
king to the pope, and the spirit of the
people, resisted it. In Venice, too, the
magistrates long refused to admit it, and
heretics were burnt on the designation of
the bishop, and by sentence of the Doge,
and of the majority of the Supreme
Council, until 1289, when the government
yielded, and the Inquisition was introduced, though with some slight restrictions favourable to the civil power.[1] In
Spain, owing to the combination of a
very strong Catholic and a very strong
national feeling, it assumed a somewhat
peculiar form. There, as elsewhere, it
was an essentially ecclesiastical institution, created, extended, and modified
under the express sanction of the Pope,
but the Inquisitor-General and the Chief
Council were appointed by the sovereign,
subject to the papal confirmation ; and
the famous prosecution of Antonio Perez,
which resulted in the destruction of the
liberties of Arragon, furnishes an example,
though perhaps a solitary one, of its employment merely as a political tool.[2] At

first its jurisdiction was confined to the
land, and many sailors of different religions had enrolled themselves in the
Spanish navy ; but in 1571 Sixtus V., at
the request of Philip II., appointed a
special Inquisitor to preside over the
navy,[1] who speedily restored its orthodoxy. By Spanish influence the tribunal
was extended to the Netherlands, to the
New World, to Sicily, Sardinia, and
Malta.

It is said in the legend of St. Dominic
that his mother, when in the season of
childbirth, dreamed that a dog was about
to issue from her womb, bearing a lighted
torch that would kindle the whole world ;
and certainly the success of the Inquisition well-nigh fulfilled the portent.[2] For
two or three centuries its extension was
the main object of the papal policy ; it
was what the struggle of the investitures
had been in the preceding age, the chief
form which the spirit of ecclesiastical
encroachment assumed ; and during this
long period there was probably not a
single pope who did not expressly eulogise
it. But although there can be no doubt
that a powerful blow was thus given to
heresy, it may well be questioned whether
the papal policy was not, on the whole,
short-sighted, for the Inquisition probably
contributed largely to the ultimate secularisation of politics. Before its institution no one doubted that the investigation
and punishment of heresy formed one of
the first duties of the civil government,
but by the Inquisition the two things
were slightly separated. The cognisance
of heresy was in a measure withdrawn
from the lay rulers, and, by a curious
inversion, that very doctrine of the religious incapacity of the latter, which was
afterwards urged in favour of tolerance,
was at this time urged in favour of the
Inquisition.[3] Nor was the new tribunal

---

[1] Sarpi, pp. 48–57 (ed. 1639).
[2] This curious episode has been lately investigated
by M. Mignet, in an interesting work called *Antonio*

Perez. One of the accusations brought against Perez
was, that he had in a moment of passion exclaimed, that
"if God the Father had ventured to say to him what
the king had said, he would have cut his nose off,"
which the Inquisitors said "partook of the heresy of
the Anthropomorphites and of the Vaudois, who maintain that the Father has bodily parts."
[1] Paramo, *De Origine Inquisitionis*, pp. 224–226.
This was perhaps one of the minor causes of the
decline of the Spanish navy.
[2] The Inquisition was not, it is true, organised till
after his death, but St. Dominic was the chief reviver
of persecution. His Order represented the principle,
and the Inquisition was, almost as a matter of course,
placed mainly in its hands.
[3] The following passage from Sarpi is very instructive : "Altre volte li santi Vescovi niuna cosa più
predicavano e raccommandavano à prencipi che la
cura della religione. Di niuna cosa più li ammonivano
e modestamente reprendevano che del trascurarla : ed

merely distinct from the civil government. It was also frequently opposed to it. Its very institution was an encroachment on the jurisdiction of the magistrate, and there were constant differences as to the exact limits of its authority. Wherever it was acknowledged it was the undisputed judge of heresy and of a large section of ecclesiastical offences, and one of these latter—the employment by priests of the confessional for the purpose of seducing the penitents—occupied a very prominent place in the writings it produced.[1] Witchcraft, too, was usually, though by no means always, regarded as within its province, but the magistrates sometimes refused to execute its sentences. Usury was said by the ecclesiastics to be an ecclesiastical offence, but the legislators refused to allow the Inquisition to try it. Perjury, bigamy, and several other crimes gave rise to similar conflicts.

While the province of persecution was thus in some degree separated from the civil government, the extreme violence of the tribunal to which it had fallen aroused a very general popular indignation. Spain, it is true, was in this respect an exception. In that country the Inquisition was always cherished as the special expression of the national religion, and the burning of Jews and heretics was soon regarded in a double light, as a religious ceremony and also as a pageant or public amusement that was eminently congenial to the national taste.[2] In other countries, however, but especially in Italy, it excited intense hostility. When the Spaniards tried to force it upon the Neapolitans, so general an insurrection ensued that even Spanish zeal recoiled from the undertaking. The north and centre of Italy writhed fiercely under the yoke. Terrific riots arising from this cause almost threatened the destruction of Milan in 1242, and of Parma in 1279, and minor disturbances took place in many other towns.[1] Although the Popes had done everything in their power to invest the office with a religious attraction—although they had granted the same indulgences to its officers as had formerly been granted to the Crusaders, and an indulgence of three years to all who, not being Inquisitors, assisted in bringing a heretic to condemnation—although, too, the sentence of excommunication was launched against all who impeded the Inquisitors in the discharge of their office—the opposition of the Italians was for centuries unextinguished. Thus we find in 1518 the district of Brescia in so wild a ferment of excitement on account of the condemnation of numerous persons on the charge of incantation, that the government could with difficulty pacify it by annulling the sentences. A similar outburst took place in Mantua in 1568, and even in Rome at the death of Paul IV. the prisons of the Inquisition were burst open, and their records burnt by an infuriated crowd.[2]

adesso niuna cosa più se predica e persuade al prencipe, se non ch' a lui non s' aspetta la cura delle cose divine, con tutto che del contrario la scrittura sacra sia piena di luoghi dove la religione è raccommandata alla protezione del prencipe della Maestà Divina." (Pp. 89, 90.)

[1] See, for example, the full discussion of the matter in Carena, *De Officio S. Inquisitionis* (Lugduni, 1649), pp. 135-161. Three Popes—Paul IV., Pius IV., and Gregory XV.—found it necessary to issue bulls on the subject, a fact which will surprise no one who has glanced over the pages of Sanchez or Dens.

[2] This appears sufficiently from the seasons in which executions took place, and from all the descriptions of them. I may notice, however, that there is in existence one very remarkable contemporary painting of the scene. It represents the execution, or rather the procession to the stake, of a number of Jews and Jewesses who were burnt in 1680 at Madrid, during the fêtes that followed the marriage of Charles II., and before the king, his bride, the court and clergy of Madrid. The great square was arranged like a theatre, and thronged with ladies in court dress; the king sat on an elevated platform surrounded by the chief members of the aristocracy, and Bishop Valdares, the Inquisitor-General, presided over the scene. The painter of this very remarkable picture (which is in the gallery of Madrid) was Francesco Rizzi, who died in 1685. He has directed the sympathies of the spectator against the Jews by the usual plan of exaggerating the Jewish nose—a device which is common to all early painters except Juannez, who, in his pictures of New Testament scenes, honestly gives this peculiarity of feature to the good as well as the bad characters. The picture is very curious from its representation of the attire of the condemned and of the penitent. Llorente has noticed this *auto da fé*, but not the picture. (*Hist. de l'Inquisition*, tom. iii. pp. 3, 4.)

Among the victims in 1680 was a Jewish girl, not 17, whose singular beauty struck all who saw her with admiration. As she passed to the stake, she cried to the queen, "Great queen, is not your presence able to bring me some comfort under my misery? Consider my youth, and that I am condemned for a religion which I have sucked in with my mother's milk." The queen turned away her eyes. (Limborch, *Hist. Inquis.* cap. xl.)

[1] Sarpi, p. 60. Gregory IX. made the admission of the Inquisition an indispensable condition of his alliances with the free towns. A monk called Friar John, of Vicenza, seems to have been the most successful in promoting the institution in Italy. He pronounced himself the apostle not of persecution, but of peace, reconciled many enemies, and burnt sixty Cathari on a single occasion in the great square of Verona. (Sismondi, *Hist. de la Liberté*, tom. i. pp. 108, 109.)

[2] Sarpi, p. 80. Llorente, *Hist. de l'Inquisition*, tom. ii. p. 272. The Inquisition at Rome was very active in the latter half of the sixteenth century—especially during the pontificate of Pius V. In April 1570 a Capuchin named Pistoggia had an interview with the Pope, in which, speaking of the repression of

All these things have their place in the history of the secularisation of politics, for they all contributed to weaken the spirit of persecution, and to separate it from the civil government. As long, however, as dogmatic interests were supreme, persecution in some form or other must have continued. How that supremacy was weakened, and how, in consequence of the decline, men ceased to burn or imprison those who differed from their opinions, the last chapter will have shown.

But, important as was this stage of the secularisation of politics, a literary censorship was still directed against heretical writings, and the system of religious disqualifications still continued. The first of these had been a very ancient practice in religious controversy. Among the pagans we find Diocletian making it one of his special objects to burn the Christian writings, and Julian, without taking precisely the same step, endeavouring to attain the same end by withholding from the Christians the means of instruction that could enable them to propagate their opinions.[1] In the same way the early councils continually condemned heretical books, and the civil power, acting upon their sentence, destroyed them. Thus Constantine ordered the destruction of the writings of the Arians when the Council of Nice had condemned them. Arcadius, following the decision of the Council of Constantinople, suppressed those of Eunomius. Theodosius, after the Council of Ephesus, prohibited the works of Nestorius, and after the Council of Chalcedon those of Eutyches.[2] At first, though the condemnation belonged to the Church, the execution of the sentence was regarded as the prerogative of the civil ruler; but as early as 443 we find

Pope St. Leo burning books of the Manichæans on his own authority.[1] All through the middle ages the practice was of course continued, and the Inquisition succeeded in destroying almost the entire heretical literature before the Reformation; but at the time of the revival of learning, these measures excited some opposition. Thus, when in 1510 the theologians of Cologne, represented especially by an Inquisitor named Hocstrat, and supported by the mendicant orders and after some hesitation by the University of Paris, desired to destroy the whole literature of the Jews with the exception of the Old Testament, Reuchlin, who was one of the chief Hebrew scholars of his age, protested against the measure, and having been on this account denounced in violent language by a converted Jew named Phefercorne, who had originally counselled the destruction, he rejoined in a work strongly asserting the philosophical and historical value of the Jewish literature, and urging the importance of its preservation. Nearly all the ablest pens in Germany were soon engaged on the same side; and the civil authority as well as many distinguished ecclesiastics having taken part in the controversy, it became for a time the most prominent in Europe, and resulted in the suspension of the intended measure.[2] The rise of the Reformation served, however, to increase the severity of the censorship. The system of licences followed almost immediately upon the invention of printing, and in 1559 Paul IV. originated the Index Expurgatorius. In England, Convocation was accustomed to censure, and the Star Chamber to suppress, heretical works. In Holland a love of free discussion was early generated by the fact that, during the antagonism between France and Spain, it suited the interests of the latter country to make the Netherlands the asylum of the French refugees, who were accustomed to publish there innumerable seditious writings which were directed against the French Government, but which had a very strong and favourable influence upon the country in which they appeared. When the Spanish yoke was broken, Holland became equally famous for the freedom of its religious press. With the exception of this country and of some of the cities of Italy, there were

heresy, he said, "Che vedeva bene ch' ella era pronta alla giustizia, e che ogni giorno faceva impiccare e squartare ora uno, ora un altro." (Cantù, *Eretici d'Italia*, ii. p. 410.) The most memorable victims of the Inquisition at Rome were Bruno, the pantheistic philosopher, and Aonio Paleario, the author of the justly famous treatise *On the Benefits of Christ's Death*. Another remarkable victim was Carnesecchi, whose trial has been printed by the Rev. E. Gibbings from the original proceedings of the Inquisition, which are now in the library of Trinity College, Dublin. Unfortunately the materials for this branch of the history of the Inquisition are still for the most part in MS.

[1] Julian did not, as is sometimes said, forbid the Christians studying the classic writings, but he prohibited them from teaching them on the ground that it was absurd for those who despised and repudiated the ancient gods to expound the records of their acts. See his *Epistle to Jamblichus*.

[2] Sarpi, pp. 192, 193. Milton gives a slight sketch of the history of censorships in his *Areopagitica*.

[1] Giannone, *Ist. di Napoli*.
[2] Sleidan, liv. ii.

scarcely any instances of perfect liberty of religious publications, till the Revolutions, first of all of England, and afterwards of France, established that great principle which is rapidly becoming universal, that the judgment of theological works is altogether external to the province of legislators.

Among the earliest advocates of toleration most accepted as a truism the doctrine, that it is the duty of every nation in its national capacity to adopt some one form of religious belief, and to act upon its precepts with the consistency that is expected from an individual. This Church and State theory, which forms the last vestige of the old theocratic spirit that marks the earlier stages of civilisation, is still supreme in many countries ; but in our own day it has been assailed or destroyed in all those nations that have yielded to the political tendencies of the age. Stating the theory in its most definite form, the upholders of the system of policy demanded that every nation should support and endow one form of religion and only one, that every other should be regarded as altogether outside the cognisance of the State, and that the rulers and representatives should belong exclusively to the established faith. This theory has sometimes been curtailed and modified in modern times after successive defeats, but anyone who will trace it back to the days when it was triumphant, and follow the train of argument that has been pursued by the Tory party for more than a century, can satisfy himself that I have not exaggerated its purport.

The two European nations which represent most fully in their policy the intellectual tendencies of the age are unquestionably France and England, and it is precisely in these nations that the theory has been successfully assailed. After several slight oscillations, the French people in 1830 finally proclaimed, as a basis of their constitution, the principle, that no State religion is recognised by France ; and as a comment upon this decision we have seen a Protestant holding the reins of power under Louis Philippe, and a Jew sitting in the Provisional Government of 1848. A more complete abnegation of the old doctrine it would be impossible to conceive, and it places France, in at least this respect, at the head of modern liberalism.[1]

The progress of the movement in England has been much more gradual, and it represents the steady growth of rationalistic principles among statesmen. The first great step was taken during the depression of the clergy that followed the Revolution. The establishment of the Scotch Kirk, whether we consider the principle it involved or the vast amount of persecution it terminated, was undoubtedly one of the most signal defeats the English Church has ever undergone. For a considerable time, however, the clergy succeeded in arresting the movement, which at last received a fresh propulsion by the Irish Parliament, and attained its full triumph under the exigencies of Irish policy.

Whatever may be thought of the purity of the Irish Parliament during the brief period in which it exercised an independent authority, there are certainly few things more absurd than the charges of bigotry that are frequently directed against it. If we measure it by the standard of the present day, it will of course appear very defective, but if we compare it with contemporary legislatures, and above all if we estimate the peculiar temptations to which it was exposed, our verdict would be very different. It would be scarcely possible to conceive a legislature with greater inducement to adopt a sectarian policy. Before 1793 it was elected exclusively by Protestants. The government had created, and most sedulously maintained, that close borough system which has always a tendency to make private interest the guiding motive of policy ; and the extraordinary monopoly the Protestants possessed of almost all positions of wealth and dignity, rendered the strictest toryism their obvious interest. There was scarcely any public opinion existing in Ireland, and the Catholics were so torpid through continued oppression, that they could exercise scarcely any influence upon legislation. Under these circumstances the Irish Parliament, having admitted them to the magistracy, to the jury box, and to several minor privileges, at last accorded them the elective franchise, which, in a country where they formed an immense majority of the nation, and where every reform of Parliament and every extension

[1] For a clear view of the successive stages of the secularising movement in France, see the memorial on the subject drawn up by the Abbé Lacordaire, and reproduced by Lamennais. (*Affaires de Rome*, pp. 37–89.)

of education must have strengthened their interest, necessarily implied a complete emancipation. It is worthy, too, of notice that the liberalism of the Irish Parliament was always in direct proportion to its political independence. It was when the events of the American War had infused into it that strong national feeling which produced the declaration of independence in 1782, that the tendency towards toleration became manifest. Almost all those great orators who cast a halo of such immortal eloquence around its closing period were the advocates of emancipation. Almost all who were the enemies of its legislative independence were the enemies of toleration.

The Irish Parliament was, in truth, a body governed very constantly by corrupt motives, though probably not more so than the English Parliament in the time of Walpole. It was also distinguished by a recklessness of tone and policy that was all the more remarkable on account of the unusually large measure of genius it produced; but it was during the period of its independence probably more free from religious bigotry than any other representative body that had ever sat in the United Kingdom. That it would have completed the measure of 1793 by the admission of Catholics to Parliament, if the Government had supported or had even refrained from opposing that measure, is almost absolutely certain. The opposition of the ministers threw out the Bill, and the recall of Lord Fitzwilliam damped the hopes of the Catholics, and was one of the chief proximate causes of the Rebellion of 1798. But although emancipation was not then conceded, the Irish Parliament directed a deadly blow against the Tory theory, by endowing the College of Maynooth, a distinctively Catholic institution designed for the education of the Catholic priesthood.[1]

The Union was, on the whole, very unfavourable to the movement. To exclude the Catholics from the Parliament of an empire in which they were a small minority did not appear such a glaring anomaly as to exclude them from the Parliament of a nation of which they formed the great majority. The national feeling that made the Irish Protestants wish to emancipate their fellow countrymen could not act with the same force on an English Parliament; and the evangelical movement which had originated with Wesley, and which was in general strongly adverse to the Catholic claims, had in a great measure pervaded English society, before it became ascendent in Ireland. Besides this, a profound change had passed over public opinion in Ireland. The purely national and secular spirit the Irish Parliament had fostered perished with its organ. Patriotism was replaced by sectarianism, and the evil continued till it made Ireland one of the most priest-ridden nations in Europe. These causes account sufficiently for the delay of more than a quarter of a century in according the boon which in 1796 appeared almost attained. On the other hand, the Whig party, which had constituted itself the representative of the secular movement, and which contained an unusually large proportion of religious latitudinarians,[1] steadily advanced, and its organ, the *Edinburgh Review*, was for some years one of the most powerful intellectual influences in England. At the same time the agitation of O'Connell gave a new and imperative tone to the demands of the Catholics, and O'Connell very judiciously maintained the claims of the dissenters as strongly as those of his co-religionists. At last the victory was achieved. By the repeal of the Corporation and Test Acts the theory of Church and State that had so long been maintained was broken. Still stage after stage of the emancipation was fiercely con-

---

[1] I may here notice that an Irishman and an ecclesiastic—Bishop Berkeley—was, as far as I know, the first Protestant who suggested the admission of Catholics into a Protestant university. He proposed that they should be admitted into that of Dublin without being compelled to attend chapel or any divinity lectures; and he observed that the Jesuits in their colleges in Paris had acted in this manner towards Protestants. (*Querist*, No. 291, published in 1735.) As early as 1725 a considerable amount of controversy took place on the subject of toleration in Ireland, occasioned by a sermon preached before the Irish Parliament by a clergyman named Synge, in which he advocated as a Christian duty the most complete toleration of the Catholics, and enunciated the principles of religious liberty with the strongest emphasis. The Parliament

ordered the sermon to be published. It was answered by a writer named Radcliffe, and defended by a writer named Weaver. Synge himself rejoined. This whole controversy, which is utterly forgotten—buried in the great chaos of Irish pamphlets, and perhaps read of late years by no human being except the present writer—is well worthy of the attention of those who study the course of public opinion in Ireland. Perhaps the most eloquent defence of toleration written in English during the last [eighteenth] century was the answer of the Irish priest O'Leary to Wesley's Defence of the penal laws; but then O'Leary was defending his own cause.

[1] See on this subject a striking letter by Southey, in Blanco White's Life, vol. i. p. 310.

tested. The Catholics were avowedly admitted through fear of a revolution, and the act was performed in such a grudging and ungracious manner as to destroy all the gratitude, and many of the benefits, it would otherwise have conferred. Even then many years elapsed before the Jews were emancipated. The invasion and partial destruction of the sectarian character of the universities represents the last stage of the movement which the earliest advocates of toleration had begun.

A necessary consequence of this movement was that the clergy were, as a body, identified either with retrogression or with immobility in politics. During the middle ages they had been the initiators of almost every progressive movement ; but in modern times, the current being directly opposed to their interests, they have naturally become the champions of the past. At the same time, and as a result of the same causes, their political influence has been steadily declining. In England the first great blow to their power was the destruction of the monasteries. Fuller has reckoned at twenty-seven, Lord Herbert at twenty-eight, and Sir Edward Coke at twenty-nine, the number of mitred abbots and priors who by this measure lost their seats in the House of Lords.[1] In the reign of Henry III. the spiritual peers had formed one-half of the Upper House ; in the beginning of the eighteenth century they formed only one-eighth, and in the middle of the nineteenth century only one-fourteenth.[2] Since the beginning of the eighteenth century no clergyman has occupied any important office in the State,[3] and the same change has passed over almost every other nation in Europe.

To those who have appreciated the great truth that a radical political change necessarily implies a corresponding change in the mental habits of society, the process which I have traced will furnish a decisive evidence of the declining influence of dogmatic theology. That vast department of thought and action which is comprised under the name of politics was once altogether guided by its power. It is now passing from its influence rapidly, universally, and completely. The classes that are most penetrated with the spirit of special dogmas were once the chief directors of the policy of Europe. They now form a baffled and desponding minority, whose most cherished political principles have been almost universally abandoned, who are struggling faintly and ineffectually against the ever-increasing spirit of the age, and whose ideal is not in the future but in the past. It is evident that a government never can be really like a railway company, or a literary society, which only exercises an influence over secular affairs. As long as it determines the system of education that exists among its subjects, as long as it can encourage or repress the teaching of particular doctrines, as long as its foreign policy brings it into collision with governments which still make the maintenance of certain religious systems a main object of their policy, it will necessarily exercise a gigantic influence upon belief. It cannot possibly be uninfluential, and it is difficult to assign limits to the influence that it may exercise. If the men who compose it (or the public opinion that governs them) be pervaded by an intensely-realised conviction that the promulgation of a certain system of doctrine is incomparably the highest of human interests, that to assist that promulgation is the main object for which they were placed in the world, and should be the dominant motive of their lives, it will be quite impossible for these men, as politicians, to avoid interfering with theology. Men who are inspired by an absorbing passion will inevitably gratify it if they have the power. Men who sincerely desire the happiness of mankind will certainly use to the uttermost the means they possess of promoting what they feel to be beyond all comparison the greatest of human interests. If by giving a certain direction to education they could avert fearful and general physical suffering, there can be no doubt that they would avail themselves of their power. If they were quite certain that the greatest possible suffering was the consequence of deviating from a particular class of opinions, they could not possibly neglect that consideration in their laws. This is the conclusion we should naturally draw from the nature of the human mind, and it is most abundantly corroborated by experience.[1] In order to ascer-

---

[1] Joyce, *Hist. of English Convocations.* p. 449.
[2] Buckle, *Hist. of Civ.* vol. i. pp. 380, 381.   [3] *Ibid.*

[1] This has been very clearly noticed in one of the ablest modern books in defence of the Tory theory. "At the point where Protestantism becomes vicious, where it receives the first tinge of latitudinarianism,

tain the tendencies of certain opinions, we should not confine ourselves to those exceptional intellects who, having perceived the character of their age, have spent their lives in endeavouring painfully and laboriously to wrest their opinions in conformity with it. We should rather observe the position which large bodies of men, governed by the same principles, but living under various circumstances and in different ages, naturally and almost unconsciously occupy. We have ample means of judging in the present case. We see the general tone which is adopted on political subjects by the clergy of the most various creeds, by the religious newspapers, and by the politicians who represent that section of the community which is most occupied with dogmatic theology. We see that it is a tendency distinct from and opposed to the tendencies of the age. History tells us that it was once dominant in politics, that it has been continuously and rapidly declining, and that it has declined most rapidly and most steadily in those countries in which the development of intellect has been most active. All over Europe the priesthood are now associated with a policy of toryism, of reaction, or of obstruction. All over Europe the organs that represent dogmatic interests are in permanent opposition to the progressive tendencies around them, and are rapidly sinking into contempt. In every country in which a strong political life is manifested, the secularisation of politics is the consequence. Each stage of that movement has been initiated and effected by those who are most indifferent to dogmatic theology, and each has been opposed by those who are most occupied with theology.[1]

and begins to join hands with infidelity by superseding the belief of an objective truth in religion, necessary for salvation ; at that very spot it likewise assumes an aspect of hostility to the union of Church and State." (Gladstone, on *Church and State*, p. 188.)

[1] The evidence of the secularisation of politics furnished by the position of what is called " the religious press " is not confined to England and France. The following very remarkable passage was written by a most competent observer in 1858, when Austria seemed the centre of religious despotism : "Tous les intérêts les plus chétifs ont de nombreux organes dans la presse périodique et font tous de bonnes affaires. La religion, le premier et le plus grand de tous les intérêts, n'en a qu'un nombre presque imperceptible et qui a bien de la peine à vivre. Dans la catholique Autriche, sur 135 journaux il n'y a qu'un seul consacré aux intérêts du christianisme, et il laisse beaucoup à désirer sous le rapport de l'orthodoxie....la vérité est que décidément l'opinion publique ainsi que l'intérêt publique ont cessé d'être chrétiens en Europe." (Ventura, *Le Pouvoir chrétien politique*, p. 139.)

And as I write these words, it is impossible to forget that one of the great problems on which the thoughts of politicians are even now concentrated is the hopeless decadence of the one theocracy of modern Europe, of the great type and representative of the alliance of politics and theology. That throne on which it seemed as though the changeless Church had stamped the impress of her own perpetuity—that throne which for so many centuries of anarchy and confusion had been the Sinai of a protecting and an avenging law—that throne which was once the centre and the archetype of the political system of Europe, the successor of Imperial Rome, the inheritor of a double portion of her spirit, the one power which seemed removed above all the vicissitudes of politics, the iris above the cataract, unshaken amid so much turmoil and so much change—that throne has in our day sunk into a condition of hopeless decrepitude, and has only prolonged its existence by the confession of its impotence. Supported by the bayonets of a foreign power, and avowedly incapable of self-existence, it is no longer a living organism, its significance is but the significance of death. There was a time when the voice that issued from the Vatican shook Europe to its foundations, and sent forth the proudest armies to the deserts of Syria. There was a time when all the valour and all the chivalry of Christendom would have followed the banner of the Church in any field and against any foe. Now a few hundred French, and Belgians, and Irish are all who would respond to its appeal. Its august antiquity, the reverence that centres around its chief, the memory of the unrivalled influence it has exercised, the genius that has consecrated its past, the undoubted virtues that have been displayed by its rulers, were all unable to save the papal government from a decadence the most irretrievable and the most hopeless. Reforms were boldly initiated, but they only served to accelerate its ruin. A repressive policy was attempted, but it could not arrest the progress of its decay. For nearly a century, under every ruler and under every system of policy, it has been hopelessly, steadily, and rapidly declining. At last the influences that had so long been corroding it attained their triumph. It fell before the Revolution and has since been unable to exist, except by the support of a foreign army. The principle of its vitality has departed.

No human pen can write its epitaph, for no imagination can adequately realise its glories. In the eyes of those who estimate the greatness of a sovereignty, not by the extent of its territory, or by the valour of its soldiers, but by the influence which it has exercised over mankind, the papal government has had no rival, and can have no successor. But though we may not fully estimate the majesty of its past, we can at least trace the causes of its decline. It fell because it neglected the great truth that a government to be successful must adapt itself to the ever-changing mental condition of society, that a policy which in one century produces the utmost prosperity, in another leads only to ruin and to disaster. It fell because it represented the union of politics and theology, and because the intellect of Europe has rendered it an anachronism by pronouncing their divorce. It fell because its constitution was essentially and radically opposed to the spirit of an age in which the secularisation of politics is the measure and the condition of all political prosperity.

The secularisation of politics is, as we have seen, the direct consequence of the declining influence of dogmatic theology. I have said that it also reacts upon and influences its cause. The creation of a strong and purely secular political feeling diffused through all classes of society, and producing an ardent patriotism, and a passionate and indomitable love of liberty, is sufficient in many respects to modify all the great departments of thought, and to contribute largely to the formation of a distinct type of intellectual character.

It is obvious, in the first place, that one important effect of a purely secular political feeling will be to weaken the intensity of sectarianism. Before its existence sectarianism was the measure by which all things and persons were contemplated. It exercised an undivided control over the minds and passions of men, absorbed all their interests, and presided over all their combinations. But when a purely political spirit is engendered, a new enthusiasm is introduced into the mind, which first divides the affections and at last replaces the passion that had formerly been supreme. Two different enthusiasms, each of which makes men regard events in a special

point of view, cannot at the same time be absolute. The habits of thought that are formed by the one, will necessarily weaken or efface the habits of thought that are formed by the other. Men learn to classify their fellows by a new principle. They become in one capacity the cordial associates of those whom in another capacity they had long regarded with unmingled dislike. They learn to repress and oppose in one capacity those whom in another capacity they regard with unbounded reverence. Conflicting feelings are thus produced which neutralise each other; and if one of the two increases, the other is proportionately diminished. Every war that unites for secular objects nations of different creeds, every measure that extends political interests to classes that had formerly been excluded from their range, has therefore a tendency to assuage the virulence of sects.

Another consequence of the intellectual influence of political life is a tendency to sacrifice general principles to practical results. It has often been remarked that the English constitution, which is commonly regarded as the most perfect realisation of political freedom, is beyond all others the most illogical, and that a very large proportion of those measures which have proved most beneficial, have involved the grossest logical inconsistencies, the most partial and unequal applications of some general principle. The object of the politician is expediency, and his duty is to adapt his measures to the often crude, undeveloped, and vacillating conceptions of the nation. The object, on the other hand, of the philosopher is truth, and his duty is to push every principle which he believes to be true to its legitimate consequences regardless of the consequences which may follow. Nothing can be more fatal in politics than a preponderance of the philosophical; or in philosophy, than a preponderance of the political spirit. In the first case, the ruler will find himself totally incapable of adapting his measures to the exigencies of exceptional circumstances; he will become involved in inextricable difficulties by the complexity of the phenomena he endeavours to reduce to order; and he will be in perpetual collision with public opinion. In the second case, the thinker will be continually harassed by considerations of expediency which introduce the bias of the will into what should be a purely intellectual process, and impart a timidity and a disingenuousness to the whole tone of his thoughts. There can, I think, be little doubt that this latter influence is at present acting most unfavourably upon speculative opinions in countries where political life is very powerful. A disinterested love of truth can hardly coexist with a strong political spirit. In all countries where the habits of thought have been mainly formed by political life, we may discover a disposition to make expediency the test of truth, to close the eyes and turn away the mind from any arguments that tend towards a radical change, and above all to make utilitarianism a kind of mental perspective according to which the different parts of belief are magnified or diminished. All that has direct influence upon the well-being of society is brought into clear relief; all that has only an intellectual importance becomes unrealised and inoperative. It is probable that the capacity for pursuing abstract truth for its own sake, which has given German thinkers so great an ascendency in Europe, is in no slight degree to be attributed to the political languor of their nation.

This predisposition acts in different ways upon the progress of Rationalism. It is hostile to it on account of the intense conservatism it produces, and also on account of its opposition to that purely philosophical spirit to which Rationalism seeks to subordinate all departments of speculative belief. It is favourable to it, inasmuch as it withdraws the minds of men from the doctrinal aspect of their faith to concentrate them upon the moral aspect, which in the eyes of the politician as of the rationalist is infinitely the most important.

But probably the most important, and certainly the most beneficial, effect of political life is to habituate men to a true method of enquiry. Government in a constitutional country is carried on by debate, all the arguments on both sides are brought forward with unrestricted freedom, and every newspaper reports in full what has been said against the principles it advocates by the ablest men in the country. Men may study the debates of Parliament under the influence of a strong party bias, they may even pay more attention to the statements of one party than to those of the other, but they never imagine that they can form an opinion by an exclusive study of what has

been written on one side. The two views of every question are placed in juxtaposition, and everyone who is interested in the subject examines both. When a charge is brought against any politician men naturally turn to his reply before forming an opinion, and they feel that any other course would not only be extremely foolish but also extremely dishonest. This is the spirit of truth as opposed to the spirit of falsehood and imposture, which in all ages and in all departments of thought has discouraged men from studying opposing systems, lamented the circulation of adverse arguments, and denounced as criminal those who listen to them. Among the higher order of intellects the first spirit is chiefly cultivated by those philosophical studies which discipline and strengthen the mind for research. But what philosophy does for a very few political life does, less perfectly indeed but still in a great degree, for the many. It diffuses abroad not only habits of acute reasoning, but also, what is far more important, habits of impartiality and intellectual fairness, which will at last be carried into all forms of discussion, and will destroy every system that refuses to accept them. Year after year, as political life extends, we find each new attempt to stifle the expression of opinion received with an increased indignation, the sympathies of the people enlisted on behalf of the oppressed teacher, and the work which is the object of condemnation elevated in public esteem often to a degree that is far greater than it deserves. Year after year the conviction becomes more general that a provisional abnegation of the opinions of the past and a resolute and unflinching impartiality are among the highest duties of the enquirer, and that he who shrinks from such a research is at least morally bound to abstain from condemning the opinions of his neighbour.

If we may generalise the experience of modern constitutional governments, it would appear that this process must pass through three phases. When political life is introduced into a nation that is strongly imbued with sectarianism, this latter spirit will at first dominate over political interests, and the whole scope and tendency of government will be directed by theology. After a time the movement I have traced in the present chapter will appear. The secular element will emerge into light. It will at length

obtain an absolute ascendency, and, ex-
pelling theology successively from all its
political strongholds, will thus weaken its
influence over the human mind. Yet in
one remarkable way the spirit of sectarianism will still survive : it will change
its name and object, transmigrate into
political discussion, and assume the form
of an intense party-spirit. The increasing tendency, however, of political
life seems to be to weaken or efface this
spirit, and in the more advanced stages of
free government it almost disappears. A
judicial spirit is fostered which leads men
both in politics and theology to eclecticism,
to judge all questions exclusively on the
ground of their intrinsic merits, and not
at all according to their position in theological or political systems. To increase
the range and intensity of political interests is to strengthen this tendency ;
and every extension of the suffrage thus
diffuses over a wider circle a habit of
thought that must eventually modify
theological belief. If the suffrage should
ever be granted to women, it would probably, after two or three generations,
effect a complete revolution in their
habits of thought, which by acting upon
the first period of education would influence the whole course of opinion.

Such then have been some of the leading tendencies produced by that purely
secular political spirit which is itself a
result of the declining influence of theology. It now remains for us to examine
the second branch of our subject—the
secularisation of the basis or principle of
authority upon which all political struc-
tures rest.

In the course of the last few years a
great many insurrections of nations
against their sovereigns have taken place,
which have been regarded with warm
approval by the public opinion of the
most advanced nations in Europe. Some
countries have cast off their rulers in
order by coalescing to form one powerful
State, others because those rulers were
tyrannical or incapable, others because
the system of their government had grown
antiquated, and others in order to realise
some historical nationality. In many
cases the deposed rulers had been bound
to their people by no distinct stipulations,
had violated no law, and had been guilty
of no extraordinary harshness. The
simple ground upon which these changes
were justified was that the great majority
of the nation desired them, and that

ground has generally been acquiesced in
as sufficient. To exhibit in the plainest
form the change that has come over
public opinion it may be sufficient to say
that for many centuries all such insurrections would have been regarded by theologians as mortal sins, and all who
participated in them as in danger of
perdition.

The teaching of the early Fathers on
the subject is perfectly unanimous and
unequivocal. Without a single exception, all who touched upon the subject
pronounced active resistance to the established authorities to be under all circumstances sinful. If the law enjoined what
was wrong it should be disobeyed, but no
vice and no tyranny could justify revolt.[1]
This doctrine was taught in the most
emphatic terms, not as a counsel of
expediency applicable to special circumstances, but as a moral principle universally binding upon the conscience. It was
taught in the midst of the most horrible
persecutions. It was taught when the
Christians were already extremely numerous, and their forbearance, notwithstanding their numbers, was constantly claimed
as a merit.[2] So harmonious and so
emphatic are the Patristic testimonies
upon the subject, that the later theologians who adopted other views have been
utterly unable to adduce any passages in
their support, and have been reduced to
the melancholy expedient of virtually
accusing the Early Christians of hypocrisy,
by maintaining that, notwithstanding
the high moral tone they assumed on the
subject, the real cause of their submission
was their impotence,[3] or to the ludicrous
expedient of basing a system of liberal
politics on the invectives of Cyril and
Gregory Nazianzen against the memory
of Julian.[4]

---

[1] See Grotius, *De Jure Belli et Pacis*, lib. i. cap. 4 ;
Taylor, *Ductor Dubitantium*, lib. iii. cap. 3, and also
the list of authorities cited by Gregory XVI. in his bull
to the Bishops of Poland, "concerning the maxims of
the Catholic Church on submission to the civil power";
Lamennais, *Affaires de Rome*, pp. 308–317. But perhaps the fullest exposition of the Patristic sentiments
on the subject is in a very able book called *Sacro-Sancta
Regum Majestas*, published at Oxford at the beginning
of the Great Rebellion.

[2] Striking instances of this are given by Grotius, *De
Jure*, lib. i. c. iv. § 7.

[3] This has been maintained among others by Milton
and Gronovius among the Protestants, and by Bellarmine and (in more modern times) by Bianchi among the
Catholics. See Bianchi, *Traité de la Puissance ecclésiastique* (trad. Peltier, Paris, 1857), tom. i. pp. 639–642.

[4] This appears to have been a favourite argument of
the French Protestants : *Avis aux Réfugiez sur leur
prochain Retour en France*, p. 43. To these the
Gallican Catholics replied that Julian was dead when

It is manifest that such a doctrine is absolutely incompatible with political liberty. "A limited monarch," as even the Tory Hume admitted, "who is not to be resisted when he exceeds his limitations is a contradiction in terms." Besides, in almost every case, the transition from an absolute to a limited monarchy has been the result of the resistance of the people, and the whole course of history abundantly proves that power, when once enjoyed, is scarcely ever voluntarily relinquished. From these considerations Grotius and many other writers have concluded that a Christian people, when oppressed by tyrants, is bound to sacrifice its hopes of liberty to its faith, while Shaftesbury and his followers have denounced Christianity as incompatible with freedom. But to those who regard the history of the Church not as one homogeneous whole but as a series of distinct phases, the attitude of its early leaders will appear very different. For the first condition of liberty is the establishment of some higher principle of action than fear. A government that rests on material force alone must always be a tyranny, whatever may be the form it assumes, and at the time Christianity became supreme the Roman Empire was rapidly degenerating into that frightful condition. Increasing corruption had destroyed both the tie of religion and the tie of patriotism, and the army was the sole arbiter of the destinies of the State. After a time the invasion of the barbarians still further aggravated the situation. Hordes of savages, fresh from a life of unbounded freedom, half-frenzied by the sudden acquisition of immense wealth, and belonging to many different tribes, were struggling fiercely for the mastery. Society was almost resolved into its primitive elements; force had become the one measure of dignity. Alone amid these discordant interests the Christians taught by their precepts and their example the obligation of a moral law, and habituated men to that respect for authority and that exercise of self-

the invectives were delivered. Hilary, however, inveighed vehemently against the Arian Emperor Constantius, in the lifetime of the latter; and Bianchi, in a very ingenious fashion, argues from this that Constantius must have been virtually deposed on account of his heresy, for respect to lawful sovereigns is among the plainest duties; and as St. Hilary called Constantius "a precursor of Antichrist," "a rascal," and "an object of malediction," &c., &c., it may be inferred that he did not regard him as his lawful sovereign. (*Puissance eccl.*, tom. i. pp. 651, 652.)

restraint which form the basis of every lasting political structure. Had they followed the example of others they might probably have more than once saved themselves from frightful persecutions, and might possibly have acquired an ascendency some time before the accession of Constantine. But, guided by a far nobler instinct, they chose instead to constitute themselves the champions of legality, they irradiated submission with a purer heroism than has ever glowed around the conqueror's path, and they kept alive the sacred flame at a time when it had almost vanished from the earth. We may say that they exaggerated their principle, but such exaggeration was probably essential to its efficacy. The temptations to anarchy and insubordination were so great that had the doctrine of submission been stated with any qualifications, had it been stated in any but the most emphatic language, it would have proved inoperative. Indeed, what cause for resistance could possibly have been more just than the persecutions of a Nero or a Diocletian? Yet it was in the reign of Nero that St. Paul inculcated in unequivocal language the doctrine of passive obedience, and it was the boast of Tertullian and other of the Fathers, that at a time when Rome was swarming with Christians, the most horrible persecutions were endured without a murmur or a struggle. Such conduct, if adopted as a binding precedent, would arrest the whole progress of society, but considered in its own place in history, it is difficult to overvalue it.

Besides this, it should be remembered that the Early Church had adopted a system of government that was based upon the most democratic principles. It can be no exaggeration to say, that if the practice of electing bishops by universal suffrage had continued, the habits of freedom would have been so diffused among the people, that the changes our own age has witnessed might have been anticipated by many centuries, and might have been effected under the direct patronage of Catholicism. This, however, was not to be. The system of episcopal election was far in advance of the age, and the disorders it produced were so great that it was soon found necessary to abolish it. At the same time many circumstances pointed out the Roman See as the natural centre of a new form of organisation. The position Rome occupied in the world, the increasing authority of the bishop resulting from the transfer of the civil ruler to Constantinople, the admirable administrative and organising genius the Roman ecclesiastics had inherited from the Empire, their sustained ambition, the splendour cast upon the see by the genius and virtues of St. Gregory and St. Leo, the conversion of the barbarians, the destruction of the rival sees of Jerusalem, Antioch, and Alexandria, and the Greek schism—all tended to revive in another form the empire Rome had so long exercised over the destinies of mankind.

When the papal power was fully organised, and during the whole of the period that elapsed between that time and the Reformation, the rights of nations against their sovereigns may be said to have been almost unnoticed. The great question concerning the principle of authority lay in the conflicting claims of temporal sovereigns and of popes. Although the power the latter claimed and often exercised over the former has produced some of the most fearful calamities, although we owe to it in a great degree the Crusades and religious persecution, and many of the worst features of the semi-religious struggles that convulsed Italy during the middle ages, there can be no question that it was on the whole favourable to liberty. The simple fact that nations acknowledged two different masters was itself a barrier to despotism, and the Church had always to appeal to the subjects of a sovereign to enforce its decisions against him. There was therefore a certain bias among ecclesiastics in favour of the people, and it must be added that the mediæval popes almost always belonged to a far higher grade of civilisation than their opponents. Whatever may have been their faults, they represented the cause of moral restraint, of intelligence, and of humanity in an age of physical force, ignorance, and barbarity.

It is not necessary to follow in detail the history of the encroachments of the spiritual upon the civil power, or to enter into the interminable controversies about the power of deposition. Such topics are only connected indirectly with the subject of the present chapter, and they have been treated with great ability by several well-known writers.[1] There are, however, two points connected with them to which it may be advisable to refer. In the first place, in judging the question as to the right of the Pope to depose sovereigns, it is evident that the advantage must have always remained with the former, in an age in which he was himself regarded as the final arbiter of moral questions. Every conclusion was then arrived at not by way of reasoning but by way of authority, and, with the very doubtful exception of general councils, there was no higher authority than the Pope. General councils too were rare occurrences; they could only be convened by the Pope, and in the majority of cases they were the creatures of his will. When a bull of excommunication had been launched, the sovereign against whom it was directed might indeed assemble a council of the bishops of his own people, and they might condemn the excommunication, but, however strong might be their arguments, their authority was necessarily inferior to that which was opposed to them. They might appeal to the declarations of the Fathers, but the right of interpreting those declarations rested with the Church of which the Pope was, in fact, the authoritative representative. Nor had he any difficulty in this respect. If it was said that the early bishops enjoined absolute submission to the pagan persecutors, it was answered that this was an irrelevant argument, for the Church only claimed the power of deposing those who by baptism were placed under her dominion. If it was rejoined that the same submission was shown under Constantius or Valens or Julian, the reply was that the weakness of the Christians was the cause of their resignation, and that the fact of the Church possessing the power of excommunication did not at all imply that she was bound on every legitimate occasion to exercise it. If, in fine, the passages in which the Fathers dilated upon the sinfulness of all rebellion against the sovereign were adduced, it was answered that the Pope exhorted no one to such rebellion,

Gallican point of view, in his *Defence of the Articles of the Gallican Church*, and from an ultramontane point of view by Bianchi, *On Ecclesiastical Power*. This last book, which is a work of exceedingly extensive learning but of undisguised and indeed dishonest partiality, was published originally in Italian in 1745, and directed especially against the opinions of Giannone. The French translation was made in 1857, and consists of two (in every sense of the word) most ponderous volumes. It is now the great standard work of the ultramontane party.

[1] A clear secular view of the subject is given by Mr. Hallam, in the chapter on the "Increase of Ecclesiastical Authority," in his *Hist. of the Middle Ages*. It has also been examined very fully by Bossuet, from a

for by the sentence of deposition the sovereign had been deprived of his sovereignty.[1] In this way the Patristic utterances were easily evaded, and the ecclesiastical authority of the Pope made it almost a heresy to question his claims.

In the next place it should be observed that this doctrine of deposition was not so much an isolated assumption on the part of the Popes as a logical and necessary inference from other parts of the teaching of the Church. The point on which the controversies between Catholics on this subject have chiefly turned is the right of the Popes to condemn any notorious criminal to public penance, a sentence which involved the deprivation of all civil functions, and therefore in the case of a sovereign amounted to deposition.[2] But whether or not this right was always acknowledged in the Church, there can be little doubt that the power which was generally conceded to the ecclesiastical authorities of relaxing or annulling the obligation of an oath necessarily led to their political ascendency, for it is not easy to see how those who acknowledged the existence of this power could make an exception in favour of the oath of allegiance.

When the rise of the scholastic philosophy had introduced into Christendom a general passion for minute definitions, and for the organisation and elaboration of all departments of theology, the attitude of hostility the Church had for some time exhibited towards the civil power was more or less reflected in the writings that were produced. St. Thomas Aquinas indeed, the ablest of all these theologians, distinctly asserts the right of subjects to withhold their obedience from rulers who were usurpers or unjust;[3] but this opinion, which was probably in advance of the age, does not appear to have been generally adopted, or at least generally promulgated. The right of popes to depose princes who had fallen into heresy was, however, at this time constantly asserted.[1] To the schoolmen too we chiefly owe the definition of the doctrine of the mediate character of the Divine Right of Kings, which is very remarkable in the history of opinions as the embryo of the principles of Locke and Rousseau. It was universally admitted that both popes and kings derived their authority from the Deity, and from this fact the royal advocates inferred that a pope had no more power to depose a king than a king to depose a pope. But, according to some of the schoolmen, there was this distinction between the cases : a pope was directly and immediately the representative of the Almighty, but a king derived his power directly from the people. Authority, considered in the abstract, is of divine origin ; and when the people had raised a particular family to the throne, the sanction of the Deity rested upon its members, but still the direct and immediate source of regal power was the nation.[2] Although this doctrine was not asserted in the popular but in the Papal interest, and although it was generally held that the people having transferred their original authority to the sovereign were incapable of recalling it, except perhaps in such extreme cases as when a sovereign had sought to betray to a foreign power the country he ruled, it is not the less certain that we have here the first link of a chain of principles that terminated in the French Revolution.

After all, however, it is rather a matter of curiosity than of importance to trace among the vast mass of speculations bequeathed to us by the schoolmen the faint outlines of a growing liberalism. Whatever may have been the opinions of a few monkish speculators, however splendid may have been the achievements of a few industrial half-sceptical republics,[3] it was not till the Reformation

---

[1] As one of the leading supporters of the Papal party put it with amusing coolness : "Certe licet Paulus dixerit 'omnis anima potestatibus sublimioribus subdita sit' nunquam addidit, etiam potestatibus excommunicatis, vel deprivatis a Papa." (Suarez, *De Fide*, lib. vi. cap. 4.)

[2] Bianchi, *Puissance ecclésiastique*, tom. i. pp. 550–571. Louis le Débonnaire seems to have been deposed in this way.

[3] "Principibus sæcularibus in tantum homo obedire tenetur in quantum ordo justitiæ requirit. Et ideo si non habeant justum principatum sed usurpatum, vel si injusta præcipiant, non tenentur eis subditi obedire, nisi forte per accidens propter vitandum scandalum vel periculum." (*Summa*, Pars. ii. Quæst. civ. art. 6.)

[1] Bossuet simply remarks that for some centuries after St. Thomas the schoolmen seem to have been nearly unanimous on this point, but that it is manifest that they were mistaken ! (See Bianchi, tom. i. pp. 135, 136.) The writer among the schoolmen who was most favourable to liberty was the Englishman William of Okham. (Milman, *Hist. of Latin Christianity*, vol. vi. pp. 470–474.)

[2] Suarez, *De Fide*, lib. iii. cap. 2 ; Bianchi, ch. i. These theologians of course endeavour to trace back their distinction to the origin of Christianity, but its formal definition and systematic enforcement are due mainly to the schoolmen.

[3] The political influence of the Italian republics upon English public opinion was very powerful in the seventeenth century, when the habit of travelling became general among the upper class of Englishmen, and

that the rights of nationalities became a great question in Europe. The spirit of insubordination created by the struggle, and the numerous important questions which Protestantism submitted to the adjudication of the multitude, predisposed the people to enlarge the limits of their power; while the countless sects that were appealing to popular favour, and the frequent opposition of belief between the governors and the governed, ensured a full discussion of the subject. The result of this was the creation of a great variety of opinions, the views of each sect being determined mainly by its circumstances, or, in other words, by the predisposition resulting from its interests.

If we begin our review with the Ultramontane party in the Church of Rome, which especially represented the opinions of the Popes, we find that it was confronted with two great facts. In the first place, a multitude of sovereigns had embraced Protestantism simply to emancipate themselves from Papal control; and in the next place, the Catholic population in several countries was sufficiently numerous to resist with some chance of success their Protestant rulers. The points, therefore, which were most accentuated in the teaching of the writers of this school were the power of the Pope to depose sovereigns, especially for heresy, and the right of the people to resist an heretical ruler. The vigour with which

when a large proportion of the highest intellects acquired in Italy a knowledge of the Italian writers on government, and an admiration for the Italian constitutions, and especially for that of Venice. The highest representative of this action of the Italian upon the English intellect was Harrington. His *Oceana*, though published under the Commonwealth and dedicated to Cromwell, was altogether uninfluenced by the inspiration of Puritanism; and it was only by the intercession of Cromwell's favourite daughter, Lady Claypole, that its publication was permitted. (Toland, *Life of Harrington*.) It is remarkable that, while Harrington's writings were avowedly based in a very great degree upon those of Italians, they also represent more faithfully than any others of the seventeenth century what are regarded as the distinctive merits of English liberty. That a good government is an organism, not a mechanism—in other words, that it must grow naturally out of the condition of society, and cannot be imposed by theorists—that representative assemblies with full powers are the sole efficient guardians of liberty—that liberty of conscience must be allied with political liberty—that a certain balance should be preserved between the different powers of the State, and that property produces empire, are among the main propositions on which Harrington insists; and most of them are even now the main points of difference between English liberty and that which emanates from a French source. Harrington was also a warm advocate of the ballot. He was answered by Ferne, Bishop of Chester, in a book called *Pian-Piano*; by Matthew Wren, son of the Bishop of Ely, and in the *Holy Commonwealth* of Baxter.

these propositions were maintained is sufficiently illustrated by the dealings of the Popes with the English Government; and the arguments in their support were embodied by Cardinal Bellarmine in his treatise *On the Supremacy of the Sovereign Pontiff over Temporal Affairs*, and by the famous Jesuit Suarez in his *Defence of the Faith*. The Parliament of Paris ordered the first of these works to be burnt in 1610, and the second in 1614.

The most ardent and by far the most able champions of Ultramontanism were the Jesuits, who, however, went so far beyond the other theologians in their principles that they may be justly regarded as a separate class. The marvellous flexibility of intellect and the profound knowledge of the world that then at least characterised their order soon convinced them that the exigencies of the conflict were not to be met by following the old precedents of the Fathers, and that it was necessary to restrict in every way the overgrown power of the sovereigns. They saw, what no others in the Catholic Church seem to have perceived, that a great future was in store for the people, and they laboured with a zeal that will secure them everlasting honour to hasten and direct the emancipation. By a system of the boldest casuistry, by a fearless use of their private judgment in all matters which the Church had not strictly defined, and above all by a skilful employment and expansion of some of the maxims of the schoolmen, they succeeded in disentangling themselves from the traditions of the past, and in giving an impulse to liberalism wherever their influence extended. Suarez, in the book to which I have just referred, devoted himself especially to the question of the mediate or immediate nature of the Divine Right of Kings.[1] It was a question, he acknowledged, that could not be decided either by Scripture or the Fathers; but the schoolmen were on the whole favourable to the latter view, and the Popes had often asserted their own authority over sovereigns, which according to Ultramontane principles was almost decisive of the question. He elaborated the doctrine of the "social contract" with such skill and emphasis as to place the sovereign altogether upon a lower level than the nation, while the Pope towered

[1] Suarez, *De Fide*, lib. iii. cap. 2. This book of Suarez was written in reply to one by James I. of England.

over all. According to these principles, the interests of the sovereign should be subordinated to those of the people. The king derived all his power immediately from the State : and in a case of extreme misgovernment, when the preservation of the State required it, the nation might depose its sovereign,[1] and might, if necessary, depute any person to kill him.[2] The case of an heretical prince was still plainer : for heresy being a revolt against that divine authority to which the sovereign ultimately owed his power, it in a certain sense annulled his title to the throne ; still, as the Pope was the arbiter of these questions, a sentence of deposition should precede rebellion.[3] The Pope had the power of issuing this sentence on two grounds—because he was the superior of the temporal ruler, and also because heresy was a crime which fell under his cognisance, and which was worthy of temporal penalties. To deny that the Pope could inflict such penalties on heretics, no matter what may be their rank, is to fall under the suspicion of heresy ;[4] to deny that death is a natural punishment for heresy was to assail the whole system of persecution which the Church had organised. In defending this doctrine against the charges brought against it on the ground of its dangerous consequences, Suarez maintained that the deposed king could only be killed by those whom the Pope had expressly authorised ;[5]

but there can be little doubt that the Jesuits looked with a very indulgent eye on all attempts at assassination that were directed against a deposed sovereign who was in opposition to the Church.

It would however be a mistake to suppose that the Jesuits advocated liberal principles only with a view to theological advantages or in Protestant countries or under the shelter of ecclesiastical authorities. More than once they maintained even their most extreme forms in the midst of Catholic nations, and, strange as the assertion may appear, it is in this order that we find some of the most rationalistic intellects of the age. Two of the leading characteristics of a rationalistic mind, as we have already seen, are a love of appealing to the general principles of natural religion rather than to dogmatic tenets, and a disposition to wrest the latter into conformity with the former : and of these two tendencies we find among the Jesuits some striking examples. The famous work of Mariana *Concerning the King and the Regal Institution* will furnish us with an illustration of these truths.

This extremely remarkable book was published at Toledo in 1599, and it bears at its commencement the approbation of the leaders of the Jesuits.[1] It was dedicated to Philip III., for whose benefit it was written : and it must be acknowledged that, among the countless works that have been dedicated to sovereigns, it would be impossible to find one more free from the taint of adulation. Its ostensible object was to collect a series of moral precepts for the benefit of sovereigns, but the really important part, and that with which we are alone concerned, is the examination of the rights of nations against their sovereigns. The cardinal point upon which this examination turns is a distinction which some of the schoolmen had derived from Aristotle, and which became very prominent in the beginning of the seventeenth century, between a king and a tyrant, as two things almost generically different. A ruler who belonged to the latter class had no right to the name of king, nor could he claim the privileges or the reverence attached to it ; and to be a tyrant, as Mariana explained, it was not necessary to be a usurper.[2] Every ruler, however legitimate, belongs

---

[1] He says that "Potestatem hanc deponendi regem esse posse vel in ipsa republica vel in Summo Pontifice, diverso tamen modo. Nam in republica solum per modum defensionis necessariæ ad conservationem suam,....tum ex vi juris naturalis quo licet vim vi repellere, tum quia semper hic casus ad proprium reipublicæ conservationem necessarius, intelligitur exceptus in primo illo fœdere quo respublica potestatem suam in regem transtulit....At vero in Summo Pontifice est hæc potestas tanquam in superiori habente jurisdictionem ad corripiendum reges." (*De Fide*, lib. vi. cap. iv.)

[2] "Ergo quando respublica juste potest regem deponere, recte faciunt ministri ejus regem cogendo vel interficiendo si sit necesse." (*Ibid.*) Suarez adds, however, that before pronouncing a sentence of deposition against the sovereign it is at least advisable and becoming (though not absolutely necessary) for the nation to apply to the Pope for his sanction. This notion has been developed at length by De Maistre, *Le Pape.*

[3] "Statim per hæresim rex ipso facto privatur aliquo modo dominio et proprietate sui regni, quia vel confiscatum manet vel ad legitimum successorem Catholicum ipso jure transit, et nihilominus non potest statim regno privari, sed juste illud possidet et administrat donec per sententiam saltem declaratoriam criminis condemnetur." (Lib. vi. cap. iv.)

[4] Bianchi has collected a striking chain of passages in defence of this proposition (tom. i. pp. 145-147).

[5] "Si Papa regem deponat, ab illis tantum poterit expelli vel interfici quibus ipse id commiserit." (*De Fide*, lib. vi. c. iv.)

[1] It is signed by Stephanus Hojeda, Visitor of the Jesuits in the province of Toledo.
[2] *De Rege et Regis Institutione*, pp. 55-65 (1st ed.).

to this category if the main principle of his government is selfishness, and if he habitually sacrifices the interests of his people to his lusts or to his pride. Such rulers are the worst of evils, the enemies of the human race. They had been figured by the ancients in the fables of Antæus, the Hydra, and the Chimæra, and the greatest achievements of the heroes of antiquity had been their destruction.[1]

This being the case, the important question arose, whether it is now lawful to kill a tyrant?[2] That there should be no equivocation as to the nature of the inquiry, Mariana takes for his text the recent assassination of Henri III. of France by Clement. He relates in a tone of evident admiration, how this young Dominican, impelled by a religious enthusiasm and having fortified his courage by the services of the Church, had contrived to obtain an interview with the king, had stabbed him to death with a poisoned knife, and had himself fallen beneath the swords of the attendants. "Thus," he says, "did Clement perish, as many deem the eternal honour of France—a youth but four-and-twenty years of age, simple in mind and weak in body : but a higher might confirmed both his courage and his strength."[3]

In examining the moral character of this act there was a great division of opinion. Very many extolled it as worthy of immortality ; others, however, whose learning and sagacity were not to be despised, severely condemned it. They said that it was not lawful for a single un-authorised individual to condemn and slaughter the consecrated ruler of a nation —that David did not dare to slay his bitterest enemy because that enemy was the Lord's anointed—that amid all the persecutions the Early Church underwent no Christian hand was ever raised against the monsters who filled the throne—that political assassinations have in the great majority of cases injured the cause they were meant to serve, and that if their legitimacy were admitted all respect for sovereigns would vanish and universal anarchy would ensue. "Such," added Mariana, "are the arguments of those who espouse the cause of the tyrant, but

the champions of the people can urge others that are not less numerous or less powerful."[1] He then proceeds, in a strain that leaves no doubt as to his own opinion, to enumerate the arguments for tyrannicide. The people had conceded a certain measure of their power to their sovereign, but not in such a manner that they did not themselves retain a greater authority, and might not at any time recall what they had given if it was misused.[2] The common voice of mankind had enrolled the great tyrannicides of the past among the noblest of mankind. Who ever censured the acts or failed to admire the heroism of Harmodius or Aristogeiton or Brutus, or of those who freed their land from the tyranny of a Domitian, a Caracalla, or a Heliogabalus ? And what was this common sentiment but the voice of nature that is within us, teaching us to distinguish what is right from what is wrong ?[3] If some ferocious beast had been let loose upon the land, and was devastating all around him, who would hesitate to applaud the man who at the risk of his life had ventured to slay it ? Or what words would be deemed too strong to brand the coward who remained a passive spectator while his mother or the wife of his soul was torn and crushed ? Yet the most savage animal is but an inadequate image of a tyrant, and neither wife nor mother has so high a claim upon our affections as our country.[4]

These were the chief arguments on either side, and it remained to draw the conclusion. The task, Mariana assures us, is not difficult, but it is necessary to distinguish between different cases. In the first place the tyrant may be a conqueror who by force of arms, and without any appeal to the people, had obtained possession of the sovereign power. In this case there was no obscurity : the example of Ehud was a guide, and the tyrant might be justly slain by any of the

---

[1] *De Rege*, &c., p. 62.
[2] *Ibid.* lib. i. ch. vi. "An tyrannum opprimere fas sit?"
[3] P. 69. Mr. Hallam observes that the words "æternum Galliæ decus" were omitted in the later editions, which, however, in other respects scarcely differed from the first. (*Hist. of Lit.*)

[1] P. 72.
[2] "Certe a republica unde ortum habet regia potestas, rebus exigentibus Regem in jus vocari posse et si sanitatem respuat principatu spoliari. Neque ita in principem jura potestatis transtulit ut non sibi majorem reservarit potestatem....Populis volentibus tributa nova imperantur, leges constituuntur ; et quod est amplius populi sacramento jura imperandi quamvis hæreditaria successori confirmantur." (Pp. 72, 73.) Very remarkable words to have been written by a Spaniard and a priest nearly a century before Locke.
[3] "Et est communis sensus quasi quædam naturæ vox mentibus nostris indita, auribus insonans lex, qua a turpi honestum secernimus." (P. 74.)
[4] Pp. 72–74.

people.[1] The next case was that of a sovereign elected by the nation, or who had obtained his throne by hereditary right, but who sacrificed his people to his lusts, infringed the laws, despised true religion, and preyed upon the fortunes of his subjects. If there existed in the nation any authoritative assembly of the people, or if such an assembly could be convoked, it should warn the sovereign of the consequences of his acts, declare war against him if he continued obdurate, and, if no other resource remained, pronounce him to be a public enemy and authorise any individual to slay him.[2] If in the last place the king who had degenerated into a tyrant had suppressed the right of assembly, no steps should be taken unless the tyranny was flagrant, unquestionable, and intolerable ; but if this were so, the individual who, interpreting the wish of the people, slew the sovereign, should be applauded.[3] Nor was this doctrine likely to lead to as many tragedies as was supposed. "Happy indeed would it be for mankind were there many of such unflinching resolution as to sacrifice life and happiness for the liberty of their country : but the desire of safety withholds most men from great deeds, and this is why of the great multitude of tyrants so few have perished by the sword." "It is, however, a salutary thought for princes to dwell upon, that if they oppress their people and make themselves intolerable by their vices, to slay them is not only without guilt but is an act of the highest merit."[4]

There was, however, one aspect of the question of tyrannicide which presented to the mind of the author considerable difficulty, and to which he devoted a separate chapter. That to slay a tyrant with a dagger was a meritorious act he was perfectly convinced, but to mingle poison with his food was a somewhat different matter. This distinction, Mariana tells us incidentally, was first suggested to him, many years before the publication of the book, by one of his scholars, when, as a public instructor, he was impressing his doctrines upon the youth of Sicily.[1] The way in which he resolves it is very remarkable as exhibiting the modes of thought or reasoning from which these speculations sprang. He in the first place shows very clearly that nearly every argument that justifies the one mode of slaughter may be also urged in favour of the other ; but notwithstanding this, he concludes that poison should be prohibited, because he says it is prohibited by that common sentiment of mankind which is the voice of nature and the test of right.[2]

The doctrine of tyrannicide, of which Mariana may be regarded as the chief apostle, is one that is eminently fitted to fascinate men who are just emerging out of a protracted servitude, and who have not yet learned to calculate the ulterior consequences of political acts. To slay a royal criminal, who, for the gratification of his own insatiable vanity, is causing the deaths of thousands of the innocent, and blasting the prosperity of his nation, is an act that seems at first sight both laudable and useful, especially if that sovereign had violated the obligations by which he had bound himself. A man who has committed an act of treason, which the law will punish by death, has incurred a penalty and retained a privilege. The penalty is that he should be put to

---

[1] "In eo consentire tum philosophos tum theologos video, eum principem qui vi et armis rempublicam occupavit, nullo praeterea jure, nullo publico civium consensu, perimi a quocumque, vita et principatu spoliari posse." (Pp. 74, 75.) A few lines lower comes the eulogy of Ehud. The "consenting theologians" are not cited—and, indeed, Mariana scarcely ever quotes an ecclesiastical authority—but the reader may find a great many given in Suarez (*De Fide*, lib. vi. cap. iv.). St. Thomas justified Ehud on this general ground, and on this point seems to have differed little or not at all from Mariana.

[2] "Si medicinam respuat princeps, neque spes ulla sanitatis relinquatur, sententia pronunciata licebit reipublicae ejus imperium detrectare primum, et quoniam bellum necessario concitabitur ejus defendendi consilia explicare....Et si res feret neque aliter se respublica tueri possit, eodem defensionis jure ac vero potiore auctoritate et propria, principem publicum hostem declaratum ferro perimere. Eademque facultas esto cuicumque privato, qui spe impunitatis abjecta, neglecta salute, in conatum juvandi rempublicam ingredi voluerit." (P. 76.)

[3] "Qui votis publicis favens eum perimere tentarit, haudquaquam inique eum fecisse existimabo." (P. 77.)

[4] Pp. 77, 78.

[1] P. 83.

[2] "Nos tamen non quid facturi sint homines sed quid per naturae leges concessum sit despicimus....Et est naturae vox communis hominum sensus vituperantium si quis in alios quantumvis hostes veneno grassetur." (Pp. 83-85.) It is said that Mariana, in his History, has treated kings with considerable deference ; but his anti-monarchical opinions appear very strongly in a short work called *Discourse on the Defects of the Government of the Jesuits*, which contains—what is extremely rare in the writings of the members of the order—a bitter attack on the General, and a fierce denunciation of the despotic principles on which the society is constituted. The following (which I quote from a French translation of 1625) is very characteristic: "Selon mon opinion, la monarchie nous met par terre, non pour estre monarchie ains pour n'estre bien tempérée. C'est un furieux sanglier qui ravage tout par où il passe, et si on ne l'arreste tout court, nous ne devons espérer de repos." (Ch. x.)

death ; the privilege is that he should only be put to death by the constituted authorities and in the legal way. But if in addition to his original crime he has paralysed the law that should avenge it, it may plausibly be argued that he has forfeited his privilege : he has placed himself above the law and has therefore placed himself out of the law and become an outlaw. Besides this, the exceedingly prominent place tyrannicide occupies in the history of the Greeks, the Romans, and the Jews tells powerfully on the imagination, and it is quite certain that none of these nations looked upon the act with the feelings of modern Englishmen.

But to those who take a wider view of the field of politics, the immense danger of encouraging individuals to make themselves the arbiters of the destinies of a nation will be far more than sufficient to counterbalance these arguments. The degree of favour that public opinion shows to political assassinations, though by no means the sole, is perhaps the principal regulator of their number ; for although the conspirator may be prepared to encounter universal obloquy, the direction his enthusiasm has taken is, in the first instance, determined by the mental atmosphere he breathes. And if it be true, as Mariana asserts, that the number of those who possess sufficient resolution to engage in such enterprises is under all cases small, it is also true that those few would usually be men preeminently unfit to adjudicate upon the policy of nations. For the amount of heroism it evokes is no test or measure of the excellence of a cause. Indeed, nothing can be more certain than that the highest displays of courage, self-sacrifice, and enthusiasm, are usually elicited not by those motives of general philanthropy which all men must applaud, but by attachment to some particular class of disputed questions or to the interests of some particular party. The excitement of controversy, the very fact that the opinions in question have but few adherents, the impossibility of triumphing by normal means, and the concentration of every thought upon a single aspect of a single subject, all stimulate fanaticism. The great majority of men will do far more for a cause they have espoused, in spite of the opposition of those around them, than for one that is unquestionably good. We accordingly find that among the many attempts that

were made upon the lives of rulers in the sixteenth century, nearly all were produced by attachment to certain religious opinions which the conspirator desired to see predominate, and from which an immense proportion of the people dissented. Never was there a spirit of more complete and courageous self-sacrifice than instigated Ravaillac to slay perhaps the very best sovereign of modern Europe. And have we not, in our own day, seen the representatives of a sect of revolutionists whose principles are rejected by the great majority of educated men attempting, again and again, to further their views by the assassination of a monarch of a different nation from their own, whose throne is based upon universal suffrage, and who, in the judgment of a large proportion of his contemporaries, has proved himself the chief pillar of order in Europe ?

These considerations, which the old Jesuit writers completely omitted, serve to show that even in the best case—even in those instances in which the conspirator is seeking only what he firmly believes to be good—the practice of tyrannicide is almost always an evil. But we have to add to this the assassinations from corrupt motives that in societies favourable to tyrannicide have always been frequent : we have to add also the danger to the State resulting from that large class of men so prominent in all criminal records who hang upon the border of insanity, who, partly from an excess of vanity and partly from natural weakness of volition, and partly under the influence of a kind of monomania, are drawn by an irresistible fascination to the perpetration of any crime surrounded with circumstances of notoriety : and when we still further consider the perpetual insecurity and the distrust between sovereign and people that must necessarily exist when these conspiracies are frequent, we shall have little hesitation in pronouncing upon the question. Political assassination is denounced, in general terms, as an atrocious crime simply because in the great majority of instances it is so ; and even in the extremely few cases that are generally recognised as exceptions, we have to deduct from the immediate advantages that were obtained the evil of an example that has been misused.

It is arguments of this kind, drawn from expediency, that are now regarded as most decisive on this as on many other questions of political ethics ; but they could have little weight in the early stages of political life, when the minds of men were still moulded by theological discussions, and were consequently predisposed to deduce all conclusions with an inflexible logic from general principles. Tyrannicide accordingly occupied an extremely prominent place in the revival of liberalism in Europe. The first instance in which it was formally supported by a theologian appears to have been in 1408, shortly after the Duke of Orleans had been murdered at the instigation of the Duke of Burgundy, when a priest and, as is generally said, a Franciscan[1] named John Petit, who was then professor of theology in the University of Paris, justified the act, and delivered a public oration in defence of the thesis, " That it is lawful, according to natural and divine law, for every subject to slay or cause to be slain a traitor and disloyal tyrant." This doctrine was afterwards energetically denounced by Gerson and condemned by the Council of Constance.[2] After the Reformation, however, it was very widely diffused. Grévin, one of the immediate successors of Jodelle, and therefore one of the founders of the French drama, brought it upon the stage in a play upon The Death of Cæsar, which was first acted in 1560, and was reprinted with an anti-monarchical preface at the time of Ravaillac.[3] A few years before the publication of the work of Mariana, no less than three Jesuits—Franciscus Toletus, Emmanuel Sa, and the famous Molina—had defended it.[4] The first, who

was made a cardinal in 1583, justified it chiefly in the case of tyrants who had usurped dominion ;[1] but intimated also, that the nation might depose a lawful sovereign, that it might condemn him to death, and that then any individual might slay him. Sa[2] and Molina[3] expressed the same opinion with still greater emphasis, and Balthazar Ayala, the most illustrious Spanish lawyer of the age, in his celebrated work on the Rights of War, which was published in 1582, though utterly repudiating their doctrine concerning tyrants with a lawful title, cordially embraced it in the case of usurpers.[4] The French Jesuits, it is true, appalled by the outcry that was raised against them on account of the work of Mariana, repudiated its principles ; but, in 1611, Mariana found a defender in another Jesuit named Kellerus,[5] who only made a single reservation—that a formal sentence was always necessary before tyrannicide was justifiable. When Henri III. was assassinated by Clement, the Catholics of the League received the news with a burst of undisguised exultation, and in many churches the image of the murderer was placed for reverence upon the altar of God. The Pope publicly pronounced the act to be worthy of ranking with that of Judith, he said that it could only have been accomplished by the special assistance of Providence, and he blasphemously compared it to the Incarnation and to the Resurrection.[6]

[1] He is called so in, I think, every history of the occurrence I have met with ; but a writer in the Journal des Sçavans of 1748 maintains (pp. 994-996) that there is some doubt upon the point. It is worthy of remark that the duke who instigated the murder, and probably inspired the apology, died himself by the hand of an assassin. (Van Bruyssel, Hist. du Commerce Belge, tom. ii. pp. 48, 49.)
[2] Mariana rejects this decree without hesitation, on Ultramontane principles, as not having been confirmed by the Pope (De Rege, p. 79). Suarez seems to think it binding, but argues (De Fide, lib. vi. c. 4) that it applies only to tyrants in regimine, because the Council condemns the opinion that "subjects" may slay a tyrant, and a tyrant in titulo has, properly speaking, no "subjects."
[3] There is a full notice of this play in Charles, La Comédie en France au Seizième Siècle.
[4] Sa was a Portuguese—the other two were Spaniards. The prominence this doctrine acquired in Spain in the reign of Philip II. is probably in part due to the contest of Spain with Elizabeth, who was regarded as a tyrant both in titulo and in regimine, and consequently naturally marked out for assassination. Mariana's book was probably written under Philip II., for the royal privilege to print it was granted only three months after the death of that king.

[1] " Adverte duplicem esse tyrannum ; unum potestate et dominio qui non habet titulum verum sed tyrannice occupat rempublicam : et hunc licet occidere, dum aliter non potest liberari respublica et dum spes est libertatis probabilis ; aliter non licet privato cuilibet occidere. Alterum administrationi qui habet quidem verum titulum sed tyrannice tractat subditos, et hunc non licet absque publica auctoritate occidere." (Summa Casuum Conscientiæ, lib. v. c. vi. p. 653.)
[2] " Tyrannice gubernans juste acquisitum dominium non potest spoliari sine publico judicio ; lata vero sententia potest quisque fieri executor : potest autem deponi a populo etiam qui juravit ei obedientiam perpetuam si monitus non vult corrigi. At occupantem tyrannice potestatem quisque de populo potest occidere, si aliud non sit remedium, est enim publicus hostis." (Aphorism. Confessariorum, verb. Tyrannus.)
[3] " Tyrannum primo modo nefas est privatis interficere ; possit tamen respublica quoad capita convenire, eique resistere, lataque sententia deponere ab administratione atque illum depositum punire. Secundo modo tyrannum quivis de republica potest licite eum interficere." (Comment, pars IV. tract. iii. disp. 6.)
[4] " Tyrannum qui per vim et illegitime principatum occupavit, si tyrannis aliter tolli non possit, occidere cuilibet licitum sit." (De Jure et Officiis Bellicis, lib. i.)
[5] In a book called Tyrannicidium, seu Scitum Catholicorum de Tyranni Internecione. This book (which was written in reply to a Calvinistic attack) contains a great deal of information about the early literature of tyrannicide. It bears the approbation of Busæus, the head of the Jesuits in Northern Germany.
[6] De Thou, liv. xcvi. The Pope was Sixtus V.

On the other hand, it would be unfair to forget the murder of the Duke of Guise in France and of Cardinal Beaton in Scotland, the justification of these instances of political assassination by the most eminent Protestants, and the many seditious works at least verging upon an approval of tyrannicide that issued from the Protestant press.

Still the main champions of tyrannicide were unquestionably the Jesuits, and it is not difficult to discover the reason. It has been said that the despotic character of their government has in these later times proved inimical to the growth of individuality among them, and that, while the institution considered as a whole has flourished, it has failed remarkably to produce originality either in intellect or in character.[1] But however this may be now, it is certain that it was not so in the early days of the society, when a few isolated Jesuits were scattered through a community of heretics waging a continued war against overwhelming numbers. All the resources of their minds were then taxed to the utmost, and they had every motive to encourage an opinion that enabled a single individual, by an act of self-devotion, to sway the destinies of a nation.

It may be said that the work of Mariana is an extreme instance of Jesuitical principles, and in a certain sense this is undoubtedly true. Mariana stands almost alone among his brethren in the directness and absence of qualifications that characterises his teaching, and he is still more remarkably distinguished for the emphasis with which he dwells upon purely political rights. In his book the interests of the Church, though never forgotten, never eclipse or exclude the interests of the people, and all the barriers that are raised against heresy are equally raised against tyranny. But his doctrine of tyrannicide, extreme, exaggerated, and* dangerous as it is, was but a rash conclusion from certain principles which were common to almost all the theologians of his order, and which are of the most vital importance in the history both of civil liberty and of Rationalism. In nearly every writing that issued from this school we find the same desire to restrict the power of the sovereign and to augment the power of the people, the same

determination to base the political system on a doctrine derived from reason rather than from authority, the same tendency to enunciate principles, the application of which would—whether their authors desired it or not—inevitably extend beyond the domain of theology. All or nearly all these writers urged in the interests of the Church that doctrine of a "social contract" which was destined at a later period to become the cornerstone of the liberties of Europe. Nearly all drew a broad distinction between kings and tyrants, nearly all divided the latter into those who were tyrants, as it was said, *in regimine* (that is to say, legitimate rulers who misgoverned), and tyrants *in titulo* (that is to say, rulers with no original authority) ; and nearly all admitted that the Papal deposition, by annulling the title-deeds of regal power, transferred the sovereign from the former class to the latter. These were the really important points of their teaching, for they were those which deeply and permanently influenced the habits of political thought, and on these points the Jesuits were almost unanimous. In the application of them they differed. Usually tyrannicide, at least in the case of a tyrant *in regimine*, was condemned, though, as we have seen, there were not wanting those who maintained that the nation as well as the Pope might depose a sovereign, might condemn him to death and depute any individual to slay him. In the case of a tyrant *in titulo* the more violent opinion seems to have predominated. If he were a conqueror or a usurper, St. Thomas Aquinas had distinctly said that he might be slain.[1] If he were a monarch deposed for heresy, it was remembered that heresy itself might justly be punished with death, and that every act of the deposed sovereign against Catholicity was a crime of the deepest dye perpetrated by one who had no legitimate authority in the State. The cloud of subtle distinctions that were sometimes raised around these questions might give scope for the ingenuity of controversialists, but they could have but little influence over the passions of fanatics.[2]

---

[1] See Suarez, *De Fide*, lib. vi. cap. iv.

[2] On the inevitable tendency of the doctrine of deposition to tyrannicide, there are some good remarks in Bossuet, *Defensio*, lib. i. c. 3. The doctrine of tyrannicide among the Jesuits seems to have died away after Suarez : the political condition of Europe no longer made it of great service to the Church, and the controversies of Jansenism diverted the energy of the Jesuits into new channels. Pascal,

---

[1] Lamennais, *Affaires de Rome*. Since the days of Lamennais the names of Ravignan and Félix have done much to rescue the order from the reproach.

If we now turn from the Jesuits to the Gallican section of the Catholic Church the contrast is very remarkable. We find ourselves in presence of a new order of interests, and consequently of new principles. The great power of the French Church and of the monarchy with which it was connected had early induced its bishops to assume a tone of independence in their dealings with the Papal See that was elsewhere unknown, and a close alliance between Church and State was the manifest interest of both. But in order that such an alliance should be effectual, it was necessary that the Pope should be reduced as much as possible to the level of an ordinary bishop, while the sovereign was exalted as the immediate representative of the Deity. In this way the bishops were freed from the pressure of Papal ascendency, and the sovereign from the worst consequences of excommunication. The advocates of Gallican principles have been able to prove decisively that in nearly all attempts to prevent the encroachments of the Pope upon secular dominion French theologians have been prominent, while their opponents have rejoined with equal truth that the Gallican authorities were by no means unanimous in their sentiments, and that the negation of the Papal claims was not usually thrown into a very dogmatic form.[1] The case of an heretical prince before the Reformation was hardly discussed,[2] and in other cases the rivalry between the two sections of the Church was rather implied in acts than expressed in formal statements. On the one side there was a steady tendency to exalt the spiritual power of the popes above that of the councils, and their temporal power above that of kings; on the other side there was a corresponding tendency in the opposite direction. As the power of deposition was in the middle ages the centre of the more liberal system of politics, and as everything that was taken from the popes was given to the kings, the Gallican teaching was always inimical to freedom. At the same time, as the interference of

in his *Provincial Letters*, barely touches this aspect of the Jesuit teaching.

[1] See on the one side Bianchi, *Puissance Souveraine*, and on the other the *Defensio* of Bossuet.

[2] According to Bianchi, the first Catholic who maintained that the Pope had no power over the temporal possessions of princes who fell into heresy was an Englishman of the time of James I.—William Barclay, the father of the author of the *Argenis*, W. Barclay wrote against and was answered by Bellarmine. (Bianchi, tom. ii. pp. 768, 769.)

an Italian priest with French politics offended the national pride, it was eminently popular; and thus, as in many subsequent periods of French history, patriotism proved destructive to liberty.

It appeared for a short time as if the Reformation were about to give rise to new combinations. The invectives of the Protestants against the papal power produced a momentary reaction in its favour, which was remarkably shown in the States General assembled at Paris in 1615. The Third Estate, either because Protestant principles were diffused among its members or because it represented especially the secular feelings of the middle classes, then proposed, among other articles, one declaring that the Pope possessed no power of deposing sovereigns, or under any circumstances releasing subjects from the oath of allegiance; but the nobles and the clergy refused to ratify it, and Cardinal Perron, probably as the representative of the clergy, asserted the Ultramontane principles with the strongest emphasis.[1]

Very soon, however, a complete change passed over the minds of the French clergy. The Huguenots, in several of their synods, had dwelt with great emphasis upon their denial of the existence of a mediate power between the Deity and a king, and there was some danger that if they possessed the monopoly of this opinion the civil power might be attracted to their side. Besides this the French Protestants made war against their rulers for the purpose of obtaining liberty of conscience, and the French Catholics naturally pronounced these wars to be sinful. In 1668 the Sorbonne asserted the absolute independence of the civil power, and the same thing was again declared in the famous Articles of 1682, which are the recognised basis of Gallicanism. In his defence of these articles Bossuet soon afterwards systematised the whole theology of the school. The general result, as far as regards civil liberty, may be briefly told. The king occupies his throne by the direct and immediate authority of the Deity, and is consequently, in his temporal capacity, altogether independent of the Pope and of the wishes of the people. Every pope who had exercised or claimed a power of deposition had exceeded his functions and been guilty of usurpation; every subject who

[1] Bianchi, tom. i. pp. 96–104.

had raised his hand against the sovereign or his agents had committed a mortal sin. The sole duty of the nation is to obey, and from this obligation no tyranny and no injustice can release it. If the rulers of the people are as wolves, it is for the Christians to show themselves as sheep.[1]

Such was the teaching of the different sections of the Catholic Church. If we now turn to Protestantism we find a diversity at least equally striking and not less manifestly due to the diversity of interests. At the same time, although the opinions advocated by any particular section at a particular time were mainly the result of the special circumstances under which it was placed, there were some general considerations that complicated the movement. In the first place, the fact that the Reformation was essentially an act of spiritual rebellion—an appeal from those in authority to the judgments of the people—gave an impulse to the spirit of insubordination which was still further strengthened by the republican form that many of the new organisations assumed. In the Early Church the ecclesiastical government had combined in a very remarkable manner the principle of authority and the principle of liberty, by magnifying to the highest point the episcopal authority, while the bishops were themselves elected by universal suffrage. But a process of gradual centralisation soon destroyed this balance, and transformed the ecclesiastical organisation from a republic into a monarchy; and although the primitive elements were revived in Protestantism, they were revived in such a way that their original character was essentially falsified. For the system of popular election and the supreme and divine authority of the episcopacy, which in the Early Church formed the two compensatory parts of a single scheme, at the Reformation were violently dissevered and thrown into the strongest antagonism—the Calvinistic Churches constituting themselves the leading champions of the one, while Anglicanism was the representative of the other.

Now it has often been observed, and is in itself sufficiently obvious, that when men have formed an ecclesiastical organisation which is intensely democratic, they will have a certain predisposition in favour of a political organisation of a kindred nature. If in Church government they are accustomed to restrict very jealously the influence of the ruler, to diffuse as much as possible the supreme power, and to regard the will of the majority as the basis of authority, they will scarcely submit without a murmur to a political system in which all power is centralised in a single man, and from which all popular influence has been carefully eliminated. Puritanism has therefore a natural bias towards democracy, and Episcopalianism, which dwells chiefly on the principle of authority, towards despotism. Special circumstances have occasionally modified but seldom or never altogether reversed these tendencies. Both forms have sometimes coalesced cordially with constitutional monarchy; but even in these cases it will usually be found that the Puritans have gravitated towards that party which verges most upon republicanism, and the Episcopalians to that which is most akin to despotism.

Another general tendency which has been much less frequently noticed than the preceding one results from the proportionate value attached by different Churches to the Old and New Testaments. To ascertain the true meaning of passages of Scripture is the business not of the historian but of the theologian, but it is at least an historical fact that in the great majority of instances the early Protestant defenders of civil liberty derived their political principles chiefly from the Old Testament, and the defenders of despotism from the New. The rebellions that were so frequent in Jewish history formed the favourite topic of the one—the unreserved submission inculcated by St. Paul, of the other. When, therefore, all the principles of right and wrong were derived from theology, and when by the rejection of tradition and ecclesiastical authority Scripture became the sole arbiter of theological difficulties, it was a matter of manifest importance in ascertaining the political tendencies of any sect to discover which Testament was most congenial to the tone and complexion of its theology.[1]

The favourable influence Protestantism was destined to exercise upon liberty was early shown. Among the accusations the Catholics brought against both Huss and Wycliffe none was more common than

[1] Defensio, lib. i. c. 15, 16. Avertissements sur les Lettres de M. Jurieu, No. 5.

[1] Hallam, Hist. of Lit.

that they had proclaimed that mortal sin invalidated the title of the sovereign to his throne ; and the last of these Reformers was also honourably distinguished for his strong assertion of the unchristian character of slavery.[1] At the Reformation the different attitudes assumed by different sovereigns towards the new faith and the constant vicissitudes of the religious wars exercised their natural influence upon the opinions of the leaders, but on the whole liberal views strongly predominated, although they were not often thrown into formal statements. Luther and Calvin both fluctuated a good deal upon the subject, and passages have been cited from each by the adherents of both views. It is probable, however, that Calvin ultimately inclined rather to the republican, and Luther—who had been greatly agitated by the war of the peasants—to 'the despotic theory. Zuinglius, without reasoning much on the subject,[2] accepted the liberal principles of his countrymen, and he died bravely upon the battle-field. Ulrich von Hutten appears to have adopted the Reformed tenets mainly as a principle of liberty, emancipating men both from intellectual and from political tyranny. " From truth to liberty and from liberty to truth " was the programme he proclaimed. The country, however, in which Protestantism assumed the most emphatically liberal character was unquestionably Scotland, and the man who most clearly represented its tendency was Knox.

A great writer, whose untimely death has been one of the most serious misfortunes that have ever befallen English literature, and whose splendid genius, matured by the most varied and extensive scholarship, has cast a flood of light upon many of the subjects I am endeavouring to elucidate, has lately traced with a master-hand the antecedents of the Scotch Reformation.[3] He has shown that for a long period before it was accomplished there had been a fierce contest between the aristocracy on the one hand, and the sovereigns and Catholic clergy of Scotland upon the other ; that this struggle at last terminated in the triumph of the aristocracy and the subversion of the Catholic establishment ; that the new clergy, called into existence by a move-

ment that was intensely hostile to the sovereign, were from the first the main promoters of sedition ; and that being hated by the Crown, and having speedily quarrelled with the nobles, they cast themselves for support upon the people, and became the most courageous and energetic of the champions of democracy. The utter contempt for ecclesiastical traditions that characterised the Puritanical sects enabled them without much difficulty to mould their theology into conformity with their wishes : for Scripture was the only guide they acknowledged, and it has been most abundantly proved that from Scripture honest and able men have derived and do derive arguments in support of the most opposite opinions. In all the conflicts with the civil authorities Knox threw himself into the foreground, and constantly asserted, with the most emphatic clearness, that it was the right and even the duty of a nation to resist a persecuting sovereign. Speaking of the persecutions that Mary had directed against the English Protestants, he declared that when they began it was the duty of the English people not merely to have deposed their queen but also to have put her to death ; and he added, with characteristic ferocity, that they should have included in the same slaughter all her councillors and the whole body of the Catholic clergy.[1]

The opinions which Knox embodied chiefly in fierce declamations, and which he advocated mainly with a view to religious interests, were soon after systematised and at the same time secularised by Buchanan in a short dialogue entitled " De Jure Regni apud Scotos," which was published in 1579, and which bears in many respects a striking resemblance to some of the writings that afterwards issued from the Jesuits. In Buchanan, however, we find none of those countless subtleties and qualifications to which the Catholic theologians commonly resorted in order to evade the decisions of the Fathers or the schoolmen, nor do we find anything about the deposing power of the

---

[1] Barrington, *On the Statutes*, p. 280.
[2] See, however, some rather strong passages quoted by Kellerus, *Tyrannicidium*, pp. 73, 74.
[3] See Buckle's *Hist. of Scottish Civilisation.*

[1] " And therfor I fear not to affirm that it had bene the dutie of the nobilitie, judges, rulers, and people of England, not only to have resisted and againstanded Marie, that Jesabel whome they call their queen, but also to have punished her to the death, with all the sort of her idolatrous preestes, together with all such as should have assisted her what tyme that shee and they openly began to suppresse Christes Evangil, to shed the blood of the saincts of God, and to erect that most devillish idolatrie, the Papistical abominations." (Knox, *Appellation.*)

Pope. The principles that were enunciated were perfectly clear and decisive : they were derived exclusively from reason, and they were directed equally against every form of tyranny. The argument is based upon "the social contract." Men were naturally formed for society : in order to arrest the intestine discord that sprang up among them they created kings ; in order to restrain the power of their kings they enacted laws. The nation being the source of regal power is greater than and may therefore judge the king ; the laws being intended to restrain the king in case of collision, it is for the people and not for the ruler to interpret them. It is the duty of the king to identify himself with the law,[1] and to govern exclusively according to its decisions. A king is one who governs by law, and according to the interests of the people ; a tyrant is one who governs by his will, and contrary to the interests of the people. An opinion had been spread abroad by some that a king being trammelled by recognised constitutional ties might be resisted if he violated them, but that a tyrant who reigns where no constitution exists must be always obeyed ; but this opinion was altogether false. The people may make war against a tyrant and may pursue that war until he is slain. Though Buchanan does not expressly defend the slaughter of a tyrant by a private individual, he recalls in language of unqualified praise the memories of the tyrannicides of antiquity.

This little tract, being in conformity with the spirit of the time, and especially with the spirit of the Scotch people, had a very great influence. Its main principles, as we have seen, differ but little from those of St. Thomas Aquinas and the schoolmen ; but by disengaging them from the crowd of theological considerations that had previously rendered them almost inoperative except when religious interests were concerned, Buchanan opened a new stage in the history of liberty. The doctrines, however, which he for the first time systematised had been at a still earlier period diffused among his fellow-countrymen. When Queen Elizabeth, in 1571, put some questions to a Scotch deputation concerning the reasons that had induced the Scots to depose their queen, she was immediately

favoured in reply with a long dissertation on the manifest superiority of nations to their sovereigns ; which, as Camden assures us, and as we can readily believe, she received with extreme indignation.[1] The same principles were no less general among the English Dissenters, and were exhibited alike in their writings and in their policy : Milton only translated into eloquent prose the no less eloquent acts of Cromwell.

It is difficult indeed to overrate the debt of gratitude that England owes both to her own non-episcopal Churches and to those of Scotland. In good report and in evil, amid persecution and ingratitude and horrible wrongs, in ages when all virtue seemed corroded and when apostasy had ceased to be a stain, they clung fearlessly and faithfully to the banner of her freedom. If the Great Rebellion was in England for the most part secular in its causes, it is no less true that its success was in a great measure due to the assistance of the Scotch, who were actuated mainly by religion, to the heroic courage infused into the troops by the English ministers, and to the spirit of enthusiasm created by the noble writings that were inspired by Puritanism. Neither the persecutions of Charles nor the promised toleration of James ever caused them to swerve. Without their assistance English liberty would no doubt have been attained, but no one can say how long its triumph would have been retarded, or what catastrophes would have resulted from the strife. For it is to Puritanism that we mainly owe the fact that in England religion and liberty were not dissevered : amid all the fluctuations of its fortune,[2] it represented the alliance of these two principles, which the predominating Church invariably pronounced to be incompatible.

The attitude of this latter Church forms indeed a strange contrast to that of Puritanism. Created in the first instance by a Court intrigue, pervaded in all its parts by a spirit of the most intense Erastianism, and aspiring at the same time to a spiritual authority scarcely less absolute than that of the Church which it had superseded, Anglicanism was from the beginning at once the most servile

---

[1] As Buchanan (imitating Cicero) tersely puts it, "Rex, lex loquens ; lex, rex mutus."

[1] Camden, *Annal.*, pars II. (ad ann. 1571).
[2] It is worthy of remark, as showing their persistence, that probably the ablest modern advocate of what may be termed the Biblical aspect of liberty was Robert Hall.

and the most efficient agent of tyranny. Endeavouring by the assistance of temporal authority and by the display of worldly pomp to realise in England the same position as Catholicism had occupied in Europe, she naturally flung herself on every occasion into the arms of the civil power. No other Church so uniformly betrayed and trampled on the liberties of her country.[1] In all those fiery trials through which English liberty has passed since the Reformation, she invariably cast her influence into the scale of tyranny, supported and eulogised every attempt to violate the Constitution, and wrote the fearful sentence of eternal condemnation upon the tombs of the martyrs of freedom.[2] That no tyranny however gross, that no violation of the Constitution however flagrant, can justify resistance ; that all those principles concerning the rights of nations on which constitutional government is based are false, and all those efforts of resistance by which constitutional government is achieved are deadly sins, was her emphatic and continual teaching. "A rebel," she declared, "is worse than the worst prince, and rebellion worse than the worst government of the worst prince hath hitherto been." "God placeth as well evil princes as good," and therefore "for subjects to deserve through their sins to have an evil prince and then to rebel against him were double and treble evil by provoking God more to plague them." St. Paul counselled passive obedience under Caligula, Claudius, and Nero, "who were not only no Christians but pagans, and also either foolish rulers or

cruel tyrants"; nay, the Jews owed it even to Nebuchadnezzar, when "he had slain their king, nobles, parents, children, and kinsfolk, burned their country cities, yea Jerusalem itself, and the holy temple, and had carried the residue into captivity." Even the blessed Virgin, "being of the royal blood of the ancient natural kings of Jewry, did not disdain to obey the commandment of an heathen and foreign prince"; much more therefore should we "obey princes, though strangers, wicked, and wrongful, when God for our sins shall place such over us," unless, indeed, they enjoin anything contrary to the Divine command ; but even "in that case we may not in anywise withstand violently or rebel against rulers or make any insurrection, sedition, or tumults, either by force of arms or otherwise, against the anointed of the Lord or any of his officers, but we must in such case patiently suffer all wrongs."[1]

"If I should determine no cases," wrote Jeremy Taylor, when treating the question of resistance in the greatest work on Moral Philosophy that Anglicanism has produced, "but upon such mighty terms as can be afforded in this question, and are given and yet prevail not, I must never hope to do any service to any interest of wisdom or peace, of justice or religion ; and therefore I am clearly of opinion that no man who can think it lawful to fight against the supreme power of his nation can be fit to read cases of conscience, for nothing can satisfy him whose conscience is armour of proof against the plain and easy demonstration of this question.......The matter of Scripture being so plain that it needs no interpretation, the practice and doctrine of the Church, which is usually the best commentary, is now but of little use in a case so plain, yet this also is as plain in itself, and without any variety, dissent, or interruption universally agreed upon, universally practised and taught, that, let the powers set over us be what they will, we must suffer it and never right ourselves."[2]

---

[1] As Macaulay very truly and very eloquently wrote, "The Church of England continued to be for more than 150 years the servile handmaid of monarchy, the steady enemy of public liberty. The divine right of kings and the duty of passively obeying all their commands were her favourite tenets. She held those tenets firmly through times of oppression, persecution, and licentiousness, while law was trampled down, while judgment was perverted, while the people were eaten as though they were bread. Once, and but once—for a moment, and but for a moment—when her own dignity and property were touched, she forgot to practise the submission she had taught." (*Essays*, vol. i. p. 60: ed. 1861.) Hallam, however, has disinterred a curious book called *A Short Treatise of Politique Power*, published by Poynet, Protestant Bishop of Winchester, in 1558, advocating the most seditious doctrines, and among others tyrannicide. But the explanation is simple : Poynet wrote during the persecution of Mary. (*Hist. of Lit.*, vol. ii. pp. 37-40.)

[2] "Eternal damnation is prepared for all impenitent rebels in hell with Satan the first founder of rebellion." "Heaven is the place of good obedient subjects, and hell the prison and dungeon of rebels against God and their prince." (Homily on *Wilful Rebellion*.)

[1] Homilies on *Wilful Rebellion* and on *Obedience*. The same doctrines were laid down in the Canons of Convocation in 1606, and by the University of Oxford in 1662, when censuring a preacher named Knight, who had said that subjects oppressed on account of religion might sometimes resist. (Hallam, *Const. Hist.*, vol. i. p. 415.)

[2] *Ductor Dubitantium*, lib. iii. cap. iii. Ussher, who was perhaps still more competent than Taylor to express the sentiments of the Fathers, was at least equally emphatic. See Elrington's *Life of Ussher*.

The teaching of which these extracts are examples was constantly maintained by the overwhelming majority of the Anglican clergy for the space of more than 150 years, and during the most critical periods of the history of the English Constitution. When Charles I. attempted to convert the monarchy into a despotism, the English Church gave him its constant and enthusiastic support. When, in the gloomy period of vice and of reaction that followed the Restoration, the current of opinion set in against all liberal opinions, and the maxims of despotism were embodied even in the oath of allegiance,[1] the Church of England directed the stream, allied herself in the closest union with a court whose vices were the scandal of Christendom, and exhausted her anathemas not upon the hideous corruption that surrounded her, but upon the principles of Hampden and of Milton. All through the long series of encroachments of the Stuarts she exhibited the same spirit. The very year when Russell died was selected by the University of Oxford to condemn the writings of Buchanan, Baxter, and Milton, and to proclaim the duty of passive obedience in a decree which the House of Lords soon afterwards committed to the flames.[2] It was not till James had menaced her supremacy that the Church was aroused to resistance. Then indeed, for a brief but memorable period, she placed herself in opposition to the Crown, and contributed largely to one of the most glorious events in English history. But no sooner had William mounted the throne than her policy was reversed, her whole energies were directed to the subversion of the constitutional liberty that was then firmly established, and it is recorded by the great historian of the Revolution that at least nine-tenths of the clergy were opposed to the emancipator of England. All through the reaction under Queen Anne, all through the still worse reaction under George III., the same spirit was displayed. In the

first period the clergy, in their hatred of liberty, followed cordially the leadership of the infidel Bolingbroke ; in the second they were the most ardent supporters of the wars against America and against the French Revolution, which have been the most disastrous in which England has ever engaged. From first to last their conduct was the same, and every triumph of liberty was their defeat.

There are contrasts that meet us in the history of Rationalism which it is impossible to realise without positive amazement. When we remember for how long a period the Church of England maintained that resistance to the regal power was in all cases a deadly sin, and that such men as a Washington or a Garibaldi were doomed "to burn together in hell with Satan the first founder of rebellion," it is hard to say whether the present condition of English public opinion shows more clearly the impotence of the theologians who were unable to prevent so absolute a rejection of their principles or the elasticity of the Church that has survived it.

Although, however, the general current of Anglican ecclesiastical opinion was on this subject extremely steady, there was one divine who forms a marked exception, and that divine was one of the ablest that Protestantism has ever produced. Hooker—not indeed the greatest, but perhaps the most majestic of English writers—was not more distinguished for his splendid eloquence than for his tendency to elevate the principles of natural right, and for his desire to make the Church independent of the State. In his discussions of the nature of the civil power both of these characteristics are strikingly shown. In examining the true origin and functions of government he scarcely ever appeals to the decisions of the Fathers, and not often to the teachings of Scripture, but elaborates his theory from his own reason, aided by the great philosophers of antiquity. His doctrine in its essential parts differs little from that of Buchanan. Individuals joining together in societies created kings to govern them. The regal power was at first absolute, but soon " men saw that to live by one man's will became the cause of all men's misery, and this constrained them to come into laws wherein all men might see their duty."[1] Although the

---

vol. i. p. 239. Berkeley made an ingenious attempt to show that passive obedience was ordained by the law of nature ; see his *Discourse on Passive Obedience.*

[1] In the clause that it was not lawful "on any pretence whatever to take up arms against the king." This clause was expunged at the Revolution (Allen's *Hist. of Royal Prerogative in England*, p. 89). Magna Charta had declared that kings who violated it might be resisted.

[2] This decree is given in full in Wodrow's *Hist. of Church of Scotland*, vol. iii. p. 506. See on this whole subject, Hallam, *Const. Hist.*, vol. ii. pp. 459-465 (ed. 1854).

[1] *Eccl. Pol.*, lib. i. sec. 10.

king received his authority from the people in the first instance, it was not on that account the less sacred, for "on whom the same is bestowed even at men's discretion they likewise do hold it of Divine right." At the same time the king was subject to the law, and as the power of enacting laws resides with the whole people, any attempt upon his part to enact laws contrary to the will of the people is a tyranny. Such laws are, in fact, a nullity.[1]

From these principles we should naturally have supposed that Hooker would have drawn the conclusion of Buchanan, and would have maintained that the will of the people is a sufficient reason for changing the government. It is, however, an extremely remarkable fact, as showing the spirit of the class to which he belonged, that this great writer, who had exhibited so clearly the fundamental propositions of modern liberalism, who had emancipated himself to so great a degree from the prejudices of his profession, and who wrote with the strongest and most manifest bias in favour of freedom, shrank to the last from this conclusion. He desired to see the power of the government greatly restricted ; he eulogised constitutional government as immeasurably superior to despotism ; he even thought that the violation of a constitutional tie was a just cause for resistance, but when he came to the last great question he dismissed it with these melancholy words : " May then a body-politick at all times withdraw, in whole or in part, that influence of dominion which passeth from it if inconvenience doth grow thereby? It must be presumed that supreme governors will not in such cases oppose themselves and be stiff in detaining that the use whereof is with public detriment, but surely without their consent I see not how the body should be able by any fresh means to help itself, saving when dominion doth escheat."[2]

[1] " The lawful power of making laws to command whole political societies of men belongeth so properly unto the same entire societies, that for any prince or potentate, of what kind soever, upon earth to exercise the same of himself and not by express commission immediately and personally received from God, or else from authority derived at the first from their consent upon whose persons they impose laws, it is no better than mere tyranny. Laws are not therefore which public approbation hath not made so." (*Eccl. Pol.*, lib. i. sec. 10.)
[2] *Eccl. Pol.*, b. viii. ch. ii. At a later period Burnet threw himself into the liberal movement as cordially as Locke, but he was almost isolated in the Church.

It is scarcely necessary, I think, to review in detail the other works which appeared in England upon this subject. A large proportion of them at least are well known : their arguments are little more than a repetition of those which I have described, and after all they were not the real causes of the development. A spirit of freedom, fostered in England by the long enjoyment of political and social institutions far superior to those of other nations, had produced both a capacity and an ambition for freedom which must inevitably have triumphed, and it is a matter of comparative insignificance what particular arguments were selected as the pretext. On the other hand the genius and the circumstances of the Anglican Church predisposed its leaders towards despotism, and they naturally grasped at every argument in its support. I may observe, however, that there was a slight difference of opinion among the English supporters of despotic principles.[1] The earliest school, which was represented chiefly by Barclay and Blackwood, appears to have acknowledged that men were born free, and to have admitted some possible circumstances under which resistance was lawful. The later school, which was led by Filmer, Heylin, Mainwaring, and Hobbes, entirely denied this original freedom. The *Patriarcha* of Filmer, which was the principal exposition of the doctrines of the last class, rested, like some of the writings of the Gallican school, upon the supposition that the political government is derived from and is of the same nature as paternal government,[2] and it concluded

[1] This change is clearly shown in Sydney.
[2] Bossuet maintained this, remarking that "Abimelech," which was a name originally common to all the kings of Palestine, signifies "My father king." (*Defensio*, lib. i. c. 3.) In England the patriarchal theory of government seems to have become especially popular under James I. (see Hallam's *Hist. of Lit.*, vol. iii. p. 439 [ed. 1854]), but there are many traces of it at an earlier period. Thus in the *Institution of a Christian Man* (1537), and in *The Necessary Doctrine and Erudition for any Christian Man* (1543), passive obedience is unequivocally enforced as a deduction from the Fifth Commandment. "I die," said Lord Capel on the scaffold, in 1649, "for keeping the Fifth Commandment, given by God Himself, and written with His own finger. It commands obedience to parents ; and all divines, differ as they will on other points, agree in this, and acknowledge that it includes the magistrate" (Marsden, *History of the Later Puritans, from 1642 to 1662*, p. 320). Milton, on the other hand, said : "Pater et rex diversissima sunt. Pater nos genuit ; at non rex nos sed nos regem creavimus. Patrem natura dedit populo, regem ipse populus dedit sibi ; non ergo propter regem populus, sed propter populum rex est." (*Defensio pro Pop. Ang.*, cap. i.)

that resistance was in all cases sinful. This book was in the first instance answered by Sydney, who opposed to it "the social compact," but rested a considerable portion of his argument on the Old Testament. At the Revolution, however, the clergy having revived the principles of Filmer,[1] Locke thought it necessary to publish another answer, and accordingly wrote his famous treatise of *Government*, which differs from that of Sydney in being almost entirely based upon secular considerations, although a considerable space is devoted to the refutation of the theological arguments of his opponent. Locke adopts almost entirely the principles of Hooker, for whom he entertained feelings of deep and well-merited admiration, but he altogether discards the qualifications by which Hooker had sometimes neutralised his teaching. All government, he maintains, is the gift of the people for the people's advantage, and therefore no legislation is legitimate which is contrary to the people's interests, and no change of government wrong which is in accordance with them.[2] Prerogative is that measure of power which the nation concedes to its ruler, and the nation may either extend or restrict it.[3] To impose taxes on a people without their consent is simply robbery.[4] Those who are appointed by the people to legislate have no power to transfer their authority to others,[5] nor may they govern except by established laws.[6] And as the sovereignty in the first instance emanates from the people, so the people may reclaim it at will. The ability with which these views

were urged, and the favourable circumstances under which they appeared, gave them an easy triumph, and the Revolution made them the basis of the Constitution.

It is well worthy of remark that the triumph of toleration and the triumph of civil liberty should both have been definitively effected in England at the same time, and should both have found their chief champion in the same man. Both were achieved by laymen in direct opposition to the Church and in the moment of her extreme depression. Both too represented a movement of secularisation: for by the first, theological questions were withdrawn from the sphere of politics, and by the second the principle of authority was removed from a theological to a secular basis. But what especially characterises the triumph of English liberty is that, although it was effected contrary to the Church and contrary to the clergy, it was not effected contrary to religion. This—which, when we consider the mournful history of Continental liberty, may perhaps be regarded as the happiest fact in English history—was no doubt due in a great measure to the success with which the Dissenters had associated religion and liberty; to the essential imperfection of the Anglican theory, which left undefined the question when allegiance may be transferred to a triumphant rebel,[1] and also to the admirable moderation of Somers and Locke: but it was still more due to the genius

[1] As Locke says, "I should not speak so plainly of a gentleman long since past answering (Sir R. Filmer), had not the pulpit of late years publicly owned his doctrine, and made it the current divinity of the times." (Preface to *Treatise on Government*.)

[2] "The end of government being the good of the community, whatever alterations are made in it tending to that end cannot be an encroachment upon anybody, since nobody in government can have any right tending to any other end." (*On Government*, c. xiv.)

[3] *Ibid.*, c. xviii.

[4] "If anyone shall claim a power to lay or levy taxes on the people without their consent, he thereby invades the fundamental law of property, and subverts the end of government." (*Ibid.*, c. xi.)

[5] "The legislature cannot transfer the power of making laws, for, it being but a delegated power from the people, they who have it cannot pass it over to others." (*Ibid.*, c. xi.) This doctrine was very justly regarded by Grattan and Plunket as decisive against the constitutional character of the Act of Union between England and Ireland, which was passed without a dissolution, by a Parliament which was notoriously corrupted and had been elected long before the measure was contemplated

[6] *Ibid.*

[1] The passages from Scripture which the Anglican divines cited as their political rules would seem to imply that allegiance should always be rendered to the sovereign *de facto*. This doctrine, however, was at the Revolution generally and indignantly repudiated by the clergy, who maintained that while King James held his court at St. Germains he alone was entitled to their allegiance. However, after the Revolution, Sancroft published a work called *Bishop Overall's Convocation Book*, which had been approved by both Houses of Convocation at the beginning of the reign of James I. This work (which had not before been published) asserted in the strongest terms the doctrine of passive obedience, based it on the patriarchal theory of government, and declared that, in case of a change of government being effected by unrighteous means, allegiance should be transferred to the new power when it was "thoroughly settled." Thereupon Sherlock declared that he considered himself bound by the voice of the Church to take the oaths of allegiance to the government of William (which, to the world at large, seemed very far indeed from "thoroughly settled"), and he accordingly accepted the deanery of St. Paul's. The explosion that followed is admirably described by Macaulay (ch. xvii.). It is evident that the doubt hanging over this part of the theory of the Anglican divines, was favourable to liberty—in the first place by weakening the logical force of that theory, and in the second place by giving those who shrank from absolutely rejecting it a pretext for joining the new government.

of the Reformation. Never did Protestantism exhibit more clearly its admirable flexibility of doctrine, its capacity for modifying and recasting its principles to meet the wants of succeeding ages, than when, without any serious religious convulsion, the political system of England was based upon the direct negation of the unanimous teaching of the Early Church and of the almost unanimous teaching of the national one. And the contrast the history of English liberty bears to that of Continental liberty becomes still more remarkable when we remember the attitude exhibited by the avowed opponents of Christianity. In England, with the exception of Shaftesbury, the most eminent of these were either indifferent or opposed to the movement. Under the government of the Stuarts, Hobbes not only maintained the most extreme views of Taylor and Ussher, but carried them to a point from which even those divines would have recoiled : for the result of his philosophy was nothing less than to make the civil ruler the supreme arbiter of the moral law. During the reaction under Queen Anne the clerical party owed its chief strength to the genius of Bolingbroke, who consolidated its broken forces, and elaborated with an almost dazzling eloquence his ideal of " A Patriot King " to counterbalance the ideal of liberty. And at a still later period, while Bishop Horsley was proclaiming that " subjects had nothing to say to the laws except to obey them," Hume was employing all his skill in investing with the most seductive colours the policy of the Stuarts, in rendering the great supporters of liberty in the seventeenth century either odious or ridiculous, and in throwing into the most plausible aspects the maxims of their opponents.[1]

It is remarkable that while England and France have been the two nations which have undoubtedly done most for the political emancipation of mankind, they have also been those in which the national Churches were most bitterly opposed to freedom. We have seen the manner in which the double movement of secularisation and of liberty was effected in the Protestant country ; it remains to trace the corresponding development in the Catholic one.

It was upon the French Protestants that the office which in England was filled by the Puritans naturally devolved. The fact that they were a minority, and often a persecuted minority, gave them a bias in favour of liberty, while at the same time their numbers were sufficiently great to communicate a considerable impulse to public opinion. Unfortunately, however, the extreme arrogance and the persecuting spirit they manifested whenever they rose to power rendered them peculiarly unfit to be the champions of liberty ; while at the same time their position as a minority of the nation, governed mainly by religious principles in an era of religious wars, rendered their prevailing spirit profoundly antinational. Wherever sectarian feeling is keenly felt it proves stronger than patriotism. The repulsion separating men as members of different religions becomes more powerful than the attraction uniting them as children of the same soil, and the maxim that a man's true country is not that in which he was born but that of his co-religionists, being professed, or at least acted on, treason is easily justified. In the present day, when the fever of theology has happily subsided, Ireland forms an almost solitary example of a nation in which national interests and even national pride are habitually sacrificed to sectarianism ; but in the sixteenth century such a sacrifice was general, and although in France at least it was made quite as much by the majority as by the minority, it naturally appeared in the latter case more conspicuous and repulsive. The atrocious persecutions the majority directed against the minority rendered the alienation of the latter from the national sympathies both natural and excusable, but it did not appear so to the persecutors. The majority have therefore usually been able to enlist the patriotic feelings of the multitude against the minority, and this has weakened the political influence of the latter.

In the political teaching of the French Protestants it is easy to detect two distinct

[1] Among the less eminent freethinkers there were, indeed, some exceptions to this tendency. Thus Tindal wrote a tract against Passive Obedience in 1694, a defence of Toleration in 1697, and a defence of a Free Press in 1698. Toland too wrote, in 1702, a somewhat remarkable book called *Anglia Libera*, in which he advocated very eloquently the political principles of Locke, denounced strongly the doctrine of Hobbes that a sovereign has a right to dictate the religion of his subjects, and maintained that " the success of the Protestant religion, politically speaking, depends on the liberty of the several States of Europe " (p. 185). Toland also edited the *Oceana*, and wrote the Lives of Harrington and Milton. But the most eminent avowed English freethinkers of the seventeenth and eighteenth centuries are those mentioned in the text, with the exception of Gibbon, who sat in Parliament as a Tory.

currents. Whenever the Pope or the Ultramontane theologians put forward a claim to the power of deposition, the Protestants constituted themselves the champions of loyalty, and endeavoured in this manner to win the favour of the rulers. Thus we find their synods condemning with great solemnity the treatise of Suarez, protesting in the most emphatic language against the disloyalty of the Catholics, and assuring the sovereign in their petitions that they at least recognised no mediate power between the king and the Almighty.[1] If we were to judge their opinions by the language of some of their petitions, we might imagine that they were no less favourable to despotism than the Anglicans. But such a judgment would do them great injustice. No body of men ever exhibited a greater alacrity in resisting persecution by force, and, with a few exceptions, the general tone of their theology as of their policy was eminently favourable to liberty. Opinions on these subjects have so completely changed since the seventeenth century, that the defence of the French Protestants is chiefly to be found in the writings of their adversaries; and, according to modern notions, it would be difficult to find a nobler eulogy than is implied in the accusation of one of the ablest of these, who declared that the general tendency of the Protestant writings was always to the effect that "kings and subjects were reciprocally bound by contract to the performance of certain things in such a manner that if the sovereign failed to perform his promise the subjects were freed from their oath of allegiance, and might engage themselves to new masters."[2]

The opinions of the French Protestants on these points may be more easily ascertained from their actions than from their writings; and the right of resisting religious persecution was naturally more considered than the right of resisting political tyranny. Jurieu strenuously asserted the first right; and although Saurin is said to have taken the opposite view,[1] the numerous rebellions of the Protestants leave no doubt as to their general sentiments. The two most remarkable works bearing upon the secular aspect of the question that issued from this quarter were the *Franco-Gallia* of Hotman, and the *Vindiciæ contra Tyrannos* of Junius Brutus.

The first of these was published in 1573. Its author (who had escaped from France to Geneva at the time of the massacre of St. Bartholomew) was one of the most learned lawyers of the day, and the chief advocate of the Protestant view of some of the legal questions that arose about the succession of the crown.[2] The *Franco-Gallia* is an elaborate attempt to prove that the Crown of France is, by right, not hereditary but elective. The arguments are drawn in part from general considerations about the origin of government, which Hotman attributed to the will of the people,[3] but chiefly from facts in French history. The writer also attempts to show, in an argument that was evidently directed against Catherine de' Medici, that the exclusion of women from the French throne implied, or at least strongly recommended, their exclusion from the regency, and that on every occasion in which they had exercised the supreme power disastrous consequences had ensued.[4]

A much more remarkable book was the *Vindiciæ contra Tyrannos*, which was published about the same time as the *Franco-Gallia*, and translated into French in 1581, and which, being written with much ability, exercised a very considerable influence. Some have ascribed it, but apparently without reason, to Hotman—others to Linguet or to Parquet. The author, whoever he may be, holds, like Hooker, that the regal authority is, in the first instance, derived from the

---

[1] Many instances of this are collected by Bianchi (tom. i. pp. 46–84), but the fullest account I have met with is in a very clever anonymous book (written from a strong Catholic point of view, and ascribed by some to an author named Pellison, and by others to Bayle), called *Avis aux Réfugiez sur leur prochain Retour en France*, par M. C. L. A. A. P. D. P. The condemnation of the book of Suarez was by a Synod of Tonneins, in 1614. On the other hand, on the extremely liberal views of Jurieu, who preceded both Sydney and Locke, see Michelet, *Hist. de Louis XIV.*, pp. 431–436. The book in which Jurieu especially expressed them is his *Soupirs de la France esclave*.

[2] *Avis aux Réfugiez*, pp. 64, 65 (ed. 1692).

[1] Michelet, *Hist. de Louis XIV.* (1860), p. 432.

[2] The works of Hotman were collected in three large volumes, in 1600. After the *Franco-Gallia* the best known are the *Brutum Fulmen*, which was written on the occasion of the excommunication of the King of Navarre; and the *Anti-Tribonius*, which was written in opposition to the revival of Roman legislation. Joseph Scaliger said he helped in the composition of the *Franco-Gallia* (*Scaligeriana*, art. *Hottomannus*).

[3] *Franco-Gallia*, lib. i. c. 9.

[4] Lib. i. c. 24. So Knox: "To promote a woman to beare rule is repugnant to nature, contumelie to God, a thing most contrarious to his reveled will and approved ordinance; and finallie it is the subversion of good order, of all equitie and justice." (*Monstrous Regiment of Women.*)

people, but that notwithstanding this it is held by divine right. From this consideration he argues that a king is bound by two pacts, on the observance of which his legitimacy depends—a pact to God that he will govern according to the divine law, and a pact to the people that he will govern according to their interests.[1] A nation may resist by arms a sovereign who has violated the divine law, because the first of these pacts is then broken, and also because it is part of the Providential system that subjects should be punished for the crimes of their ruler, which implies that they are bound to prevent them.[2] This last proposition the author maintains at length from the Old Testament. Whenever the king violated the divine command, some fearful chastisement was inflicted upon the nation, and the chief office of the prophets was to signalise these violations, and to urge the people to resistance. Every page of Jewish history bears witness to this, and at the present day the Jews are dispersed because their ancestors did not snatch Christ from the hands of Pilate. But it is impossible to go so far without advancing a step further; for if the Jewish precedent is to be applied, it is manifest the divine law is violated not merely by the persecution of truth, but also by the toleration of error. No crime was more constantly denounced or more fiercely punished under the old Dispensation than religious tolerance. No fact is more legibly stamped upon the Jewish writings than that, in the opinion of their authors, a Jewish sovereign who permitted his people to practise unmolested the rites of an idolatry which they preferred was committing a sin. Nor does the author of the book we are considering shrink from the consequence. He quotes, as an applicable precedent, the conduct of the people who at the instigation of Elijah massacred the whole priesthood of Baal, and he maintains that the toleration of an "impious sacred rite" is a justifiable cause of rebellion.[3]

The question then arose in what manner this resistance was to be organised. And here the writer separates himself clearly from the school of Mariana, for he strongly denies the right of an individual to take the life of a persecutor by way of assassination, however favourable

the people might be to the act. Resistance can only be authorised by a council representing the people. In all well-regulated countries a parliament or assembly of some kind exists which may be regarded as representative; and although each individual member is less than the king, the council, as a whole, is his superior, and the vote of the majority may depose him.[1] When such a council does not exist it may be extemporised, but the elements should, if possible, be drawn from the aristocracy and the magistrates. Nor is it simply a nation that may thus withdraw its allegiance. The author, evidently with a view to the position of the French Protestants, adds that particular districts or cities, if the inhabitants desire it and if their magistrates consent, may likewise withdraw themselves from their allegiance, and may insist upon the maintenance among them of the worship they believe to be right, and the suppression of that which they believe to be wrong.[2] The principles which were thus urged in favour of rebellion on religious grounds apply, with very little change, to rebellions that are purely political. A king who ruled in opposition to the will of his people had broken the pact that bound him, and had consequently become a tyrant. In the case of a tyrant who had occupied the throne by force against the manifest will of the people, but in this case alone, tyrannicide is lawful, and the examples of Harmodius and Aristogeiton, of Brutus and Cassius, are to be commended. In other cases, however, resistance must first be authorised by a council representing the nation, and consisting of its leading men. Like Hotman, the author contends that all monarchy was originally elective, and he adds that it still so retains its character, that the people may at any time reject the family they have raised to the throne, and that the heir-apparent is no more than a candidate for office.[3]

There is one other question treated in this remarkable book, to which I may advert for a moment, because, although not connected with the right of resistance, it throws some light upon the condition of feeling sectarian animosities produced. This question is whether, when the majority of a nation is persecuting the minority, a foreign potentate may interpose by arms to succour his co-re-

[1] *Quæst.* ii.
[2] *Vindiciæ contra Tyrannos*, p. 45 (ed. 1610).
[3] *Vindiciæ*, pp. 38–39, 60.

[1] *Vindiciæ*, p. 45.   [2] P. 60.   [3] P. 79.

ligionists. The reply is that it is his imperative duty to do so. If he does not, he is guilty of the blood of the martyrs— he is even worse than the persecutors : for they at least imagine that they are slaying the wicked, while he permits the slaughter of those whom he knows to be the just.

It is not probable that many of the French Protestants would have sanctioned all the propositions of this book, but the principles of which it may be regarded as the concentration were very widely diffused among the members of both creeds, and had no inconsiderable influence in preparing the way for the Revolution. The chief political importance, however, of the religious wars was not so much in the doctrines they produced as in the circumstances under which those doctrines were advocated. Few things contributed more powerfully to the secularisation of politics than the anarchy of opinions, the manifest subordination of principles to interests, that was exhibited on all sides among theologians. A single battle, a new alliance, a change in the policy of the rulers, a prospect of some future triumph, was sufficient to alter the whole tone and complexion of the teachings of a Church. Doctrines concerning the sinfulness of rebellion, which were urged with the most dogmatic certainty and supported by the most terrific threats, swayed to and fro with each vicissitude of fortune, were adopted or abandoned with the same celerity, curtailed or modified or expanded to meet the passing interests of the hour. They became, as Bayle said, like birds of passage, migrating with every change of climate. In no country and in no Church do we find anything resembling the conduct of those ancient Christians who never advocated passive obedience more strongly than when all their interests were against it. The apostasies were so flagrant, the fluctuations were so rapid, that it was impossible to overlook them, and they continued till the ascendency of theology over politics was destroyed. The keen eye of the great sceptic of the age soon marked the change, and foresaw the issue to which it was leading.[1]

[1] "Voyez l'horrible impudence de quoi nous pelotons les raisons divines, et combien irréligieusement nous les avons rejetées et reprises selon que la fortune nous a changez de place en ces orages publics. Cette proposition si solennelle, s'il est permis au sujet de se rebeller et armer contre son prince pour la défense de la religion, souvienne-vous en quelles bouches cette

It will probably have struck the reader in perusing the foregoing pages, and it will certainly have struck those who have examined the books that have been referred to, that, in addition to theological interests and traditions, there was a purely secular influence derived from the writings of paganism acting strongly in the direction of liberty. The names that recur most frequently in these writings are those of the great heroes of antiquity ; and whether we examine the works of Mariana or Hooker, or of the author of the *Vindiciæ*, we are transported into discussions concerning the origin of power that are drawn mainly from the pagan philosophers.[1]

The influence was, I think, of two kinds—the first being chiefly logical, and the second chiefly moral. At the close of the twelfth or in the beginning of the thirteenth century, two professors of the University of Bologna, named Irnerius and Accursius, devoted themselves to exploring manuscripts of some of the Laws of Justinian, which had for centuries been buried in the great library of Ravenna ; and they not only revived the knowledge of a legislation that was supposed to have perished, but also formed a school of commentators who did good service in elucidating its character. For a very long period the labours that were thus instituted had but little influence outside the domain of jurisprudence ; but at last, in the sixteenth century, a succession of great lawyers arose—of whom Bodin, Cujas, and Alciat were the most remarkable—who applied to the Roman law intellects of a far higher order, and, among other points, paid great attention to its historic development. The balance between the popular and the aristocratic rights and the gradual encroachment of the imperial power upon the liberties of Rome became for about a century favourite subjects of discussion, and

année passée l'affirmative d'icelle étoit l'arcboutant d'un parti, la négative de quel autre parti c'étoit l'arcboutant, et oyez à présent de quel quartier vient la voix et instruction de l'une et de l'autre, et si les armes bruyent moins pour cette cause que pour celle-là." (Montaigne, *Essais*, liv. ii. c. 12.)

[1] This tendency of the classical writings elicited a burst of extreme indignation from Hobbes : "Inter rebellionis causas maximas numerari potest librorum politicorum et historicorum quos scripserunt veteres Græci et Romani lectio.... Mihi ergo monarchiis nihil videtur esse damnosius posse, quam permittere ut hujusmodi libri publice doceantur, nisi simul a magistris sapientibus quibus venenum corrigi possit remedia applicentur. Morbum hunc comparari libet cum hydrophobia, &c." (*Leviathan*, cap. xxix.)

naturally produced similar enquiries concerning modern States. From a philosophical investigation of these questions the lawyers passed by an inevitable transition to an examination of the origin of government, a subject which they pursued, from their own point of view, as energetically as the theologians. Bodin, who was probably the ablest of those who devoted themselves to these studies, cannot indeed be regarded as a representative of the democratic tendency ; for he strenuously repudiated the notion of a social contract, maintaining the origin of monarchy to be usurpation ; he denied that the ruler should be regarded simply as a chief magistrate, and he combated with great force the distinction which Aristotle and the schoolmen had drawn between a king and a tyrant.[1] Hotman, however, in France, and, about a century later, Gronovius and Noodt, who were two of the most eminent Dutch advocates of liberty, based their teaching almost entirely upon these legal researches.[2]

But the principal influence which the pagan writings exercised upon liberty is to be found in the direction they gave to the enthusiasm of Europe. It has no doubt fallen to the lot of many who have come in contact with the great masterpieces of the Greek chisel to experience the sensation of a new perception of beauty which it is the prerogative of the highest works of genius to evoke. A statue we may have often seen with disappointment or indifference, or with a languid and critical admiration, assumes one day a new aspect in our eyes. It is not that we have discovered in it some features that had before escaped our notice ; it is not that we have associated with it any definite ideas that can be expressed by words or defended by argument : it is rather a silent revelation of a beauty that had been hidden, the dawn of a new conception of grandeur, almost the

creation of another sense. The judgment is raised to the level of the object it contemplates ; it is moulded into its image ; it is thrilled and penetrated by its power.

Something of this kind took place in Europe as a consequence of the revival of learning. In the middle ages the ascendency of the Church had been so absolute that the whole measure of moral grandeur had been derived from the ecclesiastical annals. The heroism, the self-sacrifice, the humility, the labours of the saints formed the ideal of perfection, and a greatness of a different order could scarcely be imagined. The names of the heroes of antiquity were indeed familiar, their principal achievements were related, and the original writings in which they were recorded were sometimes read, but they fell coldly and lifelessly upon the mind. The chasm that divided the two periods arose not so much from the fact that the heroes of antiquity were pagans, and therefore, according to the orthodox doctrine, doomed to eternal reprobation, or even from the different direction their heroism had taken, as from the type of character they displayed. The sense of human dignity and the sense of sin, as we have already noticed, are the two opposing sentiments one or other of which may be traced in almost every great moral movement mankind has undergone, and each, when very powerful, produces a moral type altogether different from that which is produced by the other. The first is a proud aspiring tendency, intolerant of every chain, eager in asserting its rights, resenting promptly the slightest wrong, self-confident, disdainful, and ambitious. The second produces a submissive and somewhat cowering tone ; it looks habitually downwards, grasps fondly and eagerly at any support which is offered by authority, and in its deep self-distrust seeks, with a passionate earnestness, for some dogmatic system under which it may shelter its nakedness. The first is the almost invariable antecedent and one of the chief efficient causes of political liberty, and the second of theological change. It is true that as theological or political movements advance they often lose their first character, coalesce with other movements, and become the representatives of other tendencies, but in the first instance one or other of these two sentiments may almost always be detected. It was the

---

[1] He tried, however, to establish a distinction of his own—that a king was one who governed according to the law of nature, and a tyrant one who outraged it.

[2] See Noodt *On the Power of Sovereigns*, and Gronovius *On the Royal Law*, both of which were translated into French by Barbeyrac—the first in 1707, and the second in 1714. They were both in the form of lectures, delivered near the end of the seventeenth century before the University of Leyden, and are both, I think, rather dismal performances. Noodt was a strenuous advocate of liberty of conscience, and also one of the principal assailants of the theological superstitions about usury. Gronovius is best remembered for his Annotations of Grotius, in which he strongly repudiated the servile political maxims of that writer.

sense of sin that taught the old Catholic saints to sound the lowest depths of mortification, of self-sacrifice, and of humiliation; that convulsed the mind of Luther in the monastery at Wittenberg, and persuaded him that neither his own good works nor the indulgences of the Pope could avert the anger of the Almighty; that impelled Wesley and Whitfield to revolt against the frigid moral teaching of their time, and raise once more the banner of Justification by Faith; that urged the first leaders of Tractarianism towards a Church which by authoritative teaching and multiplied absolutions could allay the paroxysms of a troubled conscience.[1] On the other hand, almost every great political revolution that has been successfully achieved has been preceded by a tone of marked self-confidence and pride, manifested alike in philosophy, in general literature, and in religion. When a theological movement has coalesced with a struggle for liberty, it has usually been impregnated with the same spirit. The sense of privilege was much more prominent in the Puritanism of the seventeenth century than the sense of sin, and a fierce rebellion against superstition than humility.[2]

Now the sense of human dignity was the chief moral agent of antiquity, and the sense of sin of mediævalism; and although it is probable that the most splendid actions have been performed by men who were exclusively under the influence of one or other of these sentiments, the concurrence of both is obviously essential to the well-being of society, for the first is the especial source of the heroic, and the second of the religious, virtues. The first produces the qualities of a patriot, and the second the qualities of a saint. In the middle ages, the saintly type being the standard of perfection, the heroic type was almost entirely unappreciated. The nearest approach to it was exhibited by the Crusader, whose valour was nevertheless all subordinated to

superstition, and whose whole career was of the nature of a penance. The want of sympathy between the two periods was so great that for the space of many centuries, during which Latin was the habitual language of literature, the great classical works scarcely exercised any appreciable influence. Sometimes men attempted to mould them into the image of the mediæval conceptions, and by the wildest and most fantastic allegories to impart to them an interest they did not otherwise possess. Thus Troy, according to one monkish commentator, signified Hell, Helen the human soul, Paris the devil, Ulysses Christ, and Achilles the Holy Ghost. Actæon torn by his own dogs was an emblem of the sufferings of Christ; the Rubicon was an image of Baptism.[1] It was not till the revival of learning had been considerably advanced that a perception of the nobility of the heroic character dawned upon men's minds. Then for the first time the ecclesiastical type was obscured, a new standard and aspiration appeared; and popular enthusiasm, taking a new direction, achieved that political liberty which, once created, intensified the tendency that produced it.

We cannot have a better example of this passionate aspiration towards political liberty than is furnished by the treatise On Voluntary Servitude, or, as it was afterwards called, the Contre-un[2] of La Boétie. This writer, who was one of the most industrious labourers in the classical field, never pauses to examine the origin of government, or to adjudicate between conflicting theologians; but he assumes at once, as a fact that is patent to the conscience, that the subordination of the interests of a nation to the caprices of a man is an abuse, and that the great heroes of antiquity are deserving of imitation. The Contre-un is throughout one fiery appeal—so fiery indeed that Montaigne, who published all the other works of La Boétie, refused to publish this—to the people to cast off their oppressors.

[1] See some striking remarks on this in Froude's Nemesis of Faith, pp. 160, 161.
[2] What, for example, could be more opposed to the spirit of the modern Evangelical party, which is supposed by some to represent the Puritanism of the seventeenth century, than those noble lines of the great poet of the latter?—

"Mortals! who would follow me,
Love Virtue, she alone is free:
She can teach ye how to climb
Higher than the sphery chime!
Or, if Virtue feeble were,
Heaven itself would stoop to her."
—Comus.

[1] Cibrario, Economia Politica del Medio Evo, vol. ii. p. 247 (2nd ed.). This tendency was turned to ridicule by Ulrich von Hutten in a very witty but very profane adaptation of the Fables of Ovid to the Christian history (Epistolæ Obscurorum Virorum [London, 1689], pp. 103-107), and also by Rabelais.
[2] The name was given during the life of Montaigne, who praised it. (Essais, liv. i. c. 27.) La Boétie, unfortunately, died when only in his thirty-second year, and nearly all his works appear to have been posthumous. They have all been republished at Paris, by Léon Fougère, in 1846.

It reads like the declamations of the revolutionists of the eighteenth century. "Wretched and insensate people," writes the author, "enamoured of your misery and blind to your interests, you suffer your property to be pillaged, your fields devastated, and your houses stripped of their goods, and all this by one whom you have yourselves raised to power, and whose dignity you maintain with your lives! He who crushes you has but two eyes, but two hands, but one body. All that he has more than you comes from you. Yours are the many eyes that spy your acts, the many hands that strike you, the many feet that trample you in the dust: all the power with which he injures you is your own. From indignities that the beasts themselves would not endure you can free yourselves by simply willing it. Resolve to serve no more, and you are free. Withdraw your support from the Colossus that crushes you, and it will crumble in the dust......Think of the battles of Miltiades, of Leonidas, and of Themistocles, which, after two thousand years, are as fresh in the minds of men as though they were of yesterday; for they were the triumphs not so much of Greece as of liberty......All other goods men will labour to obtain, but to liberty alone they are indifferent, though where it is not every evil follows, and every blessing loses its charm......Yet we were all moulded in the same die, all born in freedom as brothers, born too with a love of liberty which nothing but our vices has effaced."

During the last century language of this kind has by constant repetition lost so much of its force that we can scarcely realise the emotions it kindled when it possessed the freshness of novelty, and in a nation convulsed by the paroxysms of civil war. The French Protestants in 1578 adopted the *Contre-un* as one of the most effectual means of arousing the people to resistance,[1] and as late as 1836 Lamennais made its republication the first measure of his democratic crusade. In the history of literature it will always occupy a prominent place on account of the singular beauty of its language, while in the history of Rationalism it is remarkable as one of the clearest illustrations of the tendency of the classical writings to foster and at the same time to secularise the spirit of liberty.

Owing to the influences I have endeavoured to trace, the ascendency theology had so long exercised over politics was during the religious wars materially weakened, while at the same time the aspiration towards liberty was greatly strengthened. During the comparative torpor that followed the Peace of Westphalia, and still more after the revocation of the Edict of Nantes, the struggle was for a time suspended; and it was not till near the close of the eighteenth century that the question of the rights of nations reappeared prominently in France—this time, however, not under the auspices of the theologians, but of the freethinkers. But, before reviewing the principles that were then urged, it is necessary to notice for a moment the chief causes that were preparing the people for liberty, and without which no arguments and no heroism could have triumphed.

The first of these was the increase of wealth. Whatever may be the case with small communities and under special circumstances, it is certain that, as a general rule, large masses of people can only enjoy political liberty when the riches of the country have considerably increased. In the early periods of civilisation, when capital is very scanty, and when, owing to the absence of machines and of commerce, the results of labour are extremely small, slavery in one form or another is the inevitable condition of the masses. The abject poverty in which they live casts them helplessly upon the few who are wealthy; wages sink to a point that is barely sufficient for the sustenance of life, and social progress becomes impossible. "If the hammer and the shuttle could move themselves," said Aristotle, "slavery would be unnecessary," and machinery having virtually fulfilled the condition, the predicted result has followed.[1] The worst and most degrading forms of labour being performed by machinery, production and consequently capital have been immensely increased, and, progress becoming possible, a middle class has been formed. Commerce not only gives an additional development to this class, but also forms

---

[1] It appeared for the first time, together with the *Franco-Gallia*, in a seditious book called *Mémoires de l'estat de France sous Charles IX*. See *Les Historiettes de Tallemant des Reaux* (ed. 1834), tom. i. p. 395.

[1] See some very good remarks on this in Chevalier, *Lettres sur l'Organisation de Travail* (1848), p. 17.

a bond of union connecting the different parts of the country. The roads that are formed for the circulation of wealth become the channels of the circulation of ideas, and render possible that simultaneous action upon which all liberty depends.

The next great cause of liberty was the increase of knowledge. And here again we may discern the evidence of that inexorable fatality which for so many centuries doomed mankind alike to superstition and to slavery, until the great inventions of the human intellect broke the chain. When we hear men dilating upon the degrading superstitions of Catholicism, marvelling how a creed that is so full of gross and material conceptions could win belief, and denouncing it as an apostasy and an error, it is sufficient to say that for 1,500 years after the establishment of the Christian religion it was intellectually and morally impossible that any religion that was not material and superstitious could have reigned over Europe. Protestantism could not possibly have existed without a general diffusion of the Bible, and that diffusion was impossible until after the two inventions of paper and of printing. As long as the material of books was so expensive that it was deemed necessary to sacrifice thousands of the ancient manuscripts in order to cover the parchment with new writing, as long as the only way of covering those parchments was by the slow and laborious process of transcription, books, and therefore the knowledge of reading, were necessarily confined to an infinitesimal fraction of the community. Pictures and other material images, which a Council of Arras well called the "Book of the Ignorant," were then the chief means of religious instruction, not simply because oral instruction without the assistance of books was manifestly insufficient, but also because, in a period when the intellectual discipline of reading is unknown, the mind is incapable of grasping conceptions that are not clothed in a pictorial form. To those who will observe, on the one hand, how invariably the mediæval intellect materialised every department of knowledge it touched, and on the other hand how manifestly the peculiar tenets of Catholicism are formed either by the process of materialising the intellectual and moral conceptions of Christianity or else by legitimate deductions from those tenets when materialised

—to those who still further observe how every great theological movement, either of progress or retrogression, has been preceded by a corresponding change in the intellectual condition of society, it will appear evident that nothing short of a continued miracle could have produced a lasting triumph of Christian ideas except under some such form as Catholicism presents. It was no doubt possible that small communities like the Waldenses, shut out from the general movement of the age, inspired by a very strong enthusiasm, and under the constant supervision of zealous pastors, might in some small degree rise above the prevailing materialism ; but when we remember how readily nations, considered as wholes, always yield to the spirit of the time, and how extremely little the generality of men strive against the natural bias of their minds, it will easily be conceived that the great mass of men must have inevitably gravitated to materialism. When under such circumstances a spiritual faith exists, it exists only as the appanage of the few, and can exercise no influence or control over the people.

But while superstition is thus the inevitable and therefore the legitimate condition of an early civilisation, the same causes that make it necessary render impossible the growth of political liberty. Neither the love of freedom nor the capacity of self-government can exist in a great nation that is plunged in ignorance. Political liberty was in ancient times almost restricted to cities like Athens and Rome, where public life, and art, and all the intellectual influences that were concentrated in a great metropolis, could raise the people to an exceptional elevation. In the middle ages servitude was mitigated by numerous admirable institutions, most of which emanated from the Church ; but the elements of self-government could only subsist in countries that were so small that the proceedings of the central government came under the immediate cognisance of the whole people. Elsewhere the chief idea that was attached to liberty was freedom from a foreign yoke. It was only by the slow and difficult penetration of knowledge to the masses that a movement like that of the eighteenth century became possible ; and we may distinctly trace the steps of its evolution through a long series of preceding centuries. The almost simultaneous introduction into Europe from the East of cotton-paper by the Greeks and by the Moors, the invention of rag-paper at the end of the tenth century, the extension of the area of instruction by the substitution of universities for monasteries as the centres of education, the gradual formation of modern languages, the invention of printing in the middle of the fifteenth century, the stimulus given to education by the numerous controversies the Reformation forced upon the attention of all classes, the additional inducement to learn to read arising among Protestants from the position assigned to the Bible, and in a less degree among Catholics from the extraordinary popularity of the *Imitation* of Thomas à Kempis, the steady reduction in the price of books as the new art was perfected, the abandonment of a dead language as the vehicle of instruction, the simplification of style and arguments which brought knowledge down to the masses, the sceptical movement which diverted that knowledge from theological to political channels, were all among the antecedents of the Revolution. When knowledge becomes so general that a large proportion of the people take a lively and constant interest in the management of the State, the time is at hand when the bounds of the Constitution will be enlarged.

A third great revolution favourable to liberty is to be found in the history of the art of war. In the early stages of civilisation military achievements are, next to religion, the chief source of dignity, and the class which is most distinguished in battle is almost necessarily the object of the most profound respect. Before the invention of gunpowder, a horseman in armour being beyond all comparison superior to a foot-soldier, the whole stress of battle fell upon the cavalry, who belonged exclusively to the upper classes —in the first instance because the great expense of the equipment could only be met by the rich, and in the next place because express laws excluded plebeians from its ranks. It is, however, well worthy of notice that in this respect the position of the English was exceptional. Although St. George, who was the object of extreme reverence throughout the middle ages as the patron saint of cavalry, was also the patron saint of England, the skill of the English archers was so great that they rapidly rose to European fame, and obtained a position which in other countries belonged exclusively to the

horsemen. In all the old battles the chivalry of France and the yeomen of England were the most prominent figures; and this distinction, trivial as it may now appear, had probably a considerable influence over the history of opinions.

With this exception, the ascendency of the cavalry in the middle ages was unquestionable, but it was not altogether undisputed; and it is curious to trace from a very distant period the slow rise of the infantry accompanying the progress of democracy. The Flemish burghers brought this force to considerable perfection, and in the battle of Courtray their infantry defeated the cavalry opposed to them. A similar achievement was performed by the Swiss infantry in the battle of Morgarten. The French had always treated their own foot-soldiers with extreme contempt; but Crecy and Poitiers having been mainly won by the English archers, a slight revulsion of feeling took place, and great though not very successful efforts were made to raise a rival corps. For some time after the battle of Poitiers all games except archery were prohibited in France. More than once, too, in their combats with the English, the French cavalry were compelled to dismount and endure what they conceived the degradation of fighting on foot, and the same practice was frequent among the free-lances of Italy under the leadership of Sir John Hawkswood and of Carmagnola.

The invention of gunpowder, as soon as firearms had acquired some degree of excellence, seriously shook the ascendency of the cavalry. The mounted soldier was no longer almost invulnerable by the foot-soldier, or his prowess decisive in battle. Yet, notwithstanding this change, the social distinction between the two branches of the army which chivalry[1] had instituted continued; the cavalry still represented the upper and the infantry the lower classes, and in France the nobles alone had the right to enter the former. The comparative depression of the military importance of the cavalry had therefore the effect of transferring in a measure the military prestige from the nobles to the people. For some time the balance trembled very evenly between the two forces, until the invention of the bayonet by Vauban gave the infantry a decided superiority, revolutionised the

[1] Chivalry (*cheval*).

art of war, and thereby influenced the direction of enthusiasm.[1]

The last general tendency I shall mention was produced by the discoveries of political economy. Liberty cannot be attained without a jealous restriction of the province of government, and indeed may be said in a great measure to consist of such a restriction. The process since the Reformation has passed through two distinct stages. The first, which was effected mainly by the diffusion of Rationalism, was the triumph of tolerance, by which the vast field of speculative opinions was withdrawn from the jurisdiction of the civil power. The second, which was effected by political economy, was free-trade, by which the evil of the interference of government with commercial transactions was proved. This last proposition, which was one of the most important, was also one of the earliest of the achievements of political economists, for it was ardently professed by the French school nearly twenty years before the publication of the *Wealth of Nations ;* and as the catastrophe of Law and the ministerial position of Turgot directed public opinion in France very earnestly towards economical questions, it exercised an extensive influence. Many who were comparatively impervious to the more generous enthusiasm of liberty became by these enquiries keenly sensible of the evil of an all-directing government, and anxious to abridge its power.[2]

There were of course innumerable special circumstances growing out of the policy of the French rulers, which accelerated or retarded the advance or influenced the character of the Revolution. The foregoing pages have no pretension to be a complete summary of its antecedents, but they may serve to show that a revolutionary movement of some kind

was the normal result of the tendencies of the age, that its chief causes are to be sought entirely outside the discussions of political philosophers, and that the rise of great republican writers, the principles they enunciated, and the triumph of their arguments were all much more the consequences than the causes of the democratic spirit. In other words, these men were rather representative than creative. But for the preceding movement they would never have appeared, or, at least, would never have triumphed, although when they appeared they undoubtedly modified and in a measure directed the movement that produced them. The change must necessarily have taken place, but it was a question of great importance into whose hands its guidance was to fall.

If we take a broad view of the history of liberty since the establishment of Christianity, we find that the ground of conflict was at first personal and at a later period political liberty, and that in the earlier stage the Catholic Church was the special representative of progress. In the transition from slavery to serfdom and in the transition from serfdom to liberty she was the most zealous, the most unwearied, and the most efficient agent. The same thing may be said of the earliest period of the political evolution. As long as the condition of society was such that an enlarged political liberty was impossible, as long as the object was not so much to produce freedom as to mitigate servitude, the Church was still the champion of the people. The balance of power produced by the numerous corporations she created or sanctioned, the reverence for tradition resulting from her teaching, which perpetuated a network of unwritten customs with the force of public law, the dependence of the civil upon the ecclesiastical power, and the rights of excommunication and deposition, had all contributed to lighten the pressure of despotism. After a time, however, the intellectual progress of society destroyed the means which the Church possessed for mitigating servitude, and at the same time raised the popular demand for liberty to a point that was perfectly incompatible with her original teaching. The power of the papal censure was so weakened that it could scarcely be reckoned upon as a political influence, and all the complicated checks and counter-checks of mediæval society were swept away. On the other

---

[1] On the earlier part of the history of the comparative importance of cavalry and infantry, see the very clear account in a work of the present French Emperor, *Du Passé et de l'Avenir de l'Artillerie ;* and on the later part, and especially on the influence of Vauban, the brilliant sketch of the revolutions in the art of war in the last volume of Thiers' *Hist. de l'Empire.* M. Thiers has made some striking remarks on the effects of the sceptical movement of the eighteenth century upon war—disturbing the old traditions of the art, and culminating in the innovations of Napoleon. The democratic importance of the ascendency of infantry has been noticed by Condorcet, *Tableau de l'Esprit humain,* p. 144. Condorcet, however, has ascribed that ascendency exclusively to gunpowder. See, too, Cibrario, *Economia Politica del Medio Evo,* tom. i. pp. 334, 335.

[2] This has been noticed by many political economists, but by no one more ably than by Mr. Buckle.

hand the struggle for political liberty in its widest sense—the desire to make the will of the people the basis of the government—the conviction that a nation has a right to alter a government that opposes its sentiments—has become the great characteristic of modern politics. Experience has shown that wherever intellectual life is active and unimpeded a political fermentation will ensue, and will issue in a movement having for its object the repudiation of the divine right of kings, and the recognition of the will of the people as the basis of the government. The current has been flowing in this direction since the Reformation, but has advanced with peculiar celerity since the Peace of Westphalia, for since that event the desire of securing a political ascendency for any religious sect has never been a preponderating motive with politicians. With this new spirit the Catholic Church cannot possibly harmonise. It is contrary to her genius, to her traditions, and to her teaching. Resting upon the principle of authority, she instinctively assimilates with those forms of government that most foster the habits of mind she inculcates. Intensely dogmatic in her teaching, she naturally endeavours to arrest by the hand of power the circulation of what she believes to be error, and she therefore allies herself with the political system under which alone such suppression is possible. Asserting as the very basis of her teaching the binding authority of the past, she cannot assent to political doctrines which are, in fact, a direct negation of the uniform teaching of the ancient Church.[1] In the midst of the fierce struggle of the sixteenth century isolated theologians might be permitted without censure to propound doctrines of a seditious nature, but it was impossible ultimately to overlook the fact that the modern secularisation of the basis of authority and the modern latitude given to a discontented people are directly contrary to the teaching of the Fathers, and extend far beyond the teaching of the mediæval theologians.[2] The fact that

modern opinions have been in a measure evolved from the speculations of the schoolmen, or that the schoolmen were the liberals of their time, though important in the judgment of the rationalist, is of no weight in the eyes of those who assert the finality of the teaching of the past.

The natural incapacity of Catholicism to guide the democratic movement had in the eighteenth century been aggravated by the extremely low ebb to which it had fallen, both intellectually and morally. Nearly all the greatest French intellects of the seventeenth century were warmly attached to Catholicism ; all those of the eighteenth century were opposed to it. The Church, therefore, like every retrogressive institution in a progressive age, cast herself with more than common zeal into the arms of power, and on every occasion showed herself the implacable enemy of toleration. In 1780, but a few years before the explosion that shattered the ecclesiastical system of France, the assembly of the French clergy thought it necessary solemnly to deplore and condemn the partial tolerance that had been accorded to the French Protestants, and to petition the king that no further privileges might be granted them. Such a Church was manifestly identified with despotism, and having repeatedly asserted the evil of toleration she had no right to complain when the Revolutionists treated her according to her principles.[1]

Catholicism having thus become the representative of despotism, and French Protestantism having sunk into insignificance, the guidance of the democratic movement necessarily passed into the hands of the freethinkers. In the earlier stages of the movement, when liberty was evolved from the religious wars, they had usually stood aloof. Thus Faustus Socinus had predicted that the seditious doctrines by which the Protestants sup-

---

[1] As a distinguished Anglican divine of our own day has put it, " It is idle, and worse than idle, to attempt to restrict and explain away this positive command ('Resist not evil'), and the Christian Church has always upheld it in its full extent. *With one uniform unhesitating voice it has proclaimed the duty of passive obedience.*" (Sewell, *Christian Politics*, ch. x.)
[2] I have already referred to the bull of Gregory XVI. attesting this contradiction. I may add the following admission of a writer who may be regarded as one of the principal representatives of the Ultramontane

party, which has always been the most liberal in politics : " Quoique nous tombions d'accord que la source ou l'origine de la puissance publique réside dans la multitude, nous nions cependant que la puissance publique étant une fois transférée au prince, le peuple conserve toujours sur lui un droit de souveraineté. Nous disons, au contraire, qu'il ne lui reste plus dès lors que le devoir d'obéir, et qu'il n'existe qu'un cas où il puisse se soustraire à cette obéissance, comme en conviennent les plus ardents défenseurs de la puissance royale—savoir, celui où le prince deviendrait l'ennemi public et déclaré de tout son peuple, et où il chercherait à détruire la société civile." (Bianchi, tom. i. p. 84.)
[1] See, for some striking evidence of these sentiments, the *Discours par un Ministre patriote sur le projet d'accorder l'état civil aux Protestants*, by the Abbé de L'Enfert (Paris, 1787).

ported their cause would lead to the
dissolution of society, and in denouncing
them he especially singled out for condemnation the noble struggle of the
Dutch against Spain.[1] Montaigne, though
Buchanan had been his tutor and La
Boétie one of the most intimate of his
friends, always leaned strongly towards
political conservatism. His disciple Charron went still further, and distinctly
asserted the doctrine of passive obedience.[2] Bayle too exerted all his influence
in discouraging the revolutionary tenets
of Jurieu.[3] Nor was there anything
extraordinary in this, for the aspect
Europe presented in their time might
well have appalled any spectator who was
exempt from the prevailing fanaticism.
All the bonds of cohesion upon which
the political organisation depended were
weakened or destroyed. The spirit of
private judgment had descended to those
who by ignorance or long servitude were
totally incapable of self-government, and
it had lashed their passions to the wildest
fury. Patriotism seemed to have almost
vanished from Christendom. Neither
Catholics nor Protestants deemed it the
least disgraceful to call down a foreign
invasion upon their land, to trample its
interests in the dust, and to avow the
warmest sympathy for its enemies. Religion, which had so long formed the
basis of order, inspired the combatants
with the fiercest hatred, and transformed
every vice into a virtue. While a pope
was causing medals to be struck in
honour of the massacre of St. Bartholomew, and enjoining Vasari to paint the
scene upon the walls of the Vatican ;
while the murderer of Henri III. was
extolled as a martyr, and writings defending his act were scattered broadcast
among the people, it was not surprising
that the freethinkers, who stood apart
from the conflict, should have sought at

any risk to consolidate the few remaining
elements of order. But in the eighteenth
century their position and the circumstances that surrounded them were both
changed ; and the writings of Rousseau
and of his disciples proved the trumpet-
blast of that great revolution which
shattered the political system of France,
and the influence of which is even now
vibrating to the furthest limits of civilisation.

Assuredly no part of this great change
is due to any original discoveries of
Rousseau, though his personal influence
was very great, and his genius peculiarly
fitted for the position he occupied. He
was one of those writers who are eminently destitute of the judgment that
enables men without exaggeration to
discriminate between truth and falsehood,
and yet eminently endowed with that
logical faculty which enables them to
defend the opinions they have embraced.
No one plunged more recklessly into
paradox, or supported those paradoxes
with more consummate skill. At the
same time the firmness with which he
grasped and developed general principles,
and that wonderful fusion of passion and
argument which constitutes the pre-eminent beauty of his style, gave his eloquence
a transcendent power in a revolutionary
age. Nothing is more curious than to
observe how the revolt against the empire
of conventionalities of which he was the
apostle penetrated into all parts of French
society, revolutionising even those which
seemed most remote from his influence.
It was shown in fashionable assemblies in
a disregard for social distinctions, for
decorations, and for attire that had for
centuries been unknown in France. It
was shown in the theatre, where Talma,
at the instigation of the great revolutionary painter David, banished from the
French stage the custom of representing
the heroes of Greece and Rome with
powdered wigs and in the garb of the
courtiers of Versailles, and founded a
school of acting which made an accurate
imitation of nature the first condition of
excellence.[1] It was shown even in the

---

[1] Bayle, *Dict.*, art. *Faustus Socinus*, Remarque c.
[2] *La Sagesse*, p. iii.
[3] Many have ascribed the *Avis aux Réfugiez* to
Bayle. This charge, however, seems (as far as I know)
destitute of external evidence, and, considering the
great zeal with which Bayle threw himself into the
defence of the Calvinists when they were attacked by
Maimbourg, is rather improbable. Arguments of
style are very untrustworthy, because a great writer
always produces many imitators, and Bayle's style was
by no means difficult to imitate. However, Bayle's
aversion to democratic theories pervades all his works,
and Hallam says the presumption is strongly in favour
of his having written the *Avis*, while Gibbon and
Mackintosh speak of it as certainly his. Voltaire, as
is well known, has a far deeper stain upon his memory
—a dark damning stain which all his splendid services
can never efface : he applauded the partition of Poland.

[1] The first step, according to Madame Fusil (*Souve-
nirs d'une Actrice*, pp. 27–54), in this direction was
taken by an actress named Madame Saint-Hubert, who
discarded powder and took the ancient sculptures as
her model ; but it was the genius of Talma, warmly
seconded by the antiquarians, by the revolutionists,
and especially by the Girondins, that finally vanquished
the prevailing prejudice. The incongruity of the old
costume has, I think, been exaggerated : it was well
suited to the Greeks—of Racine.

country houses, where the mathematical figures, the long formal alleys arranged with architectural symmetry, and the trees dwarfed and trimmed into fantastic shapes, which Le Nôtre had made the essential elements of a French garden, were suddenly discarded and replaced by the wild and irregular beauties that Kent had made popular in England.[1] But though the character and the original genius of Rousseau were stamped upon every feature of his time, the doctrines of the *Social Contract* are in all essentials borrowed from Locke and from Sydney, and where they diverge from their models they fall speedily into absurdity.[2] The true causes of their mighty influence are to be found in the condition of society. Formerly they had been advocated with a view to special political exigencies, or to a single country, or to a single section of society. For the first time, in the eighteenth century, they penetrated to the masses of the people, stirred them to their lowest depths, and produced an upheaving that was scarcely less general than that of the Reformation. The history of the movement was like that of the enchanted well in the Irish legend, which lay for centuries shrouded in darkness in the midst of a gorgeous city, till some careless hand left open the door that had enclosed it, and the morning sunlight flashed upon its waters. Immediately it arose responsive to the beam; it burst the barriers that had confined it; it submerged the city that had surrounded it; and its resistless waves, chanting wild music to heaven, rolled over the temples and over the palaces of the past.

There is no fact more remarkable in this movement than the manner in which it has in many countries risen to the position of a religion—that is to say, of an unselfish enthusiasm uniting vast bodies of men in aspiration towards an ideal, and proving the source of heroic virtues. It is always extremely important to trace the direction in which the spirit of self-sacrifice is moving, for upon the intensity of that spirit depends the moral elevation of an age, and upon its course the religious future of the world. It once impelled the warriors of Europe to carry

ruin and desolation to the walls of Jerusalem, to inundate the plains of Palestine with the blood of slaughtered thousands, and to purchase by unparalleled calamities some relics for the devotion of the pilgrim. It once convulsed Europe with religious wars, suspended all pacific operations, and paralysed all secular interests in order to secure the ascendency of a church, or of a creed. It once drove tens of thousands into the retirement of the monasteries; induced them to macerate their bodies, and to mortify their affections; to live in sackcloth and ashes, in cold and poverty and privations, that by such means they might attain their reward. These things have now passed away. The crusader's sword has long been shattered, and his achievements have been idealised by the poet and the novelist. The last wave of the religious wars that swept over so many lands has subsided into a calm that is broken only by the noisy recriminations of a few angry polemics. The monastic system and the conceptions from which it grew are fading rapidly before the increasing day. Celibacy, voluntary poverty, and voluntary subjection, were the three subjects which Giotto painted over the high altar of Assisi as the distinctive characteristics of the saint—the efforts of self-sacrifice that lead to the beatitude of heaven. All of them have now lost their power. Even that type of heroic grandeur which the ancient missionary exhibited, though eulogised and revered, is scarcely reproduced. The spirit of self-sacrifice still exists, but it is to be sought in other fields—in a boundless philanthropy growing out of affections that are common to all religions, and above all in the sphere of politics. Liberty and not theology is the enthusiasm of the nineteenth century. The very men who would once have been conspicuous saints are now conspicuous revolutionists, for while their heroism and their disinterestedness are their own, the direction these qualities take is determined by the pressure of their age.

If we analyse the democratic ideal which is exercising so wide an influence, we find that it consists of two parts—a rearrangement of the map of Europe on the principle of the rights of nationalities, and a strong infusion of the democratic element into the government of each State. The recognition of some universal principle of political right powerful enough to form a bond of

[1] See a singularly curious essay on the history of Gardens in Vitet, *Études sur l'Histoire de l'Art.* Le Nôtre laid out the gardens of Versailles for Louis XIV.
[2] As, for example, when it is contended that a people with representative government are slaves, except during the period of the elections. (*Contrat Social,* 'iv. iii. ch. xv.)

lasting concord has always been a favourite dream with statesmen and philosophers. Hildebrand sought it in the supremacy of the spiritual power, and in the consequent ascendency of the moral law; Dante in the fusion of all European States into one great empire, presided over in temporal matters by the Cæsars and in spiritual by the Popes; Grotius and Henri IV. of France, in a tribunal like the Amphictyonic assembly of ancient Greece, deciding with supreme authority international differences; diplomacy in artificial combinations, and especially in the system of the balance of power. The modern doctrine of the rights of nationalities could not possibly have attained any great importance till the present century—in the first place because it is only after the wide diffusion of education that the national sentiment acquires the necessary strength, concentration, and intelligence, and in the next place because the influence of the selfish side of human nature was hostile to it. The conceptions that the interests of adjoining nations are diametrically opposed, that wealth can only be gained by displacement, and that conquest is therefore the chief path to progress, were long universal; but during the last century political economy has been steadily subverting them, and has already effected so much that it scarcely seems unreasonable to conclude that the time will come when a policy of territorial aggrandisement will be impossible. At the same time the extension of free trade has undoubtedly a tendency to effect the disintegration of great heterogeneous empires by destroying the peculiar advantages of colonies and of conquered territory; while railways and increasing knowledge weaken national antipathies and facilitate the political agglomeration of communities with a common race, language, and geographical position. The result of all this is that motives of self-interest do not oppose themselves as powerfully as of old to the recognition of territorial limits defined by the wishes of the people. And this is peculiarly important, because not only does interest, as distinguished from passion, gain a greater empire with advancing civilisation, but passion itself is mainly guided by its power. If, indeed, we examine only the proximate causes of European wars, they present the aspect of a perfect chaos, and the immense majority might be ascribed to isolated causes or to passing ebullitions

of national jealousy. But if we examine more closely we find that a deep-seated aversion produced by general causes had long preceded and prepared the explosion. The great majority of wars during the last 1,000 years may be classified under three heads—wars produced by opposition of religious belief, wars resulting from erroneous economical notions either concerning the balance of trade or the material advantages of conquest, and wars resulting from the collision of the two hostile doctrines of the divine right of kings and the rights of nations. In the first instance knowledge has gained a decisive, and in the second almost a decisive, victory. Whether it will ever render equally impossible political combinations that outrage national sentiments is one of the great problems of the future. This much at least is certain, that the progress of the movement has profoundly and irrevocably impaired the force of treaties and of diplomatic arrangements as the regulating principles of Europe.

But whatever may be thought on these subjects, it is at least certain that the movement we have traced has become a great moral influence in Europe, and, like many others, exhibits a striking synthesis of the distinctive elements of two different civilisations. The spirit of patriotism has under its influence assumed a position scarcely less prominent than in antiquity, while at the same time, by a transformation to which almost all the influences of modern society have concurred, it has lost its old exclusiveness without altogether losing its identity, and has assimilated with a sentiment of universal fraternity. The sympathy between great bodies of men was never so strong, the stream of enthusiasm never flowed in so broad a current as at present; and in the democratic union of nations we find the last and highest expression of the Christian ideal of the brotherhood of mankind.

Nor is it simply in the international aspect of democracy that we trace this influence; it is found no less clearly in the changes that have been introduced into internal legislation and social life. The political merits of democracy I do not now discuss, but no one at least can question the extent to which legislation has of late years been modified in favour of the lower classes, the sympathy and even deference that has been shown to their wants, the rapid obliteration of the lines of class-divisions, and the ever-increasing tendency to amalgamation based upon political equality and upon enlarged sympathy.

It is thus that amid the transformation or dissolution of intellectual dogmas the great moral principles of Christianity continually reappear, acquiring new power in the lapse of ages, and influencing the type of each succeeding civilisation.

CHAPTER VI.

THE INDUSTRIAL HISTORY OF RATIONALISM

THE history of labour is only second in importance to the history of knowledge. The estimate in which industry is held, the principles by which it is regulated, and the channels in which it is directed, not merely determine the material prosperity of nations, but also invariably contribute to the formation of a type of character, and in consequence to a modification of opinions. In the course of the present work I have more than once had occasion to refer to the influence of the industrial spirit upon Rationalism, but I have thought it advisable to reserve its full discussion for a separate chapter, in which the relation between the two evolutions will be clearly manifested, and the importance of commerce both as a disintegrating and constructive agent will be established.

If we examine from an industrial point of view the old civilisation, which was sinking rapidly into dissolution when Christianity arose, we shall at once perceive that slavery was the central fact upon which it rested. Whenever, in a highly-organised society, this institution is prominent, it will impart a special cast to the national character, and will in some respects invert the normal conditions of development. For labour, being identified with ignominy, will become distasteful to all classes, and wealth will be speedily accumulated in the hands of a few. Where slavery exists there is no middle class, little or no manufacturing or commercial enterprise. The slave-owner possesses the means of rapidly amassing wealth, while the freeman who is not a slave-owner, being shut out from nearly every path of industry, and being convinced that labour is a degradation, will be both demoralised and impoverished. At the same time a strong military spirit will usually be encouraged, both because the energies of men find no other sphere of action, and because in such a condition of society conquest is the chief path to wealth. In some respects the consequences of all this will appear very fascinating. A high military enthusiasm being engendered, the nation which cherishes slavery will usually prove victorious in its conflicts with the commercial communities around it. It will produce many great warriors, many splendid examples of military devotion. A combination of the high mettle of the soldier and of a chivalrous contempt for trade and the trading spirit will impart an aristocratic and refined tone to the national manners, while the national intellect will be diverted from utilitarian inventions and pursuits, and will be concentrated on sublime speculations and works of beauty. But as soon as the first energy of the conquering spirit has passed away, the hollowness of such a civilisation becomes apparent. The increase of wealth, which in a free nation strengthens the middle classes and gives a new impulse to commercial enterprise, in a slave nation produces only luxury and vice ; and the habit of regarding multitudes as totally destitute of rights, combined with the military spirit that is general, gives that vice a character of the most odious ferocity.[1]

It is of course possible that the intervention of other influences may modify this type of character, and may retard and in some degree prevent the downfall it produces, but in as far as slavery is predominant in so far will these tendencies be displayed. In the ancient civilisation they were developed to the full extent. From a very early period the existence of slavery had produced, both in Greece and Rome, a strong contempt for commerce and for manual labour, which was openly professed by the ablest men, and which harmonised well with their disdain for the more utilitarian aspects of science. Among the Bœotians those who had defiled themselves with commerce were excluded for ten years from all offices in

[1] The effects of slavery upon character have lately been treated with very remarkable ability in Cairnes' *Slave Power*. See also Storch, *Écon. politique*, tom. v., and Ch. Comte, *Traité de Législation*, liv. v.

the State. Plato pronounced the trade of a shopkeeper to be a degradation to a freeman, and he wished it to be punished as a crime. Aristotle, who asserted so strongly the political claims of the middle classes, declared, nevertheless, that in a perfect State no citizen should exercise any mechanical art. Xenophon and Cicero were both of the same opinion. Augustus condemned a senator to death because he had debased his rank by taking part in a manufacture. The single form of labour that was held in honour was agriculture ; and in the earlier and simpler periods of the national history, while slaves were still few and luxury was unknown, this pursuit proved a sufficient vent for the pacific energies of the people. But when the number and wealth of the population had been multiplied, when a long series of victories had greatly increased the multitude of slaves, and when the political privileges of a Roman citizen had been widely extended, all classes flocked within the walls, the surrounding country fell entirely into the hands of the aristocracy, and either remained uncultivated or was cultivated only by slaves,[1] and the task of supplying the overgrown city with corn devolved chiefly upon the colonies. Within the city a vast half-military population, sufficiently powerful to control the government and intent only upon enjoyment, paralysed the energies of the empire, and destroyed every trace of its ancient purity. " Bread and the games of the circus " was the constant demand ; every other consideration was sacrificed to grant it ; and industry, in all its departments, was relinquished to the slaves.

If we compare the condition of the ancient with that of the modern slaves, we shall find that they were in some respects profoundly different. The modern slave-trade has been carried on upon a scale and with circumstances of atrocity little known to the ancients, nor was there in antiquity the difference of race and colour that now prevents a fusion of the free and the enslaved classes. Aristotle, the greatest of all the advocates of slavery, recommended masters to hold out the prospect of future emancipation to their slaves ; and we know that in the latter

days of the Roman Empire the manumission of old slaves was very general, and of those who were not old, by no means rare. Besides this, the great expansion of commerce enabling the modern slave-owners to command every description of luxury in exchange for the produce of unskilled slave-labour, they have usually, in order to guard against rebellion, adopted the policy of brutalising their slaves by enforced ignorance—to such an extent that it is actually penal, in the majority of the Slave States of America, to teach a slave to read.[1] In the ancient civilisations, on the other hand, the slave produced all the articles of refinement and luxury, conducted the most difficult forms of labour, and often exercised the most important professions. His mind was therefore very frequently cultivated to the highest point, and his value was proportioned to his intelligence. Terence, Epictetus, and Publius Syrus, were slaves, as were also some of the leading physicians, and many of the most distinguished sculptors. It should be remembered, too, that while modern slavery was from the beginning an evil, slavery among the ancients was at first an unmingled blessing—an important conquest of the spirit of humanity. When men were altogether barbarous they killed their prisoners ; when they became more merciful they preserved them as slaves.[2]

Still in the later days of the republic, and during the empire, the sufferings of the slaves were such that it is impossible to read them without a shudder. The full ferocity of the national character was directed against them. They were exposed to wild beasts, or compelled to fight as gladiators ; they were often mutilated with atrocious cruelty ; they were tortured on the slightest suspicion, they were crucified for the most trivial offences. If a master was murdered all his slaves were tortured ; if the perpetrator remained undiscovered all were put to death, and Tacitus relates a case in which no less than 400 suffered for a single undiscovered criminal. We read of one slave who was crucified for having stolen a quail, and of another who was condemned to be thrown to the fish for having broken a crystal vase. Juvenal describes a lady of fashion gratifying a

---

[1] See on this subject Plutarch, *Lives of the Gracchi ;* Dionysius Halycarnassus, lib. ii. cap. 28 ; Columella, *De Re Rustica.* This whole subject has been very ably treated by M. Comte, *Traité de Législation.* See also Blanqui, *Histoire de l'Économie politique ;* Dureau de la Malle, *Économie politique des Romains.*

[1] 1863.
[2] The distinctions have been fully developed by Cairnes and Tocqueville.

momentary caprice by ordering a slave to be crucified.[1]

It was in this manner that the old civilisation, which rested on conquest and on slavery, had passed into complete dissolution, the free classes being altogether demoralised, and the slave classes exposed to the most horrible cruelties. At last the spirit of Christianity moved over this chaotic society, and not merely alleviated the evils that convulsed it, but also reorganised it on a new basis. It did this in three ways: it abolished slavery, it created charity, it inculcated self-sacrifice.

In the first of these tasks Christianity was powerfully assisted by two other agents. It is never possible for the moral sense to be entirely extinguished; and, by a law which is constantly manifested in history, we find that those who have emancipated themselves from the tendencies of an evil age often attain a degree of moral excellence that had not been attained in ages that were comparatively pure. The latter days of pagan Rome exhibit a constant decay of religious reverence and of common morality; but they also exhibit a feverish aspiration towards a new religion, and a finer sense of the requirements of a high morality than had been displayed in the best days of the republic. We have a striking instance of the first of these tendencies in that sudden diffusion of the worship of Mithra, which was one of the most remarkable of the antecedents of Christianity. About seventy years before the Christian era this worship was introduced into Italy, as Plutarch tells us, by some Cilician pirates; and at a time when universal scepticism seemed the dominant characteristic of the Roman intellect, it took such firm root that for 200 years it continued to flourish, to excite the warmest enthusiasm, and to produce a religious revival in the centre of a population that appeared entirely depraved. In the same way, about the time when Nero ascended the throne, and when the humanity of the masses had sunk to the lowest ebb, there appeared in the centre of paganism a powerful reaction in favour of the suffering classes, of which Seneca was the principal exponent, but which was more or less reflected in the whole of the literature of the time. Seneca recurred to the subject again and again, and for the first time in Rome he very clearly and emphatically enforced the duties of masters to their slaves, and the existence of a bond of fraternity that no accidental difference of position could cancel. Nor was the movement confined to the writings of moralists. A long series of enactments by Nero, Claudius, Antonine, and Adrian gave the servile class a legal position, took the power of life and death out of the hands of the masters, prevented the exposure of slaves when old and infirm on an island of the Tiber (where they had often been left to die), forbade their mutilation or their employment as gladiators, and appointed special magistrates to receive their complaints. What was done was, no doubt, very imperfect and inadequate, but it represented a tendency of which Christianity was the continuation.[1]

A second influence favourable to the slaves came into action at a later period: I mean the invasion of the barbarians, who have been justly described as the representatives of the principle of personal liberty in Europe.[2] Slavery was not, indeed, absolutely unknown among them, but it was altogether exceptional and entirely uncongenial with their habits. Prisoners of war, criminals, or men who had gambled away their liberty, were the chief slaves, and it is probable that servitude was rarely hereditary. Whenever, therefore, these tribes obtained an ascendency, they contributed to the destruction of slavery.

But when the fullest allowance has been made for these influences, it will remain an undoubted fact that the reconstruction of society was mainly the work of Christianity. Other influences could produce the manumission of many slaves, but Christianity alone could effect the profound change of character that rendered possible the abolition of slavery. There are few subjects more striking, and at the same time more instructive, than the history of that great transition. The Christians did not preach a revolutionary doctrine. They did not proclaim slavery altogether unlawful, or, at least, not until

[1] See much horrible evidence of the atrocities practised on Roman slaves in Loiseleur, *Études sur les Crimes et les Peines dans l'Antiquité et les Temps modernes* (Paris, 1863), pp. 83–98; and in Comte, *Traité de Législation*, liv. v. There is an extremely good essay on the condition of the ancient slaves—one of the best ever written on the subject—in Bodin's *Republic*, lib. i. c. 5.

[1] This movement has been well noticed by Grotius, *De Jure*, lib. iii. c. 14.
[2] Guizot.

the bull of Alexander III. in the twelfth century; but they steadily sapped it at its basis, by opposing to it the doctrine of universal brotherhood, and by infusing a spirit of humanity into all the relations of society. Under Constantine, the old laws for the protection of slaves were re-enacted with additional provisions, and the separation of the family of the slave was forbidden. At the same time the servile punishment of crucifixion was abolished; but not so much from motives of humanity as on account of the sacred character it had acquired. Very soon a disposition was manifested on all sides to emancipate slaves, and that emancipation was invariably associated with religion. Sunday was especially recommended as the most appropriate day for the emancipation, and the ceremony almost invariably took place in the church. Gregory the Great set the example of freeing a number of his slaves as an act of devotion; and it soon became customary for sovereigns to do the same thing at seasons of great public rejoicing. Under Justinian the restrictions that had been placed upon emancipation by testament were removed. For a short time the mere resolution to enter a monastery gave liberty to the slave; and the monks, being for the most part recruited from the servile caste, were always ready to facilitate the deliverance of their brethren. Even in religious persecutions this object was remembered. The Jews were early noted as slave-dealers, and among the first and most frequent measures directed against them was the manumission of their Christian slaves. In all the rites of religion the difference between bond and free was studiously ignored, and the clergy invariably proclaimed the act of enfranchisement to be meritorious.[1]

By these means an impulse favourable to liberty was imparted to all who were within the influence of the Church. Slavery began rapidly to disappear, or to fade into serfdom. At the same time the Church exerted her powers, with no less effect, to alleviate the sufferings of those who still continued in bondage. In England, especially, all the civil laws for the protection of the theows, or Saxon slaves, appear to have been preceded by, and based upon, the canon law. When, as far as can be ascertained, the power of the master was by law unlimited, we find the Church assuming a jurisdiction on the subject, and directing special penances "against masters who took from their theows the money they had lawfully earned; against those who slew their theows without judgment or good cause; against mistresses who beat their female theows so that they die within three days; and against freemen who, by order of the lord, kill a theow." Above all, the whole machinery of ecclesiastical discipline was put in motion to shelter the otherwise unprotected chastity of the female slave.[1] That Church which often seemed so haughty and so overbearing in its dealings with kings and nobles, never failed to listen to the poor and to the oppressed, and for many centuries their protection was the foremost of all the objects of its policy.

Yet as long as the old antipathy to labour continued, nothing of any lasting value had been effected. But here, again, the influence of the Church was exerted with unwavering beneficence and success. The Fathers employed all their eloquence in favour of labour;[2] but it is to the monks, and especially to the Benedictine monks, that the change is pre-eminently due. At a time when religious enthusiasm was all directed towards the monastic life as towards the ideal of perfection, they made labour an essential part of their discipline. Wherever they went, they revived the traditions of old Roman agriculture, and large tracts of France and Belgium were drained and planted by their hands. And though agriculture and gardening were the forms of labour in which they especially excelled, they

---

[1] *Cod. Theod.* lib. ii. tit. 8, lex. 1, and iv. 7, 1. For the history of the action of Christianity upon slavery, see A. Comte, *Philosophie positive*, tom. vi. pp. 43-47; Storch, *Économie politique*, tom. v. pp. 306-310; Troplong, *Influence du Christianisme sur le Droit civil.* The measures against Jew slave-owners have been noticed by Bedarride, du Lac, and many other writers. It must be acknowledged, however, that the Christian Emperor Gratian made one law which may rank with the most atrocious of Paganism. It provides, that if a slave accused his master of any crime except high treason, the justice of the charge was not to be examined, but the slave was to be committed to the flames: "Cum accusatores servi dominis intonent, nemo judiciorum expectet eventum, nihil quæri, nihil discuti placet, sed cum ipsis delationum libellis, cum omni scripturarum et meditati criminis apparatu, nefandarum accusationum crementur auctores: excepto tamen adpetitæ majestatis crimine, in quo etiam servis honesta proditio est. Nam et hoc facinus tendit in dominos."—*Cod. Theod.* ix. 6, 2. Honorius accorded

slaves the liberty of accusing their masters in cases of heresy, and Theodosius in cases of paganism.

[1] Wright, *Letter on the Political Condition of the English Peasantry during the Middle Ages.* London, 1843.

[2] Champagny, *La Charité chrétienne*, pp. 275-289.

indirectly became the authors of every other. For when a monastery was planted, it soon became the nucleus around which the inhabitants of the neighbourhood clustered. A town was thus gradually formed, civilised by Christian teaching, stimulated to industry by the example of the monks, and protected by the reverence that attached to them. At the same time the ornamentation of the church gave the first impulse to art. The monks of the order of St. Basil devoted themselves especially to painting, and all the mediæval architects whose names have come down to us are said to have been ecclesiastics, till the rise of those great lay companies who designed or built the cathedrals of the twelfth century. A great number of the towns of Belgium trace their origin in this manner to the monks.[1] For a long time the most eminent prelates did not disdain manual labour ; and it is related of no less a person than Becket that he was in the habit of labouring during harvest time in the fields with the monks at the monasteries which he visited.[2]

By these means the contempt for labour which had been produced by slavery was corrected, and the path was opened for the rise of the industrial classes which followed the Crusades. The ferocity of character that had preceded Christianity was combated with equal zeal, though not quite equal success, by the organisation of Christian charity.

There is certainly no other feature of the old civilisation so repulsive as the indifference to suffering that it displayed. It is indeed true that in this respect there was a considerable difference between the Greeks and the Romans. In their armaments, in their wars—above all, in the extreme solicitude to guard the interests of orphans and minors that characterised their legislation,[3] the former displayed a spirit of humanity for which we look in vain among the latter. Besides this, the political systems of Greece and, in its latter days, of Rome, were so framed that the state in a great measure supplied the material wants of the people, and a poor-law of the heaviest kind was, to a certain extent, a substitute for private beneficence. Still, there appears to have been no public refuge for the sick ; the infant was entirely unprotected ; and infanticide having been—at least in the case of deformed children —expressly authorised by both Plato and Aristotle, was seldom regarded as a crime.[1] The practice of bringing up orphans avowedly for prostitution was equally common. The constant association of human suffering with popular entertainments rendered the popular mind continually more callous.

Very different was the aspect presented by the early Church. Long before the era of persecution had closed, the hospital and the Xenodochion, or refuge for strangers, was known among the Christians. The epitaphs in the catacombs abundantly prove the multitude of foundlings that were sustained by their charity ; and when Christianity became the dominant religion, the protection of infants was one of the first changes that was manifested in the laws." The frequent famines and the frightful distress caused by the invasion of the barbarians, and by the transition from slavery to freedom, were met by the most boundless, the most lavish benevolence. The Fathers were ceaselessly exhorting to charity, and

[1] Hume has very ingeniously suggested, and Malthus has adopted the suggestion, that the ancient permission of infanticide had on the whole a tendency to multiply rather than to diminish population, for, by removing the fear of a numerous family, it induced the poor to marry recklessly ; while, once the children were born, natural affection would struggle to the last to sustain them.

[2] It is worthy of notice that deserted children in the early Church appear to have been supported mainly by private charity, and those foundling hospitals to which political economists so strongly object were unknown. In the time of Justinian, however, we find notices of Brephotrophia, or asylums for children ; and foundations, intended especially for foundlings, are said to have existed in the seventh and eighth centuries (Labourt, *Recherches sur les Enfants trouvés*, Paris, 1848, pp. 32, 33). A foundling hospital was established by Innocent III. at Rome. The objections to these institutions, on account of their encouragement of vice, as well as the frightful mortality prevailing among them, are well known. M'Culloch states that between 1792 and 1797 the admissions into foundling hospitals in Dublin were 12,786, and the deaths 12,561 (*Pol. Econ.* part. i. ch. viii.). Magdalen asylums, which M. Ch. Comte and other economists have vehemently denounced, were also unknown in the early Church. The first erected in France was early in the thirteenth century ; the famous institution of the Bon Pasteur was founded by a Dutch lady converted to Catholicism in 1698. A full history of these institutions is given in Parent-Duchatelet's singularly interesting work on *Prostitution in the City of Paris*. The admirable societies for the succour of indigent mothers, which complete the measures for the protection of infancy, were chiefly the work of the French freethinkers of the last [eighteenth] century. Beaumarchais dedicated part of the profits of the *Mariage de Figaro* to that of Lyons (Ducellier, *Hist. des Classes laborieuses en France*, p. 296).

[1] See on this subject Perin, *La Richesse dans les Sociétés chrétiennes*, tom. i. pp. 345-361 ; Van Bruyssel, *Hist. du Commerce belge*, tom. i. pp. 58, 59.
[2] Eden, *History of the Labouring Classes in England*, vol. i. p. 50.
[3] Grote, *Hist. of Greece*, vol. ii. p. 123.

in language so emphatic that it seemed sometimes almost to ignore the rights of property, and to verge upon absolute communism.[1] The gladiatorial games were ceaselessly denounced; but the affection with which they were regarded by the people long resisted the efforts of philanthropists, till, in the midst of the spectacle, the monk Telemachus rushed between the combatants, and his blood was the last that stained the arena. But perhaps the noblest testimony to the extent and catholicity of Christian charity was furnished by an adversary. Julian exerted all his energies to produce a charitable movement among the Pagans; "for it is a scandal," he said, "that the Galileans should support the destitute, not only of their religion, but of ours."

In reading the history of that noble efflorescence of charity which marked the first ages of Christianity, it is impossible to avoid reflecting upon the strange destiny that has consigned almost all its authors to obscurity, while the names of those who took any conspicuous part in sectarian history have become household words among mankind. We hear much of martyrs, who sealed their testimony with blood; of courageous missionaries, who planted the standard of the Cross among savage nations and in pestilential climes; but we hear little of that heroism of charity, which, with no precedent to guide it, and with every early habit to oppose it, confronted the most loathsome forms of suffering, and, for the first time in the history of humanity, made pain and hideous disease the objects of a reverential affection. In the intellectual condition of bygone centuries, it was impossible that these things should be appreciated as they deserved. Charity was practised, indeed, nobly and constantly, but it did not strike the imagination, it did not elicit the homage of mankind. It was regarded by the masses as an entirely subordinate department of virtue; and the noblest efforts of philanthropy excited far less admiration than the macerations of an anchorite or the proselytising zeal of a sectarian. Fabiola, that Roman lady who seems to have done more than any other single individual in the erection of the first hospitals; St. Landry, the great apostle of charity in France; even Telemachus himself, are

all obscure names in history. The men who organised that vast network of hospitals that overspread Europe after the Crusades have passed altogether from recollection. It was not till the seventeenth century, when modern habits of thought were widely diffused, that St. Vincent de Paul arose and furnished an example of a saint who is profoundly and universally revered, and who owes that reverence to the splendour of his charity. But although it is true that during many centuries the philanthropist was placed upon a far lower level than at present, it is not the less true that charity was one of the earliest, as it was one of the noblest, creations of Christianity; and that, independently of the incalculable mass of suffering it assuaged, the influence it has exercised in softening and purifying the character, in restraining the passions, and enlarging the sympathies of mankind, has made it one of the most important elements of our civilisation. The precepts and examples of the Gospel struck a chord of pathos which the noblest philosophies of antiquity had never reached. For the first time the aureole of sanctity encircled the brow of sorrow and invested it with a mysterious charm. It is related of an old Catholic saint that, at the evening of a laborious and well-spent life, Christ appeared to him as a man of sorrows, and, commending his past exertions, asked him what reward he would desire. Fame, and wealth, and earthly pleasures had no attraction to one who had long been weaned from the things of sense; yet the prospect of other and spiritual blessings for the moment filled the saint with joy; but when he looked upon that sacred brow, still shadowed as with the anguish of Gethsemane, every selfish wish was forgotten, and, with a voice of ineffable love, he answered, "Lord, that I might suffer most!"[1]

The third principle that Christianity employed to correct the evils of a decayed society was the principle of self-sacrifice. We have already seen some of the evils that resulted from the monastic system; but, considered in its proper place, it is not difficult to perceive its use. For the manner in which society attains that

[1] See some very striking instances of this in Champagny's *Charité chrétienne*.

[1] This is, I believe, related of St. John of the Cross. There is a somewhat similar legend of a Spanish saint of the thirteenth century named Ramon Monat. The Virgin appeared to him and offered him a crown of roses, which he refused, and Christ then gave him His own crown of thorns.

moderate and tempered excellence which is most congenial to its welfare is by imperfectly aspiring towards an heroic ideal. In an age, therefore, when the government of force had produced universal anarchy, theologians taught the doctrine of passive obedience. In an age when unbridled luxury had produced an unbridled corruption, they elevated voluntary poverty as a virtue. In an age when the facility of divorce had almost legalised polygamy, they proclaimed, with St. Jerome, that " marriage peoples earth, but virginity heaven."

The earlier portion of the middle ages presents the almost unique spectacle of a society that was in all its parts moulded and coloured by theological ideas, and it was natural that when the progress of knowledge destroyed the ascendency of those ideas a universal modification should ensue. But besides this, it is not, I think, difficult to perceive that the industrial condition of Europe at this time contained elements of dissolution. The true incitements to industry must ever be found in its own rewards. The desire of wealth, the multiplied wants and aims of an elaborated civilisation, the rivalry and the ambition of commerce, are the chief causes of its progress. Labour performed as a duty, associated with the worship of voluntary poverty, and with the condemnation of luxury, was altogether abnormal. It was only by the emancipation and development of some of the towns of Italy and Belgium that the industrial spirit became entirely secular, and, assuming a new prominence and energy, introduced an order of tendencies into Europe which gradually encroached upon the domain of theology, and contributed largely towards the Reformation, and towards the Rationalism that followed it. But before examining the nature of those tendencies it may be necessary to say a few words concerning the circumstances that gave them birth.

Although the old Roman slavery received its death-blow under the influences I have noticed, some lingering remains of it continued till the twelfth or thirteenth century;[1] and the serfdom that

followed not only continued much later, but even for a long time absorbed great numbers of the free peasants. The rapacity of the nobles, and the famines that were so frequent during the middle ages, induced the poor to exchange their liberty for protection and for bread ; and the custom of punishing all crimes by fines, with the alternative of servitude in case of non-payment, still further increased the evil. At the same time the mildness of the ecclesiastical rule, and also the desire to obtain the advantage of the prayers of the monks, induced many to attach themselves as serfs to the monasteries.[1] Although it would be unfair to accuse the Church of abandoning the cause of emancipation, it is probable that this last fact in some degree lessened her zeal.[2] The bulk of the population of Europe were emancipated between the twelfth and fifteenth centuries ; but the remains of serfdom have even now scarcely disappeared.[3] In the towns, however, personal and political liberty was attained much earlier. Something of the old Roman municipal government had lingered faintly in the South of France during the whole of the middle ages ; but the complete emancipation was chiefly due to the necessities of sovereigns, who, in their conflicts with the nobles or with other nations, gladly purchased by privileges the assistance of the towns. It is probable that the fact of many of the English kings being usurpers contributed in this way to the emancipation of the English citizens ;[4] and the struggle

bow's invasion. Bodin has noticed some passages from the bulls of the Popes relative to slaves in Italy as late as the thirteenth century (*République*, p. 43). Religion, which so powerfully contributed to the emancipation, in some cases had an opposite influence, for Christians enslaved without scruple Jews and Mahometans, who naturally retaliated. The number of Christian slaves bought up by the Jews had been one of the complaints of Agobard in the ninth century.

[1] See on all these causes Hallam's *Middle Ages*, vol. i. pp. 217-218.

[2] " The clergy, and especially several Popes, enforced manumission as a duty upon laymen, and inveighed against the scandal of keeping Christians in bondage ; but they were not, it is said, as ready in performing their own parts. The villeins upon the Church lands were among the last who were emancipated."—Hallam, *Middle Ages*, vol. i. p. 221.

[3] The decline of serfdom has been treated by Hallam, *Hist. of Middle Ages*, vol. i. pp. 222, 223. As late as 1775, colliers in Scotland were bound to perpetual service in the works to which they belonged. Upon the sale of those works the purchasers had a right to their services, nor could they be elsewhere received into service except by permission of the owner of the collieries. See a note by M'Culloch, in his edition of the *Wealth of Nations*, vol. ii. p. 186.

[4] "It wants not probability, though it manifestly appears not, that William Rufus, Henry I., and King

[1] In 1102 a Council of Westminster found it necessary to prohibit the sale of slaves in England (Eden, *Hist. of Labouring Classes*, vol. i. p. 10) ; and still later the English were accustomed to sell slaves to the Irish, and Giraldus Cambrensis tells us that the emancipation of their slaves as an act of devotion was enjoined by the Irish bishops on the occasion of Strong-

between the kings and nobles in France, and between the Popes and the emperors in Italy, had a similar effect. Whenever a town was emancipated an impulse was given to industry. The Crusades at last gave the municipal and industrial element an extraordinary prominence. The great sums for which kings and nobles became indebted to the middle classes, the rapid extension of navigation, the inventions that were imported into Europe from the East, and, above all, the happy fortune that made the Italian towns the centre of the stream of wealth, had all, in different ways, increased the influence of the towns. In the course of the twelfth century, nearly all which carried on commercial intercourse with Italy had obtained municipal government, and some of those of Belgium, and along the shores of the Baltic, almost equalled the Italian ones in commercial activity.[1] At the same time the creation of guilds and corporations of different trades consolidated the advantages that had been gained. For although it is undoubtedly true that in a normal condition of society the system of protection and monopoly, of which the corporations were the very ideal, is extremely unfavourable to production, in the anarchy of the middle ages it was of great use in giving the trading classes a union which protected them from plunder, and enabled them to incline legislation in their favour. Commerce, under their influence, became a great power. A new and secular civilisation was called into being, which gradually encroached upon the ascendency of theological ideas, and introduced a new phase in the development of Europe.

It may be observed, however, that the opposition that at last arose between the theological and the commercial spirit is not exactly what we might at first sight have expected; for in the earlier stages of society they have striking points of affinity. Missionary enterprises and com-

mercial enterprises are the two main agents for the diffusion of civilisation; they commonly advance together, and each has very frequently proved the pioneer of the other. Besides this, the Crusades, which were the chief expression of the religious sentiments of the middle ages, owed their partial success in a great measure to the commercial communities. It was the merchants of Amalfi who, by their traffic, first opened the path for Christians to Jerusalem, and, in conjunction with the other Italian republics, supplied the chief wants of the Crusaders. The spirit that made the Venetian merchants of the thirteenth century stamp the image of Christ upon their coins, and the merchants of Florence impose a tax upon their rich woollen manufactures, in order, with the produce, to erect that noble cathedral which is even now among the wonders of the world, seemed to augur well for their alliance with the Church. Yet the event shows that these expectations were unfounded, and whenever the type of civilisation was formed mainly by commercial enterprise, there arose a conflict with the theologians.

The first point in which the commercial civilisation came into collision with the Church was the lawfulness of lending money at interest, or, as it was then called, of practising usury.

In the present day, when political economy has been raised to a science, nothing can appear more simple than the position that interest occupies in pecuniary arrangements. We know that, in a society in which great works of industry or public utility are carried on, immense sums will necessarily be borrowed at interest, and that such transactions are usually advantageous both to the lender and the borrower. The first lends his money for the purpose of increasing his wealth by the interest he receives; the second obtains the advantage of disposing of a sum which is sufficient to set in motion a lucrative business, and this advantage more than compensates him for the interest he pays. We know, too, that this interest is not capricious in its amount, but is governed by fixed laws. It usually consists of two distinct elements—the interest which is the price of money, and what has been termed[1] the

Stephen, being all usurpers, granted large immunities to burghs to secure them to their party, and by the time that Glanvil wrote, which was in the reign of Henry II., burghs had so great privileges as that, if a bondsman or servant remained in a burgh as a burgess or member of it a year and a day, he was by that very residence made free; and so it was in Scotland: he was always free, and enjoyed the liberty of the burgh if he were able to buy a burgage, and his lord claimed him not within a year and a day."—Brady, *Historical Treatise on Cities* (1690), p. 18.

[1] Thierry, *Hist. du Tiers État*, pp. 24, 25. It is scarcely necessary to refer to the admirable sketch of the history of towns in the *Wealth of Nations*.

[1] By J.-B. Say, in his *Traité d'Économie politique*, where the subject of usury is admirably discussed. The term "interest of assurance," however, is defec-

"interest of assurance." The price of money, like the price of most other commodities, is determined by the law of supply and demand.[1] It depends upon the proportion between the amount of money that is to be lent and the demands of the borrowers, which proportion is itself influenced by many considerations, but is chiefly regulated in a normal state of society by the amount of wealth and the amount of enterprise. The second kind of interest arises in those cases in which there is some danger that the creditor may lose what he has lent, or in which some penalty, inflicted by law or by public opinion, attaches to the loan. For it is manifest that men will not divert their capital from secure to insecure enterprises unless there is a possibility that they may obtain a larger gain in the latter than in the former, and it is equally manifest that no one will voluntarily take a course that exposes him to legal penalties or to public reproach unless he has some pressing motive for doing so.

If, then, when the law of supply and demand has regulated the rate of interest, the government of the country interposes, and either prohibits all interest or endeavours to fix it at a lower rate ; if public opinion stigmatises the lender at interest as infamous, and if religion brands his act as a crime, it is easy from the foregoing principles to perceive what must be the consequence. As long as there are persons who urgently desire to borrow, and persons who possess capital, it is quite certain that the relation of debtor and creditor will continue ; but the former will find that the terms have greatly altered to his disadvantage. For the capitalist will certainly not lend without exacting interest, and such interest

as is at least equivalent to the profits he would derive if he employed his money in other ways. If the law forbids this, he must either not lend, or lend in a manner that exposes him to legal penalties. A great number, overcome by their scruples or their fears, will adopt the former course, and consequently the amount of money in the community which is to be lent, and which is one of the great regulators of the price of money, will be diminished ; while those who venture to incur the risk of infringing human and, as they believe, divine laws, and of incurring the infamy attached by public opinion to the act, must be bribed by additional interest. At the same time the furtive character given to the transaction is eminently favourable to imposition. The more therefore law, public opinion, and religion endeavour to lower the current rate of interest, the more that rate will be raised.

But these principles, simple as they may now appear, were entirely unknown to the ancients, and from an extremely early period the exaction of interest was looked upon with disfavour. The origin of this prejudice is probably to be found in the utter ignorance of all uncivilised men about the laws that regulate the increase of wealth, and also in that early and universal sentiment which exalts prodigality above parsimony. At all times and in all nations this preference has been shown, and there is no literature in which it has not been reflected. From the time of Thespis downwards, as Bentham reminds us, there is scarcely an instance in which a lender and a borrower have appeared upon the stage without the sympathies of the audience being claimed for the latter. The more ignorant the people the more strong will be this prejudice ; and it is therefore not surprising that those who were the pre-eminent representatives of parsimony, who were constantly increasing their wealth in a way that was so different from the ordinary forms of industry, and who often appeared in the odious light of oppressors of the poor, should have been from the earliest times regarded with dislike. Aristotle and many other of the Greek philosophers cordially adopted the popular view ; but at the same time money-lending among the Greeks was a common though a despised profession, and was little or not at all molested by authority. Among the Gauls it was

tive, because it does not comprise the opprobrium cast upon the lender, which is one great cause of the extraordinary rise of interest.
[1] As this is not a treatise of Political Economy, the reader will, I trust, pardon my adopting this old and simple formulary, without entering at length into the controversy created by the new formulary of Ricardo —that price is regulated by the cost of production. In the vast majority of cases these two formularies lead to exactly the same result, and the principal advantage of that of Ricardo seems to be, first, that in some cases it gives greater precision than the other, and secondly, that it supplements the other, meeting a few cases to which the old formulary will not apply. In determining the value of the precious metals as measured by other things—that is to say, as reflected in prices—the rule of Ricardo seems most satisfactory : in determining the normal rate of interest, the old rule is, I think, perfectly adequate. There are some good remarks on this in Chevalier, *Écon. polit.* sec. v. c. 1.

placed under the special patronage of Mercury. In Rome also it was authorised by law, though the legislators constantly sought to regulate its terms, and though both the philosophers and the people at large branded the moneylenders as the main cause of the decline of the empire. The immense advantages that capital possesses in a slave-country, and the craving for luxury that was universal, combined with the insecurity produced by general maladministration and corruption, and by frequent tumults created with the express object of freeing the plebeians from their debts, had raised the ordinary rate of interest to an enormous extent ; and this, which was in truth a symptom of the diseased condition of society, was usually regarded as the cause. At the same time the extreme severity with which Roman legislation treated insolvent debtors exasperated the people to the highest point against the exacting creditor, while, for the reasons I have already stated, the popular hatred of the usurers and the interference of legislators with their trade still further aggravated the evil. Besides this, it should be observed that when public opinion stigmatises money-lending as criminal, great industrial enterprises that rest upon it will be unknown. Those who borrow will therefore for the most part borrow on account of some urgent necessity, and the fact that interest is wealth made from the poverty of others will increase the prejudice against it.

When the subject came under the notice of the Fathers and of the mediæval writers, it was treated with unhesitating emphasis. All the pagan notions of the iniquity of money-lending were unanimously adopted, strengthened by the hostility to wealth which early Christianity constantly inculcated, and enforced with such a degree of authority and of persistence that they soon passed into nearly every legislative code. Turgot and some other writers of the eighteenth century have endeavoured to establish a distinction between more or less rigorous theologians on this subject. In fact, however, as anyone who glances over the authorities that have been collected by the old controversialists on the subject may convince himself, there was a perfect unanimity on the general principles connected with usury till the casuists of the seventeenth century, although there were many controversies about their special applications.[1] A radical misconception of the nature of interest ran through all the writings of the Fathers, of the mediæval theologians, and of the theologians of the time of the Reformation, and produced a code of commercial morality that appears with equal clearness in the Patristic invectives, in the decrees of the Councils, and in nearly every book that has ever been written on the Canon Law. The difference between theologians was not in what they taught, but in the degree of emphasis with which they taught it. There were no doubt times in which the doctrine of the Church fell into comparative desuetude : there were times when usury was very generally practised, and not very generally condemned. There are even a few examples of Councils which, without in any degree justifying usury, contented themselves with expressly censuring priests who had practised it.[2] But at the same time there is a long unbroken chain of unequivocal condemnations, extending from the period of the Fathers to the period of the Reformation.

The doctrine of the Church has been involved in some little obscurity on account of the total change that has taken place during the last three centuries in the meaning of the word usury,

[1] All the old Catholic works on the Canon Law and on Moral Philosophy show this, but I may especially indicate Concina, *Adversus Usuram* (Romæ, 1746); Concina, *Usura Contractus trini* (Romæ, 1748); Leotardus, *De Usuris* (Lugduni, 1649); Lamet et Fromageau, *Dictionnaire des Cas de Conscience* (a collection of the decisions of the doctors of the Sorbonne), art. *Usure* (Paris, 1733); and *Conférences ecclésiastiques de Paris sur l'Usure* (Paris, 1748). This last work was published under the direction or, at all events, patronage of Cardinal de Noailles, and contains a very large amount of information on the subject. It went through several editions : the first was published in 1697. See too Liégeois, *Essai sur l'Histoire et la Législation de l'Usure.*

[2] This appears to have been the case in England, where the laxity on the subject was considerable, in the twelfth and thirteenth centuries (see Anderson, *Hist. of Commerce*, vol. i. pp. 79-113). Only a month before the Council of Nice, Constantine had confirmed the old Roman law which legalised an interest of 12 per cent.; and it was probably the desire to avoid collision with the civil power that dictated the language of a curious decree of the Council, in which usury is condemned only when practised by clergymen, but at the same time is condemned on grounds that are equally applicable to laymen : " Quoniam multi sub regula constituti avaritiam et turpia lucra sectantur, oblitque divinæ Scripturæ dicentis, ' Qui pecuniam suam non dedit ad usuram,' mutuum dantes centesimas exigunt ; juste censuit sancta et magna synodus ut si quis inventus fuerit post hanc definitionem usuras accipiens.... dejiciatur a clero et alienus existat a regula." (See Troplong, *Mémoire sur le Prêt à l'Intérêt,* read before the Institute in 1844.) But the Council of Illiberis, in the beginning of the fourth century, and the Third and Fourth Councils of Carthage, expressly condemned usury in laymen.

and also on account of the many subtleties with which the casuists surrounded it ; but if the reader will pardon a somewhat pedantic array of definitions, it will be easy in a few words to disentangle it from all ambiguity.

Usury, then, according to the unanimous teaching of the old theologians, consisted of any interest that was exacted by the lender from the borrower solely as the price of the loan.[1] Its nature was, therefore, entirely independent of the amount that was asked, and of the civil laws upon the subject. Those who lent money at three per cent. were committing usury quite as really as those who lent it at forty per cent.,[2] and those who lent money at interest in a country where there was no law upon the subject, as those who lent it in defiance of the most stringent prohibitions.[3] It is not, however, to be inferred from this that everything of the nature of interest was forbidden. In the first place there was the case of permanent alienation of capital. A man might deprive himself for ever of a certain sum, and receive instead an annual revenue ; for in this case he was not receiving the price of a loan, as a loan implies the ultimate restitution of that which had been lent. There is some reason to believe that this modification was introduced at a late period, when the rise of industrial enterprises had begun to show the ruinous character of the doctrine of

usury ; but at all events the distinction was generally adopted, and became the cornerstone of a large amount of legislation.[1] In the next place there were certain cases in which a lender might claim interest from his debtor—not as the price of the loan, not as a rent exacted for the use of money, but on other grounds which were defined by theologians, and which were, or were at least believed to be, entirely distinct.[2] Such were the cases known among the schoolmen under the titles of "damnum emergens" and "lucrum cessans." If a man was so situated that, by withdrawing a portion of his capital from the business in which he was engaged, he would suffer a palpable and unquestionable loss, and if for the purpose of assisting his neighbour he consented to withdraw a certain sum, he might stipulate a compensation for the loss he thus incurred. He was not lending money for the purpose of gaining money by the transaction, and the interest he exacted was solely a compensation for a loss he had actually sustained. In the same way, if a man was able to apply money to a purpose that would bring a certain gain, and if he consented to divert a certain sum from this channel in order to lend it to a friend, it was generally (but by no means always[3]) believed that he might receive an exact equivalent for the sacrifice he had unquestionably made. The question, too, of insurances was early raised, and created a cloud of the most subtle distinctions : so too did those great lending societies, which were founded in Italy by Bernardino da Feltre, under the title of "Monti di Pietà," for the purpose of counteracting the usury of the Jews.

---

[1] The following were the principal definitions of usury employed by the writers on Canon Law : 1. Usura est pretium usus pecuniæ mutuatæ. 2. Lucrum immediate ex mutuo proveniens. 3. Usura est cum quis plus exigat in pecuniâ aut in aliquâ re quam dederit. 4. Ultra sortem lucrum aliquod ipsius ratione mutui exactum. This last is the definition of Benedict XIV. Melanchthon defined usury nearly in the same way : "Usura est lucrum supra sortem exactum tantum propter officium mutuationis." To this I may add the description given by St. Augustine of the sin : "Si fœneraveris homini, id est mutuam pecuniam dederis, a quo aliquid plus quam dedisti expectas accipere, non pecuniam solam sed aliquid plus quam dedisti, sive illud triticum sit, sive vinum, sive oleum, sive quodlibet aliud, si plus quam dedisti expectas accipere fœnerator es et in hoc improbandus non laudandus." (Sermon iii. on Psalm xxxvi.) See Concina, Adversus Usuram, pp. 32-33.

[2] In 1677, when much casuistry had been already applied to the subject, someone submitted this point to the doctors of the Sorbonne. Their decision was : "Que Titius ne seroit pas exempt d'usure en ne prenant que trois pour cent d'intérêt, parce que tout profit et tout gain tiré du prêt, si petit qu'il puisse être, fait l'usure. L'Ezéchiel, au ch. xviii, ne fait point de distinction du plus ou du moins."—Lamet et Fromageau, Dict. des Cas de Conscience (art. Usure).

[3] Thus Innocent XI. condemned the proposition, "Usura non est dum ultra sortem aliquid exigitur tanquam ex benevolentia et gratitudine debitum, sed solum si exigatur tanquam ex justitia debitum."—See Conférences sur l'Usure, tom. i. p. 100.

[1] "Tandis que le cri des peuples contre le prêt à intérêt le faisait proscrire, l'impossibilité de l'abolir entièrement fit imaginer la subtilité de l'aliénation du capital ; et c'est ce système qui, étant devenu presque général parmi les théologiens, a été adopté aussi par les jurisconsultes, à raison de l'influence beaucoup trop grande qu'ont eue sur notre jurisprudence et notre législation les principes du droit canon." (Turgot, Mém. sur les Prêts d'Argent, § 29.) Some seem to have tried to justify usury on the condition of the lender obliging himself not to demand his money till a certain period, for we find Alexander VII. condemning the proposition, "Quod sit licitum mutuanti aliquid ultra sortem exigere, modo se obliget ad non repetendum sortem usque ad certum tempus." (Conférences sur l'Usure, tom. i. p. 100.)

[2] These cases, of which I have only noticed the principal, and which were many of them very complicated, were discussed with much detail by the doctors of the Sorbonne. See Lamet et Fromageau ; see also the Mémoire of Troplong.

[3] St. Thomas Aquinas was believed to be hostile to this indulgence.

Their object was to lend money to the poor without interest, but very soon a small sum was exacted in return, in addition to what had been lent. This was very naturally stigmatised as usury, because, as we have seen, usury was entirely irrespective of the amount that was asked ; but some theologians maintained, and Leo X. at last decided by a bull, that this exaction was not usurious, because it was simply a fee for the payment of the officials connected with the establishments, and not the price of the loan.[1]

These examples will serve to show the general character that controversies on usury assumed. Above all the complications and subtleties with which the subject was surrounded, one plain intelligible principle remained—the loan of money was an illicit way of acquiring wealth. In other words, anyone who engaged in any speculation of which the increase of his capital by interest was the object, had committed usury, and was therefore condemned by the Church. It is said that after the twelfth century the lawfulness of usury was a popular tenet among the Greeks ;[2] but before this time the teaching of theologians on this subject seems to have been perfectly unanimous, and with this exception it continued to be so till the Reformation. Usury was not only regarded as an ecclesiastical crime, but was also, as far as the Church could influence the legislators, a civil one, and it was especially singled out as one that should be investigated with torture.[3]

Such then was the doctrine of theologians. It remains to examine for a moment the arguments on which it was based. The first of these in the present day appears very startling. It was said that usury, however moderate, is one of those crimes, like murder or robbery, that are palpably contrary to the law of nature. This was shown by the general consent of all nations against it, and also by a consideration of the nature of money ; for "all money is sterile by nature,"[4] and

therefore to expect profit from it is absurd. The essence of every equitable loan is, that precisely that which was lent should be returned ; and therefore, as Lactantius maintained, and as the mediæval moralists unanimously repeated, to exact interest is a species of robbery. It is true that it might naturally occur to the minds even of mediæval theologians that houses or horses were sometimes lent at a fixed rent, which was paid notwithstanding their restitution. But this difficulty was answered by a very subtle distinction, which if it was not originated was at least chiefly developed by St. Thomas Aquinas. The use of a horse may be distinguished, at least by the intellect, from the horse itself. Men borrow a horse and afterwards restore it, but the usage of the horse has been a distinct advantage, for which they may lawfully pay ; but in the case of money, which is consumed in the usage, the thing itself has no value distinct from its usage. When therefore a man restores the exact sum he has borrowed, he has done all that can be required of him, because to make him pay for the usage of this money is to make him pay for a thing that does not exist, or, perhaps more correctly, to make him pay twice for the same thing, and is therefore, said St. Thomas, dishonest.[1]

This was one branch of the argument ; the other was derived from authority. The political economy of the Fathers was received with implicit faith, and a long

of centuries during which it was incessantly asserted without being (so far as we know) once questioned is a curious illustration of the longevity of a sophism when expressed in a terse form and sheltered by a great name. It is enough to make one ashamed of one's species to think that Bentham was the first to bring into notice the simple consideration that if the borrower employs the borrowed money in buying bulls and cows, and if these produce calves to ten times the value of the interest, the money borrowed can scarcely be said to be sterile or the borrower a loser. The Greek word for interest (τόκος, from τίκτω, I beget) was probably connected with this delusion. Besides a host of theologians, the notion that usury was contrary to the law of nature was maintained by Domat, one of the greatest names in French jurisprudence. Leo X. condemned usury on the following grounds : "Dominus noster Lucâ attestante, aperte nos praecepto adstrinxit ne ex dato mutuo quidquam ultra sortem speraremus ; est enim propria usurarum interpretatio quando videlicet ex usurâ rei quae non germinat de nullo labore, nullo sumptu, nullo periculo, lucrum foenusque conquiri studetur." (*Conférences sur l'Usure*, tom. i. p. 100.)

[1] The views of St. Thomas (who was one of the chief authorities on the subject) are in the *Summa*, Pars ii. Quæst. 78. At the end of the eighteenth century they were drawn up with great elaboration by a writer named Pothier, and torn to pieces by Turgot (*Mém. sur les Prêts d'Argent*, §§ 26-27). The argument as I have stated it is, I know, very obscure, but I venture to think that is chiefly the fault of St. Thomas.

[1] Besides Lamet and Fromageau there is a discussion about "Monti di Pietà" in Escobar's *Moral Philosophy.*
[2] *Conférences sur l'Usure*, tom. i. p. 23. Salelles, *De Materiis Tribunalium Inquisitionis* (Romæ, 1651), tom. ii. p. 156. According to Cibrario (*Economia Politica del Medio Evo*, vol. ii. p. 52), a heretic named Bech, who was burnt in Piedmont in 1388, was accused among other things of having maintained that "incest and usury are not sins."
[3] Chartario, *Praxis Interrogandarum Rerum* (Romæ, 1618), p. 201.
[4] This is an absurdity of Aristotle, and the number

series of passages of Scripture were cited which were universally regarded as condemnatory of usury.[1]

As it is quite certain that commercial and industrial enterprise cannot be carried on upon a large scale without borrowing, and as it is equally certain that these loans can only be effected by paying for them in the shape of interest, it is no exaggeration to say that the Church had cursed the material development of civilisation. As long as her doctrine of usury was believed and acted on, the arm of industry was paralysed, the expansion of commerce was arrested, and all the countless blessings that have flowed from them were withheld.[2] As, however, it is impossible for a society that is even moderately civilised to continue without usury, we find, from a very early period, a certain antagonism existing on this subject between the civil law and the Church. The denunciations of the Fathers were soon succeeded by a long series of Councils which unanimously condemned usurers, and the canonical law is crowded with enactments against them; but at the same time kings found it constantly necessary to borrow for the equipment of their armies, and they very naturally shrank from suppressing a class to which they had recourse. Edward the Confessor indeed in England, St. Lewis in France,[3]

and a few other sovereigns of remarkable piety took this extreme step; but generally usury, though not altogether recognised, was in some degree connived at. Besides, to lend was esteemed much more sinful than to borrow,[1] and in the earlier part of the middle ages the usurers were almost exclusively Jews, who had no scruples on the subject, and who had adopted this profession partly because of the great profits they could derive from it, and partly because it was almost the only one open to them. It was not till the close of the eleventh century that Christian money-lenders became numerous, and the rise of this class was the immediate consequence of the commercial development of the Italian republics. The Lombards soon became the rivals of the Jews;[2] the merchants of Florence carried on usury to a still greater extent,[3] and for the first time this was done openly, with the full sanction both of law and public opinion. From Italy usury passed to France and England;[4] and the Third Council of the Lateran,[5] which was convened by Alexander III., in 1179, complained that it had so increased that it was almost everywhere practised. The same Council endeavoured to arrest it by decreeing that no notorious and impenitent usurer should be admitted to the altar, should be absolved at the hour of death, or should receive Christian burial.[6] All this, however, was in vain: the expansion of commercial enterprise became every year more marked, and the increase of usury was its necessary consequence.

In this manner the rise of an industrial

---

[1] The chief passages cited were—Lev. xxv. 36, Deut. xxiii. 19, Ps. xv. 5, Ezek. xviii., and (from the New Testament) Luke vi. 35. As Turgot notices, the popular interpretation of this last passage was peculiarly inexcusable in Catholics, who always interpret the injunctions that surround it as "counsels of perfection," not obligatory on every man. Yet Dussaut was able to say, "La tradition constante des conciles, à commencer par les plus anciens, celle des papes, des pères, des interprètes et de l'Église romaine, est d'interpréter ce verset, 'Mutuum date nihil inde sperantes,' comme prohibitif du profit qu'on tire du prêt; 'inde' c'est-à-dire de l'usure." (2nde Pastorale, contre la Version de Richard Simon.)

[2] Montesquieu, speaking of the scholastic writings on usury, says, with a little exaggeration, "Ainsi nous devons aux spéculations des Scholastiques tous les malheurs qui ont accompagné la destruction du commerce" (Esprit des Lois, liv. xxi. c. 20); and Turgot, "L'observation rigoureuse de ces lois serait destructive de tout commerce; aussi ne sont-elles pas observées rigoureusement. Elles interdisent toute stipulation d'intérêt sans aliénation du capital....Et c'est une chose notoire qu'il n'y a pas sur la terre une place de commerce où la plus grande partie du commerce ne roule sur l'argent, emprunté sans aliénation du capital." (Mém. sur les Prêts d'Argent, § xiv.). M. Sismondi has justly observed (Nouveaux Principes d'Économie politique) that the prohibition of usury in Catholic countries has also done very much to promote a passion for luxury, and to discourage economy—the rich who were not engaged in business finding no easy way of employing their savings productively.

[3] Confirming in this respect a French law of the eighth and ninth century which provided that "Usuram non solum clerici, sed nec laici Christiani, exigere

debent." Some think Justinian prohibited usury, but there is a good deal of dispute about this. Richard I. of England "Christianum fœneratorem fieri prohibuit aut quacunque conventionis occasione aliquid recipere ultra id quod mutuo concessit" (Bromton Chronicon). Some governors made it a law that the property of those who had been usurers might be confiscated by the crown after their death (Cibrario, Economia Politica del Medio Evo, vol. iii. p. 319). This arrangement had a double advantage: the government might borrow money from the usurer while he was living, and rob his children when he was dead.

[1] According to the doctors of the Sorbonne, it is sinful to borrow at usury except under extreme necessity, but the whole stress of the denunciations was directed against the lenders.

[2] Bedarride, Hist. des Juifs, pp. 186-189.

[3] Muratori, Antiq. Italicæ, dissert. xvi.—a good history of the rise of Christian usurers.

[4] Ibid.

[5] Ibid. This Council is reckoned a general one by the Catholics.

[6] Ibid. The Council of Vienne, presided over by Clement V., pronounced it to be heretical to justify usury: "Sane si quis in istum errorem inciderit, ut pertinaciter affirmare præsumat exercere usuras non esse peccatum, decernimus eum velut hæreticum puniendum." (Conférences sur l'Usure, tom. i. p. 93.)

civilisation produced a distinct opposition between the practice of Christendom and the teaching of the Church. On the one hand to lend money at interest became a constant and recognised transaction, and the more the laws of wealth were understood, the more evident it became that it was both necessary and innocent. On the other hand there was no subject in the whole compass of Catholic theology on which the teaching of the Church was more unequivocal.[1] Usury had always been defined as any sum that was exacted as the price of a loan, and it had been condemned with unqualified severity by the Fathers, by a long series of Popes and Councils, by the most eminent of the mediæval theologians, and by the unanimous voice of the Church. The result of this conflict evidently depended on the comparative prevalence of dogmatic and rationalistic modes of thought. As long as men derived their notions of duty from authority and tradition, they would adopt one conclusion ; when they began to interrogate their own sense of right, they would soon arrive at another.

The sequel of the history of usury is soon told. The Reformation, which was in a great measure effected by the trading classes, speedily dispelled the illusions on the subject, although the opinions of the Reformers were at first somewhat divided. Melanchthon, Brentius, and (perhaps) Bucer adopted the old Catholic view ;[2] but Calvin maintained that usury was only wrong when it was exacted in an oppressive manner from the poor,[3] and, with admirable good sense, he refused to listen to those who exhorted him to check it by law. In England money-lending was first formally permitted under Henry VIII.[4] Somewhat later Grotius discussed it in a liberal though rather hesitating tone, maintaining strongly that it was at least not

contrary to the law of nature.[1] Two or three other Protestant writers, who are now almost forgotten, appear to have gone still further ; but the author to whom the first unequivocal assertion of the modern doctrine of interest is due seems to be Saumaise,[2] who, between 1638 and 1640, published three books in its defence. His view was speedily but almost silently adopted by most Protestants, and the change produced no difficulty or hostility to Christianity.

Among the Catholics, on the other hand, the difficulty of discarding the past was very considerable. At the beginning of the sixteenth century the modern distinction between usury and interest had been introduced among laymen, to the great indignation of theologians,[3] in order to evade the censure of the canonical law. The casuistry of the Jesuits was soon applied to the subject, and two or three circuitous ways of obtaining interest became popular, which gave rise to long and virulent controversies.[4] Early in the eighteenth century three professors of the University of Ingolstadt, named Pichler, Tanner, and Hannold, took a further step, and contended that some forms of undoubted usury might be safely practised if the civil law permitted them ;[5] and in 1743 a writer named Broedersen wrote a book which seems to have embodied and combined nearly all the leading sentiments of the different schools of

---

[1] According to Concina, usury has been condemned by twenty-eight Councils (six of them regarded by the Church of Rome as general) and by seventeen popes (*Adversus Usuram*, pp. 112-113).

[2] See the passages in Concina, *Usura trini Contractûs*, pp. 250-251.

[3] Concina, *Adversus Usuram*, p. 2. This view was also adopted by Molinæus : "Carolus Molinæus contendit acerrime usuram, nisi fraus adsit aut debitor nimium opprimatur, licitam esse. Doctores omnes a sexcentis annis contrarium docuerunt." (Leotardus, *De Usuris*, p. 15.) Calvin was one of the very first who exposed the folly of the old notion about the sterility of money. See a remarkable passage in one of his letters quoted by M'Culloch, *Pol. Econ.*, pt. iii. ch. viii.

[4] Anderson, *Hist. of Commerce*, vol. i. p. 304.

[1] *De Jure Belli et Pacis*, lib. ii. cap. 12.

[2] Better known as Salmasius, the author of the *Defensio Regis* to which Milton replied.

[3] Le Fèvre, who was tutor to Louis XIII., mentions that in his time the term interest had been substituted for usury, and he added "C'est là proprement ce qu'on peut appeler l'art de chicaner avec Dieu." Marot also, who wrote in the first half of the sixteenth century, made this change the subject of a sarcasm :—
"On ne prête plus à l'usure,
Mais tant qu'on veut à l'intérêt."
(See *Conférences sur l'Usure*, tom. i. p. 25.) According to Concina, the first, or nearly the first (*fere primus*), Catholic theologian who cavilled at the old definitions of usury was Le Coreur, who wrote a treatise in 1682, in which he maintained that moderate interest might be exacted on commercial loans, but not on those which had their origin in the necessities of poverty (*Adversus Usuram*, p. 3). The Catholic writers at this period nearly always spoke of the modern doctrine as a Protestant heresy—the heresy of Calvin, Molinæus, and Salmasius.

[4] One of these was elaborately discussed by Concina in a treatise called *De Usura trini Contractûs* (Romæ, 1748). Others, which arose especially in the commercial communities of Belgium, are noticed in Lamet and Fromageau, and also by Troplong.

[5] Pichler was a Jesuit, and his views on usury—a perfect cloud of subtleties—are contained in his *Jus Canonicum* (Venetiis, 1730), lib. iii. tit. 19. Tanner was also a Jesuit. Of Hannold I know nothing except from the brief notice of his opinions in Concina, *De Usura trini Contractûs*, pp. 152-155.

laxer theologians. The subject had by this time excited so much agitation that Benedict XIV. deemed it necessary to interpose. He accordingly, as the head of the Catholic Church, issued an encyclical letter, in which he acknowledged that there were occasions when a lender, on special grounds, might claim a sum additional to what he had lent, but refused to pronounce in detail on the merits of the controversies that had been raised concerning particular kinds of loans, and contented himself with laying down authoritatively the doctrine of the Church. That doctrine was that usury is always a sin; that it consists of any sum that is exacted beyond what had been lent, solely on account of the loan;[1] and that the fact of this interest being moderate, or being exacted only from a rich man, or in order to further a commercial undertaking, in no degree alters its character.[2] This appears to have been the last official utterance of a Pope upon the subject, and although isolated theologians for some time attempted to stem the tide, their voices soon died away before the advancing spirit of Rationalism. Year by year what the old theologians had termed usury became more general. The creation of national debts made it the very pillar of the political system. Every great enterprise that was undertaken received its impulse from it, and the immense majority of the wealthy were concerned in it. Yet though it had long been branded as a mortal sin, and though mortal sin implied eternal separation from the Deity and the endurance of eternal and excruciating sufferings, the infallible voice continued silent. The decrees of the Councils remained indeed unchanged; the passages from Scripture and from the Fathers that had so long been triumphantly adduced continued precisely the same; but the old superstition faded steadily and almost silently away, till

every vestige of it had disappeared. Laws, indeed, against usury still continued upon the statute-book, but they were intended not to prohibit interest, but only to regulate its rate; and as the principles of political economy were elucidated, this too began to pass away. At the close of the seventeenth century, Locke protested strongly against the attempt to reduce interest by law;[1] but the full investigation of the subject was reserved for the following century. It was remarked that Catherine of Russia having endeavoured to lower the general rate of interest from six to five per cent., her enactment had the effect of raising it to seven; and that Lewis XV., in the same manner, raised it from five to six when intending to reduce it to four.[2] In England both Adam Smith and Hume threw a flood of light upon the subject, though neither of them fully perceived the evil of the laws, which the first, indeed, expressly applauded.[3] In France, nine years before the *Wealth of Nations*, Turgot had disclosed most of those evils; and he appears to have clearly seen that interest is not capricious, but bears a fixed relation to the general condition of society.[4] At last Bentham, in his famous

[1] See his *Considerations on the Lowering of Interest*, published in 1691—a tract which is, unfortunately, deeply tinged with the errors of the mercantile theory, but is full of shrewd guesses on the laws of money. Locke perceived that interest depended upon supply and demand, and that all attempts to reduce it below the natural level were pernicious or abortive. He thought, however, that the maximum should be fixed by law to prevent imposition, but that that maximum should be fixed above the natural rate. At a still earlier period Harrington saw the necessity of usury, but involved himself in great obscurity, and almost absurdity, when discussing it: see his *Prerogative of Popular Government*, c. 3.

[2] Storch, *Économie politique*, tom. iii. p. 187.

[3] Adam Smith wished the legal interest to be fixed a very little above the current rate of interest, as a check upon prodigality and rash speculation. This is still done in many countries, but Bentham has urged (Letter xiii., *On Usury*) that such a law is extremely detrimental to industrial progress, as each new enterprise is almost necessarily more hazardous than old-established ones, and therefore capitalists will only direct their capital to the former if the interest to be obtained from them is considerably higher than could be obtained from the latter. The belief that, while the ordinary commercial value of money should be unchecked by law, some restraint should be put upon the inordinate interest extorted by dishonest speculators from young and ignorant spendthrifts, has, I think, of late years been steadily gaining ground in England.

[4] Besides the *Mémoire*, Turgot noticed the subject in a very striking manner in his *Réflexions sur la Formation des Richesses*. Like nearly everyone in his time, he fell into the error of believing that the abundance of the precious metals told upon the rate of interest; but this did not affect his main argument, and on the whole there is not much in Bentham that was not anticipated by Turgot. In Italy Genovesi, who was a contemporary of Turgot, advocated the

[1] "Peccati genus illud quod usura vocatur, quodque in contractu mutui propriam suam sedem et locum habet, in eo est repositum quod quis ex ipsomet mutuo, quod suapte natura tantundem duntaxat reddi postulat quantum receptum est, plus sibi reddi velit quam est receptum." *Epistola Bened. XIV.*, in Concina, *Adversus Usuram*, p. 14.

[2] "Neque vero ad istam labem purgandam ullum arcessiri subsidium poterit, vel ex eo quod id lucrum non excedens et nimium sed moderatum, non magnum sed exiguum sit; vel ex eo quod is a quo id lucrum solius causâ mutui depositur non pauper sed dives existat; nec datam sibi mutuo summam relicturus otiosam, sed ad fortunas suas amplificandas vel novis coëmendis prædiis vel quæstuosis agitandis negotiis, utilissime sit impensurus."—*Ibid.*

Letters on Usury, gave what will probably prove a deathblow to a legislative folly that has been in existence for 3,000 years. It has been observed by a Russian political economist that the Starovertsis, and some other dissenters from the Russian Church, still maintain that it is sinful to lend money at interest[1]—perhaps the last representatives of what was for many centuries the unanimous teaching of the Christian Church.

The importance of this episode depends not so much on the question that was immediately at issue—though that question, as we have seen, was far from being insignificant—as upon its influence in breaking the authority of the Church. A second way in which the rise of the industrial classes that followed the Crusades tended towards the same object was by uniting nations of different religions in commercial relations. Before this time the intervention of the Pope had been the most effectual agent in regulating national differences, and General Councils formed the highest, and indeed almost the solitary, expression of a European federation. The benign influence of Catholicism was continually exercised in correcting the egotism of a restricted patriotism; and although this benefit was purchased by the creation of an intense animosity towards those who were without, and also by an excessive predominance of ecclesiastical influence, it would be unfair to forget its inestimable value. After the Crusades, however, a new bond of cohesion was called into existence, and nations were grouped upon a new principle. The appointment of consuls in the Syrian towns, to superintend the commercial interests of the Western nations, gave the first great impulse to international diplomacy[2] — an influence which for many centuries occupied an extremely important place in civilisation, but has of late years been in some degree waning before the doctrine of the rights of nationalities and before the increasing publicity of politics. The social and intellectual consequences of commercial intercourse were still greater. For while an intense sectarian spirit is compatible with the most transcendent abilities and with the most profound learning, provided those abilities and that learning are directed in a single channel, it can very rarely survive close contact with members of different creeds. When men have once realised the truth that no single sect possesses a monopoly either of goodness or of abilities—when they have watched the supporters of the most various opinions dogmatising with the same conviction, defending their belief with the same energy, and irradiating it with the same virtue—when they have learnt in some degree to assume the standing-point of different sects, to perceive the aspect from which what they had once deemed incongruous and absurd seems harmonious and coherent, and to observe how all the features of the intellectual landscape take their colour from the prejudice of education, and shift and vary according to the point of view from which they are regarded—when, above all, they have begun to revere and love for their moral qualities those from whom they are separated by their creed, their sense both of the certainty and the importance of their distinctive tenets will usually be impaired, and their intolerance towards others proportionately diminished. The spectacle of the contradictions around them, of the manifest attraction which different classes of opinions possess to different minds, will make them suspect that their own opinions may possibly be false, and even that no one system of belief can be adapted to the requirements of all men; while, at the same time, their growing sense of the moral excellence that may be associated with the most superstitious creed will withdraw their minds from dogmatic considerations. For human nature is so constituted, that, although men may persuade themselves intellectually that error is a damnable crime, the voice of conscience protests so strongly against this doctrine, that it can

abolition of usury laws. (Pecchio, *Storia della Economia Publica in Italia*, p. 114.)

[1] Storch, *Economie politique*, om. iii. p. 175.

[2] I use this expression because that obscure subject which Papebrochius and Mabillon have investigated, and which they have called Diplomacy, is much more what we should now term the History of Charters. The rise and influence of consulships has been traced in English by Warden, in French by Borel, and in Latin by Steck. The subject has been also well noticed by Van Bruyssel, *Hist. du Commerce belge*, tom. i. p. 140; and the influence of diplomacy as superseding General Councils, by Littré, *Révolution, Conservation et Positivisme*, one of the ablest books the Positive School has ever produced. The distinction between the old and new sense of diplomacy is expressed respectively in the words "la diplomatique" and "la diplomatie," the last of which is less than a century old. (See De Flassan, *Hist. de la Diplomatie française*, Introd.) I may add that one of the first systems of navigation law depended upon an institution

called the "Consulship of the Sea," which consisted of a tribunal of leading merchants authorised to determine disputes.

only be silenced by the persuasion that the personal character of the heretic is as repulsive as his creed. Calumny is the homage which dogmatism has ever paid to conscience. Even in the periods when the guilt of heresy was universally believed, the spirit of intolerance was only sustained by the diffusion of countless libels against the misbeliever, and by the systematic concealment of his virtues. How sedulously theologians at that time laboured in this task, how unscrupulously they maligned and blackened every leading opponent of their views, how eagerly they fanned the flame of sectarian animosity, how uniformly they prohibited those whom they could influence from studying the writings or frequenting the society of men of different opinions from their own, is well known to all who are acquainted with ecclesiastical history. The first great blow to this policy was given by the rise of the commercial classes that followed the Crusades. Orthodox Catholics came into close and amicable connection both with Greeks and with Mahometans, while their new pursuit made them, for the first time, look with favour upon the Jews. It was these last who in the middle ages were the special objects of persecution, and it was also towards them that the tolerant character of commerce was first manifested.

The persecution of the Jewish race dates from the very earliest period in which Christianity obtained the direction of the civil power;[1] and, although it varied greatly in its character and its intensity, it can scarcely be said to have definitely ceased till the French Revolution. Alexander II. indeed, and three or four other Popes,[2] made noble efforts to arrest it, and more than once interposed with great courage, as well as great humanity, to censure the massacres; but the priests were usually unwearied in

inciting the passions of the people, and hatred of the Jew was for many centuries a faithful index of the piety of the Christians. Massacred by thousands during the enthusiasm of the Crusades and of the War of the Shepherds, the Jews found every ecclesiastical revival, and the accession of every sovereign of more than usual devotion, occasions for fresh legislative restrictions. Theodosius, St. Lewis, and Isabella the Catholic—who were probably the three most devout sovereigns before the Reformation—the Council of the Lateran, which led the religious revival of the thirteenth century, Paul IV., who led that of the sixteenth century, and above all the religious orders, were among their most ardent persecutors. Everything was done to separate them from their fellow-men, to mark them out as the objects of undying hatred, and to stifle all compassion for their sufferings. They were compelled to wear a peculiar dress, and to live in a separate quarter. A Christian might not enter into any partnership with them; he might not eat with them; he might not use the same bath; he might not employ them as physicians; he might not even purchase their drugs.[1] Intermarriage with them was deemed a horrible pollution, and in the time of St. Lewis any Christian who had chosen a Jewess for his mistress was burnt alive.[2] Even in

---

[1] As their latest historian says, "Le christianisme ne prit une véritable consistance que sous le règne de Constantin; et c'est à dater de cette époque que commence, à proprement parler, pour les Juifs l'ère des persécutions religieüses." (Bedarride, *Hist. des Juifs*, p. 16.) In this, however, as in other persecutions, the Arians were quite as bad as the orthodox. Constantius persecuted at least as much as Constantine, and the Spanish Visigoths more than either.

[2] On the liberality of several Popes to the Jews, see Bedarride, p. 260; on Alexander II., pp. 114-123. St. Bernard also laboured to assuage the persecution. Alexander VI. was especially generous to the Jews, and made great efforts to alleviate their sufferings—a fact that should be remembered in favour of a Pope for whom there is not much else to be said.

[1] For a long list of these prohibitions see a curious book, *De Judæis* (Turin, 1717), by Joseph Sessa (one of the judges appointed in Piedmont to regulate the affairs of the Jews), p. 10. As early as the reign of Constantine a Council of Elvira forbade Christians holding any communication with Jews. The Council of the Lateran compelled Jews to wear a separate dress; and this very simple provision, by bringing them prominently before the people in an intensely fanatical age, contributed greatly to rouse the passions of the Catholics, and to facilitate the massacres that ensued (see Rios, *Études sur les Juifs d'Espagne* [trad. Maynabel], p. 109). St. Vincent de Ferrier persuaded the Spanish Government to enforce this decree against both Jews and Moors. (Paramo, *De Orig. Inq.*, p. 164.)

[2] *Œuvres de St.-Foix*, tom. iv. pp. 88, 89. A similar enactment was made in Spain (Rios, pp. 88, 89). It was also a popular belief that the blood of Jews was black and putrid, and the bad smell for which they were unhappily notorious, innate. There is a long discussion on this in Sessa. But perhaps the most curious instance of this order of superstitions is a statute of Queen Jeanne I., in 1347, regulating the houses of ill-fame at Avignon, in which, after providing with great detail for the accommodation of the Christians, it is enacted that no Jew shall be admitted under severe penalties (Sabatier, *Hist. de la Législation sur les Femmes publiques*, p. 103). The authenticity of this statute has been questioned, but M. Sabatier seems to have succeeded in defending it, and he has shown that in 1408 a Jew was actually flogged at Avignon for the offence in question (pp. 105, 106). This extreme horror of Jews furnished Ulrich von Hutten with the subject of one of the happiest pieces of irony he ever wrote—

their executions they were separated from other criminals, and, till the fourteenth century, they were hung between two dogs, and with the head downwards.[1] According to St. Thomas Aquinas, all they possessed, being derived from the practice of usury, might be justly confiscated,[2] and if they were ever permitted to pursue that practice unmolested, it was only because they were already so hopelessly damned, that no crime could aggravate their condition.[3]

Insulted, plundered, hated, and despised by all Christian nations, banished from England by Edward I., and from France by Charles VI., they found in the Spanish Moors rulers who, in addition to that measure of tolerance which is always produced by a high intellectual culture, were probably not without a special sympathy for a race whose pure monotheism formed a marked contrast to the scarcely disguised polytheism of the Spanish Catholics ; and Jewish learning and Jewish genius contributed very largely to that bright but transient civilisation which radiated from Toledo and Cordova, and exercised so salutary an influence upon the belief of Europe. But when, in an ill-omened hour, the Cross supplanted the Crescent on the heights of the Alhambra, this solitary refuge was destroyed, the last gleam of tolerance vanished from Spain, and the expulsion of the Jews was determined.

This edict was immediately due to the exertions of Torquemada, who, if he did not suggest it, at least by a singular act of audacity overcame the irresolution of the Queen ;[1] but its ultimate cause is to be found in that steadily increasing popular fanaticism which made it impossible for the two races to exist together. In 1390, about a hundred years before the conquest of Granada, the Catholics of Seville, being excited by the eloquence of a great preacher, named Hernando Martinez, had attacked the Jews' quarter, and murdered 4,000 Jews,[2] Martinez himself presiding over the massacre. About a year later, and partly through the influence of the same eminent divine, similar scenes took place at Valentia, Cordova, Burgos, Toledo, and Barcelona.[3] St. Vincent de Ferrier, who was then stirring all Spain with his preaching, devoted himself especially to the Jews ; and as the people zealously seconded the reasoning of the saint by massacring those who hesitated, many thousands were converted,[4] and if they

---

the exquisite description of the mental agonies of a student of Frankfort, who, mistaking a Jew for a magistrate of the city, took off his hat to him, and on discovering his error was unable to decide whether he had committed a mortal or only a venial sin. (*Epistol. Obscurorum Virorum*, ep. 2.)

[1] Michelet, *Origines de Droit*, p. 368.

[2] See a curious letter from St. Thomas to the Duchess of Brabant, given at length in Van Bruyssel, *Hist. du Commerce belge*, tom. i. pp. 239, 240. On the general doctrine that property derived from usury may be confiscated by the civil power, see Paramo, *De Orig. Inquisit.*, p. 167.

[3] There was a good deal of controversy in the middle ages about whether the Jews should be permitted to practise usury. The liberty seems to have been first openly granted in the commercial towns of Italy, but it gradually spread, and was admitted by some Popes. Sessa gives the reasons that were avowed by theologians : "Usuræ Judaicæ tolerantur quidem ex permissione Principum et summorum Pontificum in Hebræis ut de gente deperditâ, et quorum salus est desperata, et ad eum finem ne Christiani foenoris exercitio strangulentur a Christianis" (*De Judæis*, p. 9). The permission was granted in Piedmont in 1603. St. Lewis refused to permit the Jews to exercise usury (Troplong), and the Spanish rulers seem to have vacillated on the subject (Bedarride, pp. 192–194). There can be no doubt the monopoly of usury which the Jews possessed did more to enrich than all their persecutions to impoverish them. For although, as Adam Smith observes, the current rate of interest should represent approximately the average of profits, this is only when it is free, and the exertions of divines and legislators in the middle ages had raised it far above the high rate it would then naturally have borne. It seems to have usually ranged between 25 and 40 per cent. In 1430 we find the Florentines, in order to reduce the current rate, admitting the Jews into their city, whence they had previously been excluded, on the condition of their lending money as low as 20 per cent. (Cibrario, vol. iii. p. 318.) It is curious to observe how, while persecution prevented the Jews from ever amalgamating with other nations, the system of usury prevented them from ever perishing or sinking into insignificance.

[1] The Jews offered 30,000 ducats to remain. The Queen, it is said, for a time hesitated, but Torquemada, confronting her on the threshold of the palace with a crucifix in his hand, exclaimed, "Judas sold his God for thirty pieces of silver—you are about to sell him for thirty thousand" (Bedarride and Prescott). The anecdote is related by Paramo, p. 144, only he does not specify the sum.

[2] Rios, *Études sur les Juifs d'Espagne*, p. 77. Rios says that the contemporary writers are unanimous about the number.

[3] *Ibid.* pp. 79–82. Llorente *Hist. de l'Inquisition*, tom. i. p. 141.

[4] Rios gives a delightfully Spanish complexion to all this : "L'apparition de saint Vincent Ferrier devant le peuple juif avait été un fait véritablement prodigieux. Il avait apparu à leurs yeux comme un ange sauveur, et cette circonstance ne pouvait qu'être favorable à sa haute mission évangélique. Le 8 juin 1391, les rues de Valence se remplissaient du sang des Juifs, les boutiques étaient brûlées, les maisons de la Juiverie saccagées par une multitude effrénée, les malheureux Juifs couraient aux églises demandant le baptême, et ils étaient repoussés de toutes parts et ne rencontraient que la mort, quand au milieu de la populace saint Vincent Ferrier se présente, et élevant sa voix inspirée, il met un terme à cet horrible carnage. La multitude se tait. Les Juifs appelés par ce nouvel apôtre, qui se donna plus tard à lui-même le nom d'ange de l'Apocalypse, écoutent la parole divine et se convertissent.... Tout cela contribua puissamment aux merveilleux résultats de sa prédication" (pp. 89, 90). St. Vincent was a Dominican, a very great preacher, and so very good that he always undressed in the dark lest he should see himself naked. For his miracles, his

relapsed into Judaism were imprisoned or burned. Scenes of this kind took place more than once during the fifteenth century, and they naturally intensified the traditional hatred, which was still further aggravated by the fact that most of the tax-gatherers were Jews. At last the Moorish war, which had always been regarded as a crusade, was drawing to a close, the religious fervour of the Spanish rose to the highest point, and the Inquisition was established as its expression. Numbers of converted Jews were massacred; others, who had been baptised during past explosions of popular fury, fled to the Moors, in order to practise their rites, and at last, after a desperate resistance, were captured and burnt alive.[1] The clergy exerted all their energies to produce the expulsion of the entire race, and to effect this object all the old calumnies were revived, and two or three miracles invented.[2]

When we take into consideration all these circumstances, and the condition of public feeling they evince, we can perhaps hardly blame Isabella for issuing the decree of banishment against the Jews; but at the same time it must be acknowledged that history relates very few measures that produced so vast an amount of calamity—calamities so frightful, that an old historian has scarcely exaggerated them when he describes the sufferings of the Spanish Jews as equal to those of their ancestors after the destruction of Jerusalem.[3] In three short months, all unconverted Jews were obliged, under pain of death, to abandon the Spanish soil.[4] Although they were permitted to dispose of their goods, they were forbidden to carry either gold or silver from Spain, and this measure made them almost helpless before the rapacity of their persecutors. Multitudes falling into the hands of the pirates who swarmed around the coast, were plundered of all

they possessed, and reduced to slavery; multitudes died of famine or of plague, or were murdered or tortured with horrible cruelty by the African savages, or were cast back by tempests on the Spanish coast. Weak women, driven from luxurious homes among the orange groves of Seville or Granada, children fresh from their mothers' arms, the aged, the sick, and the infirm, perished by thousands. About 80,000 took refuge in Portugal, relying on the promise of the king; but even there the hatred of the Spaniards pursued them. A mission was organised. Spanish priests lashed the Portuguese into fury, and the king was persuaded to issue an edict which threw even that of Isabella into the shade. All the adult Jews were banished from Portugal; but first of all their children below the age of fourteen were taken from them to be educated as Christians. Then, indeed, the cup of bitterness was filled to the brim. The serene fortitude with which the exiled people had borne so many and such grievous calamities gave way, and was replaced by the wildest paroxysms of despair. Piercing shrieks of anguish filled the land. Women were known to fling their children into deep wells, or to tear them limb from limb, rather than resign them to the Christians. When at last, childless and broken-hearted, they sought to leave the land, they found that the ships had been purposely detained, and the allotted time having expired, they were reduced to slavery, and baptised by force. By the merciful intervention of Rome most of them at last regained their liberty, but their children were separated from them for ever. A great peal of rejoicing filled the Peninsula, and proclaimed that the triumph of the Spanish priests was complete.[1]

Certainly the heroism of the defenders of every other creed fades into insignificance before this martyr people, who for thirteen centuries confronted all the evils that the fiercest fanaticism could devise, enduring obloquy and spoliation and the violation of the dearest ties, and the infliction of the most hideous sufferings, rather than abandon their faith. For these were no ascetic monks, dead to all the hopes and passions of life, but were men who appreciated intensely the worldly

---

virtues, and the multitudes he converted, see his life in Spanish by Vincent Justiniano (Valentia, 1573). Paramo says that the Inquisitors discovered that no less than 17,000 of the converts of St. Vincent returned to Judaism (*De Orig. Inq.* p. 167).

[1] Twelve, however, who were captured at Malaga during the siege in 1485 were impaled by Ferdinand.

[2] They are detailed by Paramo.

[3] Picus Mirandola.

[4] It seems impossible to ascertain the number of the exiles with accuracy, for the Spanish historians vary greatly, from Cardoso, who estimates it at 120,000, to Mariana, who states it at 800,000. Paramo says some place it at more than 170,000, and others at 400,000 (p. 167). Justiniano says 420,000. Great numbers of the Jews avoided banishment by baptism.

[1] Bedarride, pp. 291-301; Paramo, 235. Paramo says the Portuguese decree of banishment was simply changed for one of compulsory baptism.

advantages they relinquished, and whose affections had become all the more lively on account of the narrow circle in which they were confined. Enthusiasm and the strange phenomena of ecstasy, which have exercised so large an influence in the history of persecution, which have nerved so many martyrs with super-human courage, and have deadened or destroyed the anguish of so many fearful tortures, were here almost unknown. Persecution came to the Jewish nation in its most horrible forms, yet surrounded by every circumstance of petty annoyance that could destroy its grandeur, and it continued for centuries their abiding portion. But above all this the genius of that wonderful people rose supreme. While those around them were grovelling in the darkness of besotted ignorance; while juggling miracles and lying relics were the themes on which almost all Europe was expatiating; while the intellect of Christendom, enthralled by countless superstitions, had sunk into a deadly torpor, in which all love of enquiry and all search for truth were abandoned, the Jews were still pursuing the path of knowledge, amassing learning, and stimulating progress with the same unflinching constancy that they manifested in their faith. They were the most skilful physicians, the ablest financiers, and among the most profound philosophers; while they were only second to the Moors in the cultivation of natural science. They were also the chief interpreters to Western Europe of Arabian learning.[1] But their most important service, and that with which we are now most especially concerned, was in sustaining commercial activity. For centuries they were almost its only representatives. By travelling from land to land till they had become intimately acquainted both with the wants and the productions of each, by practising money-lending on a large

scale and with consummate skill, by keeping up a constant and secret correspondence and organising a system of exchange that was then unparalleled in Europe,[1] the Jews succeeded in making themselves absolutely indispensable to the Christian community, and in accumulating immense wealth and acquiring immense influence in the midst of their sufferings. When the Italian republics rose to power, they soon became the centres to which the Jews flocked; and under the merchant governments of Leghorn, Venice, Pisa, and Genoa, a degree of toleration was accorded that was indeed far from perfect, but was at least immeasurably greater than elsewhere. The Jews were protected from injury, and permitted to practise medicine and money-lending unmolested, and public opinion, as well as the law, looked upon them with tolerance.[2]

The tolerant spirit the commercial classes manifested towards the Jews before the Reformation was displayed with equal clearness towards both Catholics and Protestants in the convulsions that followed it. In addition to the reasons I have already given, there were two causes actively sustaining the predisposition.

In the first place, the industrial character is eminently practical. The habit of mind that distinguishes it leads men to care very little about principles, and very much about results; and this habit has at least a tendency to act upon theological judgments.

In the second place, religious wars and persecutions have always proved extremely detrimental to industry. The expulsions of the Jews and Moors from Spain, and of the Huguenots from France, were perhaps the most severe blows ever directed against the industry of either country; while the nations

---

[1] The very extensive Jewish literature of the middle ages is fully reviewed by Bedarride and Rios. Maimonides is of course the greatest name. M. Renan, in his essay on Averroes, has shown that nearly all the first translations into Latin of the works of Averroes were by Jews (chiefly by those of Montpellier, who were especially famous for their learning), and that Averroism took deep root in Jewish teaching. Maimonides wrote a letter on the vanity of astrology, which two popes applauded (Bedarride, p. 151). He was also distinguished for his liberal views about inspiration (Lee, *On Inspiration*, pp. 454-459). The controversial literature of the Jews directed against Christianity was extremely voluminous. A catalogue of these works, and a description of many of them, is given in a little book called *Bibliotheca Judaica Antichristiana*, by John Bernard de Rossi (Parmæ, 1800).

[1] A very old and general tradition ascribes the invention of the letter of exchange to Jews who, having been banished from France, had taken refuge in Lombardy. Nor does there seem to be anything of much weight to oppose to it, though some have contended that the Italians were the real inventors. At all events, the Jews appear to have been among the first to employ it. The earliest notice of letters of exchange is said to be in a statute of Avignon of 1243. In 1272 there was a Venetian law, "De Litteris Cambii." Compare on this subject Villeneuve Bargemont, *Histoire de l'Economie politique*, tom. i. pp. 277-279; Blanqui, *Hist. de l'Econ. pol.*, tom. i. p. 183; Montesquieu, *Esprit des Lois*, liv. xxi. c. 20; and the tractate of Jules Thieurry, *La Lettre de Change* (Paris, 1862).

[2] Bedarride, pp. 258, 259. The magnificent synagogue at Leghorn (probably the finest in existence) was erected by the Spanish Jews who took refuge in that city.

which on these or similar occasions were wise enough to receive the fugitives, reaped an immediate and an enormous advantage. The commercial genius of the Jewish exiles was one of the elements in the development of Leghorn, Pisa, and Ancona. Amsterdam owes a very large part of its prosperity to the concourse of heretics who had been driven from Bruges and from the surrounding country. The linen manufacture in Ireland, as well as many branches of English industry, were greatly stimulated by the skill and capital of the French refugees. French commerce received a powerful and long-sustained impulse from the good relations Francis I. had established with the Turks. It is not therefore surprising that Amsterdam, and in a less degree the other centres of commercial enterprise, should have been from an early period conspicuous for their tolerance, or that the diffusion of the industrial spirit should have everywhere prepared the way for the establishment of religious liberty.

Another consequence of the rise of the industrial spirit was the decay of the theological ideal of voluntary poverty, which had created the monastic system. Immediately after the Crusades we find nearly all Europe rushing with extreme and long-sustained violence into habits of luxury. The return of peace, the contact with the luxurious civilisations of the East, the sudden increase of wealth that followed the first impetus of commerce, had all contributed to the movement. An extraordinary richness of dress was one of its first signs, and was encountered by a long succession of sumptuary laws. At the end of the thirteenth century we find Philip the Fair regulating with the most severe minuteness the number and quality of the dresses of the different classes of his subjects.[1] About the middle of the fourteenth century a parliament of Edward III. passed no less than eight laws against French fashions.[2]

Even in Florence, among the officers of the republic, in the beginning of the fourteenth century, was one especially appointed "to repress the luxury of women."[1] Bruges, which had then risen to great wealth, became very famous in this respect; and the French king and queen having visited it early in the fourteenth century, it is related that the latter was unable to restrain her tears; for, as she complained, she "found herself in presence of 600 ladies more queenly than herself."[2] The fearful depopulation that was produced by the Black Death greatly strengthened the tendency. The wages, and consequently the prosperity, of the working classes rose to an unexampled height, which the legislators vainly tried to repress by fixing the maximum of wages by law;[3] while the immense fortunes resulting from the innumerable inheritances, and also that frenzy of enjoyment which is the natural reaction after a great catastrophe, impelled the upper classes to unprecedented excesses of luxury. This new passion was but part of a great change in the social habits of Europe, which was everywhere destroying the old rude simplicity, rendering the interiors of houses more richly and elaborately furnished, creating indoor life, increasing the difference between different ranks, producing a violent thirst for wealth, and making its display one of the principal signs of dignity.

There are few things more difficult to judge than those great outbursts of luxury that meet us from time to time in history, and which, whenever they have appeared, have proved the precursors of intellectual or political change. A sober appreciation of their effects will probably be equally removed from those Spartan, Stoical, or monastic declamations which found their last great representative in Rousseau, and from the unqualified eulogy of luxury in which Voltaire, Filangieri, and others have indulged. Political economy, by establishing clearly the distinction between productive and unproductive expenditure,

---

[1] See this ordinance (which was issued in 1294) in Blanqui, *Hist. d'Economie politique*, tom. i. pp. 225–226. It provided, among other things, that dukes, counts, and barons, who have 6,000 livres rent, may have four robes a year, and their wives as many. Knights with 3,000 livres rent may have three. No member of the middle class may wear any ornament of gold or precious stone, or any dress that was green or grey. As M. Blanqui observes, articles of luxury would have been imported necessarily from foreign countries into France, which would necessitate an export of French gold—according to the current notions the greatest evil that could befall the country.

[2] Anderson, *Hist. of Commerce*, vol. i. p. 193. See, too, p. 179. More than a century later, the passion for

dress reached Scotland, when the alarmed and indignant legislators enacted (in 1457) that the wives and daughters of merchants should " be abuilzied ('dressed,' from 'habiller') gangand and correspondent for their estate, that is to say, on their heads shortcurches (a kind of cap) with little hudes as are used in Flanders, England, and other countries....and that na women weare tailes unfit in length, nor furred under but on the hailie daie." (*Ibid.* vol. iii. pp. 280–281.)

[1] Blanqui, tom. i. p. 250.
[2] Anderson, vol. i. p. 144.
[3] Wade, *History of the Middle and Working Classes*.

and by its doctrine of the accumulation of capital, has dispelled for ever the old illusion that the rich man who lavishes his income in feasts or pageants is contributing involuntarily to the wealth of the community ; and history unrolls a long catalogue of nations that have been emasculated or corrupted by increasing riches. But, on the other hand, if luxury be regarded as including all those comforts which are not necessary to the support of life, its introduction is the very sign and measure of civilisation ; and even if we regard it in its more common but less definite sense, its increase has frequently marked the transition from a lower to a higher stage. It represents the substitution of new, intellectual, domestic, and pacific tastes for the rude warlike habits of semi-barbarism. It is the parent of art, the pledge of peace, the creator of those refined tastes and delicate susceptibilities that have done so much to soften the friction of life. Besides this, what in one sense is a luxury soon becomes in another sense a necessary. Society, in a highly civilised condition, is broken up into numerous sections, and each rank, except the very lowest, maintains its position chiefly by the display of a certain amount of luxury. To rise to a higher level in the social scale, or at least to avoid the discomfort and degradation of falling below his original rank, becomes the ambition of every man ; and these motives, by producing abstinence from marriage, form one of the principal checks upon population. However exaggerated may have been the apprehensions of Malthus, the controversy which he raised has at least abundantly proved that, when the multiplication of the species is checked by no stronger motive than the natural disinclination of some men to marriage, when the habitual condition of a large proportion of the inhabitants of a country that is already thickly inhabited is so low that they marry fearlessly, under the belief that their children can fare no worse than themselves, when poor-laws have provided a refuge for the destitute, and when no strong religious motive elevates celibacy into a virtue, the most fearful calamities must ensue. Looking at things upon a large scale, there seem to be two, and but two, adequate checks to the excessive multiplication of the species : the first consists of physical and moral evils, such as wars, famines, pestilence, and vice, and those early deaths which are so frequent among the poor ; the second is abstinence from marriage. In the middle ages, the monastic system, by dooming many thousands to perpetual celibacy, produced this abstinence, and consequently contributed greatly to avert the impending evil.[1] It is true that the remedy by itself was very inadequate. It is also true that, considered in its economical aspect, it was one of the worst that could be conceived ; for it greatly diminished the productive energies of society, by consigning immense numbers to idleness, and by diffusing a respect for idleness through the whole community ; but still the monastic system was in some measure a remedy, and, as it appears to me, the increased elaboration of social life rendering the passion for wealth more absorbing, was one of the necessary preliminaries of its safe abolition. That elaboration was effected after the Crusades, and the change it has produced is very remarkable. The repressive influence upon population that was once exercised by a religious system resting on the glorification of voluntary poverty, and designed to mortify the natural tendencies of mankind, is now exercised by that increased love of wealth which grows out of the multiplication of secular aims, or, in other words, out of the normal development of society.

But, putting aside the incidental effects of luxury upon population, there can be no doubt that its effects in stimulating the energies of mankind, by investing material advantages with a new attraction, have sometimes been very great and very beneficial. For the love of wealth and the love of knowledge are the two main agents of human progress ; and, although the former is a far less noble passion than the latter, although, in addition to the innumerable crimes it has produced, it exercises, when carried to excess, a more than common influence in contracting and indurating the character, it may well be doubted whether it is not, on the whole, the more beneficial of the two. It has produced all trade, all industry, and all the material luxuries of civilisation, and has at the same time proved the most powerful incentive to intellectual pursuits. Whoever will soberly examine the history of inventions, of art, or of the learned

[1] This has been noticed in a very forcible but, of course, one-sided manner by De Maistre, who recurs to the subject again and again in his works ; also by Villeneuve Bargemont, *Économie politique chrétienne.*

professions, may soon convince himself of this. At all events, the two pursuits will usually rise together. The great majority of mankind always desire material prosperity, and a small minority always desire knowledge; but in nations that are undeveloped, or are declining, these desires are unable to overcome the listlessness that is general. There is then no buoyancy in the national character. All lively curiosity, all the fire and energy of enterprise are unknown. Men may love wealth, and even sacrifice moral principles to attain it, but they are unable to emancipate themselves from the empire of routine, and their languid minds recoil with the same antipathy from novelty, whether it comes to them in the form of industrial enterprise, or of intellectual innovation. This is even now very much the condition of Spain and of some other nations, and during the greater part of the middle ages it was the general condition of Christendom. In such a state of society, the creation of a spirit of enterprise is the very first condition of mental as of material progress; and when it is called into existence in one department, it will soon be communicated to all. The ardent passion for luxury that followed the Crusades—the new tastes, new ideas, and new fields of enterprise that were suddenly made popular—produced it in Europe; and the impulse that began in industry was soon felt in knowledge. In the Roman Empire, which rested on slavery, luxury produced idleness. In the fourteenth century it stimulated industry, and aroused a strong feeling of opposition to that monastic system, which, by its enormous development, was a serious impediment to progress.

This opposition, which was at first created by the increased energy of laymen, was intensified by the deterioration of the monks. At one time, as I have already observed, they had been the great directors of labour. But when their numbers and their wealth had immensely increased, their first enthusiasm passed away, and multitudes thronged the monasteries simply to escape the burdens of life. Besides this, the priesthood had become intimately allied with the nobles, who are always opposed to the industrial classes. The alliance was in part the result of special circumstances, for the Crusades were directed conjointly by priests and nobles; and it was during the Crusades that the aristocracy obtained its distinct

and complete organisation. It was also of part the consequence of a certain harmony which exists between the theological and the aristocratic spirit. Both raising the past far above the present, regard innovation with extreme dislike, and both measure excellence by a different rule from personal merit.

If I have been fortunate enough to carry the reader with me through the foregoing arguments, the importance of industry in influencing theological history will have become apparent. We have seen that a great religious change is effected, nòt by direct arguments, but by a predisposition to receive them, or, in other words, by a change of sympathies and bias. We have also seen that the industrial spirit which became prominent early in the fourteenth century produced such a change. It did so in three ways. It arose in a society in which the laity were crouching in abject submission to the priesthood, and it developed and raised to honour the practice of moneylending, which the priesthood had invariably anathematised. It arose in a society in which the duty of religious intolerance was regarded as an axiom, and it produced a tendency towards toleration by uniting men of different creeds in amicable intercourse, by elevating to honour on account of their commercial merits the people who were most persecuted on account of their creed, by making men concentrate their attention mainly on practice rather than on theory, and by calling into existence an order of interests which persecution seriously endangered. It, in the last place, made men look with aversion upon the monastic ideal, which was the very centre of the prevailing theology. In all these ways it proved the precursor of the Reformation, and in all these ways it harmonised with the spirit of Rationalism.

Commercial enterprise, bearing in its train these intellectual consequences, spread rapidly over Europe. The accidental discovery at Amalfi of a manuscript of Roman laws is said to have produced the navigation laws;[1] the invention of the compass rendered long voyages comparatively secure; and every shore, from the Baltic to the Mediterranean, was soon fringed with harbours. In the thirteenth and fourteenth centuries we find the

[1] Pecchio, *Storia della Economia Publica in Italia* (Lugano, 1849), p. 11.

first mercantile companies established in England.[1] At a still earlier period Belgium had entered into relations with more than thirty kingdoms or states.[2] The consular system, which emanated from the commercial republics, and which was designed for the special protection of merchants, advanced rapidly in importance.[3] As early as the thirteenth century the consuls of Italy, Spain, and France had in most countries acquired an extended and recognised authority. England, in the fourteenth century, followed the example,[4] and about the same time the jurisdiction which had formerly been confined to seaports was extended to the towns in the interior. From these consulships, or perhaps from the papal legations which were already known, arose at last the institution of resident ambassadors, which completed the organisation of diplomacy, though its influence was not fully acquired till much later, in the coalitions resulting from the rivalry of Francis and Charles V.[5] The Hanseatic League repressed piracy, associated commerce with the first efflorescence of political liberty, and by the treaty of Stralsund, in 1370, made commercial interests pre-eminent in the North; while in the South the Venetians, anticipating in some measure the doctrines of later economists, sketched the first faint outlines of the laws that govern them.[6] At last the Medici appeared, and surrounded

industry with the aureoles of genius and of art. For the first time the intellectual capital of Italy was displaced, and Rome itself paled before that new Athens which had arisen upon the banks of the Arno. An aristocracy, formed exclusively from the trading and mercantile classes,[1] furnished the most munificent and discerning patrons art had ever found ; almost every great intellectual movement was coloured by its influence, and its glory was reflected upon the class from which it sprang.

It may here be advisable to rise for a moment above the industrial movement with which we have hitherto been occupied, and to endeavour to obtain a general conception of the different streams of thought which were at this time shooting across Europe. Such a review, which will be in part a summary of conclusions I have established in previous chapters, will help to show how admirably the industrial movement harmonised with the other tendencies of the age, and also how completely the Reformation was the normal consequence of the new condition of society.

While, then, the progress of industry was producing an innovating, tolerant, and anti-monastic spirit, two great revivals of learning were vivifying the intellectual energies of Christendom.

The first consisted of that resuscitation of the classical writings which began about the twelfth century, and culminated in the labours of Erasmus and the Scaligers. This revival broke the intellectual unity which had characterised the middle ages. It introduced a new standard of judgment, a new ideal of perfection, a new order of sympathies. Men began to expatiate in an atmosphere of thought where religious fanaticism had never entered, and where the threatenings of the dogmatist were unknown. The spell that had bound their intellects was broken, and the old type of character gradually destroyed. The influence of the movement passed from speculative philosophy to art, which was then the chief organ of religious sentiments, and, under the patronage of the Medici, a profound change took place in both painting and architecture, which intensified the tendency that produced it.

[1] Anderson, *Hist. of Commerce*, vol. i. p. 117. The first English commercial companies were "the Merchants of the Staple" and "the Merchants of St. Thomas à Becket."

[2] Van Bruyssel, *Hist. du Commerce belge*, tom. i. p. 234.

[3] See the stages of its development in Warden, *On Consular Establishments*.

[4] The earliest notice Macpherson has been able to find of an English consul is in 1346 (*Annals of Commerce*, vol. i. p. 536).

[5] Before this time ambassadors were sent only on occasions of emergency. The first instance of a resident ambassador seems to have been in 1455, when Francis Sforza, Duke of Milan, established one at Genoa, and towards the close of the century the institution became somewhat common in Italy (Cibrario, *Economia Politica del Medio Evo* [Torino, 1842], vol. i. p. 319). It was also about this time that the use of cipher in diplomacy became usual. (*Ibid.* De Plassan, *Hist. de la Diplomatie française*, Introd.)

[6] M. Blanqui has collected some very remarkable evidence of this (*Histoire d'Economie politique*, tom. i. pp. 244-270). The Lombards also occasionally manifested extremely enlightened views on these subjects (see Rossi, *Économie politique*, tom. i. p. 260); and Milan, perhaps longer than any other great town in Europe, was exempt from the mediæval system of corporations. However, the first Italian writer of considerable merit on Political Economy was probably Serra, who was a Neapolitan, and it was at Naples that the first Professorship of Political Economy in Europe was established in 1754 by the munificence of the Florentine Intieri.

[1] As early as 1282, a magistracy had been constituted at Florence exclusively of merchants ; and the example was soon followed by Sienna, and in a great measure by Venice and Genoa. (See Blanqui, tom. i. p. 245 ; Rossi, tom. i. p. 266.)

The second revival was produced by the action of Moorish civilisation. It was shown chiefly in an increased passion for natural science, which gradually substituted the conception of harmonious and unchanging law for the conception of a universe governed by perpetual miracles. With this passion for science, astrology rose into extraordinary repute, and it necessarily involved a system of fatalism, which, in its turn, led the way to a philosophy of history. From the same quarter arose many of those pantheistic speculations about the all-pervasive soul of the universe, to which the writers of the fifteenth, sixteenth, and seventeenth centuries were so passionately addicted.[1] In all these ways Moorish influence contributed to shake the old faith, to produce new predispositions, and thus to prepare the way for the coming change. Roger Bacon, who was probably the greatest natural philosopher of the middle ages, was profoundly versed in Arabian learning, and derived from it many of the germs of his philosophy.[2] The fatalism of the astrologers and the pantheism of Averroes tinged some of the most eminent Christian writings long after the dawn of the Reformation. In one respect Mahometan influence had somewhat anticipated the classical revival. The Mahometan philosophers were intense admirers of Aristotle ; and it was chiefly through translations made by the Jews from the Arabic versions that the knowledge of that philosopher penetrated to Europe.

There was another influence, growing partly out of the industrial movement, and partly out of the revival of classical learning, at this time acting upon Europe, which I have not yet had occasion to mention, which many readers will deem far too trivial for notice, but which, nevertheless, appears to me so extremely important, both as a symptom and a cause, that I shall venture, at the risk of being accused of unpardonable digression, to trace some of the leading stages of its progress. I mean that change in the character of public amusements, produced chiefly by the habits of luxury, which took place about the fifteenth century, and which produced the revival of the theatre.

No one can question the immense importance in the intellectual history of mankind of an institution which has elicited the dramas of Æschylus, Sophocles, Euripides, Calderon, Lope de Vega, Corneille, Molière, Racine, Voltaire, Goethe, Schiller, Shakespeare, and Ben Jonson, and which has invariably appeared as one of the most conspicuous signs and causes of a rising civilisation. Combining the three great influences of eloquence, of poetry, and of painting, it has probably done more than any other single agent to produce that craving after the ideal, that passionate enthusiasm of intellect, out of which all great works of imagination have sprung. It has been the seed-plot of poetry and romance, and it has exercised a considerable though less direct influence over eloquence. The age of Demosthenes and Æschines was also the age in which the theatre of Athens was the object of such a passionate devotion that no politician was permitted even to propose the abolition of its subsidy.[1] The golden age of Roman eloquence was also the golden age of the Roman theatre, and the connection between acting and eloquence was one of the favourite subjects of the discussions of the time.[2] In modern days, Burke declared, in an assembly in no degree inferior to any of Greece or of Rome, that there was probably no orator among those he addressed who did not owe something of his skill to the acting of Garrick.[3] And this amusement, which has ever proved one of the chief delights, and one of the most powerful incentives of genius, had, at the same time, the rare privilege of acting with equal power upon the opposite extreme of intellect, and is even now almost the only link connecting thousands with intellectual pursuits.

But the aspect in which the history of the theatre is most remarkable is perhaps to be found in its influence upon national tastes. Everyone who considers the world as it really exists, and not as it appears in the writings of ascetics or sentimentalists, must have convinced himself that in great

---

[1] Many of these views were almost identical with those of Mesmer and his followers. (See Bertrand, *Hist. du Magnétisme animal en France*, pp. 13-17.)
[2] Sharon Turner's *Hist. of England*, vol. iv. pp. 39-40.

[1] See the *Olynthiacs*.
[2] Roscius even wrote a book on this subject, but it has unfortunately not come down to us. He kept a school of declamation, which was attended by the ablest orators of his time. The passion for the theatre is said to have come to Rome from Egypt, and Batyllus, the greatest actor of the Augustan period, was from Alexandria. See on this subject a curious dissertation, "De luxu Romanorum," in Grævius, *Thesaurus Antiq. Rom.*, tom. viii.
[3] Murphy's *Life of Garrick*.

towns, where multitudes of men of all classes and characters are massed together, and where there are innumerable strangers separated from all domestic ties and occupations, public amusements of an exciting order are absolutely necessary; and that, while they are often the vehicle and the occasion of evil, to suppress them, as was done by the Puritans of the Commonwealth, is simply to plunge an immense portion of the population into the lowest depths of vice. National tastes, however, vary with the different stages of civilisation, and national amusements undergo a corresponding modification; combats of men and animals being, for the most part, the favourite type in the earlier stages, and dramatic representations in the later ones. The history of amusements is thus important, as a reflection of the history of civilisation, and it becomes still more so when we remember that institutions which are called into existence by a certain intellectual tendency usually react upon and intensify their cause.

In this, as in most other respects, we find a strong contrast existing between the two leading nations of antiquity. The Athenians, who for a long period repelled gladiatorial spectacles with disgust, were passionately devoted to the drama, which they carried to the very highest point of perfection, and from which they derived no small amount of their intellectual culture. The Romans, on the other hand, who regarded every subject from a military point of view, had long prohibited theatrical representations, except those which formed part of the worship of the gods. The first public theatre was erected by Pompey, and he only evaded the censure of the severe moralists of his time by making it a single story of a building that was ostensibly a temple of Venus. The Stoics, and the representatives of the old republican spirit, denounced the new amusement as calculated to enervate the national character. Public opinion branded actors as infamous, and, as a necessary consequence, they speedily became so. The civilisation of the Empire made the theatre at last extremely popular; but that civilisation was the most corrupt the world had ever seen, and the drama partook of the full measure of its corruption. A few rays of genius from the pens of Seneca, Plautus, or Terence, flashed across the gloom; but Rome never produced any dramatists

comparable to those of Greece, or any audience at all resembling that which made the theatre ring with indignation because Euripides had inserted an apology for mental reservation into his *Hippolytus*, or had placed a too ardent panegyric of wealth in the mouth of Bellerophon. After a time the position of an actor became so degraded that it was made a form of perpetual servitude,[1] and no one who had embraced that profession was permitted at any future time to abandon it. The undisguised sensuality reached a point which we can scarcely conceive. Women were sometimes brought naked upon the stage.[2] Occasionally an attempt was made to amalgamate theatrical amusements with those bloody spectacles to which the people were so passionately devoted, and the tragedy was closed by the burning of a criminal, who was compelled to personate Hercules.[3] At the same time, by a curious association of ideas, the theatre was still intimately connected with religious observances; the temple was often the scene of its orgies, and the achievements of the gods the subject of representation.

It is certainly not surprising that the early writers of Christianity should have directed all their eloquence against such an institution as this. They inveighed against it as the school of profligacy, and a centre of idolatry; and they dwelt, in language which it is impossible to read without emotion, upon the duty of those who might be called, at any moment, to endure for their faith the most horrible forms of torture and of death, abstaining from whatever could enervate their courage or damp their zeal. Mingled with

[1] Nero, however, made energetic efforts to relieve the actors from the stigma attached to them (as he did also to alleviate the sufferings of the slaves), and Gibbon has noticed the great honour in which he held the Jewish actor Aliturus, and the repeated and successful efforts of that actor to obtain a relaxation of the persecutions of the Jews. Under Nero, too, lived and died (when only fourteen) a lovely and gifted actress named Eucharis—the first who appeared on the Greek stage, which Nero had instituted—who seems to have won more affection and left a deeper impression than almost any other who died so young. Her charms are recorded in perhaps the most touching of all the epitaphs that have descended to us from antiquity, and her beautiful features formed one of the last ideals of expiring art. (Visconti, *Iconographie ancienne*, p. 287.)

[2] See the evidence of this collected by Sabatier, *Hist. de la Législation sur les Femmes publiques*, pp. 45-47; Magnin, *Origines du Théâtre*, tom. i. pp. 284-287; and Lebrun, *Discours sur le Théâtre*, pp. 79-82. This last author tries as much as possible to attenuate the facts he admits, in order that the invectives of the Fathers might fall with their full force on the modern theatre. The Floral games were in this respect the worst.

[3] Tertullian, *Ad Nationes*, lib. i. c. 10.

these noble exhortations we find no small amount of that monastic spirit which regards pleasure as essentially evil, and also two or three arguments which perhaps represent the extreme limits of human puerility. Tertullian, having enumerated with great force and eloquence many of the most horrible vices of the theatre, adds that at least the Almighty can never pardon an actor, who, in defiance of the evangelical assertion, endeavours, by high-heeled boots, to add a cubit to his stature, and who habitually falsifies his face.[1]

The position of public amusements in the early history of Christianity is extremely important. On the one hand, the austerity with which the Christians condemned them was probably one of the chief causes of the hatred and consequent persecution of which the early Church was the victim, and which contrasts so remarkably with the usually tolerant character of polytheism. On the other hand, when Christianity had attained its triumph, when the intellectual and moral basis of paganism was completely sapped, and when the victorious Church had begun to exhibit something of the spirit from which it had suffered, the theatre and the circus became the last strongholds of the dying faith. Partly because they had actually emanated from the pagan worship, and partly because the Christian Councils and Fathers denounced them with an absolute and unqualified severity, they were soon regarded as the chief expression of paganism; and the people who endured with scarcely a murmur the destruction of their temples and the suppression of their sacrifices flew to arms whenever their amusements were menaced. The servitude, indeed, by which the actor was enchained for life to the theatre was soon abrogated in the case of those who desired to become Christians;[2] and the bishops refused to baptise any actor who persisted in his profession, and excommunicated any Christian who adopted it;[3] but the theatres were still

thronged with eager spectators. Indeed, one curious enactment of the Theodosian Code provides that some of the temples should be saved from the general destruction, because they were associated with public games.[1] When the bishops were manifestly unable to suppress the public games, they directed all their energies to restricting them to days that were not sacred. St. Ambrose succeeded in obtaining the abolition of Sunday representations at Milan, and a similar rule was at last raised to a general law of the empire.[2]

It is remarkable, however, when considering the relations to the theatre of Christianity and Paganism, that Julian, who was by far the most distinguished champion of the latter, formed in this respect a complete exception to his co-religionists. His character was formed after the antique model, and his antipathy to public amusements was almost worthy of a bishop. Libanius, it is true, has left a long disquisition in praise of pantomimic dances, which, he maintained, were of a far higher artistic merit than sculpture, as no sculptor could rival the grace and beauty of the dancers; but on this subject he received no encouragement from his master. It has been ingeniously, and, I think, justly remarked, that this austerity of Julian, by placing him in direct opposition to that portion of the population which was opposed to Christianity, was one of the causes of the failure of his attempts to rally the broken forces of paganism.

After a time the Roman theatre languished and passed away. The decline was partly the result of the ceaseless opposition of the clergy, who during the middle ages were too powerful for any institution to resist their anathema, but still more, I think, of the invasion of the barbarians, which dissolved the old civilisation, and therefore destroyed the old tastes. The theatre soon lost its attraction; it lingered, indeed, faintly for many centuries, but its importance had passed away, and about the end of the thirteenth century most antiquaries seem to think the last public theatres were destroyed. The amusements of men were of an entirely different, and, for the most part,

---

[1] De Spectaculis, cap. xxiii.
[2] Cod. Theod. lib. xv. tit. 7, 1, 8. If the emancipated actress turned out badly, she was to be dragged back to the stage and kept there till she was "a ridiculous old woman" (ridicula anus).
[3] Neander, Church History, vol. ii. p. 370. An old council forbade Christian women marrying actors. The actors, however, at a later period, claimed one saint as their patron. This was St. Genetus, who was an actor in the reign of Diocletian. According to the legend, he was acting the part of a Christian in a piece which was designed to turn the new religion to ridicule when, between the acts, he saw a vision, which con-

verted him, and he accordingly proclaimed his allegiance to Christ upon the stage. The emperor and the audience at first loudly applauded, imagining that this was part of the play; but when they discovered the truth, the actor was put to death.
[1] Cod. Theod. xvi. 10, 3.
[2] Lebrun, pp. 117-118; Cod. Theod. xv. 5, 5.

of a warlike character. Battle and the imitations of battle, boisterous revels, the chase, and, after the Crusades, the gaming-table, became the delight of the upper classes; while the poor found congenial recreation in bear-baiting, bull-fighting, and countless similar amuse-ments—in fairs, dances, perambulant musicians, sham fights, and rude games.[1] Besides these, there were numerous mountebanks, who were accustomed to exhibit feats of mingled agility and buf-foonery, which were probably the origin of the modern pantomime, and in which, as it has been shown by a high authority,[2] there is reason to believe a dress very similar to that of our harlequins was employed. It is probably to these mounte-banks, or possibly to the troubadours or wandering minstrels, who had then become common, that St. Thomas Aquinas referred in a passage which excited a fierce controversy in the seventeenth century. In discussing the subject of amusement, the saint suggested the question whether the profession of an "actor" was essentially sinful; and, having enumerated some special circum-stances that might make it so, he answers the question in the negative,[3] "because," as he says, "recreation is necessary to mankind," and also because "it had been revealed to the blessed Paphnutius, that 'a clown[4] was to be his companion in heaven.'"

---

[1] Strutt's *Sports and Pastimes of the English People.* Muratori, *Antiq. Ital.*, Dissert. ag. In Italy the sham fights were carried on on a vast scale, and with wooden swords, and were the cause of many deaths. Amuse-ments somewhat similar to those which were once popular in Italy are said to continue in Russia. Storch, *Econ. polit.*, tom. iii. p. 403.

[2] Riccoboni, *Hist. du Théâtre italien depuis l'an 1500 jusqu'à l'an 1660*, tom. i. pp. 4-6. The author of this remarkable book (who was known professionally under the name of Lelio) was one of the greatest Italian actors of his time. He travelled much from theatre to theatre, and in the different cities he visited ransacked the public libraries for works bearing upon his history. His book was originally written in French, and is dedicated to Queen Caroline of England.

[3] He says distinctly: "Officium histrionum, quod ordinatur ad solatium hominibus exhibendum, non est secundum se illicitum." It appears certain that when this was written there were no public theatres or dramatic representations, except the religious ones. At the same time, it is impossible to draw a clear line between the public recitation of verses or the exhibi-tions of mountebanks on the one and, hand the simplest forms of the drama upon the other. Bossuet has cited a passage from St. Thomas's work *De Sententiis*, in which he speaks of the exhibitions that had "for-merly taken place in the theatres." At all events, the saint was not very favourable to these "histriones," for he speaks of gains that have been acquired "de turpi causâ, sicut *de meretricio et histrionatu*." See on this subject, Concina. *De Spectaculis*, pp. 36-41; Lebrun, *Discours sur le Théâtre*, pp. 189-194; Bossuet, *Réflexions sur la Comédie*, §§ 22-25.

[4] "Joculator." Bossuet, however, says that the

Such, then, was the character of public amusements before the revival of learning. The time, however, was at hand when a profound change, fraught with momentous consequences to the Church, was mani-fested; and it is worthy of notice, that while that change was ultimately caused by the advance of civilisation, the Church itself was its pioneer. The first revival of the theatre is undoubtedly to be found in the religious plays. From the earliest times men seem to have been accustomed to throw into dramatic forms the objects of their belief; and the pagan mysteries, which were essentially dramatic,[1] retained their authority over the popular mind long after every other portion of the ancient worship was despised. The first Biblical play on record is on Moses, and is the composition of a Jew named Ezekiel, who lived in the second century. The second is a Greek tragedy on the Passion, by St. Gregory Nazianzen. The religious ceremonies, and especially those for Christmas, Epiphany, and Holy Week, became continually more dramatic, and the monks and nuns after a time began to relieve the monotony of the cloister by private representations. The earliest known instance of this is of the tenth century, when a German abbess named Hroswitha composed two or three dramas, with a religious object, but imitated, it is said, in part from Terence, which were acted by the nuns. The subject of one of them is curious. A hermit had brought up in the ways of piety a beautiful girl, but she rebelled against his authority, and neglected his counsels, and fled to a house of ill fame. The hermit, having discovered the place of her resort, assumed the dress and the manners of a soldier, penetrated to her retreat, supported his character so skilfully that he deceived its inmates, and at last found an opportunity of reclaiming his ward.[2]

In the extreme weariness of the con-

Acts of St. Paphnutius show that this was simply a perambulant fluteplayer. After all, Bossuet is obliged to make the following admission: "Après avoir purgé la doctrine de saint Thomas des excès dont on la chargeoit, il faut avouer avec le respect qui est dû à un si grand homme, qu'il semble s'être un peu éloigné, je ne dirai pas des sentimens dans le fond, mais plutôt des expressions des anciens Pères sur le sujet des divertissemens." (*Réflexions sur la Comédie*, § 31.)

[1] Mackay's *Religious Development of the Greeks and Hebrews*, vol. ii. pp. 286-297. Besides the drama, it is probable that the gladiatorial spectacles (which are of Etruscan origin) were originally religious. They seem at first to have been celebrated at the graves, and in honour of the dead.

[2] See Villemain, *Moyen Âge*; Martonne, *Piété du Moyen Âge*; Leroy, *Études sur les Mystères*, p. 41.

ventual life, amusements of this kind were welcomed with delight, and, though often and severely censured, they continued in some monasteries till far into the eighteenth century.[1] The form, however, which they generally assumed was not that of secular dramas with a religious tendency, but of mysteries or direct representations of scenes from Scripture or from the lives of the saints. Until the latter part of the thirteenth century they were exclusively Latin, and were usually acted by priests in the churches; but after this time they assumed a popular form, their religious character speedily declined, and they became at last one of the most powerful agents in bringing the Church, and indeed all religion, into disrepute.[2] The evidence of this is not to be found in the representations of the Almighty that were so frequent upon the stage;[3] for these, though inexpressibly shocking in our eyes, were perfectly in harmony with the intellectual condition of the time; but rather in the gross indecency which the worst days of the Roman theatre had scarcely surpassed,[4] and perhaps still more in the strange position that was assigned to Satan. At first the mysteries had probably contributed much to the religious terrorism. The glare and smoke of the fire of hell were constantly exhibited, and piercing shrieks of agony broke upon the ear. Very soon, however, Satan was made to act the part of a clown. His appearance was greeted with shouts of laughter. He became at once

the most prominent and most popular character of the piece, and was emancipated by virtue of his character from all restraints of decorum. One of the most impressive doctrines of the Church was thus indissolubly associated in the popular mind with the ridiculous, and a spirit of mockery and of satire began to play around the whole teaching of authority.

It is difficult, indeed, to say how far these rude dramatic representations contributed to that disruption of old religious ties that preceded and prepared the Reformation. At a very early period those strange festivals, the Feast of Fools and the Feast of Asses,[1] had introduced into the churches indecent dances, caricatures of the priesthood, and even a parody of the Mass; and the mysteries of the fourteenth and fifteenth centuries carried the same spirit far and wide. But what I desire especially to notice is, that their popularity had a real connection with that material prosperity which was a consequence of the industrial development we are considering. This growing passion for an order of amusements in some degree intellectual, this keen relish for spectacles that addressed themselves especially to the imagination, was the beginning of that inevitable transition from the rude, simple, warlike, unartistic, unimaginative tastes of barbarism to the luxurious, refined, and meditative tastes of civilisation. Coarse and corrupt as they were, these early plays reflected the condition of a society that was struggling feebly into a new phase of civilisation, and which at the same time, though still deriving its conceptions from the Church, was tending surely and rapidly towards secularisation.

The change was first effected in Italy and France. In those countries, which were then the centres of material prosperity, the dramatic tastes had naturally been most developed, and the mysteries had attained an extraordinary popularity. A modern Italian bibliographer has been able even now to collect more than one hundred different pieces of this kind, which were represented in Italy in the

[1] Concina, who published his work, *De Spectaculis*, in 1752, at the request of Benedict XIV., mentions that the custom still continued in some monasteries; and he devoted a dissertation to proving that monks who laid aside their ecclesiastical dress to personate laymen were guilty of mortal sin.

[2] See the collections of these by Hone, Jubinal, Jacob, &c.; and the works of Leroy, Suard, and Collier upon their history.

[3] On which see Malone, *Hist. of the English Stage*, pp. 12–13. Some curious examples of it have been collected by Hone; and also in Strutt's *Hist. of the Manners of the People of England*, vol. iii. pp. 137–140.

[4] Some striking instances of this indecency, which indeed is sufficiently manifest in most of the mysteries, are given by Jacob in his Introduction to his collection of Farces. Wherever the seventh commandment was to be broken, the actors disappeared behind a curtain which was hung across a part of the stage; and this is the origin of the French proverbial expression about things that are done "derrière le rideau." More than once the Government suppressed the sacred plays in France on account of their evil effects upon morals. In England matters seem to have been if possible worse, and Warton has shown that on at least one occasion in the fifteenth century Adam and Eve were brought upon the stage strictly in their state of innocence. In the next scene the fig-leaves were introduced. (Malone's *History of the English Stage*, pp. 15, 16.)

[1] The Feast of Fools and the Feast of Asses are said to have originated (though probably under other names) in the Greek Church about 990. (Malone's *History of the English Stage*, p. 9.) La Mère Sotte, in France, originated, or at least became popular, during the quarrel between the King of France and the Pope, at the beginning of the tenth century. (Monteil, *Hist. des Français des divers États*, tom. iii. p. 342, ed. 1853.)

fifteenth and sixteenth centuries.[1] About
the middle of the fifteenth century the
exhibitions of the mountebanks began to
be thrown into a systematic form. A
complete story was exhibited, and the
harlequin rose to great prominence as
chief actor.[2] We find, too, a few representations of pagan fables, and also some
plays that were termed impromptus, in
which the outline of a plot was sketched
by the author, but the dialogue left to the
ingenuity of the actor. Besides these,
dialogues, or discussions of the nature of
farces,[3] became common ; and having
passed from Italy to France, they there
assumed the dimensions of regular
dramas, sometimes of very considerable
merit. One of them, the famous farce of
Patelin, which was probably composed
about 1468 by Peter Blanchet, an advocate
of Poitiers, still holds its position upon
the French stage.[4] The directors of the
religious plays attempted to meet these
new rivals by the invention of semi-
religious " moralities," which were properly representations of allegorical figures
of virtues and vices,[5] and were intended
to act the part of a compromise ; but the
farces soon became the dominating form,
and all other performances sank into
secondary importance.[6] Latin plays were

also sometimes acted by the scholars
in the colleges, a practice which was
afterwards made very popular by the
Jesuits.

This was the first stage of the movement. The second was the creation of
secular plays of a higher order of merit,
which completely superseded and destroyed the mysteries.[1] Like the former,
this advance emanated chiefly from the
commercial civilisation of Florence, but
it is extremely remarkable that the leaders
of the Church in Italy were among its
most ardent supporters. The first regular
Italian comedy appears to have been the
Calandra, and its author was the Cardinal
Bibbiena, who had long been secretary to
Lorenzo de' Medici.[2] The play was probably written in the last few years of the
fifteenth century, when the author was
still young, but it at all events did not
impede his advancement in the Church.
The two first Italian tragedies were the
Sophonisba of Trissino, which was imitated
from Euripides, and the *Rosimunda* of
Ruccellai, which was imitated from
Seneca. The *Sophonisba* was acted for
the first time at Vicenza, about 1514, and
was soon afterwards represented at Rome
under the special patronage of Leo X.,
who appointed its author ambassador at
the court of the Emperor Maximilian.
The *Rosimunda* was first acted, in the
presence of the same Pope, at Florence,
in 1515.[3] The earliest instance of a secular
musical drama is the *Orpheus* of Politiano,

[1] *Bibliografia delle Antiche Rappresentazioni
Italiane Sacre e Profane stampate nei Secoli XV e
XVI*, dal Colomb de Batines (Firenze, 1852). One of
these mysteries, the *S. Giovanni e Paolo*, was written
by Lorenzo de' Medici himself (Roscoe, *Lorenzo de'
Medici*, ch. v.).
[2] Riccoboni, tom. i. p. 89. One of the most famous
of the early harlequins was Cecchino, who is also
celebrated for having published at Venice, in 1621,
perhaps the first defence of the theatre. He was
ennobled by the Emperor of Germany.
[3] These farces, in the earliest and simplest forms,
were called " contrasti" in Italian, or "débats" in
French. De Batines has made a list of several which
were translated from Italian into French—e.g., the
discussions between wine and water, between life and
death, between man and woman, &c. Italian actors
sometimes migrated to France, and in 1577 we find a
regular Italian company, called I Gelosi, there.
[4] As a comic opera, and also, I believe, as a play.
The popularity of the farce of *Patelin* produced *Le
Nouveau Patelin* and *Le Testament de Patelin*, both
of which have been reprinted by Jacob. Hallam says
(*Hist. of Lit.*, vol. i. p. 216) that the farce of *Patelin*
was first printed in 1490. There is extreme uncertainty
resting upon the early chronology of the drama ;
scarcely any two authorities agree upon the subject.
[5] The term "morality," however, was very loosely
used. Jacob has reprinted an old play, called *La
Moralité de l' Aveugle et du Boiteux*, which is nothing
more than a farce. From the religious plays the
personifications passed to the ballets, in which they
still sometimes appear. An old French poem describes
in rapturous terms the performance of a certain
Madame de Brancas, in the character of Geometry,
in a ballet on the seven liberal arts, danced before
Louis XIV. in 1663.
[6] Farces appear also to have been the chief form of
dramatic literature in Spain in the fifteenth century.

See Bouterwek's *Hist. of Spanish Literature*. They
were followed by eclogues.
[1] Some remains, however, of the mysteries continue
to the present day, especially in the villages of the
Tyrol. There is still, too, a great " passion play," as
it is termed, celebrated every tenth year at the little
village of Ober-Ammergau, in Bavaria, near the fron-
tiers of the Tyrol, which, though it is not more than 300
years old, and though it is almost entirely devoid of
grotesque scenes, may be on the whole looked upon as
a representative of the mediæval plays. It consists of
scenes from the Passion (beginning at the triumphal
entry into Jerusalem, and ending with the Ascension),
between which tableaux vivants, representing incidents
from the Old Testament typical of the Passion, are
displayed. A chorus, like those of the Greek plays,
sings hymns concerning the connection between the
type and the antitype. When I saw it in 1860, the play
lasted for 7½ hours, and commanded the attention of an
immense audience to the close.
[2] Riccoboni, tom. i. pp. 32, 33. The *Calandra* is
now nearly forgotten, but its author will always be
remembered as the subject of two of the noblest of the
portraits of Raphael—one at Florence and the other at
Madrid.
[3] Compare Riccoboni, tom. ii. pp. 9, 10 ; and Sismondi, *Hist. de la Littérature du Midi*, tom. i. pp. 188-
199. The two pieces seem to have been acted nearly at
the same time ; but the *Sophonisba* was not printed for
some years afterwards. Ruccellai also wrote a play
called *Orestes*, which, however, was not brought at this
time on the stage.

which was composed for the amusement and acted in the presence of the Cardinal Gonzaga of Mantua.[1] A few years later we find Clement VII. present with the Emperor Charles V., at Bologna, at the representation of the comedy of *The Three Tyrants*, by Ricci.[2] As a natural consequence of this patronage, the Italian theatre at its commencement does not appear to have been very hostile to the Church, and in this respect forms a marked contrast to the theatre of France. The *Eugénie* of Jodelle, which was the first regular comedy acted on the French stage, was throughout what many of the older farces had been, a bitter satire upon the clergy.[3]

One of the most important consequences of this revival of the theatre was the partial secularisation of music. This art, to which the old Greeks had ascribed so great a power over both mind and body, and which some of their states had even made an essential element of the civil government,[4] had for many centuries been entirely in the hands of the Church. Almost all the music that really deserved the name was ecclesiastical, and all the great names in musical history had been ecclesiastics. St. Ignatius, according to the legend, having heard the angels singing psalms in alternate strains before the throne of God, introduced the practice of antiphons. St. Ambrose regulated the church music for the diocese of Milan, and St. Gregory the Great for the remainder of Christendom. St. Wilfrid and St. Dunstan were the apostles of music in England. In the eleventh century the monk Guido of Arezzo invented the present system of musical notation. Nearly at the same time, the practice of singing in parts, and combining several distinct notes in a single

strain,[1] which is the basis of modern harmonies, first appeared in the services of the Church. From a very early period music had been employed to enhance the effect of the sacred plays, and as it continued to occupy the same position when the drama had been secularised, St. Philip Neri, in 1540, in order to counteract the new attraction, originated at Rome the oratorio. About twenty years later, Palestrina, a chaplain of the Vatican, reformed the whole system of Church music. These exertions would perhaps have retained for it something at least of its ancient ascendency, but for the invention in 1600 of recitative, which, by rendering possible complete musical dramas, immediately created the opera, withdrew the sceptre of music from the Church, and profoundly altered the prevailing taste. From this time the star of St. Cecilia began to wane, and that of Apollo to shine anew. Those "Lydian and Ionic strains," which Plato so jealously excluded from his republic, and which Milton so keenly appreciated, were heard again, and all Italy thrilled with passion beneath their power. Venice especially found in them the most faithful expression of her character, and no less than three hundred and fifty different operas were represented there between 1637 and 1680. In France the opera was introduced at the desire of Cardinal Mazarin; and it is remarkable that Perrin, who wrote the first French operas, was a priest; that Cambert, who assisted him in composing the music, was a church organist; and that nearly all the first actors had been choristers in the cathedrals. From this time the best singers began to desert the churches for the theatre. In England the musical dramas known under the name of masques elicited some of the noblest poetry of Ben Jonson and of Milton.[2]

Another way in which the Church exercised, I think, an indirect influence upon the stage, is not quite so obvious as the preceding one. Whatever opinion may be held on the general question of the comparative merits of the classical and the Gothic architecture, it is at least

[1] Roscoe's *Lorenzo de' Medici*, ch. v.; Hogarth's *Memoirs of the Opera*, pp. 6-8. Of course, as Hallam has observed, recitative not being yet invented, the music was confined to choruses and songs scattered throughout the piece.
[2] Riccoboni, tom. i. p. 183.
[3] See Charles, *La Comédie en France au seizième Siècle* (1862). Riccoboni, however, asserts that Molière took the character, and even some of the incidents and speeches, of his *Tartuffe* from an old Italian play called *Doctor Bachetone* (tom. i. p. 137).
[4] Among the Arcadians, for example, music was compulsory, and the one district in which this custom fell into desuetude was said to have sunk far below the surrounding civilisation. There is a singularly curious chapter on the effects ascribed to music among the Greeks, in Burney's *History of Music*, vol. i. pp. 173-194. The legends of Orpheus charming hell, Arion appeasing the waves, and Amphion moving the stones by music, as well as "the music of the spheres" of Pythagoras, will occur to everyone.

[1] Called originally "discantus." The exact date of its invention is a matter of great controversy. It is said to have been suggested by the varied tones of the organ.
[2] See Burney's *Hist. of Music*; Castil-Blaze, *Chapelle musique des rois de France*; Hogarth's *Hist. of the Opera*; Monteil, *Hist. des Français (XVIIe Siècle)*; the notice of Palestrina in Hallam's *Hist. of Literature*; and the *Essays on Musical Notation*, by Vitet and Coussemaker.

certain that the latter was immeasurably superior in suggesting the effects of immense distances—in acting, not simply on the taste, but also on the emotions, by a skilful employment of all the means of illusion which an admirable sense of the laws of perspective can furnish. The Greek temple might satisfy the taste, but it never struck any chord of deeper emotion, or created any illusion, or suggested any conception of the Infinite. The eye and the mind soon grasped its proportions, and realised the full measure of its grandeur. Very different is the sentiment produced by the Gothic cathedral, with its almost endless vistas of receding arches, with its high altar rising conspicuous by a hundred lights amid the gloom of the painted windows, while farther and farther back the eye loses itself in the undefined distance amid the tracery of the gorgeous chancel, or the dim columns of Our Lady's chapel. The visible there leads the imagination to the invisible. The sense of finiteness is vanquished. An illusion of vastness and awe presses irresistibly on the mind. And this illusion, which the architecture and the obscurity of the temple produce, has always been skilfully sustained in Catholicism by ceremonies which are pre-eminently calculated to act upon the emotions through the eye.

Now it is surely a remarkable coincidence, that while Christian architecture is thus indisputably superior to pagan architecture in creating the illusion of distance, the modern theatre should be distinguished by precisely the same superiority from the ancient one. A fundamental rule of the modern theatre is, that the stage should be at least twice as deep as it is broad. In the theatres of antiquity, the stage was five or six times as broad as it was deep.[1] It resembled the portion which is now exhibited when the curtain is down. The wall that closed it in, instead of being concealed, was brought prominently before the spectator by rich sculptures, and illusion was neither sought nor obtained. In the modern theatre, our present system of decoration only advanced by slow degrees from the rude representations of heaven

and hell, that were exhibited in the mysteries, to the elaborate scenery of our own day; but still the constant progress in this direction exhibits a conception of the nature of the spectacle, which is essentially different from that of the Greeks, and is probably in a great measure due to the influence of ecclesiastical ceremonies upon the taste.

It is not difficult to perceive the cause of the favour which Leo and his contemporaries manifested to the theatre. They belonged to a generation of ecclesiastics who were far removed from the austere traditions of the Church, who had thrown themselves cordially into all the new tastes that luxury and revived learning had produced, and who shrank with an undisguised aversion from all religious enthusiasm, from all intolerance of the beautiful. Their lives were one long dream of art and poetry. Their imaginations, matured and disciplined by constant study of the noblest works of Grecian genius, cast a new colouring upon their profession, and adorned with a pagan beauty every creation of the Church. Such men as these were but little likely to repress the intellectual passion that arose almost simultaneously in Italy, France, and Spain,[1] and created the modern theatre. But when the teaching of Luther had thrilled through Europe, a new spirit was infused into the Vatican. The intellectualist and the art critic were replaced by men of saintly lives but of persecuting zeal, and a fierce contest between the Church and the theatre began, which continued till near the close of the eighteenth century, and ended in the complete victory of the latter.

The doctrine of the Church on this subject was clear and decisive. The theatre was unequivocally condemned, and all professional actors were pronounced to be in a condition of mortal sin, and were, therefore, doomed, if they died in their profession, to eternal perdition.[2] This frightful proposition was

---

[1] The stage of Orange, which is probably the most perfect Roman theatre in existence, is 66 yards broad and 12 deep. (See Vitet's *Essay on the Antiquities of Orange*, in his *Études sur l'Histoire de l'Art*.) The length of the stage of Herculaneum is greater than that of San Carlo at Naples, but its depth is only a few feet.

[1] The Spanish theatre very early rose to perfection, and, after 1600, Spanish tragi-comedies soon became dominant, even in Italy. (See Riccoboni's history of the movement; and Bouterwek's *Hist. of Spanish Literature*.) In this review I have not entered into an examination of the English theatre, for two reasons: first, because its growth was almost entirely isolated, while the dramatic literatures of Italy, Spain, and France were closely connected; and, secondly, because my present object is to trace the relations of Catholicism and the drama.

[2] The following was the decision of the doctors of the Sorbonne in 1694: "Les comédiens, par leur profession comme elle s'exerce, sont en état de péché

enunciated with the most emphatic clearness by countless bishops and theologians, and was even embodied in the canon law and the rituals of many dioceses.[1] The Ritual of Paris, with several others, distinctly pronounced that actors were by their very employment necessarily excommunicated.[2] This was the sentence of the Church upon those whose lives were spent in adding to the sum of human enjoyments, in scattering the clouds of despondency, and charming away the weariness of the jaded mind. None can tell how many hearts it has wrung with anguish, or how many noble natures it has plunged into the depths of vice. As a necessary consequence of this teaching the sacraments were denied to actors who refused to repudiate their profession, and, in France at least, their burial was as the burial of a dog.[3] Among those who were thus refused a place in consecrated ground was the beautiful and gifted Le Couvreur, who had been perhaps the brightest ornament of the French stage. She died without having abjured the profession she had adorned, and she was buried in a field for cattle upon the banks of the Seine. An ode by Voltaire, burning with the deep fire of an indignant pathos, has at once avenged and consecrated her memory.

It is hard for those who are acquainted with the habits of modern Roman Catholic countries to realise the intense bitterness which theologians of the seventeenth and eighteenth centuries manifested towards the theatre. Molière, whose plays were continually cited as among the most signal instances of its depravity, was the object of especial denunciation, and when he died it was only with extreme difficulty that permission could be obtained to bury him in consecrated ground.[1] The religious mind of Racine recoiled before the censure. He ceased to write for the stage when in the zenith of his powers, and an extraordinary epitaph, while recording his virtues, acknowledges that there was one stain upon his memory—he had been a dramatic poet.[2] In 1696, and again in 1701, on the occasion of the jubilee, the actors entreated the Pope to relieve them from the censures of the canon law, but their request was unavailing; and when, upon the recovery of Louis XIV. from a serious illness, every other corporation at Paris offered up a Te Deum, they were especially excluded.[3] The rule of the Church depriving actors of the sacrament of marriage deliberately consigned them to concubinage. An attempt was at one time made to evade the rule, the actor who desired to marry renouncing his profession, but returning to it by an order of the king as soon as the ceremony was completed; but the Archbishop of Paris effectually prevented the evasion, refusing to accord marriage to any actor who could not produce an official paper guaranteeing him against ever returning to the stage; and the same archbishop suspended a priest from his functions because he had inadvertently married an actor.[4]

When a lawyer, named Huerne de la Mothe, ventured, in 1761, to denounce as scandalous the refusal of marriage to actors, and also to say something in defence of their profession, his work was burnt by the hand of the executioner, and

mortel."—*Dict. des Cas de Conscience*, de Lamet et Fromageau, tom. i. p. 803.
[1] See an immense mass of evidence of this collected in Desprez de Boissy, *Lettres sur les Spectacles* (1780); Lebrun, *Discours sur la Comédie*; Concina, *De Spectaculis.*
[2] "Arcendi [a sacra communione] sunt publice indigni, quales sunt excommunicati, interdicti, manifeste infames ut meretrices, concubinarii, comœdi." (Quoted by Concina, *De Spectaculis*, p. 42. See also Lebrun, *Discours*, p. 34.) Some theologians, in order to reconcile their sentiments with the passage from St. Thomas that I have quoted, said that it was actors of immoral pieces that were excommunicated, but they added that the condition of the theatre was such that all actors fell under the censure. Molière was regarded as peculiarly and pre-eminently bad. Racine was far from innocuous; and Bossuet distinctly maintained that any piece was immoral which contained a representation of love, however legitimate its character. (See his *Réflexions sur la Comédie.*)
[3] "L'Église condamne les comédiens, et croit par là défendre assez la comédie: la décision en est précise dans les rituels (*Rit. de Paris*, pp. 108–114), la pratique en est constante. On prive des sacremens, et à la vie et à la mort, ceux qui jouent la comédie s'ils ne renoncent à leur art; on les passe à la sainte table comme des pécheurs publics; on les exclut des ordres sacrés comme des personnes infâmes; par une suite infaillible, la sépulture ecclésiastique leur est déniée." (Bossuet, *Réflexions sur la Comédie*, § xi.)

[1] Lebrun relates this with much exultation. Speaking of Molière, he says: "Ce qui est constant, c'est que sa mort est une morale terrible pour tous ses confrères, et pour tous ceux qui ne cherchent qu'à rire—un peu de terre obtenu par prière, c'est tout ce qu'il a de l'Église et encore fallut-il bien protester qu'il avoit donné des marques de repentir. Rosimond étant mort subitement en 1691, fut enterré sans clergé, sans lumière, et sans aucune prière, dans un endroit du cimetière de St.-Sulpice où l'on met les enfans morts sans baptême." (*Discours sur la Comédie*, ed. 1731, p. 259.)
[2] This marvellous production is given in full by Desprez de Boissy, tom. i. pp. 510–512. Its author was named Tronchon.
[3] *Ibid.* p. 124.
[4] See on this very scandalous case Grimm et Diderot, *Mémoires historiques*, tom. iii. pp. 327–328. And yet these priests had the audacity to reproach actors with their immorality! The Council of Illiberis in the fourth century prohibited any Christian woman from marrying an actor (Lebrun, *Discours*, p. 157).

his name erased from the list of advocates.[1] Lulli, the first great musical composer of France, could only obtain absolution by burning an opera he had just composed.[2]

Yet in spite of all this the theatre steadily advanced, and as the opposition was absolute and unequivocal its progress was a measure of the defeat of the Church. In France, although the law pronounced actors infamous, and consequently excluded them from every form of public honour and employment, and although till far into the eighteenth century custom prohibited those who occupied any magisterial appointment from attending the theatre, the drama retained an undiminished popularity. In Spain it appears to have secured a certain measure of toleration by throwing itself into the arms of the Church. Calderon infused into it the very spirit of the Inquisition. The sacred plays continued after they had been abolished in almost every other country; and although Mariana and some other leading theologians denounced all dramatic entertainments, they were unable to procure their final suppression.[3] The opera, it is true, was somewhat severely treated, for, some divines having ascribed to it a period of pestilence and of drought, it was for a time abolished;[4] but it at last secured its position in Spain. The Italians at all times thronged the theatre with delight. Even the Romans exhibited such a marked passion for this form of amusement, that the popes were obliged to yield. At first dramatic entertainments were only permitted at Rome during the carnival, and Benedict XIV., while according this permission, addressed a pastoral to the bishops of his kingdom to assure them that he did it with extreme reluctance to avoid greater evils, and that this permission was not to be construed as an approval.[1] Gradually, however, these amusements were extended to other seasons of the year; and even the opera, in obedience to the wishes of the people, was introduced. At last, in 1671, a public opera-house was built at Rome; but female performers were long strictly prohibited, and their places supplied by eunuchs — an unfortunate race, which came in consequence into great request in the Holy City.[2]

The man who did more than any other to remove the stigma that rested upon actors was unquestionably Voltaire. There is, indeed, something singularly noble in the untiring zeal with which he directed poetry and eloquence, the keenest wit and the closest reasoning, to the defence of those who had so long been friendless and despised. He cast over them the ægis of his own mighty name, and the result of his advocacy was shown in the enactment by which the French Revolutionists, at a single stroke, removed all the disqualifications under which they laboured. The position actors have since conquered in almost every country, and the extent to which the theatre has become a recognised institution, must be manifest to everyone. Among the many illustrations of the impotence of modern ecclesiastical efforts to arrest the natural current of society, there are few more curious than is furnished on the opening night of the Roman theatre, when the cardinal-governor of Rome appears, as the representative of the Pope, to sanction the entertainment by his presence, to listen to the sweet songs of the opera sung by female singers, and to watch the wreathings of the dance.

I trust the reader will pardon the great length to which this disquisition on the drama has extended. It is not altogether of the nature of a digression, because, although an institution like the theatre

---

[1] See the curious Arrêt du Parlement, in Desprez de Boissy, tom. i. pp. 473-481.
[2] Hogarth, *Memoirs of the Opera*, p. 28.
[3] Philip II., however, and Philip IV. banished all actors from Spain (Boissy, *Lettres sur les Spectacles*, tom. i. pp. 483-484), and the venerable and miracle-working Father Possada, at a later period, caused the destruction of the theatre of Cordova. (Concina, *De Spect.*, p. 178.) On the extent to which actors laboured to win the favour of the Church by religious plays and by singing at the Church festivals, see the indignant remarks of Mariana, *De Rege*, pp. 406-419.
[4] Buckle, *Hist.*, vol. i. p. 347, note. In the same way Lebrun ascribes the earthquakes that desolated ancient Antioch to the passion of the inhabitants for the theatre (*Discours*, pp. 132, 133). The English bishops, in 1563, attributed the plague to the theatres (Froude's *Hist.*, vol. vii. p. 519).

[1] See an energetic extract which Concina has prefixed to his book. Some of the cardinals, however, were less severe, and in the first half of the seventeenth century the musical parties of the Cardinal Barberini were very famous. It was probably there, and certainly at Rome, that Milton met Leonora Baroni, who was one of the first of the long line of great Italian opera-singers, and to whom he, with a very unpuritanical gallantry, addressed three Latin poems (Hogarth, *Memoirs of the Opera*, pp. 17, 18). These carnival dramas excited the great indignation of the Calvinist Dallæus (Concina, pp. 302-303). The Italians do not seem to have been so violent against the theatre as the French priests, though De Boissy has collected a rather long list of condemnations.
[2] Desprez de Boissy, tom. ii. pp. 234-236.

cannot be regarded as entirely the creation of any one nation, it certainly owes its first impulse and some of its leading characteristics to that union of an industrial and intellectual civilisation which attained its culmination under the Medici. Nor is it without an important bearing on the subject of my work, because the successive transformations I have reviewed furnish one of the most striking examples of that process of gradual secularisation which, under the influence of the rationalistic spirit, is displayed in turn in each department of thought and action. Besides this, there are few more powerfully destructive agents than customs or institutions, no matter how little aggressive, which a Church claiming supreme authority endeavours to suppress, and which have nevertheless secured their position in the world. By the simple fact of their existence, they at first divide the allegiance of mankind, and at last render obsolete a certain portion of ecclesiastical teaching, and thereby impart a character of mobility and flexibility to the whole. In this respect Protestantism has been far less affected by the change than her rival ; for Protestantism does not claim the same coercive authority, and can, therefore, in a measure assimilate with the developments of society, and purify and temper when it cannot altogether control. It must be acknowledged also, that while the Calvinistic section of the Reformed Churches has ever displayed a bigotry on the subject of amusements, which is at least equal to that of the Church of Rome,[1] Anglicanism has always been singularly free from the taint of fanaticism ;[2] nor is it, I believe, too much to add that her forbearance has received its reward, and that, if we except the period of depravity that elapsed between the Restoration and the publication of the

work of Jeremy Collier in 1698, and which may be justly ascribed in a great measure to the reaction against Puritanism, the English theatre has been that in which the moralist can find least to condemn.

The creation of the secular theatre was one of the last results of the industrial supremacy of Italy. A succession of causes, into which it is not now necessary to enter, had corroded that political system, to which the world is so deeply indebted ; and the discovery of the passage round the Cape of Good Hope by Gama, and of America by Columbus, together with some other causes, directed the stream of commerce in new channels. By the time when the effects of these discoveries began first to be felt, the Reformation had divided Christendom into two opposing sections, and the important question arose, to which of these sections the sceptre of industry would fall.

It must, I think, be acknowledged that to a spectator of the sixteenth century no proposition could seem more clear than that the commercial supremacy of Europe was destined to be exercised by Catholicism. The two great discoveries I have mentioned had both fallen to the lot of the intensely Catholic nations of the Spanish peninsula. Spain especially exhibited a combination of advantages which it would be very difficult to parallel in history. Her magnificent colonies opened out a boundless prospect of wealth, and she seemed to possess all those qualities and capacities that were requisite for their development. The nation was in the zenith of its power. The glories of Granada still rested upon it. Charles V. had united the imperial sceptre with that of Spain, had organised a vast navy, had constituted himself the recognised head of the Catholic interests, had humbled that French power which alone could imperil his ascendency, and had acquired the reputation of the most consummate politician of the age. If we add to this that the passion for wealth had never been more strongly exhibited than by the Spaniards, it would seem as though no element of commercial greatness was wanting. Reasoning a priori, it would appear natural to conclude that Spain was about to embark in a long and glorious career of commerce, that she would incline the balance of material prosperity decisively to the side of the

---

[1] On the decrees of the French Protestants against the theatre, see Lebrun, p. 255. Calvin at Geneva was equally severe, and his policy long after found an enthusiastic defender in Rousseau. In England, one of the most atrocious acts of tyranny of which Charles I. was guilty, was elicited by a book called the *Histrio-mastix*, of Prynne, and one of the first effects of the triumph of the Puritans was the suppression of the theatre.

[2] I have mentioned the way in which Molière, Lulli, and Le Couvreur were treated in France. As a single illustration of the different spirits of Catholicism and Anglicanism, I may mention the fate of their English parallels—Shakespeare, Lawes, and Mrs. Oldfield. No murmur of controversy ever disturbed the grave of Shakespeare, and the great poet of Puritanism sang his requiem. Lawes and Mrs. Oldfield both rest in Westminster Abbey, to which the latter was borne with almost regal pomp.

religion of which she was the champion, but that the commercial spirit would at last act upon and modify her religious fanaticism.

None of these results followed. Although for a few years the Spanish Catholics were the arbiters and the directors of commerce, and although the effects of their ascendency have not even yet passed away, the prosperity of Spain was speedily eclipsed. At a time when she seemed on the highway to an almost boundless wealth, she sank into the most abject poverty. Her glory was withered, her power was shattered, her fanaticism alone remained.

There are several considerations that explain this apparent anomaly. The first is, I think, to be found in the erroneous economical doctrine which became the mainspring of Spanish legislation.

Although it would undoubtedly be a gross exaggeration to regard the Italian republics as having arrived at the knowledge of the true laws that govern wealth, there can be no question that their policy was far more in conformity with the principles of political economy than that of any of their successors till after the time of Quesnay and Smith. The exquisite practical skill they possessed, and also the peculiarity of their position, which made most of them entirely dependent upon commerce, and consequently the natural enemies of protective privileges, saved them from the worst legislative errors of the age; and, indeed, it has been the just boast of Italian economists, that, if we except Serra, Genovesi, and perhaps one or two others, even their speculative writers have always been singularly free from the errors of that "mercantile system" which in other countries was so long supreme. It was not until Spain had risen to power, and the stream of American gold had begun to inundate Europe, that the doctrine upon which that fatal system rests became the centre of commercial legislation.

To state this doctrine in the simplest form, it was believed that all wealth consisted of the precious metals, and that therefore a country was necessarily impoverished by every transaction which diminished its metallic riches, no matter how much it may have added to its other possessions. If, therefore, two nations exchanged their commodities with a view of increasing their wealth, the single object of each was to regulate the transaction in such a manner that it might obtain a larger amount of money than it before possessed, or, in other words, that the value of its non-metallic exports should be greater than of its imports. But as the excess of exports over imports on one side implied a corresponding excess of imports over exports on the other, it followed that the interests of the two nations were diametrically opposed, that the loss of one was the condition and measure of the gain of the other, and that to the nation which was unable to incline what was termed the "balance of commerce" in its favour, the entire transaction was an evil. It followed also that the importance of native productions was altogether subordinate to that of the export or import of gold.

From these principles three important practical consequences were drawn which contributed greatly to the downfall of Spain. In the first place, the whole energy both of the government and people was concentrated upon the gold mines, and manufactures and almost all forms of industry sank into neglect. In the next place, the colonies were speedily ruined by an elaborate system of commercial restrictions and monopolies, devised with the vain hope of enriching the mother-country, and some of them were at length goaded into successful rebellion. In the last place, an undue amount of gold was introduced into Spain, which had the very natural, but, to the Spaniards, the very astonishing effect of convulsing the whole financial system of the country. For the value of gold, like the value of other commodities, is governed by the law of supply and demand; and the fact that this metal has been selected as the general instrument of exchange, while it makes any sudden alteration in its value peculiarly dangerous, does not in any degree remove it from the law. When it suddenly becomes too common, its value—that is to say, its purchasing power—is depreciated; or, in other words, the price of all other articles is raised. After a time things adjust themselves to the new standard, and many political economists, considering the sudden stimulus that is given to industry, the particular class of enterprises the change in the value of money specially favours, and still more its effect in lightening the pressure of national debts, have regarded it as ultimately a benefit; but, at all events, the confusion, insecurity, and uncertainty of the transition constitute a grave danger to the community, and the loss inflicted on certain classes[1] is extremely serious. In our own day, although the influx of Australian and Californian gold has told very sensibly upon prices, the immense area of enterprise over which it has been diffused, the counteracting influence of machinery in cheapening commodities, and also a few exceptional causes of demand,[2] have materially deadened the shock. But the stream of gold that was directed to Spain after the discovery of America produced nearly the full measure of evil, while the economical error of the age deprived the Spaniards of nearly all the good that might have been expected. The temporary evil of a violent change in prices could only have been abated, and the permanent evil of the decay of national industry could only have been in some degree compensated, by the free employment of American gold to purchase the industry of foreign nations; but this would involve the export of the precious metal, which the government under the severest penalties prohibited. It is true that, as no prohibition can finally arrest the natural flow of affairs, the gold did issue forth,[3] but it was in the manner that was least advantageous to Spain. Charles V. and Philip II. employed it in their wars; but wars are almost always detrimental to industry; many of these were disastrous in their conclusions, and those of Charles were undertaken much more in the interests of the Empire than of Spain, while Philip sacrificed every other consideration to the advantage of the Church. The only other mode of egress was by infringing the law. After a few years, the full effects of this policy[4]

were manifested. Manufactures had languished. Prices were immensely raised. Confusion and insecurity characterised every financial undertaking. The Spaniards, to adopt the image of a great political economist, realising the curse of Midas, found all the necessaries of life transmuted into gold, while, to crown all, the government prohibited its export under pain of death.

These economical causes will help to show why it was that the material prosperity of the great Catholic power was so transient, and also why no strong industrial spirit was evoked to counteract the prevailing fanaticism. This last fact will be still further elucidated if we consider the social and religious institutions which Spanish Catholicity encouraged. The monasteries, in numbers and wealth, had reached a point that had scarcely ever been equalled; and besides subtracting many thousand men and a vast amount of wealth from the productive resources of the country, they produced habits of mind that are altogether incompatible with industry. The spirit that makes men devote themselves in vast numbers to a monotonous life of asceticism and poverty is so essentially opposed to the spirit that creates the energy and enthusiasm of industry, that their continued co-existence may be regarded as impossible. Besides this, that aristocratic system which harmonises so well with a theological society revived. A warlike and idle nobility took the place of the old merchant nobles of Italy, and a stigma was in consequence attached to labour,[1] which was still further increased by the revival of slavery.

The resurrection of this last institution is usually ascribed to Las Casas, perhaps the most eminent philanthropist Spain ever produced. In this statement there is, however, some exaggeration. Las Casas only landed in America in 1513, and he does not appear to have taken any step on the subject of slavery till some years later; but negroes had been employed as slaves by the Portuguese in their colonies in the very beginning of the

---

[1] Those who directly or indirectly depend upon fixed incomes.

[2] According to Chevalier (whose book on this subject has been translated and endorsed by Mr. Cobden), the adoption of a gold standard by France is the principal.

[3] The famous sermon of Bishop Latimer, describing the revolution of prices in England, was preached as early as 1548, only twenty-seven years after the conquest of Mexico, and at a time when the great mines of Potosi (which were only discovered in 1545) could scarcely have had any effect upon Europe. The most striking evidence of the perturbation of prices in England in the sixteenth century is given in *A Compendious or Briefe Examination of Certayne Ordinary Complaints of divers of our countrymen, by W. S.* [probably William Stafford], 1581. The greater part of this curious pamphlet has been reprinted in the fifth volume of the *Pamphleteer* (1815).

[4] Aggravated to a certain extent by the dishonest tampering with the coinage, in which Charles V., like most of the sovereigns of the time, indulged. The

chief results of this are, first, that the good coins are driven out of circulation, as men naturally prefer giving the smallest value possible for what they purchase; secondly, nominal prices are raised as the intrinsic value of coins is depreciated; thirdly, all the evils of uncertainty, panic, and suffering inflicted upon creditors and persons with fixed incomes are produced.

[1] See Blanqui, *Hist. de l'Économie politique*, tom. i. pp. 271-284, where the whole subject of the political economy of Charles V. is admirably treated.

century,[1] and a certain number were introduced into the Spanish colonies as early as 1511. They do not, however, appear to have been fully recognised by the government, and further imports were discouraged till 1516, when the monks of St. Jerome, who then administered affairs in the West Indies, recommended their employment. In the following year, Las Casas pronounced energetically in the same sense. Strange as it may now appear, there can be no doubt that in doing so he was actuated by the purest benevolence. Perceiving that the wretched Indians, to whose service he had devoted his life, perished by thousands beneath the hard labour of the mines, while the negroes employed by the Portuguese bore the fatigue without the slightest injury, he imagined that by introducing the latter he was performing an act of undoubted philanthropy; and thus it came to pass, that one whose character presents an almost ideal type of beneficence became a leading promoter of negro slavery.[2]

The traffic once organised, and encouraged by the government, spread rapidly. Its monopoly was granted to the Belgians, who sold it to the Genoese; but merchants of Venice, Barcelona, and England had all an early share in the adventure. The first Englishman who took part in it was a certain John Hawkins, who made an expedition to the African coast in 1562.[3] Scarcely anyone

seems to have regarded the trade as wrong. According to the popular sentiment of Christendom there was such an amazing, I might almost say generical, difference between those who were Christians and those who were not, that to apply to the latter the principles that were applied to the former, would have been deemed a glaring paradox. If the condition of the negroes in this world was altered for the worse, it was felt that their prospects in the next were greatly improved. Besides, it was remembered that, shortly after the deluge, Ham had behaved disrespectfully to his drunken father, and it was believed by many that the Almighty had, in consequence, ordained negro slavery. The Spanish were not in general bad masters. On the contrary, when the gold fever had begun to subside, they were in this respect distinguished for their humanity;[1] and their laws on the subject still present, in some points, a favourable contrast to those of America; but the effect of slavery upon the national character was not the less great.

Besides these considerations, we must take into account the great acts of religious intolerance of which Spain was guilty, and which recoiled with fatal effect upon her industrial system. Never did a people verify more fully the great truth that industry and fanaticism are deadly foes. Four times the Spanish nation directed all its energies in the cause of the Church, and four times its prosperity received a wound from which it has never recovered. By the expulsion of the Jews, Spain was deprived of all her greatest financiers, and of almost all her most enterprising merchants. By the expulsion of the Moors, she lost her best agriculturists; vast plains were left uninhabited, except by banditti, and some of the most important trades were paralysed for ever. By the expedition of the Armada, that naval supremacy which, since the discoveries of the Cape passage and of America had made commerce exclusively maritime, implied commercial supremacy, passed from her hands, and was soon divided between the Protestant nations of England and Holland. By her persecutions in the Netherlands, she produced a spirit of resistance that baffled

---

[1] The beginning of the trade dates from 1440, in which year some Portuguese merchants, having kidnapped some Moors on the coast of Africa, only consented to ransom them on receiving negroes in exchange. (Macpherson's *Annals of Commerce*, vol. i. p. 661.)

[2] The first writer who undertook the defence of Las Casas was Grégoire, Bishop of Blois, in a paper read before the French Institute in 1804, and the subject was afterwards treated, though in a rather different point of view, in a letter by a Mexican priest named Don Gregorio Funes, and in an essay by Llorente. They are reprinted, together with translations of all the relevant passages from Herrera (the original authority on the subject), in Llorente's edition of the works of Las Casas (1822). The first of these writers attempted to impugn the authority of Herrera, but for this there seems no sufficient reason; nor does it appear that Herrera, or indeed anyone else at the time, considered the conduct of Las Casas wrong. The monks of St. Jerome are much more responsible for the introduction of negroes than Las Casas. It is impossible to read the evidence Llorente has collected without feeling that, as a general rule (with a few striking exceptions), the Spanish clergy laboured earnestly to alleviate the condition of the captive Indians, that this was one of their chief reasons in advocating the import of negroes, and that they never contemplated the horrors that soon grew out of the trade. It should be added that the Spanish Dominican Soto was perhaps the first man who unequivocally condemned that trade.

[3] Macpherson's *Annals of Commerce*, vol. ii. p. 638. At a much later period, in 1689, the English made a

convention with Spain to supply the West Indies with slaves from Jamaica.

[1] This was noticed by Bodin in his time. See *La République*, p. 47 (1577).

her armies, destroyed her prestige, and resulted in the establishment of another State, distinguished alike for its commercial genius, its bravery, and its Protestantism.

There were, of course, other circumstances which accelerated or aggravated the downfall of Spain ; but the really dominating causes are all, I think, to be found under the economical or theological heads I have noticed. It is well worthy of attention how they conspired, acting and reacting upon one another, to destroy that political structure which was once so powerful, and which appeared to possess so many elements of stability. Nor can we question that that destruction was an almost unmingled benefit to mankind. Blind folly, ignoble selfishness, crushing tyranny, and hideous cruelty, mark every page of the history of the domination of Spain, whether we turn to the New World or to the Netherlands, or to those glorious Italian cities which she blasted by her rule. During the period of her ascendency, and especially during the reigns of Charles V. and Philip II., who were the most faithful representatives of her spirit, she was guilty of an amount of persecution before which all the enormities of Roman emperors fade into insignificance. She reorganised the accursed institution of slavery on a gigantic scale, and in a form that was in some respects worse than any that had before existed ; she was the true author of the mercantile theory and of the colonial policy which have been the sources of disastrous wars to every European nation ; she replaced municipal independence by a centralised despotism, and the aristocracy of industry by the aristocracy of war ;[1] and she uniformly exerted the whole stress of her authority to check on all subjects and in all forms the progress of enquiry and of knowledge. Had she long continued to exercise the assimilating, absorbing, and controlling influence of a great Power, the advancement of Europe might have been indefinitely retarded. Happily, however, Providence, in the laws of history as in the laws of matter, tends ever to perfection, and, annexing fatal penalties to the resistance of those laws, destroys every obstacle, confounds those who seek to arrest the progress, and, by the concurrence of many agencies, effects the objects it designs.

[1] Blanqui, *Hist. de l'Écon. pol.*, tom. i. p. 277.

Before leaving the subject of Spanish industry, I may notice one article that was at this time brought into Europe, not because it was itself very important, but because it was the beginning of a great social change that was fully accomplished about a century afterwards—I mean the introduction of hot drinks. Towards the middle of the sixteenth century the Spaniards imported chocolate from Mexico. Rather more than half a century later tea was introduced from China and Japan. It had been noticed by Marco Polo as early as the thirteenth century, but it was probably first brought to Europe by the Jesuit missionaries in the first years of the seventeenth century, and it was soon after largely imported by the Dutch. In 1636 we find it in usage in France, and enthusiastically patronised by the Chancellor Séguier. The earliest notice of it in England is in an Act of Parliament of 1660. The discovery of the circulation of the blood, which produced an exaggerated estimate of the medical value of bleeding and of hot drinks, and the writings of two physicians named Tulpius and Bontekoe, gave a great impulse to its popularity. In a letter written in 1680, Madame de Sévigné observes that the Marchioness de la Sablière had just introduced the custom of drinking it with milk. About the middle of the same century coffee began to pour in from Turkey. The properties of this berry had been noticed in 1591 by the Venetian physician Alpinus, and soon afterwards by Bacon in his *Natural History*, and the drink was introduced into England in 1652 by an English Turkey merchant named Edwards. In France the first coffee-house was established at Marseilles in 1664. A few years later, Soliman Aga, the ambassador of Mahomet IV., made the new beverage very fashionable in Paris ; and in 1672 an Armenian named Pascal established a coffee-house in that city. He had soon countless imitators ; and it was observed that this new taste gave a serious and almost instantaneous check to drunkenness, which had been very prevalent in France. Coffee-houses were the true precursors of the clubs of the eighteenth century. They became the most important centres of society, and they gave a new tone to the national manners. In England, though they were once even more popular than in France, and though they are indissolubly associated with one of the most brilliant periods of literary history, they have not taken root; but the effect of hot drinks upon domestic life has probably been even greater than on the Continent. Checking the boisterous revels that had once been universal, and raising woman to a new position in the domestic circle, they have contributed very largely to refine manners, to introduce a new order of tastes, and to soften and improve the character of men. They are, therefore, I think, not unworthy of a passing notice in a sketch of the moral and intellectual consequences of commerce.[1]

When the Spanish supremacy was destroyed, what may be termed the commercial antagonism of the two religions ceased. England and Holland were long the leaders of commerce; and if Catholic nations have since distinguished themselves in that course, it has been when their zeal had grown languid and their system of policy been secularised. The general superiority in industry of Protestant countries has been constantly noticed and often explained. The suppression of monasteries, the discouragement of mendicity, and the construction of churches that were in no degree formed upon the ascetic principle, contributed to the progress; but perhaps the principal cause was the intellectual impulse communicated by the Reformation, which was felt in every field, both of speculation and of action.[2]

But while the relative interests of Protestantism and Catholicism have not been very seriously involved in the history of industry since the seventeenth century, there is another form of antagonism which long after made that history a faithful mirror of theological progress. I mean the conflict between town and country, between the manufacturing and the agricultural interests. The question which of these two spheres of existence

is most conducive to the happiness and the morality of mankind will, no doubt, always be contested; but the fact that they produce entirely different intellectual tendencies, both in religion and politics, will scarcely be disputed. The country is always the representative of stability, immobility, and reaction. The towns are the representatives of progress, innovation, and revolution. The inhabitants of the country may be very vicious; but even in the midst of their vice they will be extremely superstitious, extremely tenacious of the customs of religions that have elsewhere passed away, and especially addicted to that aspect of those religions which is most opposed to the spirit of Rationalism. All the old superstitions concerning witches, fairies, hereditary curses, prophetical dreams, magical virtues, lucky or unlucky days, places, or events, still linger among the poor; while even the educated are distinguished for the retrospective character of their minds, and for their extreme antipathy to innovation. The general character of great towns, and especially of manufacturing towns, is entirely different.[1] It is indeed true that the great subdivision of labour, while it is eminently favourable to the increase of wealth, is for a time unfavourable to the intellectual development of the labourer; for the mind that is concentrated exclusively upon the manufacture of a single portion of a single object is far less happily circumstanced than if it were occupied with a complex subject which demands the exercise of all its faculties. But this disadvantage is more than compensated by the intellectual stimulus of association, and by the increased opportunities which greater rewards and steady progress produce. Certain it is that neither the virtues nor vices of great towns take the form of reaction in politics, or of superstition in religion. The past rests lightly, often too lightly, upon them. Novelty is welcomed, progress is eagerly pursued. Vague traditions are keenly criticised, old doctrines are disintegrated and moulded afresh by the individual judgment. Besides this, the manufacturing is also the commercial interest; and the great intellectual importance of commerce we have already seen. Such, then,

[1] The fullest history of hot drinks I have met with is in a curious and learned book, D'Aussy, *Hist. de la Vie privée des Français* (Paris, 1815), tom. iii. pp. 116-129, which I have followed closely. See, too, Pierre Lacroix, *Histoire des anciennes Corporations*, p. 76; Pelletier, *Le Thé et le Café*; Cabanis, *Rapports du Physique et du Moral*, 8me Mémoire; and for the English part of the history, Macpherson's *Annals of Commerce*, vol. ii. pp. 447-489.

[2] I do not include among these causes the diminution of Church holidays, for, although in some few countries they may have degenerated into an abuse, the number of those that are compulsory has been grossly exaggerated; and moreover, their good effects in procuring some additional recreation for the working classes appear to me to have more than counterbalanced the injury they may have done to labour. There is some correspondence between Dr. Doyle and Lord Cloncurry on this subject, which is well worthy of attention, in Fitzpatrick's *Life of Doyle*.

[1] The difference between town and country in this respect has been fully noticed by Mr. Buckle (*Hist. of Civ.*, vol. i. pp. 344-347), who ascribes it chiefly to the fact that agriculturists are dependent for their success upon atmospheric changes, which man can neither predict nor control.

being the opposite predispositions evoked by agricultural and manufacturing occupations, it becomes a matter of considerable interest and importance to trace the history of their comparative development; and in order to do so it will be necessary to give a brief outline of the progress of economical opinion on the subject.

Before the dawn of a correct political economy in the eighteenth century, Europe was for the most part divided between two doctrines on the subject of commerce. Both schools regarded money as the single form of wealth; but, according to one of them, commerce should be altogether discouraged, as at best a dangerous and a gambling speculation; while, according to the other, it should be pursued as the chief method of acquiring wealth, but only on the condition of the exports exceeding the imports. The first of these schools usually discouraged manufactures, and concentrated its attention upon agriculture; the other was eminently favourable to manufactures. Before the sixteenth century, the notions of the first school, without being systematised or formally stated, were very generally diffused: politicians laboured to make each nation entirely self-subsisting; and there was an antipathy, or at least a disinclination, to any speculation that involved an export of gold, even with the eventual object of obtaining a larger supply in return.[1] Besides this, the rude simplicity of manners which made the demand for manufactured goods very small, the superstitions about usury which fell with crushing weight on industrial enterprise, the imperfection of the means of communication, the zeal with which the monks pursued agriculture, the especial adaptation of that pursuit, on account of its comparative facility, to an early stage of civilisation, and the recollection of the peculiar honour in which it had been held by the ancients —all tended in the same direction. With the exception of the Italian republics and the cities of the Hanseatic League, which had little or no land to cultivate, and were almost forced by their circumstances into commerce, agriculture was everywhere the dominant form of labour, and the habits of mind it created contributed much to colour, intensify, and perpetuate the mediæval superstitions.

When, however, the great discoveries

[1] See M'Culloch's *Political Economy*, and his Introduction to the *Wealth of Nations*.

of gold in America created in all nations an eager desire to obtain it, industry began to assume a new form and more gigantic proportions; and although, owing to causes which I have already traced, it languished in Spain, it was rapidly developed in other countries, and the opinions of statesmen on the subject were steadily modified. Sully was probably the last minister of very considerable abilities who systematically opposed manufactures as an evil. The opposite opinion, which regarded them as the most efficient magnet of foreign gold, found its greatest representative in Colbert;[1] and although the ruinous wars of Louis XIV., and still more the revocation of the Edict of Nantes, in a great measure counteracted his efforts; although, too, the ultimate effects of the protective system have been extremely detrimental to industry; there can be little doubt that this minister did more than any preceding statesman to make manufactures a prominent form of European industry. He removed many of the impositions under which they suffered, protected their interests whenever they were menaced, and did all that lay in his power to encourage their development.

Indeed, at first sight, the school which followed that of Colbert, though in reality an immense step in advance, might appear less favourable to the manufacturing interests. The economists—as Quesnay, and those very able writers and statesmen who adopted his opinions, were termed—were not simply the precursors of political economy; they were the actual founders of many parts of it; and though their system, as a whole, has perished, and their fame been eclipsed by the great thinker of Scotland, they will always form one of the most important links in the history of the science. Perhaps their principal achievement was the repudiation of the old doctrine that all wealth

[1] See Blanqui. In England the mercantile system began under the influence of the East India Company, which, in 1600, obtained permission to export the precious metals to the amount of £30,000 per annum, on the condition that within six months of every expedition (except the first) the Company should import an equal sum. Under Henry VIII., and more than once at an earlier period, all exportation of the precious metals had been forbidden. The restrictive laws on this subject were repealed in 1663 (M'Culloch's *Introd. Discourse*). The two most eminent English defenders of the mercantile system — Thomas Mun, whose *Treasure by Foreign Trade* was published in 1664, and Sir Josiah Child, whose *New Discourse of Trade* was published in 1668—both wrote in the interests of the East India Company.

consisted of gold—a doctrine which, having lighted up the labours of the alchemists, and inspired all the Eldorado dreams of the middle ages, had become the cardinal principle of commercial legislation.[1] Almost at the same time, and about twenty-five years before the publication of *The Wealth of Nations*, this doctrine was assailed, and the possibility of the increase of wealth being in inverse proportion to the increase of gold was asserted, by Hume in England, and by Quesnay in France. But while the French economists perceived very clearly the mistake of their predecessors, when they came to establish their own doctrine they fell into an error which is a striking illustration of the difficulty with which, in one stage of progress, even the most acute minds rise to truths which in another stage appear perfectly self-evident. Nothing, according to their view, can really add to the national wealth which does not call new matter into existence, or at least introduce it to the service of men. Mines, fisheries, and agriculture fulfil these conditions, and consequently add to the national wealth. Manufactures, simply giving matter a new form, though they are extremely useful to the community, and though they may enable an individual to augment his portion of the national wealth, can never increase the great total. Practically, therefore, for the great majority of nations, agriculture is the single source of wealth; all manufactures are ultimately salaried by it, and its encouragement should be the main object of judicious policy. Raynal, it is

true, in this matter separated from the rest of the school. He saw that manufactures invested the raw material with new qualities, and making it the object of new demand increased its value; but at this point he stopped.[1] Agriculture and industry he regarded as both sources of national wealth, but not so commerce. Forgetting that an article may be far more valuable in a country into which it is imported than in that in which it is indigenous, and that, when the costs incident upon transport have been deducted from this excess, the remainder is a pure gain, he maintained that commerce, being simply displacement, could not increase the general wealth.

These doctrines were undoubtedly in some respects very unfavourable to manufactures, yet their consequences were not as evil as might have been expected. In the first place, the economists were unwittingly guilty of a grievous injustice to their favourite pursuit. All taxation, they believed, should be levied upon the net gains of the country; and as those gains were exclusively due to agriculture, they concluded, as Locke on somewhat different grounds had concluded in the preceding century, that the proprietors of the soil should bear the entire burden. Besides this, the economists, as the first great opponents of the mercantile theory, were on all occasions the advocates of free trade, the subverters of every form of monopoly, the reformers of all the means of communication. By the ministry of Turgot, and by the legislation of the revolutionary parliaments, such countless abuses of detail were swept away, and so many useful measures recommended, that it may be truly said that manufactures owe more to them than to any preceding legislators.

At last Adam Smith appeared; and while he effectually destroyed all that part of the doctrine of the economists which was hostile to manufactures, he established upon the firm basis of demonstration, and developed and irradiated with matchless skill, all that was most favourable to their progress. Proving that labour was the basis of value, that money is but a single form of merchandise which has been selected as the instrument of exchange, and that the goods of foreign countries are eventually purchased by native productions—unravelling by a

[1] The earliest writer who very clearly expounded the true nature of money was probably Bishop Berkeley, whose *Querist*, considering that it was written in 1735, is one of the most remarkable instances of political sagacity of the age; far superior in this respect, I think, to the economical writings of Locke. Berkeley very nearly broke loose from the system of "the balance of commerce." The following queries are a curious example of the struggles of an acute reason against this universal error: "Whether that trade should not be accounted most pernicious, wherein the balance is most against us? and whether this be not the trade of France?" "Whether the annual trade between Italy and Lyons be not about four millions in favour of the former, and yet whether Lyons be not a gainer by this trade?" "Whether the general rule of determining the profit of a commerce by its balance doth not, like other rules, admit of exceptions?" "Whether it would not be a monstrous folly to import nothing but gold and silver, supposing we might do it, from every foreign part to which we trade?" "Whether he must not be a wrong-headed patriot or politician whose ultimate view was drawing money into a country and keeping it there?" (*Querist*, 161, 555, 556, 557, 559.) Berkeley is an example of, perhaps, the rarest form of genius—that which is equally adapted for political speculation and for the most subtle and supersensuous regions of metaphysics.

[1] Say, *Traité d'Économie politique*, liv. i. ch. 2.

chain of the clearest but most subtle reasoning the functions of capital, the manner in which it is created by the combination of parsimony with industry, and the special facilities which manufactures and the division of labour of which they admit offer for its increase—giving, too, a fatal blow to the system of restrictions by which statesmen had long imagined that they could promote the interests of wealth—Adam Smith performed the double service of dispelling the notion that manufactures are useless or pernicious, and unfolding the true laws that regulate their prosperity. Generation after generation, and almost year by year, his principles have penetrated more deeply into the policy of Europe; and generation after generation, manufactures, freed from their old shackles, acquire a greater expansion, and the habits of thought which they produce a corresponding importance.

It is, however, an extremely remarkable fact, as showing the tenacity with which the doctrines of the " economists " clung to the mind, that even Adam Smith thought it necessary, in classifying the sources of wealth, to reserve for agriculture a position of special prominence, as the most abundant of these sources.[1] He arrived at this conclusion, not from any observation of what had actually taken place, but from two general considerations. In manufactures, he contended, wealth is produced by the unaided toil of man, whereas in agriculture nature co-operates with human exertions. Besides this, agriculture, unlike other pursuits, in addition to wages and profit, can furnish a rent. The first of these statements, as has often been observed, is palpably inaccurate, for nature is in many instances extremely serviceable to the manufacturer; as, for example, when steam or water puts his machinery in motion. The second argument lost its force when Ricardo discovered the true cause of rent, proving that it is a sign of the limited productivity of the soil, and not of its superiority to other sources of wealth.[2]

But while this steady modification of economical opinions in favour of manufactures is one great cause of the progress of the latter, it would probably have been insufficient, but for the co-operation of two other influences. The first of these was the system of credit. This remarkable agency, which has long proved one of the great moralising influences of society, by the immense importance it has bestowed upon character, and one of the great pledges of peace, by the union it has established between different nations, and, at the same time, the most powerful of all the engines of warfare, is chiefly due to the industrial genius of Holland ; for though some traces of it may be found among the Jews and the Italian republics of the middle ages, the system was not duly organised till the establishment of the Bank of Amsterdam in 1609. The immediate object was to increase the amount of money in circulation, and thus give a new impetus to industry ; and within certain limits, and subject to certain dangers, which we have not now to consider, it has fully answered its end.

The second influence is the rapid development of mechanical contrivances. Strictly speaking, machinery dates from the rudest instrument by which men tilled the soil; but its higher and more elaborate achievements are always the product of civilisation, upon which, in turn, they powerfully react. The most important machine invented, or at least introduced into Europe, in the middle ages, was probably the windmill,[1] which was an agent in the agricultural interests. In the fifteenth century, a machine for printing transformed the intellectual condition of Europe. In the nineteenth century the machines of Watt, Arkwright, and Stephenson, and the many minor inventions that are subsidiary to them, have given an impulse both to commerce

---

[1] *Wealth of Nations,* book ii. ch. 5.
[2] As long as the good land to be cultivated is practically unlimited relatively to the population, no rent is paid. When, however, the best land no longer sufficiently supplies the wants of an increased population, it will still continue to be cultivated ; but it will be necessary also to cultivate land of an inferior quality. The cost of the production of a given quantity of the best corn will necessarily be greater when derived from the latter than when derived from the former ; but when brought to the market, all corn of the same quality will bear the same price, and that price will be regulated by the cost of production which is greatest (for no one would cultivate the bad land if the sale of its produce did not compensate for his outlay), so that in the sale of corn of the same quality at the same price, the profits of the possessors of the good will be greater than the profits of the possessors of the bad land. This difference is the origin of rent, which is, therefore, not a primal element of agriculture, and which has not, as Adam Smith supposed, any influence on price.

[1] The earliest European notice of windmills is, I believe, to be found in a charter of William, Count of Mortain (grandson of William the Conqueror), dated 1105, which has been published by Mabillon. They are supposed to have been brought from Asia Minor. (D'Aussy, *La Vie privée des Français,* tom. i. pp. 62, 63.)

and manufactures which is altogether unparalleled in the history of mankind. In addition to the necessary difficulties connected with the introduction of a new form of industry, every step of the progress of machines was met by a fierce opposition, directed at one time by the ablest statesmen,[1] and long afterwards sustained by the lower classes, who very naturally regarded these inventions as prejudicial to their interests. And, certainly, the first result of machinery, by economising the labour of production, is to throw a vast number of the poor out of employment, and to reduce, by increased concurrence, the wages of the remainder. The second is to diminish the price of the article of manufacture, to the benefit of the consumer ; and in most cases this depreciation leads to an immense extension of demand, which necessitates a multiplication of machines, and usually continues till the number of persons employed is immeasurably greater than before the machinery had been introduced. At the same time, this increased facility of production and this increased demand produce an accumulation of capital far more rapid than had previously taken place ; which, as the rate of wages depends entirely upon the proportion national capital bears to the labouring classes, among whom it is to be divided, is a main condition of the material prosperity of the latter. Even in those instances in which, from the nature of the case, the demand for the manufactured article cannot be so extended as to compensate for the loss of employment which the introduction of machinery occasions, although the passing evils are very great, the change is usually an advantage ; for economical production implies increasing wealth, and the capital gained in one department finds its outlet in others.

There are, no doubt, other effects of machinery which are serious drawbacks to these advantages—some of them inherent in this mode of production, some of them partly or altogether due to the process of transition. Such are the great increase of the inequalities of fortune which results from the absorption of all production by colossal manufactures, the unnatural multiplication and agglomeration of population they occasion, the sudden and disastrous fluctuations to which manufacturing industry is peculiarly liable, the evil effects it frequently exercises upon health, and the temptation to employ young children in its service. All these points have given rise to much animated discussion, which it does not fall within the province of the present work to review ; but at all events it is unquestionable that, for good or for evil, the invariable effect of modern machinery has been to increase the prominence of manufactures, to multiply the number of those engaged in them, and, therefore, in the opposition of tendencies that exists between the agricultural and manufacturing classes, to incline the balance in favour of the latter.

Beyond all other nations, England has been in this respect distinguished. Both in the intellectual and in the mechanical influences I have reviewed, she stands without a rival ; for with, I think, the exception of Say, France has not produced any political economist of great original powers since Turgot ; and America, notwithstanding her rare mechanical genius, is as yet unable to boast of a Watt or a Stephenson. It is not surprising that a land which has attained this double supremacy, and which possesses at the same time almost unlimited coal-mines, an unrivalled navy, and a government that can never long resist the natural tendency of affairs, should be pre-eminently the land of manufactures. In no other country are the intellectual influences connected with them so powerful ; and the constant increase of the manufacturing population is rapidly verifying, in a sense that should not be restricted to politics, the prediction of Mr. Cobden, that eventually " the towns must govern England."[1]

In the preceding examination of the ways in which the successive evolutions of European industry have reflected or influenced the history of belief, I have often had occasion to refer to the different branches of political economy in their relation to different aspects of industrial progress. It remains for me now to consider in a more general point of view the theological consequences of this great science, which has probably done more than any other to reveal the true physio-

---

[1] Amongst others, Colbert.

[1] There are some striking, though now rather ancient, statistics on this point in Babbage *On Machines*, ch. i. In 1830, the non-cultivators were in Italy as 31 to 100 ; in France, as 50 to 100 ; in England, as 200 to 100. During the first thirty years of the century, the population of England increased about fifty-one per cent. ; that of the great towns, 123 per cent.

logy of society. For although political economists, and especially those of England, have often endeavoured to isolate the phenomena of wealth, all such attempts have proved entirely futile. Even Adam Smith lighted up an immense series of moral and social interests by his science. Malthus, opening out the great question of population, immensely increased its range ; and it is now impossible to be imbued with the leading writings on the subject without forming certain criteria of excellence, certain general conceptions of the aim and laws of human progress, that cannot be restricted to material interests. I shall endeavour, without entering into any minute details, to sketch the general outlines of these conceptions, and to show in what respects they harmonise or clash with theological notions.

The first important consequence of political economy I have in some degree anticipated in the last chapter. It is to contribute largely towards the realisation of the great Christian conception of universal peace. The history of the fortunes of that conception in the hands of theologians is profoundly melancholy. Though peace upon earth was at first proclaimed as a main object of Christianity, and though for about three centuries the Christian disciples displayed unwearied zeal and amazing heroism in advocating it, the sublime conception of a moral unity gradually faded away before the conception of a unity of ecclesiastical organisation, and for many centuries theologians were so far from contributing to the suppression of war, that they may be justly regarded as its chief fomenters. Certain it is, that the period when the Catholic Church exercised a supreme ascendency, was also the period in which Europe was most distracted by wars ; and that the very few instances in which the clergy exerted their gigantic influence to suppress them, are more than counterbalanced by those in which they were the direct causes of the bloodshed. Indeed, they almost consecrated war by teaching that its issue was not the result of natural agencies, but of supernatural interposition. As the special sphere of Providential action, it assumed a holy character, and success became a proof, or at least a strong presumption, of right. Hence arose that union between the sacerdotal and the military spirit which meets us in every page of history ; the countless

religious rites that were interwoven with military proceedings ; the legends of visible miracles deciding the battle ; the trial by combat, which the clergy often wished to suppress, but which nevertheless continued for centuries, because all classes regarded the issue as the judicial decision of the Deity. When these superstitions in some measure decayed, the religious wars began. The bond of Catholic unity, which was entirely insufficient to prevent wars between Catholic nations, proved powerful enough to cause frightful convulsions when it was assailed ; and one of the most faithful measures of the decay of theological influences has been the gradual cessation of the wars they produced.

The inadequacy of theological systems as a basis of European tranquillity having been clearly proved by the experience of many centuries, there arose in the eighteenth century a school which attempted to establish this tranquillity by a purely intellectual process—by giving intellectual pursuits and political principles a decisive predominance over the military spirit. I allude to the French philosophers, who in this as in many other respects were simply endeavouring to realise in their own way one of the great ideal conceptions of Christianity. They arose at a period well suited to the enterprise. France was wearied, exhausted, and almost ruined by the long wars of Louis XIV. The prestige that Condé and Turenne had cast upon the French arms had perished beneath the still greater genius of Marlborough. An intense intellectual life had arisen, accompanied by all the sanguine dreams of youth. Voltaire, after coquetting for a short time with the military spirit, threw himself cordially into the cause of peace. He employed all his amazing abilities and all his unrivalled influence to discredit war, and, with the assistance of his followers, succeeded in establishing the closest union between the intellects of France and England, and in replacing the old theological and military antipathy by the sympathy of common aspirations.

But a few years passed away and all this was changed. The long and terrible wars that were the speedy consequence of the French Revolution, and the pernicious genius of Napoleon, evoked all the reactionary influences in Europe, revived the military spirit in its full intensity, and plunged the greater part of the civilised world into the agonies of a deadly struggle.

There can, I think, be little doubt that there is a tendency in civilisation to approximate towards the ideal of the French philosophers. It can hardly be questioned that the advance of intellectual culture produces a decline of the military spirit, and that the cohesion resulting from a community of principles and intellectual tendencies is slowly superseding artificial political combinations. But at the same time it is no less certain that the bond of intellectual sympathy alone is far too weak to restrain the action of opposing passions, and it was reserved for political economy to supply a stronger and more permanent principle of unity.

This principle is an enlightened self-interest. Formerly, as I have said, the interests of nations were supposed to be diametrically opposed. The wealth that was added to one was necessarily taken from another ; and all commerce was a kind of balance, in which a gain on one side implied a corresponding loss on the opposite one. Every blow that was struck at the prosperity of one nation was of advantage to the rest, for it diminished the number of those among whom the wealth of the world was to be divided. Religion might indeed interpose and tell men that they ought not to rejoice in the misfortunes of others, and that they should subordinate their interests to higher considerations ; but still each people, as far as it followed its selfish interests, was hostile to its neighbour ;[1] and even in the best ages the guiding principles of large bodies of men are almost always selfish. Independently of the many wars that were directly occasioned by a desire to alter commercial relations, there was a constant smouldering ill-feeling created by the sense of habitual antagonism, which the slightest difference kindled into a flame.

For this great evil political economy is the only corrective. It teaches, in the first place, that the notion that a commercial nation can only prosper by the loss of its neighbour, is essentially false. It teaches still further that each nation has a direct interest in the prosperity of that with which it trades, just as a shopman has an interest in the wealth of his customers. It teaches too that the different markets of the world are so closely connected, that it is quite impossible for a serious derangement to take place in any one of them without its evil effects vibrating through all ; and that, in the present condition of Europe, commercial ties are so numerous, and the interests of nations so closely interwoven, that war is usually an evil even to the victor. Each successive development of political economy has brought these truths into clearer relief, and in proportion to their diffusion must be the antipathy to war, the desire to restrict it, when it does break out, as far as possible to those who are actually engaged, and the hostility to all who have provoked it. Every fresh commercial enterprise is therefore an additional guarantee of peace.

I know that, in the present day, when Europe is suffering to an almost unexampled extent from the disquietude resulting from the conflict between opposing principles and unequal civilisations, speculations of this kind must appear to many unreal and utopian. Most assuredly, as long as nations tolerate monarchs who, resting upon the traditions of an effete theocracy, regard their authority as of divine right, and esteem it their main duty to arrest by force the political developments of civilisation, so long must standing armies and wars of opinion continue. Nor would the most sanguine political economist venture to predict a time in which the sword would be altogether unknown. The explosions of passion are not always restrained by the most evident ties of interest ; exceptional circumstances counteract general tendencies ; and commerce, which links civilised communities in a bond of unity, has ever forced her way among barbarians by bloodshed and by tyranny. But in order to justify the prospect of a great and profound change in the relations of European nations, it is only necessary to make two postulates. The first is, that the industrial element, which, in spite of legislative restrictions and military perturbations, is advancing every year with accelerated rapidity, is destined one day to become the dominant influence in politics. The second is, that those principles of political economy which are now acknowledged to be true by everyone who has studied them, will one day be realised as axioms by the masses.

[1] Even Voltaire said, "Telle est la condition humaine, que souhaiter la grandeur de son pays c'est souhaiter du mal à ses voisins.... Il est clair qu'un pays ne peut gagner sans qu'un autre perd." (*Dict. phil.*, art. *Patrie*.)

Amid the complications and elaborations of civilisation, the deranging influence of passion, whether for good or for evil, becomes continually less, and interest becomes more and more the guiding influence, not perhaps of individuals, but of communities. In proportion to the commercial and industrial advancement of a nation, its interests become favourable to peace, and the love of war is in consequence diminished. When therefore the different states of Europe are closely interwoven by commercial interests, when the classes who represent those interests have become the guiding power of the State, and when they are fully penetrated with the truth that war in any quarter is detrimental to their prosperity, a guarantee for the peace of Europe will have been attained, if not perfect, at least far stronger than any which either religion or philanthropy has yet realised. In such a condition of commercial activity, and in such a condition of public knowledge, a political transformation would necessarily ensue, and the principal causes of present perturbations would be eliminated. At the same time two kindred movements which I have already noticed—the recognition of the principle of the rights of nationalities as the basis of political morality, and the growing ascendency of intellectual pursuits diminishing the admiration of military glory — would consolidate the interests of peace. Many years must undoubtedly elapse before such a condition of society can be attained; torrents of blood must yet be shed before the political obstacles shall have been removed, before the nationalities which are still writhing beneath a foreign yoke shall have been relieved, and before advancing knowledge shall have finally destroyed those theological doctrines concerning the relations between sovereigns and nations which are the basis of some of the worst tyrannies that are cursing mankind;[1] but as surely as civilisation advances, so surely must the triumph come. Liberty, industry, and peace are in modern societies indissolubly connected, and their ultimate ascendency depends upon a movement which may be retarded, but cannot possibly be arrested.

It should be observed, too, that while the nations which are most devoted to industrial enterprise are the most wealthy and the most pacific, they are also, as a general rule, those which are most likely to wield the greatest power in war. This, as Adam Smith has acutely observed, is one of the most important differences between ancient and modern societies. Formerly, when war depended almost entirely upon unaided valour, the military position of a rich nation was usually unfavourable; for while its wealth enervated its character and attracted the cupidity of its neighbours, it did not in the hour of strife furnish it with advantages at all commensurate with these evils. Hence the ruin of Carthage, Corinth, and Tyre, the great centres of commercial activity among the ancients. Since, however, the invention of gunpowder and the elaboration of military machinery, war has become in a great measure dependent upon mechanical genius, and above all upon financial prosperity, and the tendency of the balance of power is therefore to incline steadily to the nations that are most interested in the preservation of peace.

The influence political economy exercises in uniting different communities by the bond of a common interest, is also felt in the relations between the different classes of the same community. It is indeed no exaggeration to say, that a wide diffusion of the principles of the science is absolutely essential, if democracy is to be other than a fearful evil. For when the masses of the poor emerge from the torpor of ignorance, and begin keenly to examine their position in the gradations of society, property is almost certain to strike them as an anomaly and an injustice. From the notion that all men are born free and equal, they will very speedily pass to the conviction that all men are born with the same title to the goods that are in the world. Paley may have been wrong in regarding general utility as the ultimate basis of the rights of property, but most assuredly no other will obtain the respect of those who, themselves struggling with poverty, have obtained a supreme authority in the State. The long series of measures directly or indirectly infringing on the rights of property that have disgraced the democracy of France,[1] and the notion of the natural hostility of capital and labour which is so general among the labouring

[1] Written in 1863.

[1] There is a full description of these in Chevalier's *Lettres sur l'Organisation du Travail*—a very able, and, considering that it was written in 1848, a very courageous book.

classes on the Continent, are sufficient to cause a profound disquietude to those who have convinced themselves that democracy is the ultimate form of political development. Political economy, and political economy alone, can remedy the evil. It does not indeed teach the optimism or the fatalism that some have imagined, and there can be little question that its ascendency must give in many respects new directions to the channel of wealth, repressing forms of expenditure which have long been regarded as peculiarly honourable, and which will be regarded in a very different light when they are universally acknowledged to be useless or detrimental to society.[1] Nor does it teach that the interests of rich and poor are identical in such a sense that the wages of the workman and the profits of his employer must rise and fall together—the fact being rather the reverse. Nor, again, that a government is altogether impotent in regulating the distribution of wealth, for the laws of succession and the direction given to taxation have in this respect a gigantic influence. What, however, it does prove is, that the wages of the labourer depend so necessarily upon the proportion between the sum that is provided for the payment of labour, and the number of those among whom it is divided, that all direct efforts of the government to cause the permanent elevation of wages are, in the end, prejudicial to the very class they are intended to benefit. It proves that the material prosperity of the working classes depends upon the increase of capital being more rapid than that of population, and that this can only be ensured, on the one hand, by the continence of the labourer guarding against excessive multiplication, and, on the other hand, by the fullest encouragement of production, which implies the perfect protection of capitalists ; for he who has no assurance that he may retain what he has accumulated, will either never accumulate, or will conceal his property unproductively. In other words, political economy demonstrates, beyond the possibility of doubt, that if the property of the rich were confiscated and divided among the poor, the measure would in the end be the most fearful catastrophe that could befall the latter.

This great truth, that, in a financial point of view, with a very few exceptions, each nation, trade, or profession is interested in the prosperity of every other, has been growing clearer and clearer with each new development of political economy,[1] and cannot fail to exercise a vast moral influence upon society. For though concurrence of action based solely upon community of interests, considered in itself, has no moral value, its effect in destroying some of the principal causes of dissension is extremely important. And, indeed, human nature is so constituted, that it is impossible for bodies of men to work together under the sense of a common interest without a warm feeling of amity arising between them. Common aims and hopes knit them together by a bond of sympathy. Each man becomes accustomed to act with a view to the welfare of others, and a union of affections usually replaces or consecrates the union of interests. The sentiment thus evoked is undoubtedly a moral sentiment; and if it is not so powerful as that which is

---

[1] The main interest of the poor is that as large a proportion as possible of the national wealth should be converted into capital, or, in other words, diverted from unproductive to productive channels. Wealth in the form of diamonds or gold ornaments, retained only for ostentation, has no effect upon wages. Wealth expended in feasts or pageants does undoubtedly directly benefit those who furnish them, but is of no ultimate good to the community, because the purchased article perishes unproductively by the use. Were the sums expended in these ways devoted to productive sources, they would, after each such employment, be reproduced, and become again available for the purposes of society ; and those who now gain their living in supplying what is useless to mankind would betake themselves to the enlarged field of productive enterprise. But this train of reasoning should be corrected by the following considerations : 1st, wealth is a mean, and not an end, its end being happiness ; and therefore mere accumulation, with no further object, is plainly irrational. Some modes of expenditure (such as public amusements), which rank very low indeed when judged by one test, rank very high when judged by the other. The intensity, and the wide diffusion of enjoyment they produce, compensate for their transience. 2nd. There is such a thing as immaterial production. Expenditure in the domain of art or science, which adds nothing to the material wealth of the community, may not only produce enjoyment, but may become the source of enjoyment and improvement for all future time. 3rd. The great incentive to production is the desire to rise to the higher ranks, and the great attraction of those ranks to the majority of men is the ostentation that accompanies them ; so that the expenditure which directly is unproductive may indirectly be highly productive. Besides this, we should consider the effects of sudden outbursts of luxury at different periods of history and its different influences upon morals. So stated, the question of the most advantageous expenditure is extremely complicated, and varies much with different circumstances. As a general rule, however, political economy tends to repress the luxury of ostentation.

[1] At least till Say, whose *Théorie des Débouchés* (directed against the notion of a "universal glut," which was maintained in France by Sismondi and in England by Malthus) may be regarded as the highest demonstration of the truth. The first writer who intimated the identity of the interests of nations engaged in commerce was probably Dudley North, in his famous work on commerce, published in 1691.

elicited by agencies appealing directly to enthusiasm, it is more general, more uniform, and perhaps, on the whole, not less beneficial to mankind.

It would be easy to show that political economy, by revealing the true causes of national prosperity, has effected, or is effecting, a considerable alteration in many of our moral judgments. Such, for example, is the change in the relative position in the moral scale of prodigality and avarice, of youthful indiscretions, and of imprudent marriages ; and such too are the important modifications introduced into the conception of charity by the writings of Defoe, of Ricci, and of Malthus. It will, however, be sufficient for my present purpose, to indicate the predominating bias which these speculations produce, in order to ascertain the class of opinions and the tone of philosophy they are most likely to favour. On this point there can be little doubt. It has been again and again recognised that political economy represents the extreme negation of asceticism.

What may be termed the ascetic and the industrial philosophies have at all times formed two of the most important divisions of human opinions ; and as each brings with it a vast train of moral and intellectual consequences, their history touches almost every branch of intellectual progress. The watchword of the first philosophy is mortification ; the watchword of the second is development. The first seeks to diminish, and the second to multiply, desires ; the first, acknowledging happiness as a condition of the mind, endeavours to attain it by acting directly on the mind, the second by acting on surrounding circumstances. The first, giving a greater intensity to the emotions, produces the most devoted men ; the second, regulating the combined action of society, produces the highest social level. The first has proved most congenial to the Asiatic and Egyptian civilisations, and the second to the civilisations of Europe.

From the beginning of the fourth century, when the monastic system was first introduced from Egypt into Christendom,[1]

until near the Reformation, the ascetic theory was everywhere predominant. The movement that was provoked by the examples of St. Antony and St. Pachomius, and by the writings of St. Jerome and St. Basil, received its full organisation about two centuries later from St. Benedict. The Crusades and St. Bernard produced the military orders ; the teaching of St. Bruno, the Carthusians ; the religious struggle of the thirteenth century, the Franciscans, Dominicans, and Carmelites ;[1] the conflict of the Reformation, the Theatines and the Jesuits. With the exception of the last century, during which some opposition had arisen to the monks, this long space of time represents the continuous elevation of the ascetic principle as the supreme type with which all forms of heroism naturally assimilated or coalesced.

If we compare this period with the last three centuries, the contrast is very evident. Formerly, asceticism represented the highest point of moral dignity, and in exact proportion as a society was stimulated towards its conception of excellence the monasteries were multiplied. At present, the abolition of monasteries is an invariable concomitant of an advancing civilisation, the immediate consequence of every important movement of national progress. Protestantism was the first great protest against asceticism ; but the process of confiscation which it initiated in the sixteenth century, and which was then regarded as the most horrible sacrilege, has since been imitated by almost every Catholic government in Europe. Not only France, at a time when she had repudiated Catholicism, but even Austria and Spain, have pursued this course. No less than 184 monasteries were suppressed, and ecclesiastical property to the value of more than two millions of florins confiscated, by Joseph II. of Austria ; 3,000 monasteries are said to have been suppressed in Europe between 1830 and 1835 ; 187 in Poland, in 1841.[2] And these acts, as well as those which have recently

---

[1] The Therapeutes mentioned by Philo (*De Vitâ Contemplativâ*) were probably pagans ; and, indeed, in Asia and Africa the monastic type has always existed, and has assumed forms very similar to that among Christians. The horrible macerations of the Buddhists rival those of any Christian sect, and the antipathy to the fair sex is nearly as great among the pagan as among the Christian anchorites. Some pagan religionists of

Siam made it a rule never to keep hens, because those animals are of the female sex. (Bayle, *Nouvelles Lettres*, lettre xxi.) Some Christians of Syria, with equal wisdom, resolved never to eat the flesh of any female animal. (*Ibid.*)

[1] The Carmelites had existed before upon Mount Carmel, and had even traced their origin to the prophet Elijah ; but they were transferred to Europe, reorganised, and greatly multiplied in the thirteenth century.

[2] Montalembert, *Moines d'Occident*, ntrod. pp. 199, 200.

taken place in Italy, have been, for the most part, elicited by no scandals on the part of the monks, but were simply the expression of a public opinion which regarded the monastic life as essentially contemptible and disgraceful.

Of this industrial civilisation, political economy is the intellectual expression; and it is not too much to say that it furnishes a complete theory of human progress directly opposed to the theory of asceticism. According to its point of view, the basis of all intellectual and social development is wealth; for as long as men are so situated that all are obliged to labour for their sustenance, progress is impossible. An accumulation of capital is therefore the first step of civilisation, and this accumulation depends mainly on the multiplication of wants. When the inhabitants of any country are contented with what is barely sufficient for the support of life, they will only perform the minimum of labour; they will make no steady and sustained efforts to ameliorate their condition, and, as they will place little or no restraint upon multiplication, their numbers increasing more rapidly than the means of sustenance, the most frightful suffering must ensue. To raise that people from its barbarism, the first essential is to make it discontented with its condition. As soon as the standard of its necessities is raised, as soon as men come to regard as necessaries a certain measure of the comforts of life, habits of parsimony and self-restraint will be formed, and material progress will begin. But it is impossible for men by these means to satisfy their wants. The horizon of their ambition continually recedes. Each desire that is accomplished produces many others, and thus new exertions are elicited, and the progress of society secured. In the atmosphere of luxury that increased wealth produces, refined tastes, perceptions of beauty, intellectual aspirations appear. Faculties that were before dormant are evoked, new directions are given to human energies, and, under the impulse of the desire for wealth, men arise to supply each new want that wealth has produced. Hence, for the most part, arise art and literature, and science, and all the refinements and elaborations of civilisation, and all the inventions that have alleviated the sufferings or multiplied the enjoyments of mankind. And the same principle that creates civilisation creates liberty, and regulates and sustains morals. The poorer classes, as wealth, and consequently the demand for their labour, have increased, cease to be the helpless tools of their masters. Slavery, condemned by political economy, gradually disappears. The stigma that attached to labour is removed. War is repressed as a folly, and despotism as an invasion of the rights of property. The sense of common interests unites the different sections of mankind, and the conviction that each nation should direct its energies to that form of produce for which it is naturally most suited, effects a division of labour which renders each dependent upon the others. Under the influence of industrial occupations, passions are repressed, the old warlike habits are destroyed, a respect for law, a consideration for the interests of others, a sobriety and perseverance of character are inculcated. Integrity acquires a new value, and dissipation a new danger. The taste is formed to appreciate the less intense but more equable enjoyments, and the standard of excellence being rectified by the measure of utility, a crowd of imaginary virtues and vices which ignorance had engendered pass silently away.

This, or something like this, is the scheme of progress which political economy reveals. It differs essentially from the schemes of most moralists in the fact that its success depends not upon any radical change in the nature of mankind, not upon any of those movements of enthusiasm which are always transient in their duration and restricted in their sphere, but simply upon the diffusion of knowledge. Taking human nature with all its defects, the influence of an enlightened self-interest first of all upon the actions and afterwards upon the character of mankind, is shown to be sufficient to construct the whole edifice of civilisation; and if that principle were withdrawn, all would crumble in the dust. The emulations, the jealousies, the conflicting sentiments, the insatiable desires of mankind, have all their place in the economy of life, and each successive development of human progress is evolved from their play and from their collision. When therefore the ascetic, proclaiming the utter depravity of mankind, seeks to extirpate his most natural passions, to crush the expansion of his faculties, to destroy the versatility of his tastes, and to arrest the flow and impulse of his nature, he is striking at the very force and energy of civilisation. Hence the dreary, sterile torpor that characterised those ages in which the ascetic principle has been supreme, while the civilisations which have attained the highest perfection have been those of ancient Greece and modern Europe, which were most opposed to it.

It is curious to observe by what very different processes the antipathy to asceticism was arrived at in these two periods. In the first it is to be ascribed mainly to the sense of the harmony of complete development, and above all to the passionate admiration of physical beauty which art contributed largely to sustain. The statues of the most lovely were then placed among the statues of the goddesses, and the athletic games made the symmetry and beauty of the manly frame the highest type of perfection. "A perfect mind in a perfect body" was the ideal of the philosopher, and the latter was considered almost a condition of the former. Harmonious sustained manhood, without disproportion, or anomaly, or eccentricity —that godlike type in which the same divine energy seems to thrill with equal force through every faculty of mind and body, the majesty of a single power never deranging the balance or impairing the symmetry of the whole, was probably more keenly appreciated and more frequently exhibited in ancient Greece than in any succeeding civilisation.

Among the moderns, on the other hand, the law of development has been much more social than individual, and depends, as we have seen, on the growth of the industrial element. If we examine the history of the last few centuries, since the Italian republics revived commerce on a large scale, or since the Portuguese for the first time founded a great colonial empire in the interests of industrial enterprise,[1] we find that these interests have been steadily becoming supreme in all war, legislation, and diplomacy, and that the philosophy of utility, which is the most faithful expression of the industrial

spirit, has attained a corresponding place in the sphere of thought. It is supported by the ascendency of the inductive philosophy, which has always concentrated its efforts chiefly on material advantages. It is supported by the rapid diffusion through all classes of habits of thought derived from political life, which is the consequence of the extension of political liberty. It is supported too by the investigations of those great moralists who since Cumberland have been mainly employed in proving that virtue is a condition of happiness, from which men have illogically, but not unnaturally, inferred, that that which has no utility can have no moral value.[1]

The immense importance of utilitarianism in correcting the evils of fanaticism, in calling into action the faculties which asceticism had petrified, and in furnishing a simple, universal principle of life, has been clearly shown. Its capability of coalescing with received theological doctrines can hardly be doubtful to those who remember that Paley made it the corner-stone of his moral philosophy, maintaining that a hope of future reward was the natural principle of virtue. Indeed, one of the few political economists who have endeavoured to give their science a theological complexion, has argued that the laws of economical and of religious progress are identical, being self-denial for an end.[2] At the same time, the defects of such a system are sufficiently manifest, and they are in a great measure also the defects of Rationalism. Utility is, perhaps, the highest motive to which reason can attain. The sacrifice of enjoyments and the endurance of sufferings become rational only when some compensating advantage can be expected. The conduct of that Turkish atheist,[3] who, believing that death was an eternal sleep, refused at the stake to utter the recantation which would save his life, replying to every remonstrance, "Although there is no recompense to be looked for, yet the love of truth constraineth me to die in its defence," in the eye of reason is an inex-

---

[1] Among the ancients the Phœnician colonies, and a few others of less importance, were no doubt commercial, but the immense majority were due either to the love of migration natural to a barbarous people, or to an excess of population, or to a desire when vanquished to escape servitude, or to a fear of invasion, or to the spirit of conquest. The substitution of the industrial for the military colonial system is one of the important changes in history, and on the whole, perhaps, it cannot be better dated than from the Portuguese colonial empire, which Vasco di Gama founded, and Albuquerque consolidated.

[1] A great political economist, in a work which has now become very rare, says: "Toute vertu qui n'a pas l'utilité pour objet immédiat me paraît futile, ridicule, pareille à cette perfection de Talapoin qui consiste à se tenir sur un seul pied plusieurs années de suite, ou dans quelque autre mortification nuisible à lui-même, inutile aux autres, et que son Dieu même doit regarder en pitié." (J. B. Say, Olbie, p. 81.)

[2] Perin, La Richesse dans les Sociétés chrétiennes.

[3] Mahomet Effendi. See Bayle, Pensées diverses, § 182.

plicable folly; and it is only by appealing to a far higher faculty that it appears in its true light as one of the loftiest forms of virtue. It is from the moral or religious faculty alone that we obtain the conception of the purely disinterested. This is, indeed, the noblest thing we possess, the celestial spark that is within us, the impress of the divine image, the principle of every heroism. Where it is not developed, the civilisation, however high may be its general average, is maimed and mutilated.

In the long series of transformations we have reviewed, there are two which have been eminently favourable to this, the heroic side of human nature. The substitution of the philosophical conception of truth, for its own sake, for the theological conception of the guilt of error, has been in this respect a clear gain; and the political movement which has resulted chiefly from the introduction of the spirit of Rationalism into politics, has produced, and is producing, some of the most splendid instances of self-sacrifice. On the whole, however, it can hardly be doubted that the general tendency of these influences is unfavourable to enthusiasm, and that both in actions and in speculations this tendency is painfully visible. With a far higher level of average excellence than in former times, our age exhibits a marked decline in the spirit of self-sacrifice, in the appreciation of the more poetical or religious aspect of our nature. The history of self-sacrifice during the last 1,800 years, has been mainly the history of the action of Christianity upon the world. Ignorance and error have, no doubt, often directed the heroic spirit into wrong channels, and have sometimes even made it a cause of great evil to mankind; but it is the moral type and beauty, the enlarged conceptions and persuasive power of the Christian faith, that have, during many centuries, chiefly called it into being. The power of Christianity in this respect can only cease with the annihilation of the moral nature of mankind; but there are periods in which it is comparatively low. The decay of the old spirit of loyalty, the destruction of asceticism, and the restriction of the sphere of charity, which has necessarily resulted from the increased elaboration of material civilisation, represent successive encroachments on the field of self-sacrifice which have been very imperfectly compensated, and have given

our age a mercenary, venal, and unheroic character, that is deeply to be deplored. A healthy civilisation implies a double action—the action of great bodies of men moving with the broad stream of their age, and eventually governing their leaders; and the action of men of genius or heroism upon the masses, raising them to a higher level, supplying them with nobler motives or more comprehensive principles, and modifying, though not altogether directing, the general current. The first of these forms of action is now exhibited in great perfection. The second has but little influence in practice, and is almost ignored in speculation. The gradual evolution of societies, the organised action of great communities under the impulse of utilitarian motives, is admirably manifested; but great individualities act seldom and feebly upon the world. At the same time, the history of speculative philosophy exhibits a corresponding tone. There has always been an intimate connection between utilitarianism and those systems of metaphysics which greatly restrict and curtail the original powers of our nature, regarding the human mind as capable only of receiving, arranging, and transforming ideas that come to it from without. Those who hold that all our ideas are derived from sensation, will always, if they are consistent, make utility the ultimate principle of virtue, because by their system they can never rise to the conception of the purely disinterested;[1] and, on the other hand, it will be usually found that the sensual school and the materialism which it has produced, have arisen in periods when the standard of motives was low, and when heroism and pure enthusiasm had but little influence. In our present absolute ignorance of the immediate causes of life, and of the nature and limits of mind and matter, this consideration furnishes perhaps the most satisfactory arguments in favour of spiritualism; and it is as an index of the moral condition of the age that the prevalence of either spiritualism or materialism is especially important. At present, the tendency towards the latter is too manifest to escape the notice of any attentive

[1] As Madame de Staël said: "La morale fondée sur l'intérêt, si fortement prêchée par les écrivains français du dernier siècle, est dans une connexion intime avec la métaphysique qui attribue toutes nos idées à des sensations" (*L'Allemagne*). I believe all who are conversant with the history of philosophy will acknowledge this to be profoundly true.

observer. That great reaction against the materialism of the last [eighteenth] century, which was represented by the ascendency of German and Scotch philosophies in England, and by the revival of Cartesianism in France, which produced in art a renewed admiration for Gothic architecture; in literature, the substitution of a school of poetry appealing powerfully to the passions and the imagination, for the frigid intellectualism of Pope or of Voltaire ; and in religion, the deep sense of sin, displayed in different forms both by the early Evangelicals and by the early Tractarians, is everywhere disappearing. In England, the philosophy of experience, pushed to the extremes of Hume, and represented by the ablest living philosopher in Europe, has been rising with startling rapidity to authority, and has now almost acquired an ascendency in speculation. In France, the reaction against spiritualism and the tendency towards avowed materialism, as represented by the writings of Comte,[1] of Renan, and of Taine, are scarcely less powerful than at the close of the last [eighteenth] century; while, under the guidance of Schopenhauer and of Büchner, even Germany itself, so long the chosen seat of metaphysics, is advancing with no faltering steps in the same career.

This is the shadow resting upon the otherwise brilliant picture the history of Rationalism presents. The destruction of the belief in witchcraft and of religious persecution, the decay of those ghastly notions concerning future punishments, which for centuries diseased the imaginations and embittered the characters of men, the emancipation of suffering nationalities, the abolition of the belief in the guilt of error, which paralysed the intellectual, and of the asceticism, which paralysed the material, progress of mankind, may be justly regarded as among the greatest triumphs of civilisation ; but when we look back to the cheerful alacrity with which, in some former ages, men sacrificed all their material and intellectual interests to what they believed to be right, and when we realise the unclouded assurance that was their reward, it is impossible to deny that we have lost something in our progress.

[1] It is indeed true that a first principle of the Positive school is the assertion that the limit of human faculties is the study of the successions of phenomena, and that we are therefore incapable of ascertaining their causes ; and M. Littré, in his preface to the recent edition of Comte's works, has adduced this principle to show that Positivism is unaffected by arguments against materialism. As a matter of fact, however, the leading Positivists have been avowed materialists ; the negation of the existence of metaphysics as a science distinct from physiology, which is one of their cardinal doctrines, implies, or all but implies, materialism ; and the tendency of their school has, I think, of late years been steadily to substitute direct negations for scepticism. There are some good remarks on this in a very clear and able little book, called *Le Matérialisme contemporain*, by Paul Janet, a writer on whom (since Saisset died) the defence of spiritualism in France seems to have mainly devolved.

INDEX

PART II.

L